French Applied Linguistics

Language Learning and Language Teaching

The *LL&LT* monograph series publishes monographs as well as edited volumes on applied and methodological issues in the field of language pedagogy. The focus of the series is on subjects such as classroom discourse and interaction; language diversity in educational settings; bilingual education; language testing and language assessment; teaching methods and teaching performance; learning trajectories in second language acquisition; and written language learning in educational settings.

Series editors

Nina Spada
Ontario Institute for Studies in Education, University of Toronto

Jan H. Hulstijn
Department of Second Language Acquisition, University of Amsterdam

Volume 16
French Applied Linguistics
Edited by Dalila Ayoun

French Applied Linguistics

Edited by

Dalila Ayoun

University of Arizona

John Benjamins Publishing Company

Amsterdam / Philadelphia

™ The paper used in this publication meets the minimum requirements
of American National Standard for Information Sciences – Permanence
of Paper for Printed Library Materials, ANSI z39.48-1984.

Library of Congress Cataloging-in-Publication Data

French applied linguistics / edited by Dalila Ayoun.
        p.   cm. (Language Learning and Language Teaching, ISSN 1569–9471
; v. 16)
        Includes bibliographical references and indexes.
        1. Applied linguistics. 2. French language--Acquisition. 3. French
        language--Study and teaching. I. Ayoun, Dalila, 1963-

        P129.F74 2007
        445--dc22   2006051686
        ISBN 978 90 272 1972 5 (Hb; alk. paper)

John Benjamins Publishing Co. · P.O. Box 36224 · 1020 ME Amsterdam · The Netherlands
John Benjamins North America · P.O. Box 27519 · Philadelphia PA 19118-0519 · USA

Table of contents

Preface

Tous les moyens de l'esprit sont enfermés dans le langage; et qui n'a point réfléchi sur le langage n'a point réfléchi du tout.   Alain

When I started developing a preliminary proposal for this volume in October 2004, my main ambition was to showcase French in the vast arena of Applied Linguistics: Not only the history of the French language throughout the centuries, but also French linguists from pioneers such as J. Ronjat or Abbot Charles-Michel l'Epée to my contemporary colleagues working in so many diverse subfields of applied linguistics, from natural language and lexical creativity to French Sign Language, for instance. However, as my preliminary research progressed, I quickly realized I could not do justice to, nor include, all of the subfields of applied linguistics, even if I only attempted to focus on subfields to which French had made a contribution. Even in spite of its wide scope and thirty nine chapters, Kaplan's (2002) *Oxford Handbook of Applied Linguistics*, for instance, does not claim to "provide a definitive definition of the field. Rather, this volume offers a snapshot of some of the subfields of applied linguistics at the beginning of the third millemium – and, thus, a kind of overview of the field" (Kaplan 2002: vii).

The present volume is even more selective in its coverage of French in applied linguistics. The second introductory chapter reviews the history of the French language from a sociolinguistic perspective. Then, the six chapters of the first part cover what are most commonly considered the core aspects of the second language acquisition of any language: Phonology, semantics/syntax, syntax/morphology, pragmatics, sociolinguistics, and grammatical gender that alone encompasses lexical, semantic, and morpho-syntactic knowledge. The seven chapters that compose the second part of the volume aim at presenting less commonly researched areas of applied linguistics which also stress the contribution of the French language in various fields such as language ideology and foreign language pedagogy, corpus linguistics, or French Sign Language. A chapter also explores the role of affective variables, attitude and personality on language learning, while another investigates how computational approaches may facilitate lexical creativity. The chapters on creole studies and applied linguistics in West Africa both address issues in first and second language acquisition in complex sociolinguistic and political contexts. Finally, the last chapter – "French in Louisiana: A view from the ground" – serves as an epilogue to illustrate the past, present and future of French in a region rich in linguistic history.

My most sincere thanks and appreciation go to the numerous colleagues who served as external anonymous reviewers, providing insightful comments and invaluable suggestions. They are listed in alphabetical order: Barry Jean Ancelet, Bruce Anderson, Jonathan Beck, Kate Beeching, Julie Belz, Carl Blyth, Béatrice Boutin, Diane Brentari, Barbara Bullock, Tom Cobb, Jean-Marc Dewaele, Paulin Djité, Robert Gardner, Gaëtanelle Gilquin, Julia Herschensohn, David Hornsby, Gabi Kasper, Celeste Kinginger, Claire Kramsch, Eric Mathieu, Michael Picone, Philippe Prévost, Henry Tyne, Salikoko Mufwene, and Muriel Warga.

I would also like to thank my contributors – many of whom were colleagues I did not know prior to initiating work on this project – for their trust, patience, and professionalism throughout this journey. It was a pleasure working with all of them.

Last, but not least, I very much appreciated how prompt, professional and reliable Kees Vaes was, as usual. Sincere thanks also go to Nina Spada and Jan Hulstijn, the editors for the Language Learning & Language Teaching series, for their careful reading of the first submission and valuable comments. I truly enjoyed editing this volume, and sincerely hope it makes an important contribution to the field of applied linguistics in general, and to second language acquisition in particular.

About the contributors

Bruce Anderson is Assistant Professor of French Linguistics in the Department of French & Italian at the University of California, Davis, as well as the current director of that university's Second Language Acquisition Institute. He specializes in the acquisition of morphology and syntax in French as a second language from a generative perspective. Other research interests include corpus linguistics and their pedagogical applications. Portions of his doctoral dissertation "The Fundamental Equivalence of Native and Interlanguage Grammars" (Indiana University, 2002) are to appear in the journals *Language Acquisition* and *Applied Linguistics*. He is currently researching the acquisition of gender and number morphology among English-speaking learners of French and Spanish (as L2) and Italian (as L3). He may be contacted at bcanderson@ucdavis.edu

Dalila Ayoun is Associate Professor of French Linguistics and Second Language Acquisition and Teaching in the Department of French and Italian at the University of Arizona in Tucson. Her research focuses on the second language acquisition of French and Spanish from a generative perspective, web/computer-based elicitation task design, the development of tense/aspect morphology, and grammatical gender. Her most recent publications include a co-edited, co-authored volume with Rafael Salaberry, *Tense and Aspect in Romance Languages*, published by John Benjamins in 2005; and an article entitled "Verb movement in the L2 acquisition of English by adult native speakers of French" appeared in 2005 in the *EUROSLA Yearbook* edited by S. Foster-Cohen, M. P. Garcia Mayo, & J. Cenoz, and published by John Benjamins. Her 2003 book, *Parameter Setting in Language Acquisition*, was released in paperback in 2005 (Continuum Press). She may be contacted at ayoun@u.arizona.edu

Marion Blondel is Associate scientist, 2nd class (CR2) at the National Centre for Scientific Research (CNRS) and teaches linguistics at the University of Rouen. Her research focuses on Sign Languages and deafness. Her most recent publications deal with bilingual, bimodal acquisition (with Laurie Tuller as a co-author of an article entitled "Pointing in bimodal bilingual acquisition: A longitudinal study of LSF-French bilingual child" to appear in the Volume Leading Research in Sign Language: Selected Papers from TISLR 2004, edited by J. Quer and published by Signum Verlag) and poetic register addressed at children (with Christopher Miller and Anne-Marie Parisot, "TORTOISE, HARE, CHILDREN: Evaluation and narrative genre in LSQ", to appear in the Volume12 of the collection Sociolinguistics in Deaf Communities, edited by Ceil

Lucas, at the Gallaudet Univ. Press.) She may be contacted at marion.blondel@univ-rouen.fr

Stephen J. Caldas is Professor of Educational Leadership and Foundations at the University of Louisiana at Lafayette. He has co-authored three books on desegregation, and has just published a fourth on bilingualism entitled *Rearing Bilingual-Biliterate Children in Monolingual Cultures* (Multilingual Matters, 2006). His research interests include psycholinguistics, socio-psychometrics, race, and the socio/political contexts of education. He may be contacted at caldas@louisiana.edu

Richard Clément is Professor of Psychology at the University of Ottawa, Canada. His current research interests include issues related to bilingualism, second language acquisition and identity change in the acculturative process. He is particularly interested in the role of inter-ethnic communication in the social and psychological adjustment of minority group members and immigrants. Recent illustrative work include Gaudet, S., Clément, R., & Deuzeman, K. (2005), Daily hassles, ethnic identity and psychological well-being among Lebanese-Canadians in the *International Journal of Psychology*; and Clément, R., Baker, S. C., Josephson, G., & Noels, K. A. (2005), Media effects on ethnic identity among linguistic majorities and minorities: A longitudinal study of a bilingual setting in *Human Communication Research*. In 2001, he was awarded the Otto Klineberg Intercultural & International Relations Prize by the Society for the Psychological Study of Social Issues; in 2002, he received the Robert C. Gardner Award from the International Association of Language & Social Psychology for his work on second language acquisition; and in 2004 he was elected Fellow of the American Psychological Association. He may be contacted at rclement@uottawa.ca

Jean-Marc Dewaele is Reader in French and Applied Linguistics at Birkbeck, University of London. He published on various aspects of second language production and edited – with Li Wei and Alex Housen – in 2002, the book *Opportunities and Challenges of Bilingualism* (Mouton De Gruyter) and, in 2003, the book *Bilingualism: Basic Principles and Beyond* (Multilingual Matters). He edited *Focus on French as a Foreign Language* in 2005 (Multilingual Matters). His current research interests include the acquisition of sociolinguistic and sociopragmatic competence in a second language. He co-edited – with Raymond Mougeon – a special issue on this topic in *AILE* (2002) and a special issue in the *International Review of Applied Linguistics* (2004). A second complementary research interest is multilingualism and emotions in a variety of contexts. He guest-edited two special issues on this topic with Aneta Pavlenko in *Estudios de Sociolinguistica* (2004) and in the *Journal of Multilingual and Multicultural Development* (2004). He may be contacted at j.dewaele@bbk.ac.uk

Laurent Dekydtspotter is Associate Professor of French Linguistics and Second Language Studies at Indiana University in Bloomington, Indiana. His research addresses how semantic knowledge develops and what such development tells us about second language grammars and parsers. In the case of grammars, he is interested in the manner in which structures not licensed in the learner's native language are interpreted by second language learners. In the case of parsers, he is interested in how second language learners assign interpretations to ambiguous target language sentences. Recent publications include journal articles: Dekydtspotter, L. & Hathorn, J. (2005), Quelque chose (…) de remarquable in English-French Acquisition: Mandatory, Informationally Encapsulated Computations in Second Language Interpretation. *Second Language Research, 21*, 291–323; Dekydtspotter, L. & Outcalt, S. (2005), A syntactic bias in scope ambiguity resolution in the processing of English-French cardinality interrogatives: Evidence for informational encapsulation. *Language Learning, 1*, 1–37; and a volume co-edited with Rex A. Sprouse and Audrey Liljestrand (2005), Proceedings of Generative Approaches to Second Language Acquisition 7, Somerville, MA: Cascadilla Press. He may be contacted at ldekydts@indiana.edu

S. J. Hannahs is Senior Lecturer in Linguistics at the University of Newcastle upon Tyne. Along with interests in the acquisition of phonological structure, his primary research focus has been on theoretical phonology, morphology and morphophonology. Among his publications are *Focus on Phonological Acquisition* (John Benjamins, 1997), a volume co-edited with Martha Young-Scholten, and a highly successful introductory textbook, *Introducing Phonetics & Phonology* (Arnold/OUP, 2005 2nd ed.), co-written with Mike Davenport. In addition to French, he has long-standing interests in Celtic and Germanic linguistics. He may be contacted at s.j.hannahs@ncl.ac.uk

Julia Herschensohn is Professor and Chair of the Linguistics Department at the University of Washington in Seattle. Her research focuses on second language acquisition of French from a generative perspective, age effects in first and second language acquisition, and issues of theoretical syntax, especially in the Romance languages. Her publications include a co-edited volume with Enrique Mallen and Karen Zagona, Features and Interfaces in Romance published by John Benjamins in 2001; and Language Development and Age to be shortly published by Cambridge University Press. Recent articles include 2005, Children's acquisition of L2 Spanish morphosyntax in an immersion setting (co-authored with Jeff Stevenson and Jeremy Waltmunson), International Review of Applied Linguistics; 2004, Inflection, thematic roles and abstract Case, Bilingualism: Language and cognition. She may be contacted at herschen@u.washington.edu

Greg Lessard is Professor in the Department of French Studies at Queen's University (Canada). His research focuses on computational modelling of second language acquisition, natural language generation, and humanities computing. With Michael Levison, he has developed the VINCI natural language generation environment and has applied it to a variety of domains including error analysis, generation of narratives, modelling and testing of second language word formation, and modelling of linguistic humor (in English). Publications of the VINCI Project may be found at www.cs.queensu.ca/CompLing/. He may be contacted at lessardg@post.queensu.ca

Michael Levison is an Emeritus Professor in the School of Computing at Queen's University (Canada). Since 1958, he has conducted research in the application of computers to problems in linguistics and in literary studies, some areas of which he helped to pioneer. In his early days, he worked on the resolution of authorship problems. Since 1986, he has been engaged with Greg Lessard in natural language modelling and generation, developing with him the Vinci generation system. He may be contacted at levison@cs.queensu.ca

Anthony Lodge is Professor of French Language and Linguistics in the School of Modern Languages, University of St. Andrews, UK. He has long played a leading role in the Association for French Language Studies, and in the publication of its Journal of the same name. His research focuses on socio-historical linguistics with particular reference to Gallo-Romance. His best-known book is *French: from Dialect to Standard*, published by Routledge in 1993 (published in French as '*Le français, histoire d'un dialecte devenu langue*', Fayard, 1997), and this has been followed recently by *A Sociolinguistic History of Parisian French*, Cambridge University Press, 2004. Between these works he co-authored an introduction to French linguistics entitled *Exploring the French Language*, Arnold, 1997 and an edition of *The Earliest Branches of the Roman de Renart*, Peeters, 2001. November 2006 will see the publication by the Ecole Nationale des Chartes of the first of three volumes editing the Occitan account-books of the consuls of Montferrand (Puy-de-Dôme). He may be contacted at ral1@st-and.ac.uk

Peter MacIntyre is Professor of Psychology at Cape Breton University, in Sydney, Nova Scotia, Canada. His research focuses on psychological processes that underlie second language acquisition and communication. His publications include articles on willingness to communicate, language learning motivation, language anxiety, and personality processes in second language learning. Outside the language area, Peter has conducted research into public speaking anxiety and volunteerism. He has received awards from the Modern Language Association, the International Association for Language and Social Psychology, the Canadian Psychological Association, and others. He may be contacted at peter_macintyre@capebretonu.ca

Patrick-André Mather is Associate Professor of French and Linguistics in the Department of Foreign Languages at the Universidad de Puerto Rico (Río Piedras). His research focuses on the relationship between second language acquisition and creole genesis. His most recent articles include "Second language acquisition and creolization: Same (I) processes, different (E-) results", to appear in the Journal of Pidgin and Creole Languages, "Noun phrases in L2 French and Haitian: Clues on the origin of plantation creoles", which appeared in 2005 in the Journal of Universal Language, and "Bilingualism in Canada: Sociolinguistic aspects", published in the volume "Lenguas en contacto", edited by Lourdes Suarez (San Juan: Publicaciones Gaviota, 2005). He may be contacted at pa_mather@yahoo.fr

Florence Myles is Professor of French Linguistics in the School of Modern Languages at the University of Newcastle upon Tyne in the UK. Her research is in second language acquisition, especially of French. She is particularly interested in theories of language learning and their empirical implications, and in the interface between linguistic theory and cognitive approaches to the learning of second languages. She is well known for her co-authored best selling book on *Second Language Learning Theories*, and her work on the construction of a web-based database of French Learner Language Oral Corpora (www.flloc.soton.ac.uk), and the application of software tools to the analysis of these corpora. She is President of the AFLS (Association for French Language Studies), and she is Editor of the *Journal of French Language Studies*. She may be contacted at Florence.Myles@newcastle.ac.uk

Nathalie Niederberger is a Resource Specialist at the *Lycée Français La Pérouse* in San Francisco. Her clinical work focuses on language development and literacy of school-aged children in multilingual settings. Her research interests include typical and atypical literacy acquisition, language development of deaf children, crosslinguistic comparison of sign language development and language assessment. Among her recent publications are a chapter on deaf bilingualism and language therapy, entitled "Rééducation de l'enfant sourd profond: Bilinguisme" in *Précis d'Audiophonologie et de Déglutition*, edited by P. Dulguerov and M. Remacle and published by Editions Solal in 2005; and a contribution to the *Proceedings of the 29th Boston University Conference on Language Development*, in collaboration with U. H. Frauenfelder, entitled "Linguistic proficiency of the deaf bilingual child in French Sign Language and Written French: What is the relation between the two?", edited by A. Brugos, M. R. Clark-Cotton, & S. Ha, and published in 2005 by Cascadilla Press. She also adapted with collaborators a language test from American Sign Language into French Sign Language (TELSF) that is now used in all the schools for the deaf in the French-speaking part of Switzerland. She may be contacted at nniederberger@hotmail.com

Kimberley A. Noels is Associate Professor in the Social and Cultural Psychology area of the Department of Psychology at the University of Alberta, Canada. Her research concerns the social psychology of language and communication processes, with a focus on intercultural communication. Her publications include articles on motivation for language learning, the role of communication in the process of cross-cultural adaptation, and inter-generational communication from a cross-cultural perspective. Her research has been recognized through awards from the Modern Language Association, the International Association of Language and Social Psychology, and the Society for the Psychological Study of Social Issues. She may be contacted at knoels@ualberta.ca

Remi Sonaiya is Professor of French Language and Applied Linguistics in the Department of Foreign Languages of the Obafemi Awolowo University, Ile-Ife, Nigeria. Her research in applied linguistics started with a focus on issues relating to the lexicon. Since her doctoral dissertation – *The Lexicon in Second Language Acquisition: A Lexical Approach to Error Analysis*, Cornell University, 1988 – she has moved on to examine broader issues in language teaching and learning: The role of foreign languages in education, the appropriateness of teaching methods for particular cultural contexts, language and identity, language and development. She co-authored (with Yemi

Mojola and Tundonu Amosu) *Je démarre! Méthode de français pour débutants* (1997) and *J'Avance! Méthode de français, niveau II* (1999), the first French language teaching method written by Nigerians. She has also conducted research in the area of general linguistics, primarily on Yoruba, her mother tongue, and has published several articles with Walter Bisang of the Johannes Gutenberg University, Mainz, Germany. She may be contacted at remisonaiya@yahoo.com

Rex A. Sprouse is Professor of Germanic Studies and Second Language Studies at Indiana University. He is best known in second language studies for proposing (together with Bonnie D. Schwartz, University of Hawaii) the Full Transfer/Full Access hypothesis and for pioneering (together with Laurent Dekydtspotter, Indiana University) research on the syntax-semantics interface in English-French Interlanguage. His current research explores the hypothesis that the Language Instinct becomes 'blunted' over the course of the life span in its ability to (re-)formulate target-appropriate lexical entries, even though the fundamental architectures of grammars and processing mechanisms remain intact. Professor Sprouse's research also extends to structure and history of the languages of Western Europe (Germanic, Romance, Celtic), syntactic theory, and language contact. For further information, visit his Indiana University Department of Second Language Studies webpage at http://www.indiana.edu/~dsls/faculty/sprouse.shtml

Robert Train is Assistant Professor of Spanish in the Department of Modern Languages and Literatures and Director of the Language and Culture Learning Center at Sonoma State University. He is formerly a teacher of French in a public high school near Oakland and at the University of California, Berkeley, where he received his Ph.D. in Romance Philology. He has published and lectured on the intersection of ideologies of language and language teaching, particularly the standardization of French and Spanish and its implications for foreign language pedagogy. His research is interdisciplinary and socially engaged as it brings together insights from sociolinguistics, applied linguistics, historiography of the language, education, postmodern theory, and anthropology to consider the contours and consequences of ideologies in the lives of speakers within and beyond the classroom. Recently, he contributed a chapter ("A Critical Look at Technologies and Ideologies in Internet-Mediated Intercultural Foreign Language Education") to the AAUSC Issues in Language Program Direction volume entitled *Computer-mediated Intercultural Foreign Language Education*, edited by J. A. Belz & S. L. Thorne, and published by Heinle. He may be contacted at robert.train@sonoma.edu

Laurie Tuller is Professor of Linguistics and director of the research team "Langage & handicap", at François Rabelais University in Tours. Her current research concentrates on atypical language acquisition, and how it informs syntactic theory. Recent publications report on studies about mild-to-moderate deafness and SLI ("Développement de la morphosyntaxe du français chez des enfants sourds moyens" in *Le langage et l'homme*, with Celia Jakubowicz) and about the effects epilepsy may have on language acquisition (with C. Monjauze, C. Hommet, M.-A. Barthez, A. Khomsi) "Language in Benign Childhood Epilepsy with Centro-Temporal Spikes" *Brain and Language*. She has also collaborated with Marion Blondel in a study of the acquisition of French Sign Language ("Pointing in bimodal, bilingual acquisition: A longitudinal study of a LSF-French bilingual child". In *Leading Research in Sign Language: Selected Papers from TISLR 2004*, J. Quer (Ed.). Seedorf, Germany: Signum Verlag). She may be contacted at tuller@univ-tours.fr

PART I

Introduction

CHAPTER 1

The past, present and future of French in applied linguistics

Dalila Ayoun
University of Arizona

Résumé

Ce chapitre retrace brièvement l'histoire du français en linguistique appliquée en énumérant quelques personnes et dates marquantes comme celle de la création de AILA en 1963. La linguistique appliquée est définie comme un domaine de recherche inter-disciplinaire portant sur des questions concrètes liées à la langue et à la communication. Ses deux domaines de recherche principaux ont été la didactique et l'appropriation d'une langue étrangère/seconde mais se sont étendus à de nombreux autres sujets. Ce chapitre résume également les principaux résultats et propositions de sujets de recherche présentés dans les chapitres de la deuxième et troisième parties.

Abstract

This chapter briefly retraces the history of French in applied linguistics through key pioneer figures and significant dates such as the foundation of AILA in 1963. Applied linguistics is broadly defined as an inter-disciplinary field of research concerned with practical issues related to language and communication. Although its two main areas of research have been language education and foreign/ second language acquisition, it covers a much wider range of linguistic issues. This chapter also summarizes the main findings and directions for future research presented in the chapters that comprise Part II and III.

1. Introduction

The objective of this introductory chapter is threefold: First, to present a brief historical overview of French in applied linguistics by mentioning a few key pioneering figures who contributed to the emergence of French in various fields of applied linguistics; second, to summarize the findings of the present volume; and third, to suggest new areas of research for French in applied linguistics that would inform the discipline at large.

As illustrated by the various chapters in the present volume, applied linguistics can be broadly defined as an interdisciplinary field of research concerned primarily with practical issues of language in the community. Applied linguistics focuses on concrete problems related to language and communication, and its two main areas of research have traditionally been language education and second/foreign language (L2) acquisition. In addition, one may cite language policy and planning, the preservation and revival of endangered languages, issues in institutional and cross-cultural communication, literacy, language disorders, language variation, language conflict and discrimination, among various others. Recent large edited collections (Davies & Elder 2004; Grabe 2000; Kaplan 2002; Schmitt 2002) are a good illustration of the wide range of linguistic issues that may fall under the label of applied linguistics. This volume focuses on the second main area of research mentioned above – second/foreign language acquisition – firmly grounded in theoretical frameworks. Thus, as mentioned in the preface, following the second introductory chapter that reviews the history of the French language from a sociolinguistic perspective, the six chapters of the first part cover the core aspects of the second language acquisition of French – phonology, semantics/syntax, syntax/morphology, pragmatics, sociolinguistics, and grammatical gender. The seven chapters that compose the second part of the volume stress the contribution of the French language in a variety of subfields of applied linguistics such as language ideology and foreign language pedagogy, corpus linguistics, and French Sign Language. A chapter also explores the role of affective variables, attitude and personality on language learning, while another investigates how computational approaches may facilitate lexical creativity. The chapters on creole studies and applied linguistics in West Africa both address issues in first and second language acquisition in complex sociolinguistic and political contexts. Finally, the epilogue illustrates the past, present and future of French in Louisiana, a region rich in linguistic history.

AILA, the *Association Internationale de Linguistique Appliquée* or 'International Association of Applied Linguistics', which boasts a membership of more than 8, 000 individuals worldwide across thirty national associations grouping researchers, policy makers and practitioners (AILA website, http://www.aila.info), may be the most visible symbol of French in applied linguistics. As Valdman (2004) relates, AILA was founded in France in 1963 thanks to two French linguists, A. Culioli and G. Capelle, the latter being also the director of the BEL (*Bureau d'étude et de liaison*), created in 1959 for the teaching of French worldwide. According to Valdman (1978), the date of the conference at the *Université de Montréal* (UQAM) was a milestone for AILA as it held its first conference across the Atlantic (the first congress took place in Annecy, France, in 1964); more importantly, it also marked the beginning of the expansion of applied linguistics from the field of pedagogy into foreign/second language learning. Incidentally, the largest association of applied linguistics, the American Association of Applied Linguistics (AAAL), was also created following the 1978 AILA Conference.

AILA was preceded by another French association, the *Association française de linguistique appliquée* (French Association of Applied Linguistics) (AFLA), created in 1962, whose goal is to "promote and coordinate research in all fields of applied linguistics, as well as encourage interdisciplinary and international cooperation in these fields" (http://afla.linguist.jussieu.fr/afla_def.htm) [translation mine]. AFLA is an excellent illustration of the wide variety of fields subsumed under the label of applied linguistics: "(First) language acquisition, contrastive analysis, speech analysis and production, foreign language teaching, languages in contact and linguistic variation based on geographic, social and professional contexts, regional languages and national language, lexicology and lexicography, language planning and linguistic policy, translation, natural language generation, and so on".[1]

Unfortunately, there are no longer any French representatives on AILA's Executive Board or on its International Commission. Moreoever, French is no longer the official working language of AILA (its website is in English, and the use of local languages is encouraged at its annual World Congress, to reflect its global character).

The goal of another international association, the Association for French Language Studies (AFLS), is also to "promot[e] French language teaching and research into French linguistics in higher education" (http://www.afls.net); it organizes a yearly conference in the UK or in a francophone country, as well as workshops in practical and theoretical issues.

There are now several journals with a particular focus on French such as the *Journal of French Language Studies* (published by AFLS), *Journal International de Langue et de Linguistique Françaises, French Review, Langue Française, Langue et Langages, Lingvisticæ Investigationes, Revue Canadienne de Linguistique Appliquée, Apprentissage des Langues et Systèmes d'Information et de Communication* and *Acquisition et Interaction en Langue Etrangère*. In addition, AILA has a yearly journal, the *AILA Review*, as well as a book series , the AILA Applied Linguistics Series (AALS), published by John Benjamins.

Four recent publications (reviewed in Herschensohn 2006) illustrate the breadth of the research focusing on French from a variety of applied perspectives: Two edited volumes – Dewaele (2005b) and Prévost and Paradis (2004) – and two special issues of journals – Mougeon and Dewaele (2004), a special issue of the *International Review of Applied Linguistics*, and Myles and Towell (2004), a special issue of the *Journal of French Language Studies*.

Finally, the *Handbook of French Semantics* (Corbin & Swart 2004) takes a formal approach to semantics and its interface with syntax and pragmatics. Although it is mainly aimed at French and Romance linguists who are interested in formal semantics and cross-linguistic semantics, it is also undoubtedly of interest to applied linguists.

---

1.   Other important associations for French in applied linguistics are: ACELF (*Association canadienne d'éducation de langue française*) at http://www.acelf.ca/index.php; ALSIC (*Apprentissage des langues et systèmes d'information et de communication*) at http://alsic.u-strasbg.fr/; *Association française de linguistique appliquée* at http://afla.linguist.jussieu.fr/; *Association québécoise des enseignants de français langue seconde* at http://www.aqefls.org/; and *Associations de français langue étrangère* (FLE-ASSO) at http://fleasso.club.fr/index.htm.

2. Historical overview: A few key figures

Long before the term 'psycholinguistics' was coined in the 1940s, and was used for the first time in Osgood and Sebeok's (1954) *Psycholinguistics: A Survey of Theory and Research Problems*, scholars were doing work that would now fall within the purview of applied linguistics.

2.1 Sign language: Abbé de l'Epée

Abbot Charles-Michel l'Epée founded the first school for the deaf in France in 1760 with an innovative pedagogical approach that rapidly spread across Europe. He was the first to use FSL to teach French to deaf students (see Tuller, Blondel, & Niederberger, this volume). Later on, Thomas Gallaudet, founder of the American School for the Deaf in Hartford, Connecticut, introduced French Sign Language in the United States in 1816, and modern American Sign Language still uses some signs brought from France in the early 19th century. As Tuller et al. demonstrate, current research in French Sign Language offers the possibility to explore various questions in first and second language acquisition, as well as bilingual and bimodal language development.

2.2 Louis Braille

The Braille writing system was created in 1824 by Louis Braille (1809–1852), a French inventor who became blind from an early childhood accident. Each character in Braille is made up of an arrangement of one to six raised points used in 63 possible combinations. A universal Braille code for English-speaking countries was adopted in 1932. Braille has been adapted to almost every major language world-wide, and it is the primary system of written communication for visually impaired individuals. There is a wealth of research investigating reading and comprehension processes of Braille users suggesting they process tactile language in real time, and as rapidly as they process spoken language input (e.g., Bertelson & Mousty 1991).

2.3 Paul Pierre Broca (1824–1880) and Henry Hécaen

Paul Broca was the French physician (as well as anatomist and anthropologist) who discovered that an important speech production center of the brain is located in the left frontal lobes (subsequently named the Broca's area, although another French neurologist, Marc Dax, had made similar observations a decade or so earlier) by studying the brains of aphasic patients in the Bicêtre Hospital. It was Henry Hécaen, a French neurologist, who first used the term *neurolinguistique* in a publication in 1968, and who was instrumental in founding and developing neuropsychology as a science (Paradis 2004).

2.4 Ferdinand de Saussure (1857–1913)

Although Ferdinand de Saussure was Swiss, not French, he greatly influenced structuralist French linguists such as Emile Benveniste (1902–1976), Antoine Meillet (1866–1936), and André Martinet (1908–1999), among others. His 1916 *Cours de Linguistique Générale* ('Course in General Linguistics'), based on lecture notes and published posthumously by Charles Bally and Albert Sechehaye, was one of the seminal works of the 20th century. His *langue/parole* distinction became the Chomskyan competence/performance distinction in modern linguistics.

2.5 Gustave Guillaume (1883–1960)

Guillaume was first discovered in 1909 by Antoine Meillet who took him under his wing. His first major work, *Le problème de l'article* in 1919, is an introduction to an almost phenomenologic approach to language that sets him apart from de Saussure, whose ideas he developed: The *langue/parole* distinction is broadened to a *langue/discours* distinction (also known as a distinction between *langue/puissance* or *discours/effect*). *Psychomécanique* describes the language act of going from *langue* to *discours*, whereas *psychosystématique* is the study of *langue*. The numerous notes he left have been edited by the *Fonds Gustave Guillaume* at Laval University, and his theoretical work still inspires numerous scholars (e.g., Soutet 2002; Wilmet 1997).

2.6 Pioneers in bilingualism research

It was the French psychologist J. Ronjat who carried out the first bilingual first language acquisition study on his son Louis who was raised in French (Ronjat's native language) and German (the native language of the mother and the nanny), initiating a long European tradition of carefully documented accounts of early bilingualism. Another seminal detailed study of early bilingual development was reported in Leopold (1939–1949), with two daughters raised in a German-English environment. It was preceded by Grégoire (1937–1939) who also published a lengthy account of the bilingual development of his two children in French and Walloon. These early studies on bilingualism as the acquisition of two languages within the course of primary language development were soon followed by studies in foreign language learning or acquisition (e.g., Markman, Spilka, & Tucker 1975; Tucker, Lambert, & Rigault 1969, 1977), and of course French immersion studies (e.g., Bruck, Jakimik, & Tucker 1971).

3.   The current state of French in applied Linguistics

This section examines the current state of the research of French in applied linguistics as represented by the chapters in this volume: The second/foreign language acquisition of French firmly grounded in theoretical frameworks.

3.1   Core second language acquisition

Core second language acquisition is understood to include the acquisition of syntax, morphology, semantics, and phonology. However, as the headings for some of the chapters in this volume indicate, and as the modular approach in linguistic theory presupposes, speakers' competence of a language consists of their knowledge of the various core components of a language and their interfaces (i.e., the interface between morpho-syntactic and semantic-pragmatic components; the interface between morpho-syntactic and phonological-phonetic components). Thus, these core components, or modules, cannot be investigated in isolation, they must be investigated together, and it is more accurate to refer to the second language acquisition of syntax/morphology, or syntax/semantics, as well as phonology/morphology. The acquisition of the lexicon permeates all other subcomponents of a language.

3.1.1   *Phonological (morphological, lexical, syntactic) knowledge*
Hannahs (this volume) clearly shows how the acquisition of phonological rules closely interacts with the acquisition of syntax and morphology (in addition to lexical items) because phonological rules must be applied in the appropriate morpho-lexical-syntactic context. For instance, obligatory liaison is constrained by syntactic factors, while optional liaison is governed by stylistic factors, allowing for register variation.

The unitary phonological system of French, which of course also displays varieties due to superficial phonetic changes, is a complex and difficult system to acquire for English-speaking instructed learners. Its phonetic inventory exhibits several consonants and (oral and nasal) monophthongs which are absent from the standard English phonetic inventory, such as the high- and mid-high front rounded vowels in *lu* 'read' and *vœu* 'wish' (e.g., Levy 2004). However, it appears that even late learners can acquire native-like pronunciation (Birdsong in press). Moreover, Hannahs' critical review of the empirical literature shows that L2 French learners are able to acquire syllable structures (Beaudoin 1998; Steele 2001), liaison patterns (Mastromonaco 1999), particularly learners in immersion settings who benefit from a richer input (Thomas 2004). In spite of its importance for French phonology, variable schwa has not been directly investigated in L2 empirical studies.

3.1.2   *Syntactic-semantic knowledge*
Assuming that L2 learners construct a syntactic-semantic interface in order to pair forms with meaning, Dekydtspotter, Anderson and Sprouse (this volume) focus on idiosyncratic interpretations of various word orders in the nominal domain (e.g., *de/par*, pre- and postposed adjectives, interrogative *combien*, quantifier *beaucoup*). Once the relevant morpho-syntactic parameters are set to the appropriate L2 values, if learners are guided by Universal Grammar, they should acquire the range of subtle interpretations associated with various word orders, even if they are not taught in instructional settings. Findings indicate that English native speakers who are acquiring French in university instructional settings demonstrate knowledge of the semantic distinction

between prenominal and postnominal adjectives (e.g., *la lourde valise* vs. *la valise lourde* 'the heavy suitcase') for instance (Anderson 2002, in press a). These findings are important because they show that L2 learners go beyond basic word order patterns, and acquire subtle distinctions which are far from being obvious from the input, and which may not even be taught in foreign language classrooms. In other words, they arrive at an intuitive knowledge of the target language.

3.1.3 *Morpho-syntactic knowledge*

The term 'morpho-syntax' shows that current theoretical frameworks posit a very close relationship between these two core components of a language. Thus, the Minimalist framework (Chomsky 1995) espoused in Herschensohn (this volume) and Ayoun (this volume) posits that inflectional categories account for a variety of phenomena which are both syntactic and morphological such as tense and aspect, verb raising (yielding appropriate verb, negation, quantifier and adverb placement), and gender agreement, among others. Herschensohn focuses on the acquisition of morpho-syntactic parameters (verb raising, noun raising) with the case study of Chloé, an advanced English-speaking L2 French learner, while Ayoun investigates the acquisition of grammatical gender and agreement by English-speaking instructed learners of L2 French. In Herschensohn (this volume), the data collected during three interviews indicate that Chloé's production is almost error-free regarding verb inflection, verb raising, gender, number and adjective placement in noun phrases. Herschensohn concludes that the syntactic phenomena of verb raising, use of determiners and noun raising are mastered before the morphological phenomena of tense, person verbal agreement and number, as well as gender agreement. As in Ayoun (this volume), the residual problem in gender agreement are attributed to performance mishaps, following the Missing Surface Inflection Hypothesis, and contra the Failed Functional Features Hypothesis.

In Ayoun (this volume) – a cross-sectional study with English-speaking L2 instructed learners (n = 35) at three different levels of proficiency – the results of two elicitation tasks indicate that the participants have successfully reset the gender-marking parameter, in that they have acquired the [±masc] gender feature in nominal phrases. Their accuracy in producing determiner/noun agreement and noun/adjective agreement increases with their level of proficiency, as did their ability in detecting conflictual gender assignment. The inconsistencies in making appropriate noun/adjective agreement are interpreted as a performance issue, not a syntactic deficiency.

3.1.4 *Pragmatic and sociolinguistic knowledge*

Dewaele (this volume) adheres to the definition of sociolinguistic competence as "the ability to perform various speech acts, the ability to manage conversational turns and topics, sensitivity to variation in register and politeness, and an understanding of how these aspects of language vary according to social roles and settings" (Ranney 1992:25), while stressing the need for an interdisciplinary approach to tackle the complex cognitive, psychological and social factors that underlie sociolinguistic variation. Acquiring sociolinguistic competence in L2 French implies the acquisition of phonological variants (e.g., schwa deletion, liaison, as also reviewed in Hannahs' chapter), morpho-syntactic variants (e.g., *ne* omission in informal spoken French, tense and aspect, variants in question formation, and lexical variants), and the mastery of pronouns of address (*tu* vs. *vous*, *nous* vs. *on*). Findings consistently show an over-use of formal variants by instructed learners who are not exposed to a rich enough L2 environment, along with the noticeably positive effect that exposure to native-speaker discourse has on both immersion and instructed learners. The acquisition of sociolinguistic competence in L2 French clearly requires greater socialization and interaction with native speakers that instructed learners lack.

The acquisition of sociolinguistic competence is closely tied to the acquisition of pragmatic competence defined as "knowledge of the linguistic resources available in a given language for realizing particular illocutions, knowledge of the sequential aspects of speech acts and finally, knowledge of the appropriate contextual use of the particular languages' linguistic resources" (Barron 2003:10), as cited in Warga (this volume). Warga focuses more precisely on interlanguage pragmatics defined as "the study of nonnative speakers' use and acquisition of L2 pragmatic knowledge" (Kasper & Rose 1999:81). For L2 French, this translates mostly into longitudinal acquisition studies of speech acts (e.g., apologies, complaints, requests, refusals). Discourse ability (e.g., opening and closing remarks of discourse, discourse markers) is another important part of pragmatic competence which is under-researched in L2 French. However, a few longitudinal studies found positive instructional effects on length of discourse (Liddicoat & Crozet 2001), and several aspects of pragmatic and sociolinguistic acquisition in immersion settings such as the distinction between *tu* and *vous*, polite closings and expressions (Lyster 1994). Positive effects on the acquisition of requests by Austrian learners were also found (Warga this volume), as well as a slight but limited improvement on compliments, greetings and leave-takings by American students in a study-abroad setting (Hoffman-Hicks 1999). A teacher-fronted classroom with limited opportunities for genuine interactions in the L2 is a serious drawback to the learning of important pragmatic aspects, even if a few aspects (e.g., discourse markers, gambits) can be taught successfully.

3.2 French in applied linguistics

Due to its unique situation in several respects, French lends itself to three broad types of studies in foreign/second language acquisition and applied linguistics in the broad sense of the term: (a) Immersion studies in Canada and in Louisiana;[2] (b) French as

---

2. Unfortunately, we were not able to include a chapter on French immersion studies in Canada in the present volume. However, empirical studies conducted in French immersion settings are reviewed in Chapters 8, 10 and 11, as well as in the epilogue. In addition to the studies cited in these chapters see Calvé (1991), Cummins (2000), Lapkin, Swain and Smith (2002), Mougeon, Rehner and Nadasdi (2005), Netten and Germain (2004), Swain (2000), Swain and Lapkin (2005a, 2005b), among many

a second language in a naturalistic setting by working immigrants (e.g., Véronique & Stoffel 2003); (c) Creole studies throughout Africa (Sonaiya this volume), and the Carribbean (Chaudenson, Mufwene, & Pargman 2001; Mufwene 2005). French also finds itself at the intersection of various disciplines in applied linguistics as illustrated by the chapters under Part III of this volume.

3.2.1 *Language ideology and foreign language pedagogy*

Train (this volume) stresses the importance of examining language ideologies as a step toward a language pedagogical approach that addresses the political, sociocultural and ethical dimensions of language practice in the teaching and learning of French in global and intercultural contexts. The effects of a highly standardized French language and centralized educational system are also noted in Sonaiya (this volume) for the teaching of French in West Africa, as we will see below. The standard language is defined as a complex ideology of language and speaker identity, and its form is highly codified in the dictionaries, texts, prescriptive grammars and textbooks which make their way into the foreign language classroom. The ideology of language recognizes that language, identity and culture cannot be teased apart. Moreover, the attitudes and practices that represent French language ideology are closely tied to the ideologies of learning, teaching, identity and culture within a given community. The standard language ideology also plays an important role in what foreign language instructors view as important for their students to be exposed to and to learn. There are clear notions as to which pedagogical practices are appropriate or not. Train also proposes the notion of Pedagogic Hyperstandard (Train 2000) to investigate the various sociocultural, sociolinguistic and pedagogical attitudes toward language, culture and speaker identity, among others, in foreign language pedagogy that have been built around the ideological process of standardization.

3.2.2 *Affective variables, attitude and personality*

MacIntyre, Clement and Noels (this volume) tackle and review the literature surrounding four main themes: (1) The conceptualization of motivation and its impact on language learning; (2) The effect of social context on instructed language learning; (3) The major non-linguistic outcomes of language instruction; and (4) The role that the personality of the learner may play in language learning. Their review of the literature on models of motivation (e.g., Gardner's socio-educational model of L2 acquisition), which has played a central part in L2 acquisition research, stresses the importance of psychological processes to L2 acquisition. A variety of complex social and contextual factors come into play in shaping the psychology of the language learner be it in instructed settings, or in immersion settings in Canada. As we un-

---

others. For studies comparing the effects of contexts of learning on the L2 acquisition of French see Collentine and Freed (2004), as well as Freed, Segalowitz and Dewey (2004).

derstand them better, we can modify our pedagogical approaches to facilitate the L2 acquisition process.

They then present a new empirical study that investigates the link between personality (introverts vs. extroverts), oral communication, and French vocabulary acquisition by high-school students enrolled in grade 10, 11, and 12 core French (as an L2) courses in Nova Scotia, Canada. The findings indicate that introverts tend to obtain higher vocabulary test scores than extroverts when studying in very familiar situations, but the reverse trend was observed for somewhat familiar situations, while there was no difference in unfamiliar situations. In other words, extraversion does not appear to be a reliable predictor for vocabulary learning in different situations unless we also account for important features of those situations to better predict how extraversion will operate.

3.2.3 *Natural language and lexical creativity*

There is evidence that the typical L2 language learner tends to display a low level of lexical creativity (i.e., the use of derivationally and compositionally complex words) in spite of the fact that at least some authentic pedagogical materials contain relatively high proportions of such morphologically complex words. As part of their analysis of the problem, Lessard and Levison begin by reviewing the various word formation processes in French, and the semantic aspects of word formation, as well as the empirical literature on L2 vocabulary learning. They conclude, as have others, that there is a lack of studies focusing on lexical learning strategies beyond the beginning stages. In other words, relatively little is known about how L2 learners go about acquiring and using morphologically complex vocabulary and lexical creativity.

In addition, there is little corpus data on L2 French lexical creativity, but existing work (e.g., Broeder, Extra, van Hout, & Voionnaa 1993; Lessard, Levison, Maher, & Tomek 1994) found little evidence of lexical innovations by adult instructed learners. Analysis of additional written and oral corpus data (e.g., oral data from the Reading Corpus which is part of the FFLOC project, Myles, this volume, and their own written corpus materials) leads Lessard and Levison to conclude that the L2 learners studied show a lower incidence of use of derivationally complex forms than do native speakers. Lessard and Levison suggest that this finding may be partially explained by the lack of detailed information on word formation in traditional textbooks, and by the absence of appropriate pedagogical approaches, and they contend that the use of teaching software, as exemplified by VINCI, a natural language environment that generates and analyzes complex lexical forms, would assist in the teaching and learning of the some aspects of word formation, leading to greater lexical creativity and diversity in the interlanguage of instructed L2 French learners.

3.2.4 *Electronic corpora in SLA research*

Myles introduces the use of electronic corpora in SLA research, and related computational approaches, before reviewing the existing scant literature in SLA corpora, and proposing how electronic corpora may be used to enhance, inform, and address standing research questions in first and second language acquisition. Corpus linguistics analyzes large corpora of written and oral data from natural occurrences. It has a variety of uses from linguistic analyses of specific phenomena, to pedagogical methodologies that aim at providing the learner with authentic data in a guided environment. The French Learner Language Oral Corpora (FFLOC) is presented as a case study to illustrate the research possibilities that computerized methodologies offer in the context of L2 French acquisition. Myles first explains how the CHILDES system (with its three components and various tools) is used to organize, transcribe, tag, and codify the data, making them more easily accessible for analysis. For example, longitudinal written and oral data can be used to investigate a number of the research questions addressed in the various chapters of this volume: Morpho-syntactic, lexical, semantic development in the L2 instructed learner, the acquisition of subtle distinctions in tense and aspect, or grammatical gender.

3.2.5 *French Sign Language*
The chapter by Tuller, Blondel and Niederberger focuses on an often overlooked, and yet fascinating, area of applied linguistics: The simultaneous acquisition of French Sign Language and French, and how it may inform research questions in language acquisition in general. LSF (*Langue des signes française*, or French Sign Language) is the natural language of deaf communities in France, as well as in French-speaking Switzerland and Belgium. LSF is a natural language not only in its structure, but also in the way it emerged, evolves, and in the way it is acquired, produced and processed mentally. In other words, it is a product of the human faculty for language. After an historical overview of LSF, Tuller et al. present a review of the literature on sign language acquisition (e.g., phonological, lexical, morpho-syntactic development) which shows that it is remarkably similar to oral language acquisition. However, it appears that monolingual acquisition of sign language is much less frequent than bimodal and bilingual language acquisition by both deaf and hearing children. Tuller et al. focus on the case study of a hearing child born to deaf parents, who has acquired both LSF and spoken French in a natural environment. Tuller et al. conclude that the simultaneous language development of both languages resembles the language development of each language individually in its natural context. However, it appears that the bilingual acquisition of a signed language and a spoken language is not identical to the bilingual acquisition of two signed languages, or of two spoken languages. Deaf children are rarely exposed to sign language as early as hearing children are exposed to a spoken language, but even very young children take advantage of the bimodality between the two languages, and code-switch between the two. They appear to follow the same milestones, although deaf children who typically live in a predominantly hearing environment do not benefit from the same rich input that hearing children do. This unusual situation allows researchers to explore various questions related to bilingual and bimodal language development.

3.2.6 *Applied linguistics in West Africa*

As a language introduced in (West) Africa by colonizers, French has a heavy burden to carry on many socio-cultural and historico-political levels that deeply affect its linguistic history as well. French is in the unusual situation of being the official language and the language of instruction in a rich multi-lingual and multi-cultural environment where local, native languages are still too rarely taught. Sonaiya (this volume) explains how the intellectual elite educated in a literally foreign language has feelings of alienation to various degrees. A brief historical overview of how European languages and practices of applied linguistics were introduced in West Africa as early as the 15th century by the first Portuguese explorers shows a negativity that persists to this day, and yet multilingualism has always been characteristic of an entire continent where a variety of initially foreign languages were used and incorporated to various degrees. Thus, although standard French is restricted to the educated elite, most of the population in *Côte d'Ivoire* speaks some form of French to some degree; moreover, illiteracy has lead to the spread of a Popular French (also referred to as Nouchi, but with some distinct features) and Dyula, two *lingua francae*. From a pedagogical perspective, persistent problems are due to inappropriate textbooks and instructors whose proficiency in French is not always as good as it should be.

3.2.7 *Creole studies*

The arrival of European explorers in Africa and the Carribean created another fertile ground from an applied linguistics perspective: It is a fascinating window into the first and second language acquisition processes, sudden language change, the creation of a language by adults, a pidgin that then becomes creolized when it is acquired as a native language by children. One group of French-lexifier creoles, also known as *créole antillais*, spoken in Guadeloupe, Martinique, Dominica, St Lucia and French Guyana are largely mutually intelligible, while another group, known as *Isle de France* creoles, are spoken on islands in the Indian Ocean.

Mather (this volume) summarizes the three main competing theories of creole genesis (i.e., the substratist, superstratist and universalist theories), and argues in favor of the SLA/Gradualist Model of Creole genesis, illustrating that there is much controversy about the origin, development and typological features that creole languages share.

The SLA/Gradualist Model contends that creole genesis is best described as a gradual process involving successive stages in the acquisition of L2 French (or L2 English) over several generations, but away from the lexifier language, contra the Bickertonian view of creole genesis as the creation of a new language by children using the impoverished input from their parents' pidgin.

4. Directions for future research

As outlined in the concluding section of each of the chapters in this volume, researchers in applied linguistics still have many unexplored areas to investigate, whether they are interested in core L2 acquisition of French, or in the many facets of French in applied linguistics in the broadest definition of the term. They are briefly summarized here.

4.1 Phonological knowledge

Hannahs outlines three areas for future research in the acquisition of phonological knowledge: (a) Syllabification and syllabicity: How do English-speaking L2 French learners adapt to the differences between English and French with respect to syllabic boundaries, and which segment types can be at the nucleus of a syllable? (b) Suprasegmental prosodic structure: How do L2 learners acquire appropriate initial consonantal clusters, as well as larger prosodic structures such as phonological words or phonological phrases? (c) Variable schwa: Investigating the phonological characteristics of the acquisition of variable schwa would complement the studies conducted on it from a sociolinguistic perspective. Is the acquisition of variable schwa related to the acquisition of other phonological phenomena such as syllable structures? Additional issues would include studies of VOT, stress and the stress system, liaison, elision, latent consonants, *h-aspiré*, and nasalization among others.

4.2 Syntactic-semantic knowledge

Dekydtspotter, Anderson and Sprouse point out that the developing semantic competence of learners at various stages of proficiency is clearly understudied, and constitutes a clear area for growth. Second, they highlight several ways in which future semantic research could significantly advance theorizing about second languages. Very little research has hitherto addressed the manner in which learners access the interpretations of ambiguous sentences as they encounter them, and what information they are able to use to access these interpretations in sentence processing. A few studies of French suggest a significant role for a syntactic reflex. Another potentially fruitful area of research addresses the relationship between prosody and interpretation. We know that prosody can influence the interpretation of sentences, but it appears that this ability to use prosodic cues provided by French input develops in English-French learners. The manner and limits of these interactions have not been investigated. Generally, the way in which learners interpret structures provides information about the representations that learners posit.

4.3 Morpho-syntactic knowledge

Herschensohn suggests looking further into the differential development of the verbal domain (e.g., morphological endings on verbs) and the nominal domain (e.g., clitic pronouns), the former being acquired earlier than the latter.

Collecting cross-sectional and longitudinal data with naturalistic and instructed learners may allow us to uncover similarities in routes and rates of acquisition. L2 learners appear to have more difficulties with past tense and aspect than with present tense and aspect, and there is a lack of studies investigating the acquisition of future tenses be it with learners in immersion settings (Nadasdi, Mougeon, & Rehner 2003), or in instructed settings (Ayoun 2005b; Moses 2002). English-speaking learners of L2 French have more difficulties with gender agreement than with number agreement, although English lacks both. Conducting more comparative studies between French L1 and French L2 acquisition may help clarify current findings indicating that these two processes are alike and divergent at the same time.

Ayoun concludes her study of the acquisition of grammatical gender and agreement from a minimalist perspective by suggesting that future research look further into the initial promising results of form-focused instruction and processing instruction versus explicit instruction. Data should be collected among instructed learners with no or limited access to input outside the classroom, and instructed learners with access to input outside the classroom.

Future research into the effects of instruction could also investigate whether promoting the cognitive factors of memory, attention and awareness would affect the acquisition of grammatical gender and agreement.

Another interesting direction for future research should be into not only gender, but also number and agreement processing (following up on e.g., Dewaele & Véronique 2000). There is already a vast psycholinguistic literature of empirical data obtained with monolingual native speakers and bilingual speakers (e.g., Antón-Méndez, Nicol, & Garrett 2002; Bentrovato, Devescovi, D'Amico, Wicha, & Bates 2003; Dahan, Swingley, Tanenhaus, & Magnuson 2000; Guillemon & Grosjean 2001; Jakubowicz & Faussart 1998; Vigliocci, Butterworth, & Garrett 1996). It would be interesting to follow up on the results obtained with monolingual native speakers and bilingual speakers in the psycholinguistic literature (e.g., Antón-Méndez, Nicol, & Garrett 2002; Bentrovato, Devescovi, D'Amico, Wicha, & Bates 2003), to see how adult L2 learners process gender in picture-naming tasks or online sentence processing for example; or if the processing of number is independent of the processing of gender, as suggested in Antón-Méndez (1999), a study with L2 Spanish learners. Moreover, the following can be investigated from a pedagogical perspective or from a processing perspective: Determiner retrieval, determiner and noun gender agreement, noun and adjective agreement, subject and past participle agreement, and gender agreement with anaphora.

4.4 Pragmatic knowledge

Warga argues for more research in French interlanguage pragmatics as follows: (a) From a methodological perspective, using learners with a greater variety of L1 backgrounds, and at different levels of proficiency; collecting elicited/authentic conversational data to conduct conversation analysis; (b) Investigating different pragmatic features to expand beyond the traditional conversational functions (greetings/leave-takings, closings, responses to questions about the weekend); (c) More research in French pragmatics in general using systematically collected empirical data rather than being based on researcher introspection and informal observation; (d) Studying the degree of (in)directness in French compared to other languages; (e) Investigating the degree of formulaicity of opening sequences and other conversational functions in French as compared to other languages, as it may lead to misunderstanding in NS-NNS interactions.

4.5 Sociolinguistic knowledge

Dewaele stresses the need for future research: (a) On the acquisition of sociolinguistic competence to concentrate on differences between learners in immersion setting and learners in instructed settings. In so doing, learners' contact and exposure to the L2 outside the classroom should be carefully documented; (b) On individual differences between L2 learners and "patterns of sociolinguistic variation to psychological, psycholinguistic sociopragmatic and sociocultural variables" (Dewaele this volume); (c) By adding an emic perspective to the etic perspective to research in variationist sociolinguistics, combining both quantitative and qualitative perspectives, to gain a better understanding of the complex processes underlying variation patterns.

4.6 Foreign language ideology and language pedagogy

Train suggests that there is room for future research to take a more explicitly critical stance toward the ideologies of language and speaker identity that inform both FL teaching and applied linguistic research. He outlines several areas in which to address the consequences, possibilities, and dilemmas surrounding language ideology and speaker identity as a "necessary step in working toward a French language pedagogy and French applied linguistics that are critically responsive to the political, sociocultural, and ethical dimensions of learning and teaching French in increasingly global and intercultural contexts". First, he points out the need to go beyond (non)native and national identities of French, which have ideologically positioned L2 learners as deficient with respect to the NS, in order to highlight the value of being and doing *other-than-native* or *more-than-native*. Calling for a questioning of nativist discourse, he suggests a shift of focus away from dominant notions of competence to a more complex and observable construct of the L2 learners' intercultural performativity. In terms of teaching and learning French in the age of globalization, he argues that a *crit-*

ical reflexivity with regard to language ideologies is basic to imagining and developing viable alternatives in FL pedagogy and FL policy to the dominant discourse of national security and English hegemony. Lastly, Train foregrounds the need to critically engage with the problematic relationship between language ideology, power, and ethics in language education and in society at large, particularly in the areas of language testing and standards-based pedagogy.

4.7 Affective variables, personality and motivation

MacIntyre, Clément and Noels convincingly illustrate the relevance and importance of studying how psychological processes inform second language acquisition. In future research, they suggest placing greater emphasis on the various interactions that occur between learners and contextual situations; investigating larger scale, macro-level processes of intergroup relations, as well as smaller scale, intra-individual processes, in order to better understand all the necessary adjustments that must be made when different language groups come into contact. As in other areas of research in second language acquisition, studies focusing on affective variables will benefit from exploring new approaches such as the neurological study of emotional processes, to placing a greater emphasis on qualitative research methods. For instance, we may investigate how physiological inhibition systems are activated in the brain and the body under various situational circumstances. How do cultural differences come into play with affective variables? Another desirable consequence of better understanding the interaction of psychological processes and second language acquisition will of course be pedagogical applications in the foreign language classroom.

4.8 Natural language and lexical creativity

Lessard and Levison outline several possibilities for future research in natural language and lexical creativity: (a) First, in a similar fashion to Myles, they stress the need for better corpora of oral and written productions showing the frequency, coverage, and productivity of the various French affixes, in order to provide L2 learners with as much authenticity as possible; (b) They suggest that an enriched generative environment may allow researchers to manage the simultaneous control of the several factors involved in any L2 learning activity such as the repetition of various lexical items in any given text and the interplay of the learner's already acquired knowledge and new information included in the text; (c) They argue for further research on how cognate forms between the L1 and the L2 may be used as a means of bootstrapping lexical access; (d) They point out the need for further research on compounds which are not based on orthographic contiguity, "to measure the similarities and differences between compounds, collocations and other formulaic utterances, at both the morphosyntactic and semantic levels"; (e) Finally, they point out the absence of work dealing with lexical creativity based on semantic adjustments to base forms.

4.9 French Sign Language

Given that research on language development in the context of French and French Sign Language is relatively new, Tuller, Blondel and Niederberger outline how much work remains to be done to better understand how French Sign Language is acquired by deaf children born to hearing parents, particularly when the age of exposure, and the quality, quantity and modality of language input are quite different from the input hearing children received in oral language acquisition. Even when deaf children benefit from full scholastic integration, how do they develop oral, written and signed language in an instructional setting? How is their language development related to the development of other skills? What pedagogical approaches would be most beneficial? How would they be evaluated? And how would we assess the language development of these children?

4.10 Electronic corpora in SLA research

Myles clearly showed that so far too few studies have used computerized methodologies to analyze oral and written L2 corpora. The few existing studies are limited to written data from advanced L2 English learners. Corpus linguistics would greatly benefit from: (a) More good quality, oral and longitudinal, corpora, in a variety of L1/L2 combinations; (b) The availability of these corpora online and freely; (c) Researchers coming to an agreement for the transcription and annotation of L2 data, as well as for the documentation of learner profiles and corpora databases.

4.11 Creole studies

Mather outlines the following trends for future research in creole studies: (a) In first and second language acquisition, it would be interesting to see if the presumably unmarked characteristics of creoles are reflected in the relative ease or speed of acquisition of creoles by children (as L1s) and by adults; (b) In terms of the lexicon, more systematic comparisons between the lexicons of creoles and their putative substrates are needed; (c) In terms of syntax, comparing various stages of untutored L2 acquisition of European lexifier languages (French and English particularly) might yield interesting results in terms of the historical development of invariant preverbal tense, mood and aspect markers in creoles. More specifically, research is needed on: (a) The synchronic structure (i.e., the phonology, grammar, lexis and pragmatics) of individual creole varieties; (b) The possible sources of lexical and syntactic expressions in dialectal French; (c) The evolution and comparative typology of regional subgroups (e.g., did they develop independently or were some exported later?); (d) A variety of sociolinguistic issues could be investigated such as speakers' attitudes, diglossic situations, literacy, and so on.

4.12 Applied linguistics in West Africa

Sonaiya stresses the urgent need to address several pressing linguistic policy issues such as taking into account important socio-political and socio-economic changes and their consequences on the socio-linguistic realities of African countries. For instance, former colonial languages remain the sole official languages in countries where many other languages (including new creole languages) are spoken, and where illiteracy is on the raise. Bilingual education should be promoted, and language planners and practitioners should work together to determine what the most culturally acceptable linguistic practices would be to counter the negative effects of illiteracy, and promote more positive feelings toward mother tongues.

4.13 Immersion studies in Louisiana

Since the Council for the Development of French in Louisiana (CODOFIL) was created in 1968 to preserve the French-speaking heritage of the state, immersion schools have enrolled children from kindergarten to highschool. Caldas argues that these immersion school programs are ideal for continued research on their effects on students' academic outcomes in general. For instance, to what extent do socioeconomic status and race/ethnicity (as well as their interaction) account for the superior academic performance of immersion students? How do immersion programs impact academic achievement in general? Future qualitative research, along with classroom observations and longitudinal ethnographic studies, could provide more insight into the teacher, classroom and peer dynamics of immersion programs. Are immersion students more independent and creative, as well as able to participate in more collaborative tasks than their non-immersion peers? To what extent are immersion students using French outside of the classroom setting? Do Cajun and Creole immersion students perform better in immersion settings than students who are not heritage language learners?

5.   Conclusion

French in applied linguistics in a broad sense has come a long way from the pioneering work of Abbot Charles-Michel l'Epée, as the founder of the first school for the deaf, to Henry Hécaen, a French neurologist who first used the term *neurolinguistique* in a publication in 1968, or to Jules Ronjat who carried out the first study of bilingual first language acquisition, among others. Current research, as represented by this volume and others (e..g, Dewaele 2005b; Prévost & Paradis 2004), boasts an active agenda in both core second/foreign language acquisition in instructed, immersion and naturalistic settings, and in the various subfields of applied linguistics. Section 3 summarized the findings of empirical research into the phonological, morphological, lexical, semantic and syntactic, pragmatic and sociolinguistic knowledge of foreign language learners of French, whereas Section 4 summed up the directions for future research outlined in the chapters of the present volume with the hope that they will constitute the starting point for further research that will contribute to a greater understanding of the processes of second/foreign language acquisition in general.

CHAPTER 2

The history of French

Anthony Lodge
St. Andrews University, UK

Résumé

Ce survol de l'histoire du français replace les différentes phases de l'évolution de la langue dans le cadre des processus de standardisation identifiés par Einar Haugen. Il envisage le français standard non comme une variété réelle, mais comme un ensemble abstrait de normes. Tout en accentuant la dimension sociolinguistique de cette histoire, il décrit les principaux changements internes (phonétiques, grammaticaux, lexicaux) survenus au cours de l'évolution de la langue, et il souligne l'imbrication de ces changements linguistiques, à tout moment de l'histoire, dans la variation linguistique.

Abstract

This overview of the history of French situates the various phases of the language's evolution in the framework of the standardization processes identified by Einar Haugen, treating standard French not as a 'real variety', but as an abstract set of norms. While emphasizing the sociolinguistic dimension of this history, it describes the principal linguistic changes (phonetic, grammatical, lexical) which have occurred during the language's history, setting them firmly within the context of language variation.

1. Introduction

French has long been one of the principal languages of Europe, and in our own day still has a strong claim to the status of 'world language' (see Rossillon 1995). This chapter traces the ascent of French from its origins among the dialects spawned from Latin during Late Antiquity. We will structure the narrative around an analysis of language standardization elaborated by Einar Haugen (see Haugen 1966). In tandem with the language's sociolinguistic development, we will outline the main linguistic changes which made Latin into modern French. Standardization presupposes, of course, variation, so we will present the development of the standard language, as far as possible, in the context of other competing varieties. The bibliography on this subject is vast (see Holtus, Metzeltin, & Schmitt 1988, t. V 1:402–894), but the multi-volume *Histoire de la langue française* of Ferdinand Brunot (1966) and its subsequent updates, remains the single most accessible and comprehensive source, despite its age.

2. The Latin base

It is difficult to dissociate French from its Latin base. Not only is it impossible to establish, on linguistic grounds, when Latin stopped and French began, but also, throughout
the history of the language, Latin has influenced the development of French in a
decisive way. In its standardized, written form (commonly labelled Classical Latin),
Latin has always provided a powerful model to French speakers of what their language
should ideally be like (see Dubois 1970; Joseph 1987), and has been a constant source
of lexical renewal through the injection into French of learned borrowings. But despite
the enduring myth of its immutability, the Latin of imperial Rome was naturally subject to variation and change, and it is the vernacular form of Latin, commonly labelled
Vulgar Latin, which provides the starting point for French, as for all Romance dialects
and languages.

The label Vulgar Latin is a difficult one, not just because of its prescriptive connotations, but because of the wide range of meanings different scholars have given
to it (see Lloyd 1979). Oral vernaculars in the past are impossibly difficult to access,
for they are protean in nature and, by definition, leave only the most cursory traces
in the written record. Spoken over many centuries by a large, ethnically diverse community of speakers, Vulgar Latin was highly vulnerable to variation and change (see
Herman 2000). We might see it as a *social dialect* of Latin – the speech of the lesser
educated. Alternatively, we might see it as a *register* of Latin, the variety used in informal speech situations. However, since these two axes of variation operate conjointly,
we must ultimately define Vulgar Latin in terms of socio-stylistic *co*-variation, and see
it occupying the informal, vernacular end of that dual continuum, if we wish to retain
the label at all. Our knowledge of it is derived from a multiplicity of imperfect sources:
Literary representations of vernacular speech, the writings of inexperienced writers,
the metalinguistic comments of grammarians and, above all, from comparative reconstruction on the basis of the Romance dialects and languages which developed from
it (see Väänänen 1967: 13–20). Inscriptional evidence of regional variation in spoken
Latin is not strong, but it is unlikely that a vernacular, spoken across so broad and
diverse an area, was geographically homogeneous.

Given the importance in vernacular speech of maintaining affective relationships
between speakers,[1] the vocabulary of colloquial Latin looks to have been marked by
diminutives (e.g., *agnellum*, 'little lamb' as distinct from Classical *agnum*, *genuculum*,
'little knee', as distinct from Classical *genum*), and by jokey lexical items minimizing
the dignity of objects referred to (e.g., *caballum*, 'nag' as distinct from *equum*, *buccam*,
'gob' as distinct from *orem*). In comparison with the archaic phonetic forms retained
in Classical Latin, the sound system of Vulgar Latin was characterized by reductions
and simplifications. Consonant clusters were reduced and unstressed vowels dropped.
The ten-vowel system of Classical Latin contrasted with a seven-vowel system in Vulgar

---

1. See Brown and Levinson (1980) on 'positive politeness strategies'.

Latin. The morphology of Vulgar Latin showed a tendency towards morpho-phonemic regularity: Apophonous verb-forms were replaced, the number of noun and adjective declensions reduced from five to three, the whole synthetic conjugation of the passive was replaced, and so on. In syntax, there was a tendency towards analyticity, and an increase in the regular correspondence between content and expression: Increased use of prepositions reduced the importance of flexional endings, new analytical tenses developed (e.g., *promissum habeo,* 'I have promised', as distinct from *promisi* 'I promised', and *cantare habeo,* 'I have to sing', as distinct from *cantabo* 'I'll sing'). These vernacular forms mark the first stage in the typological drift from a synthetic structure towards the analytical structures of the modern Romance languages.

3. Dialectalization of Latin and the beginnings of Gallo-Romance

If Latin was already subject to variation and change before the Empire lost socio-economic cohesion in the fifth century, in-migration of Germanic peoples at this time accelerated the process of linguistic change. The changes in question were in many places profound: In phonology, they involved diphthongization, palatalization, and the apocope of unstressed vowels (see Pope 1952); in grammar, the gradual development of preposed grammatical markers like prepositions, articles and clitic pronouns, transformation of the demonstrative system, and restructuring of the systems of tense, voice and modality (see Price 1971; Harris 1978). These changes in Latin speech happened at different rates in different regions, leading to dialectalization.

3.1 Dialectalization

It is unlikely that the Latin spoken in Gaul was ever uniform across such a large geographical space. At the time of the Roman conquest in the first century BC, the southern half of Gaul was inhabited by a range of Celtic, Basque and Mediterranean peoples, while the north was more exclusively Celtic. The south was fully romanized a century before the north, and was engaged in the trading world of the Mediterranean, while the north was oriented economically towards the Germanic world and the North Sea. The migrations of the fifth century accentuated the north-south divide: The north was over-run by Franks who settled the area densely as farmers, whereas the south and east were taken over by Burgunds and Goths who settled more superficially, and who eventually lost control to the Franks under Clovis (507 AD). From this time on, the divergence between the two halves of Gallo-Romance increased, giving rise ultimately to the two main dialect groupings of France – *langue d'oc* in the south and *langue d'oïl* in the north (*oc* and *oïl* being the words for 'yes' in Occitan and French, respectively).[2]

---

2. A taxonomy of Gallo-Romance indicated by the Italian poet Dante in the late thirteenth century.

Table 1. Sound correspondences between Latin, Occitan and French

Latin	Occitan	French
[a]	[a]	[e]
amare (*'to love'*)	*amar*	*aimer*
[o]	[o]	[œ]
florem (*'flower'*)	*flor*	*fleur*
[e]	[ɛ]	[wa]
faenum (*'hay'*)	*fe(n)*	*foin*
[ka]	[ka]	[ʃɛ]
capitem (*'head'*)	*cap*	*chef*

Linguistic change progressed faster and further in the north than in the south.[3] This is particularly evident in the sound systems of the two nascent languages: For example, Latin vowels in stressed, open syllables and the group [ka] in word-initial syllables remained relatively stable in the south, but mutated considerably in the north (Table 1).

As time went on, morphological and syntactic differences emerged between the two languages, notably in the system of demonstratives, and in the use of subject clitics, with the northern dialects extending their use, and the southern dialects remaining closer to the 'pro-drop' structure of southern Romance. To illustrate this, here are two versions of the same Biblical text (the Parable of the Prodigal Son (Luke XV, v. 1–5)) drawn from a nineteenth-century collection of dialect texts (Coquebert-Montbret 1831:434 and 510) (Table 2).

If we examine the dialect geography of twentieth-century France (see Gilliéron & Edmont 1901–1911), we find several phonetic isoglosses following closely parallel trajectories across the country from Bordeaux to Geneva, marking the *oïl – oc* divide (see Jochnowitz 1973). However, a bi-partite division over-simplifies the situation, for a third 'transitional' zone, known as Franco-Provençal, is traditionally distinguished in the area between Lyon and Geneva (see Gardette 1983). Indeed, the whole of Gaul formed a mosaic of dialects and sub-dialects merging in a continuum (see Le Dû, Le Berre, & Brun-Trigaud 2005). While the linguistic distance between the two ends of the country (between, for example, Picard and Provençal) was large, there is no evidence on the ground to indicate an abrupt transition between *oc* and *oïl*.

Traditional explanations for the dialectalization of Gallo-Romance invoke, above all, direct interference from the languages in contact with Latin. The substrate languages undoubtedly left their mark: A large number of place-names (e.g., *Lugdunum > Lyon, Parisii > Paris*), and a small number of lexical items (e.g., *camisia > chemise* 'shirt') are Celtic (Gaulish) in origin (see Lambert 1997). Basque appears to have had a formative influence on the development of Gascon (see Rohlfs 1970). Germanic speech exerted a direct superstrate influence on the lexical development of

---

3.   On the history of Occitan, see Holtus et al. (1988, t. V, 2:1–126).

Table 2. The 'Prodigal Son' in Latin, Occitan and French

Vulgate	Occitan	French
Homo quidam habuit duos filios	*Un hommé abio dous effans*	Un homme avait deux fils.
et dixit adulescentior ex illis patri pater da mihi portionem substantiae quae me contingit et divisit illis substantiam	*Lou pu jouiné d'entre élès diguet à soun païré: Moun païré, bailat me la pourtiou dai bé que me reben, et lou païré partaget soun bé à sous effans*	Dont le plus jeune dit à son père: mon père, donnez-moi ce qui doit me revenir de votre bien. Et le père leur fit le partage de son bien.
et non post multos dies congregatis omnibus adulescentior filius peregre profectus est in regionem longinquam et ibi dissipavit substantiam suam vivendo luxuriose	*Quaouqués jours après quand lou pu jouiné aget amassat tout ce seou partiguet et s'en anet dins un païs pla liont et aqui dissipet tout soun bé en bisquen dins la debaouchou*	Peu de jours après, le plus jeune de ces deux fils, ayant amassé tout ce qu'il avait, s'en alla dans un pays étranger fort éloigné, où il dissipa son bien en excès et en débauches.
et postquam omnia consummasset facta est fames valida in regione illa et ipse coepit egere	*Et apres qu'aget tout despensat, benguet uno grando famino dins aquel païs et coummencet d'estre dins lou besoun*	Après qu'il eut tout dépensé, il survint une grande famine dans ce pays-là, et il commença à tomber en nécessité.
et abiit et adhesit uni civium regionis illius et misit illum in villam suam ut pasceret porcos	*Alors s'en anet et se louguet a un des habitans d'aquel païs que lou mandet à sa grangeo per y garda lous pourcels*	Il s'en alla donc, et s'attacha au service d'un des habitans du pays, qui l'envoya dans sa maison des champs pour y garder les pourceaux.

Gallo-Romance: It furnished various color terms (e.g., *brun* 'brown', *bleu* 'blue', *jaune* 'yellow'), words pertaining to the fields of feudalism (e.g., *maréchal* 'marshal', *baron* 'baron', *fief* 'fief'), and medieval warfare (e.g., *heaume* 'helm', *hache* 'axe', *haubert* 'coat of mail'). Germanic stress patterns may have contributed to the divergent development of stressed and unstressed vowels in north Gallo-Romance. The verb-second pattern in Germanic syntax may well have influenced the evolution of sentence word order in north Gallo-Romance (e.g., *Il viendra peut-être* ~ *Peut-être viendra-t-il* 'he will come maybe' ~ 'maybe will he come'). However, we should not overstate the effects of direct contact phenomena on dialect-fragmentation in Gallo-Romance. More fundamental explanations are to be found in social factors such as differing degrees of social/demographic disruption, ruralization, and communicative isolation between north and south. Fragmentation of social networks of the Roman world caused the breakdown of regional and supra-regional linguistic norms, giving free rein to endogenous, internally generated change.

3.2 Periodizing the history of French

Different scholars set the break-up in the unity of Latin (and thus the beginning of French) at different dates, some as early as the second century AD, others as late as the eleventh. Since there is no linguistic way of delimiting the two varieties, perhaps the only recourse we have is to pinpoint the time when speakers themselves became aware of the difference between them. This awareness dawned towards the end of the eighth century, for at that time the divergence between the Latin of the Church's liturgy and the Romance speech of the unlettered congregations, in northern Gaul at any rate, had become, for various reasons, a serious obstacle to communication (see Banniard 1992; Wright 1982). To overcome these problems, the clergy of Gaul took to conducting that part of the office designed specifically for the laity – the sermon – in the local vernacular. The decision to endorse this practice, enacted at the Council of Tours in 813, provides the first official recognition that Latin and Romance in Gaul had drifted far enough apart to be labelled separate languages (see Richter 1983).

The history of French is traditionally periodized in the following way: Early Old French from 800 to1100, Later Old French from 1100 to 1300, Middle French from 1300 to1600, Modern French from 1600 to the present. Although consecrated by usage, these divisions correlate only imperfectly with the realities of linguistic and sociolinguistic change. Moreover, they take no account of the linguistic history of the southern part of the country. In an influential article, the Norwegian linguist Einar Haugen published a taxonomy of the processes of language standardization which offers an alternative way of periodizing the history of French (Haugen 1966). Standardization has as its theoretical goal 'maximal variation in function and minimal variation in form', and involves both social and linguistic processes: At the social level, it requires the suppression of variation through the *selection* and subsequent *acceptance* by society of a single linguistic norm; at the linguistic level, it requires the *elaboration* of the linguistic structures in the selected dialect so that it may perform the full range of functions in society, and, in addition, the development of linguistic uniformity through *codification* of the norm. Of course, complete standardization of language can never be achieved – a standard language is an abstract set of norms, not a real variety – but we have here a convenient framework upon which to structure what follows.

4. The selection of vernacular norms[4]

This phase concerns modification of the status of particular Romance dialects and coincides roughly with what is known traditionally as Old French. The equivalent period in the south of the country is 'Old Provençal', though modern scholars prefer the less ambiguous term 'Medieval/Old Occitan' (see Paden 1998). In the period be-

---

4.   Here we are using the term 'norm' in a descriptive (or statistical) sense, not in a prescriptive sense.

fore 1100, textual evidence is sparse, but thereafter, it becomes increasingly plentiful, when compared with the other European vernaculars (e.g., Middle English, Middle High German).

4.1 The development of written norms

Shortly after the decision of the Council of Tours (813) to concede a small place in the liturgy to regional vernaculars, attempts were made across Gaul to devise Romance writing systems (based, of course, on the Latin alphabet). In the south of the country, Occitan forms began to appear in Latin charters of the ninth century, with the first literary texts emerging a century or so later.[5] In the north, the celebrated transcription of the Strasbourg Oaths (842) was included in a Latin chronicle of the ninth century, providing precious information about the earliest form of French (see Ayres-Bennett 1996: 16–30). Although the first literary texts followed soon after,[6] it took fully three hundred years for vernacular writing systems to become widely available. Before 1100, they were used only sporadically to record religious or semi-liturgical pieces (in verse); afterwards, they came to be used for recording a literature which was fundamentally secular in inspiration (Provençal lyric poetry, northern French epic and romance). It was only after 1200 that they started, in a small way, to be used in literary prose and in public administration, though they did not predominate in this domain until a century later (see Cerquiglini 2004).

For most of the Middle Ages, vernacular writing systems were highly variable geographically. It is likely that, as vernacular writing systems developed in the tenth and eleventh centuries, they progressively emancipated themselves from the local speech of individual writers. Indeed, the earliest manuscripts contain a mixture of forms specific to their region and forms from other regions (see de Poerck 1963). Certain scholars believe that, in the north of Gaul at least, there developed a supra-regional written koine as early as the ninth century (see Cerquiglini 1991). It is difficult to substantiate this, given the paucity of vernacular manuscripts surviving from before 1200 (see Pfister 1993).[7] Moreover, while dialect-mixing is present in the surviving early manuscripts, the mixture we find there is not stable enough for us to speak of a fully fledged written koine.[8] In fact, it is only in the middle of the fourteenth century that we can firmly assert the existence in northern France of a supra-regional written norm (see Dees 1985)

---

5. The *Chanson de Sainte Foy* was composed in the tenth century and a poem on Boethius around 1000.

6. The *Séquence de Sainte Eulalie* is usually dated around 900.

7. Many of these were copied in Anglo-Norman England.

8. We see a koine as a historically mixed but synchronically stable dialect which contains elements from the different dialects that went into the mixture, as well as interdialect forms that were present in none.

based, not surprisingly, on Parisian administrative usage (see Lusignan 2004). In the south, the lyric poems of the troubadours show a measure of linguistic uniformity, regardless of their regional provenance, but it has been demonstrated (Zufferey 1987) that this impression is created by the lateness of the manuscripts, and does not reflect the early existence of a literary koine. No such uniformity characterizes the Occitan used in the administrative sphere, where regional writtten forms survived throughout the medieval period (see Brunel 1926, 1952).

4.2 The development of spoken norms

Unstandardized languages are characterized not by the absence of norms, but by their proliferation, at various levels: Local norms, supra-local norms, regional norms. In the period before 1100, the population of Gaul was thinly dispersed, with little concentration of interaction in regional centers. It is more than likely, therefore, that at this time Gallo-Romance remained fragmented between a multiplicity of local speech-norms. Change began in the late eleventh century. Population growth and urbanization concentrated populations, in a modest way, around regional centers – Toulouse in the South, Lyon in the South-East, along the lower Loire and the lower Seine in the West, Arras in the North, Metz in the North-East and, most spectacularly, Paris. At such an early date, documentary evidence showing the linguistic effects of demographic change is entirely lacking. Moreover, extracting evidence about speech from medieval written documents is a delicate matter which inevitably causes controversy. However, when manuscript data become more plentiful in the thirteenth century, we can infer the existence of loose sets of regional speech-norms in each of the areas mentioned – Languedocian, Franco-Provençal, Tourangeau, Norman, Picard, Lorrain, and Parisian. For a summary of the diagnostic variables characterizing these dialects of Occitan and Old French see Ronjat (1941, t. 4:1–55) and Pope (1952:486–505).

Special mention must made here of the variety of Gallo-Romance which flourished in England throughout the Middle Ages: Anglo-Norman. Introduced by the followers of William the Conqueror after 1066, an insular version of the Norman dialect remained the spoken language of the feudal elites for several generations, and the written language of government and the law until the fifteenth century. Anglo-Norman, with its own insular characteristics, had a profound effect on the development of Middle English, particularly in its vocabulary (see Rothwell 1991). By the middle of the thirteenth century, it was no longer in widespread use as a spoken language, but then the cultural and political importance of Parisian French was such that we find in England the first manuals for the teaching of French to foreigners (see Kristol 1989).

In the course of the twelfth century, the city of Paris developed into an urban giant (by the standards of its day), with a population reaching 100 000, dwarfing all other urban centers in Gaul, and making the city the undisputed focus of economic and political power. Inevitably, the speech-norms of this city became pre-eminent. We now find explicit statements by contemporaries to the effect that the speech of Paris was superior to that of other areas. Indeed, in the thirteenth century, the prestige of Parisian

French was recognized outside the kingdom, not only in England, but also in Germany and Italy (see Lodge 1993:98–102). This 'selection' of Parisian speech-norms was to prove irreversible, setting in motion the whole process of standardization in north Gallo-Romance. There was no parallel development among the regional varieties in the south, where Occitan remained merely the sum of its dialects. In the right circumstances, the speech of Toulouse might have developed as a supra-regional norm, but the political and economic power of this city was destroyed by the Capetians in the Albigensian 'crusade' (1209–1229).

Which dialect of Old French forms the historical basis of the French standard language? It was for a long time believed that standard French is simply the modern projection of the dialect of the Paris region, labelled by the nineteenth-century philologist Gaston Paris *francien* (see Paris 1888). This idea has subsequently been modified, for standard French is clearly a sort of koine made up of elements drawn from other dialects as well. How this koine arose is a central problem in the history of French (see Holtus et al. 1988, t. II, 2:271–289). The fact that full standardization cannot be achieved without the development of writing has encouraged the belief that standard French was created first in writing, in the early Middle Ages, and subsequently diffused top-down through Parisian speech, and thence into the provinces. In the context of medieval French, with low levels of literacy, such a scenario is implausible. It is more likely that the norms of standard French crystallized in an empirical, haphazard way, during centuries of jostling between the competing variants in the everyday speech of Paris, before becoming fixed in the writing system during the later Middle Ages (see Lodge 2004:71–79).

4.3 Linguistic developments

To illustrate the linguistic changes leading to the formation of Old French, here are two medieval versions of the same Biblical text which we examined earlier (above §3.1) (Table 3).[9]

Space requires us to focus essentially on the Parisian version, but comparison with the Picard text will give an idea of the dialect variation present in north Gallo-Romance. An exhaustive linguistic commentary is not appropriate here, but it is worth highlighting the following grammatical features of Old French:

Morphology
–   Old French retains (superficially at least) a flexional system for nouns and their determiners:

	Singular	Plural
Subject	*li rois*	*li roi*
Object	*le roi*	*les rois*

---

9.   I am indebted to my colleague Clive Sneddon for making these extracts available, which he has edited from Rouen, Bibl. mun., MS A 211 and Zürich, Stadtsbibl., MS C 175.

- Gender marking on adjectives normally involves the addition of -*e* to the masculine (e.g., *foles femes* (3)), but adjectives derived from the Latin third declension were invariable (e.g., *grant faim* (4)).
- The Old French demonstratives could function either as pronouns e.g., *celui* (2) or as adjectives, e.g., *cele* (4), the prime distinction being that between proximity (e.g., *cel*) and distance (e.g., *cest*).

Syntax
- Word order in this passage normally follows the SV(C) pattern, but subject post-position, common in Old French, is to be found: *Lors comenca il* (4).
- Nouns frequently appear without a determiner: *Dedenz brief tens* (3), *il fu grant faim* (4), and so on.

5. Elaboration of functions

This phase in the history of French coincides roughly with the period known as Middle French (1350–1600). During the later Middle Ages, Parisian French expanded its role in society from that of a local oral vernacular to that of a supra-regional, omnifunc-

Table 3. The 'Prodigal Son' in Latin, Parisian Old French and medieval Picard

Vulgate	Parisian	Picard
Homo quidam habuit duos filios	*Uns hom avoit .ii. filz.*	*Uns homs avoit .ii. fieus.*
et dixit adulescentior ex illis patri pater da mihi portionem substantiae quae me contingit et divisit illis substantiam	*Et li plus juesnes dist a son pere: 'Pere, done moi ma porcion de[l] chatel qui m'afiert.' Et li peres devisa sa substance et dona a celui sa part.*	*Et li plus josnes dist a son pere: 'Peres donne moy la portion de la substanche qui afiert a moi.' Et il lui divisa.*
et non post multos dies congregatis omnibus adulescentior filius peregre profectus est in regionem longinquam et ibi dissipavit substantiam suam vivendo luxuriose	*Et dedenz brief tens, toutes choses assemblees ensemble, li plus juesnes filz ala fors del pais en lointiegne region, et despendi iluec sa sustance en vivant luxurieusement o les foles femes.*	*Et non apres moult de jours, li plus josnes fieus, toutes coses asamblees. alla en lontaine region, et la dissipa sa substance luxurieusement vivant.*
et postquam omnia consummasset facta est fames valida in regione illa et ipse coepit egere	*Et enprés ce qu'il ot tout despendu, il fu grant faim en cele region; lors comenca il a avoir soffrete.*	*Et apres che qu'il ot tout consumet, une grant famine fu faite en celle region; et il conmenchant de avoir indigence.*
et abiit et adhesit uni civium regionis illius et misit illum in villam suam ut pasceret porcos	*Et il ala et s'acovenanca a .i. des citoiens de cele region; et il l'envoia en sa vile por pestre les porceax.*	*S'en alla et se aherst a .i. chitoiien de celle region; et il l'envoia en sa ville qu'il gardast les pourchiaux.*

tional language, and this had far-reaching linguistic effects. Functional expansion took place on two planes: (1) The vernaculars eroded the territory of Latin in the spheres of writing and administration; (2) Parisian French nudged the regional vernaculars, notably Occitan, from whatever functions they had earlier wrested from Latin. As the use of the language expanded, so were developed the linguistic tools, lexical and syntactic, necessary to discharge these new functions.

5.1 Functional expansion

5.1.1 *The vernaculars versus Latin*
The language situation in medieval Gaul was diglossic (see Lusignan 1987). Latin, viewed by many with superstitious awe, occupied the High (H) functions in society – writing, religion, education, the law, diplomacy, serious literature – and Romance the Low (L) functions – everyday conversation, folk literature, and so on. The ascent of French in the latter half of the Middle Ages was not a smooth one, for the educated elites in the Church and in the legal fraternity were in no hurry to abandon Latin, which was at one and the same time the tool of their trade, and their badge of elite status. The ultimate beneficiary of this movement was the French of the Parisian elites, which gradually became an omnifunctional language.

The vernaculars had been challenging the grip of Latin over the H functions from the moment they began to be written down. However, this challenge did not become serious until the second half of the thirteenth century. In the twelfth century the vernaculars were widely used as a literary medium, but in literatures considered lightweight beside the writings of the great Latin *auctores*. In the thirteenth century, prose texts appear for the first time, followed by translations and vulgarizations of Latin texts. By the fifteenth century, the level of vulgarization had risen so far that advanced philosophical work was being developed in French (see Monfrin 1963). A similar pattern can be seen in the language of public administration. Here the towns led the way, maintaining their accounts, charters and council minutes in locally developed writing systems. Examples are to be found in Picardy in the north (see Lusignan 2004: 225–231; Wüest 1995), and in Auvergne in the south (see Lodge 1985). The royal chancery and the *Parlement de Paris* did not begin to shift from Latin to French until the second half of the thirteenth century, and the process was not fully completed until the fifteenth.

5.1.2 *Parisian French versus the regional vernaculars*
Parisian French acquired a particular status as a prestige-dialect by the end of the twelfth century, and this very fact meant that from then onwards, it was exerting pressure on the other regional vernaculars. This pressure could well have been oral in those areas and social groups with high levels of interaction with Paris, but it is important to understand that large-scale displacement of the regional dialects in speech did not take place until much later, in the industrial period. In medieval times, the spatial expansion of Parisian French outside the Paris region (or 'France' as it was called at

the time) occurred essentially in writing and in legal administration. The chronology of diffusion of the Parisian writing system across the country was charted by Gossen (1967), who shows how this progressed earliest in the *langue d'oïl*, with a powerful pocket of resistance in the network of towns in Picardy. Displacement of Occitan in the south took longer, notably in places only annexed by France at a later date (e.g., Roussillon in 1659).

We find a parallel development in the language of literary texts. In the north, the Picard chronicler Jean Froissart (1338–1410) was the last prominent writer to employ regional forms in a high-status literary work. In the south, Occitan literary traditions were more firmly entrenched, and, indeed, original literary production enjoyed something of a renaissance in Toulouse in the late sixteenth century (see Camproux 1953: 83–106). That said, by this time, all literary authors wishing to have a wide readership (e.g., Montaigne, Brantôme and du Bartas) knew full well that the language they needed to use was that of Paris.

The culmination of the functional expansion of Parisian French into the domains of Latin and of the regional vernaculars can be seen in article 111 of the Ordinance of Villers-Cotterêts (1539), which stipulated that:

> *tous arrestz ensemble toutes aultres procedures ... soient prononcez enregistrez et delivrez aux parties en langage maternel francois et non aultrement.*
> 'all court rulings along with all other acts of procedure ... be pronounced, registered and delivered to the parties concerned in the French mother tongue and in no other way'

The King's French was now the only language officially recognized in secular administration. Latin remained the language of the Church and of education, and at the time of the Renaissance enjoyed very high cultural status, but Parisian French, was now the dominant language of the kingdom, the symbol of a developing sense of French nationhood.

5.2 Linguistic developments

The French language underwent multiple changes between the thirteenth and sixteenth centuries (see Marchello-Nizia 1979), some of which were internally generated, others driven by the functional expansion of the language.

5.2.1 *Internally generated change*

Phonetics
- The stress accent ceased being a function of the individual word to become that of a longer sequence, corresponding, roughly speaking, to the phrase.
- The consonant reductions: Deletion of final consonants (including flexional [s], which in Old French had marked case and number), and the reduction of affricates ([tʃ] > [ʃ], [dʒ] > [ʒ]), in such words as *charme* and *juge*.

- Reduction of consonant clusters: In pre-consonantal position, [l] was vocalised to [w], eventually merging with the preceding vowel (e.g. *chevals > chevaux*), and [s] was effaced, occasionally lengthening the preceding vowel (e.g., *estre > être*).
- Old French diphthongs and triphthongs were generally simplified to monophthongs (e.g., [aj] > [ɛ], [wɛ] > [æ], [ɛw] > [ø], [eaw] > [o], in such words as *fait, coeur, peu, chapeaux*).
- All vowels followed by a nasal consonant were progressively nasalized (see Sampson 1999). However, at the end of this period, denasalization occurred when the following nasal consonant constituted the onset of the following syllable, cf. *brun* [bʀœ̃] ~ *brunette* [bʀynɛt].

Morphology
- Disappearance of the two-case declension system for nouns, determiners and adjectives, with the generalization of the Old French object case (the *cas régime*).
- Analogical re-modelling of gender-marking on adjectives: The forms of the majority of adjectives (e.g., *petit* ~ *petite* 'small') were extended to the minority group of invariables (e.g., *fort > fort* ~ *forte, grant > grand* ~ *grande*).
- Elimination of apophonous verb-forms, either through the disappearance of irregular verbs (e.g., *choir = tomber* 'fall', *gésir = se coucher* 'lie down'), or through analogical remodelling, aligning the whole verb on a single stem (e.g., Old French *truis, trueves, trueve, trovons, trovez, truevent > je trouve, tu trouves* 'I find, you find', etc.).

Syntax
- Number marked primarily by preposed determiners (articles, demonstratives, and possessives).
- Transformation of the demonstrative system, the old structure built around proximity-distance (e.g., *cest* ~ *cel*) being replaced by one distinguishing adjective from pronoun (e.g., *ce* 'this' (adjective) ~ *celui* 'the one, those' (pronoun)).
- Generalization of subject clitics (in the absence of noun subjects).
- Shift from pre-verb negation (*ne*) to double negation (*ne ... pas* 'not').
- Extension of SVO order at the expense of OVS.

5.2.2 *Lexical and syntactic expansion*
Not all linguistic changes during this period can be explained with reference to internal factors. Some were triggered by the new social role the language was acquiring. As the vernaculars replaced Latin in the H functions during the later Middle Ages, they had to develop progressively the linguistic tools for the task, entailing lexical and syntactic expansion. We must avoid placing any teleological construction upon this process. It is simply an example of the limitless extensibility of language.

The lexicon constitutes an open set of items constantly being renewed through loss of old words (archaism), and the addition of new ones (neologism). During the Middle French period, the vocabulary naturally shadowed developments in society: As the feudal practices were modernized, the accompanying vocabulary items fell out of use (see Matoré 1985 and 1988); as the prestige of Italian culture grew in the fifteenth and sixteenth centuries with the Renaissance, borrowing from Italian (e.g., *balcon* 'balcony', *banque* 'bank', *escorte* 'escort') became widespread (see Hope 1971). However, in addition to these 'natural' developments in vocabulary, the movement of French into domains hitherto reserved for Latin (the law, public administration, education and science) led to wholesale borrowing of Latin (or so-called learned) terms (e.g., *labyrinthe* 'labyrinth', *lacération* 'laceration', *laconique* 'laconic', *lacté* 'lacteal'). This process has been at work throughout the history of the language, and is ongoing even nowadays. However, Guiraud (1966: 50–72) sees it first peaking in the second half of the fourteenth century, with a second, larger peak two centuries later.

Quite commonly, learned borrowings formed etymological doublets with 'popular' words, which had been in constant use in the language since Roman times, such as:

Latin	'Popular' form	Learned borrowing	
fabricam	*forge*	*fabrique*	'manufacture'
fragilem	*frêle*	*fragile*	'fragile, weak'
hospitalem	*hôtel*	*hôpital*	'hospital'

Relexification of the vernacular, on the basis of Latin, had a parallel in *spelling*: Scribes added parasitic consonants to words of 'popular' origin, copied from their perceived Latin cognate, for example:

Latin	Old French	Middle French	
horam	*eure*	*heure*	'hour'
tempus	*tens*	*temps*	'time'
digitum	*doit*	*doigt*	'finger'

Occasionally, scribes misidentified the etymon of particular words, as in the following words:

Latin	Old French	Middle French	
sapere	*savoir*	*scavoir (scire)*	'know'
pensum	*pois*	*poids (pondus)*	'weight'

It was clearly felt that if French was to take over the rôle and status of Latin, it would have to look like Latin.

So long as the vernacular languages were consigned to the L functions in society, their syntax remained close to that of speech. Typically, this involves short utterances, inexplicit linking phenomena, coordination rather than subordination. All of these tend to be present in the French prose of the thirteenth century:

> *Ainsi s'en alla li cuens et li autre baron en Venice; et furent receu a grant feste et grant joie, et se logierent en l'isle Sain Nicolas avec les autres. Mout fu l'oz bele et de bonnes genz. Onques de tant de gens nus uem ne vit.* (Villehardouin, quoted in Caput 1972, t. 1:68)
> 'So the earl and the other lords went to Venice, and were received with much feasting and joy, and they took up residence with everyone else on St. Nicolas Island. The army

was a splendid sight with very good men in it. No one had ever seen so many men before'.

With the more widespread use of the vernaculars as written languages, traces of orality progressively disappear. This is visible in the following text from the fifteenth century:

> *Li roy feist mettre le lit de Contay dedans un grand hostevent et vieil, lequel estoit en sa chambre, et moy avec luy, afin qu'il entendist et peust faire rapport a son maistre des paroles dont usoient ledit connestable et ses gens, dudit duc; et le roy se vint seoir dessus un escabeau rasibus dudut hostevent, afin que nous peussions entendre les paroles que diroit ledit Loys de Geneville; et avec ledit seigneur n'y avoit que ledit seigneur du Bouchage.*
>
> (Commines, quoted in Caput 1972, t. 1:68)
>
> 'The king had Contay's bed set up within a large and ancient screen to keep out draughts, the which was in his bedchamber, and I was there too, in order that he might hear and report to his master the words which were used by the aforesaid duke; and the king came and sat down next to the said screen, in order that we might hear the words which the said Loys de Geneville might say; and with the said lord there was only the said lord of Bouchage'.

New subordinating devices are created, providing more specialized conjunctions than the omnifunctional *que* 'that' of medieval French: *Puisque* 'since', *parce que* 'because', *lorsque* 'when', *dès que* 'as soon as', *quoique* 'although', and so on. The notion of sentence is difficult to define with reference to medieval French, it only starts to crystallize in the sixteenth century, as written French, taking on the role of Latin, finally emancipates itself from orality (see Seguin 2003).

6. Codification

The sixteenth century did not bring to an end the elaboration of the functions of French, for speakers constantly adapt their languages to meet new conditions and situations of use. However, the most significant sociolinguistic trend in French between the sixteenth and eighteenth centuries was what Haugen calls 'codification'. Codification involves the compilation of rules designed to suppress variation in particular aspects of social behavior,[10] and in the linguistic sphere it involved the production of the early dictionaries and grammar books of French.

As we review the process of codification in French between the sixteenth and eighteenth centuries, we will see that it cannot be dissociated from the social developments of the period. Although many of the leading lights in the codification of French were provincial in origin, the movement took place essentially in Paris. The European Renaissance brought great changes in the life and culture of cities: A new polarity began to crystallize in the social psychology of the city, setting 'urbanity' against its negative

---

10.   We find the same ambiguity in the word 'rule' as we saw earlier with the word 'norm'. Here we will be using the word only in its prescriptive, normative sense.

counterpart, 'rusticity'. At the same time, there was an increase in hierarchical thought, which widened the gulf between the culture and lifestyle of the elites, and those of the population at large. This was compounded by the spread of literacy, which accentuated the divergence between high, written culture and the traditional oral culture of the masses. In this new cultural setting, Latin was removed from mainstream culture to be placed on a pedestal, and variation within French took on a symbolical importance which it appears not to have had previously. A new and very powerful ideology of language emerges (see Train this volume), which is fundamentally hostile to vernacular speech, and which has been labelled 'standard ideology' (see Milroy & Milroy 1999). Its chief tenets are the following: (1) The ideal state of a language is one of uniformity; (2) The most valid form of the language is to be found in writing; (3) The standard variety is inherently better (i.e., more elegant, clearer, more logical, etc.) than other varieties.

6.1 Early grammars and dictionaries

During the medieval centuries the focus of metalinguistic attention fell almost entirely on Latin. With the development of printing in the late fifteenth century and consequential increase in literacy, we find serious thought being given for the first time to the nature of French, and of the other vernacular languages of Europe. In *Ancien Régime* Paris, judging by the extraordinarily rich collection of dictionaries, grammar books and general observations on French published at this time, social awareness of language seems to have been exceptionally high.

In the first half of the sixteenth century, we find the first publications of ideas about the nature and current state of French. One of the earliest of these is Geoffroy Tory's *Champfleury*, which draws attention to the extent of variation in the dialects and languages of France (Tory 1529). Half a century later, Claude Fauchet produced the first history of French (Fauchet 1581). Around the same time, Henri Estienne published a series of polemical works attacking in particular the contemporary fashion of Italianism (H. Estienne 1578, 1582). In the early seventeenth century, the emphasis changes, and observers of the language, reflecting the preoccupations of *salon* society, moved beyond the observation of socio-stylistic variation to the stigmatization of linguistic forms they considered unacceptable (see e.g., Bouhours 1675; Malherbe 1630; Vaugelas 1647). It is in this context that we may set the establishment of the *Académie française* in 1635, with an explicit brief to

> *nettoyer la langue des ordures qu'elle avoit contractées ou dans la bouche du peuple ou dans la foule du Palais, ou dans les impuretez de la chicane, ou par le mauvais usage des courtisans ignorans ...*   (quoted in Chaurand 1999:235)
> 'cleanse the language of the filth it had picked up either in the mouth of the common people or in the crowds in the law-court, or in the impure elements of low-grade lawyers or the bad usage of ignorant courtiers ...'

The founding statutes of the *Académie* included the requirement to produce a dictionary of the language, a grammar, and a book of French rhetoric. The first of these was published in 1694, the second in 1935, but the third project has never been realized.

Although various French word-lists were produced during the Middle Ages to assist English-speaking learners of French, the first recognizable *dictionary* of French produced in France is probably Robert Estienne's *Dictionnaire francois-latin* (1549). The first monolingual dictionary is J. Nicot's *Trésor de la langue françoise* (1606). From the 1680s onwards, the production of dictionaries of various types became prolific. Here are some of the main ones:

1680	Richelet, *Dictionnaire françois*
1690	Furetière, *Dictionnaire universel*
1694	*Dictionnaire de l'Académie* (1st edition)
1704	*Dictionnaire universel françois et latin*
1762	*Dictionnaire de l'Académie* (2nd edition)
1765	Diderot & D'Alembert, *Encyclopédie*
1798	*Dictionnaire de l'Académie* (3rd edition)
1800	Boiste, *Dictionnaire*
1835	*Dictionnaire de l'Académie* (4th edition)

The other arm of codification is the production of *prescriptive grammars*. The first French grammar of French is Jean Dubois' *In Linguam gallicam Isagoge, una cum eiusdem grammatica latino-gallica* (1531) ['Introduction to the French language, with a Latin-French grammar of the same']. As we can discern from the title, the grammarians of the time were preoccupied above all with the relationship between French and Latin. As the century wore on, two traditions emerged in grammatical writing: The first was concerned with understanding the nature of language and grammatical system, while the second was fundamentally prescriptive. The best examples of each type are, respectively, the so-called *Grammaire de Port-Royal* of Arnauld and Lancelot (1660), and Claude Mauger's *Nouvelle Grammaire françoise* (1706).

A crucial facet of the codification movement is the role played by literary authors. The seventeenth and eighteenth centuries produced a dazzling sequence of writers – Corneille, Pascal, Racine, Montesquieu, Voltaire, Rousseau, to name but a few – whose writings are associated with a period of *gloire* in the history of the country, and served as highly prestigious models of *bon usage*. The long-term effects of codification have been profound: Prescriptive linguistic norms are probably more powerful in France, even today, than in any other European country. What gave this movement such powerful momentum?

6.2 Motivation for codification

Pressure for codification of the norms of standard French came from various directions. An important element in the production of dictionaries, grammars and general observations on French at this time was a disinterested, philosophical interest in the nature of language itself. For centuries, Paris had been one of the principal hubs in the development of European ideas. The University had provided the focus in the thirteenth century, and while this was no longer the case three centuries later, Paris, as the largest metropolis in Europe, continued to be a major intellectual center. This can be clearly seen in the size of the Paris book-trade (see Martin 1999). Throughout the *Ancien Régime* and beyond, reflection about language was a major element in intellectual exchange, and this shows through in the great sophistication of seventeenth and eighteenth century French metalinguistic discourse (see Chevalier 1968).

That said, language standardization is a political act, and we can regard the two interventions by the state we have mentioned – the Ordinance of Villers-Cotterêts (1539) and the setting up of the *Académie* (1635) – as early examples of language planning, the first being involved with status planning and the second with corpus planning. Unifying the language of government administration on the basis of the King's French had obvious political advantages, and bringing semi-public discussion of literary texts under the aegis of the *Académie* gave the prime minister Richelieu a powerful instrument for the control of ideas. As the French language became established as a symbol of royal power and as a badge of an emerging 'nation' (in the modern understanding of that word), standardization was deemed necessary to guarantee its international status, especially in comparison with Italian, but subsequently in the face of Spanish and, eventually, of English. It is worth recalling that the French *Académie* was set up in direct imitation of the Florentine *Accademia della Crusca*. It would be anachronistic, however, to see these early-modern developments as part of a long-term political project to unify the speech of the entire French population.

A third set of factors was social in nature, and they were probably the determining ones in phonology and in some parts of the lexis and grammar. The process of koineization, which we saw at work in medieval Paris, produced a relatively stable mixture of dialect forms, but the city's demographic dependence upon provincial inmigration made linguistic homogeneity impossible to achieve. Social developments initiated by the Renaissance, involving the movement into the city of important sections of the aristocracy, accentuated social division and conflict. Speakers' attitudes towards variant linguistic forms rarely remain neutral, and, as a result, residual dialect variants tend to be redistributed as stylistic variants, or as social-class variants. This seems to have been the case in the early-modern period, for example, with the variant forms [ɛ], [wɛ] and [wa] descended from the /OI/ diphthong of Old French (e.g., in *moi, toi, loi*). Broadly speaking, [ɛ] was low-status, [wɛ] high-status, and [wa] medium status and rising. Such reassignment (or 'reallocation') of variants normally takes place implicitly, even subconsciously, but it is possible to see it working itself out explicitly and consciously in the process of linguistic codification in seventeenth-eighteenth-century Paris.

6.3 Sociolinguistic variation in seventeenth-century Paris

To illustrate the linguistic distance separating upper- and lower-class speakers in Paris, we can quote the following comic pamphlet printed in 1644:

La Bourgeoise: *Parlez, ma grand'amie, vostre marée est-elle fraiche?*
La Poissonniere: Et nennin, nennin, laissez cela là, ne la patené pas tan; nos alauzes sont bonnes, mais note raye put; je panse qu'aussi bien fait vote barbue.

4   La Bourgeoise: *Je ne m'offense pas ...*
La Poissonnière: Ouy, Madame a raison, le guieble a tort qu'il ne la prend; il est vray que j'avon le mot pour rire et vous le mot pour pleuré.

8   La Bourgeoise: *Mamie, donnons trêve ...*
La Poissonnière: Vous en poirez en un mot traize francs. Et me regardez l'oreille de ce poisson là: il est tout sanglant et en vie. Est-il dodu! et qui vaut

12   bien mieux bouté là son argent qu'à ste voirie de raye puante qui sant le pissat a pleine gorge.
La Bourgeoise: *Je voy bien qu'il est excellent ...*
La Poissonnière: Parle, hé! Parrette! N'as-tu pas veu madame Crotée,

16   mademoiselle du Pont-Orson, la pucelle d'Orléans! Donnez-luy blancs draps, a ste belle espousée de Massy, qui a les yeux de plastre! Ma foy! si ton fruict desire de notre poisson, tu te peux bien frotter au cul, car ton enfant n'en sera pas marqué!

20   Un Pourvoyeur: *Ma bonne femme, n'avez-vous point là de bon saumon frais?*
La Poissonnière: Samon framan! du saumon frais! en vous en va cueilly, Parrette! Ste viande-là est un peu trop rare. Ce ne sont point viande pour nos oyseux: car j'iré bouté de seize à dix-huict francs à un meschant saumon, et vous

24   m'en offrirez des demy-pistoles. Et nennin, je ne somme pas si babillarde; je n'avon pas le loisi d'allé pardre note argent pour donné des morciaux friands a monsieur a nos despens. Si vous voulez voir un sot mont, allez vous en sur la butte de Montmartre, note homme dit que c'est un sot mon: car darnièrement,

28   quand il estet yvre, il se laissit tombé du haut en bas, et si cela ne l'y coustit rien.[11]
(see Lodge 2004:255–256)

Literary depictions of sociolinguistic variation, like this one, are based on stereotypes and cannot be read as realistic representations of vernacular speech (see Lodge 1996).

---

11.   The Lady: *Tell me, dear lady, if your fish be quite fresh?*
The Fishwife: Nay, nay give over, don't paw it about like that; our herrings are good but our skate stinks to high heaven, just like that husband of yours.
The Lady: *I'll not take offense at what you say ...*
The Fishwife: Yea, Madam is right, the devil's wrong not to take him; it's true that I've got words to make you smile you words to make us cry.
The Lady: *Dear Lady, let us call a truce there ...*
The Fishwife: Right then, you'll pay just thirteen francs for it. And just look at that fish's gills: he's still alive and bleeding. A lot of flesh on him! And it's much better sticking your money there than on that filthy stinking skate which reeks of piss.
The Lady: *I do indeed see that it is excellent ...*
The Fishwife: You don't say! Oy! Pierrette! You ain't seen mistress Crotée, miss Pont-Orson, the 'Maid' of Orléans! Give her some white sheets, that blushing bride from Massy, with her watery eyes. Bloody Hell! If your brat wants some of our fish, you can wipe your arse with it and your kid won't get a scratch!
A Merchant: *My good lady, you would not have a good fresh salmon over there?*

However, this extract gives a clear indication of the sorts of high-salience variable which were the object of reallocation at this time. Let us briefly review them:

Lexis:	*babillarde* (*24*), *bouté* (*12, 23*), *nennin* (*2, 24*), *patené* (*2*), *samon framon* (*21*), *voirie* (*12*).
Phonetics:	Reduction of consonant clusters – *note* (*3, 22, 27*), *vote* (*3*).
	Loss of final [r] – *bouté* (*12, 23*), *cueilly* (*21*), *loisi* (*25*), *pleuré* (*7*)
	[dj] + vowel > [gj] + vowel – *guieble* (*5*)
	Reduction of hiatus – *poirez* (*9*)
	[er] ~ [ar] – *Parrette* (*15*), *pardre* (*25*), *darnièrement* (*27*)
	[o] ~ [jo] – *morciaux* (*25*)
Morphology:	*je* + *-ons* – *j'avon* (*7, 23–24*), *je somme* (*24*)
	Past historics in *-it* – *lassit* (*28*), *coustit* (*28*)
	Demonstratives: *cette* ~ *ste* (*12, 17*)
Syntax:	Subject post-position
	– after initial adverb:
	aussi bien fait vote barbue (*3*).
	– in exclamitives:
	Est-il dodu! (*11*)
	Ethic datives: *Et me regardez l'oreille* (*9*).

Early evidence about sociolinguistic variation in Paris, like that admirably described by Ayres-Bennett (1990, 2004), is extremely important when we try to understand the changes which have subsequently taken place in the language. If we take post-seventeenth century developments in the standard language in isolation, it appears that much less has changed in French than, say, in English. Some minor modifications of the standard have been admitted: In orthography (e.g., the replacement of 'oi' by 'ai' in the endings of the imperfect and conditional, the suppression of pre-consonantal 's' in words like *estre, forest, feste*), and in pronunciation (e.g., realization of the /OI/ diphthong has shifted from [wɛ] to [wa], word-final schwa [ə] has been elided, and distinctions of vowel-length are no longer *de rigueur* in pairs like *lit* ~ *lie*, apical [r] has been replaced by uvular [R], l *mouillé* has been replaced by jod) (see Martinet 1969). However, the strength of the normative tradition in France has been such that the norms of the French standard language remain essentially as they were two and a half centuries ago.

On the other hand, if we take a more inclusive view of what constitutes the French language, we cannot but be struck by the wide gulf which now separates the standard

The Fishwife: Of course we have! Fresh salmon! We'll go get you one. Pierrette! That there meat is a bit too dear. It's not the sort of meat for our customers. I go spending sixteen-eighteen francs on a bloody salmon, and you just give me coppers for it. Nay, I'm not such a gas-bag; I can't go chucking our money away giving tasty morsels to some gent at our expense. If you want to see a crazy hill, get yourself off to Montmartre. That man of ours says its a crazy hill, because, the other day, when he was sloshed, he fell all the way down from top to bottom, and you can't say that didn't cost him anything.

and vernacular forms of the language. What shows up in contemporary French as linguistic variation simultaneously illustrates the linguistic changes which have been in progress since the seventeenth century (see §7.2). While some of the non-standard forms currently in use are recent innovations, many have a long history often masked from view in earlier written texts (see Bork 1975; Hausmann 1979; Hunnius 1975).

6.4 The diffusion of French

We wrote earlier that the process of codification in early-modern France took place essentially in Paris. Let us look briefly at the rest of France in the early-modern period, and then consider the spread of French beyond the borders of the kingdom. It is clear that by the seventeenth century, Parisian French had been accepted throughout the kingdom as the only language of writing, consigning Latin to the church and the schoolroom. Some serious literary activity persisted in Occitan in the region of Toulouse, but, in the rest of the country, when regional dialects and languages were used in writing, it was generally to mock them in comic or burlesque texts. In the provinces at this time, French had certainly penetrated the nobility and the upper ranks of the urban population, and was moving slowly down the urban hierarchy of France. However, in the south of the country, even among the urban elites, Parisian French was still something of a language for special occasions. Since the bulk of the population lived in small rural communities, the language of everyday speech remained the local *patois* or regional language (Breton, Alsatian, Basque, etc.). We get a snapshot of the overwhelming dominance of dialectal speech at the end of the eighteenth century in the survey conducted by Abbé Grégoire in the 1790s (see Gazier 1880). This situation did not change until industrialization.

If Parisian French served as a badge of upper-class status in the provinces of France, such was the prestige of Paris throughout Europe in the late seventeenth and eighteenth centuries, that French replaced Latin as the language of international diplomacy and became the H language of the social elites in various countries, notably Prussia, Poland and Russia. Its widespread use by the intellectuals of Europe fostered the belief in the *universalité* of French. It was believed that Standard French was the 'best' language, not because the 'best' people spoke it, but because it possessed inherent qualities of clarity and universal reason and logic which set it above all the other languages of Europe. This myth forms an integral part of standard ideology in France, and is still widely subscribed to even in our own day (see Bauer & Trudgill 1998: 23–31).

When French came to be used in other European countries at this time, it was normally as a superimposed H-language. However, in two important regions of Europe outside the borders of France the population spoke their own indigenous varieties of Gallo-Romance – in southern Belgium (Walloon) and in western Switzerland (a variety of Franco-Provençal). On the history of French in Belgium see Francard (1990), and on that of French in Switzerland see Bovet (1988). Although these regions did not fall within the French state, Parisian French diffused into these regions in the way it permeated the provinces of France itself, though with a certain delay.

Expansion in the use of French was not confined to Europe (see Chaudenson 1999; Mather in this volume; Valdman 1979). As part of a general movement of European colonization, the French began acquiring overseas territories in the seventeenth century – in the Indian Ocean, in the West Indies and in North America (Louisiana, and most importantly, Quebec). Most of these territories were ceded to Britain during the eighteenth-century colonial wars, but the French language generally survived, frequently retaining linguistic features discarded by metropolitan French.[12] In the Pacific, the Indian Ocean and in the West Indies French persists in the French-based creoles (see Stein 1987; Hull 1988; Posner 1997:91–99), and in North America in the form of Cajun and Quebecois (see Valdman, Auger, & Piston-Hatien 2005). On the linguistic characteristics of Quebec French see Morin (1994), Gauthier and Lavoie (1995), Mougeon and Béniak (1995). The case of French in Canada is particularly important for the history of French, in view of its revival in the second half of the twentieth century, when all the conditions had seemed set for its demise, in a continent where its speakers are greatly outnumbered by speakers of English (see Lockerbie, Molinaro, Larose, & Oakes 2005).

7.   Acceptance

The final stage of Haugen's taxonomy of standardization is the 'acceptance' of standard speech-norms by the community at large. It is reasonable to claim that the most striking sociolinguistic development in French over the past two centuries has been the near-eradication of the regional dialects and languages. This does not mean, however, that linguistic uniformity has been achieved: Standardization is an on-going process and, within any language, there is permanent tension between conservative and innovatory forces. In this closing section, let us examine first how the position of the traditional dialects and languages of France has been eroded over the past two centuries, and second how, despite this, the French language in our own day remains subject to variation and change.

7.1   Demise of the traditional dialects and languages of France

An invaluable picture of the distinctive rural vernaculars of Gallo-Romance, as they survived into the twentieth century, is to be found in two major sets of dialect atlases – the *Atlas linguistique de la France* (see Gilliéron & Edmont 1904–1911), and the various *Atlas linguistiques par régions* (see Séguy 1973). The main lexicological source is to be found in the remarkable 24 volume *Französisches Etymologisches Wörterbuch* (see von Wartburg 1923–1983).

---

12.   In Quebec French, the most salient example of this is the retention of the undifferentiated diphthong [wɛ̃] in contrast to metropolitan French [wa] in such words as *moi, toi, loi.*

On the basis of Abbé Grégoire's dialect survey of 1790, it has been estimated that at that time only three million of the twenty eight million population of France spoke French *correctement*, the remainder speaking various dialects and regional languages. Two centuries later, we can say that these proportions have been roughly inverted, factoring in, of course, a doubling of the total population of metropolitan France. In the 1999 census, INSEE sampled 380,000 adult people all across Metropolitan France, and asked them about the languages that their parents spoke with them before the age of five. The results were extrapolated to the population as a whole and generated the following statistics:

French:	42,100,000 (92%)
Oc languages:	1,670,000 (3.65%)
Germanic dialects:	1,440,000 (3.15%)
Oïl languages:	1,420,000 (3.10%)
Arabic:	1,170,000 (2.55%)

Given the difficulty of counting the numbers of speakers of particular languages and dialects, the absolute value of these figures is small.[13] However, they provide a general order of magnitude.

The diffusion of the standard language into the outlying provinces of France proceeded at different rates and along different pathways in different parts of the country. Parisian French cascaded down the urban hierarchy of France, hitting the towns earlier than the countryside. The chronology of diffusion followed a sort of S-curve, gathering pace in the first half of the nineteenth century, greatly accelerating in the second half, and levelling off in the twentieth century. In the areas where separate languages are spoken – Occitan and Basque in the south, Breton in the west, Flemish in the north and Alsatian in the east – the introduction of Parisian French involved a process of language shift, in the area of the *langue d'oïl* dialects, one of dialect convergence. There was a pattern of inter-generational shifting, whereby, typically, the first generation was monolingual in dialect, the second partially bi-lingual with receptive control of the standard language grafted on to the dialect, the third had fuller control of the standard, and receptive use of the dialect, and the fourth generation was monolingual in the standard language (see Maurand 1981). Once this point is reached, the traditional vernacular survives vestigially in the regional 'accent' and in regional vocabulary. These modern dialects are referred to as *français régionaux* (see Rézeau 2001).

Why has traditional dialectal speech been more effectively eradicated in France than in other European country of similar size, for example, Italy and Spain? Most observers attribute the triumph of the standard language principally to the language planning policies of the French state. We saw earlier how the monarchy had engaged in a minor way in status-planning and corpus-planning in the sixteenth and seventeenth centuries (see §5.1 and §6.1). However, we should note that the *Ancien Régime* saw no interest in spreading the standard language across the population at large. Indeed,

---

13.   These figures are drawn from the *Enquête familiale*, published by Insee in 1999.

members of the ruling class were often actively hostile to this process, fearing that the education of the poor would induce some to leave their allotted station in life and, perhaps, challenge the *régime*.

A dramatic ideological shift occurred with the Revolution of 1789. With the abolition of the monarchy, new symbols of national identity were urgently required (see Ager 1999). The standard French language slipped into this role, serving to cement internal cohesion (solidarity between all Frenchmen), and create external distinction (difference from members of other nations). Revolutionary leaders promoted a 'one language, one nation' ideology which made all non-standard speech-forms unpatriotic, and demanded a language planning policy of linguistic assimilation, the chief instrument of which would be primary education.

While the Revolution had a profound effect on the way French people thought about language, it took many decades for effective language planning policies (in the form of compulsory primary education) to be implemented. The conservative governments of the restored monarchy (1815–1848) and the Second Empire (1852–1870) put few resources into popular education. It was not until the 1880s and Jules Ferry's education acts that universal literacy programmes were finally put in place. Non-standard speech forms were seen as potential threats to the unity of the Republic and were vigorously proscribed. It is worth noting that at this time France applied analogous linguistic assimilation policies in the colonial empire it was creating in Indo-China and in Africa. The development of 'new Frenches' in the cities of Africa since de-colonization is particularly interesting (on the French spoken in Abidjan in Côte d'Ivoire see Ploog 2002; see Sonaiya, this volume, for an overview of the French spoken in West Africa).

After the Second World War, the Fourth Republic relaxed the policy, and via the Loi Deixonne (1951), allowed certain regional languages (Basque, Breton, Catalan, Occitan) to be taught in state schools (see Ager 1990). Had the use of these languages now declined so far that they no longer posed a threat to national unity? At the beginning of the twenty-first century, regional vernaculars have secured a space in the school curriculum, but whether this will create new speech communities, or whether it will serve simply to maintain the dialects as museum pieces is uncertain.

A strong *volontariste* tradition of thought leads many to believe that the 'acceptance' of the standard was brought about primarily by the will of politicians. This explanation is too simple. Political action in this sphere was driven by more profound social and economic changes. The linguistic unification of the country over this time coincides with a period of unprecedented industrialization and urbanization, accompanied by successive revolutions in transport and communications. A national market in goods and services required a common language, just as it required a common coinage and system of weights and measures. 'Dialect' diversity increases proportionately to the degree of communicative isolation between groups, and, conversely, it decreases as communication and levels of interaction increase. In an increasingly urban society, the traditional rural vernaculars were left with virtually no part to play.

Over the past century and a half, all western European countries have witnessed the triumph of their standard language over regional dialects. What is specific about the French experience is the extent to which dialect diversity has been reduced, when compared to the situation in Italy, Spain, Germany, and even the UK. We can understand this if we compare patterns of urbanization in these different countries: No country is more dominated by a single primate capital (a city which has grown disproportionately large when measured against the rest of its urban system) than France. Paris has eliminated all alternative norm centers in France in a way in which Rome, Madrid, Berlin, and even London, in their respective countries, have not.

7.2 Socio-stylistic variation

Haugen's process of 'acceptance' may now be virtually complete, but to say that the French language is fully standardized, and that variation has been banished contradicts all the evidence. To take an obvious example: In-migration from outside Europe over the past half century has brought into France large numbers of new languages, one of which, Arabic, has almost as many speakers (1,170,000) as Occitan (1,670,000). This tendency is unlikely to be halted. Furthermore, while geographical diversity within Gallo-Romance may have been curtailed, socio-stylistic variation has not (see Gadet 2003), and the gap between standard and vernacular varieties of French is particularly wide. A powerful normative tradition may slow down change in the standard language, but it is unlikely to have the same success with vernacular usage. Let us examine this further, firstly on the level of phonetics and grammar, then on that of lexis.

7.2.1 Phonetic variation and change

Although the pronunciation norms of standard French have changed since the seventeenth century (see above §6.4), they remain conservative. On the other hand, vernacular pronunciation has moved on considerably, merging several distinctions which are phonemic in formal speech-styles:

- Distinctions of vowel length cease to be phonemic, e.g.:
  [a] ∼ [aː] *chat* (short) ∼ *chats* (long)
  [a] ∼ [ɑ] merge → [a], e.g. *tâche* ∼ *tache*
  [œ̃] ∼ [ɛ̃] merge → [ɛ̃], e.g.: *brun* ∼ *brin*

The so-called *loi de position* (see Yaguello 2003: 295–297) distributes the open and closed mid-vowels in informal French not phonemically, but according to syllable type, with open vowels gravitating to closed syllables and *vice versa*:

- Closed syllables:
  [e] ∼ [ɛ] opening of [e] → [ɛ] (e.g., Modern French *père* was earlier pronounced *pére*)
  [o] ∼ [ɔ] opening of [o] → [ɔ] (e.g., *pôle* is homophonous with *Paul* in some colloquial varieties)
- Open syllables:

[ɛ] ~ [e] tensing of [ɛ] → [e] (e.g., *raisonner* becomes homophonous with *résonner*)

[ɔ] ~ [o] tensing of [ɔ] → [o] (e.g., *turbot* ~ *turbot*)

7.2.2 *Grammatical variation and change*

The development of Latin syntax into French involves a typological shift from synthetic to analytical (see Harris 1978). Various long-term changes in the French grammatical system, arrested in the formal language, have continued to progress in everyday speech. This can be seen in many areas of French grammar:

– Preposed determiners have replaced nominal flexions for marking number, e.g., *les voitures* [le vwatyʀ]. The written language continues to reflect the medieval flexional system.

– Preposed clitic pronouns have come to replace flexions in marking the person of the verb, e.g., *ils aiment* [il zɛm]. The drift towards invariable verb-forms is supported by the spread of *on* at the expense of *nous*, e.g., *nous aimons* [nu zemõ] → [õ nɛm]. Reference might be made here to pragmatically unmarked clitic doubling (**Moi, ma copine je l'aime bien** 'me, my girlfriend, I like her') which is ubiquitous in spoken French and has been discussed in the context of the increasingly prefixal status of the traditional French pronouns (i.e., it cannot be inverted, coordinated, separated from their verb, take stress, etc.).

– The tense system has seen the virtual elimination from informal usage of the past historic (*il chanta* 'he sang') and past anterior (*il eut chanté* 'he had sung'), and the progress of the periphrastic *aller* + infinitive (*il va aimer* 'he's going to like'), at the expense of the 'synthetic' future (*il aimera* 'he will like') (cf. above §2.0). Mention might be made of the extension of the present tense with future meaning alongside the periphrastic form (though admittedly with slightly different nuance).

– The expression of modality through contrasts between indicative and subjunctive verb-forms has been almost abandoned: In informal usage, the past subjunctive has disappeared completely, and use of the present subjunctive (for most persons in most verbs formally identical with the indicative) is now syntactically conditioned almost exclusively. For example, there is a theoretical difference between *le fait que tu es malade* 'the fact that you are sick' (definitely) and *le fait que tu sois malade* 'the fact that you may be sick', but for most speakers the subjunctive here is quasi-categorical in the spoken language at least.

There is a tendency for languages with analytical structures to be 'configurational languages' (languages where word order is fixed). Since medieval French, the incidence of Subject-Verb inversion has decreased progressively (see above §5.2.1). Although it still is found in formal varieties of French (e.g., *Ces étoffes sont belles, aussi coûtent-elles cher*, 'these fabrics are beautiful, thus they are expensive', and *Comment cet enfant a-t-il pu venir jusque là?* 'how could this child come all the way here'), it has been eliminated from informal usage, even in interrogatives (e.g., *Comment il a pu venir jusque là, cet enfant?* 'how could he come all the way here, this child') (see Coveney 1996:91–244).

In earlier forms of French post-position of the subject was an important tool for top-icalization. This function is carried in colloquial French by dislocation, as in *Il est allé se remarier le père* 'he went and got remarried the father', and by clefting, for example: *Ce que j'aime c'est le Piat d'Or* 'what I like is the Piat d'Or'.

The evolution of French syntax provides examples of changes involving gram-maticalization. The most striking of these is negation. We saw above (§5.2.1) how pre-verbal negation in Old French (e.g., *li cuens ne vint* 'the earl did not turn up') was occasionally reinforced by nouns like *pas* ('step'), *point* ('jot'), *mie* ('crumb'). In the later medieval period, the incidence of these nouns increased, semantic bleaching took place, and gave rise to the double negation of standard French. In the modern spoken language, however, we find almost exclusively post-verbal negation (*pas* only) (see Coveney 1996: 55–90; Martineau & Mougeon 2003).

7.2.3 *Lexical variation and change*

The lexicon is that part of the linguistic system which shows the greatest capacity to change in line with changes in society (see Colin 2003). The bulk of neologisms in French are created from native resources by affixation, compounding and semantic change. While the resources of the Classical languages continue to be drawn upon very heavily, the statistical importance of borrowing from other languages, notably English, is frequently exaggerated. National feelings are highly sensitive to English lexical influ-ence, which the state has taken energetic steps to curtail – in the *loi Bas-Lauriol* of 1975 and the *loi Toubon* of 1994 – and to replace with native equivalents.

Particularly striking in French are lexical differences between the formal and col-loquial forms of the language, where we find hundreds of paired items denoting com-monly referred to objects such as: *Fric* ∼ *argent* ('money'), *bagnole* ∼ *voiture* ('car'), *bouquin* ∼ *livre* ('book') (see Lodge 1999). It is tempting to believe that the informal variants represent innovations alongside more ancient formal items. This is not usu-ally the case, for examples of slang usage are attested as early as the thirteenth century, and many informal items have been in use for as long, if not longer, than their formal equivalent.

The most strongly marked non-standard items in French are associated with *ar-got* – originally the in-group vocabulary of thieves and vagabonds in late medieval Paris (see Guiraud 1968). Some traditional *argot* words were carried over into the speech of the Paris working class in the second half of the nineteenth century, where *argot* vocabulary was used as a badge of working-class solidarity and as a gesture of de-fiance against social norms felt to be oppressive. What makes Parisian *argot* interesting is not the fact that it is *re*lexicalised (i.e., that it creates its own technical terms), but the fact that it is *over*-lexicalized. The accumulation of alternative synonyms found in *argot* is larger than life. It presents not just one alternative word for, say, 'police', but dozens (see Guiraud 1956: 61). Such lexical exuberance is normally explained by stu-dents of slang as the result of a never-ending search for originality, for the sake either of secrecy, or of liveliness and humor. There is probably more to it than this.

The main function of *argot* seems to be to maintain the life of a group under pressure. *Argots* develop on the margins of society to foster cohesion and solidarity within the group, and a sense of separateness from the hostile world outside. Permanent renewal of *argot* vocabulary ('the never-ending search for originality') identifies those who are currently core members of the group, those who are falling by the wayside, and those who just do not belong at all (dismissed in Paris *argot* as *caves*, 'suckers'). The lexical exuberance of *argot* is not just an exotic and bizarre add-on. Its presence is essential if *argot* is to perform its central role in maintaining the life of the group and the status hierarchy within it. It is not surprising, therefore, that the second-third generation of Arab-speaking immigrants in France, known as the *Beurs* (a word derived by *verlan* from *Arabe*), should have adopted *argot* and particularly *verlan*, as a badge of ethnic identity.

8.   Conclusion

In this survey of the history of French we have considered the different phases in the evolution of the language in the framework of Haugen's taxonomy of standardization. Our approach has been a sociolinguistic one, emphasizing the importance of non-standard varieties in the development of the language, and the notion that a standard language is not a real variety but an abstract set of norms, an ideology. At the same time, we have considered changes in the internal structure of the language in its typological shift from synthetic to analytical. What does the future hold for French? There is a long-running debate in France on what is seen as *la crise du français* 'the crisis of French'-abroad, the status of French as a world language is felt to be massively threatened by English, and at home, the 'quality' of the language is perceived as being under permanent threat from the depredations of lesser-educated speakers. Such apocalyptic fears are exaggerated: Abroad, French cannot act as a global language on a par with English, but it will continue to be a key language in international organizations, like the UN, and one of the major languages of Europe, the Americas and North and West Africa, where it is the official language of twenty one states; at home, with the reduction in formality in western social behavior, compliance with the norms of the formal literary language may well decline, but the vitality of vernacular varieties, both inside and outside France, means that the future survival of the language, for all the fears of linguistic nationalists, is not seriously in doubt.

## PART II

Core aspects of the second language acquisition of French

CHAPTER 3

French phonology and L2 acquisition*

S. J. Hannahs

University of Newcastle upon Tyne

Résumé

Ce chapitre vise à examiner les aspects essentiels de la phonologie française qui ont figuré dans les débats théoriques et qui, plus récemment, ont été au centre des recherches en acquisition. Parmi les questions à considérer se trouvent les problèmes concernant les inventaires segmentaux et l'apprentissage de nouveaux segments et le réglage du VOT ('voice onset time') aux normes du français, ainsi que des questions proprement phonologiques, telles que l'apprentissage de la liaison, des consonnes latentes, du e-caduc, de la syllabification et syllabicité. Le chapitre concluera par une discussion des questions phonologiques du français qui pourraient être examinées du point de vue de l'apprentissage du français langue seconde.

Abstract

This chapter surveys some of the most salient aspects of French phonology which have figured in both the theoretical literature and, more recently, in acquisition studies. Among the issues discussed are segmental inventories and acquisition, voice onset time (VOT), stress/rhythm, syllables and syllable structure, liaison, latent consonants and schwa. The chapter ends with suggestions for further directions in examining issues in French phonology that could usefully be investigated from a second language acquisition perspective.

1. Introduction

In this paper I address the twofold task of outlining salient aspects of the phonology of French – including theoretical studies of French phonological structure – and reviewing recent investigations into the acquisition of French as a second language. That acquisition can be divided roughly into three areas: (1) The acquisition of the phonetic values of the sounds of French, in terms of both segments and phonologi-

---

* Heartfelt thanks to Dalila Ayoun, Maggie Tallerman, Martha Young-Scholten and an anonymous reviewer. Their comments have improved this paper in very many ways. They are, of course, blameless for the remaining infelicities.

cal features, including aspects such as voice onset time; (2) The acquisition of specific phonological structures, such as permissible syllable structures, syllabifications and phonotactic constraints; and (3) The acquisition of phrasal processes, such as liaison, elision and variable schwa deletion, which may be affected not only by phonological considerations and phrase-level phonological structures, but also by morphosyntax and semantics, as well as by pragmatic factors such as style and register.

To start on the theoretical side, as observed by Anderson (1982), French has long served as a proving ground for phonological theory, informing numerous and varied aspects of phonological model building. Taking only a handful of studies over the past thirty-five years or so as illustrative, a number of central issues in phonological understanding have called upon French in one way or another, including: The abstractness debate (see e.g., Klausenburger 1978; Schane 1968; Stemberger 1985; Tranel 1981; and Walker 1975, for varying positions); syllable structure and syllabicity (e.g., Bybee 2001; Clements & Keyser 1983; Encrevé 1988; Kaye & Lowenstamm 1984); phrasal phonology and the role of suprasegmental phonological structure (e.g., Hannahs 1995a; Selkirk 1978, 1980); questions of phonology and morphological relatedness among lexical items (e.g., Dell & Selkirk 1978; Farina 1984; Schane 1968,); the phonology of schwa (e.g., Anderson 1982; Martinet 1972; Morin 1982; Noske 1993; Selkirk 1978; Tranel 1988; Verluyten 1988); level ordering in Lexical Phonology (Hannahs 1995b; Johnson 1987); and more recently, issues surrounding ranking and re-ranking of optimality theoretic constraints (see Bullock 2002; Tranel 1996a, 2000). Indeed, in recent decades, very few issues of central importance to phonologists have not been investigated with reference to French phonology.

Within the study of French phonology itself there are a number of perennial problems, descriptive and analytical difficulties against which new theories are tested. These problems, some of which will be discussed below, include liaison (with and without *enchaînement*), latent consonants, *h-aspiré*, the status of nasal(ized) vowels, the alternation between high vowels and glides, and the phonological status of schwa. Investigations into these and other phenomena have yielded insights not only into the phonological relationships obtaining in French, but also into various aspects of phonological theory. There is, therefore, clearly a sense in which investigation into French continues to inform phonological theory, while at the same time phonological theory provides insights into the phonology of French.

Regarding language acquisition, French has a long history of orthoepic literature, particularly addressed to foreign learners (e.g., Valdman, Salazar, & Charbonneaux 1964; Valdman 1993; Varney 1933). Despite this tradition, there has traditionally not been a great deal of work done on L2, or indeed L1, phonological acquisition. Nonetheless, as we shall see, recent years have seen an increased interest in the second language acquisition of French phonology.

Despite the important role that French has played and continues to play in testing linguistic theory, concerns have been voiced about the data itself. As pointed out by Morin (1987), there are serious questions about which French, or whose French, is the object of analysis – to what extent is there a uniform spoken French, a *'français de référence*'? (See also Encrevé's 1988:44 discussion of data used in analyses of liaison.) Taking for instance Martinet and Walter's (1973) study of a small (n = 17) and relatively homogeneous sample of predominantly Parisian speakers, even in such a small sample, there are potentially important differences between speakers. An example of such differences arises with words judged to be *h-aspiré*, thereby failing to participate in liaison and elision. In Martinet and Walter's sample, all speakers treated the words *héros* 'hero', *héron* 'heron' and *hanter* 'haunt' as *h-aspiré* words. On the other hand, some, but not all, of their subjects treated the words *haïtien* 'Haitian', *hameçon* 'hook', and *hernie* 'hernia' as *h-aspiré*. Given this kind of inter-speaker variation, particularly in the case of a small number of speakers sharing the same dialect, it is sometimes difficult to have full confidence in the generalizations drawn (though in this case one could of course argue that any analysis is formally distinct from the question of which lexical items belong to the class of *h-aspiré* words).

One recurring issue in the descriptive literature on French is that it is not always made clear which variety of French a particular set of data comes from, or a particular analysis applies to. Given the reality of differences between dialects, and the implications of such differences for phonological analysis and acquisition, this can have important repercussions. For example, the behavior with regard to nasalized vowels is different in northern and southern varieties of continental French. Therefore, any serious account of the phonology of nasals in French, for instance, needs to be explicit about the data under analysis, and the extent to which a particular analysis may or may not be generalizable to 'French'.

To a certain extent, some of the concerns about data are beginning to be addressed by an on-going large-scale project encompassing the collection of comparable data sets from at least thirty locations throughout the francophone world. The goal of the PFC project (*La phonologie du français contemporain: Usages, variétés et structure*, available at http://www.projet-pfc.net/), under the direction of Jacques Durand, Bernard Laks and Chantal Lyche, is to establish a large corpus of descriptively accurate comparable data sets of spoken French to enable researchers to obtain a snapshot of current French phonology, in order to investigate both the unity and the diversity of varieties of the language. Initially, the emphasis will be on the description of phoneme systems, the behavior of liaison and mute-e. The ultimate aim of the project is to create a reliable database comprising some 300 to 500 speakers, with the data gathered by means of a common methodology, thus allowing comparisons to be drawn across a representative sample of contemporary French varieties. It will be interesting to see how the PFC results affect the quality and quantity of descriptive French data available over the coming years, and the theoretical insights that such a database will enable.

One of the difficulties with French phonology, which is also reflected in acquisition studies, is the fact that, to a very large extent, the phonology interacts in various ways with the other subcomponents of grammar. Many alternations, such as the alternation between oral and nasal vowels in masculine ~ feminine doublets like *fin* [fɛ̃]~ *fine* [fin], *bon* [bõ] ~ *bonne* [bɔn], *brun* [bʁœ̃]~ *brune* [bʁyn], are morphophonological in nature, rather than simply phonological; while others, like liaison, may be constrained by specific syntactic configurations. As noted by Carton (1974: 88), obligatory liaison is closely tied to syntactic integration, and may contrast with prohibited liaison, thus allowing certain semantic distinctions to be expressed. Optional liaison, on the other hand, is stylistic, constituting one of the main phonetic criteria in defining register in French. This means that purely phonological approaches are very limited in what they can account for. At the same time, it means that acquisition studies must take into consideration more than whether or not a particular learner has acquired a specific phonological rule – can that learner also apply the rule in an appropriate morpho-lexical-syntactic context? Has that learner also acquired the relevant syntactic restrictions constraining the rule? This also relates to the three-level distinction mentioned above. In those cases where phonological behavior is affected by non-phonological language considerations (e.g., syntax, semantics, word choice, register, etc.), it may be more difficult to localize a subject's phonological knowledge.

In the rest of this paper, I survey salient aspects of French phonetics and phonology, presenting an overview of some characteristics and recurring issues in French phonology. Interleaved with these issues, I consider issues in L2 French phonological acquisition, referring as well to specific studies in the literature, for example Birdsong's research (in press) on nativelikeness in late learners, Steele's (2002a) examination of the acquisition of prosodic structure in French L2, and Thomas' (1998) investigation of liaison.

2.   Phonetics, phonology and acquisition: The background

There are clearcut phonetic differences between varieties of French, even at the most general level, for instance northern varieties of French vs. Midi French vs. the French of *Québec* and that of Belgium or Switzerland, to say nothing of the variation within those broad labels. Indeed, it is often phonetic differences which alert the listener to regional varieties of French. At the same time, however, the phonological underpinnings of different varieties of French are strikingly similar. That is not to say that there are no phonological differences. Indeed, the nasalization facts, for instance, may differ from one variety of French to another, or the presence vs. absence of schwa in particular positions or in particular words. Yet, taken as a whole, there are aspects of French phonology – phonological tendencies – that do appear to be characteristic of French in general, regardless of regional variety, and about which generalizations across French do appear to be warranted.

2.1   Inventories and phonetic characterizations

2.1.1   *Phonetic inventory – segments*
In light of the differences in varieties of French alluded to above, the phonetic inventories and general remarks presented below take standard Parisian French as a reference

Table 1. French phonetic inventory – consonants

	bilabial	labiodental	dental	Palatal	Velar	uvular
Stop	p, b		t, d		k, g	
Fricative		f, v	s, z	ʃ, ʒ		ʁ
Nasal	m		n	ɲ	ŋ	
Liquid/glide			l	j (spread) ɥ (rounded)	w	

point. There are several reasons for this decision. First of all, it is beyond the purview of this chapter to examine the variation across French phonetic inventories (for pertinent information on geographic variation, see Walter 2000; for sociolinguistic variation, see Dewaele this volume). Secondly, any cogent discussion of a phonological system needs to have a starting point. Given the familiarity of 'standard' northern French, this makes it appropriate as a point of departure in discussing French phonology. (For an enlightened discussion of the nomenclature and issues surrounding 'standard French', *français de référence*, etc., see Walker 2001: 1–6.)

French is typically said to have a phonetic inventory comprising some 21 consonant sounds (including glides) as displayed in Table 1.

To illustrate the phonetic variation occurring across varieties of French, in addition to the above, note that *Québec* French has the dental affricates [tˢ] and [dᶻ] before a high front vowel (see Dumas 1987; Gendron 1966; Picard 1987); Belgian varieties typically lack the rounded palatal glide [ɥ], while some varieties (e.g., Burgundy, Wallonie, parts of *Québec*) have an apical trill [r] rather than the uvular fricative [ʁ] or trill [R] (see Carton 1974: 30). Some varieties, particularly the Parisian variety, also have voiceless vowels word finally as in *oui* 'yes' and *bu* 'drank' (see Fagyal & Moisset 1999; Smith 2003).

Phonetically, there are about eleven oral monophthongs as shown in Figure 1.

Additionally, there are three or four nasalized monophthongs, depending on the variety: œ̃, ɔ̃, ɛ̃, ɑ̃. (In those varieties with three nasalized monophthongs [œ̃] has merged with [ɛ̃], making *brun* 'brown' homophonous with *brin* 'twig'.)

Note that schwa, ə, is not included in the phonetic inventory of monophthongs given above. In French, schwa (i.e., 'mute-e', 'variable schwa', '*e-muet*' '*e-caduc*') is essentially a phonological concept in that it is used to represent not a neutral vowel (as in English and many other languages), but a vowel with particular idiosyncratic behavior, including variable presence or absence depending both on its position within a phono-

Figure 1. French monophthongs

logical phrase and on lexical specificity.[1] The phonetic value of the vowel represented by schwa is typically mid front rounded [ø] (see for instance Carton 1974: 63f.).

Regarding diphthongs in modern French, Carton (1974: 45) notes that there are no diphthongs (or triphthongs) in the standard language. However, he also observes (1974: 52) that they were used in Old French, and that regional varieties of French still have a large number of diphthongs. Picard (1987: 59ff.), for example, notes thirteen diphthongs in North American French, including [ɪj] in *admire* 'admire', [ʊw] in *bouge* 'move', [ow] in *rose* 'rose', [aj] in *arrête* 'stop'.

As with consonants, the vowels also exhibit variation, both geographic and age-related. For instance, some older Parisian speakers may still have a mid rounded nasalized [œ̃] in words like *brun* 'brown' and *un* 'one', although for many speakers that vowel has merged with [ɛ̃]; other varieties of French, such as some varieties of Canadian French and Midi French, have maintained the contrast, though even here Gendron (1966: 100) observes that the same merger is occurring in *Québec* French. Along with the diphthongs noted above, *Québec* French also has three additional lax high vowels, [I], [Y], [U] (for a recent paper on *Québec* French vowels see Martin 2002).

Despite these sorts of phonetic variation across French, however, it could be argued that French as a whole has a relatively unitary phonology – with phonology understood as the abstract organizing system underpinning the sound system of the language. The differences between varieties of French tend to be due to relatively superficial phonetic implementation, rather than fundamental structural variation. In fact, comparing *Québec* French and Parisian French nicely exemplifies Sapir's (1925) argument that two languages (or language varieties) can differ in phonetic inventory while sharing the same phonological system. By way of illustration, spoken *Québec* French tends to sound different from other, particularly northern European, varieties of French. This results from relatively minor differences in the phonetics. For instance, the affrication of /t/ and /d/ when followed by a high front vowel in *Québec* French (QF) yields [tˢy] as compared with Parisian (PF) [ty], *tu* 'you'; the laxing of high vowels in closed syllables in QF gives a contrast between QF [vɪt] with PF [vit], *vite* 'quick'; and the loss through syncope of certain unstressed high vowels leads to different syllabification, such as four-syllable QF [elɛktrɪste] compared with five-syllable PF [elɛktrisite], *électricité* 'electricity'. These differences in phonetic implementation can be seen clearly in a single word such as *difficile* 'difficult'. Whereas in standard European French this will typically be pronounced as trisyllabic [difisil], the typical *Québec* pronounciation will be bisyllabic [dᶻɪfsɪl], with an affricated initial [dᶻ], lax high front [ɪ] in the first and last syllables, and loss of the underlying /i/ of the second syllable. Although such phonetic implementation makes *Québec* French sound very different from continental French, the phonological patternings and relationships involved are remarkably similar between the two varieties.

---

1. For an excellent study underscoring the phonological rather than phonetic nature of schwa, see Bullock and Gerfen (2005).

The point of mentioning geographic variation here, and the connection to acquisition is this: Despite the undeniable influence of the standard as a prescriptive norm, the learner may nonetheless confront geographic variants (to say nothing of register levels) in the input, simply by switching on a radio, watching a film or encountering French outside the classroom.

2.1.2 *Acquiring segments*

It has become apparent in recent years that the interdependency of linguistic systems and processes requires interface studies, research that is not limited to a single linguistic component. Regarding French phonology and the acquisition of French phonology, a large number of the processes affecting the sound system of French involve not only the phonological component of the grammar, but also other linguistic subsystems of the language. Any attempt, therefore, to present a purely formal phonological account of various processes will necessarily be incomplete. This may not, of course, be a bad thing, and the interest in interface studies at the borders between various subcomponents of the grammar over the past dozen years or so provides an indication that the field may be ready to embrace analyses involving various linguistic modules in a single account, not just with respect to phonological description, but for acquisition as well (see, e.g., Archibald 1998; Sharwood Smith & Truscott 2005; Young-Scholten 1993). Indeed, it is likely that significant insights will be gained for both description and acquisition by approaching linguistic analysis from various points at once. Nonetheless, let us begin by looking at segmental acquisition.

One phonetic task facing the learner is that of acquiring the new L2 segments that is, those segments which differ from the segments of the L1 in some definable way (see e.g., Flege 1987). For instance, the coronal segments of French (e.g., /t/, /d/, /n/, /l/) are typically pronounced with a dental articulation. This is also true of Spanish, but most varieties of English produce the coronals with an alveolar articulation (thus Flege 1987 would consider these French coronals 'similar' to the English ones: The English articulation of the coronals is not identical, yet they are not entirely dissimilar). This means that a Spanish speaker, for example, should have no difficulty in transferring his or her native L1 pronunciation of coronals to achieve native-like production of French coronals.[2] The English speaker, on the other hand, will need to be aware of this difference in articulation, and reset the articulation accordingly. This, of course, assumes an ideal learner aiming to achieve native-like production. Given that alveolar articulation of French coronals results in a non-native accent, but does not impede understanding, it may well be that any particular learner will not bother to acquire the different articulatory settings.

---

2. This ignores the phonological fact that Spanish has a process of intervocalic lenition, such that /d/ has an intervocalic allophone [ð]. So although the Spanish-speaking learner should have no problems with a dental articulation of [d], the learner will also have to learn to suppress the L1 allophonic realization of intervocalic /d/ as [ð]. See also Zampini (1998).

Both the Spanish- and English-speaking learner of French will likely have some difficulty with the high- and mid-front rounded vowels of French, those in *tu* [ty] and *peu* [pø], given that neither Spanish nor English has those vowels.

The question of differences and difficulties in acquiring new L2 sounds which are not instantiated in the L1 has long been of interest in studies of phonological acquisition, at least since Weinreich (1953) and Lado (1957). Some twenty years ago, Flege and Hillenbrand (1987) revisited the question experimentally, examining, among other things, the production and perception of French /y/ and /u/ by a group of American English speakers. French /y/ was considered to be a new sound to the English speakers, whereas French /u/, despite acoustic and articulatory differences from English /u/, was considered a counterpart sound, similar enough to be available for interlingual identification with English /u/. Interestingly, they were able to show that their English-speaking subjects were able to produce French /y/ more accurately than they did the similar French /u/, that is, /y/ was produced with values closer to French norms than was /u/. Flege and Hillenbrand also showed that the more experienced subjects produced the French sounds with greater accuracy. Just as French data have been used to inform phonological theory, French acquisition data are also brought in as evidence regarding acquisition theory.

Another more recent study focusing on segmental acquisition is that of Cichocki, House, Kinlock and Lister (1999), in which they examine the acquisition of initial and final consonant production in French by Cantonese speakers. A major aim of the study is "to provide practical guidance in the pronunciation of French to Cantonese-speaking students and their teachers" (p. 97). This study is particularly concerned with [voice] as a feature, since the distribution of voicing in initial and final stops and fricatives differs between Cantonese and French. As Cichocki et al. point out, one of the interests in this sort of study is that by examining a relatively undocumented language pairing, the database of empirical acquisition studies is enhanced, thereby increasing the means of explicitly testing various acquisition hypotheses. In this particular case the researchers focus on Eckman's (1977) Markedness Differential Hypothesis (MDH), according to which target language forms which are both different from L1 forms and which are more marked (in a universal sense) will be more difficult to acquire than L2 forms which are different from L1 but less marked.

Cichocki et al.'s subjects were six native Cantonese-speaking residents of Hong Kong, 1 male, 5 female. None had spent prolonged periods outside Hong Kong and none had spent time in a French-speaking environment. Their French learning backgrounds consisted of between 1½ to 5 years of French instruction at the local *Alliance Française*. All were considered to have a proficiency of 'upper beginner' and 'lower intermediary' level. The subjects did, however, all speak fluent English. Each subject was recorded during an individual interview, a reading passage, and the production of a large number of words, the last being French equivalents of Cantonese or English words presented to the subject.

Cichocki et al.'s overall finding is that the patterns of difficulty of the Cantonese native speakers learning French are generally in line with the MDH, although there are some systematic exceptions, exceptions which the authors suggest may be related to the acquisition context itself, rather than necessarily representing counter-examples to the MDH.

In another recent study, Levy (2004) examines the acquisition of French [y] and [œ] by American English speakers. Particularly concerned with the relationship between perception and discrimination, she tested three groups of native speakers of American English, a group with minimal experience with French (n = 13), a group with moderate French experience (n = 13) and a group with extensive experience with French (n = 13). The subjects were given a Perceptual Assimilation task involving the French vowels /y, œ, u, o, i, ɛ, a/, and a three-part Categorial Discrimination task with French front vs. back rounded vowel pairs, /y~u/, /y~o/, /ø~o/, /ø~u/, front rounded vs. front unrounded pairs /y~u/, /y~o/, /œ~o/, /œ~i/, and a front rounded pair differing in height, /y~œ/. Significantly, there was overwhelming (94%) perceptual assimilation of French front rounded vowels /y/ and /œ/ to back American English vowels by all groups. Interestingly, formal instruction in French was not a predictor of perceptual success; however, extensive immersion experience did yield significantly fewer errors (4%) than formal experience alone. Levy argues that the connection between perceptual assimilation and discrimination errors in her study supports Best's (1994, 1995) Perceptual Assimilation Model, according to which a learner's perceptual assimilation of unfamiliar L2 segments into their L1 phonology is predictive of their accuracy in discriminating L2 sounds.

2.1.3 Voice onset time

One of the phonetic parameters along which languages vary, and which may be characteristic for particular languages, is voice onset time (VOT), a measurement of the time difference, if any, between the release of the closure of a voiceless stop and the beginning of vocal cord vibration for a following vowel. When the stop release is concurrent with the start of vocal cord vibration (so-called 'short-lag VOT') there is no aspiration and a 'plain stop' results. If stop release occurs in advance of the onset of vocal cord vibration the release will be accompanied by aspiration ('long-lag VOT').

Because VOT settings are language specific, and vary along a continuum from fully voiced through strongly aspirated, many language acquisition studies and studies of bilingualism have focussed on VOT where the VOT values of the two languages differ systematically. French and English differ in their characteristic VOT values for word-initial voiceless stops and have therefore been the focus of numerous first and second language acquisition studies, as well as studies investigating bilingual acquisition. French voiceless stops (like those of the Romance languages more generally) are characterized by the absence of aspiration. English, on the other hand (along with some of the other Germanic languages), has positionally determined plain and aspirated voiceless stops. The interest of acquisition studies in VOT relates to the transfer (or otherwise) of L1 VOT values to L2. Under the assumption of L1 transfer, the prediction is that the L1 English-speaking learner of L2 French, for example, will have difficulty suppressing the aspiration associated with English voiceless stops in initial position. Therefore, one of the tasks of the learner is to acquire the VOT values of L2.

There is more to the acquisition of VOT, however, than simply acquiring new values. VOT values in this case have both a phonetic and a phonological dimension. Phonetically, voiceless stops in French and English differ in VOT values word-initially and in the onset of a stressed syllable, where English alone has aspiration, that is, long-lag VOT. Elsewhere, though, the voiceless stops of French and English have very similar VOT values. In terms of the learner's task, the English-speaking learner of French will need to learn to suppress long-lag VOT; the French-speaking learner of English, on the other hand, will need to acquire long-lag voice onset timing word-initially and in the onset of a stressed syllable, but not elsewhere. So although the VOT values have a phonetic dimension, their distribution pattern, that is, the value associated with any particular position in a word, is phonological.

2.1.4 *Acquisition and VOT*

As we have just seen, the primary characteristics of voice onset time are phonetic in nature. Thus, the fundamental question in L2 studies of VOT is the extent to which the learner is able to achieve native-like production of VOT. In phonetic terms, the difficulty of the learner's task will, of course, depend on the relative VOT values of L1 compared with L2, and any differences in those values. Beyond the phonetic aspects of VOT are the phonological questions involving positional variation in VOT.

A number of studies in the literature have looked specifically at VOT, particularly with regard to bilingual learners. Moreover, some studies, such as Flege and Hillenbrand (1987), use VOT as evidence in support of proficiency characterizations arrived at by other means. In addition to the study of bilinguals (for example Mack, Bott, & Boronat 1995), a recent study of L2 French focusing on VOT is that by Birdsong (in press). Birdsong's main emphasis is on the potential of late learners to acquire native-like pronunciation. Recognizing that the perception of native-likeness depends both on global performance as well as on control of specific segmental properties, he examines the performance of late L2 French learners' VOT values and vowel length, as well as their global native-like performance.

Birdsong's subject pool of native English speakers consisted of 22 participants (7 male, 15 female). Their age at the time of immersion in French ranged from 18 to 61 years; they had all lived in the Paris area for a minimum of five years (the range was 5 to 32 years). Their ages ranged from 26 to 69 years. The French-speaking control group consisted of seventeen native French speakers (10 male, 17 female), ranging in age from 21 to 45 years. All members of the control group were residing in Paris, and all were from the Ile-de-France region or northern France. Both groups were recorded reading a list of words, which were subsequently analyzed for vowel duration and VOT values. For in-context pronunciation, the subjects were recorded reading passages from essays. These were judged on global accent by three native speakers of French from Paris, Nantes, and Amiens.

On the basis of instrumental analysis and native-speaker judgments, a significant number (+10%) of late learners in Birdsong's study were shown to have achieved nativelike control of L2 French. This calls into question specific claims with respect to the Critical Period Hypothesis, in particular the assumption that acquiring nativelike pronunciation is impossible for late learners (see for example Johnson & Newport 1989; and Long 1990). Birdsong concludes that late successful acquisition is possible.

2.2 Phonology and phonological patterns

2.2.1 *The stress system*
Lexical stress in French is assigned by syllable position in the word: The final syllable bears main stress unless that syllable contains schwa. In the latter case, the penultimate syllable bears main stress (see Walker 1975). Likewise, the last syllable of the phonological phrase bears the main phrasal stress (with the same caveat about schwa in a phrase-final syllable).

> (1)   Lexical main stress on final syllable: *deVOIR,   revendicaTION*
> 'task'   'claim'
> Phrasal main stress on final syllable: *il y fait toujours CHAUD*
> 'it's always hot there'

While characterizing primary lexical and phrasal stress is relatively straightforward, the question of secondary stress is much less so. Some (e.g., Delattre 1938, 1940; Withgott 1982) have denied the relevance of any but phrasal stress, while others have argued that secondary stress is closely linked to various phonological processes, such as vowel syncope (see Cedergren & Simoneau 1985), and the stability of schwa (see Walker 1996). See also Dell (1984) and Scullen (1997) on secondary stress.

At the foot level, French has right-headed, unbounded feet delimited by the phonological word, that is, the foot is defined from the syllable(s) bearing main lexical stress leftward to the next phonological word boundary. (On characterizing the phonological word in French see Hannahs 1995a.)

> (2)   The French foot:
> a. $[[de]\sigma\ [VOIR]\sigma\ ]_{Foot}$
> b. $[[re]\sigma\ [ven]\sigma\ [di]\sigma\ [ca]\sigma\ [TION]\sigma\ ]_{Foot}$

2.2.2 *Stress and acquisition*
Given the completely regular, positional nature of stress assignment in French, there are not surprisingly very few studies on the L2 acquisition of French stress *per se*. However, there are studies of the rhythmic properties of L2 French by native speakers of English, such as Guilbault (2002) who examines the acquisition of French rhythm by English L2 learners. One area of specific focus is on the role of duration in accounting for speech rhythm, given Guilbault's contention that inaccuracy in the speech rhythm of intermediate learners is connected to segmental duration, particularly of vowels.

Guilbault's subjects were six English learners of L2 French and six native French speakers, all staff or students at the University of Alberta. The English speakers were divided into two groups according to (subjectively measured) oral proficiency and length of contact with French, three 'low intermediate' learners, and three 'advanced' learners. All English-speaking subjects had some familiarity with another language. The French-speaking subjects were also divided into two groups: Three speakers of Canadian French and three speakers of European French.

Guilbault's data collection involved the recording of a series of controlled sentences (single sentence recall task) along with an unstructured interview (free speech). These recordings were produced in French by the L2 learners and the native French speakers. The variability of syllabic duration was measured in the controlled sentences to determine if the L2 learners exhibited greater variability than the native speakers. The unstructured interview samples were used in order to determine whether the controlled results could be generalized to free speech. In addition, the English-speaking subjects made a further recording of controlled sentences, parallel in numbers of syllables to the French corpus. In this way, Guilbault could compare the syllabic duration values of the English subjects across both English and French.

Guilbault found that the L2 learners did have greater inter-syllabic variability than the French native speakers, as predicted. Moreover, the results indicated that English-speaking learners, particularly advanced learners, do modify the temporal properties of their speech in French to approximate its rhythmic structure. Guilbault's results also suggest that syllabic duration provides a basis for accounting for the rythmic properties of French, but that language-specific phonological properties, such as segment type, also play a role in determining rhythm.

2.2.3 *Syllables and syllable structure*

The importance of the syllable in French phonological analysis is relatively uncontroversial, though the precise configuration of syllable structure is still being debated in some quarters (for a recent example see Scheer 2004). A number of scholars have examined syllables, syllable structure and syllabicity with specific reference to French, including Kaye and Lowenstamm (1984), Clements and Keyser (1983), Anderson (1982), Casagrande (1983), Plénat (1987), Noske (1993), Durand (1985), among others. One of the reasons for the importance of the syllable in French phonology is the crucial reference of a large number of phonological analyses to the syllable, to syllable structure or to syllabicity, including for example liaison and elision, latent consonants, *h-aspiré*, nasalization, and vowel~glide alternation.

Like other Romance languages, French tends to maximize onsets in its syllabification, regardless of morphological or syntactic boundaries (cf. Harris 1983 for Spanish). Thus, a word-final consonant tends in running speech to syllabify as the onset of the initial syllable of a following vowel-initial word, typically referred to as linking or *enchaînement*. Two peculiarities of French, however, belie the simplicity of this characterization: (1) The possibility in some registers of avoiding *enchaînement*, that is, keeping a word-final consonant as a coda rather than syllabifying it as an onset to a vowel-initial following word (see Encrevé 1983, 1988); (2) The fact of 'latent' consonants in French, that is, word-final consonants which are not pronounced when the word is spoken in isolation, but which are pronounced when the word is followed (in specific morpho-syntactic contexts) by a vowel-initial word. Before turning to liaison, *enchaînement* and latent consonants below, consider the list in (3) exemplifying the range of syllable types found in French.

(3)   Syllable types (from Walker 2001: 25–26)

V	/u/	*ou*	'or'
CV	/vi/	*vie*	'life'
CCV	/tʁɛ/	*très*	'very'
CCCV	/skʁy/	*scru(tin)*	'ballot'
VC	/ob/	*aube*	'dawn'
VCC	/uʁs/	*ours*	'bear'
VCCC	/astʁ/	*astre*	'star'
CVC	/paʁ/	*par*	'by'
CCVC	/priz/	*prise*	'pinch' (n.)
CCCVC	/stʁes/	*stress*	'stress'
CVCC	/pɔʁt/	*porte*	'door'
CVCCC	/mikst/	*mixte*	'mixed'
CVCCCC	/dekstʁ/	*dextre*	'right side'
CCVCC	/pʁesk/	*presque*	'nearly'
CCCVCC	/stʁikt/	*strict*	'strict'
GV	/wi/	*oui*	'yes'
GVC	/wat/	*ouate*	'cotton wool'
GVCC	/wɛst/	*ouest*	'west'
VG	/aj/	*ail*	'garlic'
CGV	/pɥi/	*puis*	'then'
CCGV	/tʁwa/	*trois*	'three'
CGVC	/djɛt/	*diète*	'diet'
CCGVC	/tʁɥit/	*truite*	'trout'
CGVCC	/sjɛʁʒ/	*cierge*	'candle'

The various syllable configurations given above are, of course, subject to more specific phonotactic constraints, that is, the restrictions on the allowable combination of particular consonants and/or glides appearing in onsets and codas. For example, an onset composed of three consonants invariably has [s] as the first consonant, a voiceless stop [p, t, k] as the second consonant and the liquid [l] or [ʁ] as the third: *Strict* [stʁ...], *sclérose* [skl...] 'sclerosis'. A CC-initial syllable will typically have a liquid [l] or [ʁ], or the nasal [n], as the second element (but see below): *Plume* 'feather', *cri* 'cry', *fleur* 'flower', *glace* 'ice', *brume* 'mist', and so on (although initial *[tl...] and *[dl...] are prohibited). Apart from the triconsonantal onsets with initial [s], in general, both onset and coda clusters in French tend to obey sonority sequencing: The more sonorant segments are nearer the syllable nucleus.

One notable difference in phonotactic restrictions between French and English, which therefore has implications for L2 French acquisition by speakers of L1 English, is the existence in French of initial clusters which English does not admit, for example [pn...] *pneu* 'tyre', [ps...] *psychose* 'psychosis', [pt...] *ptôse* 'ptosis', [gn...] *gnome* [gnom] 'gnome', [kn...] *cnémide* [knemid] 'greave' [item of classical soldiers' equipment]. Note that these onsets do, however, obey sonority sequencing, insofar as the second segment is no less sonorous than the first.

2.2.4 *Acquiring syllables and syllable structure*

A number of phenomena of specific relevance to French, such as latent consonants, liaison, nasalization, and variable schwa, are characterizable phonologically with reference to syllables, syllable structure and constraints on syllable structure. With this in mind, some recent work involving French L2 syllabification is of particular interest. Steele's (2002a) study, for example, looks specifically at the role of prosodic structure and licensing in the acquisition of L2 prosodic structure. With his study focusing primarily on the L2 French acquisition of L1 Mandarin speakers, Steele's subject group consisted of thirteen native Mandarin speakers and a control group of ten native speakers of French. The Mandarin speakers, aged between 31 and 40, were true adult learners; most had begun learning French a year before testing and had had one to four months' intensive instruction. The control group of *Québec* French speakers had an age range of 20 to 23.

In order to test the acquisition of stop+liquid onset clusters in various prosodic positions, the stimuli for Steele's examination consisted of 50 words containing stop + liquid onset clusters, 16 monosyllabic items beginning or ending in a singleton liquid, and 36 detractors. The 102 target items were divided into 34 groups, each containing three words, at least one of which was one of the stop + liquid targets. The subjects, each tested individually, were given a repetition task involving the target words; the task resulted in three tokens for each target word. The result from the study, Steele argues, is that learners' epenthesis, deletion and feature change result from the "interaction of Markedness constraints enforcing licit licensing relationships and Faithfulness constraints seeking to maintain contrast present in inputs" (p. 216).

In a different study, Steele (2001) considers the role of phonetic cues in resetting phonological parameters. Focusing on the acquisition of word-final clusters, particularly obstruent-liquid clusters, he observes that the relevant parameter settings for such final clusters differ between French and English. Moreover, the correct parameters for French are reset by the L1 English learners on the basis of phonetic cues: The absence of syllabic liquids in French leads the learners to acquire word-final obstruent-liquid clusters as onsets to empty-headed syllables, as has been argued elsewhere (e.g., Charette 1991; Dell 1995). In other words, the learners are able to acquire appropriate language-specific syllable structures in response to phonetic cues in the input.

Looking at syllabification in French as a second language, Beaudoin (1998) used a forced-choice lexical division task to examine syllable structure. Beaudoin's subject pool consisted of forty-eight volunteers (27 male, 21 female) with an age range of 18 to 40. Nine identified themselves as monolingual English speakers, nine identified themselves as monolingual French speakers, and the rest were bilingual to varying degrees.

For the test, Beaudoin devised a recorded list of 136 words with a CVCV structure meeting specific criteria; 40 were words of English, 96 were words of French. Each word was played to the subject, who was then shown three potential syllabifications of the word on a computer screen. The subjects then chose the syllabification they felt was correct.

Beaudoin's results indicted that although the L2 learners appear to acquire L2 syllable structures, their choice of L2 syllable division is nonetheless influenced by syllable structures in their L1. At the same time, however, Beaudoin found that the degree of L1 influence on L2 syllabification decreased with improved L2 performance.

2.2.5 *Liaison (with and without enchaînement) and elision*

As noted in Section 2.2.3, one of the characteristics of French, like other Romance languages, is the tendency to syllabify across morpheme and lexical word boundaries. When this happens, and a coda consonant is resyllabified as an onset to a following vowel-initial word, this is known as liaison with *enchaînement* (see Durand 1985; Encrevé 1983, 1988).[3,4]

The analysis of liaison has attracted a great deal of attention,[5] inspired particularly in the 1980s by the representational possibilities provided by autosegmental phonology on the one hand, and by the interest in syllable structure as a phonological issue on the other. The intersection of these two aspects of phonological theory led to analyses in which liaison resulted from the possibility (or necessity) of filling an unoccupied onset position with a consonant which would otherwise be a coda; the representations rely on the linking and delinking conventions of autosegmental phonology.

This type of analysis is supported both theoretically, by autosegmental representations, which easily express the delinking of a coda consonant and its reassociation as an onset, and empirically, by universal preferences for CV, rather than VC, syllables.[6]

Another phonological operation with some structural similarities is elision. In French, the form of the singular determiner and the singular pronominal clitic, feminine *la* and masculine *le*, is truncated before a vowel-initial following word: *La femme* 'the woman', but *l'amie* 'the girlfriend', for the determiner; and *je la vois* 'I see her', but *je l'aime* 'I love her', for the object clitic. Syllable structure is involved here just as it

---

3. In some, particularly formal, registers a liaison consonant may appear as a coda, rather than as an onset. See Encrevé (1988).

4. For a recent psycholinguistic perception study of *enchaînement*, see Gaskell, Spinelli and Meunier (2002).

5. Encrevé (1988:83–87) lists some seventy-five works concerning liaison published between 1965 and 1984.

6. More recently, in terms of Optimality Theory (OT; see Kager 1999; McCarthy 2004), liaison has been analyzed as resulting from the universal tendencies for CV, reinforced by constraints on syllabic well formedness (see for instance Tranel 1996a; and Bullock 2002).

is in liaison: The [l] of the determiner or clitic occupies the onset position of the first syllable of the following vowel-initial word.

There are nonetheless difficulties in accounting for this. If it were simply the case that all final consonants undergo liaison to a following vowel-initial word, or that *la* and *le* truncate before all phonetically vowel-initial words, then the analysis would be straightforward and unremarkable. However, things are not that simple for several reasons. First of all, not all orthographic final consonants behave in the same way: Some are always pronounced, some are variably pronounced, some are never pronounced. Second, the presence or absence of liaison may be conditioned by specific syntactic configurations. Third, some phonetically vowel-initial words do not participate in liaison or elision – the class of *h-aspiré* words along with a handful of orthographically vowel-initial words, for example, *onze* 'eleven', *la une* 'page one'. Fourth, register or speaking style as well as sociolinguistic context influences liaison behavior. Generally, the higher the register, the more liaison is produced (as in a poetry reading or a plenary, for instance).

2.2.6 *Liaison and acquisition*

As noted, the results of liaison can be represented with reference to phonological structure, that is, showing how an underlying final consonant may be accommodated as an onset to the first syllable of a following vowel-initial word. However, as we have just seen, the phenomenon of liaison in general goes well beyond the characterization of its result in terms of phonological structure: Liaison is conditioned not only by phonetic context (requiring a following vowel-initial word), but also by lexical considerations (some words with orthographic final consonants do not participate in liaison, e.g., *et* 'and', *chat* 'cat'), prosodic considerations (liaison occurs within but not across rhythmic groups), by syntax (i.e., the relative 'closeness' of the words: In *comment_allez-vous?* 'How are you?' liaison is expected, as compared with *comment / allez-vous au bureau?* 'How do you go to the office?' where it is not, cf. Thomas 1998), as well as by a number of sociolinguistic considerations. Indeed, as Dansereau (1995:650) notes in her pedagogical review, "Since the rules of liaison are too advanced for this level of study [i.e., beginning and intermediate], example is the best teacher here".

Thomas (1998) looks at the acquisition of liaison essentially from a pedagogical point of view, attempting to tease apart the complexities of liaison in order to reflect in the classroom the reality of modern French usage. As Thomas notes, the complexity of liaison arises, at least in part, through the incomplete correspondence between what is written and what is spoken, a correspondence that depends on phonetic and grammatical context, frequency, register, delivery, situational context and the individual, including the speaker's social background and individual preferences. Pedagogically, Thomas makes a number of suggestions concerning how best to approach liaison for L2 (immersion) students, including concentrating in particular on the highest frequency contexts and segments participating in obligatory liaison.

In a later paper, Thomas (2004) describes a large-scale ongoing study of linguistic progress in L2 French. The study compares the progress of 48 English-speaking L2 learners who spent a year abroad with a group of 39 English-speaking L2 learners who remained in anglophone Canada. The focus of the study was on liaison, as well as variable schwa deletion (see Section 2.2.10 below), and the presence or absence of *ne*. The general finding was that the group of L2 learners with high exposure levels to obligatory liaison, through participating as students in a year-abroad programme, have production levels closer to native norms than do L2 learners who did not study outside the L1 environment. Moreover, Thomas' study helps quantify the improvement of the L2 learners who studied in a French-speaking environment as compared with learners who did not.

In a dissertation-length study of the acquisition of L2 liaison in French, Mastromonaco (1999) examined the acquisition of liaison – obligatory, optional, and prohibited – by adult learners of French as a second language. The data were acquired through three tasks: A reading task, a spontaneous speech task, and a descriptive task. Her subjects comprised two groups of university students completing a second-year course in French as a second language. The first group consisted of 19 students (2 male, 17 female) in the same French class taught by the same instructor. The second group consisted of thirty students (7 male, 23 female) in a different French class taught by a different instructor. The subjects' ages ranged from 19 to 21. They were all first-language speakers of English; some may have had another language as well.

Among Mastromonaco's findings, the results showed that obligatory liaison was nearly always produced (94%) by her subjects, while prohibited liaisons were very rarely produced (< 4%). Optional liaisons were produced only infrequently (14%). Moreover, looking at syllable structure, Mastromonaco showed that more than 93% of the liaisons were resyllabified as onsets. Her overall conclusion, comparing native French speakers with her adult learners, is that while the learners in general have acquired liaison, the primary difference between the natives and the learners is the type of liaison errors which occur: The L2 speakers have problems with word-final consonants which tend to be pronounced in non-liaison contexts.

2.2.7 *Latent consonants*
There are three different behaviors of orthographic final consonants in French: Stable final consonants which are invariably pronounced, like *bis* [bis] 'repeat' and *net* [nɛt] 'clean'; those that are never pronounced, like *puis* [pɥi] 'then' and *brevet* [bʁəvɛ] 'certificate'; and those consonants that do not show up when the word is pronounced in isolation, but which nonetheless participate in liaison when the following word is vowel initial, like the second *t* in *petit* [pəti] 'small' ~ *petit ours* [pətituʁs] 'small bear'.

As with stable final consonants, syllable structure can be called on to represent the appearance of latent consonants: The consonant may appear only when there is an available onset position for it to occupy. Using the *petit ours* example, the vowel-initial *ours* may be assumed to have an unfilled onset position:

(4)

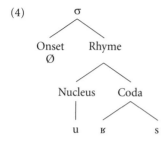

The latent final-t of *petit* surfaces because it can be accommodated in the empty onset position of the following word.

(5)

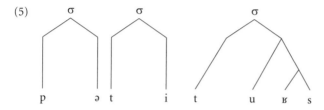

There are various analyses of the representation and behavior of latent consonants. Of primary relevance to L2 acquisition, however, are the questions of relating specific lexical items with particular latent consonants and inferring the behavior from the input.

2.2.8 *Acquiring latent consonants*

The question of latent consonants is closely related to the question of liaison, given that the participation of latent consonants in liaison is one of their defining characteristics. The primary difficulty here, from the learner's perspective, is the lexical aspect of the issue: There is no necessary correlation between the existence of an orthographic final consonant and whether or not that consonant is pronounced. Beyond that, of course, the occurrence or otherwise of a final orthographic consonant in speech is not an either/or question; compare *huit* 'eight', which may be pronounced as [ɥi] in *huit jours* 'eight days', but as [ɥit] in isolation, with *six* 'six', pronounced as [sis] in isolation, as [si] in *six jours* 'six days' and as [siz] in *six heures* 'six hours'.[7]

In light of the relationship of latent consonants and liaison (see 2.2.5 and 2.2.6, above), some of the findings of Mastromonaco (1999) and Thomas (1998, 2004) are also relevant for latent consonants. For example, as Mastromonaco (1999:275) observes, "A floating [i.e., latent] consonant that is analyzed as fixed will be anchored to the coda position and thus pronounced". For the learner, then, liaison may be a diagnostic for latent consonants – the pronunciation of the second *t* in *petit ami* 'boyfriend' through liaison but not in *petit mec* 'little guy' indicates to the learner that the second *t*

---

7. For an analysis of these see Tranel (1996b).

in *petit* is a latent consonant – but the occurrence alone of a consonant in liaison does not mean that the consonant is latent; it could also be fixed.

2.2.9 *The phonological status of schwa*

Along with latent consonants, liaison, elision, syllabicity and so on, one of the perennial descriptive and analytic challenges of French has been accounting for schwa, also referred to as *e-caduc, e-instable, e-muet,* 'mute e' and 'variable schwa'. Schwa has been the subject of a vast literature, including Anderson (1982), Basbøll (1978, 1988), Casagrande (1983, 1984), Dell (1980), Fouché (1959), Gougenheim (1935), Hansen (1994), Léon (1966), Martinet (1972), Morin (1974, 1978, 1987, 1988), Noske (1988, 1993), Schane (1968), Selkirk (1978, 1980), Spa (1989), Tranel (1981, 1984, 1988), Verluyten (1988), Withgott (1982), Walter (1990), Walker (1996), among many others.

One of the characteristics of schwa in French is that it alternates with zero. The complexity of schwa arises from the fact that its presence or absence – or indeed its variable presence – is conditioned by phonetic and phonological factors at the word level and at the phrasal level, as well as being conditioned by morphological and lexical factors. Added to this is the fact that phonetically, schwa is typically identical to mid-front rounded [œ], yet its phonological behavior (and its orthography) is different from stable /œ/. Beyond these structural aspects, there are also sociolinguistic conditioning factors along with considerations of register, speed and style relevant to the presence or absence of schwa. Taken together, all these interacting complexities give some indication of why schwa continues to be an interesting problem for both analysis and description.

Noske (1993:185ff.) outlines six types of schwa/zero alternation. By way of illustration, consider only the following examples of the most general types of schwa/zero alternation. Here the pronunciation of schwa in *devenais*, that is, the two orthographic *e* vowels, is optional: Both schwas may be pronounced as in (6a), or only one schwa may be pronounced, as in (6b) and (6c). Note, however, that at least one of these schwas must be pronounced, presumably for reasons of syllabification to avoid illicit consonant clusters. In these examples, the unpronounced orthographic *e* vowels (i.e., schwa) have been crossed out; the pronounced schwas are underlined.

(6)   *tu devenais* 'you became'
   a.   *tu de<u>v</u>enais* [ty dəvɔnɛ]
   b.   *tu dev<s>e</s>nais* [ty dəvnɛ]
   c.   *tu d<s>e</s>venais* [ty dvɔnɛ]

We see the same sort of behavior with the schwa in the initial syllable of *devrait* in the following example, where it is optionally present:

(7)   *Henri devrait partir* 'Henri should leave'
   a.   *Henri de<u>v</u>rait partir* [ãʁi dəvʁɛ partiʁ]
   b.   *Henri d<s>e</s>vrait partir* [ãʁi dvʁɛ partiʁ]

Note however that the optional appearance of schwa isn't simply a lexical characteristic of *devrait*. Compare the next example in (8):

(8) *Jacques devrait partir* 'Jacques should leave'
    a.   Jacques devrait partir [ʒak dəvʁɛ partiʁ]
    b.   *Jacques dévrait partir *[ʒak dvʁɛ partiʁ]
        'Jacques should leave'

Here schwa deletion in the initial syllable of *devrait* is impossible. Deletion would create an unsyllabifiable consonant sequence: kdv. In the case of (7b), one could argue for the syllabification [ã.ʁi d.vʁɛ] (as does Noske 1993:187) with [d] in the coda of the first syllable and a [vʁ] onset in the second syllable. With [ʒak dvʁɛ], on the other hand, [kd] is an illicit coda in French and [dvʁ] is an illicit onset, so the consonant sequence cannot be properly syllabified.

    As a further illustration of variable schwa, consider Verluyten's (1988:8) example of the possible pronunciations of the phrase *il a envie de te revoir* 'he wants to see you again':

(9)   a.   il a envie de te revoir
      b.   il a envie dé te révoir
      c.   il a envie dé te revoir
      d.   il a envie de te révoir
      e.   il a envie de té revoir

Beyond these (relatively) simple cases of the role of phonological structure, that is, syllable structure, affecting the occurrence of variable schwa, there are a number of other aspects to the behavior of schwa as a whole, including lexical, morphological and semantic considerations, as well as a great number of discourse and sociolinguistic factors influencing the presence or absence of schwa in any particular utterance.

2.2.10 *The acquisition of variable schwa*

Given the volume of interest shown in variable schwa in the theoretical literature, it is surprising that more hasn't been published from a phonological acquisition perspective. However, part of the reason for this may well be that the conditioning factors surrounding variable schwa are not exclusively phonological – a not inconsiderable role is played by other factors such as style, register, formality and sociolinguistic context. Two recent studies, however, which examine the acquisition of variable schwa, are Thomas (2004), referred to above (2.2.5) with respect to liaison, and Uritescu, Mougeon, Rehner and Nadasdi (2004). As with liaison, Thomas' (2004) primary interest is to compare the relative success in acquiring native-like behavior between two groups of L1 English university students, one of which studied in France and the other of which stayed in (anglophone) Canada. With regard to variable schwa, he finds that the group which experienced greater contact with a French-speaking environment "find themselves halfway between the official norm of standard French, high in schwa retention, and colloquial usage, which prefers deletion" (p. 373). Clearly, this sort of result is important both from a pedagogy perspective in a tutored setting, and for global aspects of L2 acquisition. At the same time, however, it does little to further our understanding of how phonological aspects of variable schwa are acquired. This is not meant to take away from the value of the study; it set out to compare two groups of learners with native norms, not to examine the phonological aspects of variable schwa.

The other recent study of variable schwa mentioned above is Uritescu et al. (2004) which targeted English-speaking French immersion students in Ontario, looking particularly at variable schwa deletion, comparing the behavior of L2 French learners with the norms of L1 French speakers. The subject pool for this study (part of a larger series of studies) consisted of 14–17 year-old French immersion students who were taped during semidirected interviews. A control group of nine L1 speakers of *Québec* French was also used. Five of the eight immersion students spoke English at home; two spoke a Romance language, while one spoke another unspecified language. Although reference is made to certain phonetic contexts, where the L2 speakers observe "the same phonetic constraints observed by L1 speakers" (p. 361), the aim of the study is to investigate sociolinguistic variation, in order to compare the use of such variation between L1 and L2 speakers.

Again, without wanting to minimize the importance of this study in terms of the acquisition of sociolinguistically relevant variables, this study does not (nor is it intended to) address the phonological issues surrounding the acquisition of variable schwa.

2.3 Phonology and acquisition

Throughout this section we have seen both phonetic and phonological aspects of French which are of relevance to the learner, in the sense that any learner of French, whether L1 or L2, must acquire these phonetic settings along with the phonological patterns (and more) to be said to have acquired French phonology. We have also seen some approaches to examining various aspects of the second language acquisition of French phonetics and phonology. The particular questions for L2 acquisition are related primarily to language-specific phonetic and phonological differences between a learner's L1 and French. On the issue of voice onset time, for example, there are unlikely to be any problems for an L1 Spanish speaker in acquiring the French values, as the L1 and L2 settings are virtually the same in any case. However, the L1 Spanish speaker's acquisition of French nasalized vowels is likely to be much more problematic, given the absence of such vowels in Spanish. The learner's task in this case would be (at least) threefold: (1) To learn to produce the appropriate nasal vowels; (2) To learn the alternation patterns between oral and nasal vowels; and (3) To learn when to and when not to de-nasalize in a liaison context.

With regard to phonetics, among the values to be acquired are the short-lag VOT values for unaspirated stops in all positions, the appropriate alternations between nasal and oral vowels, and the dental articulations of the coronals. Again, each of these is of greater or lesser importance and/or difficulty depending on the learner's L1 and the phonetic values of L1 along these dimensions.

Phonologically, the learner has a number of different patterns to acquire, including the processes and alternations discussed above, that is, word- and phrase-final stress assignment, permitted syllable types, liaison, elision, the patterning of latent consonants (to say nothing of learning which final consonants are latent and which are stable), and the behavior of schwa. These do not, of course, exhaust the task of phonetic and phonological learning involved in acquiring L2 French, and there are many areas of L2 phonological acquisition specific to French that remain to be explored, such as the behavior of *h-aspiré*, the alternation between high vowels and glides, voicing assimilation in obstruent clusters, and the acquisition of nasalized vowels.

At the same time, one of the difficulties in delimiting French phonology, and consequently one of the challenges facing studies of the acquisition of French phonology, is that very many of the phenomena that can be represented with the machinery of phonological theory – latent consonants, liaison, schwa variation, and so on – are not purely phonological. At various points in accounting for most of the phenomena at issue, reference must be made to non-phonological linguistic factors (variable schwa and vowel nasalization, for example, are affected by morphology and lexical considerations) or, indeed, to non-linguistic factors, such as speakers' social backgrounds and the social setting of the discourse.

There is a great deal of interest on the part of phonologists in the theoretical problems posed by French phonology. At the same time, there is much interest in sociolinguistic variables in French, for example, liaison and variable schwa. There is also, clearly, a pedagogical interest in helping learners achieve native-like use of French across the board, including phonology. Despite these areas of research focus, however, there has been much less interest in the acquisition of French phonology and phonological structures *per se*. This is partly due, no doubt, to the difficulty in teasing apart the phonological from the phonetic, on the one hand, and, on the other hand, distinguishing phonological aspects from syntactic, semantic, morphological and lexical ones. Nonetheless, the paucity of studies focusing primarily on the acquisition of French phonology is striking.

This apparent absence of interest in studies of French phonological acquisition has been underscored elsewhere as well. Overviews of French L2 acquisition in general, for instance Hawkins and Towell (1992), often take very little notice of phonological acquisition, ostensibly because there is little to report from the literature. Indeed, some twelve years after Hawkins and Towell's overview this was still the case; Myles and Towell (2004: 209) point out explicitly about French acquisition studies that "the field has tended to concentrate primarily on the acquisition of syntax and morphology". Thus it appears that the dearth of studies of L2 French acquisition of phonology is symptomatic of the acquisition field as a whole, rather than illustrative of any specific lack of interest in French.

Nonetheless, as we have seen, there are genuinely phonological studies of acquisition involving French, and their number appears to be on the increase. Steele (2001,

2002a, 2002b), for example, is centrally concerned with the acquisition of phonological structure; Pater (1998), while looking at French L1 learners' acquisition of L2 English stress is again concerned primarily with phonology; Mastromonaco (1999) explores theoretical and acquisition issues surrounding liaison in L2 French. Levy (2004) investigates the acquisition of French [y] and [ø] by American English speakers. Dugas (1999) examines the attrition of L2 pronunciation. Golato (1998) considers questions of limits on bilingualism, specifically studying the interaction between language dominance and markedness. Guilbault (2002) investigates the acquisition of rhythm in a 'syllable-timed' language (French) by learners of a 'stress-timed' language (English). While the basic concern of some of these studies is essentially to inform theories of language acquisition, it is to be welcomed that their empirical basis is the acquisition of L2 French phonology.

3.   Further directions

The absence of large numbers of studies of French L2 phonology does not reflect a lack of possible research topics, yet there are a number of reasons for the current state of affairs. In the first place, there have been relatively few studies of L1 phonological acquisition in general, and the vast majority of existing studies focus on English. An important exception is Vihman, Davis and DePaolis (1995) and related work, looking crosslinguistically at the early acquisition of L1 phonological structure. Without a significant breadth of studies of the acquisition of L1 French phonology, there is only anecdotal evidence of 'normal' acquisition. As a consequence, there is little reliable data against which to compare the development of L2 French phonology. The L2 learner's performance can be measured against the adult L1 speaker, but we have no way of knowing whether the L2 learner's path of acquisition bears any resemblance to that taken by the L1 learner. Thus, with our current state of knowledge, many research questions cannot be adequately addressed, since we can only compare L2 acquisition – at whatever level of achievement – with final-state L1.

In light of those considerations, one of the most important ways forward will be through serious, preferably longitudinal studies of the acquisition of L1 French. Only once those results are in place can research into L2 phonology have any confidence about the extent to which L1 and L2 acquisition are alike or are divergent, and the extent to which L1 and L2 learners invoke the same strategies to achieve their aims.

These remarks should not be taken to mean that nothing can be done on L2 phonology while we wait for results from L1 studies. There are any number of phonological aspects of L2 French which can be studied, even in the absence of L1 counterpart studies. The following list indicates areas in which much work remains to be done.[8]

Syllabification and syllabicity. As we have seen, the syllable is of great importance in allowing phonological generalizations to be expressed in French. At the same time, both syllabification and syllabicity are language-specific. Given that English syllabification respects certain morphological and syntactic boundaries, whereas French syllabification tends to ignore both, questions arise concerning the extent to which a learner's L2 French phonology reflects the English or French norms. As to syllabicity, English and French differ with respect to which segment types are permitted to occupy the nucleus of a syllable: In French, this position is restricted to vowels, while in English, sonorant consonants (liquids and nasals) may also appear as syllable nuclei. The question then is how, and how successfully, do learners acquire the French restrictions on which segment types may head syllables.

Suprasegmental prosodic structure. Beyond the question of nuclear segments, the issue of syllable structure has other L2 aspects, in light of the fact that syllable structure is language specific. In the L1 English/L2 French case, the learner is confronted with non-English initial clusters, for example [pn] in *pneu* 'tyre', [ps] in *psychose* 'psychosis', [gn] in *gnome* 'gnome', and so on. How does the L2 learner attempt to arrive at the appropriate clusters? By means of epenthesis – [pənœ] for [pnœ], [gənom] for [gnom]? Or by means of deletion – [nœ] for [pnœ], [nom] for [gnom]? Or does the learner acquire the L2 structures with no intermediate steps?

Beyond syllable structure there is the question of the acquisition of larger prosodic structures, for instance, feet, phonological words, phonological phrases, and so on. As with syllables, these structures also display language-specific characteristics. Therefore, just as with syllables, the question arises as to how the L2 learner approaches these structures, the success with which the structures are acquired, whether there are any consistent interlanguage tendencies, the factors which predict success or failure in the acquisition of any particular structures.

Variable schwa. Particularly in view of the interest in schwa in the sociolinguistic literature as a linguistic variable, it would be interesting to approach the question from a phonological point of view at the same time. For example, is there any connection between instances of successful (i.e., native-like) use of schwa and phonological characteristics? One could imagine that there might be a link between (relative) success in acquiring specific types of schwa production/suppression and particular phonological generalizations, that is, definable syllable types or other phonological structures.

Other issues. In addition to the phonological phenomena we have highlighted in this chapter, there are a number of other aspects of French phonology that have figured in the theoretical literature and which are worthy of investigation in terms of acquisition. Thus, along with studies of VOT and the acquisition of phonetically 'new' vs.

---

8. For the sake of discussion the following examples assume L1 English and L2 French. L1s other than English would, of course, raise identical kinds of issues, even if the specific questions are different.

'similar' sounds, many other sorts of L2 phonological acquisition studies are conceivable, including studies on the stress *per se* and the stress system, various other aspects of liaison, elision and latent consonants, the acquisition of *h-aspiré*, nasal vowels and vowel nasalization, vowel~glide alternation, and so on.

In light of all of the potential research areas (and possible dissertation topics) just outlined, along with innumerable permutations of the research questions raised simply by investigating learners from different L1s, one might suggest that there is enough to be done for the study of the acquisition of L2 French to become a thriving area of research for quite some time to come. It certainly has the potential to become an important field of inquiry and to inform other areas of the discipline, including acquisition in general, phonological theory and French studies.

CHAPTER 4

Syntax-semantics in English-French interlanguage

Advancing understanding of second language epistemology

Laurent Dekydtspotter*, Bruce Anderson and Rex A. Sprouse*
*Indiana University / University of California, Davis

Résumé

Ce chapitre traite de la relation entre syntaxe et sémantique en français langue seconde. Nous montrons que les anglophones adultes apprenant le français viennent à connaître bien des propriétés grammaticales subtiles du français à l'interface interprétative qui ne peuvent pas être induites de l'environnement, n'existent pas telles quelles en anglais, et ne font pas l'objet d'enseignement systématique en classe. Nous argumentons sur la base de résultats expérimentaux que le développement systématique d'une composition spécifique entre morphosyntaxe et sémantique dans l'apprentissage du français démontre que l'appropriation d'une langue seconde chez l'adulte est régie par les mêmes principes qui guident l'acquisition d'une langue maternelle. Nous considérons ensuite les implications de ces découvertes pour la recherche en langue seconde.

Abstract

This chapter discusses the relation between syntax and semantics in French as a second language. We show that adult English-speaking learners develop subtle knowledge of a broad range of grammatical properties in French that cannot be directly inferred from the input, are not straightforwardly replicated in English, and are not the object of classroom instruction. We argue, based on a review of experimental results, that the systematic development of a specific composition between (morpho-)syntax and semantics at the interpretive interface provides compelling evidence that adult second language acquisition is governed by the same principles that guide native language acquisition. We then turn to implications of these findings for second language research.

1. Introduction

The standard understanding in modern linguistics is that a linguistic expression is the pairing of a form with a meaning: A language is a set of such pairings, and the syntax of a language is the system (of rules) that mediates these pairings. This necessitates the existence of an interface between (morpho-)syntactic and (pragmatico-)semantic components and an interface between (morpho-)syntactic and phonological/phonetic components. Decades of research in generative grammar have revealed that these interfaces in native-language (L1) grammars, arising 'naturally' in human beings, exhibit many highly idiosyncratic properties that do not easily reduce to virtual conceptual necessity. That is, the interfaces in L1 grammars inhabit a small niche within the universe of logically possible interface systems. Since non-native languages (L2s) are languages, they must also have syntax-semantics and syntax-phonological interfaces. It is, however, an empirical question whether interlanguage interfaces are epistemologically equivalent to the interfaces found in L1 grammars. We explore this question in the present chapter by focusing our attention on the syntax-semantics interface.

In the L2 acquisition literature, many divergent claims have been made about the nature of L2 syntactic systems, ranging from the claim that L2 and L1 systems are epistemologically equivalent, that is, fully restricted by the principles of Universal Grammar (UG) (e.g., Epstein, Flynn, & Martohardjono 1996; Schwartz & Sprouse 1994, 1996) to the claim that L2 systems amount to simple pattern matching, linearization strategies, and/or stochastic learning (e.g., Ellis 2002a; Klein & Perdue 1997; Meisel 1997). The syntax-semantics interface in L1 grammars exhibits amazing idiosyncrasy, pointing to learners who are equipped with rich, deductive cognitive structures, given the nature of the primary linguistic evidence plausibly available in normal acquisition. To the extent that the syntax-semantics interface in interlanguage grammars can be shown to mirror these properties, serious doubt is cast upon claims that interlanguage syntax is relatively impoverished, or that its acquisition is not guided by UG.

The study of the syntax-semantics interface in English-French acquisition has proven particularly helpful in this context. English and French differ in several cases, in that French syntax licenses a morpho-syntactic alternation whereas English syntax licenses only one analogous surface pattern. The English surface pattern and its closest French analog are ambiguous, allowing (at least) two interpretations. However, in the case of the member of the French alternation without an English analog, UG blocks one of these interpretations. In the cases surveyed here, the precise semantics of the French-only pattern is never the object of classroom instruction (or even mentioned in standard reference grammars of French). If it can be shown that English-speaking learners of L2 French, once they come to cognize an interlanguage grammar that licenses the French-only pattern, also restrict the interpretation of this pattern in the target-like fashion, this result would point not only to the acquisition of French-like morpho-syntax, but also to the "acquisition" of UG-governed implications for the syntax-semantics interface.

In Section 2, we present the general research paradigm developed during the late 1990s and early 2000s at Indiana University for investigating the syntax-semantics interface in English-French interlanguage. In Sections 3 and 4, we summarize several such studies. In Section 3, we concentrate on interpretation within the nominal domain, whereas in Section 4 we deal with the clausal domain. In Section 5, we discuss the broader implications of this research for L2 studies, including the acquisition of French.

2. Research paradigm for investigating the syntax-semantics interface

All the studies surveyed in this chapter exhibit a characteristic interpretive paradigm involving two patterns, Patterns I and II, and two (relevant) interpretations, Interpretations A and B. Pattern I licenses both Interpretations A and B, and Pattern II appears to be a simple re-write variant of Pattern I. Natural analogical extension, unconstrained by UG, would lead the learner to assume that Pattern II is ambiguous in the same way that Pattern I is. Such 'reasoning' would lead to an incorrect characterization of French, where UG restricts Pattern II to licensing Interpretation A, but not Interpretation B. This basic grid of interpretative asymmetry is sketched in Table 1.

In each case, we will discuss the relevant learnability problem, arguing that English-speaking learners of L2 French could not realistically be expected to happen upon knowledge of these interpretative asymmetries on the basis of knowledge of English grammar, direct classroom instruction, or any evidence in the input. We argue that if L2 learners acquire knowledge of these asymmetries, then they are guided by the same idiosyncratic principles of UG that restrict the syntax-semantics interface in child L1 acquisition. We then summarize a study offering empirical evidence that L2 French learners indeed come to know these asymmetries, and must therefore be guided by these UG principles.

The phenomena treated in Sections 3 and 4 all share some general properties, inviting discussion of common methodological concerns. The general modality of the studies summarized here is the contextualized truth judgment task. Each participant received a booklet with approximately 50 to 100 items in one of three randomized orders. Each item consisted of a narrative in English followed by either a statement or a question-answer pair in French. Upon reading each context-stimulus sentence pairing, study participants were asked to indicate how well each test sentence described the situation in the preceding context. The choices were YES, NO, and CANNOT DECIDE. (Participants only very rarely selected CANNOT DECIDE.) Because experimental control of the interpretation was crucial, the researchers forwent the use of elicited production tasks or of pre-existing corpora, and also chose to present the narratives in English. The narratives were designed to make one or the other meaning (interpretation) maximally salient. In most of the studies, the participants were not directly asked whether a given

Table 1. Basic format of interpretive asymmetries

	Interpretation A	Interpretation B
Pattern I	✓	✓
Pattern II	✓	*

pattern was grammatical per se; rather, the focus was on the pairing of a given pattern with an interpretation. Crossing two narratives with two surface patterns yields a minimal quadruple. There was a certain task bias toward answering YES. This is because in each minimal quadruple, three of the four statements or responses to questions were indeed accurate; furthermore, without the constraining effect of UG, it would be easy to impose an interpretation of the words that make up the fourth sentence such that it would be true in the context of the given narrative as well. In order to undermine this positive response bias to some extent, fillers were included, most of which invited a negative response, because the sentence did not truly describe the narrative.

The experimental groups were generally comprised of university-level English-speaking learners of French in the United States, typically ranging from the intermediate (second year) level of study up through advanced. The most advanced learners were typically those who (a) had begun learning French through classroom instruction as adolescents or adults; (b) had spent at least 9 months (i.e., one academic year) in a French-speaking country, where they spoke French at least part of each day; and (c) had not studied French linguistics (particularly syntax) at the graduate level. Such a cross-section of learners is desirable from a developmental perspective in that a comparison of learner group behavior can allow us to extrapolate a developmental path, including the point at which such asymmetries appear in interlanguage grammars, if at all. In many instances, the researchers also used an L1 English-speaker control group whose task was to provide truth value judgments of 'sentences' based on word-for-word English glosses of the French test sentences. Another group was comprised of native French speakers who were students at French universities pursuing a general diploma in English, whose chief purpose was to establish that the testing instrument, as designed, is sensitive to the relevant distinctions in interpretation already documented in the theoretical literature. The use of French native speakers who have a good reading knowledge of English was necessary given the fact, as noted above, that the contexts were presented in English for all groups.

Given the nature of the task and the subtlety of the linguistic phenomena, it would be unrealistic to expect native speakers to accept the 'good' items at a rate of 100% and the 'bad' items at a rate of 0%. It is more realistic to expect a statistically significant difference between a 'bad' form-meaning pairing and its 'good' analog within the combined data for any given population, as shown by paired-samples t-tests. In addition, an examination of individual results should not reveal that there were individuals who accepted the 'bad' form-meaning pairings at a rate significantly higher than their acceptance rate for 'good' pairings. Furthermore, as discussed at length by Martohardjono (1993), the standard for determining whether the same cognitive mechanisms underlie L1 and L2 grammars cannot realistically be that there is no detectable difference between the performance of native and L2 participants; rather, the researchers were seeking to find the same statistically significant asymmetry between 'bad' and 'good' form-meaning pairings as was found with the target language control group. At the same time, the researchers sought to establish through the L1-only group (judging English glosses of the French sentences associated with the same contexts) that a mere glossing strategy would not yield the asymmetries under investigation.

3. Evidence from the nominal domain

In this section, we consider three interpretive asymmetries in the nominal domain: The result-process distinction in dyadic nominals, the unique-nonunique noun reference distinction in nouns modified by an adjective, and the universal-nonuniversal distinction in relative clauses.

3.1 The result-process distinction in dyadic nominals

Our first phenomenon is the process-result distinction in dyadic nominals in French, investigated by Dekydtspotter, Sprouse and Anderson (1997) and Anderson (2002), and illustrated in (1)–(2).

(1) a. *Claire choisit   l'interprétation   de la 9e symphonie par Karajan.*
Claire chooses the interpretation of the 9th symphony by Karajan
'Claire chooses Karajan's interpretation of the Ninth Symphony'

   b. *Regardez! La   destruction de Tokyo par Godzilla commence!*
Look!   The destruction of Tokyo by Godzilla begins!
'Look! Godzilla's destruction of Tokyo is beginning!'

(2) a. *Claire choisit   l'interprétation   de la 9e symphonie de Karajan.*
Claire chooses the interpretation of the 9th symphony of Karajan
'Claire chooses Karajan's interpretation of the Ninth Symphony'

   b. **Regardez! La   destruction de Tokyo de Godzilla commence!*
Look!   The destruction of Tokoy of Godzilla begins
'Look! The destruction of Tokyo of Godzilla begins!'

In French dyadic nominals, the Theme role is uniformly marked by the preposition *de* 'of': *De la 9e symphonie* in (1a) and (2a), *de Tokyo* in (1b) and (2b). However, the Agent role can be marked by the preposition *par* 'by', as in (1a) and (1b), or by the preposition *de*, as in (2a). When the Agent is marked by *par*, the nominal may be interpreted either as a result, as in (1a), or as a process, as in (1b). However, when the Agent is marked by *de*, the nominal is restricted to a result interpretation, as in (2a); attempting to combine "double-*de*" morphosyntax with a process interpretation as in (2b) leads to ungrammaticality.

Hence, we see an overall syntax-semantics interface paradigm where Pattern I (*par*-marked Agent) licenses both Interpretation A (result) and Interpretation B (process), whereas Pattern II (*de*-marked Agent) licenses Interpretation A, but not Interpretation B. Let us assume that the marking of arguments within French nominals with the preposition *de* is an instance of structural case assignment, and that French syntax allows the double-*de* pattern because French exhibits overt noun raising. Following Grimshaw (1990), we further assume that on the process interpretation, where the noun characterizes an event, nominalization entails the syntactic suppression of the external theta role. From this, it follows that on the process interpretation, the Agent cannot be marked with *de*, because it is not a syntactic argument. It may be 'reintroduced' into the nominal, however, as an adjunct marked by the preposition *par*, in analogy with the passive voice in clauses.

While *interprétation* in the context in (1a, 2a) is most naturally understood as a result and *destruction* in the sense suggested in (1b, 2b) is clearly a process, some deverbal nouns in French can readily have result or process interpretations. Consider *démonstration* 'proof' in (3).

(3) a. *La démonstration du   théorème par le professeur était très*
         the proof   of-the theorem by the professor   was   very
         intéressante.
         interesting
     b. *La démonstration du   théorème du   professeur était très intéressante.*
         the proof   of-the theorem of-the professor   was   very interesting
         'The professor's proof of the theorem was very interesting'

Both (3a) and (3b) are grammatically well-formed sentences; however, they differ in their range of interpretations. Sentence (3a), with its *par*-marked Agent, can refer either to a result, for example, the professor's proof reproduced in a textbook, or to a process, for instance, the 20-minute event in the classroom during which the professor proved the theorem. Sentence (3b), with its *de*-marked Agent, can refer only to a result, not to a process.

We summarize the interpretive asymmetry in Table 2.

We turn now to the learnability challenge for English-speaking L2 French learners posed by the asymmetry in Table 2. We note first that English generally shuns the double-*of* pattern. Consider the natural English translations of the examples in (1)–(3), as shown in (4)–(6).

(4) a. Claire chooses Karajan's interpretation of the Ninth Symphony.
     b. Look! Godzilla's destruction of Tokyo is beginning!
     c. The professor's proof of the theorem was very interesting.

(5) a. Claire chooses the interpretation of the Ninth Symphony by Karajan.
     b. Look! The destruction of Tokyo by Godzilla is beginning!
     c. The proof of the theorem by the professor was very interesting.

(6) a. *Claire chooses the interpretation of the Ninth Symphony of Karajan.
     b. *Look! The destruction of Tokyo of Godzilla is beginning!
     c. *The proof of the theorem of the professor was very interesting.

Table 2. Result-process asymmetry

	Result interpretation	Process interpretation
par-marked Agent	√	√
de-marked Agent	√	*

Dyadic nominals in English require either a prenominal genitive Agent as in (4), or a postnominal *by*-marked Agent as in (5). Postnominal *of*-marked Agents are ungrammatical in English, whether the nominal is interpreted as a result or a process, as illustrated in (6). It is thus not possible that an English-speaking L2 French learner could come to know the paradigm in Table 2 on the basis of English grammar.[1]

These facts are certainly not the object of any kind of classroom instruction, and since nominals with *de*-marked Agents and process interpretations simply do not occur, there is nothing in the input to inform the learner that this form-meaning pairing is ungrammatical. In fact, the situation is far worse for any account based on input and general cognition. Suppose that a learner has come to know that French allows dyadic nominals with *par*-marked Agents, and that this pattern is compatible with both result and process interpretations. Suppose further that the learner then encounters dyadic nominals with *de*-marked Agents. Of course, in fact, these nominals will have been uttered with an intended result interpretation. However, short of guidance by principles of UG, it is difficult to imagine that L2 learners would uniformly assume from this that dyadic nominals with *de*-marked Agents are in general restricted to result interpretations. On the contrary, natural analogical extension would lead one to assume the opposite.

As Schwartz and Sprouse (2000: 180) summarized, even if the learner were keeping track of whether each such utterance occurred in a result or process context, he or she would still have to identify what aspects of the context are relevant in the first place, a step which is fraught with potential errors. Bear in mind also that the scenes of the real world are very rich, and thus frequently underdetermine the precise interpretation of a contextualized utterance. In many circumstances where one might intend the result interpretation of a dyadic nominal, the process interpretation might be equally plausible as well. Thus, a speaker might utter (3b) with the intention that the formulation on the blackboard at the end of a given class session was very interesting. Where this is true, it is quite likely that the event during the class session was also evaluated as very interesting, although that is not what the speaker who utters (3b) wishes to express. It is difficult to see how, without the guidance of UG principles, an English-speaking learner of L2 French who would hear (3b) uttered in such a context would be guaranteed not to interpret (3b) as a comment on the event, and take this as evidence that the

---

1. Some English speakers may feel that the double-*of* pattern is worse in English with a process interpretation than with a result interpretation. As pointed out by Hale (1996), under current Minimalist assumptions about grammar, UG principles are so general that they cannot be dissociated from knowledge of particular languages. Knowledge of particular languages arises in the interaction of UG with each language-dependent parameterized lexicon. See Dekydtspotter et al. (1997) for discussion of the repercussions of intuitions like this for the UG-through-the-L1 approach and the Minimalist view that there cannot be a principle of UG that is not relevant for a particular language. Dekydtspotter et al. (1997) also provide empirical evidence that English-speakers with no knowledge of French do not approximate to the paradigm in Table 2 on the basis of English intuitions about what are essentially all ill-formed sentences in English.

<de-marked Agent, process interpretation> pairing is possible in French. Presumably, UG is required in L1 French acquisition to block such pairings. It would appear that if English-speaking learners of L2 French acquire knowledge of the asymmetry shown in Table 2, they must be guided by the same idiosyncratic principles of UG that restrict the syntax-semantics interface in child L1 acquisition.

Dekydtspotter et al. (1997) was the first published empirical investigation of the acquisition of the paradigm in Table 2 in English-French interlanguage. Anderson (2002) improved aspects of the original study design and replicated the results. Table 3, adapted from Anderson (2002, in press a), presents percentages and statistically significant differences for the study populations described above. It is based on the evaluation of 28 context-stimulus sentence pairings (7 sentences with nominals under a result interpretation, and 7 sentences under a process interpretation, presented once with a de-marked Agent and once with a par-marked Agent). Note that the context-sentence pairings utilized in Anderson represent a subset of those first used in Dekydtspotter et al. (1997); they were selected based on the clarity of the rate of acceptance/rejection data from the French native speakers in that study.

For expository purposes, we will concentrate only on the last two columns of data, as these represent the crucial distinction between conditions (a) (the first column) and (c) (the second column).

The results from the native French-speaker group, in the last row of Table 3, demonstrate that the testing instrument was highly sensitive to the distinction between result-process nominals noted in the theoretical literature: French native speakers accept de-marked Agents with result nominals significantly more than with process nominals, at 44.97% versus 7.94% ($p < .001$). As noted in Dekydtspotter et al. (1997), the 44.97% rate for dyadic result nominals most likely indicates the stylistic awkwardness of multiple de-marked arguments, noted by Milner (1977, 1982) and Ruwet (1972). Very similar acceptance rates for de-marked Agents were found for the group of French native speakers in Dekydtspotter et al. (1997) ($n = 48$; 50.42% for result and 15.65% for process nominals), thereby attesting to the reliability of the instrument developed in that study and (partially) replicated in Anderson (2002, in press a).

When presented with word-for-word translations of the French test sentences, the native English-speaker control group, as shown in the first row of Table 3, accepted

Table 3. Result-process distinction in dyadic nominal by group

| Group | n | par-marked Agent | | de-marked Agent | |
		Result	Process	Result	Process
Native English	30	81.90	63.25	23.18	14.29
2nd Year	29	77.83	62.56	61.08	44.83
3rd Year	24	87.50	83.04	63.39	41.96
4th Year	27	74.07	77.78	52.91	26.28
Advanced	20	73.57	72.86	50.00	14.29
Native French	27	78.31	73.54	44.97	7.94

multiple *of*-marked arguments at 23.18% for result nominals versus 14.29% for process nominals ($p < .05$). The low rates indicate that such dyadic nominals are clearly below the threshold of grammaticality in English. The difference in acceptance rates between the two interpretations, however, is nonetheless significant. Nearly the same acceptance rates for *de*-marked Agents were found for the English-speaker control group in Dekydtspotter et al. (1997) study ($n = 24$; 22% for result and 11% for process nominals), again attesting to the reliability of the instrument developed in that study.

Turning our attention to the learner group data, in the middle rows of Table 3, we find that the crucial distinction between result and process nominals with *de*-marked Agents is already evident at the second-year level. Thus, the 61.08% acceptance rate for result nominals is statistically different from the 44.83% acceptance rate for process nominals ($p < .01$). This remains the case at the third year (63.39% versus 41.96%; $p < .01$), fourth year (52.91% versus 26.28%; $p < .001$), and advanced levels (50.00% versus 14.29%; $p < .001$).

3.2 The unique-nonunique noun reference distinction in nouns modified by an adjective (Anderson 2002, to appear a)

We turn now to the interpretative effects of attributive adjective placement in French, interacting with the semantics of the definite determiner *le/la* 'the'. In many instances, an attributive adjective may occur in either postnominal position or prenominal position, as illustrated in (7).

(7) a. *Pierre a   dû   laisser   la   valise   lourde à   l'aéroport.*
         Pierre has had to-leave the   suitcase heavy at the airport
     b. *Pierre a   dû   laisser   la   lourde valise   à   l'aéroport.*
         Pierre has had to-leave the   heavy suitcase at the airport
         'Pierre had to leave the heavy suitcase at the airport'

When the adjective *lourde* 'heavy' appears in postnominal position with a definite article as in (7a), there may be one ($n = 1$) or more than one ($n > 1$) suitcase, as long as only one suitcase is heavy. The nominal expression *valise lourde* denotes the set of suitcases that are heavy. The determiner *la* combined with the expression *valise lourde* requires that there be a unique object in this set. The expression *la valise lourde* denotes this suitcase, but there may be other suitcases, which are not heavy. However, when the adjective *lourde* appears in prenominal position with a definite article as in (7b), the sentence can only be true for contexts in which there is a single suitcase, which of course must be heavy, notated as $n = 1$. The nominal expression *lourde valise* denotes a set of suitcases, assuming all relevant suitcases to be heavy. That is to say, this is a structure of non-restrictive modification, where heaviness of suitcases is presupposed rather than asserted. As before, the determiner *la* requires uniqueness: *Lourde valise* must denote a singleton set. Hence, *la lourde valise* refers to the unique suitcase in the set. Unlike earlier, there is no contrast set.

We summarize this interpretative asymmetry in Table 4.

Table 4. Uniqueness-nonuniqueness asymmetry

	n = 1	n > 1
Postnominal Adjective	√	√
Prenominal Adjective	√	*

Let us now consider the learnability issues for English-speaking learners of L2 French posed by the asymmetry in Table 4. First, English grammar is not likely to provide the learner with much assistance. English generally permits only prenominal adjectives, as shown in (8), and sentences containing such adjectives are freely compatible with either the presupposition of uniqueness or nonuniqueness.

(8) a. Pierre had to leave the heavy suitcase at the airport.
     b. *Pierre had to leave the suitcase heavy at the airport.

It is difficult to imagine how English grammar could assist learners in acquiring the paradigm in Table 4.

Unlike the situation with the result-process distinction discussed in 3.1, adjective placement most definitely is the object of traditional classroom instruction. However, instruction largely focuses on obligatorily prenominal adjectives, obligatorily postnominal adjectives, and adjectives with idiosyncratic meaning based on position (e.g., *ancien* as 'ancient' or 'former'). Variable adjective position on the whole is relatively rare in classroom input, especially at low and intermediate proficiency levels (Anderson 2002, in press b). The subtleties associated with the variable positioning of many adjectives are not discussed, nor does English provide precisely that kind of information.

Let us turn to contextualized input as a potential source of the knowledge of the asymmetry. Consider the examples in (9).

(9) a. *Les touristes vont visiter   le   village charmant ce   week-end.* ($n \geq 1$)
         the tourists   go   to-visit the village charming this weekend
     b. *Les touristes vont visiter   le   charmant village ce   week-end.* ($n = 1$)
         the tourists   go   to-visit the charming village this weekend
         'The tourists are going to visit the charming village this weekend'

The interpretation of the examples in (9) is that the tourists are either visiting one (relevant) village (which happens to be charming), or a number of villages, in addition to the charming one. The sentence in (9a) can therefore be uttered under either scenario, whereas the sentence in (9b) can only be uttered under the first scenario. The interpretations of the two sentences are in a subset-superset relationship so that even if we endow the learner with the ability or desire to keep track of the number of noun referents relevant to each case, she would have to know in advance what the speaker is assuming. Given that we cannot guarantee either state of affairs, there is no input to prevent learners from inferring that the permissibility of both adjective positions on one interpretation can be extended to the other interpretation.

Table 5. Unique-nonunique noun-referent distinction results by group

Group	n	Pre-N order		Post-N order	
		Unique referent	Nonunique referent	Unique referent	Nonunique referent
Native English	30	95.24	84.84	10.95	6.19
2nd Year	29	62.31	57.64	78.32	65.02
3rd Year	24	62.50	38.10	86.55	60.32
4th Year	27	50.53	35.19	82.98	68.25
Advanced	20	51.43	33.57	76.43	67.14
Native French	27	74.07	48.68	51.85	36.51

Anderson (2002, in press a) conducted an empirical investigation to determine whether English-speaking learners of L2 French typically come to exhibit sensitivity to the asymmetry in Table 4. Table 5 (adapted from Anderson 2002, in press a), presents acceptance rates for the same study population as in the study discussed in Section 3.1, and is based on the evaluation of another 28 context-stimulus sentence pairings (7 sentences with an adjective in prenominal position, and 7 with an adjective in post-nominal position, presented once in a unique noun-referent context, and again in a nonunique noun-referent context).

For expository purposes, we will concentrate only on the first two columns of data, as these represent the crucial interpretive distinction between unique reference (the first column) and nonunique reference (the second column) when the adjective appears in prenominal position.

Results in the last row of Table 5, from the native speakers of French, show that the contexts and sentences developed for the task were moderately sensitive to this distinction: Prenominal position is accepted in a unique noun-referent context at 74.07%, which is significantly more than in a nonunique noun-referent context at 48.68% ($p <$ .001). A clearly evident difference in acceptability emerges from the native English speaker results, as expected: We find in the first row of Table 5 that they accepted adjectives in prenominal position at rates of 95.24% and 84.84% regardless of interpretation (though the difference in means between the two is nonetheless significant [$p < .001$]).

Results from the learner groups, in the middle rows of Table 5, indicate that the lowest mean acceptance rate is for sentences with a prenominal adjective under a nonunique noun-referent interpretation. At the second-year level, however, the difference in means for prenominal position based on interpretation, at 62.31% versus 57.64%, does not reach statistical significance ($p = .281$), but becomes strongly significant at the third-year level (62.50% versus 38.10%; $p < .001$), and remains so at the fourth-year level (50.53% versus 35.19%; $p < .01$) and advanced level (51.43% versus 33.57%; $p < .01$). These findings from the third-year level onward are all the more surprising given that learners demonstrated knowledge of the crucial distinction concerning prenominal adjective position despite the fact that they would not normally expect such adjectives to occur in that position (on the basis of explicit rules and classroom input), and are not taught the relevant interpretive asymmetry.

3.3 The universal-existential distinction in relative clauses (Dekydtspotter, Sprouse, & Gibson 2001)

We turn now to the interpretation of cardinality quantifiers such as *peu de livres* 'few books' modified by a relative clause (RC) as in (10). There are two possibilities in French: The *de*-marked restriction of the quantifier *peu* 'few' appears either RC-externally (10a) or RC-internally (10b).

(10) a. *Le peu de livres que Marie a   lus   coûtent cher.*
          the few of books that Marie has read cost   expensive
      b. *Le peu que Marie a   lu   de livres coûtent cher.*
          the few that Marie has read of books cost   expensive
          'The few books that Marie has read are expensive'

The examples in (10a) and (10b) may appear to be simple rewrite variants, differing only with respect to the placement of the restriction *de livres* on the quantifier *peu*. However, Grosu and Landman (1998) note that RCs with internal nominal restrictions are interpreted as degree relatives, inducing a universal interpretation of the expression that they modify. This interpretation requires the definite determiner, yielding the contrast in (11).

(11) a. *Peu de livres que Marie a   lus   coûtent cher*
          few of books that Marie has read cost   expensive
      b. *#Peu que Marie a   lu   de livres coûtent cher.*
          few that Marie has read of books cost   expensive
          'Few books that Marie has read are expensive'

While (11a) is perfectly fine, pairing an RC-external restriction on the quantifier with the null indefinite article [Ø *peu de livres*], pairing an RC-internal restriction on the quantifier with the null indefinite determiner #[Ø *peu ... de livres*] is semantically odd, as shown in (11b). Thus, we have once again identified an interpretive asymmetry, sketched in Table 6.

Again, the question arises whether English-speaking learners of L2 French could plausibly be expected to come to the knowledge of this asymmetry on the basis of their knowledge of English grammar, of classroom instruction, or of contextualized occurrences of the relevant forms in the input. English grammar is an unlikely source of help for the learner, since English does not allow RC-internal restrictions, as shown by the contrast between (12a) and (12b).

(12) a. (The) few books that Marie has read are expensive.
      b. *(The) few that Marie has read (of) books are expensive.

Table 6. Universal-existential asymmetry

	Universal interpretation	Existential interpretation
RC-external restriction	√	√
RC-internal restriction	√	*

As a university student Marie is obliged to buy a very large number of books each year. For example, she bought approximately 75 books last year. Fortunately, the vast majority of these books were available in inexpensive paperback editions. However, three of the books cost over $200.

Peu que Marie a acheté de livres l'année dernière coûtent très cher.

Figure 1. Zero (indefinite) determiner with *de*-restriction internal to the relative clause

Furthermore, well-formed French examples with RC-internal restrictions like (10b) are not the object of typical classroom instruction. While learners may be exposed to such examples haphazardly, there is nothing in the input to inform them directly of the anomaly involved in (11b). Such knowledge has to be derived through specific mechanisms, from which it follows that RC-internal restrictions require a degree interpretation of the RC; that such a degree interpretation requires universal rather than existential interpretation of the NP to which it is attached; and that universal interpretation is incompatible with the null indefinite determiner preceding the quantifier. Hence, if it can be shown that English-speaking learners of L2 French come to accept (10b), but reject (11b) as anomalous, it would constitute a strong argument for the claim that knowledge of L2 French is channeled in domain-specific (UG-governed) ways.

Dekydtspotter et al. (2001) conducted an experiment involving two tasks of 50 items each: 32 experimental items and 18 fillers. Task 1 investigated interactions between determiner and RC structure. Each item included a short narrative followed by a sentence. The narrative established either an existential or a universal context, which matched the choice of determiner. Specifically, the context ensured that the null determiner was construed as existential, as in native French. A sample test item showing this is provided in Figure 1. Participants then indicated whether the sentence accurately described what happened in the narrative. If RC-internal restrictions induce a universal interpretation, a semantic clash with the existential context/determiner is induced. A rejection is therefore expected.

Table 7, adapted from Dekydtspotter et al. (2001), shows no crucial sensitivity in early learners. Third-year learners, however, accepted RCs with RC-internal restrictions paired with universal determiners at 86.76% versus 63.24% with existential

Table 7. Interaction of determiner with RC type by group

Group	*n*	RC-internal restriction		RC-external restriction	
		Definite D/ universal	Indefinite D/ existential	Definite D/ universal	Indefinite/ existential
1st Year	26	82.69	82.69	82.69	84.13
2nd Year	35	80.29	88.21	87.50	94.64
3rd Year	17	86.76	63.24	85.88	93.38
Ntv. Fr.	6	8.17	0.00	91.67	72.92

> For a university student, Marie is not very interested in reading. In fact, she bought only three books last year. Nevertheless, she spent a lot of money on these books: each of them cost over $200.
>
> *Peu que Marie a acheté de livres l'année dernière coûtent très cher.*

Figure 2. Universal context with *de*-NP internal to the relative clause

determiners ($p < .01$). Crucially, no such pattern arose in the case of RCs with RC-external restrictions. L2 learners' relative acceptance rates of definite versus indefinite determiners exhibited an emerging sensitivity to the structure of the RC despite the fact that this paradigm is not in the typical classroom input.

Task 2 investigated interactions between determiner and RC structure. In this task, participants were presented with a short narrative constituting either an existential or a universal context, controlling how the null determiner was to be interpreted. This interpretation then either clashed with or matched the interpretation induced by the structure of the RC. Figure 2 provides an example where the context requires that the null determiner receive a universal interpretation. The universal interpretation is also required by the structure of the relative clause.

Results are reported in Table 8. Because no asymmetry arose in first and second year learners, they are collapsed.

On this task, French natives provided no relevant data, because in French the null determiner cannot be induced to take a universal interpretation, and items with RC-internal restriction require the definite determiner and are rejected out of hand. We also note that learners dispreferred universal interpretations of zero determiners. But, crucially, in both universal and in existential contexts, learners produced asymmetries in acceptance rates dependent on the structure of the relative clause. Thus, in universal contexts, 1st and 2nd year learners accepted RCs with RC-internal restrictions at 44.59% versus RCs with RC-external restrictions at 34.88% ($p < .05$). An opposite asymmetry was found in existential contexts, 1st and 2nd year learners accepted RCs with RC-internal restrictions at 82.27% versus RCs with RC-external restrictions at 91.57% ($p < .05$). At the 3rd year level, similar asymmetries arose in universal contexts (46.25% versus 10.00%; $p < .05$) and in existential contexts (56.25% versus 95.00%; $p < .05$). What is interesting, therefore, is that English-French interlanguages exhibit theoretically relevant asymmetries that are obfuscated in native French. That is to say, unlike non-native speakers who can coerce a null determiner to receive a uni-

Table 8. Interpretation of zero determiner by RC type by group

Group	n	RC-internal restriction		RC-external restriction	
		Universal	Existential	Universal	Existential
1st & 2nd Year	43	44.59	82.27	34.88	91.57
3rd Year	10	46.25	56.25	10.00	95.00
Native French	6	0.00	0.00	25.00	68.75

versal/definite interpretation, native speakers cannot. What is crucial, however, is that the asymmetries show that RC-internal restrictions induced a universal interpretation, whereas RC-external restrictions did not.

To summarize the findings of this section, we found that crucial distinctions arose in English-French interlanguage grammars despite severe learnability problems. We note that the relevant data involve *asymmetries* in acceptance rates rather than in absolute terms. Studies on the interpretive interface yield somewhat murkier acceptance rates than studies of word order alone simply because one is not dealing with grammaticality per se but, more typically, the degree to which a given (grammatical) word order is acceptable based on particular and rather subtle contextual information. Consequently, participants may be able to 'defeat' the intent of certain contexts and disregard bits of information that the researcher deemed important. Generally, the bias to accept <meaning, sentence> pairings is rather high in learners. We are capturing effects of mechanisms that depress such a tendency in specific ways. We also note that respondents may also reject test sentences whose propositional content yields 'true' values in terms of truth-conditional semantics because they find them odd on pragmatic or stylistic grounds. The minimal quadruple strategy provides some protection against the many uncontrolled elements that may arise in research.

4. Evidence from the clausal domain

To guard against the possibility that the development of subtle knowledge of interpretation demonstrated in Section 3 is limited to the nominal domain, the present section discusses four interpretive properties of the clausal domain. We argue that their acquisition lends further support to the claim that the syntax-semantics composition in interlanguage is a reflex of a specific mental organization dedicated to language.

4.1 Quantification at a distance: *Beaucoup de* NP (Dekydtspotter, Sprouse, & Thyre 1999/2000)

French exhibits an alternation in the placement of certain quantifiers, such that they may occur either string-adjacent to their restriction, as in (13a), or in a position slightly to the left, presumably at the left edge of the verb phrase, as in (13b).

> (13) a. *En   cherchant   partout,   il   a   trouvé beaucoup de pièces   d'or.*
>   in   looking   everywhere   he   has   found many   of pieces of gold
>   b. *En   cherchant   partout,   il   a   beaucoup trouvé de pièces   d'or.*
>   in   looking   everywhere   he   has   found   many   of pieces of gold
>   'While looking everywhere, he found a lot of gold coins'

We refer to the order of constituents in (13a) as non-QAD and to the order in (13b) as QAD (*quantification à distance*). Given the adverbial modifier *en cherchant partout* 'while looking everywhere', the sentences in (13) are interpreted in such a way that

Table 9. Multiple event-single event asymmetry

	Multiple event	Single event
non-QAD	✓	✓
QAD	✓	*

there were multiple coin-finding events. Consider the effect of changing the context such that a single coin-finding event is involved, as in (14).

(14) a. *D'un   seul   coup, il   a   trouvé beaucoup de pièces d'or.*
          of one single blow he has found many   of pieces of gold
      b. **D'un   seul   coup, il   a   beaucoup trouvé de pièces d'or.*
          of one single blow, he has many   found of pieces of gold
          'All at once, he found a lot of gold coins'

The adverbial modifier *d'un seul coup* 'all at once' forces the sentences in (14) to be interpreted as involving a single coin-finding event. The non-QAD word order in (14a) is perfectly compatible with a single-event interpretation, but the QAD pattern in (14b) is not. We sketch the interpretive asymmetry in Table 9.

For L2 French acquisition by English-speaking learners, we have another classic poverty of the stimulus. English grammar is of no help, because it does not license QAD, as shown in (15b).

(15) a. While searching everywhere/all of a sudden, John found a lot of gold coins.
      b. *While searching everywhere/all of a sudden, John a lot found of gold coins.

Furthermore, the QAD pattern is not taught in foreign language classrooms.

In order for the learner to recognize that QAD is not simply a word-order permutation of non-QAD, he or she would need to be exposed to a situation in which the QAD construction is true in a given context while the continuous construction, uttered in the same context, would be false. Because there is no such situation, there is nothing to disabuse the learner of the assumption that QAD is simply a less frequent, stylistic version of non-QAD.

Dekydtspotter et al. (1999/2000) examined sensitivity to interpretive distinctions concerning *beaucoup* in non-QAD and QAD constructions of the type in (13) and (14) and, additionally, between QAD as in (16) and the use of the (seemingly equivalent) adverbial modifier *beaucoup de fois* 'many times' as in (17).

(16) a. *Jean a   photographié   beaucoup d'éléphants.*
          Jean has photographed many   of elephants
      b. *Jean a   beaucoup photographié   d'éléphants.*
          Jean has many   photographed of elephants
          'Jean photographed a lot of elephants'

(17) *Jean a   photographié   un éléphant beaucoup de fois.*
      Jean has photographed an elephant many   of times
      'John photographed an elephant many times'

Table 10. Multiple event-single event distinction

Group	n	QAD		Non-QAD	
		Multiple event	Single event	Multiple event	Single event
Learners	46	70.22	60.32	88.74	90.22

Sentence (16a) has an object-related (OR) reading, that is there is a number of elephants larger than some contextually-determined threshold, whereas (16b) has an event-related (ER) reading involving a contextually small number of elephants (but more than one) that are the object of a contextually large number of picture-taking events. In (16a), the number of events is irrelevant. In (16b), both the number of elephants and the number of events count. Thus, the ER reading involves quantification over <event, object> pairs. The relevant measure for the interpretation of *beaucoup* is determined by partitioning iterative events into subevents in which no part of the (plural) object is involved in two different parts of the event, and then adding up the values of the objects in each cell of the partition. The interpretation of (16b) reflects *beaucoup*'s dependence on both the verb *photographier* (which denotes a set of picture-taking events), and on the object NP *d'éléphants* (which denotes a set of elephants). Crucially, *beaucoup de fois* in (17) is not synonymous with (16b), as this adverbial expression has an event quantification (EQ) reading for which the number of objects is completely irrelevant. The QAD structure in (16b) is thus incompatible with situations in which (16a) and (17) are compatible, rendering it distinct from both (16a), the OR reading, and (17), the pure EQ reading.

Dekydtspotter et al. (1999/2000) conducted two experiments. We first consider the results of a syntactic acceptability judgment task containing 12 quadruples crossing QAD/non-QAD once with modifiers such as *d'un seul coup* inducing a "single point" view of the event ("single event" in Table 10), and once with a modifier such as *en cherchant partout* inducing an "iterative sub-events" view ("multiple event" in Table 10).

As expected, participants in the learner group made no distinction between multiple- and single-event interpretations with non-QAD (at 90.22% versus 88.74%; $p = .396$). Crucially, learners made a significant distinction between the two interpretations for the QAD construction (at 70.22% versus 60.32%; $p < .001$). Though it is clear that acceptance rates for QAD sentences are lower than acceptance rates for non-QAD, the interpretation-dependent asymmetry is not explained by a dispreference for QAD.

A second experiment therefore consisted of two interpretive acceptability judgment tasks examining (a) the interpretation of QAD sentences versus (b) the interpretation of sentences modified by *beaucoup de fois*. Each task included 13 critical pairs contrasting multiple-event and single-event contexts as well as 34 distractors. An example test item is provided below as Figure 3.

After each item, respondents were to indicate whether the sentence accurately described what happened in the scenario by marking the appropriate box.

> M. Soupçonneur is a teacher at an elementary school in Rivière-du-Loup. He is
> convinced that his pupils are always up to no good. Yesterday they had to take a test in
> English class. At one point during the exam, he cleared his throat and said, "I will say
> this once and only once. You are all a bunch of cheaters. I hate you. Good-bye!" Then,
> he stormed out of the room and did not return.
>
> *Pendant l'examen hier, M. Soupçonneur a beaucoup accusé d'élèves d'avoir triché.*

Figure 3. Single event context with QAD structure

As Table 11 shows, a difference between QAD and *beaucoup de fois* arose in single event context, but not in multiple object contexts. English-speaking learners of French accepted QAD versus *beaucoup de fois* sentences at similar rates in multiple event contexts (at 92.74% versus 94.98%, $p = .194$).

However, the same learners accepted QAD versus *beaucoup de fois* sentences at similar rates in single event contexts (at 63.78% versus 9.61%, $p < .0005$). This replicates the pattern of French natives: In multiple event contexts, the 63.86% acceptance rate for QAD sentences is indistinguishable from the 59.30% acceptance rate for *beaucoup de fois* sentences ($p = .498$); whereas in single event contexts, the acceptance rate for QAD sentences differs significantly from the acceptance rate for *beaucoup de fois* sentences (at 38.70% versus 0.96%, $p < .0005$).

This difference shows that English-speaking learners of L2 French do not treat the quantifier *beaucoup* in preverbal position in QAD sentences merely as an event modifier. It is, however, explained if both verb and object denotations are jointly implicated in the interpretation of the quantifier. In this case, the part structure of the event becomes relevant in interpreting QAD, as opposed to the number of times the same type of event happened. To the extent that respondents could construe a partology of subevents, they accepted the sentence. Event modification with *beaucoup de fois* did not permit this strategy – hence, the asymmetries in acceptance rates.

Not every system that allows quantifiers to be positioned in the preverbal position yields precisely the patterns that were uncovered, which involve a dependency on both the verb and the object. Specifically, Dekydtspotter et al. (1999/2000) also noted that basic operations of combinatory logic applied to the realm of syntactic categories do not force the interpretive particularities of QAD. These require a precise interaction of syntax and semantics.

Table 11. QAD – *Beaucoup de fois* distinction with respect to single versus multiple event interpretations

Group	n	QAD		Beaucoup de fois	
		Multiple event	Single event	Multiple event	Single event
English NSs	11	56.64	46.04	n/a	n/a
Learners	72	92.74	63.78	94.98	9.61
French NSs	24	63.86	38.70	59.30	0.96

In sum, L2 French learners' interpretation of QAD sentences suggest that their syntactic acquisition is channeled in specific ways, read off specific syntactic dependencies that guarantee certain interpretive effects. Results of an additional task with QAD sentences in English vocabulary, such as 'John has a lot photographed of elephants', also reported in Table 11 support these findings. The subjects for this experiment were college students in German-proficiency courses who had had no contact with French in at least 5 years. The acceptance rates for QAD are depressed, since the sentence is ungrammatical in English. However, the acceptances rate in single event contexts is lower than in the multiple event contexts, although the difference is not significant (at 56.64% versus 46.04%, $p = .146$). That interpretive knowledge of QAD could appear in English (albeit not in an easily measurable way) is not surprising if linguistic input must be analyzed along UG-specified dimensions, even if the resulting analyses are not licensed by the native grammar. These analyses have, however, interpretive consequences that are independent of grammaticality. This interpretive knowledge becomes more accessible to intuition with the acquisition of French morphosyntax.

4.2 Discontinuous cardinality interrogatives: *Combien de* NP (Dekydtspotter, Sprouse, & Swanson 2001)

Like the quantifier *beaucoup*, the cardinality interrogative *combien* 'how many' can appear in French together with its restriction *de*-NP as in (18a) or in discontinuous syntax as in (18b).

(18) a. *Combien   de livres   est-ce que les étudiants ont   tous lus?*
          how-many of books   Q   the students have all read
     b. *Combien   est-ce que les étudiants ont   tous lu   de livres?*
          how-many Q   the students have all read of books
          'How many books did the students all read?'

The examples in (18) include a universally quantified subject. As discussed by de Swart (1992), when a quantifier is separated from its restrictive clause in surface syntax by another quantifier, the intervening quantifier must take scope over the first quantifier. That is, *combien* in (18b) must take narrow scope, while *combien* in (18a) may take either narrow or wide scope. Again, we have an interpretive asymmetry, sketched in Table 12.

When we speak of *combien* taking narrow scope in examples like (18), we mean that the question anticipates that each student has read a number of books (not necessarily the same books) and asks for that number. When we speak of *combien* taking

Table 12. Narrow scope-wide scope asymmetry

	Narrow scope	Wide scope
Continuous	√	√
Discontinuous	√	*

wide scope, we mean that the question anticipates that there might be books that have been read by all of the students and asks for the number of those books.

Once again, the English-speaking learner of L2 French is faced with a threefold poverty of the stimulus. English grammar does not allow discontinuous quantifiers like (18b), as shown in (19).

(19)   a.   How many books did the students all read?
       b.   *How many did the student all read (of) books?

Only the continuous pattern is permitted in English, and it is indeed ambiguous in the same way as the French example in (18a). Discontinuous quantifiers are not mentioned in standard classroom instruction, let alone their interpretive characteristics. Finally, the ineffectiveness of contextualized input for this phenomenon is even stronger than what we have seen in previous sections. This is because of the nature of the acquisition of the meaning of interrogatives. Interrogatives generally occur precisely where there is an information gap. Thus, if the (non-native) hearer of (18b) should misinterpret it as intending wide scope on *combien* and answers accordingly, the learner's interlocutor will not be in a position to correct the misinterpretation, since she or he is relying on the learner for the relevant information. The same could be said for the case where the learner utters (18b) under the false assumption that *combien* could take wide scope. In this case, the answer will be taken as an answer to the intended question, since the learner does not know the information he or she is seeking. Even this presupposes interactions that not every learner will encounter, as well as the assumption that the learner would use such an interaction as an occasion for uptake.

The truth value judgment task administered in the study by Dekydtspotter et al. (2001) featured 28 test items representing seven sets of minimal quadruples. Each quadruple featured the continuous versus discontinuous version of a sentence with *combien*, as in (20) below, crossed with a scenario forcing the narrow-scope versus wide-scope interpretation.

(20)   a.   *Combien   d'animaux est-ce que ces   enfants   ont   tous voulus?*
             how-many of animals Q   these children have all   wanted
       b.   *Combien est-ce que ces   enfants ont   tous voulu   d'animaux ?*
             how-may Q   these children have all   wanted of animals
            'How many animals did these children all want?'

Each scenario consisted of a set of three individuals, all of whom select a set of items, some being selected by all three individuals and others being selected by only one individual. With respect to (20), in a scenario in which there are three children, all of whom want a dog plus one other animal (a mouse for one child, a cat for another, and a bird for the third), the answer to the question posed in (20a) could either be 'two' (narrow scope) or 'one' (wide scope), whereas the answer could only be 'two' for (20b). Participants in the Dekydtspotter et al. (2001) study were therefore asked to determine

Philippe and Monique Dupont hired a magician and her assistant to entertain at their son Jean's 10th birthday party. The magician announced that she could read minds. Her assistant brought out a white rabbit, a black rabbit, a bird, a cat and a dog. From experience, the magician and her assistant knew that the children would include the 2 rabbits in their choices. The magician then asked Jean, Marie and Paul to think of the animals they would like to have. As predicted, Jean thought of the 2 rabbits and the bird. Marie thought of the 2 rabbits and the dog. Paul thought of the 2 rabbits and the cat. Winking, the assistant asked the magician:

"*Combien est-ce que ces enfants ont tous voulu d'animaux?*"

Sure that the expected pattern had arisen, the magician answered:

"*Deux, bien sûr.*"

Figure 4. Wide scope answer with discontinuous cardinality interrogative

whether the answer to each *combien* question was correct. In the scenarios for (20), the question was asked by the assistant to a mind-reading magician, as shown in Figure 4.

For each item, the respondents were to indicate whether the given answer was a correct answer to the question, with the choices YES, NO, and CANNOT DECIDE.

The results of this study are summarized in Table 13.

On the whole, native French speakers (the last row in Table 13) more easily accessed the narrow-scope interpretation than the wide-scope interpretation irrespective of the (dis)continuous patterning of *combien*. However, despite depressed rates of acceptance for the wide-scope interpretation across both word order patterns, native speakers nonetheless distinguish to a statistically significant degree between the two syntactic constructions (at 29% versus 11.69%; $p < .01$). In a similar task in which French sentences were glossed with English words, English speakers showed a dislike for discontinuous constituents. Acceptance rates for the discontinuous syntax show that English speakers did not intuit the semantic distinction (at 33.16% versus 29.48%; $p = .476$). Echoing the English group, intermediate English-French learners did not exhibit knowledge of the discontinuous syntax (at 32.66% versus 25.99%; $p = .146$). A preference for the continuous syntax is also in evidence. In contrast, the advanced learners produced an asymmetry in their interpretation of discontinuous syntax (at 50.00% versus 28.13%; $p < .05$).

Table 13. Continuous – discontinuous *combien* distinction with respect to wide scope versus narrow scope interpretations

Group	n	Discontinuous		Continuous	
		Narrow scope	Wide scope	Narrow scope	Wide scope
Native English	21	33.16	29.48	43.88	59.59
Intermediate	71	25.99	32.66	47.75	45.51
Advanced	32	50.00	28.13	58.04	48.66
Native French	33	79.22	11.69	68.83	29.00

Table 14. Event time-speech time asymmetry

	Event time	Speech time
Continuous	√	√
Discontinuous	√	*

4.3 Adjectival restrictions on quantifiers: *Qui de* ADJ (Dekydtspotter & Sprouse 2001)

Let us consider another case of continuous and discontinuous quantifier phrases, illustrated in (21).

(21) a. *Qui de célèbre fumait au   bistro dans les années 60?*
         who of famous smoked in-the bar in the years 60

     b. *Qui fumait de célèbre au   bistro dans les années 60?*
         who smoked of famous in-the bar in the years 60
         'Which famous person used to smoke in the bar in the 60s?'

In (21a) the interrogative *qui* 'who' and its adjectival restriction *de célèbre* 'of famous' form a continuous surface constituent, whereas (21b) involves a discontinuous surface constituent. Expanding on de Swart's (1992) insight, Dekydtspotter and Sprouse (2001) point out that discontinuous constituents receive their tense interpretations in situ as well. Thus, *qui...de célèbre* in (21b) necessarily characterizes someone who was famous during the 1960s, whereas *qui de célèbre* in (21a) may characterize either such a person or someone who is famous at the time of speech. Again, this leads to an interpretive asymmetry, as sketched in Table 14.

The tripartite poverty of the stimulus discussed in the preceding sections holds: English grammar, classroom instruction, and contextualized input all fail to provide the English-French L2 learner with evidence for the asymmetry sketched in Table 14.

Dekydtspotter and Sprouse (2001) report the results of an experiment designed to probe for knowledge of this asymmetry. The stimulus consisted of a questionnaire made up of 8 quadruples crossing event-time and speech-time answers with continuous and discontinuous interrogatives and 18 fillers appearing in three random orders. However, in this experiment, scenarios supporting both event-time and speech-time answers were constant in all conditions. Thus, both (20a) and (20b) appeared in the same scenario, given in Figure 5.

> *Mrs Briggs*: Attitudes toward smoking have changes drastically since the 1960s. In the 1960s many people would go to bars and smoke every night. For example, Herman the Hermit was a famous rock star in those days and was often seen smoking with Linda Tripp, who was then totally unknown. How times have changed! It is Linda Tripp who is famous, and neither of them smokes any more.
>
> *Mme Goyette*:   *Qui fumait de célèbre au bistro dans les années 60 ?*
> *Elève*:   Linda Tripp

Figure 5. Discontinuous interrogative with speech time answer

Table 15. Event-time vs. speech-time results

Group	n	Discontinuous		Continuous	
		Event time	Speech time	Event time	Speech time
Native English [1]	23	86.95	22.28	86.95	30.98
Native English [2]	24	93.75	5.72	89.06	28.12
Intermediate	47	90.69	25.00	90.69	41.22
Advanced	11	90.90	15.90	79.55	46.59
Native French	30	96.25	5.00	88.75	12.50

The scenario was followed by an information question (21a) or (21b) asked by a character named Madame Goyette, a teacher of English, and answered by a pupil, with a speech-time answer or an event-time answer. Participants in the study were asked to determine whether this was a correct answer to the question. Results are displayed in Table 15.

Event-time answers were generally preferred and were accepted at very similar rates across constructions. Speech-time answers, however, were far less acceptable in response to discontinuous interrogatives than in response to continuous interrogatives. This was statistically significant for intermediate (at 25.00% versus 41.22%, $p <$ .005) and advanced learners (at 15.90% versus 46.59%, $p < .05$). (In the case of French natives, the difference was not statistically significant, as means were too close to zero.) This is another prime example of the poverty of the stimulus problem motivating the role of UG in L2 acquisition.

4.4 Adjectival restrictions on quantifiers and implicatures (Dekydtspotter & Hathorn 2005)

The studies reviewed hitherto have been primarily concerned with the syntax-semantic interface. We now turn to a study which focuses on the derivation of implicatures in interpretation. These are implications that are not part of the lexical semantics of the expression, but arise as part of maxims of cooperation in conversation (Grice 1975). This is especially interesting because while syntax and semantics are domain-specific grammatical modules, principles of cooperation are most certainly domain-general. The property considered touched on the interface between grammar and performance systems.

Dekydtspotter and Hathorn (2005) investigated an interpretive contrast that involves not only idiosyncrasy at the syntax-semantics interface, but crucially idiosyncrasy at the semantics-pragmatics interface. Consider the examples in (22).

(22) a. *Quelque chose de remarquable a   été   découvert par chacun des*
          Something   of remarkable has been discovered by   each   of-the
          chercheurs.
          researchers

b. *Quelque chose a   été   découvert   de remarquable par chacun des*
    something   has been discovered of remarkable   by   each   of-the
    chercheurs.
    researchers
    'Something remarkable was discovered by each of the researchers'

Examples like (22a), where the indefinite pronoun and adjectival restriction are adjacent call up situations where one and the same thing was observed by each of the scientists as well as situations where each scientist observed something different. Out of the blue, (22b) suggests that the same thing was not observed by all. This intuition requires specific interactions between syntax, semantics and pragmatics. At the syntax-semantics interface, the discontinuous quantifier *quelque chose...de remarquable* must be interpreted in situ, and thus under the quantifier *chacun des chercheurs*. The semantic interpretation, therefore, is: For each of the researchers, there is a remarkable thing that he or she discovered. At the semantics-pragmatics interface, this semantic interpretation induces an additional pragmatic inference (an implicature) excluding situations in which the discovered objects happen to be one and the same. That is to say, if you use (22b) which uniquely describes situations where each scientist observed a (potentially different) thing, it must be that the same object was not discovered by all, assuming Grice's principle of cooperation. Such reasoning can, however, be defeated. Both (22a) and (22b) can be followed by (23) without yielding a contradiction.

(23)   *En fait, la même chose a été observée par tous les chercheurs.*
        'In fact, the same thing was observed by all the scientists'

Not only do we have a rare construction with the same logical problems as before, but statements that correct implicatures confound the relevant aspects of interpretation, if the task of the learners is simply to associate a form with the range of situations that it may describe. Because corrective statements cross the continuous/discontinuous dimension, they do not specifically flag the discontinuous structure. These learning-theoretic problems are avoided if the aspects of interpretation of interest here are basic to mental organization in the area of language: The result of computations triggered by specific syntactic and semantic representations.

To find out what English-speaking learners of L2 French know of the interpretive difference between sentences in (22a) vs. (22b), they were presented with an interpretive judgment task in which crucial items crossed same or different object contexts with continuous versus discontinuous sentences. The set up was as follows: For each context-sentence pair, a first character (Mrs. Briggs) read a scenario in English; then, a second character, a teacher of English (Madame Goyette), asked an information question (*Qu'est-ce qui s'est donc passé?* 'so what happened?') to her pupils, in the context of a comprehension exercise, as shown in the sample test item in Figure 6.

A pupil would answer this question with a continuous or discontinuous answer, and participants were to indicate whether the pupil's response was adequate. An adequate response was defined as one which would not mislead a hearer about the facts. Thus, the sentence 'Someone was wearing a hat and someone was wearing a red shoe'

> *Mrs Briggs*: Having landed on the planet Omega, the three scientists of the interstellar expedition separated to begin their exploration of the planet. At exactly 1:45 in the afternoon, there was a flash of light. From their respective vantage points, each of the scientists observed a single enormous explosion on the closest moon.
>
> *Mme Goyette*: Qu'est-ce qui s'est donc passé ?
> *Elève*:   Quelque chose a été observé de remarquable par chacun des scientifiques.

Figure 6. Same object context with discontinuous syntax

would be true in a situation where Mary was wearing a hat and also a red shoe, but it would mislead a hearer to think that two people were involved. Respondents were trained with such English examples before turning to the task which consisted of 8 quadruples and 18 fillers in three random orders.

As Table 16 shows, high intermediate L2 French learners disprefer sentences with discontinuous quantifiers as descriptions of same object contexts (at 84.38% versus 66.88%, $p = .032$), whereas they accept sentences with continuous quantifiers as description of same and different object contexts at similar rates (at 84.38% versus 80.63%, $p = .645$). A difference in acceptance rates of continuous and discontinuous sentences also arose in same object contexts (t (19) = 2.60, $p = .05$). This replicates exactly the contrasts found in the native speaker data.

The results of low/mid intermediate learners on the same task do not reveal a contrast between the two constructions. This is also the case in the results of an English control group who did an English-language version of the task. Task 1 was a verbatim gloss of the French structure with 'of', while in Task 2 the preposition did not appear. In all these groups, there was a measurable response bias against same object contexts.

Thus, the behavior of low/mid intermediate learners is like that of the English natives: There is no construction-dependent effect. In contrast, the behavior of high intermediate L2 learners is native-like: A construction-dependent effect appears. The general dispreference for same object contexts by low/mid intermediates does not follow purely from semantics. This is because on all possible logical forms for the sentence, the sentence should be true. It is explained, however, if learners first access the semantic representation in which the logical object (sentential subject) is interpreted

Table 16. Continuous – discontinuous *Quelque chose+de* ADJ distinction with reference to the same or different objects

Group	n	Discontinuous		Continuous	
		Different objects	Same object	Different objects	Same object
Native English [1]	10	77.50	56.25	85.00	55.00
Native English [2]	14	78.57	70.54	91.07	66.07
Low/mid Intermediate	40	74.06	59.69	76.25	59.06
High Intermediate	20	84.38	66.88	84.38	80.63
Native French	16	71.09	61.72	82.81	82.03

in theta position in the scope of the logical subject (i.e., for every researcher there is an object that is observed), before accessing the inverse scope representation (if allowed by the syntax). The former semantic representation that for every researcher there is an object that is observed is automatically associated with a pragmatic implicature that the same objects were not observed by all. The difference between English-like and French-like response patterns can be explained if the grammaticality of the discontinuous structure (which uniquely receives the interpretation of the logical object in the scope of the logical subject) makes the inverse scope representation possible with the continuous syntax more perspicuous. These patterns in English-French interlanguage, therefore, not only suggest knowledge of specific syntax-semantics interactions, but also the computations of implicatures in the area of quantification.

5.   Broader implications for L2 research

The research surveyed in this chapter, with its focus on L2 epistemology and methods for investigating it, complements work that focuses on the analysis of learners' morphosyntactic output of an L2 in situations of language use as well as work that investigates knowledge of patterns of grammaticality in a language. Consider indeed the fact that most of the (adult) L2 participants in the studies discussed here were still obviously non-target-like in morphology and lexicon, and in general, relatively few learners manage to match native speaker norms in actual situations of language use. It is particularly interesting that these studies document that even these learners have internalized English-French interlanguage grammars with amazingly complex and subtle syntactically related interpretative paradigms.

This body of research probing L2 French learners' intuitions of particular form– meaning correspondences in the acquisition of interpretive properties in the noun phrase and in the clause strongly suggests that learners generate interpretations by virtue of domain-specific constraints on potential form-meaning correspondences at the interface between syntax and semantics. In fact, L2 learners routinely overcome significant learnability problems of the type schematized in Table 1 above, compounded in various ways by the absence of evidence for a crucial form in the input and/or too rich a context to have teachable value. In these cases, general learning principles, in conjunction with instruction and naturalistic input, do not guarantee that learners latch onto the relevant knowledge. Because the knowledge that is acquired is completely unexpected in terms of general learning strategies or input sensitivity, let alone conceptual necessity, it seems to reflect a precise grammatical organization at the interface between syntax and semantics: A 'signature' of natural language grammars. Crucially, English-French interlanguage exhibits the very type of phenomenon that motivates the assumption that UG guides L1 acquisition, showing interpretive reflexes clearly typifying the class of natural language grammars and also shared by native French. The hypothesis of (deep) epistemological equivalence becomes all the more plausible given repeated empirical demonstration involving the same basic task design administered to study populations sharing the same background (biographical factors such as L1, age, previous experience, setting of acquisition, etc.).

Following Bley-Vroman (1983), this search for specific reflexes that are prima facie the hallmark of a specific range of grammars (i.e., those specified by UG) seeks to avoid the pitfalls of the comparative fallacy associated with direct comparisons of native speakers and learners, where similar performances may, in fact, be due to different systems (and vice versa). Although Bley-Vroman (1990) is certainly correct in pointing out a myriad of differences between native and nonnative speakers, the research findings surveyed in this chapter make it implausible to attribute these differences to a "fundamental" (viz., epistemological) difference in the mental design for L1 vs. L2. Indeed, the "no UG access in L2" perspective, most prevalent during the 1980s (Clahsen & Muysken 1986; Felix 1985; Schachter 1988), but still alive in the 1990s (Meisel 1997), and even into the new millennium (Clahsen & Felser 2006), can only be maintained by ignoring the results of a large body of research. Any account claiming that L2 grammars are the exclusive result of non-language-specific abilities of the mind to analyze, categorize, and generalize from data (through, for example, low-level pattern matching and the information content in the input) offers no explanation for how learners could demonstrate knowledge of particular properties that defy domain-general learning. We have also endeavored to show that knowledge of these properties could not have been derived directly from the L1 English of the learners; indeed, we have taken great pains to demonstrate that, at least on a Minimalist conception of language design, the distinction between UG-derived knowledge and that derived by UG-through-the-L1 cannot be maintained, thereby posing problems for accounts that cast L1-L2 differences in such terms (e.g., Bley-Vroman 1990; Clahsen & Muysken 1989; Schachter 1989; Smith & Tsimpli 1995; Strozer 1994, among others).

6.   Directions for future research

In this chapter, we highlighted a research program initiated at Indiana University that addresses the epistemology of second language interlanguage in terms of the range of interpretations associated with various word orders. This is but one reason to study interpretive knowledge. After all, the development of semantic competence is a basic question that we are only now beginning to understand and that can be pursued in a variety of ways.

One possibility is to investigate the degree to which learners employ syntactic information in disambiguating the meaning of an input sentence, as the learner encounters it either orally or in writing. Dekydtspotter (2001) and Dekydtspotter and Outcalt (2005) address this issue with cardinality interrogatives. Dekydtspotter (2001) argues that, faced with ambiguous continuous cardinality interrogatives, learners who had acquired the relevant French morphosyntax (allowing discontinuous syntax) differed from learners who had not yet done so by exhibiting different disambiguation strategies. Dekydtspotter and Outcalt (2005) utilize reading time evidence in support of a structural reflex in the manner in which even intermediate learners accessed the interpretations of continuous cardinality interrogatives. Questions of (temporary) ambiguity resolution also arise in the syntactic domain (Frenck-Mestre 2002) and in the domain of lexical-semantics to syntax mapping (Frenck-Mestre & Pynte 1997).

Another issue which has only recently received attention is the interaction of prosody and interpretation (Dekydtspotter, Donaldson, Edmonds, Liljestrand Fultz, & Petrush 2005). In native speakers, there is evidence that intonation plays an important disambiguation function. The extent to which learners at various proficiency levels are able to use such information in sentence processing deserves fuller exploration, especially since English and French do not have the same prosodic structure. Liljestrand Fultz (2006) finds that the ability of learners to make use of prosodic information develops over time. Apparently, early English-French learners discriminate between possible analyses of phrasal constituents. Learners' preferred analysis of phrasal constituents, however, appears to follow basic structural strategies.

Knowledge of semantics can also provide a case study on the manner in which acquisition proceeds. A body of research argues that learners get off the ground by storing formulas – whole expressions with their semantic and pragmatic specifications – and that these formulas are later compositionally analyzed in creative construction (Myles, Hooper, & Mitchell 1999; Towell 1987; Towell & Hawkins 1994). In a recent study on the acquisition of the *ne ... que* construction expressing the meaning of *only*, Dekydtspotter and Petrush (2006) argue that learners with very little or no prior awareness of the *ne ... que* structure treat the construction compositionally. Interpretation, therefore, provides many future opportunities for empirical discoveries and for advancing theory about second languages.

## CHAPTER 5

L2 functional categories

Syntactic development and morphological mapping

Julia Herschensohn
University of Washington

Résumé

Après une présentation générale d'études d'acquisition d'une langue seconde (L2) de morphosyntaxe française dans le cadre de la Grammaire Universelle, nous abordons deux domaines: Les projections de Temps (TP) et les projections de Déterminant (DP). Nous nous proposons tout d'abord d'examiner les arguments théoriques et empiriques sur l'acquisition de catégories fonctionnelles en L2. Puis nous présenterons de nouvelles données, celles d'une apprenante anglophone avancée de français L2, dont la production (tirée de trois entrevues) est analysée par rapport aux catégories de Temps et de Déterminant. Nous considérons deux approches à l'acquisition de nouvelles valeurs fonctionnelles, la FFFH (Failed Functional Features Hypothesis ou 'l'hypothèse des traits fonctionnels en faillite') – qui prétend que les apprenants adultes de L2 sont incapables d'acquérir de nouvelles valeurs, ainsi que le démontrent leurs fautes morphologiques – et la MSIH (Missing Surface Inflection Hypothesis, ou 'l'hypothèse de l'inflection de surface manquante') – qui maintient que les apprenants en sont tout à fait capables, malgré certaines fautes superficielles de morphologie. Nos résultats nous permettent de conclure que la MSIH est mieux placée pour expliquer les nouvelles données examinées ici que la FFFH.

Abstract

After a general overview of studies conducted in the second language acquisition (L2) of French morpho-syntax in the Universal Grammar (UG) framework, this chapter will focus on Tense and Determiner projections. We will first consider the various theoretical arguments and empirical data related to the L2 acquisition of functional categories. Then, we will analyze new empirical data, the oral production data (drawn from three interviews) of an English-speaking advanced L2 French learner, from two theoretical frameworks: The Failed Functional Features Hypothesis (FFFH) – that claims that adult L2 learners cannot acquire new functional values which are not already present in their L1 – and the Missing Surface Inflection Hypothesis (MSIH) – that contends that new values are acquirable in spite of residual morphological errors. We will conclude by arguing that our results support the MSIH, rather than the FFFH.

1. Introduction

Language can be examined from the perspective of intrinsic structures – its essential components, the vocabulary and grammar that constitute it – or from the perspective of language use. From the structure perspective, the grammar of a language comprises a sound system (phonology), a word construction system (morphology), and a word combination system (syntax). The syntax in many, if not most, languages cannot be separated from morphology since inflectional morphology (often the endings on words) licenses certain syntactic combinations. The symbiotic relationship of these two components is labelled morpho-syntax. This chapter investigates the second language (L2) acquisition of morpho-syntax from the theoretical perspective of Universal Grammar (UG), a shorthand term for the linguistic properties that are shared by all the world's languages. All languages share substantive universals such as common inventories of syntactic categories, and formal universals such as similar constraints on combinations of linguistic units. All languages have categories that are noun-like, that contain words such as *dog* or *tree*; Noun is a syntactic category that labels these words. Every language also has certain constraints such as which phonological segments may be combined (these are called phonotactics); English allows the cluster [str], but prohibits the cluster [tl], which is acceptable in some other languages. Languages, in addition to lexical categories such as Noun and Verb, have grammatical or functional categories that make the lexical categories operative by fixing them in time and space. Verbs, for instance, must be anchored in time by a tense marking such as present or past ('John walks/walked'), a grammatical morpheme that is regulated by a functional category Tense.

While languages all share universal traits, certain characteristics also distinguish one language from another, often in a systematic manner. As an illustration, English and French require the presence of an overt subject in every sentence that has an inflected verb, whereas Spanish and Japanese do not require that the subject be overt (it may be null). Languages may permit or prohibit null subjects, a universal property that is determined one way or the other; this variation is delineated as a parametric choice, the Null Subject Parameter. Chomsky (1995:6) states that "language differences and typology should be reducible to choice of values of parameters"; parameters are almost entirely limited to the lexicon, and more particularly to features of functional categories (Borer 1984).

In this chapter, I address the question of L2 morphological errors through a reexamination of earlier theoretical and empirical arguments on the acquisition of functional categories, presenting evidence from a case study of an anglophone advanced L2 French learner whose production is analyzed with respect to relevant aspects of the categories Tense and Determiner. I first discuss parametric variation in French (particularly in contrast to English) as a function of differing values of features of functional categories; then I present theoretical approaches to L2 acquisition. Finally, I use the case study to evaluate the L2 approaches to functional categories.

2. Functional categories and parametric variation

2.1 Overview of parametric variation in French and English

Superficial distinctions of phonology and morpho-syntax may mask underlying universal commonalities of structure that permit infants to acquire their first language. Word order differences between French and English in both clauses and noun phrases have been shown to be a simple function of whether the verb or noun moves leftward (French) or remains *in situ* (English). This movement – as other parametric variations – is a reflex of functional features of categories such as Tense and Determiner that constitute the grammatical shell of the language. While infants set parametric values for their L1 by gaining interpretable morphology and uninterpretable functional features at an early stage, it is unclear how, or even whether, adult learners of a second language (L2) can acquire parametric values that differ from their native tongue. One theoretical position in L2 research holds that parameter resetting in adult L2 acquisition is no longer possible because the acquisition of L2 grammars is not constrained by Universal Grammar (e.g., Meisel 1997), whereas another holds that adult L2 learners can and do reset parameters (Hawkins 2001; White 2003). Since functional categories are the key to L2 grammar, the acquisition of the correct values of functional features is absolutely pivotal to L2 learning, and a topic of current discussion among researchers, some of whom restrict learning to L1 values (e.g., Hawkins & Franceschina 2004), while others (e.g., Ayoun 2003, 2005a) argue that it is possible for adult L2 learners to acquire new values. The investigation of L2 acquisition of morpho-syntactic parameters is the topic of this chapter.

In the most recent framework of UG theory, Minimalism (Chomsky 1995, 2000, 2001, 2002), uninterpretable features of functional categories such as Tense and Determiner motivate the morpho-syntax of a given language and hence determine its parameter settings. For example, it argued that the values of nominal features (e.g., Number, Gender) determine not only concord and gender marking, but also word order within the DP (Bernstein 1993; Cinque 1994; Longobardi 1994; Mallen 1990; Picallo 1991; Valois 1991). Given that functional categories are the locus of parametric variation, the mastery of new values of functional features in L2 acquisition is a question of prime importance to L2 scholars. Several articles in the past few years have examined L2 parameter setting and the morphology-syntax interface in terms of two approaches. The first approach holds that surface morphological errors indicate underlying syntactic deficits (Hawkins & Chan 1997; Hawkins & Franceschina 2004), whereas the second approach maintains that such errors are caused by problems of Phonetic Form (PF) mapping of morphology (Lardiere 2000; Prévost & White 2000a).

French morpho-syntax has already seen a substantial amount of work in areas that still remain open to further exploration (see Hawkins 2004; Myles 2004; and Towell 2004 for good overviews). Myles points to two major findings – that L2 acquisition is both systematic (in route) and highly variable (in rate and outcome) – acknowledging that UG approaches have "contributed the most to our understanding of the L2 linguistic system" (Myles 2004:218). Towell, whose interests span processing and UG approaches, asks what it is that learners know when they know a second language, and how they come to know it. Hawkins (2004) claims that the "what" of Towell's inquiries is crucial to an understanding of L2 development, and has been best addressed by the UG research paradigm. He focuses on L2 evidence unavailable in the input and only attributable to UG (poverty of the stimulus), as contrasted with L2 evidence available in the input, but not acquired. For both cases, he argues that a minimalist model using distributed morphology (Embick & Noyer 2001) offers theoretical alternatives to explain L2 grammars. "Adopting a theory of UG allows considerable progress to be made in understanding the linguistic behavior of L2 speakers as they develop knowledge of the detail of the specific languages they are acquiring" (Hawkins 2004:248).

French is a verb raising language (Pollock 1989), often compared parametrically to English, a language that raises only non-thematic verbs as 'do' or 'be', in numerous articles in the 1990s. The L2 acquisition of raising has been examined in learners of both languages (see Hawkins 2001; Herschensohn 2000; White 2003 for overviews; see also Ayoun 1999, 2003, 2005a; Hawkins, Towell, & Bazergui 1993; Hulk 1991; Myles 2005a; Prévost 2004; Prévost & White 2000a; Schwartz 1993; White 1991). Myles (2005a), in her study of 14 twelve-year-old children instructed in L2 French, and Prévost (2004), in his study of two five-year-old naturalistic learners, substantiate the proposal that child L2 acquisition resembles child L1 acquisition in including an infinitival stage without verb raising. In Myles' study, the children's instructional setting provides a kind of slow-motion view of acquisition, following a modulated structure building pattern (Hawkins 2001), in which they first use verbless utterances, then infinitival ones (the optional infinitive stage), before finally gaining verb inflection (the IP projection). In contrast, adult L2 learners of French use infinitives as default inflected forms that they raise above negation and adverbs in the earliest stages of development (Herschensohn 2000; Prévost & White 2000a; but see Ayoun 1999 for empirical data contradicting this view).

The morpho-syntax of DP, including noun raising, concord and clitic pronouns, is another area of interest that is well represented in L2 literature (e.g., Ayoun this volume; Bruhn de Garavito & White 2002; Carroll 2000; Granfeldt 2005; Granfeldt & Schlyter 2004; Herschensohn 2000, 2004; Paradis & Crago 2004; Towell & Hawkins 1994; White, Valenzuela, Kozlowska-Macgregor, & Leung 2004). As in the case of verb raising, French differs parametrically from English in raising the noun to the left of the adjective and requiring gender/number agreement (concord) on the adjective(s) and determiner, a topic explored in more detail in the current chapter. Two recent articles deal with L2 French clitic pronouns (one of the later milestones L2 learners achieve): Granfeldt and Schlyter's (2004) evaluation of 11 Swedish adults, and Herschensohn's (2004) report on two teenage anglophones. Herschensohn's intermediate subjects persist in object clitic errors even in their last interview (whereas their verb inflection accuracy is around 90%), using *in situ* (English-like) strong pronouns, null objects, or clitics attached to past participles, as well as target clitics. These same errors are repeated in Granfeldt and Schlyter's description of Swedish-speaking learners of L2 French. Both clitic inquiries conclude that adult learners have early access to a range of functional categories, but are subject to weaknesses in morphological realization. Other areas of French morpho-syntax that should be of interest to L2 researchers include CP phenomena such as relative clauses (e.g., *qui/que* 'who/which/that' alternation), and interrogatives (particularly *in situ* question words), neither of which has attracted much attention so far, and is thus a rich area for future research (to be further discussed below).

2.2 Minimalism and concord

In the bare phrase structure framework (Chomsky 2001, 2002, 2004), syntactic combinations result mainly from the operations Merge and Agree. Syntactic categories have interpretable features necessary for semantic interpretation that persist at Logical Form (LF), and uninterpretable features that must be valued and deleted before Spell-out. Merge, an operation licensed by such a match, combines two elements that mutually select one another, while Agree matches features and deletes uninterpretable ones. Chomsky (2001) describes this as a relation Agree holding between α and β, where α has interpretable features and β has uninterpretable ones, which delete. The uninterpretable features of functional categories – linked to the morphology of the language and determining the possibilities of Merge and Move – are primary syntactic properties that are subject to parametric variation. In English and French, both TP and DP show differing parametric values that I briefly outline.

Uninterpretable features of Tense determine the syntactic difference between French, a verb raising language, and English, whose main verbs do not raise. Uninterpretable features (which, as we see are linked to interpretable counterparts) are often described as [*u*features] such as [*u*tense] or [*u*gender]. Lasnik (1999) suggests that the lexical entry for main verbs in English is their bare form, with the bare form and T joined at PF by "affix hopping". French verbs enter the numeration fully inflected, with Tense specified as a feature in (1a), in opposition to the bare English forms in (1b):

(1) a. <u>Nous</u> (n')embrass<u>ons</u> *souvent / jamais* Marie.
     b. <u>We</u> *often / never* kiss Mary.

This distinction between the two languages reflects the well-accepted difference in richness of morphology that has been long cited as a criterion determining the verb raising parameter (Emonds 1978; Pollock 1989, 1997; Koeneman & Neeleman 2001). French, with its relatively rich morphology, requires raising of all finite verbs to T to check agreement, whereas English main verbs remain *in situ* in VP and only auxiliaries and modals raise (Battye & Roberts 1995; Lasnik 1999; Roberts 1998). A diagnostic for locating the position of the verb is the placement of negation, adverbs and quantifiers which are assumed to be in a left adjoined position to VP in both English and French. In English, they remain in that position as in (1b), but in French they follow the inflected verb, indicating that the verb has moved above them to T as in (1a). In infinitival clauses, French verbs cannot raise, so negation and adverbs usually precede them as in (2).[1]

(2)   French unraised infinitives

    a.   *Ne pas embrasser Marie serait   un   supplice*
            neg not to kiss   Mary would be a-M-SG torture-M-SG
            'Not to kiss Mary would be a torture.'

    b.   *Souvent embrasser Marie serait   un   plaisir.*
            often   to kiss   Mary would be a-M-SG pleasure-M-SG
            'To often kiss Mary would be a pleasure.'

To exemplify the movements involved, the tree in (3) ('John eats the red apple') shows that both the subject and verb originate in VP (the subject-internal VP); in overt subject languages such as French and English, the subject must overtly raise to the Spec of TP (ignoring the split IP with both AgrSP and TP in this tree; cf. Pollock 1989). In verb raising languages, such as Spanish and French, the verb also raises out of VP (leaving negation and adverbs to its right) to the head position T to check tense features. In English, the verb 'eats' remains in VP and checks agreement features covertly.

(3)

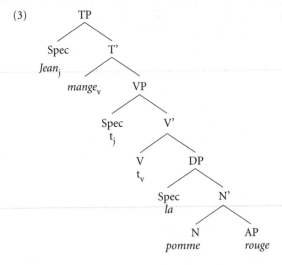

In a discussion of the parametric variation in verb raising, Thráinsson (2003: 166) provides a definition of morphological richness – "clearly separable tense and agreement morphemes in the verbal inflection" – and relates it to his Split IP Parameter (SIP):

---

1.   Infinitival verbs usually follow negation, indicating that the non-finite verbs do not raise to T (*ne pas embrasser Marie serait triste* 'not to kiss Mary would be sad'); however, auxiliary infinitives may precede negation/adverbs in French (*n'avoir jamais embrassé Marie serait triste* 'never to have kissed Mary would be sad'; see Pollock 1989, 1997).

Languages that have a positive value for the SIP have AgrSP and TP as separate functional projections whereas languages with a negative value of the SIP are characterized by an unsplit IP.   (Thráinsson (2003:164)

In the minimalist spirit of reducing the number of functional categories to v, T and C, the SIP can be interpreted as a description of features of T which allow additional projections. Using the probe-goal terminology, the verb raises in [+SIP] languages to check the uninterpretable [Agr] feature on T, which is subsequently deleted by the interpretable [+/– past] of the inflected verb; the inflected verb then raises to the second specifier of TP required by AgrS to check off that uninterpretable [Agr] feature with interpretable person features of the inflected verb. The raising of the sentential subject to the spec of AgrSP entails that the uninterpretable nominative Case feature of that DP is also deleted in the match (Pesetsky & Torrego 2001).[2] Research in L2 acquisition of verb raising in French (e.g., Ayoun 1999; Hawkins et al. 1993; Herschensohn 2000) indicates eventual mastery by anglophones, but with variation in terms of clustered properties.

In a parallel fashion, uninterpretable features of Determiner and Adjective lead to syntactic differences between French, a noun raising language, and English, whose nouns do not raise to the left of adjectives. The interpretable gender and number features of the head noun may delete more than one uninterpretable feature (since there may be several adjectives and determiners for one noun), so the syntactic operation employed is Multiple Agree (Chomsky 2004), a procedure by which the probe finds any matching Goal in the phase it heads, to delete uninterpretable features. A phase is a subarray of lexical items that constitutes a propositional stage of syntactic derivation containing a C or v; thus CP and vP are phases.

This crosslinguistic variation has led several scholars to propose a noun raising parameter distinguishing languages with respect to adjective placement and gender, number and determiner realization (Authier 1992; Bernstein 1991, 1993; Bosque & Picallo 1996; Cinque 1994; Delfitt & Schroten 1991; Knittel 2005; Longobardi 1994; Mallen 1990, 1997; Picallo 1991; Valois 1991). These works argue that noun phrases are complements of a determiner, the head of a DP that contains, in addition to the NP, other functional and lexical projections. Between D and its complement NP, Picallo proposes a gender phrase necessary for languages that mark overt gender, while Delfitt and Schroten propose a Number Phrase necessary for checking singular/plural. Valois argues for a Case Phrase and Bernstein (1993) for a "Word Marker (WM)" Phrase in addition to Number. In this chapter, I adopt Carsten's (2000) simplied notation FP. She considers agents and possessors of NP to be generated in a shell nP, similar to vP, the "light verb" shell that is the functional projection above lexical VP; likewise, nP is projected by a light noun and can be iterative.

---

2.   Thráinsson gives compelling arguments against "feature strength" of uninterpretable features of T as the trigger for verb raising.

Under these analyses, what distinguishes French from English word order is the raising of the N in French and its non–raising in English, as illustrated in (4).

(4)   Noun raising
   a.   *le voile blanc*
      [DP [D *le*] [FP [*voile$_i$*] [NP [AP *blanc*] [N t$_i$]]]]
   b.   the white veil
      [DP [D the] [FP [NP [AP white] [N veil$_i$]]]]

The tree in (5a) illustrates noun raising in French to a position above the NP-AP; in English the noun remains *in situ* in the lowest NP. Knittel (2005) proposes a similar structure to account for "NP-external" predicative adjectives (as color adjectives), but with the movement of the entire NP, not of the head N alone (5b).

(5)   a.   Noun raising

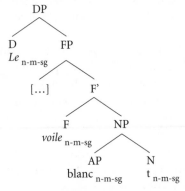

   b.   NP raising (Knittel 2005)

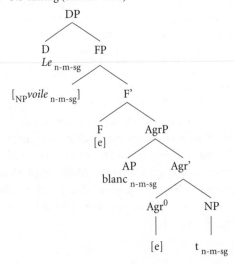

Knittel points out problems for Cinque's noun raising to NumP, and instead argues for NP movement. Her proposal is attractive in that she provides a motivated account for all classes of adjectives and the positioning of both classes pre- and post-nominally. For predicative adjectives such as *blanc* in (5b), the moved NP acts as a DP "subject" that is coindexed with its trace in the predicate phrase. Predicative or attributive adjectives usually follow the noun in French, although the most frequent adjectives (e.g., *bon* 'good,' *beau* 'handsome,' *grand* 'big,' *petit* 'small'), which also receive a semantic interpretation more dependent on the noun, precede the noun.[3]

Summarizing, main verbs in French are fully inflected, raised and checked for tense/person inflection in TP, while English main verbs do not raise and check only auxiliaries in TP. The uninterpretable feature [+Agr] is crucial to both tense and person agreement in French, with the interpretable features overtly marked on the verb valuing uninterpretable [+Agr] in the functional categories of person and tense. Nouns in French carry interpretable features of gender and number, features that may value and delete their uninterpretable counterparts on determiners and adjectives; English has no gender features and no noun raising.

2.3 French and English DP, concord

English DPs differ from French DPs according to two morphological criteria: Gender (an intrinsic feature of all nouns in French), and concord (the percolation of gender/number features throughout the DP). This section reviews the differences and presents an account of adjective placement based on the noun-raising proposals that have been put forth in several studies (Authier 1992; Bernstein 1991, 1993; Bosque & Picallo 1996; Cinque 1994; Delfitt & Schroten 1991; Knittel 2005; Mallen 1990, 1997; Picallo 1991; Valois 1991). French and English differ according to four characteristics of the DP, as demonstrated in (6)–(7).

(6) a. *Le voile blanc*
the-M-SG veil-M-SG white-M-SG
'the white veil'

b. *La voile blanche*
the-F-SG sail-F-SG white-F-SG
'the white sail'

(7) a. *Les voiles blancs*
the-PL veils-PL white-M-PL
'the white veils'

---

3. Valois (1991), Anderson (2001, 2002) and Knittel (2005) provide analyses of prenominal adjectives within the DP framework; prenominal adjectives are mainly outside the scope of this chapter. An anonymous reviewer notes that "the default position of attributive adjectives in French is after the noun, with the marked position preceding the noun governed by semantic, stylistic and contextual factors (e.g., high frequency adjectives like *bon*, whose semantic interpretation is more dependent upon the noun than color adjectives like *blanc* typically precede the noun)". Knittel points out that variable and subjective interpretation of adjectives can obtain both before and after the noun.

    b.   *Les   voiles   blanches*
        the-PL sails-PL white-F-PL
        'the white sails'

In French, nouns are masculine or feminine, a grammatical gender feature that percolates through the entire DP. Most nouns do not have a natural gender (6)–(7), and the gender of the noun is not signaled morphologically in French by a noun marker such as masculine *-o* versus feminine *-a* as in Spanish or Italian (see Ayoun this volume, for a more detailed account of lexical and grammatical gender in French).

    Number and gender are evident in French in the morphology of determiners and adjectives that agree in gender and number with the noun in the written forms. The determiner is marked for gender in the singular (e.g., *le*-M-SG / *la*-F-SG 'the') – but not in the plural (e.g., *les*-PL 'the') – and indicates gender and number. The adjective is either invariable or usually has, in the oral form, a final consonant in the feminine, and no consonant in the masculine as in *grise*-F / *gris*-M [griz / gri] 'grey'. The determiner is almost always obligatory in French, another difference with English which has a null determiner in plural generic (8) and partitive (9).

(8)   <u>*Les*</u>   *castors construisent des   digues.*
     The-PL beavers build-3-PL   some dams
     'Beavers build dams'

(9)   *Je   bois   <u>du</u>   café.*
     I-NOM drink some-MSC-SG coffee-MSC-SG
     'I drink coffee'

One treatment of concord based on Chomsky (1995) is put forth by Carstens (2000), who adopts the view that N raises to higher functional projections to check number and gender. She assumes, in the spirit of Harris (1991), that these features are interpretable on nouns, but uninterpretable on adjectives and determiners. The interpretable features of the noun are able to check and delete the uninterpretable features of the adjectives and determiners, once they are in close enough proximity (Carstens 2003). Gender is then an idiosyncratic feature that must be learned for each lexical item, and concord is a morpho-syntactic rule that operates through Agree (matching interpretable with uninterpretable or [*u*gender]) in the course of a syntactic derivation. The derivation in (10) illustrates the agreement/concord operation, assuming that the features of French nouns and determiners are N, interpretable [± fem, ±pl] and D, A uninterpretable [*u*gender, number]

(10)   Model agreement:
      {D [+Agr, +Num, +Gen], *le, voile*N-3-sg-m} = array
      → [DP [D *le*] [NP [N *voile*]]]
      Match / Agree [+interp] features on N [3-sg-m] with [–interp] features [+Agr, +Num, +Gen] on D
      Delete uninterpretable [+Agr, +Num, +Gen] on D
      Merge *le* + *voile* → *le voile*

It is the concord possibilities (with determiners and adjectives) that are a major clue to gender in French, although initially infants are sensitive to phonological cues to gender. In L1 acquisition, children exposed to a gendered language such as Swedish or French rapidly acquire gender and agreement, apparently learning gender as a feature of nouns at a very early stage, whereas L2 adult learners have difficulty acquiring gender and concord (Ayoun this volume; Bartning 2000; Bruhn de Garavito & White 2002; Dewaele & Véronique 2000; Granfeldt 2005; Prodeau 2005; several chapters in Prévost & Paradis 2004). Aside from predictable derivational suffixes such as *-tion* (F) or *-isme* (M), gender in French is idiosyncratic, and must be learned as part of the lexical information associated with a given noun. Granfeldt (2005) notes that children have early access to uninterpretable features such as gender, which they acquire by both morphophonological and semantic properties. Carroll (1989) emphasizes the lack of direct evidence for gender in French, and the subsequent challenge of mastering the feature in L1 and L2 acquisition. Harris (1991) describes the gender of Spanish nouns as distinct from word marking (e.g., the *-o*, *-a* endings) and natural gender (male, female). He argues that concord targets such as adjectives and determiners are themselves genderless and gain their gender from the head noun.

Gender and number are not comparable categories in terms of semantic function, grammatical role, acquisition and processing. While gender is invariable for a given lexical item, number is totally dependent on the actual referent. Harley and Ritter (2002) propose a feature geometry that classifies gender and number as very distinct in their morphological roles. A distinction between number and gender is also supported by processing studies (Schriefers & Jescheniak 1999) which indicate that the two are processed at different stages with only number information being processed at the initial parsing stage (Friederici, Garrett, & Jacobsen 1999:456). Guillelmon and Grosjean (2001) show that concord in French facilitates processing for monolinguals and early bilinguals (five years at onset), but is irrelevant for late bilinguals (25 years at onset) who display slower reaction times to gender anomalies. Summarizing, for DP, the two morphological differences are the French requirements of intrinsic gender and concord, and the two syntactic differences are the French overt determiner requirement and the placement of adjectives. I now turn to acquisition theory.

3.   Current second language acquisition theory

There is a chronological link between acquisition of syntax and morphology in L1 acquisition (Friedemann & Rizzi 2000), so, for example, children learn nominal agreement and noun-drop (*el* [*e*] *rojo* 'the red [one]') in Spanish in a clustering relationship, and they learn verb morphology and verb raising in tandem (Clahsen 1988). Indeed, Snyder, Senghas and Inman (2001) show that children learn agreement morphology before learning syntactic ellipsis. Likewise, Clahsen, Eissenbeiss and Vainikka (1994) find that children acquire nominal case and correct syntax in a clustered pattern in L1 German.

The mastery of this L1 syntax marks a milestone of parameter setting. Whether parameters can be reset in L2 acquisition has been a major point of L2 research in the past decade (White 2003:Chapter 4). White convincingly argues that L2 acquisition is guided by UG, and I here adopt that position (see also Hawkins 2001). In this chapter, I do not consider treatments of morpho-syntactic deficits and parameter resetting that deny or substantially restrict UG access in L2 acquisition (e.g., Clahsen & Hong 1995). Recall that it is the fixing of uninterpretable features in functional categories that determines parameter setting in L1 acquisition, and that these features constitute the locus of parametric variation cross-linguistically.

As in L1 acquisition, consistently correct morphological inflection is taken to be diagnostic of correct feature specification of the functional category in question. For example, correct tense or adjectival agreement and word order in L2 French should indicate correct specification of functional features in TP and DP. However, L2 learners' production often manifests morphology errors, so an explanation of such errors provides insight into the acquisition process. One can distinguish two views of L2 morphological deficits, characterized by the well known labels Failed Functional Features Hypothesis (FFFH) and Missing Surface Inflection Hypothesis (MSIH). The former attributes biological deterioration of the ability to acquire parameterized uninterpretable functional features (hence morpho-syntactic competence) to a Critical Period deficit. The second attributes morphological mistakes to mapping difficulties and performance errors in superficial morphology. This section critically reviews these two approaches, and then considers their predictions for the L2 acquisition of French DPs by anglophone learners.

3.1 The Failed Functional Features Hypothesis

FFFH comprises a number of studies (Beck 1998; Eubank 1996; Franceschina 2001; Hawkins 2001a; Hawkins & Chan 1997; Hawkins & Franceschina 2004), not all of which agree on every point, but which generally attribute morphological errors in the L2 to a syntactic flaw, not a morphological one. They agree that L2 functional categories are initially underspecified (and may remain so), and that there is a link between the realization of morphology and the specification of L2 uninterpretable features of functional categories.

Eubank (1996) and Beck (1998), for example, propose a defective L2 initial grammar with underspecified or local impairment of functional features respectively. They relate syntactic movement to the specification of L2 functional categories and use morphological accuracy as a litmus test for syntactic movement. Hawkins (2001a:257) notes that L2 learners have trouble establishing a gender feature not present in the native language, but also suggests that L2 acquisition may include new functional settings. He proposes a Modulated Structure Building account (drawing on Vainikka & Young-Scholten 1996a) holding that the early L2 grammar has in principle only lexical projections linked to incomplete morphology, and that the grammar is progressively built up from VP to CP, with functional projections acquired later than lexical ones.

Myles (2005a) also finds support for an initial stage of underspecification and progressive stages of development in that her teenage subjects go through a verbless, bare VP and then IP stage in their acquisition of French verb morphology.

Following a proposal by Tsimpli and Roussou (1991), and Smith and Tsimpli (1995) that parameter setting can only take place during the Critical Period, the FFFH (Hawkins & Chan 1997; Franceschina 2001) holds that parameterized L2 functional features may not be acquired past the Critical Period, leading to surface morphology errors. The authors maintain that the native values of uninterpretable functional features are available throughout life to the adult L2 learner, but that after the Critical Period, parametric values that differ from L1 cannot be acquired. Neither Hawkins and Chan, nor Franceschina, set clear chronological limits for the Critical Period, but speak generally of "postchildhood" or "older L2 learners", respectively. Hawkins and Franceschina (2004), on the other hand, suggest that the Critical Period offset is nine years of age. FFFH considers that inflectional errors are due in large part to a syntactic deficit in the underlying competence of L2 adult learners. Tsimpli and Roussou attribute superficially correct forms to misanalysis, the transfer of an L1 grammatical strategy. The interlanguage result may resemble the target L2 superficial form, but is not really target-like. For example, they discuss Greek (a null subject language) learners of L2 English who produce English sentences with overt subjects. They claim that the learners have not really reset the Null Subject parameter from the Greek to the English setting, but rather, they argue, the learners are producing the overt subjects as agreement markers on the verb (since person agreement is overtly marked on the verb in Greek). According to Tsimpli and Roussou, even though the overt subjects resemble native English overt subjects, the learners' grammatical strategy is still a null subject one.

3.2 Missing Surface Inflection Hypothesis

Schwartz and Sprouse (1996) propose that the L2 learner in the initial stage makes a full transfer of the morpho-syntactic parameter settings of the native language, but that learners also have full access to UG which helps them to evaluate the primary data they are able to use to restructure their interlanguage grammar. The MSIH hypothesis holds that the L2 grammar may access both native and L2 functional features, but that syntax is not directly dependent on the mastery of morphological inflection. Emphasizing the minimalist claim that syntax is universal, Herschensohn (2000) argues that the most salient aspects of a given parameter – those easily observable from positive evidence such as noun – adjective word order – should be the most accessible. On the other hand, morpho-lexical differences such as intrinsic gender are less obvious, and acquired later, because cross-linguistic variation is primarily in the lexicon.

Lardiere (1998a), in a longitudinal study of a Chinese-speaking L2 learner of English, shows that her subject Patty has very stable and accurate syntax, but that her morphology is consistently flawed. Patty produces tense errors at a rate greater than 50%, yet makes no mistakes in her use of nominative pronouns. Lardiere subscribes to the Missing Inflection hypothesis (Haznedar & Schwartz 1997), attributing mistakes to matching difficulties between syntactic terminal nodes and surface morphology at PF. Errors are then seen as superficial performance mistakes, not as deep syntactic deficits. Since L2 acquisition is similar for children and adults, there is no Critical Period functional deficit to examine.

Other scholars have shown that adults use default morphology, further supporting the Missing Inflection hypothesis. For example, Abdelmalek (Prévost & White 2000a: 212) produces a non-finite CP (11), while Emma uses a negated non-finite verb (Herschensohn 2001: 290) with clitic subject and post-verbal negation (12).

(11) *Combien   tu   rester   ici?*
      how much   you-NOM to stay here
      'How long are you staying here?'

(12) *Je ne   continuer   pas.*
      I neg   to continue   not
      'I am not continuing'

The use of non-finites in these contexts indicates that the L2 learners are producing correct French syntax, but fail to have the morphology at hand. Franceschina (2001) criticizes Prévost and White (2000a) as well as Lardiere (1998a), particularly for their adoption of a Distributed Morphology (DM) (Halle & Marantz 1993) treatment that is incompatible with Chomsky's (1995) assumption of pre-syntactic insertion of morphology. More recently, Chomsky (2000) has allowed for a DM approach, with morphology being realized post-syntactically.[4]

Summarizing, FFFH argues for transfer of L1 functional features with local, impermanent or global impairment for L2 functional features, while MSIH assumes transfer of L1 lexical and functional categories, with the possibility of gaining L2 functional feature values. For FFFH, errors indicate a deficit in L2 syntactic competence, but for MSIH, errors indicate a performance problem in L2 morpho-lexical realization.

3.3 Theoretical and empirical evidence from L2 DP

Several recent articles concerning L2 acquisition support native transfer and give differing answers to the question of L2 functional feature values. In this section, I review the literature dealing with uninterpretable functional features of French DP, a category that permits a good comparison of English and French, since English lacks uninterpretable gender and concord phenomena.

Research looking at acquisition of L2 DP has targeted German, French and Spanish. For instance, Parodi, Schwartz and Clahsen (1997) look at acquisition of German

---

4. Using DM, Prévost and White exploit the notion of underspecification (Lumsden 1992), whereby vocabulary items are underspecified in the interlanguage the same way they are in the lexicons of native speakers. Default forms substitute for full forms in interlanguage realization, although they would be ungrammatical for a native speaker.

DP by L1 speakers of Korean, Turkish, Italian and Spanish, through both longitudinal and cross-sectional data. Assuming a noun raising account, they examine use of
determiner, adjective placement, and number agreement. The results strongly support initial state L1 transfer in the differences between the speakers of +/–determiner
languages: Turkish and Korean (–determiner languages) speakers omit determiners at
rates greater than 50%, whereas Romance (+determiner) speakers' omission was far
less than 50%. Suppliance of determiners appears then to be a function of L1 influence (MSIH), as does adjective word order; the Romance speakers (incorrectly) place
the adjective post-nominally in the initial state, whereas the other subjects (with L1
prenominal adjectives) do not. Finally, even though their L1s have inflection for plural, all the German learners show missing plural inflection, preferring lexical means of
marking plurality. This last finding indicates that L1 transfer alone is not sufficient to
describe the developmental errors of L2 learners.

Bruhn de Garavito and White (2002), and White et al. (2004) argue against FFFH
and in support of MSIH in studies of anglophone and francophone students of L2
Spanish. Bruhn de Garavito and White show that francophone learners (with L1 gender) of Spanish have difficulty with gender, in contradiction to the arguments put forth
by FFFH concerning transfer of native language functional features. White et al., who
cross-sectionally compare L1 French and English speakers learning L2 Spanish on a
variety of tasks, find that advanced and intermediate groups do not differ significantly
from native speakers, suggesting that both interpretable and uninterpretable features
are acquirable by L2 learners (contra Franceschina's findings). They conclude that advanced adult L2 Spanish learners eventually acquire gender features on determiners
and adjectives and show concord, even when the L1 lacks grammatical gender.

However, the results also show that lower proficiency subjects of L1 English and
L1 French are more accurate on number than gender, contradicting both FFFH and
MSIH, since L1 French learners do not transfer gender at initial stages. The lack of
transfer effects for lower proficiency francophone subjects could be attributed to the
idea that gender and number are not comparable, for, as in the Parodi et al. study, L1
transfer alone cannot account for the interlanguage data.

Granfeldt (2005), in a comparison of three bilingual first language learners of
Swedish and French with seven Swedish adults learning L2 French, documents a case
study of Karl, an L2 subject followed longitudinally. Over 27 months, he goes through
a period of default determiner (a mixed double gender *le/une*, 'the-M-SG'/ 'a-F-SG'),
before converging on a single gender for a given noun. Granfeldt convincingly argues
that L2 learners begin with a lexical entry unspecified for gender (indicated by default
determiners), and later modify the entry to be specified for consistent gender (which is
occasionally incorrect). However, he remains agnostic as to the FFFH claim of gender
unavailability to learners with non-gendered L1s: "It is not quite clear whether there
is a longitudinal difference between anglophones and Swedish learners such that only
the latter will develop both an assignment and an agreement system for French gender
at all" (ibid.: 185).

Noting, as Granfeldt, that L2 learners have more difficulty with adjective than determiner concord, Prodeau (2005), in a study of 27 adult L2 learners, investigates L2
gender processing through controlled production tests (gender assignment to words,
sentence repetition, gender transformation) and elicited discourse (film retelling, character description). She notes that even when gender is known, for L2 learners "the
information is not systematically available, more so when the constraints of the task
imply too heavy a cognitive load" (ibid.: 148). Bartning (2000) finds greater accuracy
for determiner concord than adjective concord (cf. Dewaele & Véronique 2000), that
definite determiners are mastered sooner than indefinite ones, and that masculine is
acquired before feminine.

Using data from French processing, Hawkins and Franceschina's (2004) theoretical account of adult/child gender acquisition differences attributes the distinction to a
Critical Period loss of ability to gain parameterized uninterpretable syntactic features.
Guillelmon and Grosjean's (2001) study indicates that native speakers of French and
early French-English bilinguals use gender marking to facilitate lexical access (while
wrong gender inhibits access, creating longer reaction time). However, adult learners
of L2 French do not show the same facilitation/inhibition. Hawkins and Franceschina
suggest that very young children situate gender concord in vocabulary on the basis of
phonological shape, whereas nine-year-olds shift concord to the syntax on the basis
of concord cues (cf. Karmiloff-Smith 1979). Thus, children initially have no uninterpretable feature, but gradually establish [$u$gender] on D by age nine. Adults, on the
other hand, are able to acquire L2 [$u$gender] only if their L1 has the parameterized
feature: Anglophones should not be capable of acquiring [$u$gender], while L1 gendered hispanophones or Swedes should (see also Ayoun this volume). The authors
also cite Franceschina's (2001) analysis of a near-native L2 learner of Spanish, Martin,
whose L1 English lacks gender agreement. Franceschina concludes that anglophone L2
learners show this contrast because they are permanently impaired in acquiring an L2
functional feature that is not instantiated in their native language.

Summarizing, the studies reviewed support L1 transfer, greater accuracy on interpretable features present in L1 (e.g., number) than on features different in L2 (e.g.,
gender), and eventual mastery of gender in some fashion (for FFFH it's lexical, not syntactic; whereas for MSIH it can be syntactic). For intermediate and advanced stages, the
studies by Franceschina and White et al. present contradictory results: White et al. find
that advanced learners are indistinguishable from native speakers in their knowledge
of gender (as demonstrated on their experimental task), whereas Franceschina finds
that her expert Spanish speaker's 90%+ accuracy rate on gender is far lower than that
of the native Spanish controls who showed 100% accuracy on gender. The results from
White et al. and Franceschina do not shed light on the availability of uninterpretable
gender features in adult L2 acquisition.

4. Current study: TP and DP in L2 French

In order to reexamine the two approaches with respect to French morpho-syntax, and particularly to test the contrasting findings of earlier studies of French DP, I evaluate the production data of an advanced French L2 learner. To consider the relationship of explicit morphology and functional categories in the emerging L2, this study looks at the development of morphological competence – specifically verb inflection and DP structure – in an advanced anglophone subject who spent nine months in France as an English language teaching assistant in a French *lycée* ('highschool'). The corpus consists of three interviews conducted before, during, and after the period spent abroad. This section describes the subject, the data collection, and presents a summary of the findings.

4.1 Subject and data collection

Chloe, who was first interviewed at age 22, had studied French for nine years, with two years in middle school and two years in high school before she spent six months immersion at age 16 in France (Herschensohn 2001, 2003). Subsequently, she studied French in college, spent six months in France her junior year (age 20), and then became an *assistante d'anglais* (English teaching assistant) in the French overseas department of *Réunion* after college graduation. During her nine months in France, she was in a nearly total francophone environment, living with a French roommate and working with French speakers in the *lycée*.[5] Three interviews over nine months document Chloe's development of French verb inflection, her syntactic control of verb raising, as well as her ability to use gender, number and adjective placement in DP.

Chloe's use of verb inflection and TP syntax is indicated in Table 1 which tallies tokens of non-finite (all correct) and finite verbs, and errors in use of finite verbs (Appendix); Table 2 tallies tokens of VP negation, adverbs, and quantifiers, the diagnostics of verb raising (VR).[6] These are all correct, so she makes no errors of verb raising (VR errors). The small number of tokens of adverb and quantifier diagnostics are supplemented by grammaticality judgments discussed below. The errors include only conjugational mistakes, not lexical errors such as the use of a null subject (one error), a pronominal verb as a non-pronominal (two errors), an incorrect past participle (two errors), all included in Appendix, or mistakes in choice of aspect; her non-finite verbs are all correct. She makes no errors by selecting a non-finite form instead of a finite form.

---

5.   The length of each interview increases during the nine month period, specifically, Sept. 15, 1020; Dec. 20, 1528; May 26, 2479 words.

6.   Parts of the TP data were presented at the GALA conference (September 2005) in Siena, Italy, and at the SLRF conference (October 2005) in New York City.

Table 1. Chloe's TP data and errors

Interview	V-fin	V+fin	Total	Err's+fin	% Error
I	29	150	179	5	2.8%
II	33	231	264	4	1.5%
III	85	372	457	3	0.6%
Total	147	384	900	12	1.3%

Table 2. Chloe's VR diagnostics

Interview	Negation	Adverb	Quantifier	Err's VR	% Error
I	18	1	2	0	0%
II	28	5	0	0	0%
III	50	6	1	0	0%
Total	96	12	3	0	0%

Although Chloe produces numerous lexical and other grammatical errors, she uses all persons of verbal inflection and a range of tenses including present, *passé composé*, imperfect, pluperfect, future, and conditional. As Table 1 indicates, she increases her productive use of correct verbal morphology and reduces the percentage of errors from the first to the third interview. Her principal finite verb error (7/12) is third person singular for third plural (13), but she makes other errors as in (14). The Roman numeral indicates the interview.

(13)   Examples of singular-plural mistakes

a.   *Les   voitures qui   traversaient la   rue   dans l'autre   sens   a*
the-PL cars-PL that crossed   the street in   the other direction has
écrasé (I)
run over
'the cars that crossed the street in the other direction has run over' = *ont écrasé*

b.   *Des   chaussures qui   me plaît* (II)
some shoes-PL   that me please-3-SG
'shoes that pleases me' = *me plaisent*

c.   *Les   cyclones   a   passé* (III)
the-PL cyclones-PL has passed
'the cyclones has passed' = *ont passé*

(14)   Other errors

a.   *ça   vais* (I)
it   go-1-SG
'things are fine' = *ça va*

b.   *ils   prendent* (II)
they-M take-3-PL
'they take' = *ils prennent*

The singular for plural appears to be a default since the mistake only goes in one direction; error (14c) can be seen as an example of overregularization of an irregular verb *prendre* to the regular *rendre* ('render') paradigm (15); in the singular persons, the regular and irregular verb are identical for the present tense.

(15) *rendre / prendre*
  a. *ils   rendent*
      they render-3-PL
      'they render'
  b. *il   rend*
      he renders-3-SG
      'he renders'
  c. *il   prend*
      he takes-3-SG
      'he takes'

The one instance of a null subject (*comment se fait* [*le vin*] 'how [wine] is made') is in the context of a middle voice construction which would prohibit an expletive subject in null subject languages; in spoken French null subjects are licit in certain impersonal constructions (16).

(16) *Faut   faire   attention!*
      be necessary-3-SG to make attention
      'It is necessary to pay attention/be careful'

Chloe's inflectional mistakes diminish to less than 1% by the third interview (the only mistake is number at that point), pointing to her consistently target-like morphological inflection that indicates mastery of person/number/tense inflection in L2 French. The mistakes she makes often seem related to added processing load, as for example (13b) which is a long distance agreement, or (14c) which she repeats twice, obviously searching for the correct irregular form.

As for the syntax interface, Chloe always uses nominative subjects, is 98% accurate for tense and person agreement, and consistently raises the thematic verb/auxiliary to Tense, as indicated by the 111 tokens of negation, adverb placement and quantifiers. The placement of these adverbials, which start out in a left adjoined VP position (as indicated by infinitival forms and by languages with no verb raising), serves as a clear diagnostic for raising. Often omitting *ne*, as is common in spoken French, Chloe uses not simply *pas* 'not,' but a number of other negations, including *jamais* 'never,' *aucun* 'not one,' *rien* 'nothing'and *plus* 'no more' (17). The examples in (17) contain other errors such as wrong gender (17b) and lack of elision (17d), indications of non-nativeness unrelated to the essentially accurate tense.

(17) Negations
  a. Interview I
      j'ai   jamais compris
      I have never   understood
      'I never understood'

b. Interview III
   il   y   aurait   aucune   problĕme
   it   there would have not-one-F problem-M-SG
   'there would be not one problem'

c. Interview III
   on   avait   rien   à leur   donner
   one   had-IMP-3-SG   nothing to them   to give
   'we had nothing to give them'

d. Interview III
   on   avait   plus ...   de essence
   one   had-IMP-3-SG   no-more of gasoline
   'we had no more gasoline'

Likewise, adverbs and quantifiers indicate correct placement of both thematic verbs and auxiliaries in French, even when the placement is different from English as shown in (18).

(18)   Adverbs and quantifiers

a. Interview II
   le   vol   s'   était   bien passé
   the-M-SG flight-M-SG   SELF was-IMP-3-SG   well passed
   'the flight had gone quite well'

b. Interview II
   j'évite   un   peu plus la   politique   américain
   I avoid-1-SG a-M-SG little more the-F-SG politic-F-SG American-M-SG
   'I avoid American politics a little more'

c. Interview III
   on   étudie tous   les   mêmes   sujets
   one   studies all-M-PL   the-PL   same-PL subjects-M-PL
   'we all study the same subjects'

After the second interview, Chloe completed a grammaticality judgment (GJ) task. On 37 GJ items (modeled after Hawkins et al. 1993) using negation, adverb and quantifier placement as in (19), she correctly identifies and corrects 35 sentences as grammatical and ungrammatical, and makes two mistakes with quantifier placement, one grammatical as ungrammatical and vice versa as shown in (20).

(19)   Grammaticality judgment examples

a. *Marie n' écoute jamais ses   disques.*
   Mary neg listens never her-PL records
   'Mary never listens to her disks'

b. **Marc et Jeanne probablement viendront.*
   Mark and Jean   probably   will come-FUT-3-PL
   'Mark and Jean will probably come.'

c. *Ils relisent   tous   leurs   notes.*
   they reread-3-PL all-M-PL   their-PL notes-F-PL
   'They all reread their notes'

Table 3. Chloe's DP data and errors

Interview	Lexical DPs	DP+adj	Errors-adj	% Err-A
I	94	11	0	0%
II	152	22	0	0%
III	302	62	0	0%
Total	548	95	0	0%

Table 4. Gender and number of adjectives

Interview	Adj-m	Adj-f	Adj-pl	Errs	% Errs
I	2	3	2	4	36%
II	5	9	5	3	14%
III	21	23	11	7	11%
Total	28	35	18	14	15%

(20)   Grammaticality judgment errors

    a.   *Les   photographes   quittent tous   leurs   voitures pour*
         the-PL photographers-M-PL leave   all-M-PL their-PL cars   for
         suivre   P.
         to follow P
         'The photographers all leave their cars to follow P'

    b.   **Les   spectateurs tous regardaient   la   famille   royale.*
         The-PL spectators all   watched-IMP-3-PL the-F-SG family-F-SG royal-F-SG
         'The spectators all were watching the royal family.'

Her GJs are essentially correct, with a very small amount of indeterminacy for quantifier placement.

The interviews also document Chloe's development of her ability to use gender and number concord on determiners and adjectives, as well as correct placement of elements in DP. Table 3 tallies tokens of full lexical DPs, tokens of lexical DPs modified by adjectives, and adjective errors in placement (there are none; both pre- and post-nominal adjectives are used correctly). Table 4 gives the breakdown of genders and number for the adjectives that are correctly inflected, as well as the adjective concord errors. These numbers include both attributive and predicative adjectives.

Over the three interviews she makes a total of six gender errors that are clearly performance errors (because she uses the correct gender in other tokens) as in (21).

(21)   Incorrect gender:

    a.   Interview I
         ma,   *mon   voiture; *un   maman
         my-F-SG my-M-SG car-F-SG; a-M-SG mom-F-SG
         'my, my car; a mom'

    b.   Interview III
         *aucune   problème;
         not-one-F-SG problem-M-SG

le   système   scolaire français,   française;
the-M-SG system-M-SG school French-M-SG French-F-SG
*tous   les   écoles
all-M-PL the-PL schools-F-PL
'no problem; the French school system; all the schools'

Not included in the tally are four mistakes of invented words (e.g., *la remonte* 'the going back up,' a non-existent word modeled after *la descente* 'the descent'), or two mistakes of wrong gender (e.g., *aucune enseignement pédagogique* no-F-SG teaching-M-SG pedagogical-M/F-SG) where there is no way of knowing if Chloe simply had the wrong gender for the word.

Chloe uses a range of determiners (definite, indefinite, singular and plural, quantifiers, possessives, demonstratives) all correctly, numerous nominal complements correctly introduced by a preposition and following the head noun, as well as adjectives correctly placed either before or after the noun, as the examples in (22) show. The [...] indicate intervening material, usually a copula.

(22)   Examples of DP with adjective

a.   Interview I
     le   style   romain;
     the-M-SG style-M-SG Roman-M-SG
     'the Roman style'
     des   familles   israéliennes
     some-F-PL family-F-PL Israeli-F-PL
     'some Israeli families'

b.   Interview II
     des   vols   directs;
     some-PL flights-M-PL direct-M-PL
     'some direct flights'
     une   solution   évidente;
     a-F-SG solution-F-SG evident-F-SG
     'an obvious solution'
     un   accent   trop fort;
     a-M-SG accent-M-SG too strong-M-SG
     'an accent too strong'
     la   bonne   taille
     the-F-SG good-F-SG size-F-SG
     'the right size'

c.   Interview III
     les   gens...   conservateurs;
     the-PL people-M-PL conservative-M-PL
     'the conversative people'
     le   plus fort   cyclone;
     the-M-SG most strong-M-SG cyclone-M-SG
     'the strongest cyclone'
     un   petit   bateau;
     a-M-SG little-M-SG boat-M-SG
     'a little boat'

> *une   situation   chaude;*
> a-F-SG situation-F-SG hot-F-SG
> 'a hot situation'
> *son   pire   défaut;*
> his-M-SG worst-SG flaw-M-SG
> 'his worst flaw'

While the percentage accuracy of gender agreement is lower than for the use of tense, Chole's DP syntax is 100% accurate. Her problems appear to relate to lexical lapses and cognitive overload. The six errors of adjective concord in Interview III (which constitute the double percentage-wise of Interview II) mostly occur at the end of the nearly 2500 word interview when her conversational skills are clearly taxed as she admits "*Je suis fatiguée*" 'I am tired.' The two areas of L2 French morpho-syntax, the TP and DP, offer us the opportunity to revisit the two approaches to interlanguage morphological mastery and deficits in the next section.

4.2 Discussion

What do the current results indicate for the two approaches to L2 morphosyntax that have been considered earlier? FFFH holds that verb inflection, gender knowledge and DP concord should show surface inaccuracies (since the uninterpretable gender feature is non-existent in L1 English, and the Tense setting is different in the two languages), and that morphological errors are due to syntactic deficits. In contrast, MSIH assumes that intermediate stages demonstrate differential acquisition of syntax and morphology, with syntactic mastery earlier and more completely than acquisition of concord, which may surface as default or missing inflection. The importance of primary linguistic data to both approaches implies that experience in the target environment should result in higher mastery scores for syntax and morphology with more extended input.

The importance of PLD is indeed borne out by Chloe's nine month immersion, since she generally increases accuracy in most domains over the year, as well as acquires greater fluency and production capacity. Her target-like L2 morphological inflection and word order indicate mastery of person/number/tense inflection and correct raising of thematic verbs and auxiliaries to check the tense and agreement features. The nearly 100% accuracy of the verbal aspects of her L2 grammar (contrasted, for example, with the lexical and gender agreement errors she makes) support the view that the functional features in French T and AgrS are correctly specified, hence favoring MSIH over FFFH. Given the rather stipulative nature of the FFFH claim, however, with misanalysis as a potential explanation of correct production, it is difficult to come to a clear conclusion regarding the two hypotheses. Chloe's virtually error-free production and nearly perfect GJs, give no indication of misanalysis, and it would seem more complicated to devise a misanalyzed interlanguage grammar than to infer that she had simply reset the verb raising parameter to the French value. Indeed, the results seem to indicate she has gained the L2 split IP (T and AgrS), to which she accurately raises all verbs, and which are correctly inflected. Providing additional support for MSIH, her singular-plural and overgeneralization errors suggest mapping mistakes of performance, not permanently impaired morpho-syntax. Her judgment errors corroborate Hawkins et al.'s (1993) observation that clustered properties of a parameter are not acquired simultaneously in L2 acquisition (see also Ayoun 2003, 2005a), and that acquisition of core negation precedes the acquisition of peripheral quantifiers (Herschensohn 2000).

Likewise, Chloe's DP word order is completely accurate, indicating correct use of noun raising. In contrast, her production of gender agreement is less accurate than the verb inflection, perhaps supporting Hawkins and Franceschina's hypothesis of impaired functional features. On their account, nonnative uninterpretable functional features are unavailable for concord between N, D and A, and use of inconsistent gender can be interpreted as lack of acquisition of the target features. They maintain that what appears to be concord in correct uses of D-N-A agreement is simply a sort of lexical agreement (misanalysis), not syntactic concord. If this were the case, we would expect that a known lexical item (e.g., *le système* 'the-MSC system-MSC') would either consistently have correct concord (Chloe does repeatedly demonstrate knowledge of its masculine gender), or be randomly incorrect. But in fact, while she correctly uses masculine concord for D and A with this very noun in most instances, she breaks down late in Interview III and starts using inconsistent and wrong gender with it. Her inconsistent production appears to be impacted by processing demands and fatigue (cf. Prodeau 2005 on processing gender), characteristics that should not influence performance if the deficit were purely syntactic. It would seem that for FFFH, inconsistent gender should occur with equal randomness throughout the interview, not strictly at the end, although one might assume that the underlying syntactic deficit could – in the words of a reviewer – "start to show signs of wear and tear at the end of a long elicitation interview". Chloe's mostly correct concord indicates almost 90% accuracy of number/gender inflection by the third interview, a very high percentage that corroborates the observed mastery of gender by L2 learners found in other studies (Ayoun this volume; Bartning 2000; Bruhn de Garavito & White 2004; Franceschina 2001; Granfeldt 2005; White et al. 2004). These accounts document eventual acquisition by advanced learners, but always with residual problems with knowledge of intrinsic gender and with total mastery of concord.

The interviews provide evidence that Chloe masters word order before concord, acquiring rule-governed syntax fairly definitively, yet still making some inflectional errors. FFFH's proposal that overt morphology triggers syntactic development is not supported by the marked contrast between the mastery of syntax and that of lexical gender. While Chloe does show better mastery of number concord than gender, the cause is not self-evident. Rather than a Critical Period defect, as Franceschina argues for FFFH, it may be that other characteristics of gender distinguishing it from number (Friederici et al. 1999; Harley & Ritter 2002; Schriefers & Jescheniak 1999) contribute to the discrepancy between the two features. The TP/DP developmental differences support other research indicating that parameterized functional features from different domains are not all acquired at a comparable rate or with analogous errors (see several chapters in Prévost & Paradis 2004). Dewaele and Véronique (2000), who also find a disjunction in inflectional accuracy between adjectival concord and verbal agreement, corroborate the importance of primary linguistic data to gender acquisition as well as its vulnerability to processing demands. The differential development of TP and DP suggests that future studies must take into account differential domains and unique characteristics of a given grammatical phenomenon in evaluating transfer and L2 development of uninterpretable functional features.

5. Conclusion

This chapter has reported on a study of the acquisition of TP and DP in L2 French by an advanced anglophone learner in terms of two theoretical approaches to interlanguage morphosyntax, the Failed Functional Features Hypothesis and the Missing Surface Inflection Hypothesis. The analysis of three interviews over nine months of L2 immersion supports the latter hypothesis in the differential development of syntax and morphology and the character of morphological errors, which appear to be random mapping mistakes of performance, but not a reflection of misanalyzed morpho-syntax. Overall, the syntactic phenomena of verb raising, determiner suppliance and DP word order (noun raising) are mastered earlier than L2 morphology (tense, person verbal agreement and number, gender concord for DP), with idiosyncratic gender, an inherent lexical feature of nouns and its uninterpretable functional counterparts of D and A, acquired later than tense features. While the evidence from Chloe indicates mastery of the new parametric values for TP and DP in her L2 French, there is still evidence of residual problems, as for example the gender lapses and obvious lexical lacunae. Evidence of distinct processing patterns when L1 and L2 differ in functional features (e.g., Guillelmon & Grosjean 2001) also suggest that parameter resetting is not a simple procedure, and that L1 influence can be quite persistent. The areas examined in this chapter then merit further exploration in future research.

6. Directions for future research in morpho-syntax

This chapter has examined the development of TP and DP in L2 French using earlier studies and a new corpus of interview data from an advanced anglophone learner. The existing evidence in cited literature has documented the possibility of gaining new parametric values related to T and D in terms of verbal and nominal word order in L2 French as opposed to L1 English, as well as the correct agreement patterns of both TP and DP elements. Future research can, nevertheless, pursue additional studies of TP and DP to be outlined below, and can also develop to a much greater degree investigation of CP-related phenomena.

One area to consider for future research is the differential development of the nominal and verbal domains which has been amply documented in a variety of learning contexts (Prévost & Paradis 2004). For example, verbal morphology and syntax are mastered earlier than clitic pronouns or adjectival concord in the nominal domain. Differential development could be profitably followed in longitudinal studies, perhaps along the lines of the European Science Foundation (Klein & Perdue 1992) of naturalistic learners, or the studies by Myles (2005a) of instructed ones. Only closely followed trajectories will reveal the commonalities of route and rate among various L2 French learners. Accurate documentation will then permit researchers to seek reasons for differential development between domains, or to discern disparities within a domain. For anglophone learners of L2 French, gender concord is more difficult than number concord, even though English has neither in its adjectival-determiner system. Likewise, studies of more advanced L2 learners (Labeau 2005) indicate that all verbal features are not created equal, for learners have more difficulty with aspect and complex tenses than with present indicative. A related area to consider is a comparison of French L1 and L2 acquisition; some comparative studies exist, but they indicate that the two processes are both alike and divergent (Herschensohn 2006), so clarification would be quite welcome.

As for the CP realm, it is mainly unexplored territory in L2 French, yet it offers rich possibilities for research into relative and complement clauses, interrogatives, and discourse related focus and topic elements. Aside from a few oblique references to that-trace phenomena in French from a decade past, there has been no systematic investigation of the acquisition of relative clauses or verbal/adjectival complement clauses in L2 French by anglophones (or anyone else); the clear morpho-syntactic differences between the two languages makes the investigation quite compelling. Likewise, interrogatives differ substantially between the two languages with French including both the QU-movement (in formal register) and *in situ* (in informal register) options, while English only allows the movement possibility. Finally, questions of discourse phenomena such as topicalization and focus, also present a nearly untouched area of study. French offers a distinct range of syntactic devices that are not matched one to one in English (e.g., left and right dislocation) and that engage the CP domain, relating the sentence to the larger discourse. These CP related areas are among the most difficult to master in a second language (Sorace 2005), and demonstrate interface effects not only with discourse, but also with prosody.

There is then no lack of topics to be explored in the acquisition of L2 French morpho-syntax. Once information on the many facets of CP is amassed, the finer grained questions posed about TP and DP can then be asked about CP. The *embarras de richesses* is only cumbersome in being a list of research yet undone rather than a list of accomplishments. But Towell (2004:357) is encouraging in his observation of contributions in the past decade or so: "Now the colleagues who have written the articles in this volume and the many more whose work is referred to throughout, have been able to provide accounts, from a variety of persepctives, on research which *has taken* place. I take this as a sign of significant progress".

Appendix

Errors of TP

Interview I

Ça <u>vais</u>-1-sg = ça <u>va</u>-3-sg 'it's going'

Comment se fait-3-sg <u>null subject</u> = se fait <u>le vin</u> 'how [wine] is made'

Qui <u>a</u> arrêté = qui <u>s'est</u> arrêté 'who stopped' (pronominal)

Les voitures [...] <u>a</u>-3-sg écrasé = <u>ont</u>-3-pl écrasé 'the cars ran them over'

Tous les trois ne <u>va</u>-3-sg pas marcher = ne <u>vont</u>-3-pl pas 'all three are not going to walk'

Interview II

Ils <u>prendent</u>, ils <u>apprendent</u> = ils <u>apprennent</u>-3-pl 'they learn'

Ils prend-3-sg = ils prennent-3-pl 'they take'

Des chaussures qui me <u>plaît</u>-3-sg = me <u>plaisent</u>-3-pl 'shoes that please me'

N'inquiétez-2-pl pas = ne vous inquiétez pas 'Don't worry.' (pronominal)

Interview III

Les cyclones <u>a</u>-3-sg passé = <u>ont</u>-3-pl passé 'the cyclones passed through'

Qu'ils <u>veut</u>-3-sg = ils <u>veulent</u>-3-pl 'they want'

Des sujets qui <u>doit</u>-3-sg être enseignés = <u>doivent</u>-3-pl être 'subjects that must be taught'

CHAPTER 6

The second language acquisition of grammatical gender and agreement

Dalila Ayoun
University of Arizona

Résumé

La première partie de ce chapitre décrit les particularités du genre grammatical en français; puis l'explication théorique et les prédictions pour les apprenants de langue seconde (L2) sont formulées dans le cadre minimaliste qui présuppose que le genre grammatical est une propriété lexicale des noms, alors que le nombre et la personne sont des propriétés des déterminants. L'approche minimaliste des traits paramétrisés du genre présuppose que les apprenants L2 ont accès aux catégories fonctionnelles et à leurs traits, que ceux-ci soient présents dans leur première langue ou pas. L'étude empirique présentée dans la section 5 teste trois prédictions: (a) Les participants seront plus précis dans les accords déterminant/nom que nom/adjectif; (b) Leur performance dépendra de leur niveau en L2; (c) Leur niveau en L2 leur permettra de mieux détecter les conflits de genre. Les trois prédictions sont confirmées par les résultats de deux tâches (jugement grammatical et production) effectuées par des anglophones apprenants de français L2 à trois niveaux d'appropriation, indiquant qu'ils ont réussi à acquérir la valeur du paramètre du genre associé avec Num, ayant acquis le trait [± masc] dans les phrases nominales. Les difficultés à effectuer l'accord nom/adjectif de façon consistente sont expliquées par un manque d'attention et de motivation de ces apprenants pour qui le genre grammatical a une faible valeur communicative, est fortement redondant, et doit être appris à partir de données ambiguës et complexes, comportant de nombreuses exceptions.

Abstract

This chapter starts with a descriptive account of grammatical gender in French, outlining its idiosyncrasies in Section 1. The theoretical account and learnability predictions for L2 French learners presented in Section 2 are couched in the minimalist framework in which is is assumed that grammatical gender is a lexical property of nouns, while number and person features are generally assumed to be a property of the determiner. The minimalist approach of parameterized gender features has clear learnability implications for L2 adult learners. Assuming that they have access to functional categories and their features, whether they are instantiated in their L1 or not, the empirical study presented in Section 5 tests three predictions: (a) Participants will perform more accurately on determiner/noun agreement than on noun/adjective agreement; (b) Participants will become more accurate with their increasing level of proficiency; (c) The higher the level of proficiency, the more likely will the participants be able to detect conflictual gender assignment. The results of a grammaticality judgment task and production task performed by English-speaking L2 French learners at three different levels of proficiency confirmed all three predictions, indicating that they have successfully reset the gender-marking parameter associated with Num, in that they clearly seem to have acquired the [±masc] gender feature in nominal phrases. The difficulties in consistently making N/Adj agreement are attributed to a lack of attention and motivation on the part of L2 learners for whom grammatical gender carries a low communicative load, is highly redundant, and must be learned from an ambiguous, complex input with numerous exceptions.

1.   French grammatical gender

1.1   Lexical gender and grammatical gender

French is one of the numerous languages that exhibit both inherent lexical gender and grammatical gender. Inherent lexical gender refers to the fact that, quite logically, inherently female nouns are feminine, while inherently male nouns are masculine. Thus, *neveu* 'nephew' and *frère* 'brother' are masculine nouns, while *nièce* 'niece' and *soeur* 'sister' are feminine nouns. Grammatical gender, also referred to as arbitrary gender, applies to all nouns, animate or inanimate, concrete or abstract. Thus, *vélo* 'bicycle' and *esprit* 'spirit' are masculine nouns, whereas *coccinelle* 'lady bug' and *foi* 'faith' are feminine nouns.

Whether grammatical gender is an inherent property of all nouns which then dictates agreement (Carroll 1989), or whether gender classes are defined by agreement (Corbett 1991), it is required of all nouns in French as in the other Romance languages, among many other languages. Greenberg (1978: 50) proposes that grammatical gender is a combination of classification and agreement, "the two being in a relation of mutual determination, the gender being defined by the agreements, and the agreements being determined by the genders". Thus, French is said to have a formal gender system with a weak semantic component (Corbett 1991): Some animate nouns are assigned a grammatical gender based on natural gender, while the majority of other nouns are assigned a grammatical gender arbitrarily. According to Séguin (1969), semantically motivated gender categories account for only 10.5% of all French nouns.

In contrast to French, English has a semantic gender system: A noun's gender is not formally marked. Instead, it is determined through its meaning (Corbett 1991). Thus, 'grandmother' and 'uncle' are respectively feminine and masculine, whereas 'friend', 'cousin' or 'doctor' are neither, and their meaning will depend on their referents in a specific context. English also has gender marked pronouns ('he/she', 'him/her', and even 'it' for neuter), but there is a strong tendency to neutralize the gender distinction with the widespread use of 'they/them', even when the gender of the referent is known, and clearly masculine or feminine (e.g., 'Paul is looking for a new girlfriend. But they would have to love sports'). English lost its three genders over time along with its case system: As phonetic changes eliminated final syllables and nominal inflectional endings, English gradually relied more on word order rather than on agreement to indicate the syntactic functions of words, and gender lost its grammatical role (e.g., Bolton 1982). Similarly, phonological changes and the disappearance of the Latin case system resulted in the loss of the neuter gender in Romance languages (e.g., Posner 1966).

1.2   How is grammatical gender assigned in the lexicon?

French is traditionally described as a language with an opaque gender system because of the arbitrariness of grammatical gender. However, various gender assignment rules were proposed very early on. First, there were rules based on semantics and orthography along with a detailed count of nouns (Bidot 1925); then rules based on phonological endings for about 85% of frequently occurring nouns were suggested (Mel'čuk 1958); and finally, the combination of phonological and semantic rules provided in Tucker, Lambert and Rigault (1969, 1977) constitute the most extensive system of rules for gender assignment of French nouns.[1] Tucker et al. established that the majority of the rules are phonological, but there are also some semantic rules which take precedence over morphological rules. All these rules overlap and present exceptions, but overall form a coherent and relatively reliable system, albeit a complex one. For instance, Séguin (1969) lists 570 distinct endings for masculine alone, and as we will see below, there is a high degree of variability in the predictive value of these multiple endings.

The rules proposed by Tucker et al. (1977) were tested on a large number of French speakers who were asked to assign grammatical gender to a variety of common, rare, and pseudo-nouns in various conditions.[2] For example, words ending in -ais, -oi, -illon, -eur were found to be reliable markers of masculine nouns, while -ation, -ité, and -stion were found to be reliable markers of feminine nouns. The word endings exhibit a clear overlap between morphology and phonology.

Orthography also plays an important role in determining gender. Tucker et al. (1977:33) mention that the phone [e] spelled -é and -ée yields both masculine and feminine nouns such as le comité 'committee' and la bonté 'kindness', or le musée 'museum' and la mosquée 'mosque'. Words with a final consonant (phonetically speaking) are usually feminine, while words with a final vowel are often masculine, but there are many exceptions to that rule as well, and it depends on the final consonant: For instance, one says un crabe 'crab', but une syllabe 'syllable', or un verbe 'verb', but une courbe 'curve'. To see more precisely how reliable this general rule is, I randomly se-

---

1.   The studies by Tucker and his colleagues have been reviewed in more detail elsewhere (e.g., Antes 1993; Warden 1997).

2.   See also Mel'čuk (1958), Levy (1983), and Tucker, Lambert, Rigault and Segalowitz (1968) for similar analyses to establish gender assignment rules.

Table 1. Gender assignment by phonological ending (vowel)

Phonological ending	Total number of tokens	% Feminine	% Masculine
[ã]	1963	0.72%	99.28%
[ɛ̃]	938	0.96%	99.04%
[i]	2337	75.39%	24.61%
[o]	865	2.78%	97.22%
[ø]	189	2.65%	97.35%
[œ̃]	17	0.0%	100.0%
[y]	201	28.35%	71.64%
average	930	15.83%	84.16%

Table 2. Gender assignment by phonological ending (consonant)

Phonological ending	Total number of tokens	% Feminine	% Masculine
[k]	833	33.30%	66.70%
[d]	714	61.90%	38.09%
[f]	300	11.00%	89.00%
[l]	1581	41.55%	58.44%
[n]	1204	68.02%	31.97%
[s]	980	84.59%	15.40%
[t]	2269	48.78%	51.21%
average	1126	49.87%	50.11%

lected seven consonantal endings and seven vowel endings from their frequency tables. The total number of tokens for each phonological ending and the percentage of feminine nouns and masculine nouns are displayed in Tables 1 and 2, for vowels and consonants respectively.

Table 1 shows that 84.16% of the total number of tokens ending in a vowel are masculine ([i] is a notable exception at 75.39% feminine), but Table 2 reveals that only 49.87% of the tokens ending in a consonant are feminine as expected. Of course, one may point out that 84.59% of nouns ending in [s] are feminine, a reasonably high percentage. Note also that the ending with the highest number of tokens, [t], is almost evenly split between feminine words (48.78%) and masculine words (50.11%).[3]

We now turn to the numerous idiosyncrasies and exceptions French displays in assigning grammatical gender.

3. Her analysis of the tables presented in Tucker et al. (1977) leads Andriamamonji (2000) to conclude that 5% of the endings are ambiguous (40 to 50% exceptions), 6% have a low predictive value (30 to 40% exceptions), and 89% have a high predictive value (less than 30% exceptions); 63% of words have a predictive value for gender, but the probability of that value is not given.

1.3   Idiosyncrasies and exceptions

1.3.1   *Epicene nouns*

Epicene nouns are nouns used with only one grammatical gender regardless of the gender of the referent. For instance, the following words are always grammatically feminine: *Une victime* 'victim', *une sentinelle* 'sentinel' (although it usually refers to a male soldier), *la personne* 'person', *une vedette* 'star', including some animal referents such as *une souris* 'mouse', *une abeille* 'bee', and at least the inaminate word *une étoile* 'star' referring to a celebrity; conversely, the following animate nouns are always grammatically masculine: *Un bébé* 'baby', *un génie* 'genius', *un ange* 'angel', *un mannequin* 'model' (although it usually refers to a female model), among others, regardless of the referent.

The most difficult cases from a learnability perspective are those where grammatical gender and natural gender clash. Thus, *ascendant,* a masculine form, applies also to feminine referents as in the following example:

(1)　a.　*Sa*　　　　　　　*grand-mère*　　　*maternelle*　　*est*
　　　　　3rd-POSS-FEM-SG　grand-mother-FEM-SG　maternal-FEM-SG　is

　　　　　son　　　　　*seul*　　　*ascendant*　　　*survivant*
　　　　　3rd-POSS-MSC-SG　only-MSC-SG　ascendant-MSC-SG　surviving-MSC-SG
　　　　　'Her maternal grand-mother is her only surviving ascendant'

It appears that even epicene nouns generally follow the regular patterns of gender assignment based on phonological rules. Thus *chameau* 'camel' and *éléphant* 'elephant' are only used with the masculine, like most nouns ending in *-ant* [ã]; on the other hand, *abeille* is feminine but its ending [a bɛj] is similar to masculine nouns such as *le miel* [mjɛl] 'honey', *le ciel* [sjɛl] 'sky' or *un partiel* [par sjɛl] 'midterm exam'.

1.3.2   *Gender change according to number*

Most French nouns can be used at the singular (*le livre* 'the book') or the plural (*les livres* ' books'), and in general, gender and number are independent (Corbett 1991:154). However, three French nouns – *amour, délice, orgue* – considered as exceptions and labelled as such in the lexicon, change gender according to number as illustrated in (2):

(2)　a.　*Un*　　　*bel*　　　　　　　*amour*
　　　　　a-MSC-SG　beautiful-MSC-SG　love-SG
　　　　　'A beautiful love'

　　　b.　*De*　　　*belles*　　　　／ **beaux*　*amours*
　　　　　some-PL　beautiful-FEM-PL ／ *MSC-PL　love-PL
　　　　　'Beautiful loves'

　　　c.　*Un bel*　　　　／ **une belle* *orgue*
　　　　　a　beautiful-SG-MSC ／ *SG-FEM　organ
　　　　　'A beautiful organ'

　　　d.　*De*　　　*belles*　　　　／ **beaux*　*orgues d'église*
　　　　　some-PL　beautiful-FEM-PL ／ *MSC-PL　organs-PL of church
　　　　　'Beautiful church organs'

e. *Ce   vin   est un   délice*
   this-MSC-SG wine-MSC-SG is a-MSC-SG delight-MSC-SG
   'This wine is a delight/is delicious'

f. *Les   délices   orientales   / *orientaux*
   the-PL delights-FEM-PL oriental-FEM-PL / *MSC-PL
   'The Oriental delights'

Délice had two genders in Latin as well: Singular neuter (*delicium*), and feminine plural (*deliciae*). *Amour* was feminine until the 17th century when prescriptive grammarians decided it should be masculine.[4]

1.3.3 *Fluctuating gender*

At least two very high frequency nouns, *gens* 'people' and *après-midi* 'afternoon' fluctuate between masculine and feminine. *Gens* always remains plural but it may be feminine or masculine as follows:

(3) a. *Les   vieilles   / *vieux   gens*
      the-PL old-FEM-PL / *MSC-PL people-PL
      'The old people'

   b. *Ces   gens   sont vieux   / *vieilles*
      these-PL people are old-MSC-PL / *FEM-PL
      'These people are old'

   c. *Curieux   / *curieuses, les gens s'approchaient pour mieux voir*
      curious-MSC-PL / *FEM-PL,   people got closer   to   better see
      'Curious, people were getting closer to see better'

Gens was feminine in Old French, and took on the masculine gender as well when it started to be used with the meaning of 'men, young men', whereas *après-midi* fluctuates between the two genders without a clear preference, as illustrated in (4):

(4) a. *Nous avons passé un   bel   / une belle après-midi*
      we   have spent a-MSC-SG beautiful-MSC-SG / FEM-SG afternoon
      'We had a beautiful afternoon'

Similarly, *personne* is a feminine noun even with male referents as in (5a); but when used as a pronoun in negative constructions in the sense of 'nobody, no one', it is masculine, as in (5b, c):

(5) a. *Mon   frère   est une   personne   amusante / *amusant*
      my-MSC brother-MSC is a-FEM person-FEM fun-FEM / *MSC
      'My brother is a fun person'

   b. *Personne n'a été   surpris   / *surprise*
      nobody   has been surprised-MSC / *FEM
      'Nobody was surprised'

---

4. Italian, another Romance language, has many more forms (twenty five to thirty nouns) left over from the neuter gender in Latin that are masculine in the singular and feminine in the plural: *Braccio* (MSC-SG), *braccia* (FEM-PL) 'arm(s)', *uovo* (MSC-SG), *uova* (FEM-PL) 'egg(s)'.

    c. *Personne n'est venu*   / *venue*
       no one is   came-MSC / *-FEM
       'Nobody came'

    d. *La personne n'est pas venue*   / *venu*
       the person is not   came-FEM / *MSC
       'The person did not come'

Thus, the examples in (5c) and (5d) allow us to contrast the use of *personne* as a noun, always feminine, and as a pronoun, always masculine.

1.3.4 *Grammatical homonyms*

Some nouns with different etymologies became homonyms, and are only differentiated by their gender (Wagner & Pinchon 1991), yielding grammatical homonyms:

(6) a. *un moule* < (Lat.) *modulum* vs. *une moule* < (Lat.) *musculum*
      'mould'   'mussel'

    b. *un poêle* < (Lat.) *pallium* vs. *une poêle* < (Lat.) *patellam*
      'stove'   'pan'

    c. *un vase* < (Lat.) *vas* vs. *une vase* < (Dutch) *wase*
      'vase'   'mud'

For other homonyms, gender is used to distinguish between inaminate and animate nouns as in (7), among others:

(7) a. *une aide* 'help' vs *un aide* 'aid'
    b. *une manœuvre* 'manoeuvre' vs *un manœuvre* 'worker'
    c. *une enseigne* 'sign' vs *un enseigne* 'ensign'

To sum up, French presents numerous idiosyncrasies in their gender assignment to nouns, from epicene nouns to grammatical homonyms, as well as nouns with fluctuating gender based either on number or semantic shift, all of which contribute to a rather complex and ambiguous input for L2 learners, as will be discussed below.

1.4 Agreement and gender resolution

Grammatical gender has syntagmatic consequences in that gender marking is also required on determiners, adjectives, and past participles.[5] Here we will only mention an idiosyncrasy of the quantifier *combien* 'how many'. Agreement is optional when there is overt *wh*-movement of *combien* as in (8a), but it is not allowed when *combien* remains *in situ*, as shown in (8b):

---

5. The past participle of intransitive verbs agrees in number and gender with the subjects, while the past participle of transitive verbs agrees in number and gender with direct objects that precede these verbs.

(8) a. *Combien   en   avez-vous acheté(es)?*
         how many of them have you   bought-(FEM-PL)
         'How many did you buy?'
     b. *Vous en   avez acheté(*es)   combien?*
         you of them have bought-(*FEM-PL) how many
         'How many did you buy?'

Boivin's (1998) suggestion that the lack of agreement is an indication that there is no movement of the object through [Spec, AgrO] is plausible, but the examples in (8) are bound to be confusing for L2 learners (or even for native speakers), particularly given the fact that *en* does not agree with past participles, contrary to other direct object pronouns, as illustrated in (9):

(9) a. *Les roses? Oui, Sophie les   a   achetées   / *acheté*
         the roses? Yes, Sophie them has bought-FEM-PL / *SG
         'The roses? Yes, Sophie bought them'
     b. *Les roses? Oui, Sophie en   a   acheté / *achetées*
         the roses? Yes, Sophie them has bought / *FEM-PL
         'The roses? Yes, Sophie bought some'

Determiners include definite (*le, la, les*), indefinite (*un, une, des*), and partitive (*du, de la*) articles; demonstrative (*ce, cette, ces*), possessive (*mon, ma*, etc.), and interrogative (*quel(s), quelle(s)*) adjectives (see more detailed discussion below). The terms of concord and agreement will be assumed to refer to the same phenomenon (see Corbett 2003 for a discussion).

Corbett (1991:269) also shows that a syntactic gender resolution of conjoined nouns operates in French: "[T]he syntactic principle operates according to the gender of the conjoined items, irrespective of their meaning". The masculine is the unmarked gender in that it is used when masculine nouns are conjoined as one would expect, but also when nouns of both genders are conjoined. The feminine is only used when all nouns are feminine. Contrast the examples in (10):

(10) a. *Un frère   et   une soeur obéissants   / *obéissantes*
          a   brother and a   sister obedient-MSC-PL / *FEM-PL
          'An obedient brother and sister'
      b. *Un frère   et   une soeur obéissante*
          a   brother and a   sister obedient-FEM-SG
          'A brother and an obedient sister'
      c. *Une soeur et   une cousine obéissantes   / *obéissants*
          a   sister and a   cousin obedient-FEM-PL / *MSC-PL
          'An obedient sister and cousin'

Although acceptable and grammatical, (10b) sounds a little odd at first and constitutes the marked case, while (10a) is definitely the unmarked, expected case. Inanimate nouns follow the same rules as illustrated in (11):

(11) a. *Le piano et   le   violon sont neufs*
           the piano and the violin are new-MSC-PL
           'The piano and the violin are new'
      b. *Le piano et   la   flûte sont neufs   / *neuves*
           the piano and the flute are new-MSC-PL / *FEM-PL
           'The piano and the flute are new'

Because gender resolution favors the masculine for both animate and inanimate nouns, Corbett (1991) concludes that it is a syntactic resolution, as opposed to a semantic resolution, whereas Wechsler (in press) suggests that French uses both types of resolution: Animate nouns use semantic resolution, whereas inanimate nouns use syntactic resolution.

1.4.1 *Nominal affective constructions*

Hulk and Tellier (1998, 2000) distinguish between internal agreement (between the nominal head of the DP and the functional (D) head of the DP), and external agreement (between the lexical head of the DP and any DP external adjectives or past participles) to account for the so-called N1 *de* N2 affective constructions. They suggest that when the N1 is masculine and the N2 feminine, the external adjective or participle agrees in gender with the animate N2, which is then taken to be the nominal head of the construction. Consider the examples in (12) (Hulk & Tellier 2000: 55):

(12) a. *Ton   phénomène   de fille est bien distraite   / *distrait*
           your-MSC phenomemon-MSC of girl is quite distracted-FEM / *MSC
           'That character of a daughter of yours is quite absent-minded'
      b. *Son abomination   de beau-père   est craint   / *crainte*
           his abomination-FEM of father-in-law is feared-MSC / *FEM
           'His abomination of a father-in-law is feared'
      c. *Ce que ta   tornade   de fils peut être étourdissant   / *étourdissante*
           how   your tornado-FEM of son can be dizzying-MSC / *FEM
           'How your tornado of a son can be dizzying'

When the N2 is inanimate, they argue that the external adjective or participle may or may not agree with it, as shown in the following examples (Hulk & Tellier 2000: 56–57):

(13) a. *Ta   saleté   de toit   a   été repeint   / *repeinte*
           your dirt-FEM of roof-MSC has been repainted-MSC / *FEM
           des dizaines de fois
           tens   of times
           'Your dirt of a roof has been repainted tens of times'
      b. *Les marins trouvent cette saloperie de vent   particulièrement*
           the sailors find   this filth-FEM of wind-MSC particularly
           *exaspérant   / *exaspérante*
           exasperating-MSC / *FEM
           'The sailors find this filth of a wind particularly exasperating'

Hulk and Tellier (2000: 56–57) propose the sentences in (14) as examples of the external adjective agreeing with the N1 instead of the N2:

(14) a. *Je peux vous garantir que ce bijou de symphonie sera*
I can guarantee that this jewel-MSC of symphony-FEM will be
*désormais inscrit / *inscrite dans tous les répertoires*
from now on included-MSC / *FEM in all the repertories
'I can assure you that from now on this jewel of a symphony will be included in all the repertories'

  b. *Ce chef-d'œuvre de fresque Michelangelo l'a peint / *peinte*
this masterpiece-MSC of fresco-FEM Michelango it painted-MSC / *FEM
dans des conditions très difficiles
in some conditions very difficult
'This masterpiece of a fresco Michelangelo painted it in very difficult conditions'

  c. *Je trouve ce chef-d'œuvre de robe absolument ??exquis /*
I find this masterpiece-MSC of dress-FEM absolutely ??exquisite-MSC /
??exquise
??FEM
'I find this masterpiece of a dress absolutely exquisite'

According to Hulk and Tellier, in (14a) and (14b), the participles used as adjectives agree in gender with the N1, not the N2, while in (14c) native speakers' judgments fluctuate between the masculine and the feminine. They suggest that this "striking un-ease with the data suggests that the masculine form on the adjective/participle in (14) is not a reflex of agreement with N1, but rather the default gender choice" (2000: 57). Although they do not specify how the NS judgments were obtained (they may just be referring to anecdotal evidence), the study presented below includes stimuli exempli-fying these affective constructions in a grammaticality judgment task.

1.4.2 *Past participles used as adjectives*

Most past participles used as adjectives behave like other adjectives in that they agree in number and gender with the noun they modify (e.g., *prétendu(e)* 'supposed', *promis(e)* 'promised', *respecté(e)* 'respected'). However, several other of these adjectives derived from past participles have the particularity of agreeing with the noun they modify only when postposed: *Ci-joint* 'attached', *approuvé* 'approved', *attendu* 'expected', *étant donné* 'given', *excepté* 'excepted', *(y-, non-) compris* 'included', *passé* 'passed', *supposé* 'supposed', *vu* 'seen/given', as illustrated in the following examples:

(15) a. *Il est onze heures passées / *passé*
it is eleven hours past-FEM-PL / *MSC-SG
'It is past eleven p.m.'

  b. *Passé / *passées onze heures, il sera trop tard*
past-MSC-SG / *FEM-PL eleven hours, it be-FUT too late
'After eleven p.m. it will be too late'

  c. *Veuillez lire les pièces ci-jointes / *ci-joint*
please read the documents-FEM-PL attached-FEM-PL / *MSC-SG
'Please read the attached documents'

  d. *Ci-joint / *ci-jointes les pièces envoyées par le secrétaire*
attached / *FEM-PL the documents-FEM-SG sent-FEM-PL by the secretary
'Attached are the documents sent by the secretary'

Agreement is usually optional with *fini* 'finished' and *mis à part* 'except for':

(16) a. *Fini*   / *finies*   les   vacances!
        finished-MSC-SG / FEM-PL the vacations
        'The vacations are over'
     b. *Mis*   / *mise à part ma maladie, je vais bien*
        excepted-MSC-SG / FEM-SG   my sickness, I go   well
        'Except for my sickness, I'm doing well'

Ci-inclus is an exception in that it never agrees in gender or number with the noun it modifies, be it preposed or postposed.

1.5 Anaphora

Gender features are also present in various forms of anaphora (subject, direct and indirect objects, and emphatic pronouns), though very few of them are gender-marked. Thus, only *elle(s)* 'she-SG-PL' and *il(s)* 'he-SG-PL' are gender-marked among the personal subject pronouns (the remaining pronouns being: *Je* 'I', *tu* 'you-SG', *nous* 'we', *vous* 'you-SG-PL'). The singular direct object pronouns *le* 'it, him' and *la* 'it, her' are gender-marked, but the plural form *les* 'it, them' is not. None of the indirect object pronouns is gender-marked (*me, te, lui, se, nous, vous, leur*). And among the emphatic pronouns, only the third person singular (*lui* 'him', *elle* 'her') and plural (*eux* 'them', *elles* 'them') are gender-marked. *Lui* 'him, her' is particularly difficult for L2 learners because it is both an indirect object pronoun and an emphatic pronoun, but it is only gender-marked as an emphatic pronoun.

Note that *on* 'one' a third person singular personal subject pronoun that very often replaces *nous* 'we' will agree in number and gender with its past participle when the context clearly establishes the number and gender of its referent as illustrated in (17):

(17) a. *On y est allées*   / *allé   avec les filles*
        one/we went-FEM-PL / *MSC-SG with the girls
        'We went with the girls'
     b. *On s'est embrassés*   / *embrassé   et on est tous   partis*
        one/we kissed-MSC-PL / *kissed-MSC-SG and we   all-MSC-PL left-MSC-PL
        / *parti   en courant
        / *MSC-SG running
        'We kissed and we all left running'

As seen in 1.4 above, the masculine is always selected in the syntactic gender resolution of conjoined nouns as exemplified in (18):

(18) a. *Ma   nièce et   mes   neveux, eux,   ils   sont*
        my-FEM-SG niece and my-PL nephews, them-MSC-PL, they-MSC-PL are
        tous   venus   me voir
        all-MSC-PL came-MSC-PL me see
        'My niece and my nephews, they all came to see me'

b. *J'ai   une   sœur et   quinze frères: ils   sont tous*
   I have a-FEM-SG sister and fifteen brothers: they-MSC-PL are all-MSC-PL
   mariés
   married-MSC-PL
   'I have one sister and fifteen brothers: They are all married'

c. *Mes soeurs   et   mes cousines,   elles   sont toutes*
   my sisters-FEM-PL and my cousins-FEM-PL, they-FEM-PL are all-FEM-PL
   célibataires
   single-FEM-PL
   'My sisters and my cousins are all single'

As example (20c) shows, anaphoric elements are feminine only if all the referents are feminine. In other words, the masculine is used as the default gender, as discussed in the next section.

1.6 Masculine as the default gender

In French, masculine appears to be the default (or unmarked) gender in a binary system that contrasts masculine and feminine for at least the following three categories of nouns: (a) Nominalized verbs (*le boire* 'drinking', *le manger* 'eating'), adjectives (*le vrai* 'truth'), adverbs (*le oui* 'yes', *le non* 'no'), present participles (*un penchant* 'tendency') or phrases (*le qu'en-dira-t-on* 'what will people say'); (b) Most compounds, particularly those with a verbal stem, even if one or both morphemes are feminine as simple words (*porter* 'to carry' + *la monnaie* 'change') = *le porte-monnaie* 'wallet'); (c) Borrowings from other languages (*le baby-sitting, le sake, le tennis*), with the exception of words already marked for the feminine as *la paella* 'paella', and a few others such as *une star* 'a star'.

Moreover, colors are always masculine: *Le bleu* 'blue', *le marron* 'brown', *le vert* 'green', *le rouge* 'red', and so on. And *un truc, machin, bidule,* even *un chose* (which is normally *une chose*), which are all words meaning 'a thing', and which are used to refer to an unknown word, are masculine.

Finally, while anecdotal evidence suggests that L2 French instructed learners rely heavily on the ending *-e* as a marker of feminine gender, corpus analysis shows that it has a surprisingly low predictive value since only 58% of the nouns ending in *-e* are feminine (Desrochers, Paivio, & Desrochers 1989; Desrochers & Paivio 1990). Thus, *pluie* 'rain' is feminine, but *parapluie* 'umbrella' is masculine. Moreover, contrary to expectations, a few nouns ending in *-ée* are masculine, such as *musée* 'museum', *mausolée* 'mausoleum' or *scarabée* 'beetle'.

2. Theoretical background: Grammatical gender and minimalism

In languages with a nominal classification system, the lexical entry of nouns includes a feature indicating its class. That feature is labelled [±fem] for expository purposes.

In languages with grammatical gender, [±fem] is one of the required features in the construction of N roots sometimes referred to as the narrow lexicon (Marantz 1997).[6] The phonological lexicon, also called the vocabulary component, which consists of lists of phonological forms partially specified for grammatical features (Halle & Marantz 1993), provides phonological content to the lexical roots. When a nominal root enters syntactic derivations, it merges with other categories to create an extended nominal projection which includes at least Number and Determiner (e.g., Ritter 1991, 1993). Lexical N may also merge with the functional head *n* to form an NP shell where the Agent is generated in [spec, *n*P], and where Adjectives are outer specifiers of projections within DP (Carstens 2000). Thus, grammatical gender is a lexical property of nouns while number and person features are generally assumed to be a property of the determiner D (e.g., Carstens 2000; Ritter 1991).

There are two competing accounts of gender agreement in the current minimalist literature. On one hand, Halle and Marantz (1993) suggest that gender agreement is a property of the vocabulary component of the grammar. It applies after the derivation has been created by the syntactic computational component. On the other hand, Chomsky's (1995, 2001) account (which is extended and slightly modified in Carstens 2000) assumes that gender agreement is a syntactic property: The feature checking mechanism is thus a syntactic operation.

In Chomsky's (1995, 2001) checking theory, the interpretable, hence non-erasing, phi-features of gender and number enter into multiple checking relations with modifiers and arguments inflected for these features. These features are said to be interpretable in that they include information that is required for semantic interpretation. Gender agreement on adjectives (and past participles) is thus the overt reflection of either Specifier-Head or Head-Head agreement within the maximal projection of the functional category AgrP.

We will adopt this account to be consistent with the most recent accounts in the L2 minimalist literature (Franceschina 2005; Hawkins & Franceschina 2004; White, Valenzuela, Kozlowska-MacGregor, & Leung 2004). Determiners and adjectives are assigned [*u*gender] features on their root entries: The [±fem] feature checks and erases the uninterpretable [*u*gender] features on determiners and adjectives from the derivation to LF to satisfy the principle of Full Interpretation. Then, determiners and adjectives are attributed the appropriate [±fem] feature (e.g., *la petite* with [+fem] nouns and *le petit* with [−fem] nouns).

The Determiner Phrase includes the functional category Number (Num) between Det and NP, and number features (e.g., Ritter 1993). In French and other Romance languages, because of the strong features in Num, nouns overtly raise from N to Num, while they raise covertly in languages like English because of its weak features, creating the well-known prenominal position for adjectives in English in contrast to the

---

6.   It is assumed that nouns, determiners and adjectives have so-called roots used by the syntactic-computational system in building syntactic derivations.

typically postnominal position for adjectives in French. As N raises, it enters into a head/head or specifier/head relationship with the adjective and determiner for its interpretable [±fem] features to check and erase the corresponding uninterpretable [*u*gender] features on the determiner and the adjective.

To sum up, functional categories in the minimalist framework are associated with features such as tense, number, person, gender, and case. These features vary cross-linguistically in that they may or may not be present, and if they are present, they may differ in values. Thus English lacks the gender feature that French instantiates, and while both languages have Infl features, these features are weak in English but strong in French.

Feature strength is particularly important and relevant for English and French in an L1-L2 relation, because it accounts for several word order variations that must be acquired by L2 learners. For instance, number features are strong in French, and nouns must raise overtly from N to Num over adjectives to check and delete the uninterpretable features. The resulting word order in French is typically Noun Adjective, whereas in English it is always Adjective Noun, because nouns do not raise, since the Num features are weak. Moreover, French displays gender agreement on nouns, adjectives and determiners, as do other Romance languages, whereas English lacks such overt gender features and agreement. Finally, French verbal forms are inflected for person, number and tense, whereas English verbal forms typically exhibit zero derivation.

The L2 learnability implications of parameterized gender features made available by Universal Grammar will be examined below in Section 3. We will adopt the position that adult L2 learners can acquire gender features in their L2 whether they are instantiated in their L1 or not, following White et al. (2004), and most notably *contra* Hawkins and Franceschina (2004), and Franceschina (2005).

3. Learnability implications for L2 adults

3.1 General theoretical considerations

The minimalist approach of parameterized gender features has clear learnability implications for L2 adult learners depending on whether one assumes that their L2 grammars are constrained by Universal Grammar or not. The question is whether adult L2 learners can acquire new functional categories which do not exist in the L1 at all, or functional categories existing in the L1 but with different values in the L2. In the case of grammatical gender, English-speaking learners of L2 French must acquire a gender feature that is not instantiated in their L1. In other words, and as suggested by Hawkins (2001:254), there may be a "gender-marking parameter associated with Num in French", since the "presence or absence of a gender feature in nominal phrases appears to be a parameter of variation allowed by UG".

The current literature offers diametrically opposed views on the L2 acquisition of functional categories in general. At one end of the spectrum, there is the view that adult learners cannot acquire functional features at all because their acquisition of L2 grammars is no longer constrained by Universal Grammar (e.g., Meisel 1999, 2000). Then, an intermediary position contends that the L2 acquisition of functional categories and features is either limited to the features already available in the L1 (e.g., Hawkins & Chan's (1997) Failed Feature Hypothesis), or is impaired because the features remain "valueless" or "inert" (e.g., Beck 1998). Another limitation would be that functional categories are part of a sub-module of Universal Grammar subjected to a critical period, preventing their representation in the L2 when they are not already present in the L1 (e.g., Franceschina 2005; Tsimpli & Roussou 1991; Smith & Tsimpli 1995).[7] This is similar to the No Access/Partial Access hypotheses proposed earlier for L2 acquisition in general (e.g., Clahsen & Muysken 1986).

At the other end of the spectrum is the position that allows for the L2 acquisition of functional categories and their features such as the Full Access Hypothesis (e.g., Epstein, Flynn, & Martohardjono 1996; Schwartz & Sprouse 1994, 1996), or the Full Functional Hypothesis (Gess & Herschensohn 2001). There is still some disagreement as to the initial representation of the functional categories, that is, whether they are present from the very beginning, or whether they develop in stagelike fashion. Generally, child L2 acquisition research suggests that functional categories are present and operative from the very beginning (see e.g., Grondin & White 1993; Haznedar 2003; Lakshmanan & Selinker 1994), but others argue that functional categories are initially absent in interlanguage grammars, and gradually develop in discrete stages on the basis of input. For instance, the Minimal Trees Hypothesis (Vainikka & Young-Scholten 1994, 1996a, 1996b, 1998) states that only lexical categories are available to adult L2 learners from the beginning, and that they project the relevant functional categories progressively, starting with a bare-VP stage. In a similar vein, Eubank's Weak Transfer/Valueless Features (1993/1994, 1996) Hypothesis contends that there is partial transfer from the L1, and that the L2 initial state is incomplete.

An alternative approach, the Missing Surface Inflection hypothesis, (e.g., Haznedar & Schwartz 1997; Haznedar 2001; Lardiere 1998a, 1998b, 2000; Prévost & White 2000b), assumes that abstract functional categories and features are present in L2 grammars, but that the difficulty lies in mapping the abstract features to their morphophonological forms on surface morphology. A study by Duffield, White, Bruhn de Garavito, Montrul and Prévost (2003) also challenges impairment hypotheses with em-

---

7.   It is important to point out that the claims that Smith and Tsimpli (1995) make, are based on the data collected with Christopher, a person who was clearly impaired cognitively, at least partially, but who nevertheless seemed to be able to acquire several languages. Based on their analyses, Smith and Tsimpli concluded that parameter resetting was not possible when the L1 and L2 settings differed, but that Christopher's L2 grammar appeared to be constrained by Universal Grammar principles anyway. It seems that generalizing Christopher's case to non-cognitively impaired language learners would be unwarranted.

pirical evidence from Spanish-speaking and English-speaking L2 learners of French. The Spanish native speakers' grammar has clitic projections, while the English native speakers' grammar does not. The results of a sentence matching task indicated that L2 learners can indeed acquire clitic projections which are not present in their L1, as well as reset feature values from weak to strong.

Following previous work (Ayoun 2003, 2005a, 2005c) and others (e.g., Duffield et al. 2003; Franceschina 2005), I will argue that L2 grammars are constrained by Universal Grammar, and that consequently, functional categories and features, including gender features, are in principle acquirable. However, this does not imply that L2 acquisition will be effortless, quite the contrary. L2 learners will encounter difficulties in the mapping of abstract features to the appropriate L2 surface morphology, as for the Aspect Phrase (Ayoun 2005c).

3.2 Learnability considerations for L2 French learners

Most of the L2 studies reviewed above assumed that the input offers not only sufficient but unambiguous positive evidence of gender assignment and agreement, arguing that the determiner is the most obvious and clear clue to L2 learners, particularly for instructed L2 French or Spanish learners. I would like to argue quite the opposite by carefully considering the various clues that L2 French learners may get from the input.

Semantic clues – Can L2 French learners rely on the semantic assignment rules (Corbett 1991:57) establishing that sex-differentiable nouns denoting males are masculine, and sex-differentiable nouns denoting females are feminine? Section 1 above clearly established that they cannot: Semantically motivated gender categories account for only 10.5% of all French nouns (Séguin 1969). Learners are left to figure out the correct grammatical gender of almost 90% of the rest of the lexicon.

Morpho-phonological clues – The numerous gender assignment rules based on morpho-phonological clues proposed by Tucker et al. (1977) among others, rest upon the crucial assumption that the L2 learners have an accurate phonetic representation of these elements, which may be problematic particularly with lower level proficiency learners. This assumption is also problematic for the determiners, in particular the indefinite articles *un, une*, which display a phonetic contrast particularly difficult to distinguish and produce for English-speaking learners of French: Neither the nasal vowel in *un*, nor the high front rounded vowel in *une* are part of the English phonemic inventory (see Hannahs this volume).

Determiners – Do French determiners provide reliable clues to the gender of lexical items? It is important to consider vowel-initial and consonant-initial words separately because in a type count of the BRULEX database (Content, Mousty, & Radeau 1990), it was found that about 21% of the nouns begin with a vowel. If the frequency of occurrence of each noun is taken into account (by doing a token count), the percentage goes up to 27%; again, based on a token count, 51% of vowel-initial nouns are feminine while 49% are masculine. Table 3 lists all the determiners that may occur in front

Table 3. Determiners used with consonant-initial words

Consonant initial words	Feminine words	Masculine words	Plural	Negation
Definite article	la [la]	le [lə]	les [le]	No change
Indefinite article	une [yn]	un [œ̃]	des [de]	de [də]
Partitive article	de la [də la]	du [dy]		de [də]
Demonstrative adjective	cette [sɛt]	ce [sə]	ces [se]	No change
Possessive adjectives	ma [ma], ta [ta], sa [sa], notre [nɔtr], votre [vɔtr], leur [lœr]	mon [mõ], ton [tõ], son [sõ], notre [nɔtr], votre [vɔtr], leur [lœr]	mes [me], tes [te], nos [no], vos [vo], leurs [lœr]	No change
Interrogative adjective	quelle [kɛl]	quel [kɛl]	quels [kɛl], quelles [kɛl]	No change

of French consonant-initial nouns: Definite, indefinite and partitive articles; as well as demonstrative, possessive, and interrogative adjectives.

The darkened cells, morphemes or phonetic forms, represent non gender-marked forms. The first observation is that none of the plural forms is gender-marked with the exception of the interrogative adjective *quel(s)/quelle(s)* in its written form, but not its phonetic form that is unique for the feminine, masculine, and plural. Secondly, both the written and phonetic forms of all articles are gender-marked in the singular. But the gender distinction is neutralized with the form *de* [də] that replaces the indefinite and definite articles in negative sentences (unless the predicate is *être* 'be'). Third, the first three persons of the possessive adjectives are gender-marked in their written and phonetic forms, but the singular/plural forms of the other three persons are not. Finally, the interrogative adjective has different gender-marked forms in the singular and the plural, but they are always phonetically identical.

Next, Table 4 lists the same determiners as in Table 3 but for vowel-initial words. Again, none of the plural forms of the determiners is gender-marked. The interrogative adjective *quel(s)/quelle(s)* constitutes the sole exception in its written form, but not its phonetic form, which is unique for feminine, masculine, and plural. Second, the elided singular forms of the definite article *l'* and the partitive article *de l'* are no longer gender-marked in their written or phonetic forms. Moreover, the only phonetically realized gender distinction is neutralized with the form *de* [də] that replaces the indefinite articles *une/un* in negative sentences (unless the predicate is *être* 'be').

In addition, *de*, a non-gender-marked form, typically replaces *des* in front of a preposed adjective (*des roses jaunes* 'some yellow roses' vs *de jolies roses* 'some pretty roses'); and after an expression of quantity (*beaucoup, peu, assez, trop de fleurs* 'many, few, enough, too many flowers'); a determiner may or not may be used (*beaucoup trop de (ces) fleurs* 'too many (of these) flowers').

To sum up, only 3 out of 11 singular determiners are gender-marked morphologically for vowel-initial words; phonologically there is a single form, *une*, that is neutral-

Table 4. Determiners used with vowel-initial words

Vowel initial words	Feminine words	Masculine words	Plural forms	Negation
Definite article	l' [l]	l' [l]	les [le]	no change
Indefinite article	une [yn]	un [œ̃]	des [de]	d' [d]
Partitive article	de l' [dəl]	de l' [dəl]		d' [d]
Demonstrative adjective	cette [sɛt]	cet [sɛt]	ces [se]	no change
Possessive adjectives	mon [mõ], ton [tõ], son [sõ], notre [ntr], votre [vtr], leur [lœr]	mon [mõ], ton [tõ], son [sõ], notre [ntr], votre [vtr], leur [lœr]	mes [me], tes [te], nos [no], vos [vo], leurs [lœr]	no change
Interrogative adjective	quelle [kɛl]	quel [kɛl]	quelles [kɛl], quels [kɛl]	no change

ized to *de* in negative contexts. Only 2 out of 10 plural determiners are gender-marked morphologically, but not phonetically (*quels/quelles* [kɛl]). As for consonant-initial words, 8 out of 11 singular determiners are gender-marked morphologically, as well as phonologically. But as for vowel-initial words, only 2 out of 10 plural determiners are gender-marked morphologically, but not phonetically (*quels/quelles* [kɛl]).

These facts combined with the various idiosyncrasies outlined above in Sections 1.3 through 1.8 clearly show that L2 French learners are confronted with a complex and ambiguous input when it comes to grammatical gender and assignment, not with the clear and unambiguous positive evidence as others contend (see the literature review below), and that they must learn: (a) That French has inherent as well as grammatical gender; (b) The proper gender assignment of each lexical item; (c) Proper D-N agreement: Using that noun with the proper determiner, that is, selecting a [+fem] determiner for a [+fem] noun; (d) Proper A-N agreement: Selecting the [+fem] form of an adjective modifying a [+fem] noun; (e) The proper word order placement of N Adj reflecting a strong Num feature.

4. Literature review

This section will only review empirical studies conducted within the minimalist framework. Studies conducted within other frameworks have already been extensively reviewed and are summarized in Appendix A.

Shelton (1996) focused on past participle agreement adopting an account involving interaction of the functional category AgrO with either A-chains (for passives, unaccusatives and pronominal verbs), A'-chains (for wh-movement and relative clauses), and head-chains (for clitic constructions). A grammaticality judgment task and four production tasks were administered to three groups of English-speaking French learners in England. A small group (n = 6) of French native speakers served as controls. The results are quite surprising in that in general the scores decreased from the first year group (n = 16, averaging 8 years of L2 exposure), to the second year group (n = 16, averaging 9 years of L2 exposure), and the third year group (n = 29, averaging 10 years of L2 exposure). However, the results must be considered with caution because the stimuli used in the various tasks are problematic. The 74 stimuli of the grammaticality judgment task are not controlled for length and test many different types of agreement, while the distractors also include a wide variety of structures, but the results do not break down the different types of agreement. The second task, a correction test, is a very long text that includes a large number of different types of errors. In contrast, the opposites test includes only 10 stimuli and it is unclear what the researcher was trying to elicit. The passives test had also only 10 stimuli, which were not always controlled for length. Passive structures in French are notoriously difficult for L2 learners, so although its design was quite simple, the task was very difficult in terms of processing and structural complexity. The pronouns test was also difficult in that participants had to both use the proper direct object pronoun, and then provide the agreement with the past participle. Anecdotal evidence suggests that even French native speakers do not consistently make proper past participle agreements.

Hawkins (1998a; as cited in Hawkins 2001; and Hawkins & Franceschina 2004)[8] obtained production data elicited from English native speakers (n = 10 from the UK, n = 10 from Canada) who were advanced learners of French and who had spent at least six months in immersion programs. Oral data (about 3 minute transcripts) were obtained by asking the participants to describe an animated film. Appropriate gender assignment was operationalized as target-like use of definite and indefinite articles. Data reported show a greater percentage of errors on definite articles than on indefinite articles: 7% for the UK group, and 11% for the Canada group on definite articles; 14% for the UK group, and 27% for the Canada group on indefinite groups. It is interesting to note that the Canada group, who spent the most time in French immersion programs, was outperformed by the UK group who did not benefit from such an intensive exposure. Individual data show overgeneralized article use, but it could be either the masculine or the feminine form of the (in)definite articles. Hawkins and Franceschina (2004) contend that the consistent pairing of the articles for the native speakers is due to a [ugender] feature on D. In the absence of such a feature, each lexical entry would be associated with a given article without taking into account the phonological forms of nouns. They conclude that the L2 learners' interlanguage grammar resembles the early child L1 grammar in that they lack an uninterpretable [ugender] feature on D.

Gess and Herschensohn (2001) set out to investigate the variation between French and English with regard to the Determiner Phrase (DP) parameter by contrasting two approaches to L2 acquisition: The Full Functional Hypothesis (FFH) and the Structure Building Hypothesis (SBH). The FFH contends that initial L2 grammars have access to all functional projections independently of morphological inflection, in a similar vein

---

8.   Hawkins and Franceschina (2004) do not present new empirical data but review data from other studies in language processing, code-switching and language impairment.

to the Full Transfer/Full Access Hypothesis (Schwartz & Sprouse 1994, 1996). It also implies that syntax is acquired before idiosyncratic lexical elements following the Constructionism approach (Herschensohn 2000). In contrast, the SBH claims that initial L2 grammars lack functional categories altogether or instantiate only underspecified functional categories (see the Minimal Tree Hypothesis, Vainikka, & Young-Scholten 1996, 1998); the activation of the functional categories is tied to morphology (Eubank & Grace 1998); and the activation of functional categories takes place in stages (see the modulated structure building presented in Hawkins 1998a, 2001). Anglophone foreign language learners at 5 different levels of proficiency (from true beginners to immersion students) were administered a sentence completion task intended to elicit determiners, properly placed adjectives, as well as gender and number agreement markers on all these elements. As stated by the researchers, this was a simple, familiar task for instructed learners who, moreoever, were provided with rather explicit instructions since they were told that they would "need to add any necessary changes such as agreement, articles, etc." (p. 116). Results indicate that these instructed learners quickly learn to use obligatory determiners and nouns-adjectives (above 90% accuracy by the second year), while agreement accuracy goes from 76% for half of the first year group to 98% for the highest proficiency level. It is argued that these results provide support for the FFH over the SBH, and they may; but the authors do not provide sufficient information about the data, nor are the results detailed enough. For instance, the Agreement category is not broken down by gender or number. Moreover, they do not consider accuracy in gender assignment, just proper agreement.

Bruhn de Garavito and White (2002) tested the L2 acquisition of Spanish DPs by 42 high-school French-speaking students, divided in a low proficiency group and a low intermediate proficiency group based on the grades they were in (not on an independent measure of proficiency). The participants were tested individually in an oral production task (communicative game consisting in describing pictures) in order to elicit determiners, nouns and adjectives. The results showed that: (a) The participants overwhelmingly used the appropriate N Adj order, indicating that their IL possesses a strong Num feature; (b) A relatively high accuracy in gender agreement on determiners (and a higher accuracy on definite than on indefinite determiners); (c) A greater accuracy on nouns with arbitrary gender (90% to 84.4%) than on nouns with inherent gender (75.3% to 85%); (d) Both groups were less accurate in gender agreement on adjectives than on determiners.

White et al. (2004) administered four oral tasks (production tasks, vocabulary test, picture identification task) to elicit DPs and adjectives from adult French native speakers (n = 48), and English native speakers (n = 68) (Spanish native speakers acted as controls) to test the L2 acquisition of Spanish gender and number agreement. Spanish and French share the same gender and number features. The results showed that learners at all levels of proficiency were highly accurate on both gender and number, but less so with adjectives. The low proficiency group was also much less accurate on the picture identification task than on the other task, and had a high failure percentage on the vocabulary test. But there was no L1 effect, and White et al. argue that their results provide strong support for the Full Transfer/Full Access Hypothesis (Schwartz & Sprouse 1994, 1996), contra the Failed Functional Features Hypothesis (Hawkins & Chan 1997), and in favor of successful parameter resetting of gender features.

Finally, Franceschina (2005) focused on the acquisition of the functional feature [ugender] in L2 Spanish by adult learners from a variety of L1 backgrounds classified into two groups, based on whether they instantiated the [+gen] feature (Arabic, French, German, Greek, Italian and Portuguese), or the [–gen] feature (English). Native speakers of Spanish were used as a control group. The participants were administered a battery of written and oral elicitation tasks (production, comprehension or metalinguistic judgments). Franceschina tested the null hypothesis that "[t]here is no significant difference between Spanish NSs, advanced L2 Spanish speakers of +gen L1s and advanced L2 Spanish speakers of –gen L1s in the production/interpretation of Spanish grammatical gender" (p. 123). She set out to test the strong version of the Failed Functional Features Hypothesis that she claims is supported by the findings suggesting that adult L2 learners can reach a native-like knowledge of grammatical gender, but only if their L1 already instantiates gender features. Extralinguistic factors seem to account for some of the variability found in the participants' performance but apparently cannot eliminate the L1 effects.[9] Franceschina concludes that adult L2 learners and child L1 speakers do not use the same Universal Grammar functional features, but that the development of both the child L1 and adult L2 grammars is nonetheless constrained by Universal Grammar.

To summarize, the results of the few empirical studies conducted within the minimalist framework can be divided between those that found L1 effects (Franceschina 2005; Hawkins 1998a), and argue that adult L2 learners cannot fully acquire gender features if they are not already present in their L1; and those that contend that L2 adult learners can achieve ultimate attainment in their acquisition of grammatical gender regardless of whether it is instantiated in their L1 or not. However, two studies (Bruhn de Garavito & White 2002; Franceschina 2005) tested the acquisition of L2 Spanish, another Romance language, but with perceptually more salient gender features than French (e.g., greater number of gender-marked determiners such as *el, la, los, las, uno(s), una(s)*, and distinct masculine endings in *-o* and feminine endings in *-a*, albeit also with exceptions). Moreover, these empirical studies entail a few caveats. First, oral elicitation tasks are not always successful in eliciting sufficient tokens (e.g., White et al. 2004), and learners can simply produce the lexical items they know well, avoiding others. Second, oral data may not always be an accurate reflection of the participants' knowledge of gender features in French because they may not consistently

---

9. See also Sabourin (2001) who found L1 effects for the acquisition of grammatical gender: The results of three experiments revealed a hierarchy of performance among L2 Dutch learner groups with different L1 backgrounds. The two groups with gender in their L1 (the German group and Romance group) outperformed the English-speaking group. The fact that the German group performed better than the Romance group led Sabourin to further argue that similarity in grammatical gender was important as well. Sabourin, Stowe and Haan (2006) obtained very similar findings.

mark the phonetic distinctions between the masculine and the feminine as in [pə ti] *petit* 'small' and [pə tit] *petite* 'small', and because there are many non-gender marked contexts such as [bō na ni vɛr sɛr] *bon anniversaire* 'happy birthday' or [də ʒo li flœr] *de jolies fleurs* 'some pretty flowers'. This brings us to the last point: None of these studies considered learnability implications specific to English-speaking L2 French learners in detail. As mentioned above, the acquisition of L2 French is no easy task for English native speakers because a lack of congruence between an L1 lacking gender features and the L2, a lack of perceptual salience that makes for a complex and ambiguous input as outlined above, and a low communicative load. The lack of perceptual salience is compounded by the estimate that only according to Desrochers et al. (1989), only 20–25% of words are inflected for gender (based on a corpus of 300 sentences from first page of *Le Devoir* and *Le Monde*).

Again, English-speaking learners of L2 French are faced with acquiring: (a) The fact that French has grammatical as well as inherent gender; (b) The proper gender assignment of each lexical item; (c) Proper D-N agreement: Using that noun with the proper determiner, that is, selecting a [+fem] determiner for a [+fem] noun; (d) Proper A-N agreement: Selecting the [+fem] form of an adjective modifying a [+fem] noun; (e) The proper word order placement of N Adj reflecting a strong Num feature.[10]

Adopting the position that adult L2 learners are guided by Universal Grammar, and rejecting the hypothesis that functional categories or features can be partially impaired, lead us to assume that adult L2 learners can acquire gender features in their L2 whether they are instantiated in their L1 or not. However, it is also assumed that the lack of perceptual salience of the input combined with multiple idiosyncrasies requires extensive exposure to achieve near-native competence. L2 learners' performance will be tested on their ability to: (a) Correctly assign gender to nouns operationalized by correctly gender-marked determiners; (b) Realize proper gender agreement on adjectives (c) Detect conflictual gender assignment.

Based on the results of previous studies, the following predictions can be made: (a) Participants will perform more accurately on determiner/noun agreement than on noun/adjective agreement; (b) Participants will become more accurate with their increasing level of proficiency; (c) The higher the level of proficiency, the more likely will the participants be able to detect conflictual gender assignment in the GJT.

---

10.   There are a handful of adjectives which are preposed and may be postposed as well but with a semantic change such as *ancien* in *j'ai rencontré mon ancien professeur*' I met my former professor', and *j'ai acheté un meuble ancien* 'I bought an antique piece of furniture'. In these cases, the adjective is generated in Num, or in another functional projection between D and Num. See Knittel (2005) for a detailed account of adjectives in French.

5.   Methodology

5.1   Participants and elicitation tasks

Two groups of participants were used for this study: Native speakers of English who were acquiring French as an L2 in an instructed setting in a North-American University, and native speakers of French who were living in France at the time of the data collection. The L2 learners first filled out a background questionnaire to gather information related to personal information (see Appendix B). The majority of the participants were women (80% combining all groups), the average age was in the 20s for all four groups. The main difference between the L2 groups is the length of time they spent abroad in a Francophone country. Although 64% of the participants in the Low group had spent time abroad, they only averaged 3.45 weeks, whereas participants in the Intermediate group (82% of them) averaged a stay of 15.27 weeks, and all the participants in the Advanced group had spent time in a Francophone country averaging 4 years.

They were then asked to complete two pre-test tasks, a grammaticality judgment task and a preference/grammaticality task (see e.g., Ayoun 2005a, c) used as an independent measure of proficiency. Based on their pre-test performance, the thirty-five participants were placed in one of three groups: Low (n = 11), Intermediate (n = 11), or Advanced (n = 13). The means and standard deviations obtained on the pre-test scores are presented in Table 5. A one-way ANOVA indicated that there was a significant difference between the three groups as displayed in Table 6.

Then, both the French native speakers and L2 French groups completed a grammaticality judgment and correction task (GJT). In addition, the L2 learners were instructed to complete a production task which consisted in three short compositions

Table 5.   Pre-test scores' means and SDs

Group	n	Mean	SD
Low	11	51.23	8.34
Intermediate	11	69.77	2.71
Advanced	13	85.72	7.19

Table 6.   ANOVA on pre-test scores

	SS	df	MS	F	Sig.
Between groups	7086.712	2	3546.356	81.474	.000
Within groups	1391.694	32	43.450		
Total	8478.406				

with given elements.[11] The tasks were written and computerized (see Ayoun 2000 for the advantages of web-based data collection).

The GJT included 25 stimuli exemplifying agreement mismatches or conflicts between two nouns and/or a noun and an adjective as in (19):

(19) Votre   enfant   est belle   comme un   ange
      your-NG child-NG is   beautiful-FEM like   an-MSC angel-MSC
      'Your child is as beautiful as an angel'

The stimulus in (19) presents a number of difficulties: (a) *Enfant* 'child' can be used with both the masculine and the feminine genders (*un enfant, une enfant*); (b) *Votre* 'your' is not marked for either gender; (c) *Ange* is an epicene noun (see 1.2.1 above) that is always used with a masculine determiner regardless of the natural gender of the referent.

Another example of stimuli displaying conflictual genders exemplified the N *de* N affective constructions discussed above. The NSs are expected to accept these stimuli because they are grammatical, but if they are aware of obligatory gender agreement in French, L2 learners should reject them if they notice the gender-marked determiners but are unfamiliar with the lexical items.

The semi-controlled production task consisted in three short compositions about the participants' real or fictive parents in order to test for the production of determiners with animate and inanimate nouns, adjective placement and agreement, determiner/noun agreement (see Appendix C). The participants were first instructed to describe their parents' physical appearance in the first composition, then their personalities in the second composition, and finally what their parents would be wearing on a special occasion such as an anniversary, in the third composition. They were provided with adjectives and nouns (without determiners to avoid giving clues to grammatical gender), all of which were familiar to them from beginning level French classes.

The next section will examine the results of the two elicitation tasks based on the three predictions made above and repeated here for convenience: (a) Participants will perform more accurately on determiner/noun agreement than on noun/adjective agreement; (b) Participants will become more accurate with their increasing level of proficiency; (c) The higher the level of proficiency, the more likely will the participants be able to detect conflictual gender assignment in the GJT.

5.2 Results of the grammaticality judgment/correction task

The raw data were computed to yield percentages of accepted sentences, rejected sentences and sentences classified as 'I don't know' by the L2 learners and '3' by the NSs (taken to indicate that they were 'undecided') on the scale they used to judge the

---

11. Both the French NS group and L2 French groups also performed a gender assignment task with common and less common nouns, as well as a preference/ grammaticality judgment task, but the results will not be reported here.

Table 7. Results of the GJT

GJT	Accepted	Rejected	Undecided
Low (n = 11)	57.81%	20.36%	21.81%
Intermediate (n = 11)	53.81%	28.36%	17.81%
Advanced (n = 13)	59.38%	22.15%	18.46%
NS (n = 20)	67.8%	25.8%	6.4%

Table 8. Oneway ANOVA with GJT results

	SS	df	MS	F	Sig.
Reject					
Between groups	412.01	3	137.339	.556	.646
Within groups	12595.98	51	246.980		
Accept					
Between groups	1637.43	3	545.811	1.986	.128
Within groups	14017.55	51	274.854		
Undecided					
Between groups	2393.22	3	797.741	7.117	< .0001
Within groups	5716.30	51	112.084		

stimuli (from '1', completely incorrect, to '5' completely correct). The percentages for 'accepted', 'rejected' and 'don't know'/'undecided' are presented in Table 7.

The results indicate that the higher the level of proficiency, the greater the number of stimuli were accepted as grammatical. All groups, included the NS group, rejected a similar percentage of sentences (from 20.36% to 28.36%), but the L2 learner groups have a much greater percentage of 'undecided' stimuli than the NS groups.

A oneway ANOVA did not reveal a significant difference between groups (F (3, 51) = 1.986, p = .128). Moreover, a oneway ANOVA on the percentages for 'accept', 'reject' and 'undecided' revealed a significant difference between groups only for the undecided percentages as shown in Table 8 (F (3, 51) = 7.117, $p <$. 0001).

Tukey post hoc analyses revealed that the significant differences were between the NS group and the three L2 learner groups: Low group (mean difference = 15.91, SD = 3.9746.15, p = .001); Intermediate group (mean difference = 11.91, SD = 3.97, p = .021); and Advanced group (mean difference = 12.56, SD = 3.77, p = .009).

There was also a significant correlation between age and the 'undecided' percentage for the NSs. The younger NSs (17 to 18 year old) selected 'undecided' significantly more often than the older NSs (Pearson correlation = .509, significance (two-tailed) = .022).

The data were also computed to show results for each stimulus by group (see Appendix D for complete data) to see if the participants accepted or rejected the same stimuli in a similar fashion. The results of a chi-square analysis showed a significant difference for 9 out of the 25 stimuli as displayed in Table 9.

These stimuli are given in (20) with their respective number as displayed in Table 10.

Table 9. Chi-square analysis on GJT

Stimulus	Pearson chi-square	df	P
# 1	14.552	6	.024
# 3	12.381	6	.054
# 5	13.836	6	.032
# 8	14.128	6	.028
# 9	13.345	6	.038
# 12	14.896	6	.021
# 19	13.284	6	.039
# 20	26.922	6	< .0001
# 21	22.713	6	.001

Table 10. Significant differences on GJT stimuli

Stimulus	Low (n = 11)			Inter. (n = 11)			Advanced (n = 13)			NSs (n = 20)		
	A	R	DK	A	R	DK	A	R	DK	A	R	DK
# 1	27.27	54.54	18.18	36.36	36.36	27.27	46.15	15.38	38.46	80.0	10.0	10.0
# 3	27.27	18.18	54.54	45.45	27.27	27.27	23.07	61.53	15.38	45.0	50.0	5.0
# 5	63.63	9.09	27.27	9.09	45.45	45.45	30.76	15.38	53.84	35.0	50.0	0.0
# 8	45.45	36.36	18.18	54.54	45.45	0.0	84.61	7.69	7.69	90.0	10.0	0.0
# 9	54.54	9.09	36.36	36.36	9.09	54.54	69.23	7.69	23.07	90.0	10.0	0.0
# 12	45.45	18.18	36.36	63.63	36.36	0.0	84.61	7.69	7.69	90.0	5.0	5.0
# 19	36.36	9.09	54.54	72.72	9.09	18.18	84.61	7.69	7.69	90.0	0.0	10.0
# 20	63.63	18.18	18.18	72.72	9.09	18.18	46.15	7.69	46.15	15.0	70.0	15.0
# 21	54.54	0.0	45.45	45.45	27.27	27.27	15.38	0.0	84.61	60.0	30.0	10.0

(20)   GJT stimuli with significant differences

      Stimulus #1   *Cette   femme   est un   vrai   laideron*
              this-FEM woman-FEM is   a-MSC real-MSC   ugly duckling-MSC
              'This woman is a real ugly duckling'

80% of the NSs accept this stimulus in which *femme*, an inherently feminine noun, conflicts with *laideron*, a masculine noun.[12] The majority of the learners in the Low group rejected it (54.54%), a equal number of Intermediate learners (36.35%) rejected it or did not know, while the Advanced learners accepted it (46.15%), or did not know (38.46%). The participants in the Low group offered these corrections or explanations for rejecting these stimuli: *une vrai laideronne, une vrai laideron, une vraie laideron.*

      Stimulus #3   *Mais que tu   es   con,   ma   fille!*
              but   that you are stupid-MSC my-FEM girl-FEM
              'But how stupid can you be, girl'

The Low group appeared to be at a loss with stimulus #3 which exemplifies a common lack of agreement in spoken familiar French between *con* and *fille*. Exactly 50% of the

---

12. *Laideronne*-FEM exists but it is generally not used.

NSs rejected it; 45.45% of the Intermediate learners accepted it, against only 23.07% who indicated in their corrections that *con* [−FEM] should be *conne* [+FEM]. Only one participant in the Low group suggested *conne* as a correction.

> Stimulus #5 *Ton   phénomène   de fille est vraiment*
> your-MSC phenomemon-MSC of girl is   quite
> *discret*
> discret-FEM / *MSC
> 'That character of a daughter of yours is quite discret'

One participant in the Low and Intermediate group suggested *discrète* as a correction. Only two Advanced learners did, while one proposed *ta phénomène*. One native speaker suggested *discrète*, while another switched the word order to *ta fille est vraiment un phénomène discret*; most noticeably, 50% of the NS rejected this stimulus (15% were undecided), supporting Hulk and Tellier (1998, 2000).

> Stimulus #8 *Cette   femme   ressemble à   un   vrai   boudin*
> this-FEM woman-FEM looks   like a-MSC real-MSC sausage-MSC
> *dans cette   robe*
> in   this-FEM dress-FEM
> 'This woman looks really fat in that dress'

Almost all the NSs (90%) and most of the Advanced learners (84.61%) accepted this stimulus, while a much smaller percentage of participants in the lower proficiency groups accepted it (45.45% and 54.54%). Two participants in the Low group suggested *une boudin*, while *une vraie boudine, une vraie boudin* were proposed by two different participants in the Intermediate group. One advanced learner asked whether *boudin* could be feminine.

> Stimulus #9 *Mon   frère   se   montre têtu   comme une*
> my-MSC brother-MSC himself shows   stubborn-MSC as   a
> *bourrique*
> donkey
> 'My brother is being as stubborn as a donkey'

Again almost all the NSs (90%) accepted this stimulus, while the L2 learners did not (36.36% to 69.23%). One participant in the Intermediate group suggested *un bourrique* as a correction, showing that s/he noticed the gender mismatch between the two nouns.

> Stimulus #12 *Son   Excellence voudrait-elle se   reposer?*
> his-MSC Excellency would   she-FEM rest
> 'Would his Excellency like to rest?'

The NSs and the Advanced learners performed the same way on stimulus #12 as on stimulus #8, accepting it overwhelmingly, whereas it was rejected by lower proficiency levels. Corrections included *il, sa excellence, son majesté Louis XIV n'était pas satisfait*, and even *sa majesté Louis XIV n'était pas satisfait*, clearly an attempt to have the adjective agree with the noun.

Stimulus #19 *Celles   qui   deviennent psychologues ont du mérite*
             those-FEM who become   psychologists have   merit
             'Those who become psychologists are deserving'

The NSs (90%) and Advanced learners (84.61%) consistently accept this stimulus, a greater percentage of Intermediate learners do as well (72.72%), while a puzzling low percentage (36.36%) of Low proficiency learners do, most of them (54.54%) indicating they did not know what to do with stimulus #19. They may have been thrown off by the sentence structure or maybe did not know the word *mérite*.

Stimulus #20 *Les nouvelles sentinelles? Toutes   des glandeurs!*
             the new-FEM sentries?   All-FEM lazy bums-MSC-PL
             'The new sentries are all lazy bums'

Most of the participants in the Low and Intermediate groups accepted Stimulus #20 (63.63% and 72.72%, respectively), contrary to the Advanced learners (46.15%, who were equally undecided), and the NS group (15%) who overwhelmingly rejected it (70%), presumably objecting to *toutes* (FEM) modifying *glandeurs* (MSC), and proposing either *toutes des glandeuses* (n = 3), or *tous des glandeurs* (n = 4), as corrections. The first correction was also proposed by one learner in the Low group and in the Advanced group. One participant in the Intermediate group also proposed *tous des glandeurs*, either knowing or guessing that *glandeurs* was masculine (*-eur* is typically a masculine ending with exceptions such as *la peur* 'fear' or *l'ardeur* 'ardor'), or that *sentinelles* referred to male soldiers.

Stimulus #21 *Les recrues   de l'empereur se tenaient tous   penauds*
             the recruits-FEM of the emperor stood   all-MSC sheepish
             'The recruits of the emperor were all standing there looking sheepish'

The NS and L2 learners groups performed very differently on stimulus 21 in which *recrues* is feminine, but *tous* and *penauds* are masculine. Learners may not have known *penauds* (or even *recrues*, although it is a cognate of 'recruit') as indicated by the extremely high percentage of 'don't know' for the Advanced learners (84.61%). Only 60% of the NSs accepted #21 (30% rejected it), and the lower proficiency levels tended to accept it (54.54% and 45.45% for the Low and Intermediate groups, respectively). A single correction from a participant in the Intermediate group suggested *toutes penaudes*.

5.3 Results of the production task

The descriptive statistics presented in Table 11 combine the participants' production for the three texts to show how many tokens, nouns, adjectives and determiners they used. The noun/adjective ratios indicate that all three groups produced a relatively high number of adjectives (83.79% of all tokens for the Low group, 91.18% for the Intermediate group, and 72.56% for the Advanced group).

Table 11. Production task results

		Low (n = 11)	Intermediate (n = 11)	Advanced (n = 13)
Tokens	Total	3429	3360	5634
	Average	311.72	305.45	408.90
	Range	184–868	159–370	233–728
Nouns	Total	537	488	882
	Average	48.81	44.36	64.63
	Range	23–120	26–66	35–103
Adjectives	Total	450	445	640
	Average	40.90	40.45	49.23
	Range	27–74	29–52	28–74
	Noun/Adj Ratio	.83	.91	.72
Adjectives Gender errors	Total	41	52	23
	Ratio	.091	.116	.037
Adjectives Number errors	Total	33	21	7
	Ratio	.073	.047	.013
Determiners	Total	490	455	776
	Average	44.54	41.36	56.90
	Range	21–110	25–64	33–90
Determiners Gender errors	Total	25	18	12
	Ratio	.051	.039	.015
Determiners Number errors	Total	6	2	2
	Ratio	.012	.004	.004

There are slightly fewer determiners than nouns because determiners can be omitted in a variety of structures as illustrated in (21):

(21) a. *Ma mère   est sociologue*
          my mother is   sociologist
          'My mother is a sociologist'
      b. *Il sortira   sans   chapeau, sans   gants et   sans   parapluie*
          he go out-FUT without hat,   without gloves and without umbrella
          'He will go out with a hat, without gloves and without an umbrella'

There are very few gender errors on the determiners, indicating that the participants knew the appropriate gender of most of the nouns they used: Only 5.1%, 3.9%, and 1.5% of the total number of determiners produced by the Low, Intermediate and Advanced groups respectively, were erroneously gender-marked. Table 11 also displays the number errors produced on the determiners, which are negligible for all three groups.

Participants made more gender and number errors on the adjectives than on the determiners, but these numbers are low as well. Thus the Low group failed to make the proper agreement on 9.1% of the adjectives produced, the Intermediate group made gender agreement errors on 11.6% of the adjectives they used, while the learners in the Advanced group failed to make the proper gender agreement on only 3.7% of the total number of adjective tokens they produced. The percentage of number agreement errors on adjectives is even lower than the percentage of gender agreement errors: 7.3%, 4.7%, and 1.3% for the Low, Intermediate, and Advanced groups, respectively.

These errors appear to be performance errors as illustrated in the following examples in (22) for gender agreement errors, and in (23) for number agreement errors:

(22) a. *Une   robe   *long   et   élégante*
          a-FEM dress long-MSC and elegant-FEM
          'A long and elegant dress'

    b. *Ma   mère   est très   *élégant   et   jolie*
          my-FEM mother is very elegant-MSC and pretty-FEM
          'My mother is very elegant and pretty'

    c. *Elle est tres passionnante   et   *compétent   mais elle n'a jamais*
          she is very passionate-FEM and *competent-MSC but she has never
          été   *sportif   comme mon père   et   moi
          been athletic-MSC like   my   father and me
          'She very passionate and competent but she has never been athletic like my father and me'

In (16a, b, c), the participants clearly knew the grammatical gender of *robe* and, of course, the inherent gender of *mère*, as indicated by the use of the feminine form of the determiners (*une, ma*), or anaphora (*elle*). And yet, they failed to consistently indicate that gender agreement on the adjectives they chose.

(23) a. *Ses   cheveux n'étaient pas longs, mais très *court   et   *raide*
          her-PL hairs-PL were   not long, but very short-SG and straight-SG
          'Her hair was not long, but very short and straight'

    b. *Ses   cheveux sont *long   et   *frisé*
          her-PL hairs-PL are long-SG and curly-SG
          'Her hair is long and curly'

    c. *Elle portera   des   chaussures *noir*
          she wear-FUT some-PL shoes-PL black-SG
          'She will wear black shoes'

The output in (23c) is an example of failing to make the appropriate number agreement on the adjective *noir* when the determiner shows the participant knew the noun *chaussures* was plural, but maybe not feminine since *des* is not gender-marked.

Finally, nouns were consistently raised above adjectives, yielding the appropriate word order N + Adj, which shows that participants' IL instantiates strong features for Num.

6. Discussion and conclusion

6.1 Summary and discussion

The results of two different elicitation tasks, a GJT and a production task, confirmed the three predictions made above: (a) Participants performed more accurately on determiner/noun agreement than on noun/adjective agreement; (b) Participants were more accurate as their level of proficiency increased; (c) The higher the level of proficiency, the more likely were the participants able to detect conflictual gender assignment in the GJT, as indicated by the rejection percentages.

The results also showed that these participants were successful in the various tasks required in acquiring gender in L2 French: (a) They demonstrated that they learned that French has grammatical as well as inherent gender; (b) The high accuracy percentage of determiner/noun agreement showed that they could assign the proper gender to a large number of lexical items; (c) They were less accurate in indicating proper noun/adjective agreement though, as also found in other studies (e.g., Bartning 2000; Bruhn de Garavito & White 2000; Dewaele & Véronique 2001), and as in L1 acquisition; (d) There was not a single instance of improper word order placement of N Adj, reflecting that they indeed have acquired a strong Num feature, along with the gender features necessary for appropriate gender agreement on nouns.

Thus, from a generative perspective, it appears that these L2 French adult learners have successfully reset the gender-marking parameter associated with Num in French, in that they clearly seem to have acquired the [±masc] gender feature in nominal phrases, *contra* the Failed Feature Hypothesis (e.g., Hawkins & Chan 1997), and *contra* the weak or strong version of the Failed Functional Features Hypothesis (Franceschina 2005). English-speaking learners of L2 French can indeed acquire gender features which are not instantiated in their L1.

However, the L2 acquisition of grammatical gender is far from effortless, as discussed above. L2 learners do encounter difficulties in the mapping of the abstract features to the appropriate surface morphology, as for the Aspect Phrase (Ayoun 2005c), and in processing difficulties probably mostly due to the complex and ambiguous input, as well as the numerous idiosyncrasies and exceptions. The inconsistencies in performance noted above may be due to a lack of motivation and attention on the part of instructed learners or immersion students (see review below). Grammatical gender carries a low communicative load, is often highly redundant, and is far less salient in the input than previously argued. The cognitive factors of attention, noticing and memory (e.g., Ellis 1995; Leow 1999a, 1999b, 2000; Schmidt 1990, 1993, 1995, 2001; Tomlin & Villa 1994) may thus be relevant not only to the acquisition of grammatical gender, but more specifically to gender agreement, as will be briefly discussed below.

Even NSs do not always know about some of these idiosyncrasies, as revealed by the GJT results. The GJT included the following three stimuli:

(24) a. *Les vieilles   gens   se couchent toujours tôt*
          the old-FEM people go to bed   always   early
          'Old people always go to bed early'
      b. *Je trouve ces   amours enfantines vraiment adorables*
          I find   these loves   children   really   adorable
          'I think that these children's lovestories are really adorable'

    c.   *L'église   résonnait du   son   des orgues   chrétiennes*
        the church resounded from the sound of the organs Christian-FEM
        'The church resounded with the Christian organs'

Only 55%, 50% and 55% of the NS correctly accepted (24a, b, c) respectively. In (24a) a preposed adjective modifying *gens* is correctly feminine, while *gens* is normally masculine. The sentences in (24b, c) illustrate the interdependence of number and gender in French: Both *amours* and *orgues* are feminine when plural, but masculine when singular (see Section 1.3.2). When provided, the corrections indicated that the NSs thought the adjectives should be masculine: *Vieux* (n = 2), *enfantins* (n = 5), *chrétiens* (n = 4).

    Another stimulus exemplified a different type of gender clash between a noun and its adjective in (25):

(25)   *Le   capitaine   est tombé   enceinte*
       the-MSC capitain-MSC is   fallen-MSC pregnant-FEM
       'The captain got pregnant'

The stimulus in (25) illustrates the fact that standard French is still working on the feminization of words depicting professions or positions traditionally held by men because *juge* 'judge', *ministre* 'minister', *psychologue* 'psychologist' and so on are still overwhelmingly used with masculine determiners even when they refer to women. Most of the NSs (55%) rejected (25) though, and in their corrections stated that a man could not be pregnant, while one participant wrote *le capitaine est tombée* (FEM) *enceinte*, and another proposed *madame le capitaine est tombée enceinte*, thus indicating that the captain had to be a woman but maintaining the masculine determiner *le*. The L2 learners noticed the clash between the noun and the adjective as well and proposed *enceint* (an inexisting masculine form) at least once in all three groups; or *la capitaine*, especially among the Low group (n = 4); Advanced learners noted that there could not be an agreement between the noun and the adjective (n = 4), asked if *le capitaine* was a woman, or proposed *la* (FEM) *capitaine* (n = 1), *le capitaine est tombée* (FEM) *enceinte* (n = 1), or *la* (FEM) *capitaine est tombée* (FEM) *enceinte* (n = 2). Only 27.27%, 36.36% and 23.07% of the Low, Intermediate and Advanced learners, respectively, accepted (25).

    One may argue that these L2 learners benefitted from the formal instruction they received in their foreign language classes, but empirical studies that directly tested the effect of instruction present mixed findings.

6.2 Effect of formal instruction

In Warden (1997), sixty-two grade 11 French immersion students were divided into one experimental classroom in which they practiced form-focused tasks during 8 weeks, and two control classrooms. The form-focused instruction provided activities designed to raise awareness of word-ending regularities, and to practice making gender agreements. The results of immediate and delayed post-tests indicated that the experimental group's performance on three tasks (listening test, written endings test, agreement test) was significantly better than the control groups' performance. The experimental group also outperformed the control groups on the other two tasks (written assignment and oral production task), but not significantly. Warden concludes that these findings provide tentative support for the positive effect of form-focused instruction in immersion settings.

Harley (1998) investigated the effect of focus-on-form instruction in French immersion settings but among younger learners (7- to 8-year-olds, grade 2). She found that focus-on-form produced better results than no instruction, but it appeared that the learners failed to extend their knowledge to new words. Harley (1998: 168) suggested that "the experiment was more successful in inducing 'item learning' than 'system learning'".

More recently, Lyster (2004) investigated the effects of form-focused instruction and corrective feedback (recasts, prompts, or no feedback) with eight classes of 179 fifth-grade (10–11 year-old) immersion students by drawing their attention to reliable noun endings, and by providing opportunities to practice associating these endings with nouns. The results of immediate and delayed post-tests revealed that students exposed to form-focused instruction significantly improved in their ability to correctly assign grammatical gender, particularly in the written tasks.

Dewaele and Véronique (2001) did not find a correlation between the L2 and accuracy rates for gender agreement among L1 Dutch/L2 French speakers, although the frequency of L2 use in authentic communication outside the classroom had a positive effect on how accurately the participants performed. This is also a finding of the present study in which the Advanced learners had spent a much greater length of time in a Francophone country than the participants in the lower levels of proficiency. Granfeldt (2000) did not find a positive effect for instruction in the acquisition of L2 French gender by two L1 Swedish naturalistic learners and an instructed learner.

Finally, to test for effects of processing instruction (VanPatten & Oikkenon 1996), Benati (2004) divided English-speaking beginning learners of L2 Italian into three groups: Processing instruction, structured input, and explicit information. The results of an immediate post-test revealed that processing instruction and the structured input groups made significant gains on an interpretation test and a production task, while the explicit information group made no gains on either.

6.3 Directions for future research

First, further research into form-focused instruction and processing instruction versus explicit instruction should be pursued as some of the initial findings are promising, even if it is still premature to propose pedagogical applications for foreign language classrooms since the studies that investigated the effect of instruction have so far yielded mixed results. More empirical data are needed with adult learners, preferably by comparing instructed learners with no or limited access to input outside the classroom, and instructed learners with access to input outside the classroom via study abroad programs for instance.

Future research into the effects of instruction could also investigate whether promoting the cognitive factors of memory, attention and awareness would affect not only the acquisition of grammatical gender, but also the acquisition of gender agreement. Studies investigating other difficult elements to acquire for adult L2 learners obtained positive results. For instance, Rosa and O'Neill (1999), who presented Spanish conditional sentences to L2 learners, showed that the higher the level of awareness, the stronger the effect on intake. Their findings were similar to those reported in Leow (1997, 2001).

Another interesting direction for future research should be into gender (as well as number) and agreement processing. There is already a vast psycholinguistic literature of empirical data obtained with monolingual native speakers and bilingual speakers (e.g., Antón-Méndez, Nicol, & Garrett 2002; Bentrovato, Devescovi, D'Amico, Wicha, & Bates 2003; Dahan, Swingley, Tanenhaus, & Magnuson 2000; Guillelmon & Grosjean 2001; Jakubowicz & Faussart 1998; Vigliocci, Butterworth, & Garrett 1996). It would be interesting to see how adult L2 learners process gender in picture-naming tasks or online sentence processing for instance; or if the processing of number is independent of the processing of gender, as suggested in Antón-Méndez (1999) in a study with L2 Spanish learners.

The following can be investigated from a pedagogical perspective or from a processing perspective:

– determiner retrieval;
– determiner and noun gender agreement;
– noun and adjective agreement;
– subject and past participle agreement;
– gender agreement with anaphora.

Finally, grammatical gender can be investigated from a variety of different perspectives that would include, but are not limited to the following:

– the feminization of standard French and other varieties of French (for instance, it appears that feminized forms are much more frequent in *Québécois* French than in Standard French);
– gender and conversational analysis in French;
– gender and discourse analysis in French;
– the analysis of gender-inclusive or gender-neutral discourse in various jargons (politics, media, business world, military, advertising, etc.);
– gender stereotyping in the teaching of French.

Appendix A: Empirical studies in chronological order

Study	L1 CHILD STUDIES	Main findings
Karmiloff-Smith (1979)	Children 3;2 to 12;5 years 5 conditions with nonsense words	Reliance on phonological clues over semantic and syntactic clues; gender system mastered before articles
Karmiloff-Smith (1986)	Older children tested mostly on determiner system and conflict between inherent and grammatical gender	Older children use semantic clues sooner than younger children; they maintained syntactic agreement within NP but allowed semantic overriding on pronouns
Kail (2004)	3 age (6;8, 8;6, 10;10) groups of French children and adults were asked to detect grammatical violations in an online processing experiment	Children were slower than adults; morphological violations (number and gender agreement) were more rapidly detected by all

Study	L2 CHILD STUDIES	Main findings
Ervin-Tripp (1974)	31 children aged 4 to 9 in Swizertland; comprehension tasks, elicited imitation, translation; diary notes, recorded speech samples with 2 children	Older children made faster progress than younger children in acquiring gender and number; little difference between masculine and feminine determiners although children never made mistakes in elicitation tasks
Spilka (1976)	Comparative error analysis of free speech samples of immersion students in grades 1 to 6, along with their francophone peers	Examined rate of production, complex sentences, flexible structures (clefts, topicalized sentences, incidental clauses), errors of omission and commission in use of gendered articles, possessive determiners, verbs, pronouns. Major differences between groups except for flexible structures; anglophone learners do not seem to improve on gender.
Tarone et al. (1976)	Grade 2 immersion students; oral data (conversations, picture description, story telling)	Overgeneralization of masculine especially with 3rd person pronouns
Harley (1979)	Anglophone and francophone children grades 2 to 5 in either immersion programs, bilingual community or francophone community; speech samples analyzed for errors in gender usage	Correlation between L2 exposure and accuracy of gender assignment in oral production; unilingual francophones and bilinguals from dominant French backgrounds consistently accurate, much more than others; massive overgeneralization of masculine forms and use of neutralized form of definite article as avoidance strategy
Stevens (1984)	Canadian immersion programs – partial replication of Karmiloff-Smith	Use of phonological clues before semantic clues; acquisition in stages similar to NSs; constant reliance on phonological clues

Study	L1 CHILD STUDIES	Main findings
Taylor-Browne (1984)	Early, continuing partial and late immersion students; 11 experimental tasks partially replicated from Karmiloff-Smith (1979) and Tucker et al. (1977)	Overgeneralization of masculine; inability to use phonological, semantic or syntactic clues in determining gender of novel nouns
Lyster (2004)	Grade 5 immersion students; 3 groups received form-focused instruction (recasts, prompts or FFI only) for 5 weeks; 1 control group	Results of pretest, immediate posttest and delayed posttest (2 written and 2 oral tasks) showed students exposed to FFI-prompts outperformed other groups particularly for the written tasks

Study	L1 ADULT STUDIES	Main findings
Tucker et al. (1968)	Gender assignment task with non-words; range of typical endings	Gender given to a non-word was correlated with the proportion of times its ending was actually associated with masculine or feminine
Desrochers, Pavio, & Desrochers (1989)	60 French NSs, university students; 20 read a text outloud, 40 did a gender identification task from 2 list of words (common and experimental)	Faster gender decision responses to visually presented words with higher predictive value ending than other words; interaction between predictiveness effect and word frequency on error rates, but predictiveness effect on response times was as great for high- as for low-frequency words
Desrochers & Paivio (1990)	Adult university students assigned gender to lists of nouns with F/M labels or with articles	Gender identification was faster and more accurate for words beginning with a consonant than with a vowel, and with strong predictive value endings
Desrochers & Brabant (1995)	Adult university students assigned gender to lists of animate and inanimate nouns	Gender identification faster and more accurate with consonant initial than vowel initial words; faster responses when providing *un/une* than M/F labels
Jakubowicz & Faussart (1998)	Two experiments tested effects of gender agreement on lexical decisions; 2 groups of French NSs (n = 64, n = 52); masculine nouns only	Exp. 1: lexical times are faster in congruent condition (determiner/noun pair agree); Exp. 2: lexical times were faster in congruent condition with variable and invariable adjective
Taft & Meunier (1998)	Gender decision task (exps 1, 2) and gender verification task (exp. 3) (16 and 30 adults) to investigate how grammatical gender is represented in the lexical memory of NSs	Grammatical gender doesn't appear to be stored with each lexical item; determiners and orthographic form of endings play a role; a neural network model could account for these relationships

Study	L1 ADULT STUDIES	Main findings
Guilford (1999)	32 francophone speakers; gender assignment task to 55 English loanwords taken from written popular music corpus	Greater consistency in assigning MASC gender to MASC loanwords in corpus than FEM; but uncertainties and hesitations; semantic analogy and literal translations most common processes; MASC as the unmarked gender. Suggested that determiners are main source of agreement processing for NP
Alario & Caramazza (2002)	3 picture naming experiments with simple or complex NPs to contrast two accounts of determiner retrieval	There must be a mechanism activating semantic/syntactic, lexical, and phonological features relevant to determiner selection but determiner selection is delayed until all required information is available
Dahan et al. (2000)	Adult French NSs; eye movement experiments to investigate whether a gender-marked definite article affects what the participants initially considered for recognition of the following noun	Clear evidence that when a gender-marked definite article preceded a noun, initial activation of a gender-mismatching cohort competitor was eliminated; implying that language processing system exploits contingency between article and noun in word recognition
Chevaux & Meunier (2004)	Cross-modal semantic priming experiments to test processing of homophones in two conditions	For homophones presented in isolation, there was priming only for semantic representation associated with most frequent meaning; in gender marked context, facilitation effect found only for targets preceded by congruent definite article that is the less frequent meaning
Colé et al. (2003)	Lexical decision times and eye movements were recorded to determine whether grammatical gender can influence the visual recognition of isolated French nouns	Gender information can influence both the activation stage and the selection stage of the word recognition process
Irmen & Rossberg (2004)	3 experiments to investigate how grammatical gender and gender stereotypicality influence the way person information is mentally represented	Stereotypicality varied within studies; 2nd sentence reading times differed depending on fit between grammatical gender and stereotypicality of the 1st sentence's subject and subsequent information's gender-relatedness; strong grammatical input may override influence of stereotypicality; influence of FEM seems weaker than MASC's

Study	L2 ADULT STUDIES	Main findings
Tucker, Lambert, & Rigault (1977)	139 anglophone university learners at the introductory, intermediate or advanced level; real and invented nouns with high PVE	Advanced learners performed within NS range on gender assignment task; group provided with organized lists and explicit information on endings was only group to improve
Surridge & Lessard (1984)	113 university students; gender assignment task	High accuracy for frequent nouns; decreasing accuracy from less frequent nouns but with high PVEs to infrequent nouns with low PVEs
Carroll (1989)	English NSs (n = 88), beginning learners, exposed to auditory stimuli (learning and guessing phases with word lists) to test their initial sensitivity to gender classes	Learners were more sensitive to natural semantic and morphological patterns than phonological patterns and could generalize from learned instances to novel exemplars
Myles (1990)	Correction test for study on error and order	Systematic development towards target-like gender agreement, but constrained by distance between elements and direction of agreement
Hardison (1992)	3 studies to test Tucker et al.'s (1977) rules with students in college courses with frequent and rare nouns	Participants use gender of most salient element of each phonetic category to formulate rules of gender-noun endings, even with exceptions; high levels of accuracy
Sokolik & Smith (1992)	Connectionist model applied to corpus of 450 words; input coded in terms of orthographic structure	After several learning trials model could accurately classify a high percentage of target and new nouns
Antes (1993)	Longitudinal study with college students	Participants in enhanced input condition outperformed participants in analogical enhancement condition and control group
Vuchic (1993)	Claims that French NP agreement is perceived and processed analogously to Vowel Harmony within autosegmental model; adolescent learners	Findings of quantitative and qualitative analyses show that learning NP agreement is constrained by principles of autosegmental theory, and L2 learners use both linguistic principles and learning strategies during acquisition process
Marinova-Todd (1994)	18 English-speaking and 8 German-speaking university students were administered gended assignment tasks to test critical period hypothesis	Post-puberty learners outscored learners who had been in immersion programs before reaching puberty
Holmes & Dejean de la Bâtie (1999)	Gender assignment/verification task of regular and exceptional nouns with and without determiners, and invented nouns; spontaneous written data (determiner and adjective agreement); FNSs and L2 French learners	L2 learners were much more accurate with regular than exceptional words, as were NSs who also took longer. L2 learners relied extensively on ending-based rules whereas NSs seem to rely more on lexical associations.

Study	L2 ADULT STUDIES	Main findings
Bartning (1999)	Longitudinal study of 4 L1 Swedish speakers	Accuracy agreement for attributive adjectives not higher than for predicative adjectives
Bartning (2000)	Follow-up study (within Pienemann's 1998 Processability Theory) with pre-advanced and advanced learners; corpus of 1352 forms of gender agreement on determiners and adjectives	Advanced learners display very high levels of accuracy with definite DETs (93%), indefinite DETs (93%) and possessive DETs (97%), with 81% average on Adj agreement; preadvanced learners average 74% on DETs and 80% on Adj; MASC may be used as a default until FEM is acquired
Dewaele & Véronique (2000)	Advanced university learners, Dutch L1 speakers, recorded conversations transcribed and coded for lexical and morphological errors	Negative relationship between the number of gender errors and fluency variables; No relation between gender errors and other agreement errors explained by processing difficulties
Dewaele & Véronique (2001)	Advanced university learners, Dutch L1 speakers; recorded conversations transcribed and coded for lexical and morphological errors	Accuracy of gender agreement not higher for DETs and attributive Adjs than for predicative Adjs; large inter- and intra-individual variation explained by variety of psycholinguistic factors
Guillelmon & Grosjean (2001)	2 experiments in gender processing (lexical naming task) in early vs late English-French bilinguals with French NS controls; congruent/neutral stimuli, incongruent/neutral stimuli; both masculine and feminine determiners with 36 nouns, adjectives	Results of first exp. revealed congruency (facilitation) and incongruency (inhibitory) effects with French monolinguals; similar strong effects for early bilinguals. 2nd exp. showed late bilinguals to be insensitive to both gender congruency and incongruency. Processing and perception problems not linked to production
Taraban (2004)	5 experiments with artificial language to test hypothesis that syntactic-context models are sufficient for category induction if they include processes for drawing learners' attention to the related subsets of grammatical morphemes defining the categories	Hypothesis was supported by 4 of the experiments without negating learners' ability to use phonological and semantic noun cues induction of linguistic gender; learners probably draw on multiple resources
Prodeau (2005)	English L1, French L2 adult instructed learners; gender assignment, comprehension and production tasks; film retell task	Participants generally knew the gender of common nouns but were not always able to retrieve it or to make the proper agreement with adjectives
Granfeldt (2005)	Swedish-speaking L2 French naturalistic and instructed adult learners; bilingual Swedish-French/French-Swedish children	analysis of gender agreement with articles, articles with nouns, and adjectival agreement. Quick acquisition for children, progressive increase in agreement on articles and adjectives for adults

Appendix B: Participants' background information

Group	n	Gender	Age	L2 stay	L2 stay length
Low	11	1 male, 11 females	23.36 (19–45)	no = 4 yes = 7	3.45 weeks (1–8 weeks)
Intermediate	11	1 male, 11 females	25.09 (18–42)	no = 2 yes = 9	15.27 weeks (1–108 weeks)
Advanced	13	7 males, 6 females	29.46 (19–54)	no = 0 yes = 13	48.23 weeks (5–108 weeks)
NS	20	3 males, 17 females	26.8 (16–54)	n/a	n/a

Appendix C: Production task

I will probably never get to meet your parents in person, so please tell me about them (you can also imagine fictive parents if you prefer).

1. First, please describe their physical appearance. Please use all the adjectives listed below, feel free to also use other adjectives to write a minimun of 10 sentences.

> *jeune / vieux*
> *petit / grand / moyen*
> *joli / beau*
> *élégant*
> *mince / gros / musclé*
> *frisé / long / court / raide*
> *souriant*
> *sportif*

2. Second, describe their personalities. Please use at least 10 of the adjectives listed below, feel free to use other adjectives in addition if you like. Then tell me also what they do professionally and what they like to do for fun.

> *gentil*   *ennuyeux*   *énervé*
> *distrait*   *ambitieux*   *généreux*
> *passionnant*   *intelligent*   *patient*
> *travailleur*   *amusant*   *compétent*
> *sportif*   *organisé*   *vieux jeu / moderne*

3. Finally, imagine that your parents are going out to dinner to celebrate their anniversary. Please describe what they are wearing using as many of the adjectives and nouns listed below (with a minimun of 10 sentences, with 10 adjectives), and feel free to use others as necessary. Hint: you may need to use a few negative sentences for some items... Have fun!

> *pantalons*   *robe*   *veste*   *jupe*
> *chemise*   *shorts*   *bikini*   *chemisier*
> *chaussettes*   *chaussures*   *bijoux*   *chapeau*
> *bottes*   *foulard*   *ceinture*   *lunettes de soleil*

cravate	jeans	manteau	blouson de cuir
joli / beau	ridicule	fleuri / uni	blanc / noir /crème
rose / violet	gris / vert bleu / jaune		élégant / soigné
long / court / mini	glamour / sexy		

Appendix D: GJT results by stimuli

Stimulus	Low (n = 11)			Inter. (n = 11)			Advanced (n = 13)			NSs (n = 20)		
	A	R	DK	A	R	DK	A	R	DK	A	R	DK
# 1	27.27	54.54	18.18	36.36	36.36	27.27	46.15	15.38	38.46	80.0	10.0	10.0
# 2	45.45	18.18	36.36	63.63	18.18	18.18	61.53	15.38	23.07	80.0	10.0	10.0
# 3	27.27	18.18	54.54	45.45	27.27	27.27	23.07	61.53	15.38	45.0	50.0	5.0
# 4	81.81	9.09	9.09	81.81	18.18	0.0	76.92	23.07	0.0	90.0	10.0	0.0
# 5	63.63	9.09	27.27	9.09	45.45	45.45	30.76	15.38	53.84	35.0	50.0	0.0
# 6	54.54	36.36	9.09	36.36	54.54	9.09	15.38	84.61	0.0	35.0	65.0	0.0
# 7	63.63	27.27	9.09	36.36	54.54	9.09	61.53	23.07	15.38	50.0	30.0	20.0
# 8	45.45	36.36	18.18	54.54	45.45	0.0	84.61	7.69	7.69	90.0	10.0	0.0
# 9	54.54	9.09	36.36	36.36	9.09	54.54	69.23	7.69	23.07	90.0	10.0	0.0
# 10	81.81	18.18	0.0	54.54	36.36	9.09	76.92	7.69	15.38	90.0	10.0	0.0
# 11	63.63	36.36	0.0	45.45	36.36	18.18	15.38	61.53	23.07	70.0	25.0	5.0
# 12	45.45	18.18	36.36	63.63	36.36	0.0	84.61	7.69	7.69	90.0	5.0	5.0
# 13	27.27	36.36	36.36	36.36	45.45	18.18	23.07	69.23	7.69	35.0	55.0	10.0
# 14	45.45	27.27	27.27	54.54	18.18	27.27	76.92	7.69	15.38	90.0	10.0	0.0
# 15	45.45	18.18	18.18	81.81	9.09	9.09	84.61	7.69	7.69	80.0	15.0	5.0
# 16	54.54	18.18	27.27	63.63	27.27	9.09	84.61	7.69	7.69	75.0	15.0	10.0
# 17	81.81	27.27	18.18	63.63	27.27	9.09	76.92	15.38	7.69	95.0	5.0	0.0
# 18	54.54	18.18	27.27	63.63	18.18	18.18	92.31	0.0	7.69	85.0	10.0	5.0
# 19	36.36	9.09	54.54	72.72	9.09	18.18	84.61	7.69	7.69	90.0	0.0	10.0
# 20	63.63	18.18	18.18	72.72	9.09	18.18	46.15	7.69	46.15	15.0	70.0	15.0
# 21	54.54	0.0	45.45	45.45	27.27	27.27	15.38	0.0	84.61	60.0	30.0	10.0
# 22	81.81	18.18	0.0	45.45	45.45	9.09	69.23	23.07	7.69	55.0	45.0	0.0
# 23	81.81	18.18	0.0	63.63	18.18	18.18	38.46	15.38	7.69	50.0	40.0	10.0
# 24	63.63	9.09	27.27	54.54	18.18	27.27	69.23	7.69	23.07	55.0	35.0	10.0
# 25	54.54	18.18	27.27	63.63	18.18	18.18	84.61	15.38	0.0	60.0	30.0	10.0

Note: A(ccepted); R(ejected); DK (don't know).

CHAPTER 7

Interlanguage pragmatics in L2 French*

Muriel Warga
University of Graz

Résumé

Ce chapitre a pour objectif de présenter d'une part le domaine de la pragmatique de l'interlangue, générale et française, et d'autre part, une étude empirique sur le processus de l'évolution pragmatique en français L2. Dans la première partie, nous ferons le point sur l'état actuel de la discussion dans le domaine de la pragmatique de l'interlangue (PIL), et en particulier de la PIL française. A cette fin, nous présenterons différentes positions théoriques, et passerons en revue les études disponibles à propos des méthodes de recherche, des différences entre natifs et apprenants et de l'acquisition pragmatique. Le survol de la littérature sur la PIL en français L2 présentera, de façon aussi actuelle et complète que possible, les recherches effectuées à ce jour dans ce domaine. Dans la seconde partie, nous présenterons une étude empirique portant sur l'une des principales questions de recherche, à savoir le processus de l'évolution pragmatique.

Abstract

This chapter has two aims: (1) To provide a thorough overview of the field of general and French interlanguage pragmatics; and (2) To present an empirical study on the path of pragmatic development in L2 French. In the first part, this chapter offers a state-of-the-art discussion of interlanguage pragmatics (ILP), with a particular focus on French ILP. It presents specific theoretical positions, and reviews the data-based research on a variety of issues, such as research methods, differences between native speakers and learners, as well as pragmatic acquisition. The review of the literature on interlanguage pragmatics in L2 French provides a general and encompassing up-to-date overview of studies that have been conducted so far in the field of French ILP. In the second part, an empirical study addressing one of the standing research questions in French ILP, namely the path of pragmatic development, is presented.

1. Introduction

Every learner of French or other second or foreign languages knows anecdotes of intercultural misunderstandings. Most of the time, these misunderstandings can be

---

* I would like to thank the two anonymous reviewers for their helpful comments and suggestions.

ascribed to the violation of a language's rules of use, that is of a language's pragmatic rules. The discipline concerned with the comprehension, production and acquisition of pragmatics in a second or foreign language is interlanguage pragmatics (ILP).

Compared to other areas of second language (L2) research, interlanguage pragmatics (ILP) is still a young discipline, and few studies have as yet focused on French. Therefore, this chapter first aims to present the field of interlanguage pragmatics, and to highlight French interlanguage pragmatics as an area of inquiry within this field; and, second, to present an empirical study designed to address one of the standing research questions in French interlanguage pragmatics, that is, the path of pragmatic development.

The chapter sets out by presenting the theoretical underpinnings of interlanguage pragmatics in Section 2. In Section 3, the field of interlanguage pragmatics is defined, and its scope is discussed. Section 4 focuses on various theories offering alternative accounts of pragmatic acquisition. Then, methodological issues are outlined in Section 5. In Section 6, emphasis is on pragmatic differences between learners and native speakers. Section 7 discusses acquisitional pragmatics, an under-researched area of interlanguage pragmatics. In Section 8, the focus shifts to French interlanguage pragmatics. First, I present a very general and exhaustive review of the literature outlining what is known about how L2 learners comprehend, produce, and acquire pragmatic aspects in L2 French. Based on the research gaps identified in this review, one standing research question, namely the path of pragmatic development, is finally addressed on the basis of empirical data. The chapter concludes with suggestions for further research in Section 9.

2.   Defining pragmatics

Since the philosopher Charles Morris introduced the modern usage of the term *pragmatics* as the study of "the relation of signs to interpreters" (Morris 1938:6), pragmatics has become an important branch of linguistics. An array of distinct definitions of this research area has been put forward since, the most frequent sees pragmatics as "the study of language usage" (e.g., Levinson 1983:5), while Crystal (2003:364) defined pragmatics as:

> [...] the study of *language* from the point of view of the users, especially of the choices they make, the *constraints*[1] they encounter in using language in social inter-

---

1.   For instance, a well-known constraint for English speaking learners of French is the use of the two pronouns of address *tu/vous* 'you' in French as there is only one such form in English. For German-speaking learners of French, on the other hand, the French pronouns of address do normally not cause problems as there are also two pronouns in German (*du/Sie*). However, the fact that a polite form of address requires the mentioning of *Monsieur/Madame* in French (e.g., *Excusez-moi, Madame, quelle heure est-il?* 'Excuse me Madam, what time is it?'), is a well-known constraint for German native

action, and the effects their use of language has on the other participants in an act of *communication.*   [original emphasis]

Traditionally, the study of pragmatics has been dominated by speech act theory, a theory of language developed by the British language philosopher John L. Austin whose set of lectures given at Harvard University was posthumously published as *How To Do Things With Words* (Austin 1976 [1962]). Austin suggested that, when we talk, we do not only *say* things with words, we also *do* things with words. For instance, to make the statement "I promise to help you" is to perform the act of promising. In John Searle's words, a language philosopher who modified and further developed speech act theory (cf. Searle 1969, 1976), the basic assumption of speech act theory is that:

> [...] the minimal unit of communication is not a sentence or other expression, but rather the performance of certain kinds of acts, such as making statements, asking questions, giving orders, describing [...] etc.   (Searle, Kiefer, & Bierwisch 1980:vii)

Speech act theory has, however, been criticized for its exclusive focus on the sentence level. The most convincing and influential critique dates back to the 1970s, and comes from conversational analysts who have shown that the functions utterances perform in a context are mainly due to their place within specific conversational sequences (e.g., Sacks, Schegloff, & Jefferson 1974).[2]

The other main areas of pragmatics are deixis, conversational implicature, and presupposition (Levinson 1983). Deixis is a form of 'pointing' via language that is tied to the speaker's context. Depending on whether what is referred to is 'near speaker' or 'away from speaker', different deictic expressions are used (*je* 'I', *tu* 'you'; *ici* 'here', *là* 'there'; *maintenant* 'now', *après* 'after').

Conversational implicature is a concept developed by the language philosopher Paul Grice who states that the basic assumption in conversation is that the participants are cooperative (cooperative principle and conversational maxims). Consequently, the listener can assume that the speaker wants to communicate meaning when his/her contribution violates the requirements of the maxims. The inference calculated on the basis of the maxims of conversation is called implicature. If, for example, A asks *"Tu as emmené le pain et le fromage?"* 'did you take the bread and the cheese', and B answers *"Oui, j'ai emmené le pain"* 'yes, I took the bread', A can assume that B wants to communicate a meaning by not mentioning the cheese (example taken from Yule 1996:40).

Presupposition is a field of enquiry that used to play a more central role in pragmatics in the past than it does now (Yule 1996:25). A presupposition is something a speaker assumes in saying a particular sentence. For example, in producing the utterance *Où est le sel?* 'where is the salt', the speaker will normally have the presupposition

---

speakers as there is no such equivalent in German (*Entschuldigen Sie, wie spät ist es bitte?* 'Excuse me, what's the time, please?').

2.   For more information on the critique of speech act theory, see Levinson (1983:Chapter 6).

that the salt is not present to the speaker, and that there is a person who knows where the salt is, and so on.

The purpose of this chapter, which is to investigate the L2 pragmatic competence of learners of French, requires a definition of the term 'pragmatic competence'. Since pragmatic competence is a sub-concept of communicative competence, we will first turn briefly to this latter concept. As a response to Chomsky's (1965) notion of competence, the anthropologist and sociolinguist Hymes (1972) introduced the concept of communicative competence encompassing not only the knowledge of the rules of grammar, but also their appropriateness in a communicative context. The concept of communicative competence was further developed by Bachman (1990), Bachman and Palmer (1996), Canale (1983), and Canale and Swain (1980). Pragmatic competence is included in Canale and Swain (1980), and in Canale (1983) under sociolinguistic competence, and to a certain degree, under discourse competence as well. However, the first to mention pragmatic competence explicitly was Bachman (1990). On the basis of these concepts of pragmatic competence (Bachman 1990; Bachman & Palmer 1996; Canale 1983; Canale & Swain 1980; Hymes 1972), Barron (2003:10) proposes a working definition of pragmatic competence as

> Knowledge of the linguistic resources available in a given language for realizing particular illocutions, knowledge of the sequential aspects of speech acts and finally, knowledge of the appropriate contextual use of the particular languages' linguistic resources.

Given that becoming communicatively competent in the target language is the aim of most language learners, Hymes' (1972) introduction of the concept of communicative competence has also aroused interest in the field of L2 acquisition. As a consequence, pragmatic aspects of L2 learning were investigated for the first time at the end of the 1970s. The first two studies concerned with L2 pragmatic competence (Borkin & Reinhart 1978; Hackman 1977) marked the beginning of the conception of a whole new area of research, the field of interlanguage pragmatics, briefly outlined in the next section.

3.   Interlanguage pragmatics

3.1   Definition

"[...] The study of nonnative speakers' use and acquisition of L2 pragmatic knowledge [...]" (Kasper & Rose 1999:81) has been defined as interlanguage pragmatics (ILP). Kasper and Blum-Kulka (1993:3) characterize ILP as "second generation hybrid":

> [...] ILP belongs to two different disciplines, both of which are interdisciplinary. As a branch of L2 Acquisition Research, ILP is one of several specializations in interlanguage studies [...]. As a subset of pragmatics, ILP figures as a sociolinguistic,

psycholinguistic, or simply linguistic enterprise, depending on how one defines the scope of "pragmatics".

However, the theoretical background, the methodology and the research questions have come directly from cross-cultural pragmatics, ILP's 'real parent discipline'.[3]

Researchers concerned with L2 acquisition adopted a primarily psycholinguistic perspective for a long time. However, since the early 1990s, research into L2 pragmatics has begun to perceive pragmatic development from a more socio-cognitive perspective. In response to the need to pay more attention to language acquisition as social phenomenon, the prior exclusive focus on language learning as an internal process of the individual learner has begun to lose ground (cf. Section 4 for a discussion of these perspectives).

3.2 Scope

There is now a substantial body of research on interlanguage pragmatics (for review, see e.g., Bardovi-Harlig 1999b, 2001; Kasper & Rose 1999, 2002; Rose & Kasper 2001). Topics investigated in these studies refer to two main categories of learning objectives, namely speech acts on the one hand, and various aspects of pragmatic and discourse ability, on the other hand (Kasper & Rose 2002: 117). Let us first address discourse ability.

3.2.1 *Discourse ability*
Discourse ability refers to how learners structure continuous stretches of speech. Recent approaches in cross-cultural and interlanguage pragmatics (e.g., constructivism) have highlighted the *joint* accomplishment of speech act performance throughout the whole discourse through a sequencing of implicit illocutionary acts, rather than any explicit expression of the communicative intent.

When studying discourse ability, researchers have mainly looked at opening and closing sequences of discourse (e.g., Edmondson, House, Kasper, & Stemmer 1984; Omar 1992, 1993), as well as on turn-taking phases and adjacency pairs (e.g., Jaworski 1994; Kasper 1984).

Here is an example of an opening sequence of a native speaker doctor-patient conversation (A = doctor, P = patient). It is shown that the opening of the conversation is constructed jointly over several turns. For nonnative speakers, this task is not straightforward:

(1) A: *Bien. Alors, qu'est-ce qui vous amène?*
      P: *Ben, c'est pour [...?]*
      A: *Oui. Alors c'est A.*

---

3. One of the consequences of the fact that cross-cultural pragmatics has served as a model for ILP is the prevalence of comparative studies (native speakers vs. nonnative speakers) over acquisition studies in ILP research (cf. 6).

P: *Oui*
A: 'Well. What brings you to me?'
P: 'Well, it's because of [...?]'
A: 'Yes. OK it's A'
P: 'Yes.'   (Hölker 1988: 183)

The ability to use discourse markers (*alors, bon, donc, enfin, quoi,* etc.) appropriately is another important aspect of the learners' discourse competence (e.g., House 1993; Müller 2004; Sawyer 1992; Scarcella 1983; White 1989; Wong 2000; Yoshimi 2001). The following example illustrates the use of *enfin* et *quoi* in a native speaker utterance, and shows how the two discourse markers are used in order to make a self-correction:

(2)   *Maintenant tu tournes à droite, **enfin** à gauche, **quoi**.*
      'Now, you turn to your right, I mean to your left'   (Hölker 1988: 56)

For nonnative speakers, the difficulty in acquiring discourse markers and using them appropriately lies in their poly-functional nature (Koch & Oesterreicher 1990: 72). *Enfin*, for instance, is not only used as self- and other-correction signal but also to structure discourse (cf. Beeching 2001 for a discussion of the particle *enfin*). This applies to most discourse markers and makes them difficult to acquire for learners.

Kanagy (1999), Kanagy and Igarashi (1997), Schmidt (1983), and Schmidt and Frota (1986) investigated more than one discourse phenomenon. Further studies in this field include Bardovi-Harlig (1992), Bardovi-Harlig, Hartford, Mahan-Taylor, Morgan and Reynolds (1991), DuFon (1999, 2000), House (1993, 1996), Kasper (1981, 1986), Ohta (2001), Warga (2001), Wildner-Bassett (1984, 1986), and Zuengler (1993).

3.2.2 *Speech acts*

As in general pragmatics, the main focus in ILP research has been on speech acts, the second area of ILP. The studies conducted so far in this field have yielded a wealth of knowledge about speech act strategies and resources for mitigating and aggravating the illocutionary force, the relationship between indirectness and politeness, and the influence of social variables such as social power and social distance on the linguistics realization of the speech act. The speech acts investigated thus far include: Apologies (*Je suis désolée de ne pas pouvoir t'aider* 'I'm sorry I can't help you'), complaints (*Tu ne ranges jamais ta chambre!* 'you never clean up your room'), compliments (*Ta nouvelle coiffure est très belle* 'your new haircut is beautiful'), compliment responses (*Merci, c'est très gentil de ta part* 'thank you, it's very nice of you'), expressions of gratitude (*Je te remercie de m'avoir aidé* 'thanks for helping me'), invitations (*J'aimerais t'inviter à dîner pour en parler avec toi* 'I would like to take you out to dinner to discuss it with you'), offers (*Je peux faire les courses pour toi, si tu veux* 'I can do the grocery shopping for you if you want'), refusals (*Non, je suis désolé, je n'ai pas le temps* 'no, I'm sorry, I don't have time'), requests (*Tu pourrais m'aider avec ça?* 'could you help me with that'), and suggestions (*Et si on allait au cinéma?* 'how about a movie').[4]

The standard approach of speech act researchers has been to isolate the speech act in question from the context, to investigate its linguistic design, and to relate it to discourse-external context factors. However, recent studies, such as Golato (2003) and Kasper (2004), have tried to increase the analytical benefits that derive from the study of interlanguage pragmatics by bringing together traditional speech act analysis and conversation analysis, as well as drawing on both approaches in an integrated way.

A rather limited number of studies have investigated the perception and judgment of speech acts (e.g., Bardovi-Harlig & Dörnyei 1998; Bouton 1988; Niezgoda & Röver 2001). One main finding of these studies is that learners do not always make use of their inferencing ability; thus, they may understand the literal meaning, for instance, but not the indirectly conveyed pragmatic meaning of an utterance. Another finding concerns the important role of the L1 culture for the assessment of politeness in the L2. Also, it has been shown that learners' convergence to L2 politeness norms tends to increase with the time spent in the target community.

4.   Theoretical positions[5]

Theories of importance in the investigation of interlanguage pragmatics are among others speech act theories, politeness theories, the concept of communicative competence and discourse analysis. All existing ILP studies draw on these theoretical orientations in one way or another. However, as Kasper and Rose (2002: 13) argue, these theories concern "the object of the study, not the learning process". Regarding the learning process itself, most studies have been descriptive without being related to an explanatory framework of pragmatic acquisition. Few investigations have been guided by a theory, and only rarely has a study been designed to test a certain theoretical approach explicitly. Therefore, in the following, different theoretical positions that have been drawn upon to account for pragmatic acquisition will be discussed.

4.1 Acculturation model

Developed by Schumann (1978) in the late 1970s, the acculturation model claims a relationship between the success in L2 learning and the degree of acculturation, that is the social and psychological integration in the L2 language group. Schumann argues that the lower the learner's social and/or psychological distance to the target com-

---

4.   Cf. Barron (2002) for a list of cross-cultural and interlanguage pragmatics studies relating to various speech acts.

5.   This section is based on Kasper (2001b) and on the chapter "Theories of Second Language Pragmatic Development" in Kasper and Rose (2002: 13–61).

munity is, the higher the probability of successful second language acquisition and vice versa. Schmidt's (1983) famous "Wes-study" was designed to test Schumann's acculturation model. Based on a range of social and psychological factors, Schmidt established Wes' acculturation profile according to which it was predicted that Wes would be rather successful in learning the L2. However, the results showed that Wes' morphological and syntactical systems showed no significant improvement, and that he relied heavily on formulaic expressions over the entire observation period of three years. In contrast, his oral discourse competence progressed considerably. Therefore, it can be said that although Schmidt's (1983) study challenged the acculturation model in so far as grammatical accuracy is concerned, the study demonstrated the model's value for explaining the pragmatic development.

4.2 Cognitive processing

Cognitive-psychological theories accounting for pragmatic acquisition emerged at the beginning of the 1990s. Both Schmidt's (1993a) noticing hypothesis, and Bialystok's (1993) two-dimensional model of L2 proficiency development take a cognitive perspective, and are perfectly compatible as they address different phases of L2 learning. While Schmidt's noticing hypothesis is concerned with the initial phases of L2 learning, Bialystok's model applies to later stages of learning. Schmidt takes up the issue of the role of consciousness in the development of L2 pragmatics, stating that relevant input features have to be noticed, that the learner is consciously aware of them, in order to make them available for further processing.

Evidence for the noticing hypothesis in interlanguage pragmatics comes from a study by DuFon (1999). Her six informants kept a journal over their four month study-abroad experience in Indonesia. All informants commented extensively on address terms and greetings in their journals, which reveal that features of address terms and greetings were noticed. However, there were considerable differences between the learners' level of language production. Whereas one learner made an effort to use the appropriate address term on every occasion, another learner cared much less about the appropriateness of a certain address term. Consequently, this study shows that noticing is a necessary condition but not a guarantee for pragmatic acquisition.

In her two-dimensional model of pragmatic acquisition, Bialystok (1993) claims that learners do on the one hand have to develop representations of pragmatic knowledge, and on the other hand gain control over processing. In Bialystok's view, for children, the primary task is to acquire new representations, whereas adult L2 learners have to "develop the control strategies to attend to the intended interpretations in contexts and to select the forms from the range of possibilities that satisfy the social and contextual needs of the communicative situation" (Bialystok 1993:54).

Empirical evidence supporting Bialystok's two-dimensional model comes from research which demonstrates that adult learners rely strongly on L1 or universal pragmatic knowledge. Such findings show that for adults the task of developing representations[6] of socio-pragmatic and pragma-linguistic knowledge is already largely accomplished. Further support comes from studies showing that accessing the linguistic forms required to formulate a certain speech function requires much time and effort. House (1996), for instance, found that her advanced German EFL learners experienced difficulties with their uptaking and responding behavior. In her analysis, House states that the learners' responding problems cannot be found in deficits in discourse representation but rather in a lack of "control of processing" (p. 249). Gaining expertise in processing pragmatic information easily and quickly in a wide variety of contexts is therefore one of the main learning tasks of adult L2 learners.

The cognitive processing approach has also been the framework for a range of classroom studies on pragmatic instruction. Investigating the effect of implicit vs. explicit teaching, these studies show a clear advantage for explicit teaching, that is the provision of meta-pragmatic information (e.g., House 1996; Tateyama, Kasper, Mui, Tay, & Thananart 1997; cf. also Norris & Ortega's 2000 meta-analysis).

As opposed to the acculturation model and the cognitive processing, socio-cultural theory and language socialization have in common their inter-psychological approach. Arguing that the acquisition of language and culture is not only transmitted, but also created through social interaction in concrete socio-historical contexts, both theories reject the view of creating knowledge as an individual intra-psychological process.

4.3 Socio-cultural theory

According to socio-cultural theory, social interaction between children and adults, or more generally between novices and experts, is not only viewed as a tool for L2 learning but also as a skill in its own right. Therefore, social interaction is learning. A number of studies have shown that the learning opportunities are considerably affected by the interlocutor's way of shaping learners' contributions to the discourse. However, in contrast to Neo-Vygotskyan views of participation and apprenticeship (e.g., Lave & Wenger 1991; Rogoff 1990) which claim that assisted performance requires a more competent and a less competent partner in order for learning to take place, studies by Ohta (1995) and Donato (1994) have demonstrated that both participants can take on alternating roles as expert and novice in the same task. This finding has important implications for L2 learning in the classroom as it highlights the positive role of learner-learner collaboration.

Studies guided by the social interaction theory (e.g., Antón 1999; Hall 1998) have also addressed the learning opportunities in the teacher-fronted Initiation-Response-Follow-up (IRF) classroom, and have found that it is not necessarily the IRF structure which obstructs learning. Hall (1998:308) notes that "rather, it was both the amount

---

6. Cf. Bialystok (1993:49–50) for a detailed discussion of "representation".

and qualitative nature of the opportunities for participation in the exchange that the teacher made available to each of the students".

In sum, then, socio-cultural studies have come to the result that the reservations regarding two forms of classroom structure, namely IRF and NNS-NNS collaboration, are not entirely justified, as it has been shown that both forms of instruction can be extremely fruitful if they offer high-quality opportunities for participation.[7]

4.4 Language socialization

Similar to socio-cultural theory, language socialization views language as the means and one of the goals of socialization (Schieffelin & Ochs 1986). Socialization is seen in concrete activities in which novices interact with experts, and gain socio-cultural knowledge of the concrete activity and society in general through language use in interaction. As opposed to socio-cultural theory, which has a psychological/psycholinguistic orientation, language socialization is anthropologically oriented and, as a consequence, adopts a comparative perspective. Studies on language socialization in adult L2 teaching investigate the teachers' socialization goals, and make explicit comparisons between target practices in different contexts (e.g., Falsgraf & Majors 1995; Poole 1992). Language socialization research on children often has a developmental focus and studies the increasing participation in particular activities (e.g., Kanagy 1999).

Having briefly discussed four theoretical perspectives from which L2 learners' development of pragmatic ability have been studied, we will now consider the relation between these theories. First, it is rather obvious from the characterization of socio-cultural theory and language socialization that these two theories converge in a central point, namely in their close attention to interactional processes and are therefore mutually compatible. The same applies to cognitive processing and the acculturation model which adopt an intra-individual perspective in that they view the creation of knowledge as an individual process. Second, given their conflictive perspectives, theories with an inter-personal orientation on the one hand, and theories with an intra-personal orientation on the other hand, are incommensurable. However, Kasper (2001b: 525) argues that there is a need for both theoretical perspectives in interlanguage pragmatics as they "do not only examine the same object of investigation from different perspectives, but focus on different aspects of a complex research object".

---

7.   For the examination of how Vygotsky's zone of proximal development can be applied to the teaching and learning of interlanguage pragmatics, see Ohta (2005).

5. Research methods

Methodological issues have been addressed extensively in ILP. However, while there is a rather large number of theoretical accounts on data collection methods (Bardovi-Harlig 1999a; Kasper 2000; Kasper & Dahl 1991; Kasper & Rose 2002), the issue of data analyzing methods has been largely neglected (Kasper 1993:53; Warga 2004:11). The reason for this is pointed out by Kasper and Dahl (1991:216):

> [...] data collection is primary in relation to analysis: Not only because it comes prior to analysis in the sequential organization of the research process, but also because it is a more powerful determinant of the final product.

However, in a later article, Kasper (1993:53) acknowledges the importance of dealing with data analyzing issues on a theoretical level:

> It would therefore be helpful if authors reported on solutions to categorization problems in their publications. This would make it easier for other researchers to use existing coding systems consistently, and it would also improve the degree of replicability and comparability of studies. These methodological questions have to be addressed actively before we can expect more reliable results.   [translation mine]

Despite Kasper's exhortation, which dates back to the early 1990s, the ILP literature is practically devoid of studies that address data analyzing issues.[8]

Regarding data collection methods in ILP, much criticism has been voiced in terms of authenticity of the collected material. However, authenticity is only one of the requirements of 'good' data. The other one is the possible control of the contextual variables, such as social distance and dominance, but also age, gender, and so on. As one data collection instrument can never guarantee authenticity and control of the variables at the same time, the researcher faces a dilemma. He or she can either choose an instrument which allows for control but does not produce authentic data, or the other way around. Therefore, as Bardovi-Harlig (1999a:238) puts it: "We need to get away from the best-method mentality, and return to the notion of customizing the research design to fit the question".

---

8. This critique does not apply to the field of L1 pragmatics. In their much-cited publication on pragmatic development in children, Ninio and Snow (1996:15–44) do not only discuss in great detail the limitations of existing coding systems, but also present the advantages of the "Ninio and Wheeler taxonomy", a systematic typology of communicative acts (Ninio & Wheeler 1984). According to the constructivist account of social behavior, talk derives its meaningfulness from having a systematic relationship with the interactive context. Based on the assumption that a finite system of distinct and separate types of social-cognitive concepts underlies utterance meanings, the Ninio and Wheeler taxonomy classifies speech acts based on how an utterance relates to its context. Comparable discussions on data analysis do not exist in interlanguage pragmatics, but see Meier (1998) and Warga (2004:82–86) for some remarks on this issue.

The most commonly used data collection instrument in ILP is the discourse completion task (DCT).[9] It was first used in ILP by Blum-Kulka in 1982, and became popular as the instrument employed in the CCASRP (Cross Cultural Speech Act Realization Project, Blum-Kulka, House, & Kasper 1989) to investigate native and nonnative requests, as well as apologies.

Barron (2003: 83) describes the DCT as "a series of short written role-plays based on everyday situations which are designed to elicit a specific speech act by requiring informants to complete a turn of dialogue for each item". Before each interaction, a short situational description is given. The description is designed to set the general circumstances and the situational parameters (social distance, social dominance, etc.). Respondents are instructed to write down in the space provided below the description what they would say in each respective situation. Here is an example of a DCT item taken from Warga (2004: 272):

> *Dans les jours qui viennent tu dois faire un grand exposé en anglais. Tu as de grandes difficultés avec la préparation. Tout à coup tu te souviens d'une élève de terminale (tu ne la connais pas bien) qui est bilingue. Tu voudrais qu'elle t'aide à préparer ce travail. Cela durerait une après-midi ou deux. Tu sais que cette fille n'a pas beaucoup de temps parce qu'elle doit préparer le bac. Le lendemain tu vas la voir dans la salle de classe et tu dis:*

> 'In the next few days you have to give a presentation in English. You have great difficulties with the preparation. Suddenly, you remember a student (you do not know her well) who is bilingual. You would like her to help you with the preparation of your presentation. That would last one or two afternoons. You know that this girl does not have much time because she has to prepare for her final high-school examinations. The next day you go to see her in her classroom and you say:'

Validation studies investigating method effects between DCTs and other data collection instruments have demonstrated that, when carefully designed, the DCT is a highly effective tool for studying the stereotypical semantic formulas and strategies of speech acts (Beebe & Cummings 1996 [1985]; Eisenstein & Bodman 1993; Hartford & Bardovi-Harlig 1992; Rintell & Mitchell 1989; Sasaki 1998). Moreover, DCTs have been found useful for obtaining information on the speakers' socio-pragmatic knowledge because they allow researchers to keep the speech act constant while varying social variables, such as social distance, social dominance and the degree of imposition. Furthermore, it has been claimed that data elicited by a DCT reflect the content of oral data despite its written form (Rintell & Mitchell 1989: 270).

However, in spite of these numerous advantages, a number of drawbacks need to be borne in mind: First, neither DCTs nor role-plays elicit authentic data. In both cases, the respondents write what they believe they would say in an authentic situation. Furthermore, features related to the dynamics of a conversation, such as turn-taking

---

9.   Due to space restrictions, other data collection instruments such as role-plays, multiple-choice and scaled-response questionnaires are not discussed here. See Bardovi-Harlig (1999a) and Kasper (2000) for more information on these instruments.

and sequencing of action cannot be investigated. All paralinguistic elements (e.g., intonation, volume, speed) and non-verbal elements (e.g., gestures, facial expression, eye movement) are also excluded from investigation given the written character of the DCT. Despite these disadvantages, the DCT has been found to be a very suitable data-gathering instrument when it comes to investigating what learners know, as opposed to what they are able to perform under the demanding conditions of a conversational encounter (Kasper & Rose 2002:96).[10] In other words, it is a suitable instrument for tapping into the learners' competence.

In the last few years, researchers have begun to use the computer as data collection instrument in order to improve the quality of the elicited data. The Multimedia Elicitation Task (MET) (Schauer 2004), for example, is a computer-based production questionnaire focusing on requests. While providing rich audiovisual context information through a computerized presentation format, the MET is designed to ensure equal conditions for every participant. Moreover, the instrument elicits oral rather than written data. It can be assumed that instruments of this type will be further developed in the next years, and that data collected through such an instrument will be of higher quality than those produced by the 'classic' DCT.

From L2 acquisition research, ILP has inherited the practice of collecting three sets of data, namely data from: (a) Native speakers of the target language; (b) Learners of the target language; (c) Native speakers of the learners' first language (Selinker 1972). The comparison of these three sets of data makes it possible for the researcher to identify learner specific linguistic behavior. However, this methodology has been criticized for assuming implicitly that the linguistic performance of the native speakers of the target language represents the prescriptive norm against which the learners' performance is to be measured (cf. House & Kasper 2000). House and Kasper (2000:112–114) cite ten reasons why the communicative practices of native speakers are a questionable norm for learners. Three of these reasons are: (1) Given the multitude of language varieties (e.g., Standard French vs. *Québécois* French), it is difficult to choose which variety should be adopted as the norm; (2) Communication among native speakers is often partial, ambiguous and fraught with misunderstandings; (3) Opting for partial divergence from the L2 community, learners may not aim at adopting the pragmatic norms of the L2.

Consequently, it has been suggested that intelligibility among educated native and nonnative speakers of English, French or Spanish is a more realistic aim than pushing L2 learners of English, French or Spanish to sound like native speakers from Great Britain, France or Spain (Kasper 1997).

However, even if the concept of native speaker norm needs to be reconsidered for pedagogical purposes, the adoption of a native speaker norm against which the learner's competence can be measured continues to be appropriate in empirical research. In the next section, we will adopt this perspective of considering the native

---

10. For a summary of the strengths and weaknesses of DCTs, see Beebe and Cummings (1996).

speaker pragmatic behavior as norm to expose and discuss the pragmatic differences between native speakers and L2 learners.

6.   Differences between native speakers and learners

Bardovi-Harlig (2001: 14–20) identifies four main categories of differences between native speakers and learners: (1) Choice of speech acts: Learners may choose a different speech act than native speakers in the same context, or they may prefer not to perform the speech act at all. Bardovi-Harlig and Hartford (1993) found, for example, that in authentic academic advising sessions, learners produced more rejections whereas native speakers used more suggestions. For both groups of students, the aim of their utterances was the same, namely gaining control over the course schedule; (2) Choice of semantic formulas: Learners and native speakers may also differ in their choice of semantic formulas, that is in the strategies that can be used to perform a certain speech act. For instance, many studies found that learners show a tendency to use more direct strategies than native speakers (Billmyer & Varghese 2000; Hill 1997; Kasper 1981; Rose 2000; Yu 1999); (3) Choice of content: A third way in which learners and native speakers may differ is the choice of content.[11] Hartford and Bardovi-Harlig (1992) observed, for example, that native speakers and learners used different content with the same semantic formula, namely that of grounder.[12] For instance, whereas learners gave reasons such as "The course is too difficult, or too easy, or uninteresting", the native speakers avoided this kind of face-threatening reasons and invented other reasons for rejecting the course; (4) Form: Learners may also differ from their native speaker counterparts regarding the form, that is grammatical and lexical modification devices. As far as the most frequent request strategy is concerned, the query preparatory, Warga (2004: 156–160) observed in her DCT data that native speaker query preparatories were hardly ever used without any downtoning element. Usually, the native speaker query preparatories were downtoned using a *conditionnel* in (3) or an *imparfait* in (4):

(3)   *Tu pourrais* [conditional form] *m'aider à rattraper mes cours?*[13]
      'Could you help me to catch up with the material from class?'

(4)   *Je me demandais* [past tense form] *si tu pouvais m'aider.*
      'I was wondering whether you could help me'

---

11.   Bardovi-Harlig (2001: 18) explains the difference between semantic formula and content as follows: "Whereas a semantic formula names the type of information given, content refers to the specific information given by a speaker".

12.   A grounder is a supportive move by which the speaker gives reasons, explanations, or justifications for his or her potentially face-threatening speech act (cf. Blum-Kulka, House, & Kasper 1989: 287).

13.   The examples are presented as they appeared on the questionnaires. No orthographical, morphological, syntactical or other errors were corrected for either the native speaker or learner data.

By contrast, the learners' query preparatories contained considerably less conditional and past tense forms.

(5)   *Est-ce que vous **pouvez** [indicative form] corriger mon travail bientôt?*
      'Can you mark my paper as soon as possible?'

(6)   *Peut-être que tu **peux** [indicative form] m'aider *au week-end.*
      'You can probably help me over the week-end'

ILP has become a well-established discipline in the last twenty-five years or so, and despite the large number of existing ILP studies, many research questions have not even been touched upon. One important reason for this is that mainstream ILP is characterized by very homogeneous studies:

–   Most studies have investigated second – not foreign – language learners.[14]
–   Almost all studies have examined college/university students between 20 and 25 years of age.
–   In many studies, only one data collection instrument has been used, predominantly the discourse completion test.
–   Most studies have focused on L2 use rather than acquisition.
–   The majority of the research carried out has been limited to English as the target language.

Two of these under-researched areas, acquisitional pragmatics and French ILP, will be discussed in the following sections.

7.   Acquisitional pragmatics

As opposed to developmental pragmatics, a branch of developmental psychology and first language acquisition research which has always put the focus on the development of the pragmatic competence in children (Ninio & Snow 1996), ILP has long been "fundamentally not acquisitional" (Bardovi-Harlig 1999b: 679). The research gap for acquisitional research was first pointed out by Kasper (1992: 204). Later on, other researchers made similar claims (Bardovi-Harlig 1999b; Kasper 1998a; Kasper & Blum-Kulka 1993; Kasper & Rose 1999; Kasper & Schmidt 1996), but despite an upsurge in developmental studies at the beginning of the 21st century (Achiba 2003; Barron 2003; Martínez Flor 2004; Rose 2000; Schauer 2004; Warga 2004), L2 pragmatic development is still an under-researched area.

---

14.   In this chapter, a clear distinction between second and foreign language acquisition/learning will be made. If the L2 is learned in a target language environment mainly through direct communication (but also through instruction), the term second language acquisition will be used. If, however, the L2 is learned in an L1 environment mainly through instruction, the term foreign language learning will be used.

Regarding methodology, acquisitional research can be conducted through cross-sectional or longitudinal studies. In contrast to the studies of pragmatic competence in children, which have been predominantly longitudinal, the majority of ILP studies have used a cross-sectional design. Reasons for that are not only that longitudinal studies are time-consuming, but also because it may be difficult to keep the same participants over the length of the study.[15]

In a much-cited publication which intended "to profile interlanguage pragmatics (ILP) as an area of inquiry in L2 acquisition research", Kasper and Schmidt (1996: 149) asked fourteen guiding questions about ILP. Three of them have been particularly influential for the constitution of L2 pragmatics as an issue of L2 development:[16]

- Does the L1 influence L2 learning (discussed in 7.1)
- Is there a natural route of development, as evidenced by difficulty, accuracy, acquisition orders, or discrete stages of development? (discussed in 7.2)
- Does instruction make a difference? (discussed in 7.3)

The next three sections (7.1, 7.2, 7.3) are devoted to the discussion of these guiding questions.

7.1 Pragmatic transfer

Pragmatic transfer may be defined as "the influence exerted by learners' pragmatic knowledge of languages and cultures other than L2 on their comprehension, production and learning of L2 pragmatic information" (Kasper 1992: 207). Pragmatic transfer can operate on different levels, namely on the pragmalinguistic or on the sociopragmatic level depending on whether it concerns primarily the linguistic or the sociological side of pragmatics (Leech 1988 [1983]). Moreover, transfer can be divided into positive and negative transfer: As Kasper (1992: 210) points out, "transfer resulting in IL outcomes consistent with L2 patterns (positive transfer)" has hardly been investigated up to now. This is presumably due to methodological difficulties: It is impossible to differentiate between positive pragmatic transfer on the one hand, and universal pragmatic knowledge or generalization from already existing interlanguage pragmatic knowledge on the other hand. Unlike positive transfer, negative transfer has been studied extensively (e.g., Cohen 1997; Hill 1997; Takahashi & Beebe 1987; Warga 2004). The reason for this is that negative transfer is more visible as it results in deviation from the L2 norm.

---

15.   See Hoffman-Hicks (1999: 273–276) on measures one may take to minimize the attrition of subjects.

16.   The other questions refer to issues such as the universals of language underlying cross-linguistic variation, potential advantages of children over adults in L2 learning, the type of input, motivation, personality, learners' gender, and chunk learning.

The relationship between transfer and development is addressed by Takahashi and Beebe (1987) who proposed the hypothesis that pragmatic transfer from the first language correlates positively with the proficiency in the target language. In other words, according to the so-called 'positive correlation hypothesis', less proficient learners are less likely to transfer from their L1 than more proficient learners who already have at their disposal the linguistic resources in the target language in order to transfer. Support for Takahashi and Beebe's (1987) hypothesis comes from Cohen (1997), Hill (1997), and Warga (2004).[17]

However, Maeshiba, Yoshinaga, Kasper and Ross (1996) do not lend support to the 'positive correlation hypothesis'. Investigating the production of apologies by two proficiency groups of Japanese learners of English, one group of NSs of English and one group of NSs of Japanese, Maeshiba et al. (1996) found that the more proficient learners showed less negative and more positive transfer than the latter.

How could one explain the different outcomes of these studies? One possible explanation is that the relationship between transfer and proficiency depends on the environment in which the language is learned. It is striking that the participants in the studies providing support to the 'positive correlation hypothesis' are all foreign language learners (Cohen 1997; Hill 1997; Warga 2004) whereas the participants in Maeshiba et al.'s (1996) study are L2 learners. The role of the environment for the amount of pragmatic transfer needs further investigation, but it is rather plausible that pragmatic transfer decreases in the speech of L2 learners who have ample opportunities for participating and obtaining L2 pragmatic input in different types of authentic discourse, and that it increases in the speech of foreign language learners who do not have access to the same range and amount of pragmatic input.

It has been claimed in the literature that more research needs to be done in the field of transferability of pragmatic aspects, that is the conditions of transfer (how, why, when?) and its interaction with other factors (e.g., Kasper & Schmidt 1996). However, to the best of my knowledge, Takahashi (1996) is the only ILP study focusing explicitly on transferability.

Finally, when discussing pragmatic transfer issues, one should keep in mind that (negative) transfer results in differences from the target language but that it does not necessarily lead to miscommunication. More research is clearly needed in the area of the communicative effects of negative pragmatic transfer. For instance, Carroll (1987) found evidence of different socio-cultural rules in greeting and leave-taking behavior of French people and Americans. Based on this study, it would be interesting to examine what happens when American learners of French transfer their American way of greeting and leave-taking into French. Studying the communicative effects of such non-target like production in terms of politeness, (mis)understanding and so on, would be of particular interest.

---

17. Interestingly enough, Takahashi and Beebe's (1987) own study did not support their hypothesis.

7.2 Developmental path

A second central question asked in Kasper and Schmidt (1996) concerns the developmental path of pragmatic competence in L2. Despite more than two decades of research in the field of ILP and despite a recent upsurge of acquisitional studies, little is known about the road to L2 pragmatic competence.

In a volume focusing on L2 pragmatic development, Kasper and Rose (2002:140) propose five developmental stages of request development in an L2: Pre-basic, formulaic, unpacking, pragmatic expansion and fine-tuning.[18] It could be argued that the studies on which the stages have been developed, are based on very few cases (Achiba 2003: n = 1; Ellis 1992: n = 2; Schmidt 1983: n = 1), and that consequently, the results cannot be generalized. However, given the fact that the participants in these studies differ considerably in terms of L1 backgrounds (same in Schmidt and Achiba, different in Ellis), age, gender, L2 proficiency, social situation and context of observation, it is quite impressive that their requests display a common developmental pattern.

Regarding further speech acts, such as apologies, expressions of gratitude, and refusals, for instance, no such developmental stages have been proposed so far. However, this is not surprising as the bulk of studies has always centered on requests. Consequently, the next step must be to delineate the developmental trajectories of each speech act separately. Once robust speech act specific sequences have been established, researchers can examine whether there are more abstract developmental principles underlying the substantive differences.

There is another area of pragmatic competence, namely that of pragmatic routines, where developmental stages have been proposed. With respect to the role of routines, a growing body of research suggests that routines play a major role not only in language production, but also in language acquisition (Kecskes 2003; Warga 2005; Wray 2002) because they not only promote people's feelings of belonging to a socio-cultural group, but also allow speakers to greatly accelerate the planning of their consecutive conversational moves (Coulmas 1981). The development of routines was among others investigated by Bahns, Burmeister and Vogel (1986:719f.), as well as Kecskes (1999:304) who proposes a three-stage development: First, the routines are transferred from L1; second, the routines are used creatively which often results in linguistically incorrect and/or pragmatically inadequate utterances; third, the routines are used in accordance with the target language.[19] Whether routines contribute to the

---

18.   The identification of the five stages is based on Achiba (2003), Ellis (1992) and Schmidt (1983). The authors do not mention Schmidt [1983] in the title of the table. However, it is clear from the context that the five stages have been developed on the basis of all three studies.

19.   However, Barron (2003:239–240) reports that although most developments regarding pragmatic routines were progressive, such as the decrease in the use of "*Ich wundere mich...*" 'I am surprised...', a non-L2-like literal translation of "I wonder...", there were also instances where the use of pragmatic routines did not move in the direction of the target language norm.

mastery of rule-based individual stretches of speech or not is still a matter of discussion (see Wray 2000 for an overview).

Two more observations regarding pragmatic development are in order. First, just as in developmental pragmatics, it has been found in ILP that learners do not develop the same competence level in all speech acts within the same amount of time. Competence in some speech acts may develop relatively slower or faster as compared to other speech acts (e.g., Barron 2003; Trosborg 1995). Barron (2003: 250), for example, found that her learners were more advanced in realizing requests than in realizing refusals. She ascribes the different competence levels according to speech act types to the rather routinized head-act form of requests, to the learners' familiarity with the speech act of request, and to the low cognitive complexity of requests as initiating move.[20]

A second finding which can be generalized is the non-linear character of L2 pragmatic development. Several studies have found that even if many of the learners' pragmatic developments move in the direction of the target language norm, there are also developments which reveal the opposite trend, that is, developments away from the target language norm (e.g., Barron 2003; Hill 1997; Warga 2004). Warga (2004: 150–152), for instance, found that the number of query preparatory-strategies (e.g., *Pourriez-vous...?* 'could you') increased continually, moving in the direction of the French native speaker norm. However, closer examination revealed that the development regarding the distribution of two query-preparatory substrategies (simple vs. combined)[21] was regressive. While the less advanced learners showed, just as the French native speakers, a clear tendency towards using the simple query preparatory (cf. (7)), the more advanced learners tended to opt for the combined query preparatory (cf. (8)), a strategy rarely found in the French data. One possible reason for instances of regressive development is the growth of transfer as proficiency increases (Takahashi & Beebe 1987; cf. 6.1 for further details).

(7) *Est-ce que vous pouvez corriger mon travail bientôt?* (LNI)
     'Can you mark my paper as soon as possible?'

(8) *Je voulais te demander si tu pouvais m'aider.* (LNIII)
     'I wanted to ask you whether you could help me'

Let us now turn to the third guiding question, namely the role of instruction in pragmatics.

---

20. It has been argued that responding speech acts are cognitively more complex than initiating acts as the former require not only full concentration on the speaker's own imminent utterance but also on the interlocutor's preceding utterance (House 1997). Moreover, observational and self-report evidence attests to the *social* difficulty that interlocutors often experience when refusing a co-participant's proposed course of action.

21. A simple query preparatory is an utterance which consists of a query preparatory strategy (cf. (7)). A combined query preparatory is a combination of a performative and a query preparatory (cf. (8)).

7.3 Instruction

Studies from SLA research have shown that instruction has positive outcomes on acquisition in terms of: (1) SLA processes; (2) SLA route; (3) SLA rate; and (4) level of ultimate SL attainment (Long 1983, 1988; cf. Doughty 2003; Ellis 1994:611–663; Norris & Ortega 2000 for an overview). Regarding the relationship between instruction and pragmatic competence, there has been a growing interest in this subject since the beginning of the 1990s.[22]

As mentioned in Section 4, research has identified a number of areas where learners differ considerably from native speakers in their pragmatic competence. This seems to be particularly true for foreign language learners who have only limited access to authentic pragmatic input in the target language, and lack the opportunities to be engaged in genuine communication in the target language. It is well-documented that teacher-fronted classroom discourse displays a narrow range of speech acts, a lack of politeness markings, a limited range of gambits used for turn-taking and politeness marking, and shorter and less complex openings and closings (Kasper 1997). The latest textbooks contain pragmatic information but it has been found that there is often a mismatch between textbook dialogues and authentic discourse (Kasper 1997). For this reason, it is essential to create the conditions that would allow the learners to develop their pragmatic competence. As Kasper (2001a) notes, an L2 setting offers more advantages than a foreign language context for developing pragmatic competence. However, depending on the quantity and quality of contact with the target language community, pragmatic instruction may be useful in both the foreign language and the L2 environment.

Having demonstrated that learners do not (always) develop a satisfactory pragmatic competence on their own, and that pragmatic instruction might therefore be useful, we will now turn to the question of whether such instruction is actually possible and effective. In her overview, Kasper (2001a) discusses classroom-based studies investigating pragmatic learning. In doing so, she distinguishes between observational and interventional studies, the former not being specifically arranged for research purposes, the latter being designed for experimental research.

The observational studies with a developmental focus[23] are all longitudinal case studies based on participant and nonparticipant observation and self-study diaries (e.g., Cohen 1997; Ellis 1992; Kanagy & Igarashi 1997). One of the findings of these studies is the limitation of teacher-fronted teaching for pragmatic learning. According to these studies, priority should be given to peer interaction. However, there are also

---

22. See Kasper (2001a) and Rose (2005) for an overview of studies on pragmatic instruction. For a recent collection of papers on pragmatics in instructed language learning, see Alcón Soler and Martínez Flor (2005).

23. The first observational studies focused on pragmatic use rather than development and are therefore not discussed here. Cf. Kasper (2001a: 34–40) for an overview of non-developmental classroom-based research.

contradictory findings from recent studies which give rise to a re-evaluation of the teacher-fronted Initiation-Response-Follow-up (IRF) routine. Hall (1998), for example, suggests that if the students' opportunities for participation are carefully planned, an IRF routine can be beneficial for the learners' pragmatic competence.

Interventional studies usually adopt a pretest-posttest design. However, as Kasper (2001a:57) notes critically, very few studies include a delayed posttest, and studies comparing different experimental teaching approaches often lack the control group which does not receive particular pragmatic treatment.

Many interventional studies focus on a comparison between approaches including explicit metapragmatic instruction (explicit instruction), and those where a rich amount of pragmatic input and abundant practice opportunities are offered but no meta-pragmatic instruction is given (implicit instruction)[24] (e.g., Alcón Soler 2005; House 1996; Koike & Pearson 2005; Martínez Flor 2004; Martínez Flor & Fukuya 2005; Rose & Ng 2001; Takahashi 2001; Tateyama 2001; Tateyama et al. 1997; Wildner-Bassett 1984, 1986).

In sum, studies investigating the teachability of pragmatic aspects have shown that a range of different features, such as discourse markers, gambits, pragmatic routines, pragmatic comprehension, and a variety of speech acts can be taught successfully. As far as different teaching approaches are concerned, it has been found that explicit instruction is more effective than the implicit variant (e.g., House 1996; Tateyama et al. 1997; but see also Koike & Pearson 2005 for a more differentiated result). However, *contra* earlier research, Martínez Flor (2004) comes to the conclusion that both teaching conditions, explicit and implicit, are equally effective in developing learners' pragmatic ability when properly implemented. Martínez Flor (2004:295) attributes this conflicting result to the fact that she has employed a systematic combination of two implicit techniques, namely input enhancement and recasts, which was not the case in the previous studies.

Some pedagogical implications can be derived from the results of the research on pragmatic development in the classroom so far. First, research has shown that integrating pragmatic instruction in the L2 classroom considerably improves the learners' pragmatic competence (e.g., Alcón Soler 2005; Koike & Pearson 2005; Lyster 1994; Martínez Flor 2004; Martínez Flor & Fukuya 2005; Yoshimi 2001). Bearing this in mind, it seems essential to cease relegating pragmatic instruction to a second-best slot in the lesson plan to be included only if there is time at the end of the class. On the contrary, pragmatic instruction has to begin as early as the level of primary or the beginning of secondary education. This is particularly relevant for foreign language learners.

Second, in order to raise learners' pragmatic awareness of pragma-linguistic and socio-pragmatic features of the target language, it has been claimed that it is fun-

---

24. Kasper and Rose (2002:263) note that the operationalization of the constructs 'explicit' vs. 'implicit' varies from study to study.

damental to bring relevant authentic input into the classroom (e.g., by means of videotaping authentic conversation, using scenes from films or sitcoms).

Third, concerning the aim of improving learners' productive competence, it has been found useful to reduce teacher-fronted instruction and to increase student-centered activities in order to create opportunities for communicative practice.[25] However, this may not be enough, as conversation alone does not guarantee that students practice a wide variety of speech acts and conversational routines. It therefore seems to be essential to include activities, such as drama, simulations and role-play, so that a wide range of speech acts may be practiced (Kasper 1997).

Fourth, studies have shown that the acquisition of pragmatic competence can be improved by consciousness-raising techniques, such as giving learners meta-pragmatic information (House 1996: 250) or, as shown in Martínez Flor's (2004) study, by using a combination of input enhancements and recasts.[26] As a consequence, there is an urgent need for teaching materials (particularly in French), that provide explicit information about, for example, requesting appropriately.

In terms of future research, more data-based studies are needed in order to examine foreign language learners' ability to perform speech acts in French. It is, however, equally important to adapt teaching materials to the conversational needs of foreign language learners, as well as to teach students the performance of speech acts, such as requests, complaints and apologies, from the beginning of their learning.

After presenting the theoretical underpinnings and outlining the discipline of interlanguage pragmatics, the first part of this chapter has focused on acquisitional research within ILP. In doing so, special emphasis has been given to the discussion of three particularly important issues for the constitution of ILP as a research field in SLA, namely pragmatic transfer, developmental path, and instruction. In the second part of this chapter, we shift our focus from general to French L2 pragmatics. As with general ILP, the perspective will be an acquisitional one. Consequently, the themes discussed will cover the developmental path, the role of instruction, formulaic language and pragmatic transfer.

8.   Empirical focus on French

8.1 Literature review

Table 1 shows that, contrary to ILP studies with different target languages, the bulk of French studies is acquisitional in nature. Only one out of five studies, namely Kraft

---

25.   Recent findings suggest, however, that the IRF structure can also promote certain areas of pragmatic development (e.g., Hall 1998).

26.   There is a vast literature on various types of recasts, input enhancement, etc. (e.g., Ayoun 2001, 2004; Doughty & Williams 1998; Gascoigne 2003; Leeman 2003; Spada 1997).

Table 1. Interlanguage pragmatic studies with L2 French (FL=foreign language)

Study	Pragmatic feature	Data	Informants	L1	Time frame
Hoffman-Hicks (1999)	greetings and leave-takings, compliments	dialogue completion task; case studies: authentic data, open role play	study abroad students (n = 14), NS of French (n = 25), non-study abroad students (n = 10)	English	longitudinal, 16 months
Kraft and Geluykens (2002)	complaint	Discourse Completion Task	LN (n = 87), NS of French (n = 81), NS of German (n = 84)	German	not acquisitional
Liddicoat and Crozet (2001)	responding to *T'as passé un bon week-end?*	open role play	second-year university-level French students (n = 10)	English	longitudinal, 1 year
Lyster (1994)	*tu/vous*, conditional, politeness expressions/ questions, polite closings	written and oral production test, multiple choice test	grade 8 French immersion students (n = 106), NSs (n = 81)	English	longitudinal; 11 weeks
Warga (2004, 2005)	request	Discourse Completion Task and closed role play	LNI (n = 27), LNII (n = 27), LNIII (n = 30), NS of French (n = 45), NS of German (n = 20)	German	cross-sectional

and Geluykens (2002), takes a single moment perspective. Moreover, it is striking to note that the longitudinal studies outweigh the cross-sectional ones. This is in clear contrast to what has been observed in ILP (e.g., Bardovi-Harlig 1999b). Regarding the participants' age, it is noticeable that two out of the five studies, namely Lyster (1994) and Warga (2004), consider school-aged participants. This is noteworthy as a lack of research for participants at school age has been pointed out (e.g., Warga 2004). The participants' L1 background in the French studies is either German (Kraft & Geluykens 2002; Warga 2004) or English (Hoffman-Hicks 1999; Liddicoat & Crozet 2001; Lyster 1994). As far as the data collection instrument is concerned, Table 1 shows that all studies but one, Liddicoat and Crozet (2001), use variants of the DCT. This is in line with research on target languages other than French. However, only one study, Kraft and Geluykens (2002), does not use oral data elicitation instruments. This is because three of the French studies combine different data elicitation methods (Hoffman-Hicks 1999; Lyster 1994; Warga 2004).[27]

---

27. This so-called "triangulation of data" has many advantages, such as the reduction of any possible task-bias (Kasper 1998b: 105).

Having identified relevant themes in the previous section, namely developmental patterns in SL pragmatics with or without instruction, formulaic language and transfer, we will now examine what the French studies have to say about them.

8.1.1 *Developmental patterns without instruction*
The only studies on L2 French addressing the question of developmental patterns without specific pragmatic instruction are those by Hoffman-Hicks (1999) and Warga (2004).

Hoffman-Hicks (1999) investigated American learners' French pragmatic development during the course of a study abroad experience in Strasbourg, France. Pragmatic development is examined through the learners' production of the conversational functions of greetings and leave-takings, as well as through the speech act of compliment. The objective of the study was to determine whether, and to what extent, the study abroad students show approximation to native speaker norms over time. Data were collected from fourteen students over a period of sixteen months. The subjects ranged in age from 19 to 21. In addition, ten students who did not participate in the study abroad program but were enrolled in third- and fourth-year French courses at Indiana University served as a control group. All participants had begun their study of French prior to university-level, and averaged between seven and eight years of study. French baseline data were also collected from native speakers of French.

Learner data were collected through a dialogue construction task:[28] (1) Prior to the study abroad experience; (2) Early in the study abroad experience; (3) At the end of their study abroad program. The construction task was open-ended, without any prompts or rejoinders to constrain or guide the response. In the questionnaire, participants were asked to provide a complete dialogue, rather than a one-sided response to the various items. Participants were also offered the choice to opt out of responding if they felt they would not say something in that situation in real life. The questionnaire included 24 items. The three acts investigated – compliments, greetings and leave-takings – were equally represented with eight situations each.

For analysis, all responses were systematically analyzed for both content and form. Each response was broken down into meaningful elements which were coded following a detailed coding scheme. In order to examine development over time, the data had to be analyzed to determine the group's progress from the Time 1 of the administration of the questionnaire to Time 2, and, again, to Time 3. The learners' responses were compared with those of the native speakers which served as the norm. Finally, their performance was also compared to those learners who did not spend a year abroad in France.

---

28. The primary data collection instrument for the study was a production questionnaire. In addition, a series of additional questionnaires was administered to the respondents. Finally, the researcher conducted retrospective interviews with the respondents.

Quantitative and qualitative analyses revealed that study abroad students progressed pragmatically during the sixteen months of the study. However, Hoffman-Hicks (1999: 256) points out that "their development was generally slight and limited in scope". This applies particularly to the compliments which remained quite different from the French native speaker compliments. Regarding the structure and the content of compliments, the study abroad students continued to follow American English norms. As expected, more significant development was observed in the analysis of greeting and leave-taking data than in the compliment data. After only a few months in the target culture, the students improved significantly their use of discourse particles, votive expressions, and other formulaic speech. For instance, discourse particles were absent in the Time 1 responses provided by nonnative speakers. However, beginning at Time 2, the experimental subject group showed an increased use and expanded range of French discourse particles. Not only *bon* et *alors*, but also *(eh) ben, bon ben, écoute, allez, bon alors* occurred in the experimental subject data beginning at Time 2 and continuing to Time 3 (ibid.: 168–175). Here is an example of a Time 3 dialogue showing that discourse particles were incorporated in the response:

(9) Moi: *Ben, ça c'est mon train. Merci de m'avoir accompagné. T'es vraiment un pote. Je t'enverrai des cartes postales.*

     Lui: *Alors, bonnes vacances. Salut.*

     Moi: *Salut.*

     Me: *Well,* that's my train. Thanks for coming with me. You're really a buddy. I'll send you post cards.

     Lui (sic)   *Well,* have a good vacation. Bye.

     Me: Bye.   (Hoffman-Hicks 1999: 173)

In short, then, although the gains they made were not spectacular, they performed in a more native-like fashion in the questionnaires at Time 2 and Time 3 than the nonnative speaker control group did. In other words, the experimental group clearly made improvements their colleagues who stayed at home did not make.

Warga (2004) investigated the effect of increasing proficiency on the pragmatic development of Austrian learners of French as a foreign language. A combined data elicitation technique (discourse completion task and closed role play) was used to compare the requests of three levels of Austrian learners of French (n = 84), native speakers of French (n = 45), and native speakers of Austrian German (n = 20), all high school students. The data were analysed using an adapted version of the Cross Cultural Speech Act Realization Project (CCSARP, Blum-Kulka et al. 1989; cf. 8.2 for more detailed presentation of the methodology).

The quantitative and qualitative findings revealed that increasing proficiency does not necessarily lead to a higher level of pragmatic competence, except in the case of specific aspects of requesting behavior, such as internal modification. Interestingly, however, pragmatic transfer from Austrian German into the foreign language was found to increase with proficiency (cf. 8.2 for further discussion of this study).[29]

8.1.2 *Developmental patterns with instruction*

Turning from the investigation of pragmatic development without instruction to the investigation of developmental patterns with instruction, we will discuss two studies on L2 French, namely those by Liddicoat and Crozet (2001) and Lyster (1994).

Liddicoat and Crozet (2001) investigated the acquisition of French interactional norms through instruction. Previous cross-cultural research has shown that the question "Did you have a good weekend?/*T'as passé un bon week-end?*" initiates in Australian English "a ritualistic exchange which forms a part of a greeting sequence on Mondays" (p. 128), whereas, in French culture, it gives rise to a "specific talk about a specific occasion between specific interlocutors" (p. 130). This study thus focused on the effects of instruction Australian learners of French as a foreign language received about how to respond to a question about a weekend.

Participants in this study were ten Australian university students who had completed one year of study of French. Data were collected prior to instruction, immediately after instruction (10 weeks later), and approximately one year after having completed instruction, using an open role-play. The instructional treatment consisted of four phases, namely awareness raising, narrative reconstruction, production, and feedback. The features examined in the open role-plays included those relating to the content of talk (e.g., question leads directly to talk on topic, detail, lively/dramatic) and to those relating to the form of talk (feedback, repetition, overlap) (p. 133). The analysis of these features is based on a comparison of the role-plays at Time 1, 2, and 3 of data collection.

Liddicoat and Crozet found that it was possible to acquire interactional norms in a foreign language context where there are fewer opportunities for exposure to authentic pragmatic input. In particular, elements related to the content side of talk were shown to be more amenable to teaching in a language classroom than elements related to the language form of talk. For instance, regarding content, the role-plays immediately after instruction clearly differed from those before instruction in terms of formulaicity: After instruction, the dialogues had become considerably longer, and this difference in length is due to the fact that the conversation had moved away from the status of formulaic insofar as the weekend had become the topic of talk (see Appendix for an extract of the conversation).

Lyster (1994) is another study on pragmatic development with instruction. Situated at the interface of pragmatics and sociolinguistics, this study investigated the

---

29. The analysis involves both quantitative and qualitative aspects. For the quantitative analysis, descriptive statistics are employed in the presentation of results. However, it was not possible to submit the data to rigorous quantitative comparisons as the study includes a number of rather close detailed analyses. Consequently, the instances of one type of strategy in one group may be rather small and do not always permit statistical analyses.

effect of instruction on aspects of French immersion students' pragmatic and soci-olinguistic competence (*tu/vous*, conditional, politeness expressions/questions, polite closings). Using three types of data collection materials – a written production test, an oral production test, and a multiple choice test, in a pre-test, immediate post-test and delayed post-test design – Lyster found that the experimental classes performed signif-icantly differently from comparison classes over time, regarding the variation of their language between formal and informal situation. More precisely, the results indicate that instruction improved the students' pragmatic and sociolinguistic competence by significantly increasing their ability to: (1) Appropriately and accurately use *vous* in formal situations; (2) Use polite closings in formal letters (only in the short run); and (3) Recognize contextually appropriate language.

Lyster concludes that instruction focusing on the above mentioned pragmatic/so-ciolinguistic features is effective. Based on his findings, he suggests that improvement is more likely in the case of explicit than implicit instruction. However, he also points out that the features examined may be successfully taught only to a certain degree (p. 281).

Regarding pragmatic development with or without instruction, the review has shown that all but one study note a progressive development towards the French prag-matic norm. However, these studies also indicate that not all elements can equally suc-cessfully be learned. Thus Hoffman-Hicks (1999) and Liddicoat and Crozet (2001) in particular emphasize that important pragmatic aspects have not been learned. Warga (2004) differs from the other studies insofar as her learners did not make considerable progressive developments in the course of the study. Rather, her learners showed an in-crease in transfer from L1 German with higher proficiency levels. The fact that Warga (2004) is the only study in a foreign language context with no pragmatic instruction for the learners explains at least to some extent the divergent result (cf. 8.2 for a further discussion of this study).

8.1.3 *Formulaic language*

Several studies have examined implicitly or explicitly the role of formulaic language in L2 pragmatic competence. Hoffman-Hicks (1999) observed that the learners' ten-dency towards verbosity was particularly striking in her data. For instance, by Time 3, the experimental group's responses were longer than the native speaker responses in seven out of the eight scenarios. In three of them, the responses were substan-tially longer by up to 17 words (p. 118–119). A closer analysis revealed that this could be attributed to an overuse of terms of address, such as *Madame/Monsieur*, and to longer and creatively constructed expressions where native speakers would use shorter formulaic routines.

A similar observation was made by Kraft and Geluykens (2002) who investigated the speech act of complaint in nonnative and native French from a non-developmental perspective. DCT data were elicited from 87 German learners of French, 81 native speakers of French, and 84 native speakers of German. Similar to Hoffman-Hicks (1999), Kraft and Geluykens found significantly longer complaints in the learner data than in the NS data. The authors explain this observation by stating that learners seem to be aware of their shortcoming in realizing accurate and appropriate complaints and try therefore to compensate for this by using repetitions and variations of strategies (p. 235).

A third study considering formulaic sequences was conducted by Warga (2005). Based on the corpus elicited in Warga (2004), it was found that learners use formulaic sequences significantly less frequently in request-closings than native speakers. Moreover, the data demonstrate that learners employ complex, situation-specific request-closings as a strategy to compensate for their lack of appropriate formulaic sequences. For example, native speakers offer a reward, so to speak, by saying in very general terms *Je te rendrai ça* 'I will make it up to you'. In exactly the same situation, learners, on the other hand, have been found to produce utterances such as *En contrepartie, je t'aiderai avec l'interrogation en maths* 'In return, I will help you with your math test' (p. 67).

Regarding formulaic language, the review has demonstrated that learners are very often not familiar with the appropriate formulaic sequences for expressing a communicative intent. Instead, learners have been shown to use creatively constructed and situation-specific expressions in order to compensate for this shortcoming. The learners' verbosity is a consequence of this behavior.[30]

8.1.4 *Transfer*

Although transfer has not been an explicit research question in the French ILP literature, it plays an important role in most of the studies. Thus Liddicoat and Crozet (2001) found that their participants transferred the formulaic character of the response to a question about the weekend from L1 Australian English to L2 French. As mentioned above, Warga (2004) found in her study that more advanced learners showed a stronger tendency to transfer request strategies from their L1 German than less advanced learners. In contrast to these studies, Kraft and Geluykens (2002:241) conclude in their analysis of learner complaints that the differences between learners and native speakers cannot be attributed to transfer from L1 German. However, they point out that their complaint data revealed some occurrences of the rather unidiomatic use of *pardon* 'pardon me', an apology which is not used at all by the French native speakers in the study (p. 239). *Pardon* is an expression which is also used in German for apologizing. Consequently, there is reason to believe that the use of *pardon* is indeed a transfer from L1 German.

This short overview has demonstrated that transfer from L1 does play an important role in pragmatic development. It has been shown that transfer not only operates at the speech act strategy level, but also at the level of interactional norms. More research in the area of transfer at the level of discourse is urgently needed.

Despite the small number of studies on French ILP to date, the findings of the present literature review would seem to be in line with previous research on ILP deal-

---

30.   In ILP, this so-called "waffle phenomenon" has been a well-known feature of learner language for a rather long time (e.g., Blum-Kulka & Olshtain 1986; Edmondson & House 1991).

ing with other L2s: Hoffman-Hicks (1999), Liddicoat and Crozet (2001), and Lyster (1994) found that learners' pragmatic competence can be improved by either pragmatic instruction or a study abroad program. This finding corroborates similar ILP studies investigating languages other than French (e.g., Barron 2003 for German,[31] and Martínez Flor 2004 for English). Moreover, in Lyster's (1994) study, explicit instruction turned out to be more effective than implicit instruction. Similar results can be found in studies focusing on L2s other than French (e.g., House 1996 for English; Tateyama et al. 1997, for Japanese, but cf. Martínez Flor 2004 [English] for a conflicting result). Hoffman-Hicks (1999), Kraft and Geluykens (2002), and Warga (2004) found their learner speech act realizations to be considerably more verbose than their French native speaker counterparts'. Regarding directness level, Kraft and Geluykens (2002) found their learner head acts to be more direct than the native speaker head acts. This finding is in line with previous research on directness (Billmyer & Varghese 2000; Hill 1997; Kasper 1981; Rose 2000; Yu 1999).

Let us now briefly highlight the pragmatic practices that are specific to French. One such practice that has been shown to be particularly challenging for English learners of French is the system of pronouns of address (see Dewaele this volume, for a detailed discussion). From the perspective of learners with German as L1, another French pragmatic practice is the use of query preparatories as standard request strategy. In Warga (2004), advanced learners have been shown to resort to rather complex request strategies that are not used by the French native speakers, as for instance *Je voulais savoir si tu pourrais m'aider* 'I wanted to know whether you could help me'. The French native speakers used mostly less complex strategies, namely query preparatories, as for example *Tu pourrais m'aider?* 'Could you help me?' It becomes clear from the data that transfer from L1 German plays an important role for this learner behavior. Therefore, German-speaking learners of French should be made aware of the fact that in the French cultural context, the standard request strategy is the query preparatory.

Another noteworthy feature of the French language concerns the conversational style. Béal (1992) and Peeters (1999), for instance, found that the question "Did you have a good weekend?" is that of a greeting ritual in Australian English. The response to this question is, therefore, ritualistic. In the French cultural context, however, the question is not ritualized, so that it requires a considerably more elaborate response. Whether the same is true for "How are you (doing)?" vs. *Ça va?* cannot be definitely said because there has not been any cross-cultural research on this subject. However, it seems indeed to be the case that "How are you (doing)?" is interpreted as a ritualistic greeting to a higher degree than is *Ça va?* Kerbrat-Orecchioni (2001:110–122), for instance, comments on the role of *Ça va?* in France and points out that one of the conditions of use is that the interlocutors have already met (p. 113). This is not a prerequisite for the English "How are you (doing)?" Therefore, it could be argued that this

---

31. The language indicated between brackets is the target language of the respective study.

question is less ritualized in the French than in the English-speaking context. As a consequence, English-speaking learners of French have to be cautious when interpreting opening sequences as pure greeting rituals. However, these considerations can only be a starting point for the further investigation of the formulaicity of opening sequences in English and French.

As can be seen from the literature review, a number of important issues in interlanguage pragmatics such as developmental patterns, instruction, formulaic language and transfer has already been addressed by the French studies and some pragmatic practices that are specific for French have been identified. However, the studies conducted so far are small in number and limited in scope. Only three speech acts, namely complaints, compliments, and requests and a few conversational functions, namely greetings/leave takings, closings, responses to a question about the weekend have been studied so far in French L2 pragmatics. Many areas of pragmatic competence have not yet been researched.

8.2 Development of requesting behavior in L2 French

This final section explores one of the standing research questions in ILP: The path of pragmatic development. As mentioned above in 7.2, we still do not know very much about the developmental path of pragmatic competence in L2, particularly in French. Warga (2004) will be used to address this question in more detail.

Warga (2004) investigated the development of request behavior in L2 French using cross-sectional data from high school students after three, four and five years of study of French. Based on this study, we will focus on whether the learners' requesting behavior moves in the direction of the target language norm with increasing proficiency. Three instances of pragmatic development will be discussed: Number of words per request, frequency of query preparatories, and number of grammatical modality markers per request.

8.2.1 *Methodology*

Three groups of students took part in the study: One group of Austrian learners of French as a second language at an intermediate level (n = 84), one group of French native speakers (n = 45),[32] and one group of native speakers of Austrian German (n = 20). All subjects were high school students aged between 15 and 18 years. Learners had studied French for either four (n = 27), five (n = 27) or six years (n = 30) through formal education in Austria (3 to 4 hours a week). Except for one, none of them had been in French-speaking countries for more than one month.

A discourse completion test (DCT) and a closed role-play were used to elicit requests from the L2 learners and native speakers. The situations in the DCT and closed role-play were controlled for three major situational variables, namely social

---

32. The French native speakers are from Cannes (n = 24) and from Rennes (n = 21).

dominance, social distance and degree of imposition. All situations were carefully designed to facilitate participants' identification with the roles they had to play. Female participants had only female interlocutors, while male participants only had male interlocutors, in order to exclude the possible influence of cross-gender effects.

For the data collection procedure, all 149 subjects filled in the written DCT. Then, 50% of the subjects responded to the oral closed role-play. Before the subjects started to fill in their requests, the following instructions (in the subjects' L1) were given, in both written and spoken form:

> Please read the situational description before writing what you would say in the described situation in a natural conversation. Try to write down the exact words you would use in an authentic situation. If you would not say anything, please write down your reasons. The situations are set in France and the language to be used is therefore French.

In order to make sure that all subjects had understood the task, the answer to one item was worked out by the whole group as an example. For the oral role-play, the instructions were the same. For the DCT, each student had to respond to six situational descriptions in written form. All students in each class took the DCT at the same time. For the oral closed role-play, each student was tape-recorded individually. In order to make the situation more authentic, a technique developed by researchers at the *OISE* (Ontario Institute for Studies in Education) (Harley, Cummins, Swain, & Allen 1990) was used: Students taking the oral test were shown photographs of people in four different situations while the investigator described a specific context and asked students to respond as if they were actually addressing the person pictured in the photograph (cf. Lyster 1996).

In total, the questionnaires elicited 1,182 requests (660 learner requests; 346 French native speaker requests; 176 Austrian native speaker requests).[33] Accordingly, the learner corpus consists of 27,100 words, the French native speaker corpus of 10,400 words, and the Austrian native speaker corpus of 9,300 words.

The requests were analyzed according to a coding system which is largely based on the CCSARP coding scheme in Blum-Kulka et al. (1989:273–294) and the coding scheme in Held (1995:473–486).

8.2.2 *Results and discussion*

Regarding the first instance of pragmatic development which will be discussed, namely the number of words per request, we have pointed out above (in 8.1.4) that learners have been shown to 'waffle' as compared to native speakers. Does this waffle diminish as learners become more proficient? Do learners use fewer words when improving their language skills?

---

33. Please note that instances where individual students chose not to react verbally ("opting out") are also included in these frequencies.

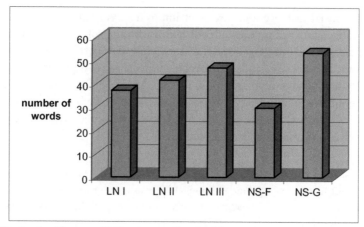

Note. LNI = low level learners; LNII = intermediate level learners; LNIII = advanced level learners; NS-F = native speakers of French; NS-G = native speakers of Austrian German

Figure 1. Number of words used per request

Figure 1 illustrates the number of words in the learner and native speaker groups. As can be observed, learners use more words than French native speakers, across all proficiency levels. Whereas learners employ between 37.14 and 46.91 words per request, French native speakers employ only 29.69 words. This phenomenon is illustrated in (10) with an example from a native speaker, and in (11) with an example from a learner:

(10)   French native speaker (NS-F)
Excusez-moi, mais je trouve que vous m'avez noté sévèrement par rapport à mon camarade. Pourriez-vous relire ma copie, s.v.p.?
'Excuse me but I think that you have graded me harshly in comparison to my friend. Could you please read my essay again?'

(11)   L2 Learner (LN I)
Excusez-moi, Madame, mais je crois que ma note du contrôle est injuste. Quelques autres ont écrit les choses similaires et ils ont des meilleures notes. Pouvez-vous relire mon test encore une fois? Si vous voulez, je peux vous apporter un test d'une autre élève de ma classe et vous pouvez comparer.
'Excuse me, Madam, but I think that the grade of my essay is unfair. Others have written similar things and they got better grades. Could you read my essay once again? If you want, I can give you an essay of another student so that you can compare.'

As can be seen from Figure 1, the number of words used by the learners gradually increases from level I to level III. This is a regressive movement away from the French native speaker norm. This suggests that learners' performance in L2 is related to their L1 style. In other words, as proficiency increases, learners show regression as to the target language norm and move in the direction of their L1 norm. But why is it that transfer increases with the proficiency level? It may be the case that more advanced

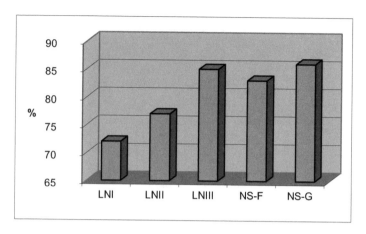

Figure 2. Frequency of query preparatories

learners, who already have at their disposal the linguistic resources in the target language, are in the position of using the same amount of supportive strategies (e.g., introductions, grounders, closings) in their speech acts as they do in their L1 (cf. Takahashi & Beebe's 1987 'positive correlation hypothesis' in 7.1). This would explain why more advanced learners use even more words than less advanced learners.

The development of the most frequent head act strategy, the query preparatory, is illustrated in Figure 2. It can be seen that the number of query preparatories gradually increases from 72% at level I to 85% at level III. The French native speakers employ a query preparatory in 83% of all requests. Therefore, the learners' development from level I to level III is a movement towards the French native speaker norm. However, the high percentage of query preparatories in the Austrian native speaker data (86%) leads us to wonder whether the increasing use of query preparatories over time is a deliberate development towards the French native speaker norm, or if it is caused by an approximation to the Austrian native speaker norm. Here are examples of query preparatories from both NS speech and L2 learner speech:

(12) French native speaker (NS-F)
  Serait-il possible de laisser mon chien à la conciergerie?
  'Would it be possible to leave my dog at the porter's lodge?'

(13) L2 Learner (LN I)
  Est-ce que tu peux faire cet exposé?
  'Can you do this presentation?'

The third example of pragmatic development concerns the morphological and syntactical modification devices used to downtone a request, such as the conditional form.

Figure 3 shows that the number of learners' grammatical modifications increases slightly and discontinuously from level I (0.5) to level III (0.62). This is a movement in the direction of the norm of the French native speakers who employ 1.11 grammatical modification devices per request. However, as with the query preparatories,

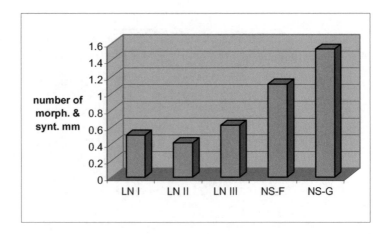

Figure 3. Number of morphological and syntactical modality markers (mm) per request

the high percentage of grammatical modification devices on the part of the Austrian native speakers (1.53) makes it impossible to find out whether the learners' development is a deliberate approximation towards the French norm, or is rather a matter of convergence to the Austrian native speaker norm (for examples, see (1) to (4) above).

The discussion of three instances of pragmatic development has shown that the issue of pragmatic development – particularly in a foreign language context – is not straightforward at all, as we are confronted with progressive and regressive developments at the same time (e.g., Barron 2003; Hill 1997).

Why does pragmatic competence develop in such a non-linear way? Transfer from L1 German obviously plays an important role in the interlanguage of the Austrian learners. This seems particulary true for features situated at the level of strategy. These features tend to develop primarily towards the L1 norm instead of the target language norm. That is, as soon as the learners have at their disposal the linguistic means, they seem to start to transfer at both the strategic (e.g., number and type of query preparatories) and linguistic level (number and type of grammatical modification devices) from their L1. The reason for this is that foreign language learners are usually not familiar with the pragmatic norms of the target language, as they do not have access to a wide range of authentic pragmatic input, nor do they normally get pragmatic instruction. By contrast, pragmatic features that are situated at the linguistic level, such as grammatical modification devices (e.g., conditional), are taught in the language classroom and show a stronger tendency to move towards the target language norm over time. It is possible that the features which have been shown to move away from the French native speaker norm will move 'back' at a more advanced level, as future research with more proficient learners may show.

Another reason for the non-linear character of L2 pragmatic development is accounted for by the "complexification hypothesis" (Meisel, Clahsen, & Pienemann 1981). Warga (2004: 141–143) found in her study that the proportion of the more complex hedged performatives (*Je voudrais vous demander de...* 'I would like to ask you to') increased to the disadvantage of the less complex explicit performatives (*Je vous demande de...* 'I'm asking you to') from level I to level III learners. Similarly, the proportion of the more complex possibility question (*Serait-il possible de...?* 'would it be possible to') increased, whereas the less complex ability question (*Pourriez-vous...?* 'could you?') decreased during the same period of time (Warga 2004: 154–155). Both these instances of pragmatic development seem to lend support to the "complexification hypothesis", since it appears that less complex structures are used earlier than more complex structures which appear later. It is, however, important to note that the complexity does not only refer to the linguistic level, but also to the pragmatic level. For instance, the above mentioned explicit performatives are not only grammatically easier to form than hedged performatives, they are also more transparent from a pragmatic point of view, as there is a direct, 'non-hedged' link between the form of the utterance and its illocutionary force. Concerned with expressing themselves in the L2, less advanced learners seem to appreciate this clarity which facilitates the process of encoding and reduces the cognitive effort.

Further support to the "complexification hypothesis" in interlanguage pragmatics comes from the numerous studies which have found an overuse of direct strategies in the initial phases of learning (Billmyer & Varghese 2000; Hill 1997; Kasper 1981; Rose 2000; Yu 1999). The high frequency of direct strategies, such as imperatives, can again be explained by the pragmatic transparency, that is the direct relationship between the structural form (e.g., imperatives) and the communicative function (e.g., requests).

In sum, then, the developmental path in ILP is still a matter of debate. French acquisitional ILP studies (e.g., Hoffman-Hicks 1999; Lyster 1994; Warga 2004) have contributed to the finding that pragmatic development takes a non-linear path. However, we are only just beginning to understand why some features develop towards and others away from the target language norm. More research is clearly needed in this field.

9.   Directions for further research

French ILP is still a very young field of inquiry. As we have seen, there is only a handful of studies, one of them focusing on use, another one on the influence of proficiency, a third one on the effects of a study abroad program on acquisition, and two studies on acquisition through pragmatic instruction. Consequently, the opportunities for research in the field are vast and many aspects of French ILP urgently require investigation. More precisely, the goals for future research can be summarized as follows:

–   Widening the scope of the learners' first language: In the existing studies, the first languages are either English (Hoffman-Hicks 1999; Liddicoat & Crozet 2001; Lyster 1994), or German (Kraft & Geluykens 2002; Warga 2004).

- Expanding learner populations to include lower-proficiency learners: Apart from Warga (2004), the existing studies investigate solely higher-level learners.[34]
- Expanding data collection instruments to integrate elicited/authentic conversational data which allow for the analysis of the dynamics of conversation: The majority of the existing studies used the DCT as a data collection instrument (Hoffman-Hicks 1999; Kraft & Geluykens 2002; Lyster 1994; Warga 2004). Although some of these studies employed a second or even third data collection instrument, Hoffman-Hicks (1999) was the only one to add authentic data to her DCT data.
- Widening the scope of pragmatic features: In the studies conducted so far, only three speech acts, namely complaints, compliments, and requests and a few conversational functions, namely greetings/leave-takings, closings, responses to a question about the weekend have been investigated.
- Implementing acquisitional studies (cross-sectional as well as longitudinal).
- Investigating the main request strategy used by learners of French with other first languages than German: In Warga (2004), it has been shown that Austrian learners of French resort to a rather complex strategy, the so-called "combined query preparatory" (see 7.2 for a definition), when it comes to formulating a request. French native speakers, on the other hand, use a "simple query preparatory". Investigating learners with other first languages than German would make it possible to find out whether the use of complex request strategies by learners is a typical learner behavior or whether it is specific to L1 German learners.
- Moreover, apart from interlanguage pragmatics, we need to learn more about French pragmatics. Empirical data currently available in the area of French pragmatics are strikingly limited. What is more, the research investigating realizations of speech acts and conversational functions by native speakers of French are mainly based on researcher introspection and informal observation. Therefore, there is not much, if any, research available which investigates French pragmatics using systematically collected empirical data.
- Studying the degree of (in)directness of the French language as compared to other languages: In the framework of the Cross Cultural Speech Act Realization Project (CCSARP; Blum-Kulka et al. 1989) it was found that speakers of Canadian French and German occupy the mid-point in the cross-cultural scale of indirectness, that is, they are more direct in their requestive behavior than speakers of English. Future studies should investigate whether speakers of French also opt for higher levels of directness than speakers of English. If so, the consequences of this difference in (in)directness for English-speaking learners of French and French-speaking learners of English should be investigated.
- Investigating the degree of formulaicity of opening sequences and other conversational functions in French as compared to other languages: It has been argued that

---

34.   Kraft and Geluykens (2002) do not comment on the proficiency level of their learners.

the conditions of use for French *Ça va?* are not the same as for English "How are you (doing)?" (Kerbrat-Orecchioni 2001:110–122). Given that the interpretation of opening sequences and other conversational functions (e.g., greeting, closing sequence) as too ritualistic or insufficiently ritualistic can lead to serious misunderstandings in learner-native speaker and learner-learner conversation, this area of pragmatic competence needs to be addressed.

Appendix

Conversation extract taken from Liddicoat and Crozet (2001:138–139):

Extract 5

Amy: *Eh salut Angela, salut. Le week-end a été bon?*
Angela: *Ah oui en fait le weekend a été vraiment fantastique=ma mère m'a rendu visite*
Amy: *oui ta mère. Est-ce que c'est ça j'ai pensé qu'elle était à Sydney en ce moment.*
Angela: *Oh non non elle est rentrée à minuit donc euh nous avons passé le week-end ensemble e[uh euh nous avons=*
Amy: *[bien*
Angela: *=euh vu deux films puis alors nous avons visité le musée des beaux arts.*
Amy: *Oh là là quel jour.*
        (.)
Amy: *J'ai- j'ai été euh là aussi avec ma sœur elle éta[it-*
Angela: *[Oui oui*
Amy: *Samedi matin.*
Angela: *Tu as été là samedi?*
Amy: *Oui.*
Angela: *Quel dommage j'étais là dimanche.*
((Continues for 68 more lines))

Translation

Amy: Eh hi Angela, hi. The weekend was good?
Angela: Ah yes the weekend was really fantastic=my mother visited me
Amy: Yes your mother. Is that it I thought she was in Sydney at the moment.
Angela: Oh no no she got back at midnight so euh we spent the weekend together e[uh euh we=
Amy: [well
Angela: =euh saw two films then we visited the art gallery.
Amy: Oh, my, what a day.
        (.)
Amy: I w- I was euh there too with my sister. she wa[s-
Angela: [yes yes
Amy: Saturday morning.
Angela: You were there Saturday?
Amy: Yes.
Angela: What a pity I was there Sunday.

CHAPTER 8

Diachronic and/or synchronic variation?

The acquisition of sociolinguistic competence in L2 French*

Jean-Marc Dewaele

Birkbeck, University of London

Résumé

Une majorité des premières études en acquisition de langues étrangères a porté sur la variation diachronique dans l'interlangue des apprenants, c'est-à-dire des différences dans l'interlangue liées à une augmentation graduelle du savoir linguistique de l'apprenant (cf. Tarone 1988). La dernière décennie a vu une véritable éclosion d'études combinant une perspective diachronique avec une perspective synchronique, c'est-à-dire, une perspective dans laquelle la variation est perçue comme étant la conséquence de différences individuelles entre apprenants (sexe, degré d'extraversion, attitudes, motivation, variables sociobiographiques liées à l'expérience d'apprentissage, type et fréquence des contacts avec la langue cible). Selon cette perspective, l'absence d'isomorphie avec le comportement linguistique des natifs n'est pas automatiquement attribuée à des lacunes de connaissances. D'autres causes possibles sont prises en considération telles que l'inaccessibilité temporaire à l'information dans des situations stressantes, ou même une décision consciente de la part de l'apprenant de dévier de la norme standard de la langue cible.

Abstract

A majority of the early research in second language acquisition focused on diachronic variation in the learners' interlanguage (IL), that is, differences in the IL linked to a supposed increase in knowledge between two points in time (cf. Tarone 1988). The last decade has seen an increase in studies combining a diachronic perspective with a synchronic one, that is, where variation in production is seen as the consequence of individual differences among learners (gender, extraversion, learning strategies, attitudes, motivation, sociobiographical variables linked to the language learning experience and the use of the target language (TL)). In this perspective, non-native-like patterns are not automatically assumed to be the result of incomplete knowledge, but

* The present chapter is a revised and updated version of the review article "The acquisition of sociolinguistic competence in French as a foreign language: An overview". In F. Myles and R. Towell (2004, Eds.), *The acquisition of French as a second language*. Special issue of the *Journal of French Language Studies*, 14, 301–319. The present work benefited from a Small Research grant from the British Academy (SG-32409).

other possible causes are taken into consideration, such as temporary inaccessibility of information in stressful situations, or even a conscious decision by the L2 user to deviate from the TL norm.

1. Introduction

The study of sociolinguistic competence in second language acquisition (SLA) started to attract the attention of a growing number of researchers in the late 1980s (Preston 1989), and was broadly situated within a quantitative Labovian tradition (Labov 1972b, 2001). Several colloquia at international conferences (NWAVE in 2000, 2001; Sociolinguistic Symposium in 2002 and 2004), and special issues in international journals have been devoted to the development of sociolinguistic competence in the second language (L2) (Bayley & Regan 2004; Dewaele & Mougeon 2002; Mougeon & Dewaele 2004). Several review articles on the acquisition of sociolinguistic competence in French L2 have been published recently (Dewaele 2004e; Mougeon, Nadasdi, & Rehner 2002; Mougeon, Rehner, & Nadasdi 2004). These reviews have mostly focused on the studies carried out in the quantitative sociolinguistic framework that looked at French L2 learners in Europe (often in study abroad contexts) and French L2 learners in immersion schools in Canada.

The current understanding of sociolinguistic research is linked to the seminal work of Labov (1972b) and Hymes (1974). Both researchers reacted against the powerful paradigm of purely theoretical linguistics. Labov complained that "[t]he great majority of linguists had resolutely turned to the contemplation of their own idiolects. We have not yet emerged from the shadow of our intuitions (. . .)" (1972:xix). He further wrote in his introduction that he long resisted the use of the term *sociolinguistic* "since it implies that there can be a successful linguistic theory or practice which is not social" (1972:xix). Hymes (1974) also attacks Chomsky's definition of linguistic competence, arguing that it is both too narrow and inadequate:

> An adequate approach must distinguish and investigate four aspects of competence:
> (a) *systemic potential* – whether and to what extent something is not yet realized, and, in a sense, not yet known, it is to this that Chomsky in effect reduces competence; (b) *appropriateness* – whether and to what extent something is in some context suitable, effective, or the like; (c) *occurrence* – whether and to what extent something is done; (d) *feasibility* – whether and to what extent something is possible, given the means of implementation available. (Hymes 1974, reprinted in 1997:13)

We define the notion of sociolinguistic competence as the "ability to perform various speech acts, the ability to manage conversational turns and topics, sensitivity to variation in register and politeness, and an understanding of how these aspects of language vary according to social roles and settings" (Ranney 1992:25).

Labov (1972b, 2001) has linked linguistic variation to independent variables such as the situation in which an interaction takes places, the type of task being performed and speaker's social characteristics. Following this approach, variationist sociolinguists deal with probabilities of particular variants appearing in specific contexts. Preston (2000:11) illustrates the probabilistic approach as follows: "For a two-way variable, a speaker [...] is equipped with a coin, the two sides of which represent the options for that variable; it is flipped before the product appears". He points out that in this context "fair" tosses are unlikely, the chances of obtaining 50% occurrences of each variable are remote. Indeed, several factors contribute to the probability of one variable being selected. The individuals might not be aware of the pattern of their choices as they "are not monitoring their overall performance with some tallying device. They are evidencing the influence of a set of probabilistic weights which come to bear on each occurrence" (Preston 2000:11). The factors that have been considered in this type of approach are linguistic, sociobiographical and situational. In an L2 context, these might also include time spent abroad, amount of instruction in the TL, first language(s), attitudes towards the TL, and so on. Variationists' preferred tool is a logistical regression analysis, the VARBRUL program (Bayley & Preston 1996) that allows for simultaneous analysis of a variety of factors. The program calculates which factors have a statistically significant effect, as well as the relative importance of each factor. Each factor suspected of influencing the variation is assigned a probability weight, when all the factor groups are applied simultaneously. A higher weight indicates a stronger influence of a factor: If a probability weight exceeds 0.5, it is said to favor the application. If, on the other hand, the weight falls below 0.5, it is interpreted as disfavoring the application.

The deterministic nature of variable rule probabilities has been criticized (see Young 1999) as well as "the failure of the approach to engage such 'real' psycholinguistic factors as memory, attention, access, processing and the like" (Preston 2000:28). The psychological concept presented by Labov as the cause of style-shifting, namely *attention to form*, was first criticized by Wolfson (1976) who stated that "it would seem to be a good idea to measure attention to speech independently in order to find out just what it involves. At present we have no idea WHAT people monitor when they pay attention to their speech" (Wolfson 1976:203) (original emphasis). This criticism has been reiterated ever since (Bell 1984; Dewaele 1995a; Gradol & Swann 1989; Rickford & McNair-Knox 1994). Later psycholinguistic research has shown that speakers constantly shift the focus of their attention as they speak in order to avoid communication breakdown (Levelt 1989). Models of interlanguage variation based on the concept of *attention to form* (for example Tarone's 1989 Chameleon Model) were found to be defective (Dewaele 1995b).

The problem is that too few researchers approach sociolinguistic questions from a psycholinguistic or a psychological perspective. I have argued that only interdisciplinary approaches can hope to provide a complete description of linguistic phenomena (such as sociolinguistic variation), and begin to understand the complex cognitive, psychological and social causes underlying that variation (Dewaele 2005a).

Other methodological and ideological aspects of variationist sociolinguistics have been criticized. Postmodernist feminist researchers like Pavlenko (2002a) have attacked the use of discrete categories like sex, age, and social class as independent variables. Referring to Cameron (1990), Pavlenko states that the assumption that "people behave in certain ways because they are members of certain groups is a correlational fallacy, because the purported explanation is in reality nothing but a descriptive statement" (Pavlenko 2002a: 282). Labov (1972b) has also been criticized for the criteria used to determine the socio-economic status of the subjects. This was based largely upon occupation for men; but for women, it was based on the occupation of their husbands (if married or widowed), or their fathers (if single). Cameron and Coates (1989) argue that this method of not classifying women in their own right could quite easily lead to inaccuracies in the results of any subsequent research findings. Much of this early research studied male groups of subjects (Coates 1986), and those that did include female subjects were often based on limited data and led to many stereotyped presumptions about female and male speech (Freed & Greenwood 1996).

Despite the concerns expressed about the variationist approach, a large amount of research into the acquisition of sociolinguistic competence in the L2 has been situated within this paradigm. Dickerson (1975) was among the first to adopt the variationist approach to account for variable phonological production in the English interlanguage (IL) of Japanese learners. She postulated, "Like native speakers, second language speakers use a language system consisting of variable rules" (1975: 407).

The interest was fuelled not only by purely theoretical considerations – that is the need to situate SLA within a social context (Tarone 1997) – but also by practical and political concerns. Bayley and Regan (2004: 327) point out that there is a need in SLA research to move beyond the focus on the standard language to consider "the vernaculars that constitute the input for most immigrants who are acquiring a second or nth language with little or no formal instruction". Having spent years learning "the orthoepic standard norm" (Valdman 2003), instructed L2 learners might find themselves at a loss when they suddenly become L2 *users* (Cook 2002) unable to produce vernacular speech (see also Nadasdi, Mougeon, & Rehner 2005). Valdman (2003: 13) describes the difficulty facing learners as follows:

> To speak like a native requires the ability to select among several norms on the basis of the total situational context and in light of varying communicative intents. In addition, the norms for prestigious planned speech are usually complexified with respect to those that characterize vernacular unplanned speech. At the phonological level, they require finer discriminations; at the grammatical level, they involve numerous lower-level and highly specific constraints. Consequently, to approximate these norms learners are likely to produce more deviant forms, both inaccurate from a linguistic perspective and inappropriate from a sociopragmatic one.

Beginning to intermediate learners might, for example, be distressed when placed in an authentic situation that requires the use of a highly formal speech. Learners appear to be monostylistic at first, stuck somewhere in the middle of the speech style continuum, only gradually do they start to explore both ends of the continuum (Dewaele 2001; Tarone & Swain 1995; Tyne 2005). Learners in these early stages typically use one sociolinguistic variant (generally the formal one) categorically. It is only at a later stage that alternation between two sociolinguistic variants starts to emerge (Adamson & Regan 1991). This synchronic variation is often non-systematic or "free" variation, oscillating between overuse or underuse of particular variants compared to native speaker (NS) norms. Highly advanced L2 learners/users (i.e., non-native speakers, hence NNS) start to conform to NS variation patterns.

The crucial problem that faces any researcher interested in analyzing the development of sociolinguistic competence in the L2 is the interpretation of the variation observed for specific sociolinguistic markers. As Beebe (1988) underlined in her overview of sociolinguistic approaches to SLA, there is an important limitation in importing sociolinguistic methods designed to measure subtle variation in the speech of NSs as L2 performance "involves using a repertoire that is both limited and in a state of flux" (Beebe 1988:44).

The state of flux might be linked, as Rehner (2005) pointed out, to the larger number of independent variables that affect the variation in the L2, and not simply the social characteristics of the speaker combined with situational variables. Additional independent factors include the students' first language(s), the degree of curricular and extra-curricular exposure to the L2, and the type of input received through teachers and pedagogical materials. Rehner (2005) further warned that L2 studies should not blindly adopt the Labovian approach in equating 'correct' L2 forms with 'standard' or 'prestige' L1 forms. She suggests a differentiation between two kinds of variable production observable in L2 data, namely 'Type 1' variation, that is, an alternation between native-like and non-native like forms (errors), and 'Type 2' variation that manifests itself via an alternation between forms that are each used by NSs of the TL (Rehner 2005:14–15).[1] She argues that the measure of learner success in relation to 'Type 1' variation is increasingly error-free production. Measuring success is more difficult in relation to 'Type 2' variation. It can be made in terms of: "(a) learners' use of the same expressions as NSs; (b) their use of such expressions at levels of discursive frequency similar to those found in the speech of NSs in the same situation; and (c) the correlation of such uses with similar independent factors, both social (e.g., social class, sex, and style), and linguistic (e.g., the surrounding lexical and syntactic context), affecting the uses by NSs" (Rehner 2005:15).

Yet, as will be demonstrated in the present chapter, even 'Type 2' variation can be linked to incomplete grammatical knowledge, or to limited input, and only among the highly advanced speakers does 'Type 2' variation truly reflect an awareness of sociolinguistic rules in the L2. Finally, some very advanced NNSs may possess full sociolinguistic competence, and yet consciously wish to avoid informal variants, thereby creating a false impression of incomplete competence, or at least a different presentation of the self (Koven 1998, 2006; Dewaele 2005a).

---

1.   Nadasdi et al. (2003) proposed yet another type of variation which partakes of both 'type 1' and 'type 2', namely an alternation between forms that are used by L1 speakers and forms that are non-native.

Any overview is by nature incomplete and arbitrary. Beebe (1988:45) decided to include five approaches while admitting that it is "simplistic to lump sociolinguistics (broadly defined) into five (and only five) traditions", arguing that it is "equally misleading to treat every researcher as a totally independent voice" (p. 45). Most research has been carried out in the Labovian tradition, which has gradually been expanded to combine ideas and methodologies from other approaches. Beebe criticized the variationists for emphasizing the *what* and ignoring the *why* (p. 44). Recent sociolinguistic research in L2 pays more attention to both the *what* and the *why*. The present study will concentrate primarily on studies that borrowed from the Labovian theory. However, these variationist studies will be complemented by a number of sociocultural case studies of individual learners/users that present interesting observations and speculations on the *why* of sociolinguistic variation.

The focus will be on advanced learners of French who are typically instructed learners in European and American contexts. They may have occasional contact with NSs for a determined period through study abroad programs. Some Canadian learners share that profile, while others are in daily contact with French through immersion education (Lapkin 1999). The only study in our overview dealing with naturalistic learners is that of Véronique (2005). In the first part of the chapter, some key concepts will be defined. In the second part, a series of empirical studies on French IL will be reviewed that include situation, type and frequency of exposure to French as independent variables. The studies have been ordered roughly by function of the type of dependent variable that was investigated (phonological, morphological, morphosyntactic, and lexical). The third and final part will present some general patterns that emerge from these studies, and will consider some pedagogical implications.

2.   Empirical studies

2.1   Studies on phonological variants

French pronunciation is often considered to be equivalent of the Mont Blanc for NSs of English engaged in deciphering and reproducing complex clusters of phonemes (see Hannahs this volume). Thomas (2004) observed that while some simple phonemes such as /y/ or /ø/, are stable throughout the French-speaking world (they are normally not deleted and essentially realized the same way everywhere), some features are extremely variable, going from full retention to full deletion, depending on a myriad of linguistic and extra-linguistic factors. Striking differences between official norm and actual usage add a further challenge for the exhausted learners. Learners who have been taught the "orthoepic norm", that is, an imitation of the native-speaker norm (typically middle class Parisian French) are suddenly confronted with a perplexing array of schwa deletions for which they need to identify the sociolinguistic constraints. Schwa deletion, defined by Thomas as an orthographic *e* which is deleted, is particularly popular among the young NSs of French (*j'pars* instead of *je pars*). Thomas' Canadian learners were found to omit the schwa much less frequently than NSs. Thomas (2004) found that after eight months in a French Second Language program in a university in France, the L2 learners had not changed their rate of schwa deletion in a significant way. However, Uritescu, Mougeon and Handouleh (2002) found that Canadian immersion students who had had the opportunity of staying with a Francophone family displayed significantly higher rates of schwa deletion than the remaining students.

Similar patterns emerged in Uritescu, Mougeon, Rehner and Nadasdi (2004) who analyzed the presence or absence of schwa in unaccented open non-final syllables of 8 anglophone students in French immersion programmes in Ontario. Immersion students were found to employ the mildly-marked variant of schwa deletion much less often than L1 speakers but observed the same phonetic constraints as L1 speakers. Schwa deletion was positively correlated with exposure to spoken NS French outside the school context. The authors also found that immersion students did not attach a clear social value to schwa deletion.

Sax (2003) compared levels of sociolinguistic competence among 35 American students at three different levels of French study: Second year university French, fourth year French and graduate students. None of the second year students had spent time abroad, half of the fourth year students had spent time abroad, and all of the graduates had spent time abroad (from several weeks to four years). She also obtained data from a control group of 5 NSs. She gathered her data through two role-plays: One was a simulated formal situation, and the other was a simulated informal situation. She found that the learners as a combined group deleted /l/ less frequently than NSs, but that they were sensitive to stylistic variation, deleting slightly less in the formal role-play than in the informal role-play. Time spent abroad in France emerged as the strongest predictor of /l/ deletion. The longer the time learners had spent abroad, the more they deleted /l/. Advanced learners were found to delete much more frequently than less advanced peers. The former also showed evidence of stylistic variation between the formal and informal contexts while no such variation appeared in the latter group.

A study by Howard, Lemée and Regan (2006) on /l/ deletion in the French IL of 19 classroom learners in Ireland showed distinct similarities to findings of Sax. Deletion of /l/ was virtually absent before the stay abroad but soared to 33 per cent after the stay abroad. The authors conclude that "living in the native speech community does what the classroom cannot do for the acquisition of native speaker variation patterns" (Howard et al. 2006: 20).

Howard (2004a) reported an unusual preference for informal variants in his study of variable use of the liaison in French IL by a group of 18 classroom learners in Ireland. Use of the obligatory liaison was found to pose less difficulty to the learners than variable liaison: In a range of syntactic contexts, the learners greatly underused the liaison which constitutes the formal variant of this variable and overused the informal variant, that is, non-use of the liaison. Comparing the learners' data with that of NSs, Howard noticed that learners' use of the liaison was non-existent in some contexts, and when it was used "those contexts (dis)favoring its use are not the same as in the case of the native speaker" (2004a: 159). In a further study on the topic, Howard

(2005b) underlines that his findings on the liaison diverge from the general conclusion (cf. Mougeon et al. 2002) that advanced learners respect the linguistic constraints of variation, and overuse formal variants. His learners ignored the use of variable liaison in a wide range of syntactic contexts.

2.2 Studies on morphosyntactic variants

2.2.1 *Omission of* ne

Negation in French is expressed through a pre-verbal *ne*, a verb form and one of many possible post-verbal items (*pas, jamais, plus, rien, personne, point*). These post-verbal items used to have a much stronger semantic content and reinforced preverbal *ne*. The weakening of the particle *ne* and the phrase-final stress on the post-verbal item made the *ne* more or less redundant (Englebert 1984). Although still required in written speech and formal oral speech, *ne* is omitted in more than 80% of the cases in informal speech (Coveney 1996: 30).

The following extract (example (1)) was presented in Dewaele (2004b: 440–441) as an illustration of the variation in the omission of *ne* within the same exchange. The researcher (JM) and Henry (H), a 21 year-old student English native speaker who spent 6 months in France during the previous academic year as part of his study abroad experience, discuss Henry's perception that language teachers in the UK do not allow him to use the vernacular French that he picked up in France. Proud as he is of his newly acquired knowledge of informal speech styles, he is frustrated not to be able to demonstrate the progress he has made. The exchange also illustrates micro-stylistic variation. The exchange is mostly a monologue by Henry, with 5 omissions of *ne* in all 5 negations.[2] The only retention of *ne* occurs in the last turn, which involves a micro-style shift, that is, a direct question asked to the researcher with a polite third person pronoun of address *vous*.

(1) H: *J' ø aime pas j' ø aime pas trop les cours de français parce que je trouve ça ennuyant.*
          'I don't like, I don't like the French courses very much because I find them boring.'
     JM: *Pourquoi ?*
          'Why?'
     H: *Parce que je sais déjà parler français assez bien mais euh c' ø est pas seulement ça c'est euh il faut qu'on parle différemment parce que moi quand je suis allé euh en France j'avais vraiment envie de parler exactement comme un Français.*
          'Because I speak French quite well already and but it is not only that it's that we have to speak differently because me, when I went err to France, I wanted to speak exactly like a Frenchman.'
     JM: *Ah oui.*
          'Ah yes.'

---

2. The symbol "ø" indicates the omission of *ne*.

H: *Mais je ø sais plus le faire et quand on est en cours en Angleterre tout le monde parle en français évidemment avec le le prof est Français.*
       'But I can't do it anymore and when one is in England everybody speaks French of course with, the the teacher is French.'

JM: *Mmm.*
       'Mmm.'

H: *Et quand même il faut parler dans le registre soutenu et j' ø aime pas ça c'est tellement euh artificiel.*
       'And still one has to speak in a formal register and I don't like that, it's so artificial.'

JM: *Ah hmm.*
       'Ah hmm.'

H: *Vous n'êtes pas d'accord ?*
       'Don't you agree?'

JM: *Haha.*
       'Ha ha.'

The main problem with the analysis of morphosyntactic variants lies in the interpretation of the presence and absence of the variant. The case of the negative particle *ne* in French IL provides an excellent illustration of how something apparently simple can in fact be fiendishly complex. The mastery of French negation involves a long circuitous route for English-speaking learners of French. First, they need to realize that negation in French involves a pre-verbal and a post-verbal element. Research on negation in the pre-basic-variety shows an anaphoric negator expressed by *non*, followed later by a non-anaphoric negator inserted in complex utterances, and the emergence of *pas* in modal formulae (*je (ne) sais pas; je (ne) comprends pas*) and presentationals (*c'(n) est pas, il y a pas*) (Véronique 2005:132). Target-like use of the preverbal particle *ne* coincides with the emergence of explicit lexical verbs. Véronique (2005:132) argues that the "analysis of TL verb morphology paves the way for correct placement of the negator". In other words, syntactic and semantic issues need to be resolved in the acquisition of the negation (during which free variation may occur) before the learner can address the issue of variable omission of *ne*.

Course book material and formal grammar instruction leads learners to grasp the functioning of negation resulting in an almost categorical use of a pre-verbal and a post-verbal element. At this point, learners have the necessary grammatical competence to use negation correctly in written French and in formal speech. They may start noticing the omission of the *ne* in informal oral French, and analyze the sociolinguistic constraints on this variant. Poorly written textbooks may also affect learners' understanding of the degree of markedness of the variant. Mougeon et al. (2002) found that the only characters to omit the *ne* in an Ontario textbook for English-speaking learners of French were negatively portrayed. This could have induced the learners in error, they may have concluded that the omission of *ne* is a stigmatized variant. Different options are possible once learners grasp the functioning of the negation: Either they opt for categorical use of the standard variant everywhere (preferring to be too formal rather than risk inappropriate informal use), or they may opt for categorical use of the informal variant (extending it to written language and formal speech), or they may gradually approximate NS variation patterns. For example, the retention of *ne* in Henry's last turn could be linked to a pragmatic fact, namely the occurrence of an interrogative turn addressed to the researcher in a slightly more formal style, after a long series of declarative turns in a more informal style.

Research on the omission of *ne* has shown the crucial effect of authentic interaction in French on this specific variation pattern. Irish learners of French were found to omit the *ne* considerably more in sociolinguistic interviews after spending a year in a francophone region (65% versus 38%) (Regan 1995, 1996, 1997, 2004, 2005). She observed a great deal of inter-individual variation, especially in the corpus collected before the year abroad. Some students had overgeneralized the omission of *ne* after their stay abroad, which Regan interprets as a sign that they were eager to adopt TL sociolinguistic norms and 'sound native' in order to integrate into the TL community (1997:206). Similar patterns were observed in a study by Rehner and Mougeon (1999) based on a corpus of oral IL of 41 young immersion students in Ontario. The amount of time spent in a francophone environment, and the amount of contact with French media as well as amount of formal instruction in French correlated positively with omission rates. Thomas (2004) found that 48 Anglophone Canadian students who spent their third year of university study in France came back with significantly higher omission rates compared to those of the control group who had remained at home.

Sax (2003) also analyzed the omission of *ne*. A VARBRUL analysis revealed showed that time spent in a French-speaking environment contributed to the omission of *ne*. Learners who had spent little to no time abroad almost never omitted *ne* in both an informal and a formal situation. However, mean omission rates for the intermediate group were 25% and 23% respectively, and they rose to 75% and 63% respectively for those who had spent the longest time abroad. Length of pre-university French study also affected the use of *ne*; learners with more than 5 years of instruction deleted *ne* less frequently (23%) than learners who had only 3 to 4 years of previous instruction in French (55%).

Prolonged authentic use of French with NSs thus seems to kickstart the development of stylistic variation. Students who had never been abroad did not adapt their omission rate according to the situation. Stylistic variation appears in the intermediate group, and it becomes statistically significant in the group that spent most time abroad. Finally, Sax found that the 5 NSs displayed both higher omission rates and more stylistic variation than the group of learners.

Dewaele and Regan (2002) analyzed omission rates of *ne* in a cross-sectional corpus of oral IL of 27 Dutch L1 students at the Free University of Brussels. Participants were interviewed in an informal (conversation), and a formal (oral exam) situation. Omission rates in the formal situation (12%) were not significantly different from those in the informal situation (15%), which was interpreted as an indication of the incomplete mastery of sociolinguistic rules in the TL by the learners. Omission rates were lower in the formal situation for a majority of participants but they went up for a small number of participants. Length of formal instruction in French did not affect omission rates of *ne* but the amount of authentic use of French outside the classroom and contact with French through radio and television were linked with higher omission rates. More extraverted participants also tended to omit *ne* more frequently. The amount of inter-individual variation was very high. Looking at the data such as the examples presented below (Dewaele & Regan 2002:141), we realized that it is close to impossible to make a *post-hoc* guess as to whether an omission of *ne* had been a deliberate choice or not.

(2) Anton: *Euh j'étais français troisième langue donc je n'ai français.*
'Err, I was French third language so I didn't have French'.

(3) Anton: *Non je ne pense ça.*
'no I don't think so'.

(4) Anton: *Je ne sais pas.*
'I don't know'.

(5) Anton: *Oui j'ai choisi deux heures parce que normalement c' ø est pas mathématiques.*
'Yes I've chosen two hours because usually it is not mathematics'.

(6) Filip: *Là j'ai dû commencer avec jouer avec lui mais j' ø ai jamais entré au club.*
'There I have been forced to start playing with him but I've never become a member of the club'.   (Dewaele & Regan 2002:136)

Anton is a speaker with a low level of overall morpho-lexical accuracy, who does not produce the obligatory *pas* in examples (2) and (3), produces the standard variant (*ne* + *pas*) in example (4), and omits (or forgets) *ne* in example (5). Filip, on the other hand, is a more advanced speaker who is more likely to be aware of the possibility to omit *ne* (see example (6)); he also produces utterances with both *ne* and *pas* such as in example (7):

(7) Filip: *Et je ne pouvais pas euh participer parce que je n'étais pas membre d'un club.*
'And I couldn't err participate because I wasn't member of a club'.
(Dewaele & Regan 2002:135)

Looking at proficiency levels and omission rates, we realized that the omission of *ne* in French IL follows a U-shaped development. Beginning and intermediate learners typically opt for the more salient post-verbal particle to express negations. The absence of *ne* could thus be linked to incomplete grammatical knowledge rather than complete sociolinguistic competence. In the former case, the absence of *ne* reveals a gap in knowledge, whereas in the latter case, it could be interpreted as a conscious omission. As learners progress, they may gradually understand the morpho-syntactic rules for the negation in French, and start to produce pre-verbal and post-verbal particles categorically. Highly advanced learners finally grasp the sociolinguistic rules that allow the particle *ne* to be omitted in certain situations. Given the heterogeneous nature of learner groups in terms of linguistic development, the causes underlying omission are likely to be varied, which would account for the large within-group variation in omission rates. Alternatively, Dutch learners for whom French is an L3 (as was the case for Anton) may be tempted in the first stages to use only the preverbal *ne* as in their English L2 until they realize that it does not function like that in French. Being unable to produce a two-part negative, they may seize on the *pas*-only version because it feels more native and allows them to integrate only one word into their sentence plan, which is less effortful (Foster-Cohen 2002, personal communication). Given the heterogeneous nature of learner groups in terms of linguistic development, the causes underlying omission are likely to be varied, which would account for the large within-group variation in omission rates.

Dewaele (2004a) analyzed inter-individual variation in omission rates of the preverbal particle *ne* in 991 negations produced in conversations between 73 NSs and NNSs of French who were students at Birkbeck College, London. Both endogeneous (user internal) and exogeneous (user external) extralinguistic factors were found to be linked to omission rates of *ne* (mean = 64% for the 9 NSs, and 27% for the 64 NNSs). Whereas age and gender were found to have little effect, the degree of extraversion of the speaker, the frequency of use of French and the native/non-native status of the speakers were significantly correlated with omission rates. Among the exogeneous factors, the composition of the dyad was found to be linked to omission rates: NSs interacting with NSs omitted *ne* more frequently than NNSs in conversation with other NNSs. It was argued that this accommodation effect among NNSs might in fact trigger a development towards native-like omission rates.

2.2.2 *Pronouns of address*

The choice of an appropriate pronoun of address (the formal *vous* or the informal *tu*) in French interactions has been linked to dancing on a sociolinguistic tightrope (Dewaele 2004b). One small misstep means a bad fall with little chance of (sociolinguistic) recovery. Pronouns of address are also notoriously difficult to master as speakers must resolve the inherent socio-pragmatic ambiguity whereby the same linguistic behavior may be interpreted as following either from perceived status difference or from desire to index social distance (Kinginger 2000: 24). The *vous* can be used as a form of respect, but it can equally serve to indicate a social distance between the interlocutors and the superiority of one of them. The *tu* on the other hand, can be perceived as a sign of solidarity, but it can also carry a value of familiarity or inferiority (or even contempt).

The following extract from the novel *Dieu et moi* (2001) by the Belgian author Jacqueline Harpman provides an apt illustration of the link between pronoun choice and power relations between interlocutors. Conscious violation of the sociolinguistic rules allows an interlocutor to challenge the position of the addressee. The following exchange is situated at the beginning of the story, when the narrator, an old lady and author of many books, has just passed away, surrounded by her family. She had been a fervent non-believer for all her life, and is therefore quite surprised to see an angel fetching her for an interview with God. Facing God (a male), she decides to ask him for a little more time to finish her latest novel. God is magnanimous but he rejects her plea. The choice of pronouns of address reveals the tension between the narrator and God:

Monsieur, dis-je en soupirant. Dieu qui m'écoutait, vous me rendez nerveuse (…) Je voudrais… dis-je. – C'est impossible. Les morts n'écrivent pas de romans. – Vous avez donc lu ma pensée ? – Oublies-tu encore qui je suis ? (…) A la fin, dis-je, que me veux-tu ? Il ne me parut aucunement dérangé par mon propre tutoiement. Au fond, international comme il devait logiquement l'être, peut-être que pour lui le tutoiement n'était qu'un singulier et, si cela se trouve, j'avais eu tort de me formaliser.   (p. 35)

'Sir, I say with a deep sight. God who were listening, you (V) make me nervous. I would like to… I say. Impossible. The deceased don't write novels. Have you (V) read my thoughts? – Do you (T) forget who I am? (…) In the end, I say, what do you (T) want from me? He didn't seem one bit perturbed by my own use of *tu*. On reflection, international as he had to be logically, maybe *tu* was a simple singular address form, and, in that case, I had been wrong to be so formal'.   (translation mine)

The *tu* form used by God with the narrator is indicative of his higher status. Being God entails certain linguistic privileges such as the right to use *tu* with all mortals. God declares later: *Je tutoie toutes les créatures* ('I use *tu* with all creatures'). The connotation of the *vous* of the narrator in the beginning is more ambiguous. It shows respect but also polite defiance. It shows that she is not ready to give up easily, and that even as a mere mortal, she expects to be treated with respect. Her use of *tu* in the second paragraph shows her losing her temper, and has the same negative connotation as the previous *vous*. It is also the only *tu* uttered by the narrator in the story.

It takes a while before learners of French understand the functioning of the system of pronouns of address and become capable of inferring the intention underlying a particular choice correctly. Only at that point can they start using them appropriately.

The analysis of a corpus of oral interviews between NSs and NNSs of French showed that a significant number of participants used either *tu* or *vous* categorically while others used both pronouns in free variation within the same utterance (Dewaele 2002, 2004b). An illustration of this free variation can be seen in the examples (8) and (9).

(8)   Tara: *Bon d'accord, et euh quand **tu** finis votre examen **vous** voulez travailler où et faiser quoi ?*
'Good OK, and err when you (T) finish your exam you (V) want to work where and do what?'

(9)   Rachel: *Et votre **vous vous** avons dit euh **tu** as dit euh euh avant que **vous** êtes une Catalane ?*
'And your (V) you you (V) have said err you (T) have said err err before that you (V) are Catalan?'

These NNSs who switch back and forth between *tu* and *vous* are typically less advanced speakers. They are struggling with verb morphology and try to express "you" with whatever means at their disposal. Their sociolinguistic rules are clearly still in state of flux. Dewaele (2002b) argued that the phenomenon of instability or free variation in the choice of pronouns of address can be approached through Chaos and Complexity Theory (CCT). The system of pronouns in IL is a complex, dynamic and non-linear system. It is first determined by learners' levels of grammatical competence, and secondly by the amount of sociolinguistic knowledge. Using the CTT metaphor, one could say that the developing pronoun system goes through stable states or "equilibrium points" (categorical use of a variant), before varying freely without any apparent systematicity, and finally reaching a state where the variation becomes more NS-like.

We reported instances of this moment of sudden understanding on the part of NNSs in Dewaele (2002b, 2004b). Most interviews started with an implicit or explicit negotiation phase on the choice of pronoun. This phase was always implicit in NS-NS interactions, and between highly advanced NNSs and NSs. In some cases, explicit negotiation occurred on the appropriate pronoun. This is illustrated in example (10) where Aman (a female NNS) starts the interview with Angela (a female NS from France) using the formal possessive adjective *votre*. Angela tells her explicitly to use *tu* instead. As Aman does not seem to understand the meaning of the verb *tutoyer*, Angela repeats the verb in the infinitive, urging her to use *tu*: *Il faut me tutoyer* 'you need to say *tu* to me', and after a short pause adds the pronoun *tu*. Aman agrees but uses the *vous* form again. Angela insists on being addressed with *tu*. Clearly confused, Aman avoids using either pronoun in the following sentence. She then switches effectively to *tu* but persists in the second person plural for the verb (*dites*). She does use the correct possessive adjective (*ton*) but does not agree the gender correctly (*ta*) with the noun *famille*.

(10)   Aman (NNS):   All right *d'accord je suis en compagnie de Angela aujourd'hui, maintenant nous parlons de **votre** famille.*
'All right, OK, I'm in the company of Angela today, now we speak about your (V) family.'

          Angela (NS):   Oui **tutoie**-moi, non.
'Yes, use (T) tu with me # no.'

          Aman (NNS):   *Pardon ?*
'Sorry?'

          Angela (NS):   *Il faut me tutoyer # euh **tu**.*
'One has to use tu with me # err tu.'

          Aman (NNS):   *Tu oui # d'accord si **vous** voulez.*
'Tu yes # OK if you want (V).'

          Angela (NS):   *Non non **tu** # si **tu** veux oui.*
'No no tu # if you (T) would be so kind yes.'

          Aman (NNS):   *Aujourd'hui on parle de toi et moi, de toi et moi, d'accord **tu** me dites euh de quelle chose de **ton** famille ?*
'Today we speak about you and me, you and me, OK, you (T) tell (2nd person plural) me err about what thing about your (T) family?'
(Dewaele 2004b: 394–395)

We argued that this exchange could be an indication that Aman's unwillingness to switch to *vous* may be linked to her unease with the verb morphology of the second person singular. As Aman continues to use *vous* (example (11)), Angela insists again on the use of *tu*, explaining that she does not like to be addressed that way. Aman then admits that she does not know the meaning of the verb *tutoyer*. Angela code-switches to English to make herself clear.

(11)   Aman: *Oui vous êtes trop gentille excusez-moi.*
               'Yes you (V) are too kind forgive (V) me.'

       Angela: *Tutoie-moi.*
               'Use *tutoiement* (T) with me.'

       Aman: *Haha?*
               'Haha?'

       Angela: *Tutoie-moi.*
               'Use *tutoiement* (T) with me.'

       Aman: *Tutoie-moi qu'est-ce que c'est ?*
               "*Tutoie-moi*" what does it mean?'

       Angela: *Oui* you know don't be *ne sois pas trop formelle avec moi.*
               'Yes you know don't be (T) don't be too formal with me.'

       Aman: *Ah d'accord.*
               'Ah OK.'

       Angela: *Il faut me tutoyer.*
               'One (i.e., Aman) has to use *tu* with me.'

       Aman: *Ah "tu" ah d'accord.*
               'Ah "*tu*" ah OK.'   (2004b: 395)

An illustration of this gradual understanding of the different values attached to the pronouns of address can be found in Kinginger (2000), Belz and Kinginger (2002), and Kinginger and Belz (2005), who explored the effect of tele-collaborative learning via electronic interaction on the development of L2 pragmatic competence in American learners of French. The researchers, who work within the sociocultural paradigm (cf. Lantolf & Pavlenko 2001) argue that tele-collaborative language classes allow learners to interact and negotiate social meaning with NS peers and thus develop a wider range of registers. The NS partners pointed to instances of inappropriate use of address pronouns during email exchanges, and this led to changes in the learners' language use. A microgenetic analysis of a limited number of learners showed that increased opportunities for interaction and assistance from peers led to a disambiguation of the numerous sociopragmatic meanings of the pronouns of address. Learners became more aware of the use of the informal forms of solidarity (Belz & Kinginger 2002).

Kinginger and Farrell (2004) explored the development of meta-pragmatic awareness and, more specifically, social indexicality of the address pronouns in French among eight American students in study abroad programs. The authors used a Language Awareness Interview to investigate learners' awareness of pronouns of address in French before and after a sojourn in France. Results suggest that the greatest area of growth was in development of address-form awareness in relation to age-peers. In a follow-up study, Kinginger and Belz (2005) focused on the development of the system of pronouns of address among two participants. They found that the development of T/V use and awareness reflects the nature of the language learning experience. One participant, Bill, who engaged in frequent interactions with NSs of French in a variety of social contexts, understood that *tu* is a sign of solidarity among peers, and used both pronouns appropriately. Another participant, Deidre, who did not engage in frequent interactions with NSs of French, except in service encounters, understood the relevance of *vous* but remained unaware of the social meaning of the *tu* form with peers.

Appropriate use of pronouns of address can be taught within the classroom with some success. Lyster (1994) showed that learners who had had 7 weeks of instruction based on a combination of an analytic approach with its focus on correctness, awareness of the variable rules through explicit instruction, and a communicative approach outperformed a control group, which had received standard experiential instruction, in appropriate use of the address pronoun *vous* in formal written and oral French (Lyster 1994:279).

Lyster and Rebuffot (2002) further investigated the acquisition of pronouns of address in French in Canadian French immersion programs. An analysis of a corpus of audio recordings of teacher-student interaction in immersion classrooms revealed an absence of singular *vous* from classroom discourse. The authors show that *tu* serves as a second-person pronoun of address to indicate singular and familiar reference, but it also indicates indefinite reference along with plural reference. The latter adds to the difficulty already experienced by these young learners of French whose L1, English, uses only one pronoun to encode the functions fulfilled by *tu* and *vous*. The authors also point to a morphological explanation: The over-use of *tu* might be the result of the learners' preference for the morphologically simpler and more frequent verb forms with *tu* which are homophonous for the first, second, third person singular and third person plural in regular verbs, whereas the second person plural is a different verb form (i.e., *je/tu/il(s)/elle(s) aime* versus *vous aimez*) ('*I / you (T) / she / he / they love* versus *you* (V) *love*').

What independent variables are linked to the choice of the address pronoun in the oral French of NSs and NNSs? The analysis of the spoken corpus revealed that the 9 NSs used *tu* more frequently than NNSs in that specific interview-type interaction (Dewaele 2004b). Age and gender of the speaker had no effect. Frequency of use of French was clearly positively correlated with the use of *tu*. NNSs with a system of multiple address pronouns in their L1 were also found to use more *tu*. Among the exogeneous variables, gender of the interlocutor was not to linked to the use of *tu*, but a strong effect for age of the interlocutor emerged, with higher use of *tu* in same-age dyads. These data were complemented with self-reported pronoun use in five situations collected through a written questionnaire from 24 NSs and 102 NNSs. Both groups were found to differ in their reported use of *tu*. More specifically, the NSs used *tu* much more frequently with known interlocutors, but almost never with unknown interlocutors. The NNSs followed this pattern, but not as consistently: They reported occasional use of *vous* with known interlocutors, but also of *tu* with unknown interlocutors. Older NSs and NNSs reported using fewer *tu*, frequent users of French reported a slightly higher use of *tu* overall. NNSs with a system of multiple address pronouns in their L1 were also found to use more *tu*. The results showed that the exogeneous variables had similar effects on NNSs and NSs. A strong interlocutor effect was discovered, with female and younger interlocutors being reportedly addressed more often with *tu* than male and older interlocutors. Both NSs and NNSs reported using *vous* almost exclusively with strangers.

Our questionnaire on self-reported pronoun use also contained one item concerning the perception of difficulty of the use of pronouns of address. We investigated the individual differences in these judgments in Dewaele and Planchenault (2006). Unsurprisingly, the 102 NNSs judged the system to be "quite difficult" on average, while the 24 NSs described it as "easy" on average. Unexpectedly, independent variables such as frequency of use of French and length of stay in a francophone environment – linked to increased native-like use of pronouns of address – did not significantly affect the perception of difficulty of the system of address among NNSs. A closer analysis revealed that increasing use of French and longer stays in a francophone environment was not linked to a linear decrease in the values reflecting perception of difficulty. While NNSs at intermediate levels of contact judged the system to be easier than those with less intense contact, difficulty scores peaked again for NNSs who used French most frequently. This non-linear relation suggests that at some point in the development of their sociolinguistic competence, NNSs feel quite confident about their mastery of the system, but at a later stage they realize that some aspects still elude them. NNSs whose L1s instantiate multiple address pronouns judged the address system in French to be more difficult compared to NNSs whose L1 exemplifies a single address pronoun.

2.2.3   *Subject pronouns* 'nous' *versus* 'on'

The variable use of subject pronouns *nous* and a subgroup of *on* (which designates a group of persons including the speaker) is another pronominal puzzle that learners of French have to solve. In L1 French, '*nous* + 1st person plural verb' is characteristic of formal styles while '*on* + 3rd person singular verb' is typical of informal styles. Both mean 'we'. The utterance *Nous allons à la mer* ('we go to the sea') is thus the formal standard variant, while the utterance *On va à la mer* ('we go to the sea') is the informal variant. A number of studies have been carried out on the use of *nous* versus *on* in the French IL of Canadian students in French immersion programs. Swain and Lapkin (1990) found that students in a late immersion program used *on* much more frequently than students in an early immersion program.

Harley (1992) compared the use of *on* firstly in groups of learners from early immersion, late immersion and extended French, and proceeded then to a comparison of the learner corpora with a corpus of NSs from Quebec. Harley found that the early immersion students used substantially more *nous*. Late immersion students appeared to use *on* more frequently, but the NSs used *on* exclusively in the first person plural context.

Rehner, Mougeon and Nadasdi (2003) analyzed the proportion of *nous* versus *on* in their corpus of spoken French gathered among 41 immersion students in Ontario. It contained 810 tokens of *on*, and 642 tokens of *nous*. The formal variant *nous* thus accounted for 44% of the 1st person plural contexts, the informal variant *on* for the remaining 56%. Exposure to French, through radio and television or through extended stays with Francophone families or in Francophone environments, was found to be linked, though not linearly, to a proportional increase in the use of *on*. Students speaking Spanish or Italian at home were also found to favor the use of *nous*, which could reflect the presence of *noi* and *nosotros* in these languages and the absence of variants similar to *on*. The authors speculate that preference of the English L1 students for *on* could be linked to the fact that English use a subject pronoun *one*. It might not be frequently used in English but its mere existence could facilitate its use in French L2 because of their morpho-phonetical similarity and semantic relatedness. It is also possible that the English L1 students simply did not have another L1 variant pulling them in the direction of *nous*.

Sax (2003) investigated the use of *nous* versus *on* by her American learners of French. Time abroad emerged as the most significant factor. Learners having 2 weeks or less abroad used very few *on* (9%); this proportion jumped to 47% for the intermediate group and reached 93 % for the learners having spent the most time abroad. The three groups used *on* more frequently in the informal situation, which suggests that awareness at some level of stylistic variation exists even before the learners have fully grasped the extent of use in NS speech. Comparing the emergence of *nous/on* variation with the other variables in her study, Sax concludes that *on* is the first stylistic variable to appear.

Lemée (2002) analyzed the *nous/on* variation in the French IL of 48 Irish students. The participants belonged to four proficiency groups ranging from intermediate (high school leavers) to highly advanced (at the end of three years of university study and a year in France). She found relatively little variation across groups, but students who had spent little time in France used more *nous*. Male participants favored *on* but there was no effect for social class. The author argues that the relatively high proportion of *on* in the low proficiency groups was due to incomplete grammatical competence, while the proportion of *on* in the highest group was linked to their growing sociolinguistic competence. Surprisingly, the choice of variant did not vary with the formality of the topic, which suggests that the participants still had some way to go before achieving a full understanding of socio-stylistic variation.

Dewaele (2002a) investigated the use of *nous* versus *on* in both the advanced oral and written French IL of 32 Dutch L1 speakers. A quantitative analysis of the oral corpus revealed that the amount of authentic interaction in the TL positively correlated with use of *on*, as did greater morpho-lexical accuracy rates, fluency, omission of *ne* in negations and use of colloquial vocabulary. A similar analysis of the written corpus revealed proportions of *on* equal to the oral corpus, which suggests that as a group, the learners had not yet completely acquired the variable constraints on the use of *nous/on*.

The research on the variable use of *nous* and *on* shows very clearly so-called pendulum effects in French IL. Initial over-use of the formal variant is often followed by over-use of the informal variant. Learners are keen to sound native, meaning "informal", and are thus tempted to generalize informal variants in formal oral styles or in their formal written work where they are inappropriate from a prescriptive point of view.

2.2.4 *Tense and grammatical aspect*

Even highly advanced learners of French continue to experience difficulties with tense and aspect in French (Ayoun & Salaberry 2005). So-called 'fragile zones' persist in advanced IL reflected in under- and over-use of past time forms in certain contexts (Ayoun 2001, 2004; Bartning 1997; Howard 2002b, 2002c, 2005d; Labeau 2005). The appropriate functional use of certain morphological forms also remains a challenge (Howard 2005a). Howard (2001, 2002a) focused on the adjustment of functional use of aspectuo-temporal morphology of 18 Irish instructed learners of French in conversations with the researcher. The learners were university students specializing in French and who had been learning French for 5–6 years at secondary school. Three groups were distinguished according to amount of instruction in French at the university level, and time spent in France: (a) Two years of classroom instruction; (b) Three years of classroom instruction; (c) Two years of classroom instruction, and an academic year at a university in France. One such analysis concerns the internal development on use of such forms as the *imparfait* (imperfect) at various stages within the advanced learner variety. Overall, it appeared that use of the *imparfait*, the imperfective marker, is less advanced than the use of *passé composé* (perfect), the perfective marker. He found that study abroad students attained a higher level of accuracy across a more expansive range of aspectual contexts (Howard 2001). The study abroad learners were also found to be less likely to overuse the present in past imperfective contexts. Howard (2005a) found that the *plus-que-parfait* (pluperfect) develops later still, which he attributes to the functional complexity of its aspectual value. Also, learners who had had extra instruction showed relatively similar levels of use of the *plus-que-parfait* (pluperfect) compared to study abroad learners. This finding was balanced however by the fact that the study abroad learners did demonstrate an increased development on use of the *imparfait*.

Howard (2004a) used the same population to consider the interaction between linguistic factors in the case of aspectuo-temporal variation in L2 French. He focused on the question of how the learner expresses temporal reference in linguistic contexts where the predictions of the hypothesis at work behind a particular factor (inherent lexical aspect) are at odds with another factor (discourse grounding). He argues that an analysis of such contexts ultimately allows an investigation of the question of which factor(s) might exert a more dominant influence in the learner's aspectuo-temporal system. His results suggest that both factors interact in their effect: The occurrence of each form varies not only between the foreground and the background, but also across the verb types within each ground.

Harley (1992), Lyster (1996) and Swain and Lapkin (1990) reported that the grammatical complexity of verb forms might limit their use in French IL. Their immersion students clearly preferred the present tense although this is the informal option rather than using the more formal *conditionnel* in requests. In the case of the Swain and Lapkin study the students had no trouble associating *s'il vous plaît* ('please') or polite openers such as *pardon* ('pardon'), or *pardonnez-moi* ('excuse me') with the formal register.

Nadasdi, Mougeon and Rehner (2003) studied the expression of future in a corpus of oral IL of 16 French immersion students. They looked at three constructions in
particular: The *futur périphrastique* (periphrastic future) and the *présent de l'indicatif*
(present), which are considered informal, and the *futur fléchi* (synthetic future), considered to be more formal. Overall the *futur périphrastique* accounted for 78% of the
cases, with 11% for the two other variants (p. 205). A VARBRUL analysis revealed that
length of stay in a francophone environment (ranging from 0 to "more than 3 weeks")
had a strong effect, with a linear positive relationship between length of stay and use
of the *futur périphrastique*, an equally negative relation emerged between length of
stay and the use of the *future fléchi*, and, to a lesser degree, the present tense. Girls
were found to use more *future fléchi* than boys. Students from non-Anglophone backgrounds used more *futur périphrastique*. The second part of the study focused on the
use of informal French-Canadian variants of the *futur périphrastique*, *(je vais, je vas*
and *m'as)*. A negative correlation was found between length of stay in a francophone
environment and the proportion of the marked variant *je vas*. No student used the
stigmatized variant *m'as*.

2.3 Studies on syntactic variants

The developing knowledge of phonology, morphology, and the lexicon has to be
supported by a concomitant understanding of syntactic rules that allow the L2 learn-
ers/users to string words together and produce grammatical utterances. The learner
who notices superficial similarities between syntactic rules in his/her L1 and French
syntax could conclude prematurely that getting the words in the right order is less of
a challenge than pronouncing them correctly. Indeed, SVO word order (Subject-Verb-
Object) exists both in English and in French; verb agreement with the subject (person
agreement) functions in similar ways, but at that point English L1 learners of French
may suddenly realize that agreement in gender is also necessary between the head noun
and its adjectives. Then, crucially, learners need to remember that the adjective precedes the noun in English (as in 'the great white cliffs of Dover'), while they can both
precede or follow the noun in French (*les grandes falaises blanches de Douvres*). Moreover, some adjectives in French can be placed pre-nominally or post-nominally but
their meaning changes according to their position (*un grand homme* = a great man,
versus *un homme grand* = a tall man) (see Ayoun, and Herschensohn this volume).
Once learners of French have memorized the syntactic rules governing interrogative
structures and are able to produce grammatically accurate questions, they have to start
sensing the stylistic connotations of the different structures and use them appropriately. This may take a while and widespread variation occurs at that stage. Dewaele
(1999) looked at variation in the use of 8 direct interrogative structures (Yes/No questions and WH-questions) in a corpus of spoken French produced by 5 NSs and 15
NNSs, all living in London, and compared these results with data from existing cor-

pora of oral native French. Examples of every structure are presented in the examples (12) to (19).[3]

(12)   [SV] Mary (NNS):   *Vous n'avez pas de difficulté avec l'anglais ?*
                                'Don't you have difficulties with English?'

(13)   [ESV] Djé (NNS):   *Mais est-ce qu'il y a des cours que vous préférez ?*
                                'But are there courses that you prefer?'

(14)   [V-CL] Steven (NNS):   *Pouvez-vous donner une description ?*
                                'Can you give a description?'

(15)   [QSV] Xenia (NNS):   *Donc pourquoi tu as choisi d'euh d'étudier à Birkbeck ?*
                                'So why have you chosen to err to study at Birkbeck?'

(16)   [QESV] Christine (NS):   *Qu'est-ce que tu vas aller faire à un cours pareil ?*
                                'What are you going to do in such a course?'

(17)   [SVQ] Tanguy (NS):   *Tu habites où à Londres ?*
                                'Where do you live in London?'

(18)   [QV-CL] Karine (NS):   *Ben pourquoi as-tu continué tes études ?*
                                'Well why have you continued your studies?'

(19)   [QV-NP] Martin (NNS):   *Quelle est votre motiv, motivisat, motivation ?*
                                'What is your motiv, motivisat, motivation?'

                                                              (Dewaele 1999: 163)

The structures [V-CL], [QV-CL] and [QV-NP] are generally considered to belong to the careful style, the structures [ESV] and [QESV] are considered neutral, but rather inappropriate in writing, the structures [SV] and [SVQ] are considered colloquial but correct in speech, the structure [QSV] is generally labelled "working-class" and incorrect (Grevisse 1980).

A large amount of variation in the proportions of these structures was found in the NS corpora, making comparisons with NNS corpora very difficult. While the analysis of variation between two variants is quite straightforward, patterns of variation between eight variants are inherently more fluid and complex, and hence harder to compare. A comparison of group averages for NS and NNS revealed no difference between Yes/No questions, but a significant difference emerged for the WH-questions. The NNSs avoided WH-variants that ranked low on the socio-stylistic scale and used more formal WH-variants with clitic inversion instead. We speculated that the higher proportion of inversion could be linked to the influence of English, where there is systematic inversion in interrogatives, strengthening the probability among both NNSs and NSs to opt for inversion in interrogatives when speaking French. No single sociobiographical variable was linked to variation in the proportions of the various interrogative structures. One pragmatic factor, however, was found to strengthen the probability of interrogatives structures with inversion. The 13 participants (3 NSs and

---

3.   S = subject clitic or Noun Phrase; CL = subject clitic; NP = subject Noun Phrase; V = verb; E = est-ce que/qui; Q = WH word or phrase.

10 NNSs) who used [V-CL] and [QV-CL] structures chose them in more than 95% of cases to introduce a new topic or a new theme within a topic. In other words, inversion in the question signalled the shift to a new topic or theme in the interview.

Sax (2003) also considered interrogatives in her investigation on the development of sociolinguistic competence in the French IL of American learners but she focused only on partial interrogatives (WH-questions). The learners showed a strong awareness of the stylistic value of the formal variant with subject-verb inversion (*avez-vous?* 'have you', instead of the less formal *vous avez?* 'you have'), using it at a rate of 21% in the formal context versus only 14% in the informal context. Learners who had spent little to no time abroad used *est-ce que* (question tag) most frequently (44%), followed by inversion, fronting (**Quoi/Que tu fais?* 'what you do'), and finally pronominalization (*tu fais quoi?* 'you do what'). Students who had spent some time abroad used similar proportions of *est-ce que* and inversion, but their use of fronting decreased, while their use of pronominalization increased. Those who had spent most time abroad used fewer *est-ce que* and inversion. The NS control group was found to avoid inversion completely, preferring *qu'est-ce que* and pronominalizations.

2.4 Studies on lexical variants

The vocabulary taught in the French as a foreign language class is inevitably an emasculated version of the rich and vibrant vocabulary used daily by Francophones. Learners wishing to engage in peer interaction with NSs often discover that they are totally outgunned. Their limited stylistic range and ignorance of social, sexual, racial vocabulary as well as colloquial idioms leave them stranded. The reasons for this are linked to ethical and practical concerns, and to the inherent difficulty of acquiring a deep understanding of words with a limited input and relatively little authentic use of the words.

First, one might wonder whether colloquial words that are so frequent in informal interactions between NSs can legitimately be included in teaching manuals. A lot of high frequency colloquial words refer to sexual acts for example, and their inclusion in the foreign language curriculum would probably lead to more than a raising of eyebrows.

Secondly, the teaching system is traditionally more concerned with word phonology, morphology, lexico-syntax and denotative word meaning rather than with associative word meaning (consisting of connotations and stylistic properties) (Bijvoet 2002). The priority in the classroom is given to basic vocabulary learning (denotative word meaning), suitable for the widest possible range of social situations rather than the more fickle and elusive associative word meaning which is inherently more difficult to teach. While denotations are shared by large groups of speakers, connotations are shared by particular communities of practice and are much more dynamic. In order to produce socially appropriate speech, an L2 user needs to master the connotations and the stylistic nuances of particular words (see also Levison & Lessard's chapter in the present volume).

Mougeon and Rehner (2001) and Rehner (2005) considered the development of discourse and linguistic competencies by Ontario French immersion students. Both studies focus on polysemous and polyfunctional words. Mougeon and Rehner (2001) considered *juste* versus *seulement* versus *rien que*; Rehner (2005) studied *comme/like*; *donc/alors/(ça) fait que/so*; *bon*; *là*) which play key roles in the expression of fundamental semantic notions and discursive functions. She compared the students' discursive and non-discursive uses of these expressions with native and teacher norms. The students' frequency of use of the expressions and the range of discursive functions this use fulfills were found to be influenced by the existence of equivalent expressions in their L1. Students' gender and/or social class appeared only to affect the use of those expressions with English discursive equivalents. Frequency of exposure for the students was positively correlated with use of four of the six French expressions. Rehner (2005) showed that, while the students' rank order of frequency of use of the expressions matches almost exactly that of the immersion teachers, it is far from approximating NS norms. In a further study based on the same corpus, Rehner and Mougeon (2003) focused on how the students express the notion of consequence inter-sententially. The students were found to use *alors* and *donc*, as well as a variant in English, *namely so*. The variant (*ça*) *fait que*, which is a very frequent vernacular variant in Quebec French, was absent in the students' educational input and in their speech production.

Dewaele and Regan (2001) addressed the issue of under-representation or avoidance of colloquial words in the advanced French IL of 29 Dutch L1 speakers and of 6 Hiberno-Irish English L1 speakers before and after spending a year in a Francophone environment. Colloquial words (i.e., words which were coded as stylistically colloquial by the French monolingual dictionary *Le Petit Robert* 1979) were found to be very rare in the two corpora as learners preferred more formal synonyms (the word *argent* instead of *fric* 'money', *travailler* instead of *bosser* 'to work'). Even learners who reported frequent active authentic communication in French used significantly fewer colloquial words in the cross-sectional corpus than in a comparable corpus from a control group of 6 NSs of French. While the proportion of colloquial words increased significantly after a year abroad in the longitudinal corpus, the values remained significantly below those obtained from the control group. It was argued that only prolonged authentic contact with the TL community might allow learners to develop the kind of implicit, proceduralized socio-pragmatic knowledge that would allow an increased use of colloquial words. An additional explanation for the relative infrequency of colloquial variants in the speech of advanced learners of French may be that the social-psychological costs of using them inappropriately is higher than that of using formal variants inappropriately, since the use of formal variants is what is expected of L2 learners (Mougeon 2002, personal communication).

In a further study on colloquial vocabulary in French, Dewaele (2004d) analyzed the Birkbeck corpus of interviews between 62 NSs and NNSs of French. Statistical analyses revealed a positive relation between the use of colloquial words and extraversion level, frequency of contact with French and proficiency level in French. It was argued that the extraverts' inclination to take risks, combined with lower communicative anxiety, might explain the higher use of colloquial words. Proficiency seems to be a prerequisite, but not the only factor, for actual use of colloquial vocabulary. Indeed, NSs were found to use only marginally more colloquial words than NNSs.

Evans and Fisher (2005) found that short but intense contact with a TL seems to be linked to an increase of expressive use of that language among elementary level students. They showed that short exchange visits (up to 11 days) by 68 young British pupils in France lead to significant increases in listening skills and in expressive use of language in writing: "verbs of likes and dislikes (e.g., *j'aime, j'aime pas* 'I like, I don't like'), set phrases (e.g. *c'est super* 'it's great', *c'était ennuyeux* 'it was boring'), or use of adjectives of evaluation (e.g., *elle est sympa* 'she's nice')" (Evans & Fisher 2005: 187).

The Evans and Fisher study corroborates the findings for the use of emotion words in our study of advanced Flemish learners of French and advanced Russian learners of English (Dewaele & Pavlenko 2002). Dutch L1 learners of French and Russian L1 learners of English under-used emotion vocabulary in informal conversations and film retellings in their IL. The Dutch L1 learners of French with higher levels of morpho-lexical accuracy – who also happened to be the ones using their IL most frequently outside the classroom (Dewaele 1994) – were found to use a significantly larger pro-portion of, and a greater diversity of, emotion words in their conversations with the researcher. Two other variables were found to be significantly linked to the use of emo-tion words in the French IL corpus: Gender and degree of extraversion. Female and extravert participants used a wider range of emotion lemmas and a greater number of emotion word tokens than male and introvert participants.

Kinginger and Farrell (2005) have presented a completely different approach to the study of lexical competence in French IL. They investigated the effect of the confronta-tion with gendered practices and ideologies on the development of communicative competence in a sample of three American students who spent their study abroad semester in France. Two female and one male student, who kept a diary of their expe-riences, were interviewed before and after their stay abroad. The linguistic instruments used in the study were a standardized test of general proficiency in reading and listen-ing (*Test de Français International*), and a Language Awareness Interview focusing on knowledge of colloquial words. The stay abroad did not boost the linguistic develop-ment of the first female student, Deirdre: Her score went down on the reading test, while it improved only marginally on the listening test and on the colloquial word test. The authors link this finding to her early rejection of French gender practices which she perceived as sexual harassment. This resulted in sense of alienation from the social context and interrupted her investment in the language learning process. The second female student, Jada, saw the French gender practices as a challenge but engaged in numerous social interactions with French men. The authors connect this to her dra-matic gains on the three linguistic tests. The male student, Bill, did not question his performance of gender in light of the new social environment, was successful in the classroom as well as in interactions of NSs of French, and made spectacular gains on the linguistic tests. The authors are careful not to attribute causality to the relation be-tween the students' stories and the quantitative data, but their study sheds a welcome light on the baffling issue of the huge amount of inter-individual variation in the rate of acquisition of sociolinguistic competence after a period abroad.

3. Discussion

This final section will first consider some methodological issues about the studies that were reviewed. Some general trends in the results will then be identified and interpreted by considering the complex interaction between dyad characteristics and individual factors.

The first methodological point to be made is the general preference for cross-sectional studies on relatively large samples rather than longitudinal studies. This means that groups of different proficiency levels are distinguished, and the results are interpreted as an illustration of on-going development. Longitudinal studies tend to have smaller sample sizes, which could lead to questions about the generalizability of the results, as outliers might obscure or accentuate group patterns. More longitudinal studies with large groups are needed (cf. Howard 2005a; Regan 2004; Thomas 2002, 2004).

Another methodological difficulty lies in the sample size of the NS baseline data. As the researchers usually work in French departments with L2 learners, they usually have access to larger numbers of learners than NSs, which are typically language teachers or assistants who might be tempted to produce hyper-correct speech when recorded in interviews. Authors generally refer to studies carried out in native French, allowing them to compare values for certain variables. However, inter-corpora comparisons are often difficult to carry out because of the different methodologies used to collect the data, different categorizations of dependent and independent variables, different times, populations and tasks. Using someone else's corpus means that one is in the dark about certain aspects that might be crucial for the interpretation of data and results. The inclusion of even a small number of NSs in the original design provides a valuable base-line value. Some statistical tests such as t-tests are quite robust and can be used to compare samples of unequal size.

A final methodological problem resides in the fact that researchers can never be entirely certain that the variation they observe in the use of sociolinguistic variants is synchronic or diachronic in origin. The use of certain variants may increase over time, but their use in certain contexts may suddenly drop, not because the L2 user has forgotten the variant, but because it may suddenly be judged too risky, or because it may have morphological implications that the L2 user wishes to avoid (for example a L2 user may wish to avoid the formal pronoun *vous* in combination with the verb *dire* in order to avoid the irregular form *dites*, and feel safer to use the regular *tu dis*). One possible way to overcome the limitation in the interpretation of quantitative data is through supplementary qualitative data. While L2 users may not always be aware of every single choice of a sociolinguistic variant, they may have developed general strategies linked to speech styles in specific situations, and they may have established their own personal list of the degree of markedness of certain variants. Researchers who tap into the personal experience of the learner/user through diary studies or meta-linguistic and meta-pragmatic interviews can obtain strong clues on why individuals act in certain ways. The research shows that issues of identity, attitudes and self-perception are linked to sociolinguistic choices. By combining this emic perspective (participant-centered) with the traditional quantitative analyses (typically researcher-centered, hence etic), sociolinguists could obtain a more global understanding of variation patterns among learners and L2 users.

One fairly consistent finding in our overview is the over-use of formal variants. It has been linked to restricted access to sufficiently diverse linguistic input. Lack of access makes it very difficult for L2 users to pick up the linguistic characteristics and variation patterns of their chosen community of practice within the larger group of TL speakers. Instructed L2 learners are mainly exposed to formal speech styles and written material (see Mougeon et al. 2002).

A consistent and systematic finding in the literature is that authentic interactions with NSs of the TL have a noticeable effect on the learners' IL. A more prolonged stay in the TL community, or intense contact with members of that community, is necessary to develop sociolinguistic and pragmatic competence. Some of the changes seem to happen without the user noticing, such as specific lexico-syntactic choices in the formulation of emotional speech acts (Pavlenko 2002b), which the author attributes to conceptual restructuring linked to the process of L2 socialization.

However, learners might consciously reject linguistic variants common in certain communities of practice. Dewaele (2004c) reported that L2 users often refrain from using swear words in the L2 because they feel that NSs display a proprietary attitude towards these words. L2 users who betray their non-nativeness through their accent but do use these words that characterize "in-group" membership may be surprised by the unwanted illocutionary effects. The development of advanced language learners' sociolinguistic competence allows them to identify not only gender-specific variants, but also social or generational speech patterns used by groups of NSs with whom they may wish to identify. The young learners' desire to stop sounding like their teachers at some point in their linguistic development probably reflects a similar process in the L1 where it is perceived 'uncool' to speak like one's parents. By consciously traveling up and down the continuum of speech styles learners can show their linguistic independence. However, learners may also consciously decide not to adopt certain variation patterns from the NS community if they judge them to be in conflict with their own ideological and cultural beliefs or sense of self. Tensions can also arise between L2 learners and NSs on 'appropriate' topics of conversation. Kinginger (2004) reports the case of a young American working-class woman from a migrant family, Alice, who spends a year studying in France, and slowly acquires sociolinguistic and socio-cultural competence in French. Alice expresses frustration in her diary about her companion Cedric who refuses to respect her decision to ignore politics and who criticizes the political actions of the US:

Moi, je fais pas la politique, je m'en fous (…) j'ai demandé si on pourrait changer de sujet… j'ai essayé au moins 3 fois de changer mais chaque fois il a continué.

(Kinginger 2004: 236–237)

'I, I don't do politics, I don't care (…) I've asked whether we could change topic…I tried to change it at least 3 times but every time he has continued'. (translation mine)

Variation patterns can extend to non-verbal areas of self-expression. Kinginger and Farrell (2005: 9) illustrate the resistance of Deidre to conform to French gender patterns. Deidre perceives herself as an athletic American woman for whom it is perfectly acceptable to go to class in sweat pants. She can't understand what she perceives as French women's obsession with their looks: "Monday morning rolls around and the girls dress up like they're going out Friday night, and it just – it looks ridiculous to me" (Interview, May 2003).

Another recurrent finding in the literature is the relatively small amount of inter-stylistic variation which suggests that the L2 users have not yet identified (or differentiated) the socio-stylistic value of the various sociolinguistic variants and do not style-shift in a native-like way. However, inter-individual variation between L2 users is generally much larger than such variation between NSs. One possible explanation is that the L2 user's probability of choosing a variant will always differ from that of the NS as an extra set of independent variables enters the equation. Beebe (1988) was right to advocate caution in the use of sociolinguistic methods for the analysis of variation in the L2. Superficially similar patterns of variation may be the result of different underlying mechanisms. In the L1, the choice of a particular variant can be the result of a conscious or unconscious decision between instantaneously accessible alternatives of which the illocutionary effects are perfectly clear. It is unlikely that L2 users always have much liberty, their choice may sometimes be guided by L1 or IL transfer, and they may be unsure about the exact illocutionary effects of a variant.

The findings do have some important didactic implications. Valdman (2000, 2003) has advocated the inclusion of a variety of speech styles in French instruction in order to provide learners with a realistic linguistic diversity. Rather than sticking to the "standard" norm in French classes using contrived and inauthentic materials, Valdman proposes to introduce the more dynamic "pedagogical" norm that would "offer learners changing targets that lead them progressively toward the full range of TL variants" (2003: 13). It would adhere to standard French expected of learners, but it would account for sociolinguistic considerations, for attitudes of NSs toward sociolinguistic variants, and for the own students' acquisitional patterns. Training in the pedagogical norm rather than the standard norm would allow the transition from L2 learners to L2 users to be much smoother. Daily interactions and service encounters happen generally in a relatively informal style, it thus makes perfect pedagogical sense to prepare L2 learners appropriately for these interactions.

Hedgcock and Lefkowitz (2000) refer to Valdman's notion of pedagogical norm in their study on overt and covert prestige in the French language classroom. Their starting point was that social status and prestige as instantiated in the classroom setting are important socio-affective factors linked to the acquisition of effective pronunciation skills in the L2. An analysis of the performance and perceptions of 100 American university students in a French class showed the wide range of perceptions of what it means to "sound good" when speaking French. After a detailed study of phonemic and phonological errors combined with students' perceptions, beliefs and attitudes, the authors conclude that a fairly homogeneous value system (i.e., a pedagogical norm) exists among their students. The authors do point out that the chief concern of the students was to establish group solidarity and please their peers.

4. Conclusion

To conclude, both the investigation of the acquisition and performance of sociolinguistic competence in the L2 and the teaching of sociolinguistic rules present considerable theoretical, methodological and practical obstacles. First, because the target is an abstract set of complex native variation patterns, it takes a while before learners understand what they are aiming for. In other words, it is a moving target that no single book or grammar can capture. One difficulty for the learners is that once they have decided on what the appropriate style should be, they may feel overwhelmed by the sheer amount of choices that have to be made instantaneously about appropriate variants - ranging from phonology to syntax, and even discourse. Inevitably, when juggling with too many balls, they will occasionally drop a few, so to speak, which could have embarrassing consequences. Code-switching to a vernacular style in the L1 was one effort- and embarrassment-avoidance strategy observed by Tarone and Swain (1995) in immersion education. Another difficulty facing the learner is the huge variability that exists within the NS community (both socially and geographically), and the learners' need to identify the sociolect that will suit them best. Secondly, the sociolects are ever-evolving. As a consequence, stigmatized variants may lose their stigma and become appropriate in more informal speech styles (such as the omission of *ne* or the use of *on* instead of *nous*). This makes it harder to capture them and present them as pedagogical norm to language learners. Thirdly, no amount of classroom instruction can suffice to instill the intuition of what sociolinguistic variant is appropriate in a specific situation. The English L1 learner of French who is used to a single pronoun of address will struggle to form an accurate conceptual representation of a system that involves two pronouns. That learner will quickly realize in authentic communication that this choice of pronoun in French is not just a trivial matter. While no NS would complain about the inappropriate omission of *ne*, interrogative structure or liaison, there would probably be a much stronger reaction on the part of the NS for an inappropriate use of *tu*. The fact is that every NS of French recalls instances of inappropriate use of pronouns in exchanges with other NS of French (Dewaele 2004b). Acquiring sociolinguistic competence in French equates the ability to navigate a social minefield. It may become easier and automatic after sufficient practice, but nobody can ever feel completely safe.

What is a minefield for learners is a rich area of investigation for researchers. Further research on the acquisition of sociolinguistic competence could concentrate on differences in the trajectories followed by learners in immersion education and those in purely instructed settings, following the example of studies like those by Thomas (2004). It is equally important that researchers studying the IL development of instructed learners enquire in sufficient detail about the learners' contact and exposure to the TL outside the classroom. In this age of global communication, learners have many more opportunities to use their IL skills than ever before. The likelihood of being exposed to the TL is also much greater for learners living in big multilingual and multicultural cities. Much more detailed research is also needed on individual differences between learners/users and these need to be linked to patterns of sociolinguistic variation to psychological, psycholinguistic (cf. Preston 2000), socio-pragmatic and socio-cultural variables. The addition of an emic perspective to the traditional etic perspective of variationist sociolinguistics could lead to a better understanding of the complex processes underlying variation patterns. Sociolinguistic variation reflects L2 users' choices, which can be unconscious or conscious. Ideally, researchers could combine quantitative and qualitative perspectives. Rigorous quantitative analyses could identify the effect of specific independent variables and establish probabilities of occurrence of the dependent sociolinguistic variables. A complementary phase could then include the L2 users' metalinguistic intuitions on their use of the dependent variables (conscious choices), their social and personal context, their perception of belonging to different groups within the TL and the L1 community. The qualitative information might help interpret the quantitative findings and hence escape the correlational fallacy (Pavlenko 2002a). The argument for a combination of etic and emic perspectives is not new (see Eckert 1989; Trévise & Noyau 1984) but it seems worth restating it in order to avoid the fragmentation of our field into isolated fiefdoms.

The productivity of a field can be estimated through the amount of output it generates. It is more difficult to judge its impact on a larger scale. Didactic implications of sociolinguistic research have found their way to the teaching profession. In my opinion, the best illustration of the impact of the sociolinguistic enterprise within social sciences would be through the incorporation of sociolinguistic variables and issues in the work of psycholinguists, psychologists and pragmaticists. To achieve this goal, sociolinguists need to communicate their findings not only to their own community, but also to their peers outside their field. By drawing them in, old problems could be solved or discarded, and new broader research agendas could be established.

PART III

French in applied linguistics

CHAPTER 9

Language ideology and foreign language pedagogy*

Robert W. Train
Sonoma State University

Résumé

Ce chapitre propose une perspective à la fois critique, réflexive et sociolinguistique des idéologies autour de 'la langue française' en ce qui concerne les implications des recherches effectuées sur l'idéologie de la langue pour la linguistique appliquée et la pédagogie des langues étrangères. Ce chapitre expose la notion de Langue standard native (NSL) comme un ensemble d'idéologies langagières qui, par le processus complexe de la standardisation, arrive à définir les 'réalités' culturelles, linguistiques, et identitaires pour les apprenants et les enseignants du français aussi bien pour les locuteurs dits natifs que pour les non-natifs. Afin de mieux comprendre le rôle de la standardisation dans la pédagogie du français langue étrangère, l'auteur présente aussi les concepts jumellés de l'hyperstandardisation et de la Langue hyperstandard pédagogique. Pour les recherches futures, examiner les idéologies langagières offre une voie vers des pédagogies du français qui répondent aux dimensions politiques, socioculturelles et éthiques de l'enseignement et de l'apprentissage de la langue dans des contextes globaux et interculturels.

Abstract

This chapter outlines a critical perspective on the ideologies surrounding 'the French language' in terms of the implications of research on language ideology for applied linguistics and foreign language pedagogy. Language ideology is discussed in light of research on practice and reflexivity. This chapter critically examines the Native Standard Language (NSL), a constellation of hegemonic ideologies of language, (non)standardness, and (non)nativeness that has come to define through standardization the constructed 'realities' of language, culture, and identity inside and outside the French-as-foreign-language classroom. The concepts of hyperstandardization and Pedagogic Hyperstandard are also explored. It is shown in socio-historical perspective that applied linguistics and FL pedagogy have participated in the inventing of languages and the imagining of communities, as well as in a monolingual nativism

* I would like to thank Dalila Ayoun for her patience, perseverance and encouragement in bringing this chapter and volume into being. I also extend many thanks to Claire Kramsch and two anonymous reviewers who provided insightful and useful comments and suggestions on various drafts of this chapter.

attached to the Native Speaker construct. In considering directions for future research, it is suggested that addressing language ideologies in the classroom and in applied linguistic research is a fundamental step in working toward a French language pedagogy that is critically responsive to the political, sociocultural and ethical dimensions of language practice, pedagogical practice and identity in the teaching and learning of French in global and inter-cultural contexts.

1. Language ideology and problem framing in foreign language pedagogy and applied linguistics

This chapter presents an overview of some of the issues and approaches raised by the intersection of two important bodies of interdisciplinary research into language as social and pedagogical practice: Language ideology and standardization. In particular, I will critically examine the construct of (Non)Native Standard Language (NSL) (Train 2003) – a constellation of ideologies of language, (non)standardness, and (non)nativeness that has come to define the sociohistorically – and discursively-constructed 'realities' of 'the French language' inside and outside the FL classroom. This chapter is intended to provide insight into how foreign language (FL) pedagogy and applied linguistic research shape, and are shaped by, language ideology.

A greater understanding of language ideology in pedagogy and research responds to the emergence of applied linguistics as an interdisciplinary field that mediates between the theory and the practice of language acquisition, socialization and use, in order to provide insight into the teaching and learning of foreign language (Kramsch 2000). From this perspective, pedagogy comes to be understood in theoretically-grounded terms as sociocultural, historical, and semiotic practice informed by the rich interplay between micro-level research into what happens in classrooms, and macro level inquiry into broader educational and social contexts involving language planning and policy.

The increasing focus on connections between research and practice also highlights a basic "problematicity" (Bygate 2004) in applied linguistics, that is, a concern for posing real-world problems, and for engaging in meta-reflection on the relevance of those theorized problems for practice, in both research and pedagogy. However, questions have been raised as to how far applied linguistic theory is "independent of – and/or indifferent to – the concern for responsive action" (Bygate 2004:7) with respect to the concerns of learners, teachers, and society at large.

In this chapter, I will make the case for an applied linguistics that is centrally involved in promoting a critical awareness of what FL educators and applied linguists do, and how we conceptualize what we do. This mutually reflexive project has the goal of working toward a more critical and responsive pedagogy (Apple, Kenway, & Singh 2005; Bowers & Flinders 1990) through which educators are aware of, and capable of responding in educationally constructive ways to the ecology of FL education with its complex relationships between classroom practices and the multifarious contexts of human experience in an increasingly globalized world.

This perspective is intended to be a broadly contextualizing approach to "problem framing" (Block 1999) in applied linguistics that recognizes that the framing of problems and the generation of solutions often depend on metaphors underlying the narratives which generate problem-setting and orient the direction of problem-solving. In identifying problems for applied linguistic research, the study of language ideology can shed light on whether a second language problem that is manifested as a classroom problem might not be perhaps more of a language policy issue (Bygate 2004:7). For instance, language choice, code-switching, and orthography are all examples of canonical classroom problems that are embedded in larger ideological contexts of language use (see Blyth 1995; Cerquiglini 1995; Jaffe 1999; Pavlenko 2003b).

Bringing the study of language ideology and standardization into the theory and practice of FL pedagogy assumes a broadly sociolinguistic vision of applied linguistics that incorporates an ethical dimension intended to prepare applied linguists to address actual inequalities in the lives of real speakers (see Rampton 1997).[1] This chapter will explore some of the connections between the teaching and learning of French and standardization as socio-historically and culturally embedded ideology and practice constituted at many levels in society and in the lives of individual speakers. This complex interplay between ideology and language offers a fruitful place from which to critically look at the practices of French and FL pedagogy in terms of their multi-faceted role in the construction of sameness and difference, as well as inequality.

Problematicity and problem-framing come to the fore because discursive practices of variation have generally been represented as the supposed problem in applied linguistics and FL pedagogy for which the Native Standard Language (NSL) construct offers a solution. However, I will argue that variation is not the problem, but rather standardization and its often troubling educational and social consequences. As a response to variation and diversity, each standardizing solution has generated as many problems as it has ostensibly solved. The problematicity imperative of applied linguistics can be critically directed toward grappling with the dilemmas engendered by the NSL as a deeply problematical construct of learner competence, identity, and communication.

---

1.   Drawing on Hymes' characterization of "socially constituted linguistics" (Hymes 1974), Rampton (1997) articulates a view of applied linguistics as a social and cultural semiotics which foregrounds cultural and social organization. The socially constituted study of language re-conceptualizes the conventional notion of language-as-grammar in terms of language as a repertoire of ways of speaking shaped through social action and communicative practice.

2.   (Standard) French and beyond: Ideology and reflexivity

French offers applied linguists an important site for critically exploring *language ideology* as a far-reaching phenomenon encompassing specific ideologies of language[2] in FL education and applied linguistic research. As "probably the most highly standardized of European languages" (Haugen 1972: 247), 'the French language' has come to be conventionally confused with that of *standard language* (SL). The reduction of 'French' to standard language entails a notion of 'the language' as a set of linguistic forms and structures, such as 'words' and 'grammar', codified in dictionaries, grammar manuals, and textbooks. These standardizing codifications are seen to objectively provide the accepted rules for the 'correct' or 'appropriate' use for a given language, as well as assuring the basis for efficient 'transmission' of 'information' and 'communication' between speakers of the 'same' language, and translation between 'different' languages. French has been an attractive case study for standardization, and its political, cultural and educational consequences (e.g., Dannequin 1988; Fishman 1972; Grillo 1989; Joseph 1987; Lodge 1993; Schiffman 1996). This considerable body of research has described French as being constructed by an ongoing socio-political, socio-cultural and socio-linguistic process of *standardization* involving the codification and institutionalization of the dominant linguistic and cultural norms of privileged speakers in the social, political, cultural and historical contexts of nation-state and empire.

As research into language ideology and standardization has made clear, the socio-historically-situated and ideological-constructed practices surrounding standard languages are not unique or exclusive to French. In somewhat paradoxical terms, a greater understanding of the specificity of French can lead us to a larger critical awareness of how language and ideology shape, and are shaped by educational practices in a diversity of languages. The salience of standardization with respect to French highlights significant connections between notions of 'the language' and the FL language education context in which French is part of a constellation of ideologies and practices attached to English, Spanish, and other (standard) languages taught in schools.

Standardization is, in fact, not unique to the French language, but a potent force throughout linguistic and educational landscapes both nationally and globally, as has been amply shown for English (e.g., Bonfiglio 2002; Milroy & Milroy 1999) and Spanish (e.g., Mar-Molinero 2000). Perhaps, the notion of a primordially standardized French, the *exception française* ('French exception') taken to an extreme in language, has more to do with another fundamental misconception: That ideology always resides *chez les autres* ('with the others'), and that from a US perspective in which 'our' English language is seen as somehow more 'open' (see Pennycook 1998) and less standardized than 'their' language, promulgated by the Academy and a highly centralized

---

2.   I will use *language ideology* as a broad term pertaining to ideas and practices surrounding language structure, language use, and speaker identity in relation to social context. *Language ideology*, then, is the superordinate term subsuming *ideologies of language*, *linguistic ideology*, and *linguistic ideologies*.

educational system. In order to challenge this we/they dichotomy, I will outline a practice-focused perspective on ideology for applied linguists and educators working with French as a foreign language (FFL).

A more critical view of ideology has emerged. It conceptualizes *ideology* not as the polar opposite of *reality*, but rather as both constitutive and reflective of complex socially- and discursively-constructed realities of language, its speakers, and the culture in which speakers live (e.g., Blommaert 2005; Gee 1990; van Dijk 1998; Woolard & Schieffelin 1994). This crucial conceptual and methodological issue in theorizing language and ideology can be expressed, drawing on Hasan (1996), in the following terms: While ideology left unexamined and unquestioned can mask the socio-cultural and historical contingency of 'reality', the examination of ideology through a critical lens can powerfully reveal this same constructed view of the world as it is, or may be, lived by a significant number of persons in society.

From a critical discourse perspective, language is "always and everywhere ideological" (Gee 1990:104). Given the ubiquity of language, all accounts of language, including those that form the basis of applied linguistics and FL pedagogy, are fundamentally ideological. They are claims for the reality and validity of certain 'authentic', 'legitimate', and/or 'authoritative' views of language and its speakers. These claims are constructed and represented through an ongoing reflexive discourse involving complex processes of evaluation, prescription, creativity, awareness, obfuscation, imagination, value, and identity.

Ideology can also be a powerful basis for reflection and action, because it is about how we understand, enact, and judge what we do as human beings in relation to others. In terms of language, ideology is bound up with *reflexivity*, which is manifested in a set of meta-discursive or metalinguistic vocabulary, concepts, techniques, and stances that allow us "to use language to communicate about the activity of using language" (Lucy 1993:9). In turn, reflexivity is basic to the awareness of language that makes it possible to comment and reflect on what '(the) language' and '(the) culture' are, and how they should be, how they are used, and by whom. The reflexive dimension of language ideology implies engagement and/or non-engagement in certain practices through the interplay of individual speaker's agency and normative structures of language with their constraints on behavior in given contexts.

The fundamental reflexivity of language has been identified in at least three broad areas. First, reflexive discourse can be focused within a given linguistic code (Lucy 1993), such as the comments in French about French (e.g., *parler correctement* 'speak correctly') that are a feature of the standardizing constraints that children typically encounter beginning with their first experiences in school (Dannequin 1988). Second, reflexivity can be observed in the meta-discursive practices surrounding two or more distinct named codes (Lucy 1993), as in the case of the discourse in English on American television concerning French. Third, linguistic reflexivity has emerged as central to the process of "language constructing language" (Taylor 2000), without which "there could be no language policies or language planning, no linguistic prescription, no language mavenry, no language politics, and no national ideologies of language" (Taylor

2000:489). This line of inquiry has consistently noted that there could not be any standardized languages without the ideologically-constitutive role of reflexive language, because standardization requires that "the language users be able to talk about, characterize, evaluate, recommend, prescribe, ask questions about, and refer to language" (Taylor 2000:489).

From the standpoint of French-language pedagogy, the critical study of language ideology highlights several important inter-related issues that will be discussed in the following section in terms of standardization. First, language ideologies have both symbolic value and practical consequences for learner and teacher practices both inside and outside the French language classroom. Second, language is deeply reflexive and ideological in everyday uses and conceptions of language as well as in the structural account of mainstream linguistics, supported by the formal description of the real or imagined utterances of idealized native speakers, sometimes the linguists themselves. To critically reflect on ideology as part and parcel of language is to also acknowledge that language, identity, and culture are fundamentally inseparable. From there, it is possible to discern the problematic relationship between the complex language-culture practices as they can be observed in the "context of situation" (Malinowski 1923),[3] and what is thought, or assumed, or imagined, or represented to be '(the) French language' and its speakers. Third, the constellation of attitudes, beliefs, experiences and practices that constitute French language ideology are not isolated from other ideologies such as those concerning learning, teaching, identity, and community.

3.   Standardization and Native Standard Language

I will outline the notion of (Non)Native Standard Language (NSL). The (non)standardness dimension frames variability and diversity as a 'problem' that applied linguistics and FL pedagogy has for the most part addressed in terms of the standardizing constructs of language that "make language" (Harris 1980) and "make it safe for science and society" (Bauman & Briggs 2003). The standard language (SL) is ideologically fused with (non)nativeness through an ongoing process of standardization by which is constructed the supposed authority, validity and reality of the SL and its speakers.

Problematizing the 'reality' imposed by SLs, contributions from diverse research traditions (including applied linguistics, sociolinguistics, anthropology, education, and cultural theory) have increasingly portrayed standardization as the *ideological* construction of a language (e.g., Crowley 1990; Lodge 1993; Milroy 2001; Makoni &

---

3.   An influential figure in anthropology and linguistics, Malinowski expressed what he called the "Ethnographic view of language" in which "utterance and situation are bound up inextricably with each other and the context of situation is indispensable for the understanding of the words. Exactly as in the reality of spoken or written languages, a word without *linguistic context* is a mere figment and stands for nothing by itself, so in the reality of a spoken living tongue, the utterance has no meaning except in the *context of situation*" (Malinowski 1923:307).

Pennycook 2005). The SL is not limited to 'the language' in any narrow formal and structural sense. The validity, authority, and reality attached to the SL construct do not reside solely in the codifications (e.g., dictionaries, literary texts, grammars) that give material existence to the language. These codifications and the very notion of a language are artifacts of standardization, and they must be reframed to emphasize that the SL always involves a complex cultural context of standardization.

The SL construct has been shown to be part of a linguistic culture with practices that entail significant socio-cultural, political and pedagogical implications, including tensions and conflicts. Speakers of SLs can be said to live in "standard language cultures" in which certain languages are believed by their speakers to exist in standardized forms, affecting the way in which they think about their own language and language in general (Milroy 2001:530). Given the globalization of SL culture, it is virtually impossible to find speakers who are unaffected by standard language practices, generally associated with Western notions of schooling and literacy (Mühlhäusler 1996). Therefore, the practices surrounding the SL can be said to provide a powerful, if not hegemonic, normative metadiscourse that comments on the perceived reality of language in society by defining what counts as 'a' or 'the' language, and profoundly shapes the discursive practices surrounding that constructed idea of language and speakers in a given sociocultural context.

In terms of pedagogy, the SL ideology (Lippi-Green 1997; Milroy & Milroy 1999) is central to what language professionals, students and the public generally believe to be important about teaching and learning, as well as what is deemed irrelevant to the educational endeavor. Since, for example, language and schooling often coalesce around notions of 'appropriate' behavior, educators and learners commonly assume that SL practices must be privileged over all others by virtue of their 'correctness' or 'appropriateness' (Fairclough 1992).

4. Hyperstandardization and Pedagogic Hyperstandard

I will use the term Pedagogic Hyperstandard to conceptualize the standardized object of FL pedagogy that is distanced from both the Native Standard Language (NSL) and the complexity of actual speaker practices (Train 2000). The notion of Pedagogic Hyperstandard is intended as a way to critically examine the sociocultural, sociolinguistic and pedagogical stances toward language, culture, speaker identity, competence, and communication in FL pedagogy that have been constructed around the complex ideological process of standardization.

As the NSL is constructed through standardization, the Pedagogic Hyperstandard results from hyperstandardization (Cameron 1995; Train 2000). Hyperstandardization has been described as the desire for uniformity taken to an extreme, or "the mania for imposing a rule on any conceivable point of usage, in a way that goes beyond any ordinary understanding of what is needed to ensure efficient communication" (Cameron 1995:47). For example, unrelenting focus by a teacher on the 'rules' of normative grammar and 'accuracy' assumes that the learners' speech, in order to be 'accurate,' should conform to the written standard French with its orthographical rules, as in the case of past participle agreement (e.g., *je l'ai [l' = la fourchette] mise sur la table*). Standardization and hyperstandardization can be seen as part of a larger ideological phenomenon of "verbal hygiene", a set of practices based on "an urge to improve or 'clean up' language" (Cameron 1995: 1). In addition, this attempt to sanitize the language of the French classroom can lead teachers to systematically suppress or marginalize common L2 learner and bilingual practices, such as code-switching and language-mixing, which are deemed outside the SL with its monolingual NS ideology (see Blyth 1995).

Cameron (1995) crucially points out that it is necessary to examine the larger goals of standardization (e.g., linguistic uniformity, communicative efficiency) in terms of "the more specific interests of people who made a living from linguistic production", those she calls "craft professionals" (Cameron 1995: 42) and elsewhere termed "language controllers" (Joseph 1987) and "language guardians" (Milroy & Milroy 1999). In asking whose professional interests have been served by standardization and hyperstandardization, one must include traditional grammarians, language teachers, and linguists (applied, theoretical, descriptive and prescriptive alike), all of whose livelihood centers on authoritative knowledge of the language in the construction of which they participate. Dannequin (1988: 26), in her study of French language teaching to French-speaking children in 3 "traditional" *Cours Préparatoire* classes in France (first grade in the US), offers a stark demonstration of the control wielded by a teacher over the language practices of 6 year olds: "Now you will tell me what happened in the story I have just read to you. *Think carefully so you can say it quite correctly and not speak nonsense.* So now who has something to say?"

The construction of 'the French language' as the Pedagogic Hyperstandard of FL classroom discourse and pedagogical materials involves a complex process of recontextualization, briefly outlined here. The "imaginary discourse" (Bernstein 2000: 33) of French in the FL classroom is constructed and reconstructed through a chain of ideological transformations involving shifting contexts of use. First, the complexity of discursive practices of French speakers in a number of contexts are selectively appropriated, relocated, and refocused (to use Bernstein's terminology) from their original sites to constitute the discourse of Native Standard French, as seen above in the teacher's instructions to the class. Next, these standardized practices of French take on a life outside or on the margins of the French speaking (national) community, where they are recontextualized as a discourse of Pedagogic Hyperstandard for the purpose of French-as-foreign-language within the various global, national, local contexts of education, such as in the case of French taught in American schools.

Textbook publishers, content consultants, and educational authorities act together as "recontextualizing agents" in the process of symbolic control and authority to create school knowledge in the form of pedagogic discourse and practice (Bernstein 2000). This "official knowledge" (Apple 2000) can be seen in terms of the "monological knowledge" (Giroux 1981) that privileges 'scientific facts', including 'the language', and acts against the incorporation and validation of students' unofficial knowledge into classroom discourse.

5.   Visions of unity, acts of exclusion: A critical sociohistorical perspective on the ideology of variation-as-problem

Situated within a culture of standardization (Train 2002), the NSL and Pedagogic Hyperstandard represent and validate a standardizing view of the perceived or imagining reality of language, community, and identity in which variability and diversity are problematic. The culture of standardization has been most visible in terms of language and schooling where standardness reigns largely undisputed, as evidenced in the apparent acceptance by educators and the public of the basic assumptions surrounding standards in education in the United States (see Darder 2005; Reagan 2002). From a critical socio-historical perspective, applied linguists and educators must engage in a problematization of the standard stance toward variation and diversity. In this section, I will turn the question around and address the problem of standard French in terms of an ideology of variation-as-problem.

Standardization has been said to suppress present and future variability in language that does not conform to the language-culture practices of adult educated speakers or writers codified in, for example, grammars or dictionaries (Milroy & Milroy 1999). Applying Irvine and Gal's (2000) terminology, the NSL as linguistic ideology provides an interpretive structure of language and culture which seeks to erase or devalue the observable complexity and variability of language-culture practices deemed to be outside standardized practices. For instance, commenting on departures from standard French as '*ce n'est pas du français*' amounts to the erasure of non-authorized lexical items from what is seen to constitute the valid language. Common terms used by many French-speakers in France are borrowings from English (e.g., *zapper, se crasher, shopping*) that have been marginalized from the ideologically native and standard French language by being designated as *franglais* or *franglicismes* – as if French or any other language could or should somehow be 'pure,' that is, 'untouched' by 'foreign' influences and unaltered by changes in society (see Ager 1999: 98–115; Yaguello 2000). In a socio-historical context, standard French was built upon a sort of textual silence and absence that was already present in the putative linguistic unity of Latin model language. Latin was preserved in extant written texts which demonstrated a surprising uniformity and conformity to codified norms despite the certainty of variation among Latin speakers in the linguistically and culturally heterogeneous Roman empire (Herman 1991).

For all its exclusionary and silencing power, however, standardization does not eliminate variability. Rather, standardization constructs variation as a salient and problematic category. The ideology of variation-as-problem has been constructed and reproduced in large part by the reflexivity and agency of language professionals who institutionalize a set of authoritative meta-discursive stances toward practices of vari-

Table 1. Some French discourse practices of variation, with examples

world, national, and continental practices of Francophonie	e.g., Canadian/Quebec French, French as official language in African nations
diglossia	Modern French vs. spoken "New French" (Joseph 1988)
inter-speaker variation	dialects, sociolects, argot, *patois*, slang, child language, teen language, *verlan*, non-native, foreign, accent
intra-speaker variation	formal/informal register, genre, *francais de référence*, *style littéraire*
unassimilated borrowings and neologisms	English loan words, *franglais*
inherent variability	no two speakers speak exactly alike, idiolect
diachronic, temporally-bounded practices	archaisms, pre-standard French, Old French
bilingual and multilingual practices	code-switching, mixing, bilingual language play, contact languages, creoles, heritage languages
digitally-mediated discourse	"Netspeak" (Crystal 2001); *textos*
second language learner practices	interlanguage, transitional competence, approximative system, pedagogical error, non-native

ation in opposition to a standardized language and its cultural practices. The standard notion of a language could not exist without those same discourse practices of variation, which are marked for departure from the legitimating standard practices, and which define, and are defined by those standard practices. Some of the observable and overlapping discourse practices of variation from the French as NSL construct are summarized in Table 1.

While the concept of discourse practices of variation is a useful way for educators and applied linguists to begin to address diversity and variability in language, it must also be taken critically because the very notion of variation is in fact a residue of standardization, as will be discussed further below. In sociolinguistic terms, the NSL is the assumed zero degree of variation (Chambers 2003:25) from which other discourse practices are marked either explicitly or implicitly as 'non-standard.' Speech can be marked for non-nativeness and/or non-standardness in terms of 'accent' (Lippi-Green 1997). The notion of diglossia partitions French into a hierarchy of high standard attached to the written practices of Modern French in distinction to a low vernacular variety of the *same* language in spoken "New French."[4] The assumption that standard

---

4. Joseph (1988) describes an emerging diglossic situation in which the spoken practices that constitute a socially-marked variant, tentatively named "New French," are increasingly divergent from the "unusually" conservative practices surrounding the standard dialect used in writing, Modern French. Examples of New French include the "loss of special interrogative word order" typical of the standard language (*d'où viens-tu?* ∼ *tu viens d'où?*), the replacement of *nous* by *on* (*nous sommes contents* ∼ *on est content/s*), and the elimination of *ne* (*il n'aime pas Marie* ∼ *il aime pas Marie*) (Joseph 1988:33).

French and spoken French are separate entities is grounded in a linguistic ideology that has reduced the complex, changing and dynamic phenomenon of language into discrete varieties that can be neatly classified into historical periods, such as Old French, Middle French, Modern French, and New French. The concepts of intra-speaker and inter-speaker variation (Lodge 2004: 230) likewise assume a problematic segregation of speakers into identifiable and bounded communities which does not necessarily recognize the inherent variability of language. No one in the same situation, the same utterance, or even the same context, can use the same structure or lexical item in exactly the same way (Gadet 1996). If we accept at some level the inherent variability among "linguistic individuals" (Johnstone 1996), then it follows that no two speakers use language identically, nor is anyone always part of 'the same community' of speakers, even given the pervasiveness of standard language practices. From a critical perspective, the very existence of SL practices seriously compromises the notion of 'sameness' in language and community.

6.   The chimera of universality: Ideologies of correctness, communication, and competence

In conjunction with variation-as-problem, the standardness of French has been constructed and institutionalized around an ideology of correctness (Corson 2001) that assumes a universalizing notion of communicative efficiency based on the expertise and competence of NSL speakers. In this section, I will present a critical view of these interlocking ideologies of correctness, communication, and competence in order to better address the dilemmas posed by them for FL education.

The standardizing practice of European printers during the 14th to 17th century was inseparable from their role as the "inventors of *bon usage*" (Trudeau 1992) in the emerging European national languages and cultures. The standardization of printing technologies in early modern Europe made possible the print-languages (Anderson 1991) and print-cultures (Eisenstein 1983) that are seen as central to many national identities today. The technological standardization of printing went hand in hand with increasingly standardized orthography and the diffusion of the first codifications of European national SLs upon which FL education has been constructed (Auroux 1994; Joseph 1987; Train 2000). Centuries later, correctness can still be seen as necessary for communication. Models for the legitimized communicative competence (Bourdieu 1982) of 'speaking and writing the language correctly' have been diffused over the centuries through printed manuals, textbooks and treatises on any number of language-related topics including grammar, orthography, elocution, and education.

Much linguistic research and traditional accounts of the history of the French language claim that standardization has served the interests of society as a whole by enhancing communicative efficiency and promoting national unity. Standardness has been seen to impart superior communicative power on a language, by virtue of its perceived uniformity and "the codification and acceptance, within the community of users, of a formal set of norms defining 'correct' usage" (Stewart 1968:534). As a central assumption within the foundational discourse of modern language planning (Williams 1996), the SL as the most "useful" and "efficient" variety of language within a national community, due to its idealization as a vehicle for maximum communication, became the "remedy" to the communication "problem" raised by linguistic diversity within the national space (Stewart 1968). The assumption that standardized language is necessary for efficient communication is basic to the dubious deficit view *vis-à-vis* non-standard practices, critiqued by Labov (1972a), whereby the SL is seen as a requirement for the expression of cogent thought. In historical context, this ideologized clarity (Swiggers 1990) is revealed, for example, in Rivarol's famous trope extolling the communicative and cognitive virtues of (standard) French: "*Ce qui n'est pas clair, n'est pas français*" ('what is not clear is not French').

Critical accounts view standardization as serving the interests of dominant groups in society by reinforcing their linguistic, cultural, economic, professional, and political privilege (Bourdieu 1982; Cameron 1995, 2002). Cameron (2002) observes that an ideology of communication has given new legitimacy to the long-lived idea that linguistic diversity is a problem, while linguistic uniformity is a desirable ideal:

> [...] a standard for 'effective communication' is always in practice based on habits and values which are not cultural universals, but are specific to a particular cultural milieu.
> [...] the effect of institutionalizing some people's preferred practices as norms will be to define large numbers of other people as inadequate or 'substandard' communicators. (p. 80)

Cameron suggests that an ideologized notion of standard communication is becoming a feature of global language teaching practices (Cameron 2002:81).

The constellation of standardized language, culture, and identity are increasingly yet problematically identified with global communicative practices. The emerging notion of global standard communication highlights a fundamental paradox for language teaching: Although sociolinguistic research has shown that effective communication does not necessarily require standardized language practices, it may be that the ideologies surrounding these standardized practices have exacerbated the prejudice and bias toward the users of perceived non-standard practices so as to impede comprehensibility and communicative effectiveness. The ideology of communicative efficiency attached to standardized practices shapes dominant notions of interaction between speakers both within and between supposedly their communities. The 'global' has long been associated with speaker participation in the supposedly modern practices of the national or world SL culture that is constructed in opposition to devalued and/or marginalized 'local' varieties, whether indigenous or regional languages, or the so-called dialects or sociolects defined by the standard (e.g., *patois* 'patois', *le français populaire* 'popular French', *les parlers ruraux* 'rural dialects').

Globalization has given rise to the notion of world (standard) languages. Historically, the SL construct has been exported throughout the world through European imperialism, and, more recently, through language planning attached to development and modernization projects in Third World nations. The French-as-world-language construct is derived from its universalizing force, by which a prestige norm associated with the language-culture practices of politically powerful groups of Parisians becomes the language of the nation that can be imposed on colonized populations, or exported as a model to other parts of the world.

The globalness of a world language exacerbates the multi-layered tension between a standard Hexagonal French, the various Francophone varieties of French undergoing pluricentric standardization, and the non-standardized practices that in effect define and are defined by standardizing practices. As Heller (1999, 2002) has demonstrated for the Canadian bilingual context of French and English, the ideology of monolingual national SL has morphed into an "ideology of commodification" that differentially values the language and culture practices of standard French over the diversity of observable practices among bilingual Canadians. In a globalizing ideology, the school contributes to the notion of bilingualism as a commodity for exchange in an internationalized job market. But only a certain type of "parallel" or "double" bilingualism is valued, one in which the student is expected to "speak each 'language' as though it were a homogeneous monolingual variety" (Heller 2002:48). In doing so, the school "promotes the socio-economic advancement of one set of francophones", those who command the standard, "but marginalizes another set and narrows and normativizes the definition of what it means to speak French" (Heller 1999:273).

The Pedagogic Hyperstandard of French as FL is distanced from its colonial past. This is partly due to a desire to present an attractive subject matter for students, but it is also consistent with the general injunction on questioning the authority of the language and its speakers that is built into the notion of the NSL. The worldliness of the French language is often presented in terms of instrumental orientation (e.g., tourism, career). But membership in a foreign colonial structure, or the political role of FL instruction in larger geopolitical networks and balances of power is not generally highlighted, nor are language policies or educational policies with respect to language within the target nations usually a part of the curriculum. In historical perspective, *L'Alliance française* was founded in 1883 in the go-go years of the Republican colonialism of the Third Republic as an "*association nationale pour la propagation de la langue française dans les colonies et à l'étranger*" ('a national association for the spread of the French language in the colonies and abroad'). Spaëth (1998) demonstrates that colonial language ideologies served as the basis for *Français langue étrangère* (French as a FL), as a discipline and methodological approach. While issues of colonization have taken on an increasingly important role in the study of Francophone literatures in conjunction with French studies at American universities, the relationship between colonial language ideologies (Errington 2001; Pennycook 2000) and the teaching of French in the United States has remained largely unexplored.

7. Imagining communities of French: Monolingual ideologies of national space

Standardization involves the complex interrelationship between the invention of unitary languages and the imagining of human communities (Anderson 1991) on the level of nation-states in the larger context of globalization. In this section, I will develop a critical angle on standardization that problematizes the assumption of one nation-one-language-one-culture-one self as the only desirable model. This critical perspective challenges the standardized imagining of community, language, culture, and identity in FL education: An ideologically monolingual national community inhabited by putative native speakers of the NSL.

Research into the construction of SLs has revealed that Nation and Language are not immutably fused from time immemorial. While ideologically national, NSLs are in fact only relatively recent and problematical components of national identity. The notion of a French-speaking France is a recent invention, situated in the specific ideological and material context of political transformations (e.g., revolution, republic), and changing social and economic conditions of life (e.g., education, transportation, capitalism) in the 19th century (Lodge 1993; Weber 1976).

Standardization studies have also increasingly challenged the assumption that the relationship between Nation, Language, and Identity is a simple one. As Joseph (2004) has observed, national languages and identities are dialectically constructed in a complex process that should be the focus of research. In examining the historical and ideological creation of a French national language, Julia and Revel (2002:429) similarly remark that language policy and language politics (*"une politique de la langue"*) represent a complex set of positions from which constructions of social reality were fashioned (*"un jeu complexe de positions à partir desquelles des constructions de la réalité sociale étaient élaborées"*).

In early standardization studies, the NSL construct was framed in largely uncritical terms as being instrumental in overcoming the 'problem' of linguistic diversity by creating "contrastive self-identification" (Fishman 1972) at the individual and societal levels between speakers of different languages within and between national borders. In distinction to other varieties, a SL has been celebrated as being invested with the symbolic power accrued from the synergy of the standardized formal properties of the language, its social functions, and the attitudes the language inspires in speakers (e.g., language loyalty, pride, and awareness of the norm) (Garvin & Mathiot 1968).

More recent critical discourse perspectives, in contrast, foreground the discursive construction of the national identities (Wodak, de Cillia, Reisigl, & Liebhart 1999) that constitute and support the ideologies and technologies underlying national communities, languages, literatures, and cultures. From a critical perspective, the national unity embodied in SLs cannot be disassociated from the troubling phenomena of ethnocentrism, xenophobia, racism and purism (Bonfiglio 2002).

The ideology of one-nation-one-culture-one-language-one-self presents a view of reality where practices of variation are excluded or marginalized. The NSL becomes the locus of monolingual identity to which speakers aspire both collectively and individually. Within this ideology, bilingual and multilingual identities are seen as threats to the unitary structures of language, nation, culture, and self. In response to the undeniable existence of variability and diversity in language and culture, the monolingual exclusivity of the standard positively values bilingualism only in terms of an idealized competence by which speakers will move from one monolingual national standard norm to another, without any of the variations (such as language mixing or codeswitching) that have been so abundantly documented in actual bilingual discourse, particularly in minority language situations.

Education is central to this ideological landscape of standardizing and essentializing discourses of identity, community, language, and culture. As "technologies of a nation," schooling and teaching remain "about, within, and for the nation, tacitly about the protection and production of its Culture (and, by implication, its preferred ethnicities and races, languages, and codes) and committed to the production of its sovereign subjects" (Luke 2004:24). The monolingual exclusivity of the linguistic, cultural and educational space of the nation is connected to what Heller (1999) has identified as "an ideology of monolingualism". Based on extensive ethnographic research at a French-language high school in Toronto, Canada, Heller (1999:139) observed that this ideologized monolingualism is grounded in a normative bilingualism that requires the student to "collaborate with the construction of a French monolingual public face" in contrast to their actual bilingual practices.[5]

In very real terms, the ideologically monolingual zone of the school (within a larger devaluing of linguistic diversity) generates forms of symbolic violence (Bourdieu & Passeron 1970) by which the imposition of one language or a single standard variety of a language can create pain and anguish for human beings. In his poem *Schizophrénie linguistique* ('linguistic schizophrenia'), Jean Arceneaux offers a poignant expression of the violence of assimilation and marginalization, as well as the decisive role of monolingual schooling in that process from the perspective of a French speaker in Louisiana.

> I will not speak French on the school grounds.
> I will not speak French on the school grounds.
> I will not speak French...
> I will not speak French...
> I will not speak French...
> *Hé! ils sont pas bêtes, ces salauds.*

---

5.   Heller further describes the role of the school in the construction of an ideologically monolingual national space: "The school, as a key site for the production of the nation, must create within its walls a monolingual zone, in order to produce bilinguals (who are, in effect, meant to be double monolinguals, that is, people who can act like monolingual Francophones as well as monolingual Anglophones). It manages the tension between fictive monolingualism and real bilingualism by creating a barrier between the monolingual, public discourse of the school and bilingual marginal discursive spaces" (Heller 1999:19).

Après mille fois, ça commence à pénétrer
Dans n'importe quel esprit.
Ça fait mal; ça fait honte;
Puis là, ça fait plus mal.
Ça devient automatique,
Et on speak *pas* French on the school grounds
Et anywhere else *non plus.*   (Arceneaux 1980 quoted in Ryon 2005:64)[6]

For Ryon (2005:64), this poem is an example of local knowledge on language loss that reveals an "undocumented side of linguistic assimilation" and the "emotional and mental violence involved in the formation of a new 'linguistic habitus'". In short, monolingualism for many minority language speakers ceases to be fictive and becomes very real. This characterization is consistent with the present discussion according to which the poem is also testimony to the marginalization of speakers' non-standard knowledge of bilingual language practices (Cajun French and codeswitching) both in school and in the larger social context. This poem also stands as witness to the internalization by speakers of a strong version of the NSL ideology: That speaking more than one language, particularly in non-standard ways, is not a 'normal' state, a sort of schizophrenia representing a discursively-expressed disorder in the monolingual regime.

In FL settings, French exists within a larger professional, educational and social context in which "the preferred route to bilingualism is that of a monolingual speaker of an L1 learning the L2 from zero as an adult, and the ideal goal is eventually to be able to 'pass for' a monolingual speaker of the learned language" (Ortega 1999a:249). The French as FL classroom is generally an ideologically monolingual space (Blyth 1995) in which only the target language is supposed to be used, and students will be discouraged from using their L1. Bilingual dictionaries, a fundamental component of FL

---

6. My translation of Arceneaux's "Linguistic Schizophrenia" (codeswitching between French and English is marked by italics):

> *I will not speak French on the school grounds.*
> *I will not speak French on the school grounds.*
> *I will not speak French …*
> *I will not speak French …*
> *I will not speak French …*
> See, they're not stupid, those bastards.
> After the thousandth time, it begins to sink in
> In anyone's mind.
> It hurts, it makes you ashamed;
> And suddenly, it doesn't hurt anymore.
> It becomes almost natural,
> And we don't *speak French on the school grounds*
> And *anywhere else* either.

pedagogy, provide a condensed codification of the lexicon of the two SLs. Cognates represent the authorized zone of interference between the languages, but language mixing is generally not encouraged. The standard-to-standard move is ideally to be accompanied by the corresponding shift in identity as the student assumes the appropriate cultural norms, generally based on a highly stereotyped view of the target (i.e., 'foreign') culture of the idealized NS. In this pedagogical and ideological context, the default value for unmarked French is the SL and culture associated with native speakers in France, with only very limited sociolinguistic and cultural information about other French-speaking regions of the world (Wieczorek 1994:493).

8.   Inventing languages: Linguistic and textual ideologies

The dubious premise of national unity mirrors the assumption of a linguistic unity that in fact never existed and in all likelihood never will. The construction of Native Standard French through standardization involves the invention of languages, that is, "an ideology of languages as separate and enumerable" (Makoni & Pennycook 2005:138). The NSL construct has a profound languaging effect (i.e., providing the prestige of language status to a variety through standardization), as in the case of (standard) French in Canada and Africa (see Moreau 1998). However, the NSL's dynamic of hierarchization and exclusivity has also been shown to exert a powerful 'de-languaging' force, referred to in various contexts as "dialectization", "near-dialectalization" (Kloss 1967) and "destandardization" (Joseph 1987) on other varieties within the nation. Such has been the case for French on Occitan, once the most important vernacular (i.e., non-Latin) literary language in medieval Europe until the political and military conquest and annexation by France of the major centers of Occitan culture and power.

Like other SLs, French is based largely on the Graeco-Latin model (Joseph 1987) with its ideologized relationship between spoken and written discourse that grants primacy to the written word. Critical perspectives on the ideological construction of linguistics have recognized the overt and covert normativity (Taylor 1990) that the written SL exerts on our notions of what constitutes a language. This written language bias in linguistics (Linell 2005) has been basic to the idealization, abstraction, and codification of variable and complex discursive practices into so-called descriptive and prescriptive accounts of language. The premise of homogeneity in language assumes that *a* or *the* language is a whole that can be described, codified, and analyzed according to its constituent parts, which serve as objects of research and subjects of knowledge.

The Graeco-Latin standard model is inseparable from a subset of language ideologies or "textual ideologies" (Collins 1996) characterized by particular, historical, and institutional forms. This textualism constitutes "a general complex of ideas about written language," the central features of which are "beliefs in the fixity of text, the transparency of language, and the universality of shared, available meaning" (Collins 1996:204). This textualist ideology is deeply implicated in the "pedagogization of literacy" (Street 1995:114) that involves the construction and internalization of a particular form of language corresponding to the "autonomous model" of literacy (Street 1984) in which individuals come to conceptualize literacy as a separate, reified set of 'neutral' competencies, autonomous of social context. The notion of a universalistic, schooled literacy (Cook-Gumperz 1986) is basically standardizing as it constructs a supposedly uniform set of capabilities, rather than diverse, historically contingent, specific writing practices. In terms of current educational practices, this standard view of literacy is supportive of assessment in which learners are evaluated by tests under prior assumptions of differential achievement. It is "a stratified literacy" in which achievement is "calibrated by technical (standardized) measures of skill, and with hierarchy and segregation as basic principles" (Collins 1996:205). The teaching of French as a FL has been deeply influenced by these ideologies of text and literacy that have constructed French on the basis of a formal written language of great writers as a "*langue universelle, la langue de l'universalité*" ('universal language, the language of universality') that can be taught and learned in the same way, by all learners and teachers, in all contexts (Porcher 1995:10).

Shaped by the ideologies that have constructed popular and scientific notions of language, the French pedagogic hyperstandard of FL education is a product of the "induced homogeneity" (Davies 2003) that the NSL undergoes as it becomes the pedagogical object of teaching to non-native speakers. In terms of both (applied) linguistics and FL pedagogy, language is transformed into the object and the subject of instruction, learning and analysis that can be studied, tested, controlled, and taught. As the model for a teachable and testable language, the hyperstandard is thus seen as a manageable body of objective, universal, and authoritative knowledge. The hyper-standardization of the FL makes this knowledge amenable to educational standards and standardized assessment. The hyperstandard is also associated with commercial pressures. It can be conveniently packaged for the pedagogical and commercial purposes of textbook and dictionary publishing, given that to 'know the language' has been constructed in terms of knowing a relatively restricted number of forms and structures within a limited set of uses in a relatively small range of functions and situations.

The Pedagogic Hyperstandard has come to be characterized by the covertly normative influence of the written language in response to the ascendancy over the past 40 years of the research and methodological agendas focusing on spoken language, such as the audiolingual method (e.g., Lado 1964) and Communicative Language Teaching (e.g., Canale & Swain 1980). In pedagogical settings, the spoken language of FL 'communication' undergoes tremendous normative pressure to conform to the written standard (e.g., the teacher admonishes students to speak in complete sentences). Even more than the NSL, the Pedagogic Hyperstandard is distanced from a wide range of real-life communicative settings, thus making the teaching and learning of the pragmatics of communication highly problematic. In spite of the emphasis in FL pedagogy on the communicative uses of language, questions arise as to how much communication is really going on in the classroom, and what is being communicated beyond the traditional focus on the correctness.

A central concern for more discourse-/sociolinguistic-oriented views of French language pedagogy has been the gap between the 'real-life' spoken contexts in which French is used (in which students should be prepared to function as proficient speakers), and the fact that the bulk of French college textbooks, particularly at the introductory level, have been largely based on the written forms of the language (Walz 1986). From a curricular perspective, the FL hyperstandard is associated with a restricted content that tends to focus on the language itself, whether as grammar (i.e., focus on form(s) or explicit grammar instruction), vocabulary (i.e., lexical items isolated from discursive context), or communication, with generally poorly integrated lessons on culture. As Wilkinson (2001) notes, French as FL curricula have given relatively little attention to teaching students how to recognize and use target language discourse norms, that is, the conventionalized ways of carrying on a conversation through turn-taking, shifting topics, and so on, in a given cultural situation (see Warga this volume).

9.   The Native Speaker question: Questioning the ideology of monolingual nativism

In modern linguistics, the fiction of the SL has been a stock theme, famously stated by Vendryès (1921), echoing Saussure: "*Il y a beaucoup d'hommes qui parlent français, il n'y a personne qui parle le français et qui puisse servir de règle et d'exemple aux autres. Ce que nous appelons le français n'existe dans le langage parlé d'aucun être humain*".[7] Following the premise of artificiality, the SL has been characterized by linguists as no one's native language insofar as it is a set of cultural practices that cannot be learned until after the period of normal first language acquisition (Joseph 1987; Milroy & Milroy 1999).

While linguists may agree that the SL is no one's native language, it comes to define in ideological terms the language of native speakers with respect to the imagined communities of nation-states with all the assumptions of nativeness and foreignness that surround national identities on both individual and collective levels. This ideologized (non)nativeness, that is, the seemingly simple, but highly problematic, identity between one's native language and standardizing constructs of language, culture, community, and identity are given a 'flesh and blood' reality in the notion of the Native Speaker (NS). Embodied in the real or imagined practices of speakers, the omnipresent NS concept is central to much of what language researchers and educators have come to (dis)believe about language structure, use, development, and acquisition. However, a significant and growing body of scholarship has problematized the concept of NS as the most salient ideology of identity and language use connected to second and FL

---

7.   'There are many men who speak French, but there is no one who speaks the French language and who might serve as a model and example for others. What we call French does not exist in the spoken language of any human being'.

education (see Cook 1999; Davies 2003; Kramsch 1997; Rampton 1990; Train 2003; Valdman 1982). In this section, I will outline some of the ways applied linguistics and FL pedagogy have shaped and been shaped by this nativist orientation to the theory and study of language.

The NS construct, ideologically fused with that of SL in the NSL, presupposes a *monolingual nativism* constructed in terms of standardizing individual and collective identities. The ideologically monolingual NS identity is bound to a homogeneous speech community in which NSs are assumed to 'speak the same language' (Silverstein 1998). However convenient this monolingual nativism may seem, a critical perspective poses the fundamental question: Whose language? (Mey 1985).

The nativist conception of language was formulated as that of an "ideal speaker-listener, in a completely homogeneous speech-community" (Chomsky 1965:3). Much linguistic analysis in this vein depends on grammaticality judgments supplied by the intuitions relating to the linguistic production of selected NSs. The power and authority as to what is included or excluding from the language (as grammatical or not) resides in this tacit and unquestioned privileging of the linguist's own beliefs and language practices or those of other authorized NSs. Chomsky inherited and embraced the nativist view of language underlying the NS from the prescriptive tradition of grammarians who codified their idea of authoritative language practices (often conforming to their own) into national SLs, and European rationalist thinkers who turned sociohistorically-contingent practices of language into universalized notions of human language and modern structural linguists (Bauman & Briggs 2003; Train 2000). In particular, Saussure offered nativists a scientific description of language based on an idealized state of the language (*langue*) that resembled the SL, abstracted from the observable language practices (*parole*) of educated NSs, as represented by the linguist (Crowley 1990). The Chomskyan idealization of competence relegates the way people actually use language (performance) to a theoretically lesser status.

For FL education and research, the NS has been, and continues to be, the implicit and explicit model for competence in L1 as well as for ultimate attainment for L2 learners. The NS construct thus embodies the "monolingual bias" of SLA theory and education that "elevates an idealized 'native' speaker above a stereotypical 'nonnative', while viewing the latter as a defective communicator, limited by an underdeveloped communicative competence" (Firth & Wagner 1997:285), thus contributing to "the myth of the deficient communicator" (Belz 2002). This ideology of (in)competence is discursively constructed through the term NS and its binary opposite, the NNS, along with a host of even murkier concepts of speaker identity that index notions of (in)competence marking the NNS as deficient or as less-than-native: "Near-native speaker" (see Valdés 1998), "the pseudo-native", "quasi-native" speaker.

The NS construct is vital to the systematizing and recontextualizing of knowledge (Bernstein 2000) of the NSL construct as a Pedagogic Hyperstandard for the purposes of teaching the language to non-native speakers (see Section 4). The codified formal and appropriate communicative elements attributed to native speakers of the standard (foreign) language come to constitute a pedagogical norm representing the supposed reality of the language and the culture that are distanced from the learners' actual language-culture practices as well as those of the target language speakers. As such, learner and teacher identity have been grounded in the ideologized concept of the NS as an educated monolingual speaker of the target language living in an ideologically homogeneous national French culture.

Significantly, the NS represents a universalized norm that in the FL classroom settings is almost entirely controlled by the educational institution through teachers, instructional materials, and assessment. As locus of control and discipline, the NS construct shifts power away from the language learner to NS norm-bearers such as teachers, testers, NS interlocutors, and textbook authors. In this context, learners are expected to conform to and, ideally, internalize the monolingual native norm based on relatively little linguistic input, and in a relatively reduced range of settings in which the language is presented. For the most part, textbooks and course materials have only begun to explore the possibilities for presenting a greater range of discourse practices in French based on empirical language use data and corpora analysis (see Barnes 1990).

The ideology of the NS as the ideal target of FL competence is linked to a traditional definition of multiculturalism that seems to include only cultures outside the United States, while marginalizing American immigrant or indigenous language communities (Ortega 1999b). This is supported by the fact that FL programs in higher education place a great emphasis on study abroad experience, and FL textbooks have traditionally focused on the mainstream culture of the target-language countries with little or no reference to minority or heritage language communities in the United States where French is spoken (e.g., for Louisiana, see Caldas this volume). Language educators have only recently addressed how to integrate heritage learners into classroom-based instruction in ways that benefit both the NNS learners and the heritage learners (see Blake & Zyzik 2003). The bilingual and extra-SL practices of the 'native' communities are often stigmatized in FL classrooms resulting in labeling some learners as 'near-native' (Valdés 1998) or 'inadequate' with respect to the idealized native standard speaker norm of competence. For instance, the complex discursive practices and transnational linguistic identity among multilingual (French-Creole-English) Haitian immigrants to the United States (see Zéphir 1996) seldom enter into the teaching materials and curriculum of French programs. In many cases, the Haitian immigrants who are designated as 'near-native' speakers of French are poorly served by French-as-FL programs and there are few heritage language programs available (Katz 2003).

In light of the hegemony of the NSL ideology, it is not surprising that the variability and diversity of French language practices have not become a significant part of FL programs and standardized FL textbooks, despite the efforts of some applied linguists and educators to the contrary (see Auger 2003; Auger & Valdman 1999; Blyth 1995; Valdman 2000). Practices of variation have typically appeared as 'factoids' and lexical features isolated from any meaningful discussion of the variants other than in terms of supposed geographical range of use or their implied departure from the Native Standard (e.g., 'In Québec they say *char* for *voiture*', 'In... they say *X* for *Y*'). For example, students in the US are seldom exposed to the variation of French spoken across the border in Canada because teachers of French have "either ignored, frowned upon, or ridiculed" Quebec French (Salien 1998:95). In general, FL programs seem unable to provide learners of French with an adequate appreciation of the complex practices within and between multilingual speakers and communities that are typical throughout the Francophone world, most notably in the language ecologies of Africa (see Calvet 1999). FL pedagogy generally has not addressed larger sociolinguistic issues of variation with respect to appropriateness, such as: Who uses the variant? In what settings? With what meaning? As Valdman (2000) remarked, *Québecois* French tends to be reduced to *le joual*, the popular variety most distanced from Hexagonal standard French, when in fact *Québecois* language practices are sociolinguistically complex, including a *norme locale* 'local norm' that is situated between Hexagonal standard French and more distinctively *Québecois* traits.

10. Directions for future research: Toward a critically responsive French language pedagogy

10.1 Beyond (non)native and national identities of French

The discursive construction of ideologies of national identity has emerged as a vital piece in critical research agendas for applied linguists. From this perspective, second language education research must find ways of generating "new ways of being and communicating beyond the nation", otherwise "it will remain a technology for domesticating the Other into nation, whatever its scientific and humanist pretenses" (Luke 2004:28). Ideologies of nation cannot be separated from the construction of (non)native identities around the NSL. The question of (non)native identity among language learners and teachers remains a topic of debate in applied linguistics.

An increasingly important body of research in applied linguistics throws into question the sociolinguistic, socio-cultural, and pedagogical validity of the NS and the ideologically monolingual NSL as a suitable goal for competence in L2 learners (e.g., Belz 2002; Blyth 1995; Cook 1999, 2002; Kramsch 1997, 1998; Rampton 1990; Train 2003; Valdman 1982, 1992, 2000). The basic insight in this line of inquiry is that language learners, whether in the context of second-language, foreign-language, or heritage-language education, are not monolinguals, and therefore they do not, nor should they be expected to, speak, behave, or even think in exclusively monolingual ways. Proficient L2 users are not "failed monolinguals" vis-à-vis the NS, but rather successes in their own right (Cook 1999:204). Proponents of a more sociolinguistically-informed pedagogical norm (Gass, Bardovi-Harlig, Magnan, & Walz 2002; Valdman 1982, 1992, 2000) have also rejected the idealized Native Speaker norm. These positions destabilize the ideological basis of the NS and NSL that defines the L2 speaker as deficient and defective because as a NNS she or he does not conform to an arguably unattainable NS norm. Moreover, this critical perspective asserts that an understanding and valuing of the diverse bilingual or multilingual practices of language learners (such as code-switching, language-mixing, multilingual language play) are fundamental to language learning, and therefore ought to be to incorporated into language education and pedagogy.

Resolutely focused on the NS construct as the source of authoritative knowledge and expertise, the nativist orientation seems ill-suited to the educational needs of L2 learners for whom native-like competence may be neither a realistic nor desirable goal. Porcher (1995:41) reminds teachers of French as a FL that "[p]arler le français comme un natif, tel est le fantasme qui, comme pour toutes les autres langues, régit notre domaine. Mais ce n'est qu'un fantasme" ('speaking French like a native is the delusional fantasy that, as is the case for all other languages, controls our field. But it is only a fantasy').

The NS question goes to the ideological core of foreign and SL education. Challenges to the hegemony of the NS have attempted to re-appropriate and subvert the discourses of nativism in ways that break down the binary native/non-native construct and highlight the value of being *other-than-native* or even *more-than-native*. Rather than acquiesce to the ideological positioning of L2 learners as deficient, the "privilege of the non-native speaker" enables foreign language learners to "construct linguistic and cultural identities in the interstices of national languages and on the margins of monolingual speakers' territories" (Kramsch 1997:368). Taking a similar critical discourse stance, "intercultural speakers" (Kramsch 1998) and intercultural learners can be seen to inhabit a "critical third place" in which language study is an initiation into a kind of social practice that is at the boundary of two or more cultures and languages (Kramsch 1993).

The desire to somehow unobtrusively assimilate to dominant norms of identity and language by 'passing' as a native standard speaker still seems to be a powerful ideological component of what is valued by many FL educators and learners, as well as by FL education in general. However, the valuing of intercultural thirdness is one of the few non-assimilationist responses to the ideologically-shaped prejudices directed at non-native speakers, of whom few could conceivable 'pass as native'. Given the *imaginaire linguistique* surrounding the NSL, even highly proficient non-native speakers continue to be the object of exoticism and marginalization as attested by common NS judgments such as *j'aime ton accent, il est charmant* 'I love your accent, it's charming', or *qu'est-ce que vous parlez bien français* 'you speak French so well', with the expressed or tacit coda *pour un étranger* 'for a foreigner'.

While it is vital to move beyond the native/non-native dichotomy, it is equally important that applied linguists avoid the time-worn "end of ideology" (Aron 1955) mindset in which the very present ideologies surrounding language, identity and education are condemned to the margins of applied linguistic inquiry and language pedagogy. It is at our risk that those of us engaged in researching and/or teaching French take a *fin de l'idéologie* ('end of the ideology') view that amounts to a *politique de l'autruche* ('policy of hiding one's head in the sand') with respect to the ideologically constructed realities of competence, communication, and identity. Failure to engage critically with language ideologies risks to expose French to an increasingly precarious position in FL education. A case in point is the French prescriptivism associated with the NSL construct that has significant implications for the FL classroom:

> When teachers of French uncritically represent puristic, native-speaker attitudes to-wards language in the American classroom, these behaviors can create a discourse of exclusion. Examples include an automatic-correction reflex, a fetishistic banishing of English (and perceived anglicisms) from the classroom, and a visceral intolerance of error.   (Siskin 1999: 148–149)

This discourse of exclusion becomes even more troubling given the continued institutional erosion of French in FL education.[8]

10.2   From nativist competence to intercultural performativity

In the last half century, applied linguists have relied on various formulations of 'competence' as a way of conceptualizing and describing, even prescribing and analyzing what language is, how speakers know a language, and how this knowledge is related to the learning and teaching of FLs. Chomskyan linguistic competence with its nativist view of speaker identity seems very much alive in the reliance in education and research on the NS as the model for competence. This nativist view of competence has informed cognitive views of language acquisition according to which increasing numbers of researchers and theorists "focus their attention on SLA as an internal, individual, in part innately specified, cognitive process" (Long & Doughty 2003: 866). In constituting SLA as a cognitive science, "the object of inquiry, broadly conceived, is the mind of the second language learner" (White 2004: 704), and that "what has to be explained includes the L2 learner's underlying linguistic competence and how such competence is acquired" (White 2004: 705). Some cognitive approaches have shifted the locus of competence from the NS to the L2 learner such that "the goals of an SLA theory include understanding the nature of interlanguage competence (what is knowledge of language?), as well as how L2 learners come to know what they know (how is that knowledge acquired?)" (White 2004: 704). However, SLA has been reluctant to abandon the NS as the model for ultimate attainment (see White & Genesee 1996). In the few cases where competence is largely conceptualized in terms of a bilingual "multi-competent" speaker (Cook 1992), researchers reject the "monolingual bias of SLA" and assert that "the 'ultimate attainment' of second language is not, and could never be, monolingual competence" in the L2 (Cook 1997: 46).

---

8.   Welles (2004) reported that although French enrollments in United States institutions of higher education remained stable from 1998 to 2002, the enrollments for French also show a steady decline relative to the total number of students enrolled in FLs at US post-secondary institutions, from 34.4% in 1968 to 16.7% in 1998 to 14.5% in 2002. Steward (2004), citing a number of factors including a general "flight from the arts and sciences" (79), found that the French Master's Degree programs (unlike Spanish programs) in the US faced "the problem of not attracting students" (77) as evidenced by the slow but continual erosion of the percentage of Master's degrees granted in French in recent decades.

In response to the dominant cognitive focus of linguistics, more socially and culturally-contextualized approaches to language have re-appropriated competence in terms of "communicative competence" (Hymes 1972, 1992), originally defined as a form of "cultural competence". This line of inquiry has generated a considerable body of research in applied linguistics on what it means for L2 learners to know a language in broader interactional and communicative terms of 'competence' (Bachman 1990; Canale 1983; Canale & Swain 1980; Savignon 1972). "Grammatical competence" has been conceived of as one element within the larger communicative competence (Canale & Swain 1980), "language competence", or "knowledge of language" (Bachman 1990) in which the language learner demonstrates the ability to use this grammatical competence in conjunction with sociolinguistic competence, discourse competence, strategic competence (Canale & Swain 1980), and pragmatic competence (Bachman 1990) in order to communicate appropriately according to the variable contexts in which language is used. Particularly in Europe, "intercultural communicative competence" (ICC) has emerged as an influential model that ever further extends the notion of L2 "competence". ICC is grounded in complex skills of discovery, interpreting, relating, and understanding that can lead to a meta-linguistic awareness and critical cultural awareness by which learners and teachers begin to realize and relativize the cultural-situatedness and constructedness of their own way of seeing the world and the worldviews of others (Byram 1997).

Although these socially-grounded views of competence have been valuable in questioning the NS model of identity and language, they have stopped short of bringing critique to bear on the foundational notion of competence itself as a central linguistic and pedagogical construct. Due to its preponderance, competence remains a deeply ideological and, therefore, unsettled concept. In bringing language ideology into the mix, one must ask what are the ideological underpinnings of competence, its socially and educational consequences, and whether or not FL pedagogy, applied linguistic research, and society might be better served by a more skeptical and critical stance toward the very notion of competence?

Bernstein (2000) offers a trenchant critique of "the social logic of competence" as it has been theorized in linguistics, psychology, anthropology, sociology and sociolinguistics. For Bernstein, the apparent "universal democracy of acquisition" and "idealism of competence" are bought at the price of "abstracting the individual from the analysis of distribution of power and principles of control" surrounding the acquisition and realization of competence (p. 43). In this sense, applied linguistic research and FL pedagogy has generally assumed this idealized view of competence and thereby ignored macro-level issues of ideology, such as those surrounding the NSL.

But if not competence, then what? A basic problem for applied linguistics centers on how to critically address in educational and linguistic terms the relative fixity of standardizing notions of competence in light of the observable variability of performance. In rehabilitating and reformulating the concept of performance, the neglected twin of Chomskyan linguistics, some broadly sociolinguistic approaches have extended Bernstein's critique. In his study of multilingual adolescent FL learners in a school in inner London, Rampton (1999) demonstrates how the "aesthetics of performance" play a significant role in the negotiation of identities and in the repositioning of an official code (i.e., the FL) at school. Rampton foregrounds the metalinguistic awareness and reflexivity involved in performance, described by Bauman (1986) in terms of "the assumption of responsibility to an audience for a display of communicative skill, highlighting the way in which communication is carried out, above and beyond its referential content" (Bauman 1986:3; cited in Rampton 1999:497). The learners in Rampton's study played with their limited exposure to and proficiency in the foreign language and "reconstituted" it as "unofficial talk" through their performance with peers outside of class as a sort of "unpredictably mobile resource" for identity construction.

In terms of French as a FL, applied linguists have not yet begun to explore how learners with limited access to and proficiency in French perform the language outside of class as they engage in meaningful and complex instances of language use that are on the margins of what would conventionally be termed competence. On the other end of expertise in L2 use, passing as a NS of French can be re-conceptualized in terms of a temporary, context-, audience- and medium-specific performance (Piller 2002) rather than as a model of nativized competence for a NNS.

Since the dominant FL pedagogies and their associated ideologies privilege a notion of (in)competence based on the NSL, they have not adequately addressed the larger question of language performance in the enactment of complex and variable multilingual and intercultural identities (Kramsch 1998; Pavlenko 2003a). In theory and practice, the primacy of competence must give way to performance, or other alternative concepts, if education is to seriously engage with the variability and diversity of discursive practices. A shift to performance then offers a basis on which applied linguists and educators may explore the possibilities and concerns of French language pedagogy within a larger educational, social, and affective space. On the one hand, the notion of performativity (in the critical sense described here, not in the standard educational terms discussed in 10.4) undermines the ideological foundations of the NSL. I do not take lightly the discomfort that teachers and learners may experience as we exit the comfort zone afforded by the familiarity of normative grammar, orthography, and national identities. However, I suggest that these familiar and secure places are, upon closer scrutiny, neither so comfortable nor secure as may often be assumed. On the other hand, the challenge of critical performativity also presents teachers of French with new paths toward understanding and valuing their students and themselves as complex intercultural individuals who learn and 'do' French in diverse ways that do not necessarily conform to an unrealistic model of monolingual competence.

10.3 Teaching and learning French in the age of globalization

The theme of language study in the age of globalization (Modern Language Association no date) has emerged prominently in the discourse of FL education. Similarly, communication in global contexts offers abundant opportunities for applied linguists to explore what it means to be a speaker of French in global cultural contexts. French, then, can be characterized in terms of an ongoing construction of standardizing practices on the international and national level as well as local variability involving the complex appropriation and contestation of those standardizing global practices.

While the ecology of French FL education is complex, French like all FLs taught in the US must contend with the ideological domination of English as *the* language of the Nation and the World. Evoked in concerns of linguistic imperialism (Phillipson 1992) and the specter of an English-Only Europe (Phillipson 2003), the ideologies of English language as *rex imperator,* or even *Tyrannosaurus rex* (Swales 1997), present singular challenges to the well-being of FL education as a pluralistic endeavor involving a diversity and multiplicity of languages. This amounts to the ideological construction of the irrelevance of learning languages other than English. If the world speaks English, one must pose the question, then why learn another language?

Ideology is all about what is valued and what is not. Spanish, for example, has enjoyed increasing enrollments in US schools and universities due, it would seem, to a perceived instrumental value for students as a career asset ('you'll have better job opportunities if you speak Spanish'). French, however, has apparently benefited less in recent times from this commodification of FL learning. Traditionally, French occupied a privileged position as the language of Culture and Diplomacy (both tied to the universalizing ideology of world language). As such, French succeeded Latin in the early twentieth century as the preeminent FL at the apex of the educational hierarchy in the US and in a number of other nations. However, French has perhaps fallen victim to a New Latin syndrome by which it is no longer seen by many as relevant to the education of Americans. This unfortunate view has been exacerbated by the post-9/11, post-diplomacy context that FL education in general and French in particular (as a language of the "Old Europe") must confront in the United States.[9] In this latest version of the New World Order ideology, FL education has seen its *raison d'être* skewed in institutional and political terms toward national security and defense, thus prioritizing the 'language of our enemies' and further diverting interest and funding away from the traditional European languages, particularly French and German. In a salient example of the ideological confluence of FL education policy and US foreign policy, the supposed value of FL learning and teaching are defined in terms of "our national security" and Americans' ability to "confront the new threats we face" (*National Se-*

---

9.   In January 2003, the US Secretary of Defense Donald Rumsfeld referred to France and Germany as "Old Europe", a comment clearly designed to discredit those nations that did not support the invasion of Iraq. While motivated by the immediate and long-term goals of US imperialism, Rumsfeld's remark also attests to a larger stance that has gained some currency in recent years in conjunction with the world-wide dominance of English by which the two most powerful continental European countries are ideologically positioned as somehow irrelevant to global matters, whether linguistic, cultural or political. The ideological counterpoint to this view can be seen in the discourses surrounding *la Francophonie* that attempt to maintain the viability of French as both a global language and a vehicle for French culture and influence throughout the world.

curity Language Act 2003). Of course, one could cynically or opportunistically make the case that even the European world languages are 'strategic' since 'terrorists' (real or imagined) also speak French or German or Spanish, as well as English. There is more at stake than enlisting the expertise of language educators and applied linguists in educating future spies and soldiers, although there is also a long history of doing just that through military funding (see Newmeyer 1986). At issue is the ideological refocusing of FL education, with far-ranging ethical, social and educational implications in both national and global terms.

In both the short and long term, a *critical* awareness of language ideologies is at heart a matter of imagining and developing viable alternatives to the dominant discourse of national security. Pratt (2003, 2004), for example, has openly questioned the ideological underpinnings of language education and policy in the US that discourage individual bilingualism and societal multilingualism. Instead, she calls for "building a new public idea about language" (Pratt 2003) that requires a "public commitment" and "public investment" in FL education based on the "understanding that studying other languages and cultures serves a deeper understanding of our world, and of ourselves and others in it" (Pratt 2004: 291).

Within the context of transcultural global flows (Appadurai 1996), global languages such as French and English are used "to perform, invent and (re)fashion identities across borders" through "acts of semiotic reconstruction" (Pennycook 2003: 528–529). Pennycook (2003, 2004) asserts that the notion of performativity in conjunction with that of "semiotic reconstruction" opens up several important dimensions of language use. A performativity-oriented view suggests that languages themselves are better viewed from an anti-foundational perspective, such that it is no longer useful to look for varieties of French or English (e.g., world Englishes, francophone Frenches) as "variants on a central linguistic monolith" (Pennycook 2003: 528). In this sense, the ideological character of the NSL is fully exposed as a problematic construction that marginalizes the complexity of observable uses of language. Pennycook observes that "performativity questions the notion of prior, pre-given identities," such that it is "not that people use language varieties because of who they are, but rather that we perform who we are by (amongst other things) using varieties of language" (ibid.: 528).

Applied linguists and FL educators would do well to consider how French learners semiotically reconstruct their identities in the performance of language and how language is created in the performance of identity. As a case in point, Kinginger's (2004) compelling story of 'Alice' problematizes French as an object of desire for foreign language learners in the US and affirms that "foreign language learners are people too" (p. 241). In performing her multifaceted and dynamic identity as a learner of French in the US and France, Alice demonstrated a complex engagement and investment into her learning of French. While Alice appears to have bought into the standard ideology of French as language of culture and prestige, the uniqueness and complexity of her language learning experience defies the standard notions of identity and competence. Another promising area in which to explore performativity is in Internet-mediated intercultural FL education (see Belz & Thorne 2006) as a site of intercultural discourse in which FL learners and teachers may begin to critically engage with ideologies of language and learning through telecollaborative exchanges with French speakers at home and abroad (Train 2006). From an intercultural perspective, all communication, as Scollon and Scollon (2001) argue, is to some extent inter-discourse communication, given the multiplicity and complexity of discourse systems with their normative expectations that make it unlikely that one will be considered a full member of most of the discourse systems in which one will participate (p. 134). The question becomes: what shapes learning French as "global communicative practice" (Kramsch & Thorne 2002) or "glocal" practice (Robertson 1995) constituted within "a contact zone, a space where the local meets the global" (Koutsogiannis & Mitsikopoulou 2004:83)? One pressing task for applied linguistics is to search for ways of understanding individual learners' engagement with the ideological contours and conflicts of the emerging global, local and intercultural contexts of teaching, learning and language use.

10.4 Language ideology and ethics: Language testing and standards-based education

Critical, ethnographically informed notions of performance and performativity, such as those suggested above, must contend with an educational ideology, evident in theory, policy and practice, that has increasingly engaged in very different "performativity discourse" (Ball 1997; Jeffrey 2002). In conjunction with the National Curriculum and National Standards movements in Britain and the US respectively, this dominant performativity stems from the importation of a competitive economic market structure for schools in order to ostensibly improve the perceived effectiveness and efficiency of the outputs of learning and to increase the opportunity of choice for educational "consumers" (Jeffrey 2002:531). This dominant performativity criterion of efficiency and effectiveness is an optimization of the relationship between input and output which supports a standardizing notion of competence codified in educational Standards, institutionalized by professional and governmental bodies, marketed through textbooks, and enforced by standardized assessments.

In the context of teacher education, Kinginger (2002) critically examines the notion of (in)competence in French that is situated with respect to the prevalent concepts of proficiency and standards in US education (entextualized in the ACTFL Oral Proficiency Guidelines and codified in the National FL Standards). Both proficiency and standards share an ideological stance, typical of a modernist/utilitarian discourse (Scollon & Scollon 2001), toward language competence as "a product that can be gauged through objective measurement of its effectiveness" (Kinginger 2002:203). While both proficiency and standards appear to value performance (i.e., language use), they are ideologically grounded, as Kinginger points out, in the measurement of discrete quantities of competence and the quality (i.e., 'accuracy') of the final product of instruction according to the "basic structures" of the SL confirmed by native speaker judgment (203–204). Therefore, an error in French comes to be seen as "a defect in the product that reduces its effectiveness but (presumably) can be improved through closer attention to the production process" (Kinginger 2002: 204).

In the area of language testing, applied linguists have begun to rethink the nativist conception of competence underlying the standardizing practices which have guided testing. Spolsky, for instance, draws an analogy between knowing a friend and knowing a language:

> [...] knowledge of a language is dynamic (at different times of day, I know more or less French), is contextualized as to domain (place and topic, certainly), and person (my language ability varies with my interlocutor). (Spolsky 1995: 358)

The observable variability within and between speakers-as-test-takers highlights many of the language ideologies that are part of the dominant culture of standardization (Train 2002) which interfaces with a "culture of measurement" (Padilla 2005).

This measurement imperative raises the possibility that the test may not be measuring what matters most, even "measuring what matters least" (Kohn 2000). In relying heavily on discrete item questions focusing on the orthography, lexicon, morphology, and syntax of the SL, as well as narrow views of literacy, do standardized language tests measure what is most important for learners to be able to do with language? Moreover, what are the social and ethical implications of testing a given set of language practices?

The matter of what is considered important or valuable is very much the terrain of ideology, with which applied linguists and educators must engage in order to address the need for an "ethical evaluation and justification of the intended and probable use" of any given test (Spolsky 1995: 358). This argument has been continued by Shohamy (2001, 2005) in her work on critical and ethical language testing. Shohamy (2001) identifies an "ideology of testing" that is grounded in the notion of symbolic power (Bourdieu 1982) that perpetuates and guarantees the continued status and roles of both the dominators and the dominated in society.

Much work remains to be done by applied linguists working on FL pedagogy regarding the pervasive problem of (in)equality in society and education in the US that has become increasingly linked to standardized and standardizing educational practices (Valenzuela 2005). In fact, the absence of controversy surrounding the National FL Standards project (see Reagan 2002: 38–39; Train 2002, 2003) has been hailed as an achievement of "strong national" and "professional consensus" among FL educators (Phillips 1999: 2), including a number of applied linguists. Perhaps some of the acquiescence, even enthusiasm, for the National FL Standards stems from the fact that French and the other FLs have enjoyed the dubious luxury of being a 'non-core' subject in US schools, and therefore able to pursue what has been seen as necessary educational change on the margins of the standards-driven accountability movement with its large-scale, high-stakes testing of students in core subjects (e.g. Math and English). Or perhaps, there have been few critical perspectives available to FL educators from which to question the underlying assumptions of standards in education. Nevertheless, the National FL Standards movement is a significant step in aligning instruction, curriculum and assessment in ways that make broad-based standardized testing inevitable within the ideological context of 'educational reform' in a United States characterized by the linkage of educational inequalities with socioeconomic status and race (Berliner 2005; Darder 2005). These standardized inequalities, because they are woven into the ideological fabric of the US, beg for a critical reflexivity that will explicitly recognize the agency of French language teachers and learners in the face of standardizing 'solutions' to social and educational inequality.

11. Conclusion

The critical perspective outlined in this chapter calls for moving beyond the ideological confines of the language, with its assumptions of (non)nativeness and (non)standardness. However, this approach ultimately points beyond a critique of ideology. As Luke (2002) observes, new conditions of economic and cultural globalization have created theoretical and empirical challenges for critical discourse analysis (CDA) and, more generally, for a critical applied linguistics. Luke argues that these challenges will require that critical applied linguistics augment its long-standing focus on ideology critique with the study of texts that model the productive uses of power and discourse in these new conditions.

In his recent critique of the teaching of language and culture as "hegemonic practice", Scollon (2004:274) calls for an "open forum about the nature of language and culture among scholars and practitioners in linguistics, education, anthropology, and the other fields in which language works as a central focus and tool of change." The discussion, Scollon explains, should focus on "the sociopolitical consequences of our concepts of language and culture" so that we may take "a sociopolitical position of opposition to the hegemony of the First World, its nation-state apparatuses, and its monolingual/monocultural views of human life" (Scollon 2004:274). Scollon poses a fundamental question for language professionals:

> Are we working in the service of the nation state, a domain in which the dominant ideology of the modern period is an equation of the tripartite entity, state, language, and culture, or are we working in the service of ordinary people throughout the world for whom language and culture are diverse, multifarious, complex, continuous, semiotic resources which do not parse into neat formal and structural entities?
>
> (Scollon 2004:271)

Linked to standardization, this "hegemonic 'tripartite' ideology" of state, language and culture constructs a reality that "somehow languages come in nicely packaged units with names and that those named units correspond exactly to the similarly named units of their cultures" (Scollon 2004:272). Scollon (2004:274) concludes:

> I believe that language pedagogy, far from being a neutral academic subject, is a significant tool of political power. I believe that only where the tools of power are

openly known, openly critiqued, and accessible to everyone can anything like a true democracy work.

I agree that the critical inquiry into language that Scollon articulates so well has a vital role to play in better addressing the problematic relationship between language and power in language pedagogy and the world at large. However, I would also offer a word of caution that is perhaps consistent with but not explicit in Scollon's argument: It would be a mistake to position ourselves as enlightened applied linguists with respect to the so-called ordinary people. Lest we become too self-congratulatory, critiques of ideology and hegemony have increasingly pointed to the ways in which ordinary people, teachers, and linguists are not mutually exclusive categories. We must realize that the ideological premises of standardization go very deep and have shaped how all of us view the practices and ideologies of state-language-culture-self, with schooling in general and language teaching in particular being the most influential forces in promoting these ideologies. As scholars and practitioners, we have an ethical responsibility to recognize and challenge how we come to support the ideological foundations of the state and the dominant assumptions of inequality by engaging willingly, reluctantly, or unknowingly in asymmetrical power relations through language.

The critical perspective advocated in this chapter points to a *French* applied linguistic research agenda that will be actively engaged in questions of language ideology and FL pedagogy in sociocultural, sociolinguistic and sociohistorical context. By foregrounding the specificity of French, applied linguists will be well positioned to critically explore the consequences of the "*l'invention de la langue et la nomination corrélative des langues*" (the invention of the language and corresponding naming of languages) (Calvet 1999:289). Applied linguists working with French will also be better equipped to work with FL educators toward (1) A critical understanding of how language pedagogy in theory and practice has been connected to the exclusive and univocal naming of language as 'the *x* language' (French, English, etc.) with the attendant issues of power, authority and inequality; and (2) Ways of reconceptualizing and reconstituting the learning, knowing, using, and teaching of French and other languages as a complex of sociocultural practice and intercultural performativity that by virtue of multiple historical, social, cultural, sociolinguistic, semiotic, and affective factors can be considered part of the discourse(s) of French.

CHAPTER 10

Affective variables, attitude and personality in context*

Peter MacIntyre, Richard Clément and Kimberly A. Noels
Cape Breton University / University of Ottawa / University of Alberta

Résumé

Ce chapitre offre une perspective de l'apprentissage du langage à travers le contexte plus spécifique des caractéristiques individuelles. Nous désirons mettre l'accent sur les variables affectives qui ont un impact général sur l'apprentissage des langues en général et, plus particulièrement, sur l'apprentissage du français. Nous organisons le chapitre autour de plusieurs variables et processus essentiels. Les relations intergroupes et leur effet sur les attitudes et la motivation ont reçu beaucoup d'attention. Dans cette foulée, les approches éducationnelles de la motivation ont récemment proposé d'inclure des processus liés à l'enseignement proprement dit, tels que la motivation auto-déterminée et la promotion de l'autonomie en salle de classe. Nous poursuivons avec une discussion de la confiance langagière et de l'anxiété, soulignant leurs effets académiques et sociaux. Sur le plan psychologique, l'apprentissage d'une langue remet en cause l'identité ethnolinguistique et a des conséquences différentes pour les membres de minorités et de majorités. Ces changements sont reliés au contact entre les groupes, et à la volonté de communiquer dans une langue seconde. Nous nous attardons par la suite à décrire les variables individuelles, particulièrement l'extraversion, afin d'introduire de nouvelles données expérimentales intégrant les effets de cet aspect et de la volonté de communiquer sur l'apprentissage du vocabulaire français. Interprétées en fonction de leur contexte, les variables affectives contribuent donc à la complexité de l'apprentissage des langues et aident à expliquer leurs conséquences.

Abstract

The focus of this chapter is on research into the affective factors that impact language learning. We organize the chapter around several key variables and processes. Intergroup relations and their effect on attitudes and motivation have been well studied.

---

* Preparation of this manuscript was facilitated by a grant from the Social Sciences and Humanities Research Council of Canada to the three authors. We would like to thank Sean MacKinnon and Kristie Saumure for their contributions to the preparation of this chapter. We are very grateful to Leanne Standing and Leslie Donovan for collection and analysis of the data reported in Section 7. Correspondence may be directed to Peter MacIntyre, Department of Psychology, Cape Breton University, PO Box 5300, Sydney NS Canada B1P 6L2 or peter_macintyre@capebretonu.ca

Educational approaches to motivation have more recently been proposed that implicate classroom processes in motivation, including the effects of self-determination motives, autonomy in the classroom, and related factors. From self-determination we move on to discuss self-confidence and language anxiety, highlighting their academic and social effects. The language learning context exerts significant influences on the learning process and its outcomes via the operation of the pedagogical and social psychological milieu. A key social psychological outcome of language learning is change in identity, a concern that plays out differently in minority and majority groups. These changes are related to the contact between groups and the willingness to communicate in the second language. We consider the research into learner personality attributes, particularly introversion-extraversion in order to introduce new experimental data that integrates the effects of personality and willingness to communicate on a specific vocabulary learning task. Considered in context, affective variables contribute to the complexity of the language learning process and help to explain the diversity of its outcomes.

1.   Introduction

Language learning is accomplished within the complex systems that make up each person. The various factors that comprise the affective system impact language learning in a number of obvious and subtle ways that can be viewed from interacting macro and micro-perspectives. From a macro-perspective, intergroup relations and their effect on attitudes and motivation have been well studied, notably by R. C. Gardner and colleagues, including studies that involve the present authors. Educational approaches to the study of motivation that explicitly consider classroom processes and their effect on self-determination motives, autonomy in the classroom, and related factors are becoming more widely studied. The focus on conditions that create self-determination leads directly to a consideration of more micro-perspective issues such as an individual's level of self-confidence and language anxiety, which in turn have demonstrable effects on that person's academic and social life. The context in which language learning occurs, including the relationships among language groups and the pedagogical processes underway within any given context encroach upon the learning process and its outcomes. For example, the effect of language learning on identity is a concern that plays out very differently in minority and majority groups when linguistic groups are in contact. On the individual level, contact itself is related to the willingness to communicate in the second language. Communication processes have long been studied in relation to the personality attributes, particularly introversion-extraversion. Although extraversion has been called the unloved variable in applied linguistics research (Dewaele & Furnham 1999), it is difficult to believe that it has no impact on language learning. We attempt to shed light on this particular issue with new experimental data that examines both extraversion and willingness to communicate in a vocabulary learning task. Although the results are complex, and in one condition seem counter-intuitive, we argue that the complexity of the interactions among affective variables, if understood in terms of the experiences of the learner, can lead to a rich description of the role of affective processes.

Knowledge about the psychology of language learning, and individual differences in second language (L2) acquisition in particular, owes a debt of gratitude to students learning French. Studies conducted around the world have shed light on the fascinating, complex psychological processes that underlie L2 acquisition. The literature on individual differences is expansive and cannot be completely covered in a single chapter. We focus instead on enduring questions that will help organize our discussion of the literature. The questions we will consider are:

- How can we conceptualize motivation and understand its impact on language learning?
- What is the effect of social context on instructed language learning?
- What are the major non-linguistic outcomes of language instruction?
- Does the personality of the learner play a role in language learning?
- The final section will offer new empirical evidence, not published elsewhere, that addresses the link between personality, communication, and French vocabulary acquisition.

We should note, at the outset, that the discussion below does not limit itself exclusively to studies of the French language, though the bulk of the work we discuss has been done with French.

2.   Second language motivation and its impact

The concept of motivation has been a fundamental element of the explanation of second language acquisition (SLA) for close to half a century. In fact, because the only other element of significance, linguistic aptitude, was deemed to be more or less part of the genetic makeup of the individual, and therefore more or less fixed, aspects of motivation have attracted researchers, and educators' attention. Because motivation is likely to respond to situational contingency, it can be enhanced by external interventions. Although all of motivation is social, the focus of past and current research has cast the phenomenon as emerging from, and contributing to, the fabric of its sociopolitical context. This characteristic distinguishes L2 acquisition from the study of other subjects, and has served to orient virtually all research in the field. In the following pages, we will review some of the models and research which, in our view, represent various turning points in the thinking about SLA motivation as it particularly pertains to French as a foreign or second language. It should be clear at the outset, however, that our review is by no means exhaustive. Clément and Gardner (2001) list ten models dealing with social aspects of SLA, without pretending to have covered the field. However, they conclude that "no one model is inherently better or more meaningful than the others" (p. 494). In spite of disagreements between their authors, it appears that no one model makes predictions that contradict the others.

2.1 Intergroup relations and motivation

Historically, models of SLA have emphasized the relation between attitudes toward the second language speaking group and the classroom on the one hand, and motivational variables on the other hand. An early study using this approach was conducted by Gardner and Lambert (1959) who found that achievement in French as a second language was related to two independent factors: Social motivation (defined primarily by indices of attitudes, orientation, and motivation), and language aptitude (defined by measures of language learning abilities and verbal intelligence). They advanced the notion that proficiency in a second language was a function of two independent factors: Language aptitude and a socially-based motivation that involved a "willingness to be like valued members of the (second) language community" (p. 271).

From these results and other similar studies, Gardner developed the socio-educational model of SLA (see Gardner 1979, 1985; Gardner & Lambert 1972). The early versions of the model emphasized motivation as a function of attitude toward the second language community and an integrative orientation – that is, an interest to become similar and even identifying with members of that community. The model, more recently summarized by Masgoret and Gardner (2003), identifies attitudes and the integrative orientation as defining *integrativeness*, which, together with attitudes toward the learning situation, determine L2 acquisition motivation. The three components, integrativeness, attitudes toward the learning situation, and motivation constitute a cluster identified as the *integrative motive.*

Considerable empirical research supports the idea that intergroup attitudes and motives play an important part in sustaining motivated effort. In addition to L2 acquisition achievement, the integrative motivation has been shown to predict language classroom behavior (Gliksman, Gardner, & Smythe 1982), motivational intensity (MacIntyre & Charos 1996), language class dropout (Gardner 1983), and the rate of learning (Gardner, Lalonde, & Moorcroft 1985; Gardner & MacIntyre 1991; see Masgoret & Gardner 2003, for a meta-analytic overview of this research program).

Intergroup attitudes in second language learning and use continue to be at the center of current research on motivation. Since the 1990s there has been an elaboration of motivational models that inform our understanding of language learning and bilingualism (see Dörnyei 2003, 2005, for an overview). It has been argued that models developed in the Canadian context, often emphasizing the acquisition of French and the intergroup relations between Anglophones and Francophones in Canada, might not apply in other parts of the world where contact with members of the target language community is rare. There also was concern that models of motivation were not applicable to social dynamics within the classroom, and provided little insight into how teachers and program developers could improve students' motivation, as found

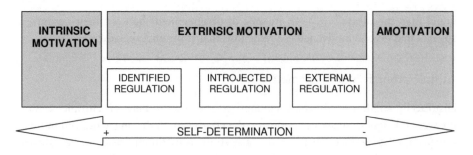

Figure 1. Schematic representation of the self-determination continuum

in the literature on motivation in education. The calls for an expanded motivational framework have led to novel lines of research.

2.2 Self-determination and motivation in L2 acquisition

Noels and her colleagues (e.g., Noels 2001a, 2001b, 2005a, 2005b; Noels, Clément, & Pelletier 2001) have introduced tenets of a well-studied motivation model, Deci and Ryan's self-determination theory (Deci & Ryan 1985, 2002; Deci, Vallerand, Pelletier, & Ryan 1991), into a model that also recognizes intergroup processes. In this approach, motivation can be categorized in terms of three orientations organized along a continuum: Amotivation, intrinsic motivation, and extrinsic motivation (see Figure 1). At one end of the continuum, amotivation refers to the lack of motivation and intention to act (Deci & Ryan 2002). At the other end of the continuum, intrinsic motivation refers to the desire to perform an activity for its own sake, because it is seen as interesting or enjoyable. These feelings of pleasure derive from the fulfillment of three basic needs: Autonomy, competence, and relatedness. Intrinsic motivation is best sustained when learners feel that all three needs have been met, that is, when they have voluntarily chosen an activity wherein they can feel both competent and supported by others.

Located conceptually between amotivation and intrinsic motivation are various forms of extrinsic motivation. Extrinsic motives involve goals that support the performance of an activity but that are external to the activity itself. Deci and Ryan (1985) highlight three types of extrinsic motivation that vary in the extent to which the goal is controlled by internal or by external contingencies. External regulation is the least self-determined form of extrinsic motivation. This motive is governed by instrumental ends, such as to gain a reward or to avoid punishment. Noels argues that students whose motivation is externally regulated (e.g., by parents, teachers, peers, etc.) have not chosen the activity of their own free will, and will be unlikely to incorporate second language learning into their identities. Introjected regulation is more internally determined. It involves a self-induced pressure, such as a desire to avoid guilt or to enhance one's prestige. Identified regulation refers to more self-determined reasons for learning a language, whereby the learning activity may not be interesting on its own, but is undertaken because it serves a desirable purpose. Integrated regulation, the fourth and most internally regulated form of extrinsic motivation, refers to actions that fit in with the rest of the person's values and aspirations, where performance of the activity expresses who that person is. In such a case, the reason for performing the activity still remains external to the activity per se.

The motivational basis for behavior may change over time. The introduction of extrinsic rewards for an intrinsically motivated activity can change the perception of why a person engages with an activity, a phenomenon sometimes called the "hidden cost of reward". But it is also possible that an externally regulated activity may become more internally regulated if persons feel that they voluntarily choose to engage in the activity, a sense of competence is developing, and other people support them in the activity. To the extent that the needs for autonomy, competence, and relatedness are being met, even in an externally regulated activity, students are likely to engage in the activity longer, and therefore be more productive.

The relevance of the self-determination framework for L2 acquisition has received support from a growing body of research. More self-determined and/or intrinsically oriented language learners have been shown to be more persistent, and/or exhibit greater motivational intensity (Noels, Clément, & Pelletier 1999; Noels 2001b, 2005b; Ramage 1990), use the second language more often, and have greater speaking and reading proficiency (Ehrman 1996; Noels et al. 1999, 2001a; Tachibana, Matsukawa, & Zhong 1996), have greater grammatical sensitivity and better language learning strategy preferences (Ramage 1990), feel less anxiety, have more positive attitudes towards language learning and increased feelings of self-efficacy (Ehrman 1996; Schmidt, Boraie, & Kassabgy 1996); and are more likely to pursue post-secondary education in the second language, as well as identify with the second language community (Goldberg & Noels 2006).

These motivational orientations have been shown to be somewhat independent of intergroup motives. Noels and her colleagues (Noels 2001a; Noels et al. 2001; Noels 2005b) found that although integrative orientation correlates significantly with intrinsic and self-determined orientations, the two categories of motives predict different outcomes: An integrative orientation predicts longer term intergroup outcomes, such as contact with the second language group and ethnic identity, whereas intrinsic/self-determined orientations more strongly predict immediate outcomes, such as effort, persistence and positive attitudes towards language learning. Among heritage language learners, Noels (2005a) found a unique substrate of intergroup motivation that included identified regulation and the integrative orientation. Such evidence suggests that the introduction of self-related motives can enhance our understanding of the variety of language learning processes.

Although Ushioda shares with Noels and others a concern for self-determination and learner autonomy, she has proposed to investigate second language motivation with a methodology that starts with the learner's point of view, that is, she argues for the use of qualitative approaches that reflect the role of learner autonomy in the language learning process. Ushioda (2001) draws a comparison between quantitative and qualitative research by noting that, on the one hand, a quantitative approach examines differences in the *level* of motivation, and their relative impact on behavior. On the other hand, motivation from a qualitative viewpoint "[...] may be defined not in terms of observable and measurable activity, but rather in terms of what patterns of thinking and belief underlie such activity and shape students' engagement in the learning process" (p. 96).

Ushioda's (2001) study of a small group of Irish students learning French demonstrates that intergroup attraction, highlighted by an interest in spending a summer in France, provides motivational support for language learning. Her results expand on number and type of motivational processes, including academic interest, enjoyment of the language itself, desired levels of L2 competence, personal goals and satisfactions, external pressures and incentives, as well as positive learning history. Not all of these processes were correlated with achievement measures, but two noteworthy observations can be made. First, less successful students maintained motivation by a focus on external incentives and pressures, consistently attributing difficulties to factors outside themselves and their control (e.g., quality of the French department, appropriateness of academic regulations, etc.). Successful students engaged intrinsic motivational processes more often, integrating both language learning success and motivation into the self. Learners are able to regulate their motivational processes to some extent by rekindling their interest through conscious thought about future aspirations, past successes, reasons for enjoyment, and so on, actions that Ushioda labels "self-motivation".

Another recent development within the self-related conceptual sphere is Dörnyei's (2005) proposed "reinterpretation" of integrativeness, locating that familiar concept within the concept of self (see Markus & Nuirius 1986; Higgins 1998). Drawing upon the work on self-determination (Noels 2003), self-motivation (Ushioda 2001), and imagined communities (Norton 2001), as well as bringing in his own thoughts on integrative motivation in learning situations where the target language group is not in contact with the learners (see also Yashima 2000; Yashima, Zenuk-Nishide, & Shimizu 2004; Kimura, Nakata, & Okumuram 2001), Dörnyei's (2005) L2 Motivational Self System is made up of three dimensions. The first is a concept of the *Ideal L2 Self* that captures a future-oriented desire to become a person who masters the L2. It represents a vision of oneself as a member of an imagined L2 community with access to the social and instrumental incentives that community provides. Interacting with this self is a more externalized construction, the *Ought-to L2 Self*, that refers to attributes that ought to be possessed if one wants to avoid negative outcomes. Finally, these two teleological visions of the self are balanced against a causal dimension captured by *L2 Learning Experience* which concerns situation-specific motives in the present learning situation. As noted earlier, this theoretical scheme does not make predictions that contradict previous formulations, but rather is an attempt to locate language learning motivation within the broader system of the learner. The motivational properties of the self have been implicated in other ways as well, including the notion of self-confidence and its link with anxiety in L2 acquisition.

3.   Self-confidence and anxiety

Pursuing the investigation of attitude and motivational factors among Francophones learning English as a second language, Clément and his colleagues (Clément 1986; Clément, Gardner, & Smythe 1977, 1980; Clément & Kruidenier 1985) have proposed that a major dimension underlying second language acquisition is self-confidence with the language. In the original findings (Clément et al. 1977, 1980), two factors related to motivation: Integrative motive and second language confidence, that is, the belief in one's capacity to interact in a meaningful and efficient manner in second language usage situations. This L2 confidence was defined as a combination of low levels of language specific anxiety, confidence in one's language skills, and self-perceptions of high levels of proficiency, and was linked to quantitative and qualitative aspects of contact with members of the second language speaking group.

Following these results and the apparent discrepancy with the Anglophone learners of French studied by Gardner, Clément (1980, 1984) proposed a model later dubbed "the social context model" according to which two processes might intervene in the definition of SLA motivation. In unicultural situations, where majority group members would be learning the language of a minority or absent group, such as those typically studied by Gardner and his collaborators, it would be expected that integrativeness would be the main determinant of SLA motivation. In contexts where there are opportunities to interact with the L2 group, however, integrativeness would orient the individual to enter in contact with members of that group and, to the extent that this contact is positive and frequent, develop language confidence, which would then sustain motivation.

Clément's model also drew implications for non-linguistic aspects of SLA which we will review later. But regarding the dynamics of language mastery, it also introduced an additional element to the components of the integrative motive. A product of studies of Canadian Anglophones learning French as a second language, the original integrative motive was defined in terms of the attractiveness of the L2 group. The analysis of the Canadian Francophone situation, however, revealed that these minority group members also felt reluctant about sharing the Anglophone reality because of the fear that, as a result, they might lose their first language and culture (Clément & Kruidenier 1985). Integrativeness was, therefore, re-defined as the result of two antagonistic forces: Perceived attractiveness of the second language group, and fear of assimilation. Of course, in the specific Canadian or North American context, French may be considered a minority language which would not evoke among its learners any strong fear of assimilation. It remains to be seen if, in a situation where French is the dominant language (e.g., in France), its acquisition by minority members would result in the same reactions witnessed in Canada among the Francophone Canadians.

Wherever language learning takes place, the demands of acquisition and usage provide fertile ground for the development of anxiety among learners. Cohen and Norst (1989:61) state the issue well: "[...] there is something fundamentally different about learning a language, compared to learning another skill or gaining other knowledge, namely, that language and self are so closely bound, if not identical, that an attack on one is an attack on the other". Concern over the effects of language anxiety emanates from its effects on the learning process, the individual learner, and the social consequences of anxiety arousal.

3.1 Academic effects

The effects of language anxiety in the classroom are well documented. There are a number of studies that show strong negative correlations between measures of language anxiety and course grades (e.g., Horwitz, Horwitz, & Cope 1986; Young 1986). One study reported a correlation as high as –.65 in a university-level French class (MacIntyre & Gardner 1994b), indicating that over forty percent of the variation in course grades is associated with anxiety in that sample.

In an extensive study reported by Gardner, Smythe, Clément and Gliksman (1976), and subsequently detailed in a monograph by Gardner, Smythe and Lalonde (1984), the relation between attitudes, motivation, anxiety and language learning (in French as a L2) was investigated in seven locations across Canada. Language anxiety consistently was among the strongest predictors of second language achievement (Gardner et al. 1976). Language anxiety was negatively related to both actual and perceived L2 competence (Gardner et al. 1984).

The source of these effects lies in the cognitive, emotional, and behavioral disruptions caused by anxiety arousal. Eysenck (1979) proposed that anxiety arousal has a complex set of effects, including (1) An increase in activity levels as the "fight or flight" response of the sympathetic nervous system is engaged, and (2) A disruption in ongoing cognition caused by distracting self-related thoughts. The combination of these effects leads to the possibility that anxiety arousal can be facilitating or debilitating to performance, depending on the demands of the task and the level of anxiety arousal. The concepts of facilitating and debilitating anxiety were highlighted by Scovel (1978) in his review of the early literature, based primarily on data collected by Klienmann (1977). Performance on a relatively easy task, that otherwise might be boring for students, can be facilitated when some anxiety is aroused, as when task performance is done in public or evaluated by a teacher. Yet one risks going too far in creating anxiety, pushing students beyond the level where performance is facilitated. Indeed, the vast majority of research to date has shown a negative correlation between anxiety and academic performance in language courses, indicating that language anxiety is predominantly of the debilitating variety (MacIntyre 1999).

Tobias' (1986) three-stage analysis of learning tasks focuses attention on the various ways anxiety arousal can affect learning. Tobias breaks tasks into input, processing and output stages. At the input stage, anxiety acts like a filter preventing some information from getting into the cognitive processing system. Anxious students lose information because of the distraction caused by anxiety, especially when listening to a second language speaker. An anxious student might re-read a written text, but the social conventions and conversation constraints of language classrooms make it difficult for an anxious learner to repeatedly ask for clarification, repetition, and so on. During the processing stage, anxiety can influence both the speed and accuracy of learning as attention is distracted from the process of making connections between new material and existing knowledge structures. Anxiety arousal at the output stage can influence the quality of second language communication. Anxious learners report 'freezing-up' on an important test, or having words on the 'tip-of-the-tongue' but being unable to speak them. The frustration of such experiences can heighten anxiety, creating a vicious cycle that maintains heightened anxiety even among learners whose level of proficiency is improving.

Several studies support this three-stage model (Onwuegbuzie, Bailey, & Daley 2000; MacIntyre & Gardner 1991; MacIntyre & Gardner 1994a, 1994b; Onwuegbuzie, Bailey, & Daley 1999, 2000). For instance, in a study of L2 French learners, MacIntyre and Gardner (1994a, 1994b) reported significant correlations of language anxiety with the amount of time required to recognize words, the ability to hold words in short term memory, recall of grammar rules, paragraph translation, the amount of time needed to studying new vocabulary items, memory for new vocabulary items, time to complete a test of vocabulary, retrieval of vocabulary from long term memory, ability to repeat items in L1 and L2, ability to speak with an L2 accent, complexity of sentences spoken, as well as the fluency of speech. Results on complex, multi-stage tasks show that extra effort can reduce the effects of language anxiety in cases where a learner can compensate for distractions at earlier stages of processing (e.g., by re-reading a passage, or practicing a response). Such compensation is not always possible because of the structure of a task.

In an experimental task using a video camera to arouse anxiety during learning of French vocabulary items, MacIntyre and Gardner (1994a) found that the effects of anxiety are strongest immediately after it is aroused, dissipate with time, and can be overcome if opportunity for the use of compensation strategies is given. MacIntyre and Gardner (1994b: 301) conclude that "[t]he potential effects of language anxiety on cognitive processing in the second language appear pervasive and may be quite subtle".

3.2 Social effects

The social effects of language anxiety influence ways in which second language interaction takes place, and begin within the individual. Price (1991: 104) reported strong emotion from students, one of whom said "I'd rather be in a prison camp than speak a foreign language". Although the severity of this reaction probably is not typical, avoidance of communication is a pervasive reaction to anxiety, one that has important social consequences. Anxious individuals often engage in self-deprecating cognition (Schwarzer 1986), and this has an impact on the ways in which the learner relates to other people. Students worry that others think that they are "stupid," "a total dingbat", or "a babbling baby" (Price 1991: 105), because they are having trouble using simple vocabulary and grammar structures.

There are many ways in which the social context can influence language anxiety. A competitive classroom atmosphere (Bailey 1983), difficult interactions with teachers (Young 1991), risks of embarrassment (Ely 1986), opportunity for contact with members of the target language group and tension between ethnic groups (Clément 1986), may all influence language anxiety.

Perhaps the most frequent finding in the literature on language anxiety, and one of its most important social effects, is that anxious learners do not communicate as often as more relaxed learners (MacIntyre & Gardner 1994b; MacIntyre & Charos 1996; MacIntyre, Baker, Clément, & Donovan 2003), and the simple prospect of communicating in a L2 appears to be the major source of language anxiety. Although there has not been much research on the interpersonal effects of avoiding communication in an L2, it is clear that avoiding communication in the native language generates a number of negative assumptions about a reticent speaker (Daly & McCroskey 1984). How anxious L2 communicators are perceived by others would be an interesting avenue for future research, especially considering the important role played by situational context (e.g., inside versus outside the classroom; control versus affiliative situations; novel versus familiar contexts).

4.   Contextual effects in L2 acquisition

Context can of course be understood along varied dimensions from the context of a particular language to the wider societal context. Because of their greater relevance to social and motivational issues, we will here consider the pedagogical and the social-political context.

4.1   The pedagogical context

The pedagogical context for language learning lies at the interface of social and individual processes, the language classroom is a potentially powerful force for changes in social context and intergroup relations. Early versions of the socio-educational model (Gardner & Smythe 1975) explicitly incorporated attitudes toward the learning situation (the teaching and course). Even so, calls for a stronger focus on education-friendly approaches to motivation have been made (e.g., Crookes & Schmidt 1991), and the issues have been taken up (e.g., Ushioda 2001). However, there remains an unfortunate lack of empirical data on many of these developments (MacIntyre, MacMaster, & Baker 2001).

For our purposes, we will contrast intensive and non-intensive programs. Intensive programs, such as immersion and study abroad, are based on the notion that intense, authentic communication in the L2 will facilitate learning. The notion of inter-ethnic contact was at the heart of the establishment of the French immersion programs in Canada, first in Montreal and later throughout Canada (Genesee 1998). The outcomes of these programs have been well studied and reviewed elsewhere (Clément 1994; Noels & Clément 1998). In general, immersion programs produce greater comfort with passive language skills, and a greater capacity for L2 production than non-intensive programs, although the speech production of immersion students frequently does not reach native-like levels (Hammerly 1989). This is not necessarily a surprising outcome, given the limited range of contact and exposure to conversation in the classroom (Allen, Swain, Harley, & Cummins 1990; Genesee 1987; Liskin-Gasparro 1998). If the language classroom could provide a microcosm of authentic interactions with native speakers, then we might expect it to yield a more complete range of linguistic and non-linguistic outcomes (Firth & Wagner 1997). Although some researchers focus on the limitations of the linguistic capabilities of immersion students, the non-linguistic outcomes – including more positive attitudes toward the L2 community (Genesee 1987), lower levels of anxiety and a greater willingness to communicate in the L2 (MacIntyre et al. 2003) – suggest that immersion programs have been at least partially successful in meeting the goal of improved intergroup relations behind the original concept of immersion education (Genesee 1998).

4.2 The social context

As the above discussion suggests, the issue of contact with the second language speaking group in naturalistic contexts is a key issue to understanding L2 acquisition. It does appear that aspects of inter-ethnic contact in the context of L2 programs serve to develop more positive attitudes and greater self-confidence in the ability to use the second language efficiently (for reviews, see Clément 1994; Gardner 1985; Clément & Gardner 2001). The assumption that such interaction could occur, and has consequences that would be independent of the wider structural context in which it occurs is, however, challenged in a number of ways.

4.2.1 *Structural aspects*

An important theme here is the idea that positive benefits from language acquisition will only be achieved to the extent that the first language and culture are well established within the individual (Carey 1991; Clément 1984; Cummins & Swain 1986; Hamers & Blanc 1988; Landry & Allard 1992). This presupposes a familial, educational, and social context which allows the development and transmission of the first language and culture. Although such conditions may be present for majority group members, they may not characterize the situation of many minority group members, immigrants, refugees, and sojourners. The relative status of the first and second language speaking groups and the linguistic composition of the community are key determinants of the linguistic and cultural outcomes of L2 acquisition.

Under the concepts of additive and subtractive bilingualism, Lambert (1978) proposed that language learning outcomes could be very different for members of majority and minority groups. Additive bilingualism expected among members of a majority group learning the language of a minority group corresponds to the capacity to use two languages as cognitive and social tools. Subtractive bilingualism corresponds, however, to the loss of the first language as a result of the acquisition of the L2, and would result from minority group members learning the language of a dominant or majority group.

As a further formalization of the concepts of minority and majority as pertains to language issues, Giles, Bourhis and Taylor (1977) proposed the concept of ethnolinguistic vitality which encompasses demographic representation of the communities, their institutional representation, and the socio-economic status of their members. These factors were further developed by Prujiner, Deshaies, Hamers, Blanc, Clément and Landry (1984) in terms of the relative demographic, political, economic and cultural capital of the in- and out-group communities. The results obtained to date show a consistent relation between these structural factors and first language retention and competence (e.g., Landry & Allard 1992; Landry, Allard, & Henry 1996).

The above would imply the shorter or longer term disappearance of languages with lesser vitality. This problem has come to be a key issue for governmental authorities in countries promoting a pluralist approach to ethnic diversity. Language planning (cf., Haugen 1959; Maurais 1987) has been the political and administrative instrument used to promote and protect language according to predetermined societal options (e.g., Martin 1997). Accordingly, the State may determine the goals of language education, the medium of interaction with government agencies, tribunals and schools, and the relative visibility of different languages in public and commercial signs – the *linguistic landscape* (Landry & Bourhis 1997). The effectiveness of such measures depends to a large extent on conditions already present in the communities on which it is imposed. Promoting English as the only language among Americans seems to be relatively easy (cf., Frendreis & Tatalovitch 1997). In fact, the promotion of English outside the United States and England has been referred to as "linguistic imperialism" (Boyle 1997; Clachar 1998), and has raised some concerns about the local, demographically-dominant languages. Likewise, the promotion of French as the only official language by the Quebec government has had a direct impact on the usage of French as a public and working language in a province which is no more than a French enclave in the North American continent (Pagé 2006).

4.2.2 *Psychological aspects*

To understand the effects of structural aspects requires an array of psychological constructs likely to mediate their influence on individual characteristics and behavior. A first step towards bridging the structural-psychological gap has been to recast ethnolinguistic vitality as the perceived counterpart of "objective vitality" (Bourhis, Giles, & Rosenthal 1981). Subsequent studies tended to show a stable relation between objective and subjective measures of vitality (e.g., Bourhis & Sachdev 1984; Landry & Allard 1992), and subsequent studies suggest a number of direct and indirect effects through the influence of vitality on interethnic contact experiences (e.g., Cenoz & Valencia 1993; and a review by Harwood, Giles, & Bourhis 1994).

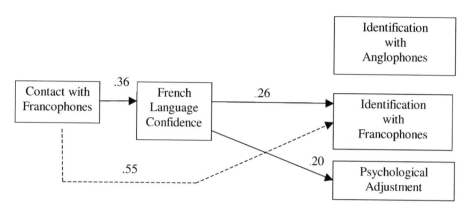

Figure 2. Path analytic solution: Majority Anglophones (from Noels & Clément 1996)

4.3 Identity processes

The preceding discussion suggests that acquiring an L2 involves certain costs and benefits which are directly related to the relative status of the communities in contact. Following the additive/subtractive bilingualism hypothesis (Lambert 1975, 1978), for majority group members learning a minority language – whether the minority language group is represented or not in the community – benefits in terms of personal enrichment might well outweigh the cost incurred by a momentary culture shock and communication anxiety. It is possible, however, that teaching a second dominant language to help in the adaptation of minority group members entails the disappearance of the minority community as a distinct cultural entity of a nation. This would certainly defeat the purpose of an important goal of pluralist societies. A better understanding of identity and adaptation patterns is, therefore, deemed useful.

As illustrated above, shifts in identity as an outcome of L2 competence was not unforeseen by social psychologists dealing with bilingualism. The social context model (e.g., Clément 1980, 1984; Clément & Noels 1991) described earlier applies the same construct to the development of L2 competence as it does to the maintenance or loss of ethnic identity. Following the original model, confidence in the L2 developed through frequent and positive contacts with outgroup members is hypothesized to mediate the effects of intergroup contact on identity. Since the development of adequate identity profiles is hypothesized to be related to adjustment, it would be expected that well-being would be related to L2 confidence as well. The results obtained by Noels and Clément (1996) support both this hypothesis and the preceding considerations regarding status. As can be seen in Figure 2, majority Anglophones (i.e., Anglophones originating from settings where they are a majority) show an additive pattern: Better identification with the Francophones, and better psychological adjustment as a result of greater language confidence in French and no erosion of English identity.

These results contrast with those obtained with Francophones from majority Francophone settings currently evolving in an Anglophone setting as illustrated in

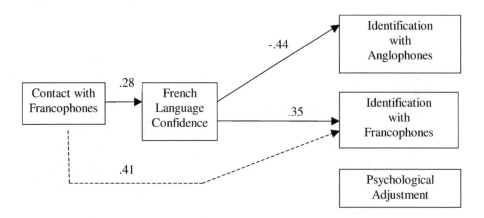

Figure 3. Path analytic solution: Majority Francophones (from Noels & Clément 1996)

Figure 3. Increased English language confidence results in increased identification with Anglophones and decreased identification with their own group. Furthermore, in this case, increased language confidence is not related to psychological adjustment. This illustrates the most pernicious effect of a minority situation. These students come from majority settings, and yet, develop a subtractive profile as a result of a brief immersion in a context where they are a minority.

The research reported above supports the original contention pertaining to the subtractive effects of second language competence. It further demonstrates its implications for psychological adjustment. Finally, the results obtained with majority Francophone students support the powerful impact of L2 confidence as a determinant of identity shift.

At the root of the process is an intergroup contact situation which entails the actual use of a L2. Contact can be defined as direct, such as any face-to-face situation, or indirect when the presence of the other group is symbolic or mediated. For example, under the label 'linguistic landscape', Landry and Bourhis (1997) showed that a number of factors defining the linguistic environment such as road signs, shop signs and the media contributed to the maintenance of minority languages. Clément, Baker, Josephson and Noels (2005) reported results supporting cultivation (Gerbner 1969) and erosion (Varan 1998) theories, to the effect that media have an immediate impact on culture. Specifically, their longitudinal design showed that L2 audio-visual and written media had an impact on degree of identification with the outgroup, mediated by L2 confidence. These results buttress the hypothesis that it is not so much competence in the L2, as measured by standard tests that is important, but rather the actual usage of the language in a communication situation, to which we now turn.

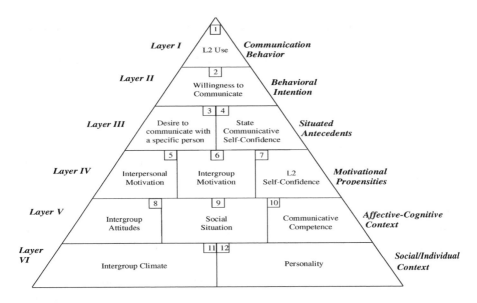

Figure 4. The pyramid model of WTC

5. What factors lead to a willingness or unwillingness to communicate?

Communication processes occupy a central place in both intergroup contact and L2 pedagogy. Fostering willingness to communicate (WTC) in the L2 is both an outcome of SLA and a strategy for learning (MacIntyre, Clément, Dörnyei, & Noels 1998). The pyramid model of WTC provides a framework to integrate research from disciplines including communication, psychology, a spectrum of applied linguistics domains (including sociolinguistics and language acquisition models), and education. The model is organized into six layers, proceeding from the most distal to most proximal components, as displayed in Figure 4.

At the base of the pyramid are two wide-ranging sets of influences, intergroup climate and personality. The intergroup climate is defined by the broad social context in which various language groups operate. The relative ethnolinguistic vitalities (Giles et al. 1977) of the language communities may be moderated by the interpersonal communication networks in which individuals participate. Processes of acculturation and adaptation will play out differently in conditions of contact or isolation, harmony or prejudicial discrimination, as well as when groups perceive competition or disadvantage (Guimond & Tougas 1994). Tensions and attractions among groups potentially predate nation-states making individual language learners tiny threads in a complex fabric of social relations. Yet within this context, individuals themselves differ significantly in their reaction to social situations, reactions that stem, in part, from basic personality traits, including sex differences (Lin & Rancer 2003). Evidence for the heritability of basic traits demonstrates that genetic endowment plays a key role in temperamental reactions, such as nervousness or shyness (Pedersen, Plomin, McClearn, &

Friberg 1988). Given the interaction of basic personality traits with the social environment, the base of the pyramid is formed by long term individual differences operating within various social structures and networks, providing highly stable patterns that predate the individual.

Moving to a more proximal level, the next layer of the pyramid captures the individual's typical affective and cognitive context. Setting the tone for motivation to learn the L2 is the tension between a desire to approach the target language group, and a sense of hesitation or fear of the implications of doing so. The evolution of Gardner and Lambert's (1959) concept of integrative orientation into the more comprehensive integrative motive, as part of the socio-educational model (Gardner 1985), has captured for applied linguists the tendency for approach toward the other group. Tension within the self is often created with the L1 or heritage group as a learner begins adapting to a new group. Therefore, L2 communication must take into account the predictable avoidance tendencies as reflected in the fear of assimilation and its conceptual cousin, subtractive bilingualism (Lambert 1975). The motivations emerging from such tensions sustain or impair the action necessary to develop competencies in the L2 (Clément 1986). It almost goes without saying that linguistic competence, knowledge of syntactic and morphological rules, lexical resources, and the phonological and orthographic systems needed for communication, both spoken and written, is fundamental. Building upon the linguistic dimension are competencies to handle discourse appropriately, to accomplish communicative actions, to deal with situational variation, and when all else fails, to strategically compensate for deficiencies in any of these areas. Such motives and competencies play out within social situations with an almost infinite number of permutations of participants, settings, purposes, topics, and channels of communication. The pyramid model is not so specific as to be formulaic in the application of these factors, and it is understood that their operation in situ will depend on interactions with variables from other layers.

Moving to the last of the layers of enduring influences, we find highly specific motives and self-related cognition. Intergroup motives stem directly from membership in a particular social group and interpersonal motives stem from the social roles one plays within the group. Both intergroup and interpersonal motives arise from two classic sources: Affiliation and control. Harmonious intergroup relations are a fundamental, explicit objective of supporters of intercultural communication (Kim 1988) and a firmly established motive in the research literature. Control motives encompass L2 communicative behavior aimed at asserting the power and autonomy of the speaker, and often simultaneously limiting the freedom of the interlocutor. Taken broadly, this includes events such as directives from a supervisor, instruction from a teacher, and requests for assistance in the L2. The final set of influences at this level includes L2 self-confidence; perceptions of communicative competence coupled with a lack of anxiety define the self-confident L2 speaker. This concept is somewhat more specific than the linguistic competencies described at the lower level to capture the idea that learners may overestimate or underestimate their capabilities, and how they may be applied.

When we move to the next layer of the pyramid, we make a transition from enduring influences to situational ones. The sense of time is coming to focus on the here-and-now. At this level of the pyramid model is the desire to communicate with a specific person as well as a state of self-confidence. The general attitudes and motives found at lower levels find their embodiments in persons immediately present, and exceptions to the rules can be made. At this level, power motives are reconciled with affiliation, task and relationship orientations find their expressions, and persons are accepted or rejected as communication partners. The self-confidence expressed in a given situation is based on actual competencies possessed by a speaker, any systematic biases in perception of abilities (MacIntyre, Noels, & Clément 1997), and salient elements of the situation.

The culmination of the processes described thus far is the willingness to communicate, that is, to initiate L2 discourse on a specific occasion with a specific person. This represents the level of behavioral intention to speak (Ajzen & Fishbein 1980) if one has the opportunity. The prototypical event in the language classroom is a group of students indicating a willingness to communicate by raising their hands to respond to a teacher's question. Dörnyei and Otto (1998) have likened this sort of event to "crossing the Rubicon", a point of no return where one commits to act in the L2. At times one crosses such a threshold with reluctance, hesitation, even trepidation (MacIntyre 2005) because the course of future conversations can be quite unpredictable.

The empirical work on WTC in the L2 has centered around Skehan's (1989) notion that the willingness of language learners to "talk in order to learn" was a fundamental, yet elusive, individual difference variable. Prior work has supported the key relationships proposed in the pyramid model. Both components of self-confidence, perceived competence and anxiety, consistently have been shown to relate to WTC (MacIntyre et al. 2003; Yashima 2002; Yashima et al. 2004), although their interrelationships have been shown to change over time in adolescents (Donovan & MacIntyre 2004), and with experience in the second language (MacIntyre, Baker, Clément, & Donovan 2002).

Generally, anxiety takes on greater importance as learners gain experience (see also McCroskey & Richmond 1991). WTC correlated, as expected, with both the key motives for communication: The desire for control (MacIntyre & Donovan 2004) and affiliation (Clément, Baker, & MacIntyre 2003) tend to increase WTC. The key role of WTC – its prediction of the initiation of communication – also has been demonstrated in several studies, both in the L1 (MacIntyre, Babin, & Clément 1999) and the L2 (Dörnyei & Kormos 2000).

In further work, WTC has been studied as a non-linguistic outcome of Canadian immersion programs (MacIntyre et al. 2003). More broadly, social context has been shown to affect WTC, and its role in generating L2 communication differs between majority and minority groups in a bilingual context (Clément et al. 2003). As might be expected, ethnocentrism has been shown to reduce intercultural WTC (Lin & Rancer 2003). Perceiving social support from friends and siblings, but not necessarily parents and teachers, enhances WTC in high school students (MacIntyre, Baker, Clément, & Conrod 2001). Finally, attempts to integrate WTC with existing literature on motivation demonstrate that WTC shares common variance with both Gardner's (1985) integrative motive and mainstream academic motivation factors (MacIntyre et al. 2001).

6. Personality

The personality of the learner has been implicated in WTC and it is one of the foundations on which the 'pyramid' is built because personality represents the enduring character of an individual. Definitions of personality often emphasize the uniqueness of each individual created by various modes of interaction between genetic endowment and learning experiences. Personality is a wellspring from which flows the consistency of thoughts, feelings, and behaviors. At a more humanistic level, personality can be thought of as the mask we wear in social situations, as the core of our being, or as the process of actualizing our true potentials. Clearly the term 'personality' has a wide variety of connotations, among them the adaptive function of personality is often under-emphasized in its definition.

The study of personality has been significantly informed by the study of language. Almost 70 years ago, Allport and Odbert (1936) reasoned that the adaptive nature of personality would lead to vocabulary terms to describe the main traits or dimensions on which people differ, and to the extent that personality is universal, different languages will code terms for the same traits. This has been called the lexical hypothesis (Goldberg 1993). In practice, we characterize people by their traits. When we know someone is lazy, kind, smart, serious, nervous, and so on, we can better predict how they will act and react with us. The almost infinite possible combinations of even a few basic traits allows for the diversity observed in personality, akin to the way combinations of basic colors in paint or light lead to a plethora of observable colors.

There has been surprisingly little research directed at determining the personality correlates of L2 achievement. According to Gardner (1990: 184), the research that has been done has yielded "generally poor results". Intuitively, it seems difficult to believe that a trait such as extraversion-introversion is not somehow related to success in a second language. Yet Dewaele and Furnham (1999: 509) label extraversion as the "unloved variable" in applied linguistics research, because of its poor reputation in empirical research. In spite of these disappointments, it seems almost axiomatic that the personality of the language learner would have an impact on the process of L2 acquisition, yet the empirical evidence appears to be lacking. Why would that be?

We can identify four plausible explanations for the sparse results linking extraversion and language learning. First, Dewaele and Furnham (1999) cite misinterpretation of early work, such as Naiman, Frolich, Stern and Todesco's (1978) classic study of the Good Language Learner, as a reason for the neglect of extraversion among applied linguistics researchers. Although extraversion may not be linked to written linguistic outcome measures (Dewaele & Furnham 1999), it appears to be reliably associated with the achievement of oral fluency in the L2 (Dewaele & Furnham 2000). Thus, one possible explanation for the disappointing results of most work on personality and language learning might be that researchers have been measuring outcomes that do not lend themselves to influence by traits such as extraversion.

Ehrman (1990) presents a second view of why the link between personality and language learning, more specifically, between extraversion and language learning, has been elusive. She argues that much of the time, people are using the language in dyadic situations, which are likely to be just as comfortable for introverts as for extraverts, and thus an advantage for extraverts fails to emerge.

A third argument, offered by Skehan (1989), holds that for academic achievement in general, and verbal learning in particular, it is the introverts who usually have the advantage over extraverts. However, for SLA and communication, extraversion has been taken as the desirable personality orientation (Wakamoto 2000). It can be suggested that, on the one hand, a formal classroom setting where achievement is based primarily on rote memory for vocabulary and grammar rules might favor the introvert. On the other hand, language learning emphasizing naturalistic communication opportunities would likely favor the extravert. A classroom that blends the two pedagogical styles might wash out the advantages gained by extraverts or introverts, yielding a near zero correlation. In the literature, the correlation between extraversion and language achievement has been nonsignificant or slightly positive, and the results seem to be related to the particular measures employed in the studies (Skehan 1989).

We offer an elaboration on Skehan's argument as a fourth explanation for the relative scarcity of consistent research results linking personality and L2 learning: Much prior research does not consider the adaptive nature of personality as it interacts with situations. According to Mischel (1999:233), "knowledge of individual differences alone often tells us little unless it is combined with information about the conditions and situational variables that influence the behavior of interest".

Previous studies (Chastain 1975; Naiman et al. 1978; Pritchard 1952; Riding & Banner 1986; Robinson, Gabriel, & Katchan 1994; Smart, Elton, & Burnet 1970; Swain & Burnaby 1976) have assumed that L2 achievement and individual difference variables should correlate, though the assumption of a *direct* link between personality and language learning seems to be unwarranted (Lalonde & Gardner 1984; MacIntyre & Charos 1996). Personality traits impinge on behavior in context, helping to shape our adaptation to that context. To emphasize the person by situation interactions, then, is to shift the focus onto the fit between the demands of language learning and the personality of the student. We now offer new empirical evidence demonstrating the interaction of personality and contextual effects in the expression of WTC.

7.   Original empirical data: Extraversion and studying French vocabulary[1]

One of the most fundamental of all personality traits is captured by the terms introvert and extravert. Given the tendency of introverts to prefer quiet solitary study environments while extraverts tend to choose more social environments (Campbell & Hawley 1982), one could predict that introverted L2 students would tend to study better alone, while extraverted L2 students might demonstrate better progress when learning in groups. Introverts' greater tendency to be socially anxious (Cheek & Buss 1981) might also lead to an advantage for introverts in solitary study environments. Wilson and Lynn (1990) have argued that the classroom settings where students are expected to complete assignments on their own, without social interaction, favor introverts over extraverts.

Given the discussion of personality in the preceding section, these assumptions appear to be consistent with theory, but likely are too simplistic to describe the action of personality on learning in practice. Lacking is an account of the individual's familiarity with the context itself or in other words, the learner's degree of actual experience in a given situation. Personality certainly is not the only determinant of an individual's study habits, especially if the development of those practices depends on cooperation from other persons. For example, a given teacher might employ a great deal of group work in the classroom, to introverts and extraverts alike. Extraverts are more prone to boredom than introverts (Ahmed 1990), tend to be higher in sensation-seeking than introverts (Eysenck & Zuckerman 1978), and prefer to build more variety into monotonous tasks than do introverts (Hill 1975). It is possible to imagine that even an extravert might not attain optimal levels of arousal in a group setting, if he or she is bored from repeated exposure to the same set of classmates and group work tasks. In such a case, the novelty of being permitted to study alone actually might benefit the extravert. Similarly, introverts who become accustomed to studying in dyads or small groups might become overly aroused when placed in a solitary study setting because of their lack of familiarity with the situation.

Given the concern we noted earlier about communication processes in the classroom, we also were curious about the differences between studying in groups and studying alone, both in achievement and WTC. With the present study we are developing a new measure of WTC, defined with reference to each of the specific vocabulary items under study. This novel approach will be maximally sensitive to contextual effects, such as prior knowledge of related content.

---

1.   These results were presented at the annual conference of the Canadian Psychological Association by MacIntyre, Donovan and Standing (2004).

7.1 Methodology

We sought to create conditions under which introverts and extraverts might differ in two language learning outcomes: Vocabulary acquisition and willingness to use each of the new vocabulary items in a sentence. Using a laboratory analog approach (Gardner, Day, & MacIntyre 1992), and focusing on one key element of L2 learning, vocabulary acquisition, allows for examination of the effects of personality on a specific task. Having both a measure of WTC and a vocabulary test in the present study will allow for examination of the link between test scores and willingness to use the new vocabulary items in oral communication. The laboratory analog approach also allows for manipulation of the study situation with the aim of creating conditions that might facilitate learning among introverts, and other conditions that might favor extraverts. Based on the extant literature, however, we do not expect strong effects.

7.1.1 *Participants*
Participants were 127 high school students enrolled in grade 10, 11, and 12 core French-as-a-second-language courses in Nova Scotia, Canada. As is typical in language classes, approximately two-thirds of the sample was female (n = 91), and one-third male (n = 36). Students ranged in age from 15 to 19 years with a mean age of 16.5 years. All of the students in the sample indicated English as a first language, and the high schools were located in predominantly Anglophone communities. The study was conducted during regularly scheduled French classes with the permission of the school board, school administrators, teachers, and parents.

7.1.2 *Measures*
Measures administered to the students included a demographics questionnaire with questions about age, sex, and previous experience learning French, Eysenck and Eysenck's (1975) 23-item extraversion scale, a fifteen-item vocabulary test, and a measure of state WTC. The vocabulary test was scored on a 3-point scale, with one point awarded for the definite article, and 2 points awarded for a close approximation of the root word (as used by MacIntyre & Gardner 1989). As a measure of reliability of the extraversion scores, Cronbach's alpha was calculated and deemed acceptable ($\alpha = .73$). Students were classified as either introverts or extraverts based on a median split of extraversion scores. Following the advice of classroom teachers, vocabulary items were selected from concrete nouns of the type the students might learn in their courses. Prior to the study, we asked students to translate as many of the items as possible. The mean and maximum numbers of correct English translations ($\underline{M} = 0.72$, $\underline{SD} = 0.83$, maximum obtained score = 3 of a possible 45 points) suggest that the words were indeed unfamiliar to the students in our sample.

7.1.3 *Procedure*
After giving informed consent, students completed the extraversion scale, the trait WTC scale, the vocabulary pretest, and the demographics questionnaire. Next, each

class was randomly divided such that some students were assigned to study either (a) Alone in a separate room, or (b) In small groups of three to four students in their regular classroom. Following a fifteen-minute study period, all students returned to their classroom, and completed a five-minute filler task consisting of writing about their study methods, after which they completed the vocabulary posttest, as well as the state WTC measure. Following the vocabulary posttest, students were asked "Is this [study method] similar to how you usually study?" The available responses were "very similar", "somewhat similar", and "not at all similar".

7.2 Results

The data analysis reported below first examines the effects of extraversion and assigned study situation on two dependent variables, vocabulary learning scores on the posttest, and state willingness to communicate. The second analysis utilizes post-hoc t-tests to more directly test the hypothesis that familiarity of study situation interacts with extraversion to affect the same two dependent variables. The third analysis examines whether extraverts and introverts differ in their familiarity with assigned study contexts. Our final set of analyses examines the relationship between vocabulary acquisition and WTC at the level of the individual vocabulary word.[2]

To examine the effects of extraversion and similarity of the study situation a 2 (introvert, extravert) × 3 (very similar, somewhat similar, not at all similar) MANOVA was performed with the dependent variables posttest scores and state WTC. At the multivariate level, the main effects of extraversion (Hotelling's = .001, F (2, 120) = 0.09, p = .92) and similarity of study situation (Hotelling's = .021, F (4, 238) = 0.62, p = .65) are not significant, but the interaction is significant (Hotelling's = .093, F (4, 238) = 2.76, p < .03). Examining this interaction at the univariate level we observe a significant interaction on state WTC (p < .05), and the interaction on posttest scores approaches significance (p < .07). The results are shown in Figures 5 and 6.

Post hoc t-tests (displayed in Table 1 below) indicate that extraverts are more willing than introverts to use the vocabulary words to communicate when students have studied in a somewhat similar situation. However, when the participants have studied in very similar situations, the reverse pattern holds, that is, introverts are more willing than extraverts to use the words for communication. When students have studied in situations that are not at all similar to those to which they are accustomed, no significant difference between state WTC of introverts and extraverts is found. A similar

---

2.   Given the possible influence of prior familiarity with the vocabulary words on posttest scores and state WTC, the two MANOVAs were also done as multivariate analyses of covariance (MANCOVAs) with pretest scores as a covariate. The inclusion of pretest scores as a covariate removed a significant amount of variance at the multivariate level in both analyses. The univariate analyses of covariance (ANCOVA) results are similar to the univariate results without the pretest score covariate, and the adjusted means follow the same pattern. For ease of presentation and interpretation, only the ANOVA results are reported.

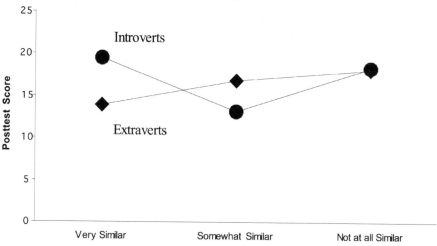

Figure 5. Interaction of personality and similarity of study situation on Vocabulary Posttest Scores

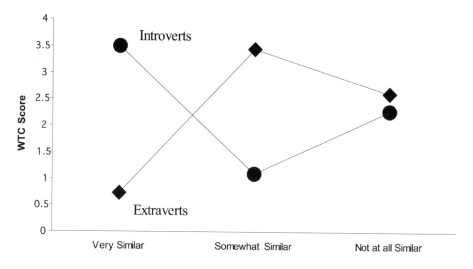

Figure 6. Interaction of personality and similarity of study situation on State WTC

pattern may be noted for the effect of the interaction between introversion and similarity of study situation on posttest scores. That is, there is a trend for introverts to obtain higher vocabulary test scores than extraverts when studying in very familiar sit-

Table 1. Learning outcome and willingness to use each of the 15 vocabulary items

Word	Num Correct (a)	Willing & Able (b)	Able but unwilling (c)	Unable but willing (d)	Unwilling & Unable (e)	% willing if able (f)	Chi-square, sig	Cramer's V, sig
Blackbird	74	16	58	3	50	21.6%	6.2,	.221,
	(58.3%)	(12.6%)	(45.7%)	(2.4%)	(39.4%)		.021	.013
Swan	31	6	25	6	90	19.4%	4.7,	.192,
	(24.4%)	(4.%)	(19.7%)	(4.7%)	(70.9%)		.07	.030
Greenhouse	62	15	47	1	64	24.2%	14.8,	.341,
	(48.8%)	(11.8%)	(37.0%)	(0.8%)	(50.4%)		.000	.000
Otter	66	13	53	5	56	19.7%	3.45,	.165,
	(52.0%)	(10.2%)	(41.7%)	(3.9%)	(44.1%)		.077	.063
Lighthouse	39	10	29	2	86	25.6%	17.25,	.369,
	(30.7%)	(7.9%)	(22.8%)	(1.6%)	(67.7%)		.000	.000
Circulation	63	10	53	4	60	15.9%	2.997,	.154,
	(49.6%)	(7.9%)	(41.7%)	(3.1%)	(47.2%)		.097	.083
Stork	36	10	26	2	89	27.8%	19.73,	.394,
	(28.3%)	(7.9%)	(20.5%)	(1.6%)	(70.1%)		.000	.000
Partridge	44	8	36	6	77	18.2%	3.52,	.166,
	(34.6%)	(6.3%)	(28.3%)	(4.7%)	(60.6%)		.077	.061
Hanger	45	10	35	6	76	22.2%	5.862,	.215,
	(35.4%)	(7.9%)	(27.6%)	(4.7%)	(59.8%)		.024	.015
Fashion	119	32	87	0	8	26.9%	2.88,	.150,
	(93.7%)	(25.2%)	(68.5%)	(0%)	(6.3%)		.200	.090
Monkey	97	30	67	3	27	30.9%	5.22,	.203,
	(76.4%)	(23.6%)	(52.8%)	(2.4%)	(21.3%)		.030	.022
Octopus	24	4	20	5	98	16.7%	4.125,	.180,
	(18.9%)	(3.1%)	(15.7%)	(3.9%)	(77.2%)		.065	.042
Tub	89	20	69	2	36	22.5%	5.51,	.208,
	(70.1%)	(15.7%)	(54.3%)	(1.6%)	(28.3%)		.021	.019
Artist	58	21	37	5	64	36.2%	16.233,	.358,
	(45.7%)	(16.5%)	(29.1%)	(3.9%)	(50.4%)		.000	.000
Tile	85	19	66	3	39	22.4%	4.541,	.189,
	(66.9%)	(15.0%)	(52.0%)	(2.4%)	(30.7%)		.045	.033

Note: Percentages in columns (a) through (e) use N = 127 as the denominator. Percentages in column (f) divide column (b) by column (a).

uations, the reverse trend holds for somewhat familiar situations, and no difference is observed in unfamiliar situations.

We did not wish to assume that extraversion would be a reliable predictor of the students' typical study situations. Therefore, in order to examine whether extraversion is related to familiarity with specific study settings (i.e., group versus solitary), a 2 (group, alone) × 3 (very similar, somewhat similar, not at all similar) ANOVA was performed using extraversion as a dependent variable. The analysis yielded no significant main effects of study situation ($F(1, 121) = 0.47$, $p > .05$) or similarity of study situation ($F(2, 121) = 0.12$, $p > .05$), and no significant interaction between study situation and similarity of study situation (F (2, 121) = 0.09, p > .05). Whereas one must be cautious in interpreting non-significant results, the fact that the interaction did not even approach statistical significance suggests that extraversion does not reliably predict whether students will be accustomed to studying alone or in a group setting.

For each of the 15 words learned in the study we have an assessment of whether the learner is able to use the word, based on a correct response to the posttest item, and an assessment of whether the learner is willing to use the word in a sentence, based on their 'yes' or 'no' response to the WTC question. For each of the 15 words, a 2 by 2 cross-tabulation was performed and evaluated using chi-square test of independence. In cases where the chi-square is significant, we have evidence of a dependency between being willing and able to use the words; in cases where chi-square is non-significant, we must conclude that we have not obtained evidence of a relationship between being willing and able. In each case, the strength of the relationship will be evaluated with Cramer's V statistic (see Table 1 above).

In the case of four words, evidence was obtained for a strong relationship (all chi-square > 14.8, Cramer's V > .34, p < .001) between learning and willingness to use the word ('greenhouse', 'lighthouse', 'stork', and 'artist'). For 5 other words, we find evidence of a significant relationship (all chi-square between 4.5 and 6.2, Cramer's V between .19 and .22, p between .013 and .045) between learning and willingness ('blackbird', 'hanger', 'monkey', 'tub', and 'tile'). In the remaining six cases, there is a non-significant relationship (chi-squares < 4.7, p > .05) between learning and willingness to use the word ('swan', 'otter', 'circulation', 'partridge', 'fashion', and 'octopus').

At the word level, a wide range of learning was evident. The word *le pieuvre* 'octopus' was learned by only 19% of the students, while *la mode* 'fashion' was learned by 94%. When students had learned the words, a mean of only 23% were willing to use that word in a sentence. That is, if we take only those students who correctly produced the French word, the data are highly consistent in showing that less than one quarter of the students are willing to use that word in a sentence soon after learning it.

7.3   Discussion of the results

The major results of this study indicate the complexity of the person by situation interaction in vocabulary learning. We found that introverts are more willing to communicate than extraverts in the familiar setting, and this idea is somewhat counter-intuitive. We obtained the reverse pattern, wherein extraverts are more willing to communicate than introverts, when assigned study conditions were somewhat unfamiliar. It may be commonly assumed that the introvert, who is often less sociable and outgoing than his or her extraverted counterpart (Eysenck & Eysenck 1975; Wilson 1978), should be less willing to communicate than an extravert across a wide variety of contexts. Studies conducted with reference to the L1 (McCroskey, Burroughs, Daun, & Richmond 1990; McCroskey & Richmond 1990; Sallinen-Kuparinen, McCroskey, & Richmond 1991), and to the L2 (MacIntyre & Charos 1996) have consistently found positive relationships between extraversion and trait-level WTC. Yet, there are conditions under which this tendency can be reversed.

The effects of extraversion and similarity of study situation on posttest scores were marginally significant. Given the very brief amount of time available to students for learning the vocabulary items, the interaction warrants consideration. Figure 5 shows a pattern of means that matches the pattern evident in the state WTC scores. That is, there is a tendency for introverts to show optimal posttest performance when they have studied in very familiar situations, but extraverts perform best under conditions involving a moderate degree of novelty. The pattern of means obtained here suggests that, over a longer time span, the person by situation interaction would be expected to produce noticeable effects on language achievement. This indicates that some learning situations will favor the introvert and others will favor the extravert, as Skehan (1989) has suggested. It is interesting, and somewhat surprising, to note that extraversion was not predictive of whether students were accustomed to studying in either a group or solitary setting. We would suggest that researchers who wish to examine how interactions between personality and situations affect language learning keep in mind that their participants may not have the expected experience one would predict based on their personality traits alone.

If willingness to use the L2 for authentic communication is to be a central goal of L2 instruction (MacIntyre et al. 1998), it is important to understand the factors that encourage or discourage the L2 learner from speaking up at any particular moment. In the present study, there clearly is a difference between being able and being willing to communicate at the word level. In response to the request to use the words in the present study, on average, approximately 77% of learners appear to be linguistically competent, yet unwilling to use the new words in the L2. In contrast, a small percentage of learners indicated a willingness to use the words even though they had responded incorrectly on the vocabulary test. It is possible that those respondents were overestimating their competence (MacIntyre et al. 1997), thinking that they had correctly responded on the test, or perhaps those students are the sort of adventurous risk-takers who seem willing to try anything (Beebe 1983; Clifford 1991; Ely 1986).

When learners can be categorized as (1) willing and able, (2) willing but unable, (3) unwilling but able, or (4) unwilling and unable to communicate, a more sophisticated analysis of the link between learning and communication becomes possible. Such a categorization scheme has potential pedagogical applications in the classroom for task-based communication and motivation processes (see Dörnyei 2001). Of particular interest are the categories 'willing but unable', and 'unwilling but able.' On the one hand, one can imagine the positive effects of occasions where students willingly use inadequate L2 skills for the potentially embarrassing purpose of receiving error correction as a means of accelerating learning. The second category with special pedagogical relevance is the situation wherein students are able, but unwilling to communicate. No doubt this represents a source of concern for second language educators. Psychologically, this is an interesting phenomenon given the emphasis in the motivation literature on communication-dependent reasons for language learning including friendship, travel, career-goals, and so on (Clément & Kruidenier 1983; Ushioda 2001). Perhaps anxiety reduction strategies can be tried (Baker & MacIntyre 2000; MacIntyre & Charos 1996), and special efforts can be made to encourage students to communicate in the L2 outside class with supportive friends as a means to increase WTC (MacIntyre et al. 2001), provided the intergroup situation does not constrain such interaction (cf. Norton 2000, 2001).

The results of our study indicate that, despite the status of extraversion as an "unloved variable" (Dewaele & Furnham 1999:509) in the literature on language learning, the investigation of how personality relates to L2 acquisition can indeed be rewarding. Researchers must bear in mind that relationships between broad personality traits and specific language learning outcomes are likely to be indirect and influenced by complex processes and past experiences.

8.   Conclusion

The study of the psychology of individual differences has produced a broad literature demonstrating the relevance of psychological processes to SLA. The current elaboration of the literature on motivation promises to add richness to our understanding of those processes. Contextual effects, including relative language status, ethnolinguistic vitality, pedagogical setting and so on, play an important role in shaping the psychology of the language learner. In addition to the linguistic outcomes so often emphasized in the literature are a host of non-linguistic outcomes that must be taken into account, if the learning process is to be understood fully. Whereas it would be easier theoretically if individual differences did not exist and psychological process played no role, that simply does not reflect the reality of the language learning process as it unfolds in context. Our discussion of the difficulties encountered in the study of personality traits, and extraversion in particular, demonstrate the folly of too simplistic an orientation. The data presented demonstrate that even a statement as seemingly self-evident as "extraverts will be more willing to communicate than introverts" can be shown to be true, untrue or even true in reverse because of the interaction of the person and the learning situation.

With respect to future research, we suggest that placing greater emphasis on the interactions of the person and situation, as we attempted to do in our study of personality and WTC in vocabulary learning, may yield further interesting, pedagogically useful, and perhaps surprising results. Examining the patterns of association between psychological processes and SLA processes, wherein research is designed to look beyond simple correlation coefficients, allows future research to study the complexity of these relationships. We suggest that there is a need for further research on both the larger scale, macro-level processes of intergroup relations, and the smaller scale, intra-individual processes, if we are to arrive at a more complete understanding of the various forms of adjustment that take place when language groups come into contact.

In the future, studies of the affective system in SLA will require increasingly diverse methodologies, spanning the study of brain-based emotional processes to a more prominent role for qualitative research methods. For example, studies of WTC may examine the physiological inhibition systems that are activated in the brain and the body when a person experiences a threat within his or her surroundings. Yet at the same time, it is to our advantage to understand also the felt experience of apprehension and the reluctance of some learners to use their highly developed L2 communication system. To do so will require an explicit recognition of cultural differences in understandings of key concepts, such as identity and anxiety. If this idea is at all attractive, researchers in the field must continue to expand their comfort level with a variety of methodologies. Further developments in SLA theory and a widening of the research agenda to include studies of the complex learner in context are required. As our partial review of the literature has indicated, we have learned much about the psychology of SLA, but we have much more to learn.

## CHAPTER 11

Lexical creativity in L2 French and natural language generation*

Greg Lessard and Michael Levison
Queen's University

Résumé

Dans un contexte où les aspects lexicaux de l'acquisition d'une langue seconde font l'objet d'un nombre croissant d'études, les recherches sur la créativité lexicale parmi les apprenants d'une langue seconde, c'est-à-dire la dérivation, la composition et d'autres mécanismes analogues, ainsi que l'enseignement de ces mécanismes, sont toujours rares, ceci malgré un certain nombre d'indications que la performance des apprenants dans ce domaine est loin d'approcher celle des locuteurs natifs, en termes de qualité et de quantité, que ce soit à l'oral où à l'écrit, et malgré le fait que beaucoup de textes authentiques utilisés dans l'enseignement des langues secondes comprennent un nombre non négligeable de formes complexes. Nous croyons que l'étude et l'enseignement de la productivité lexicale devraient prendre leur place à côté de l'analyse de la fréquence, des relations sémantiques, des 'bons amis' et d'autres dimensions lexicales dans l'ensemble des outils utilisés par les enseignants d'une langue seconde. L'analyse des corpus fournit un mécanisme utile et intéressant pour la découverte d'exemples de créativité lexicale; par contre, à cause de la complexité des corpus et de la nature disparate des données qu'ils contiennent, la constitution d'un ensemble cohérent de mécanismes dérivationnels représente un défi de taille. Comme complément à l'étude des corpus (mais non pas comme solution de rechange) nous proposons une autre approche basée sur un environnement de génération qui rend possible la génération et l'analyse de formes lexicales complexes en français, avec ou sans contexte, et nous illustrons l'approche et le logiciel au moyen d'une série d'exemples.

Abstract

The lexical aspects of second language (L2) acquisition have gained increasing prominence in recent years. However, the analysis, teaching, and learning of L2 lexical creativity in the form of derivation, compounding and other word-formation devices have received relatively little attention, despite evidence that L2 learners tend to fall short of native speakers in terms of the quantity and quality of the complex lexical

* The research described here was made possible by grants from the Social Sciences and Humanities Research Council of Canada. We would also like to thank the anonymous reviewers and the volume editor whose comments allowed us to improve this chapter.

forms used in their oral and written productions, and despite the fact that authentic texts frequently used in second language teaching make frequent use of such devices. We argue that lexical productivity should take its place alongside frequency, semantic relations, cognate forms and other dimensions of the lexicon in the arsenal of tools available to the second language teacher and learner. Finding examples of lexical creativity for teaching and research is now feasible using corpus technology. However, because of the complexity and disparate nature of corpus data, distilling these into sets of coherent and comparable examples is harder. As a complement, but not a replacement for corpus data, we describe a natural language generation environment capable of generating and analyzing complex lexical forms in French, both in isolation and in context, and we illustrate some uses of the program by means of sets of generated productions.

1. Introduction

At the lexical level, second language (L2) learners are often confronted with a 'poverty of resources' problem: They are called upon to produce and understand utterances dealing with a complex reality by means of a set of lexical items which falls short of their needs. Most L2 learners can recall, often with a vivid sense of the frustration involved, instances where they were attempting to name an object or a need, and found themselves incapable of finding a label shared with their interlocutor, or where a new word was encountered in speech or writing and where, despite the context, the meaning remained elusive or was misinterpreted.

Of course, such difficulties are not peculiar to L2 learners: The observation of children acquiring their first language provides ample evidence of similar phenomena. The development of new technologies also gives rise to problems of the sort (see e.g., Guilbert 1965, 1967, 1975). In fact, all native speakers find themselves occasionally stuck for words, and will resort to various linguistic devices to resolve these difficulties. For instance, a young native speaker of English, recently confronted with his inability to spell *fire extinguisher*, wrote instead *fire putter-outer*. The set of such strategies is quite broad. The phenomena we will discuss below are based on word-formation, primarily derivation and compounding. However, we will not deal with semantic extensions, lexical borrowing from another language, the formation of acronyms or abbreviations, or gestural devices (pointing at or mimicking the shape of the referent). We will also leave aside the use of circumlocutions, syntactic resolutions, or higher-level discursive devices used to deal with lexical gaps. In other words, we will be primarily interested in the within-the-lexicon machinery available to those using a language.

Most of the discussion which follows will deal with lexical creativity in the case of L2 French. However, this will be embedded in the larger context of L1 French, both in terms of oral and written productions, and in terms of reception and interpretation. Since they represent the vast majority of the current research, data and theories based on work in English will also be discussed. We will also present some current pedagogical approaches to lexical creativity as manifested in language teaching and testing materials, and we will conclude by describing a variant approach based on a computational-generative framework demonstrated by means of the VINCI generation environment.

2.   Word formation in French: Some basic distinctions

Traditionally, morphology is divided into derivational morphology and inflection. Inflectional morphology consists in adding a grammatical affix to a base form, with the resulting complex form retaining the semantic core and part of speech of the base (as in *achet-* 'buy' + *-aient* 'IMPERF', *table* 'table' + *s* 'PLUR', *grand* 'large' + *e* 'FEM'). With the exception of defective forms, all members of the inflectional paradigm may apply. Derivational morphology, on the other hand, produces new lexical forms (derived and compound words) whose semantic transparency cannot be predicted with certainty, and the application of one affix to a base is often sufficient to block the use of others.

Derived and compound forms fall in the mid-point of a spectrum between mono-morphemic lexical units (*pomme* 'apple', *mensonge* 'lie', *vif* 'lively') on the one hand, and on the other hand, more or less fixed sequences of simple lexical items designated in the literature by a variety of terms, including formulaic or institutionalized utterances or collocations (see e.g., Lewis 1997; Schmitt 2004; Wray 2002). Specifically, derived forms are based on some combination of affixes (lexical formants which do not occur independently), and lexical bases (lexical formants which do). Examples of French affixes include prefixes (*in-/im-/ir-/il-*, *re-/ré-*, *pré-*) and suffixes (*-isme*, *-eur*, *-iser*), while examples of lexical bases include mono-morphemic lexical units such as those shown above, as well as complex forms built up from bases and affixes which are themselves the starting point for further derivation, as in *pesanteur* 'weight', based on *pesant+eur*, which is the basis for the further derived form *apesanteur* 'weightlessness'.

Prefixation represents the combination of an affix and a following lexical base, while suffixation represents the combination of a lexical base followed by an affix. Most analyses treat as a distinct class examples of parasynthetic forms, where a prefix and suffix are added simultaneously to a lexical base (as in *re+froid+ir* 'to cool down or chill', where one finds the prefix and suffix together, but neither is found separately with the base form: **re+froid* or **froid+ir*, at least in modern French). Of course, it is also possible to identify sequences of derivational steps, as in *apesanteur* discussed above.

Compounds may be of two types: Native compounds are formed from lexical bases found elsewhere in native speaker productions, as in *taille-crayon* 'pencil sharpener' or *porte-fenêtre* 'patio door', while learned compounds are built up from Latin or Greek roots which may be combined with other learned roots, as in *carn+i+vore*, or with native bases, as in *joujou+thèque* 'toy lending library'. For technical reasons, we will restrict our attention here to compounds which form contiguous strings, leaving aside constructions such as *pomme de terre* 'potato' and *table de travail* 'workbench' which are based on a sequence of orthographic strings separated by spaces. Although the latter have a number of semantically predictable traits – for example, the base noun tends to represent a class rather than an individual – formal tests for the existence of such complex entities are not easy to find, and represent a significant research area in their own right. The list in (1) summarizes the mechanisms and structures we will be studying here:

(1)   Word formation processes   Examples
      prefixation   *antigel* 'antifreeze', *refaire* 'redo', *surestimer* 'overestimate'
      suffixation   *acheteur* 'buyer', *laideur* 'ugliness', *livresque* 'bookish'
      parasynthesis   *empoisonner* 'to poison', *refroidir* 'to chill'
      native compounding   *coupe-ongles* 'nail clipper', *taille-crayon* 'pencil sharpener'
      learned compounding   *fratricide* 'fratricide', *omnivore* 'omnivorous'

These word formation processes give rise to a number of problems of analysis, to which we now turn.

2.1   Degrees of motivation

One of the long-recognized differences between inflectional and derivational affixes is the semantic predictability of the former (the inflection *-aient* produces essentially the same semantic effect in all cases) versus the semantic variability found in forms produced by means of the latter. One case of this is found where derived forms have undergone restriction of meaning. Consider, for example, the following set:

(2)   a. *enseignant*   'teacher'
      b. *surveillant* 'guard, overseer'
      c. *protestant*   'protestant' (as in Presbyterian, Methodist, etc.)

Although the deverbal suffix *-ant* has the meaning 'one who performs the action represented by the base verb', and while this is more or less transparently the case for *enseignant* and *surveillant*, it is clear that in the case of *protestant*, a meaning restriction has occurred, and the protest in this case was against the Roman Catholic Church. As a result, to represent the meaning of 'one who protests against something', in Modern French it is necessary to change the verbal base and use *manifestant*. In fact, many if not most cases of derivation result in some degree of semantic narrowing. Thus, to take the examples above, *enseignant* typically designates not just anyone who happens to teach, but rather someone who does so professionally at the elementary or high school level. A similar effect is found in the case of *surveillant*.

In more extreme cases, this semantic shift can lead, by degrees, to total opacity, as can be seen by comparing the following examples in (3):

(3)   a. *parlementaire* 'member of a parliament'
      b. *fonctionnaire* 'office worker in public administration'
      c. *annulaire*   'third (ring) finger'

In (3b), the complex lexical entry *parlementaire* suggests that the suffix signifies 'one who is a member of the entity designated by the base form'. The meaning of *fonc-*

tionnaire is more restricted, since it is limited to 'one who works in a government administration *(fonction publique)*', as opposed to someone who is associated with just any function, while in the case of *annulaire*, the meaning is entirely opaque.

It is clear that such variations present a real problem for L2 production, since learners must be in a position to judge whether possible derived forms they might create, do or do not carry the transparent meaning they intended. Only knowledge of the lexical items themselves will answer this question, which to some extent defeats the use of derivational mechanisms. In fact, it can be argued that an important aspect of lexical acquisition involves internalizing the semantic narrowing resulting from derived forms and taking account of blocking mechanisms (cf. Aronoff 1976). A number of studies of first language acquisition have illustrated the steps in restricting use of derivational forms (see e.g., Clark 1993, who surveys studies of lexical creativity in young native speakers of French). On the other hand, from the point of view of reception, an incorrect interpretation based on a transparent application of derivational rules (as in taking *protestant* to mean just any protestor, or *annulaire* as meaning someone who has something to do with annulling some ceremony) has at least the chance of being shown to be implausible by the surrounding context.

Despite the role of blocking, it is important to recognize the role of continuing lexical productivity in the spontaneous and lively use and ongoing evolution of a language. Thus, new derived or compound forms are occasionally created alongside existing forms in order to produce or emphasize a semantic difference. For example, there exists in Canadian French the form *ontarien* with the meaning 'having to do with the province of Ontario'. Some years ago, the form *ontarois* was created, on the model of *québécois*, to designate the francophone population and culture of the province, and thereby distinguish them from their English-speaking counterparts.

The question of how morphologically complex lexical items are stored remains a hotly-debated issue (see e.g., Babin 2000, for an overview). There seems to be agreement that at some point they are stored as units in memory, but that mechanisms may exist for their reanalysis as required. Baayen and Renouf (1991) show that productivity of an affix appears to be related to the proportion of hapax forms it is involved in. Hay and Baayen (2003) make this model more precise by showing that productivity (and thus, lexical transparency) appears to be related to the ratio of the frequency of derived forms to the frequency of the bases from which they are built. Much simplified, their model suggests that if a derived form is more frequent than its base, then it is likely to be accessed directly from memory. See also Bauer (2001) for additional discussion of these issues. Such analyses are complicated as well by the fact that derivational systems change over time. For example, Dubois and Dubois (1971) compared two successive editions of the *Petit Larousse* dictionary to show relative numbers of derived forms, and thereby study the relative productivity of a set of suffixes. They found, for instance, that the agent suffix *-ier* tended to be displaced by its competitor *-eur*.

It is also important to distinguish active and passive knowledge of word formation devices and products. Active vocabulary is typically defined as the set of those items which a speaker uses in speech or writing, while passive vocabulary may be defined as those items which a speaker is capable of understanding. However, while active vocabulary may in principle be measured by the collection of corpus data, at least over some time frame and in some contexts, passive vocabulary requires that subjects indicate their degree and level of knowledge. Moreover, knowledge of a word is a notoriously fuzzy concept. For one thing, learners are not always capable of determining their level of knowledge with precision (see e.g., Schmitt & Zimmerman 2002), and for another, context is a dangerously elastic concept. Some contexts provide almost definitional levels of information, while others provide almost none. In what follows, we will be concerned primarily with actual production of derivationally complex lexical items by L2 learners, either in speech or writing. We will not address issues of reception or understanding (although these certainly merit study).

Finally, it is important to recognize that much of the debate on word formation has centered around native-language speakers. L2 learners, by their more limited vocabulary, but their access to an existing linguistic structure, including in some cases cognate forms with their first language, represent a more complex case which has been relatively little studied, as we will see below.

3. Word formation in the context of L2 lexical learning

Recent years have seen a significant upsurge in work devoted to vocabulary learning by L2 learners (see e.g., Bogaards & Laufer 2004; Cook 2002; Nation 2001; Singleton 1999), on the characterization of the cognitive state, strategies and context of L2 learners (see e.g., Dewaele 2005b); on overviews of what is currently known about L2 acquisition (see for instance Ritchie & Bhatia 1996), and on strategies for attaining a maximal level of proficiency (see for example Leaver & Shekhtman 2002). However, with rare exceptions, the description and analysis of the role of word-formation devices and lexical creativity remain conspicuous by their absence in English, and even more so in French. As Arnaud and Sauvignon (1997:159) put it: "Generally speaking, the literature is comparatively poor on the subject of learning strategies for words beyond the first two or three thousand, outside the subject of mnemonics".

Although both are based on English data, two pieces of work merit special mention. Nation (2001) shows that something on the order of one eighth of the words in a written text can be expected to have an affix, a figure comparable to one we will present later for French (Nation's figure, and more generally, Nation's discussion, does not appear to include compounds). Using earlier work (Bauer & Nation 1993) which ranked English suffixes by their frequency, productivity, regularity and semantic predictability, as well as the results of other studies, Nation proposes a five stage presentation of derivational affixes, beginning with the most transparent and productive (-'able', -'ish', -'ness' and others) to others which are much more opaque and rare (like -'ar' in 'circular'). After some discussion of the debate on mental storage of derived forms, Nation provides some possible exercises for teaching and testing such forms. A second important piece of work is the article by Schmitt and Zimmerman (2002), a careful study of productive knowledge of L2 English, which showed that learners tended to know (i.e., claimed to know, but also were capable of producing in context) only some members of most word families tested, with derived nouns and verbs more likely to be better known than adjectives or adverbs, and that L2 performance fell short of that found in native speakers, although the latter also showed gaps. On the basis of their findings, Schmitt and Zimmerman argue for the explicit teaching of derivational mechanisms to L2 learners.

Clearly, word formation represents a problem area. However, it is less clear which approaches are most useful for teaching and learning it. There would appear to be evidence that, on a purely formal level, in English at least, patterns of prefixation and suffixation present a high degree of predictability. Thus, Baroni (2003) shows how a computational mechanism based on three heuristics (substrings occurring in a high number of different words are likely to be morphemes, substrings which tend to co-occur with other potential morphemes are more likely to be morphemes, and low-frequency words are more likely to be morphologically complex than high frequency words) is capable of discovering in a list of untagged English words drawn from the Brown corpus a set of prefixes comparable to those identified by human speakers. As Baroni points out, this does not demonstrate that humans use distributional information to identify prefixes. In fact, it is more than likely that semantic factors play a significant role. However, it does show that distributional factors are sufficient to provide such an analysis. There is evidence that L2 learners sometimes make use of such information. For example, Nassaji (2003) used a think-aloud protocol to establish strategies and knowledge sources used by L2 learners of English in order to establish the meaning of unknown words encountered in a short passage. Of the 199 inferential responses found in the study, only 51 were successful, amounting to a success rate of 25.6%. The most used strategy was world knowledge (46.2%), followed by morphological knowledge (26.9%), with the latter being based on "[...] knowledge of word formation and word structure, including word derivations, inflections, word stems, suffixes and prefixes" (Nassaji 2003:656). However, of all the knowledge sources, morphological knowledge had the highest rate of association with successful inferencing (35.7%). A caveat of the study was that it was of relatively limited scale. However, given that, like others, it shows a low success rate for context (see e.g., similar results found by Bensoussan & Laufer 1984), it seems clear that morphological factors can at least do no worse, and have the potential of doing better. This appears to be accepted by other researchers. Thus, in another study on strategies in reading, Haynes (1993) encourages the use of guessing based on word formation clues, and Chern (1993) finds evidence of successful use of the strategy by Chinese learners of English.

There is also some neurolinguistic evidence that morphological and lexical knowledge is acquired very quickly after exposure. McLaughlin, Osterhaut and Kim (2004) tested groups of L2 learners of French with varying degrees of exposure (means of 14 hours, 63 hours, and 138 hours) and using N400 potentials, which in native speakers have been shown to be sensitive to lexical status (words versus non-words) and context (anomalous or not). They found that even after 14 hours of instruction, Event Related

Potentials (ERPs) measured from the scalp showed L2 ability in discriminating words from non-words, even though subjects still performed no better than chance in behavioral tests. They conclude that the first stages of L2 vocabulary learning happen surprisingly early, and more importantly for our purposes, that learners are sensitive to formal traits of lexical items very early on. Given this, early attention paid to this aspect of vocabulary may have the potential for assisting learning later on.

It is also possible that improved knowledge of complex lexical structures might play a role in other aspects of L2 language acquisition. For example, in her presentation of the Autonomous Induction Theory, Carroll (2004) proposes that the L2 learner's skill in word segmentation involves building up sets of language-specific phonetic patterns, as well as the correspondence rules for matching particular patterns to morphosyntactic structure. For example, stressed syllables in English tend to signal the existence of content words as opposed to function words. We would argue that at least in some languages, similar phenomena exist which permit the identification of derivationally and compositionally complex lexical items, as in the case of English head-final compounds such as *fire truck*, with its stressed first syllable, and unstressed second syllable.

A fundamental issue of vocabulary learning has to do with the order in which words are taught and learned. It is well-recognized that learners benefit from learning first the most frequent forms in a language. This is predicated on the observation first made by Zipf (1935) that the words of a language follow a distribution such that the 1000 most frequent words will represent approximately 75% of the occurrences in a typical text, while the 2000 most frequent forms will represent on the order of 80% of the occurrences. Unfortunately, the rate of coverage falls off sharply thereafter, so that coverage of 95% of the occurrences of a typical text requires a vocabulary of 12,000 words. The high coverage provided by high-frequency words is the motivation behind lists such as the *Français fondamental* (Gougenheim 1967).

A recently-proposed complement to frequency data in English is the *Academic Word List* (see Coxhead 2000; and also http://www.vuw.ac.nz/lals/research/awl/awlinfo. html). Based on a 3,500,000 word Academic Corpus, the AWL includes words which occur in four 'Faculties': Arts, Science, Commerce and Law, and in over half of the 28 subject areas. Words in the list are divided into 'families' which include both inflected and derived forms, as the following example illustrates:

(4)   assist
      assistance (the word in italics represents the most frequent of the members of the 'family')
      assistant
      assistants
      assisted
      assisting
      assists
      unassisted

Families had to occur over 100 times in the entire corpus and at least 10 times in each Faculty to be included in the list.

Despite its obvious value, the AWL fails to distinguish derived from inflected forms in the context of word families, which reduces the salience of the derivational mechanisms. In fact, the notion of word families, which is quite general in discussions of acquisition of L2 English, is arguably an unfortunate choice, unless supplemented by means of a discussion of word formation.

The logic behind the AWL lies partly in the presence in English of a core of frequently latinate academic vocabulary. There is some question whether an AWL would work similarly in other languages. In the case of French, Cobb and Horst (2004) argue that it would not, and that similar coverage of 90% of a typical academic text would be provided by the 2000 most frequent words of French. On the other hand, work by researchers such as Kocourek (1991), who does not use frequency as a criterion, would appear to illustrate the existence of a well-developed lexical underpinning of scientific and technical French, including a large set of word-formation devices.

Another approach to vocabulary learning and teaching suggests that words should be presented in semantic groupings (synonyms together, antonyms as pairs, etc.). The rationale is that learners will better discriminate items by opposition with the cohort of related words. However, Finkbeiner and Nicol (2003), based on a study of one and two-syllable pseudo-words used as labels for objects appearing in pictures, found that translation times from L1 to L2 and L2 to L1 were slower for subjects who had learned the pseudo-words in semantic sets, and that performance was also lower, although not to a statistically significant extent. The authors admit that it is possible that semantic sets produce deeper learning, but on the surface, their data suggest that semantic grouping may not be a powerful solution for vocabulary learning.

Reading is often mentioned as another means of lexical acquisition, and there is no doubt that it has a crucial role to play. However, Cobb and Horst (2004: 17) show the limits of this method. They claim that while incidental lexical acquisition is important, and does occur, there exists a large gap between the results of L1 and L2 reading. In the case of the former, they assume exposure to something on the order of a million words per year, and they make the point that no current L2 reading program comes close to approaching this level. In addition, it has been suggested that optimal acquisition of new vocabulary will occur when the ratio of known to unknown items is on the order of 20:1 (Nation 2001). However, L2 learners faced with authentic texts are unlikely to find such a ratio.

Even after all these solutions to lexical improvement are considered, there remains the gap between 90% coverage and full coverage. Of course, for most speakers, this gap will be filled for some domains, but not for others. Nevertheless, we will argue that the use of lexical creativity, and in particular word-formation devices, provides one element of the set of solutions to this problem.

4. Corpus data on L1 and L2 French word formation

There has been relatively little work done on determining the extent to which L2 learners produce new forms. Lessard, Levison, Maher and Tomek (1994) studied a written corpus produced by L2 learners of French in the context of second and third year literature courses and showed that lexical innovations (words unattested in French lexicographical resources) were rare. Similarly, Broeder, Extra, van Hout and Voionmaa (1993) found relatively little evidence of lexical creativity in a large multilingual corpus of L2 adult speech. They noted that derivation was exceedingly rare, with many instances based on imitation or lexical recall, and compounding tended to overshadow derivation in the languages they studied. However, this predominance of compounding may not apply in all languages. Thus, Clark (1998), working on a compilation of data concerning L1 learners of French, found that suffixation was far more frequent that compounding, and our results for L2 French support this finding. Vizmuller-Zocco (1985) mentions the existence of a number of creations in L2 Italian, but gives no figures on relative frequencies of different word formation mechanisms.

In what follows, we extend these findings by analyzing some additional materials from oral and written corpora. Our goal is to determine, in a preliminary fashion, whether L2 learners of French employ derivationally complex lexical items to the same degree, and in the same fashion as native speakers. Clearly, this is a large-scale problem, and the work presented here represents only the first step in an attempt to understand it more clearly.

We begin be examining the Reading Corpus, made available through the FFLOC Project (see Myles this volume and http://www.flloc.soton.ac.uk/), and based on oral interviews with L2 and L1 speakers of French. L2 learners were secondary school students, all native speakers of English, aged 16, (n = 34) who had been learning French for five years, receiving four 35-minute lessons a week. Their proficiency varied significantly, as did the number of words produced, which ranged from 35 to 808. L1 speakers were 15 year old French students (n = 26). They were all native speakers of French, except for one Vietnamese student who had learned French as a second language.

In all cases, data were elicited by means of a conversational format and transcribed using the CHILDES formalism (http://childes.psy.cmu.edu/). The corpus was downloaded, then analyzed by means of several Unix programs (freq, awk, uniq, sort). Word counts were established using spaces, ends of line and apostrophes as delimiters. L2 learners produced 2,101 word-tokens representing 468 word types. L1 speakers produced 6,949 word-tokens representing 1,049 word-types. In other words, L1 productions contained more than three times the number of tokens, and more than twice the number of types than L2 learners' productions.

The wordlist for each subcorpus (L1 and L2 speakers) was analyzed manually, using the following criteria. Suffixes were determined by the existence of an independently existing base form (noun, verb, or adjective), and a clearly delimited suffixal ending with a coherent semantics. Thus, *amusant* 'amusing' was identified as a suffixal form since there is a verbal base (*amus-*), and an affix (*-ant*) with the meaning 'performing the action associated with the verbal base'. Prefixes were identified in an analogous fashion. Thus, the form *international* may be divided into an adjectival base (*national*) preceded by an affix (*inter-*) with the meaning 'between elements identified by the base form', in this case, *nation*. In all cases, we have based our classification on the 'outermost' layer of derivation. Thus *international* should be analyzed as *nation* + -*al* and to this derived form is subsequently added the prefix *inter-*. This analysis is supported by the fact that we find the form *national* but not the form **interna-tion*. However, it is important to note that this way of proceeding, while it allows for each lexical item to be assigned to a single class (suffix, prefix, etc.), has the disadvantage of 'hiding' layers of derivation which fall inside complex forms. Since suffixes are frequently the last layer of derivation, one result is to artificially inflate the relative number of suffixed forms. However, the overall number of complex forms is not affected.

Examples of parasynthesis were identified by the existence of complex lexical items where both a prefix and suffix are added to a base, but where there exists no prior form containing only the prefix or the suffix with the base. In the case of compounds and learned compounds, several points bear mentioning. First, the criterion whereby lexical items are restricted to those forming a single uninterrupted sequence of orthographic symbols (letters and hyphens) has the effect of removing from consideration multiword compound nouns such as *chemin de fer* 'railroad' and *autobus scolaire* 'school bus'. As a result, the relative frequency of compounds is artificially reduced. However, since as we have shown earlier, the criteria for compounds are not clear, we have opted for this artificial clarity here. By the criteria used here, compounds are lexical items in which it is possible to identify two or more base forms (noun, verb or adjective) where each has a definable meaning, where the contribution to the whole is transparent, and where each element is found in at least one other context. Thus, to take the example *grands-parents* 'grandparents', we find a base noun (*parents*) and a preceding adjective with the meaning 'of a prior generation to the generation identified by the base form'. The analysis of learned compounds is similar, in that each case involves two or more forms of Greek or Latin origin, each of which carries a distinct and identifiable meaning, and each of which may be found in at least one other context. Thus, *biologie* may be decomposed into *bio-* with the meaning 'life', and -*logie*, with the meaning 'study of'. In fact, the distinction between regular and learned compounds is not always clearcut, since frequent learned bases may be considered to have entered the language. Thus, we have counted *télévision* as a learned compound, but it might well have been considered a native compound instead. However, again, such distinctions have no bearing on the total number of complex forms found.

Using these criteria, we analyzed the two subcorpora and obtained the results shown in Table 1 below.

Consideration of the table reveals that both L1 speakers and L2 learners produced a predominance of suffixes, although as we mentioned earlier, this is to some extent an artefact of the analysis. In fact, the relative frequency of the different word-formation

Table 1. Relative frequency of word formation devices in spoken L1 and L2 French (Reading Corpus)

Word formation type	L1 corpus (1,049 forms, 6949 tokens)				L2 corpus (468 forms, 2,101 tokens)			
	No of forms	% of all forms	No of tokens	% of all tokens	No of forms	% of all forms	No of tokens	% of all tokens
Suffixation	83	7.9%	134	1.9%	11	2.4%	17	0.8%
Prefixation	3	0.3%	4	0.6%	0	0%	0	0%
Parasynthesis	0	0%	0	0%	0	0%	0	0%
Composition	2	0.2%	3	0.04%	3	0.6%	5	0.2%
Learned forms	7	0.7%	15	0.2%	5	1.1%	10	0.5%
All types	95	9.1%	156	2.2%	19	4.1%	32	1.5%

types is broadly similar between the two subcorpora, with suffixes coming first, followed by learned forms, then prefixation and composition, and finally parasynthesis.

More importantly, for all word-formation types taken as a whole, complex words represent a greater proportion of the L1 corpus than of the L2 corpus, both in terms of forms and tokens. In other words, these native speakers used a greater variety of word-formation devices than did learners (9.1% of all forms against 4.1% for L2 speakers), and the relative number of times these devices were used was also higher (2.2% of all word tokens against 1.5% for L2 speakers).

In addition, analysis of the actual forms used shows that L2 learners used exclusively lexicalized items (i.e., those found in standard dictionaries), many of which have cognates in English. In other words, the L2 subcorpus shows no evidence of the use of word formation. In the case of L1 speakers, we find a greater proportion of complex forms and tokens and the set of devices is also greater; thus, while L2 speakers used a total of 6 different suffixes, L1 speakers used 27, as illustrated in Table 2 below. Some of this difference can be attributed to the larger size of the L1 corpus, but it is also clear that these native speakers are employing a derivationally richer language. On the other hand, all of the forms used by L1 speakers are well-attested lexical items. In other words, even with their richer derivational mix, the L1 speakers still show little evidence of lexical creativity. This may be due, among other things, to the possibility that L1 speakers in their teens do not yet have access to the full range of derivational mechanisms of their language. For example, Singleton (1999:42) reports work by Smedts (1988) on a small number of young Dutch learners of English which suggests that even the oldest learner studied, aged 17, had access to only around two-thirds of the word formation devices of their language. In addition, the oral context probably provides less incentive for lexical creativity.

However, even with these caveats, two conclusions bear mentioning. First, there would appear to be value in a method whereby the linguistic production and specifically the rate of use of morphologically complex words by L2 learners is compared to that of native speakers in a similar context. Second, comparison of these two corpora suggests that differences of the sort do exist and can be measured.

Table 2. Morphologically complex forms found in Reading Corpus (L1 and L2)

	L1 subcorpus	L2 subcorpus
Suffixed forms	*ambiance, américains, assistante, association, associations, autrement, buanderie, championnat, chauffeur, cinquième, coiffure, colonie, correspondante, correspondants, couramment, dessinateur, distractions, dramatique, économiques, énormément, équitation, enseignement, espagnol, exceptionnel, exposition, expositions, familiaux, formation, français, française, girondins, historique, hôtesse, hôtellerie, individuel, informatique, ingénieur, intéressant, italien, japonais, légiste, maternelle, natation, national, naturelles, normalement, nourriture, observations, organisation, originales, pédagogiques, policiers, pratiquement, professeur, professeurs, professionnel, proximité, préférences, psychologique, publicitaire, pâtissier, quatorzième, rattrapages, récemment, redoublement, rééducation, reportage, scientifique, scientifiques, scolaire, scolaires, seulement, soirées, spécialement, sportives, supplémentaire, sympathique, synthétiseur, troisième, vietnamien, vivante, vraiment*	*amusant, camping, cinquante, correspondant, éducation, historique, historiques, natation, professeur, professeurs, soixante, éducation*
Prefixed forms	*déménageons, extraordinaire, international*	
Native compounds	*autocar, kilomètres*	*grand-père, grands-parents, kilomètres*
Learned compounds	*biologie, géographie, technologie, télévision*	*biologie, discothèque, discothèques, géographie*

In an attempt to extend this analysis to a broader context, we now turn to two larger corpora composed of written French texts. The first dataset, DiploFreq, compiled by Jean Véronis (http://www.up.univ-mrs.fr/~veronis/donnees/index.html), is a wordlist based on ten years (1987–1997) of the *Monde diplomatique*, a French newspaper which deals with diplomatic and political questions. The entire DiploFreq corpus contains 11,139,376 word tokens divided among 127,452 distinct forms if case is ignored. Words are delimited by spaces, ends of line and punctuation, including hyphens. The DiploFreqMaj wordlist based on the corpus includes for each word form the number of occurrences found in the corpus and the number of distinct typographical variants (upper and lower case) associated with each word form.

The second dataset, the VINCI Corpus, was compiled by Lessard, Levison and others (see Lessard et al. 1994 for details). It is based on a set of handwritten and type-

Table 3. Relative frequency of word formation devices in written L1 and L2 French

Word formation type	L1 corpus (DiploFreq-1%) (1274 forms, 53,556 tokens)				L2 corpus (Vinci) (8000 forms, 70,972 tokens)			
	No of forms	% of all forms	No of tokens	% of all tokens	No of forms	% of all forms	No of tokens	% of all tokens
Suffixation	249	19.5%	11,281	21.1%	1187	14.8%	2,886	4.1%
Prefixation	56	4.4%	798	1.5%	181	2.3%	281	0.4%
Parasynthesis	23	1.8%	164	0.3%	35	0.4%	45	0.1%
Composition	5	0.4%	10	0.01%	39	0.5%	56	0.1%
Learned forms	28	2.2%	1000	1.9%	36	0.5%	59	0.1%
All types	361	28.3%	13,253	24.8%	1478	18.5%	3,327	4.7%

written essays produced by second year and third years students in French Studies at Queen's University in 1985–1987. Essays were written in the context of several literature courses and represent discussion of sets of literary texts in a social and cultural framework. In the form used here, the corpus contains 70,972 word tokens and 8,000 distinct word forms. Like the DiploFreq corpus, lexical items are delimited by spaces, punctuation and ends of lines, except that complex items like multiword prepositional units (*en dessous de*), proper names (*Le Grand Meaulnes*), and hyphenated compound words (*texte-miroir* 'mirror-text', *reine-dragon* 'dragon-queen') are treated as units. In all, the VINCI Corpus contains 47 essays, the longest having 4,087 words, the shortest 519 words, with an average essay length of 1512 words. Although this information was not used here, the corpus has been tagged for part of speech and error type.

For the purpose of the present chapter, the entire VINCI Corpus was retagged for derivational structure using the model described earlier for the Reading Corpus. In other words, it is marked for suffixation, prefixation, parasynthesis, compounding and learned compounding. For practical reasons, it was not possible to tag the entire DiploFreq wordlist. Instead, the entire list was sorted into random order: Using the awk program, a random number was assigned to each line and the entire corpus sorted on the random number field. Subsequently, the first 1% (1274 lines) were selected and tagged. It is the product of this sample which is used below. As a check on the coherence of the sample, it was subsequently divided into two halves of 637 lines each and the relative frequencies of the two halves were compared between each other and with the value obtained for the entire 1274 forms. Results found were comparable in all three cases, which suggests that the sample provides a reasonable representation of the wordlist as a whole. The entire sample includes 1274 forms and 53,556 tokens, and is thus roughly comparable in size to the VINCI Corpus. Table 3 presents the results obtained when the two datasets were analyzed.

As was found in the oral subcorpora, native speakers in these cases use a higher proportion of complex word forms (28.3% of all word forms) than do L2 learners (18.5% of all word forms). This difference was found in the case of suffixation (19.5% versus 14.8%), prefixation (4.4% versus 2.3%), parasynthesis (1.8% versus 0.4%), and learned compounds (2.2% versus 0.5%). On the other hand, the L2 corpus contains marginally more cases of composition (0.5% versus 0.4%), but this fact is probably due to the inclusion of hyphenated forms as units in the VINCI Corpus and their exclusion from the DiploFreq wordlist. As well, the number of complex word forms in the VINCI Corpus is artificially inflated by the fact that spelling errors were counted as distinct forms. When this is taken into account, the overall number of complex word forms in the VINCI Corpus is reduced by 87, although the number of tokens remains the same.

The underuse of complex wordforms by these L2 learners becomes even more marked at the level of word tokens. Thus, we find that complex words represent 24.8% of all word tokens in the DiploFreq list, but only 4.7% of tokens in the VINCI list. This difference is found in all subclasses, except for composition for the reasons outlined above.

These results appear to confirm those found for the oral corpora analyzed earlier: The L2 learners studied use a relatively smaller number of complex word forms than do the native speakers studied, and these forms are much more thinly scattered through their texts. It would seem likely that such a difference would have an effect on how L2 texts are perceived, although this has not been measured. At the least, it seems clear that further research is warranted, firstly to determine whether such differences are found in other comparable L1 and L2 corpora, and secondly to establish whether there are norms or expectations for the use of morphologically complex words, and whether these vary by modality (oral versus written), genre, and so on, in the case of L1 productions. This would make possible the establishment of targets for L2 learners.

5. Pedagogical approaches to word formation in L2 French

If, as the previous results suggest, L2 learners of French differ significantly from their native-speaker counterparts in their use of complex word forms, one would assume that this shortfall would be recognized and dealt with in foreign and second language textbooks. Unfortunately, this would appear not to be the case. The following table is based on a survey of materials currently or recently used in the undergraduate program in French Studies at Queen's University, which we have taken as typical of North American (or at least Canadian) undergraduate programs of the sort. Most students in such programs are assumed to have some previous knowledge of French from primary or secondary school studies, and by the end of a three or four year program, students are expected to be able to speak and write with some fluency. Although no claims can be made for exhaustivity, or even representativity, the results shown in the following table suggest that none of the standard grammar textbooks used in the four years of the undergraduate program provide detailed information on word formation.

In some cases, where they do appear, elements of word formation are hidden among other grammatical devices. Thus, for example, in the text by Théoret, a page is devoted to the question of the hyphen in compound nouns and adjectives, and in an exercise book not included in the above list (Loriot-Raymond et al. 1996, *À vous d'écrire*), one exercise involves choosing the correct preposition linking a base noun

Table 4. Treatment of derivation in a sample of L2 French textbooks

Year	Target audience	Author	Title	Number of pages devoted to word formation
1	L2	J. Olivier	*Grammaire française*	0
1	L2	A. Favrod	*Mise en pratique*	<1
1	L2	J.-P. Valette	*Contacts*	0
1	L2	J. Barson	*La grammaire à l'oeuvre*	0
3	L1?	M. Théoret	*Grammaire du français actuel pour les niveaux collégial et universitaire*	1

and its complement. However, the list includes, without any distinction, compound nouns such as *pomme de terre* 'potato' and *bateau à voiles* 'sailboat' inter-mixed with grammatical structures such as *une boîte de chocolats* 'a box of chocolates', and *la fille aux cheveux d'or* 'the girl with the golden hair'.

There exist textbooks with more detailed treatment of word formation, but they are the exception rather than the rule. A good example is the *Grammaire pédagogique du français d'aujourd'hui* by Chartrand et al. (1999), which is targeted at francophone primary and secondary school students, and which claims to follow the guidelines of the Québec Ministry of Education. Of a total of 397 pages, no fewer than 37 (just under 10%) are devoted to a detailed presentation of word formation, including separate chapters on prefixation and suffixation, composition, learned compounds, acronyms, and truncation and *téléscopage* ('mots-valises').

The other element of the equation in the teaching of derivation is instructors themselves. We performed a small survey of faculty involved in the teaching of L2 French in several Ontario universities. Respondents were asked to reply to three questions dealing with the nature and level of the each course they taught, the total number of contact hours, and the number of hours devoted to teaching or discussion of word formation. In almost all cases for which a response was received, little or no time was devoted explicitly to the discussion of word formation. One of the reasons for this may lie in the fact, pointed out in one of the responses, that many language teachers, who are not linguists, feel unqualified to discuss the mechanisms of word formation in any detail. These results are very limited in scope and should be taken only as indicative of a possible state of affairs. A broad general survey would be needed to provide accurate information across languages and in different countries. Nevertheless, it would seem at least probable that the systematic teaching of word formation devices is rare in the university-level curriculum for L2 French.

A similar state of affairs can be found in the tests used to diagnose language skills as a prelude to admitting students to a particular level of study in French. For example, according to online documentation at http://www.collegeboard.com/student/testing/sat/about.html, the US-based SAT and subject tests are taken by approximately 2 million students per year as part of the requirement for admission to college. Based on the sample questions included in the published documentation concerning the French test at http://www.collegeboard.com/prod_downloads/sat/SAT2_Chi_Fr_Ger_

Heb.pdf, it would appear that word formation is not one of the elements analyzed. The France-based DELF/DALF test is comparable to the English-language TOEFL test, and is used in evaluating admission to French universities (see http://www.ciep.fr/delfdalf). It is based primarily on simulated language interactions, production of short texts, and reactions to authentic texts. There is no special emphasis on word formation. Finally, the *Chambre de commerce et d'industrie de Paris* has a detailed test used by numerous organizations, including the Government of Canada, which uses it to evaluate requests for immigration (http://www.cic.gc.ca/francais/qualifie/ qual-3-1.html). Based on the documentation provided (http://www.fda.ccip.fr/), the test includes a test of unscrambling sentences, comprehension tests of oral and written documents, and production of short passages. No particular facet of the test appears to deal specifically with word formation.

There are exceptions: For example, an early proficiency test, the *Test Laval*, developed in Canada, and still quite widely used, does include a section on the comprehension of complex lexical items. Of the 30 multiple-choice questions in the Vocabulary section of the test, 16 questions are devoted to word-formation, including deverbal nouns, denominal and deadjectival verbs, formation of adverbs, and suffixes of nationality.

6. Use of word formation in authentic documents

If it is true that lexical creativity occupies at best a marginal position in the teaching and testing of French, this is doubly unfortunate in that it coexists with a long tradition of providing L2 learners with authentic materials designed to improve their language skills. These may take a variety of forms, ranging from immersion in a linguistic milieu, to the reading of written materials, including newspapers, textbooks, novels, and short stories. There is evidence that such exposure brings positive results. For example, Dewaele and Regan (2001) show that colloquial words, despite their formal simplicity, are under-represented in the L2 French of two groups of learners they studied, but that a year abroad tended to increase proportions of such forms. In a later study, Dewaele (2002a) found that the use of the informal *on* as opposed to the more formal *nous* is strongly correlated with the degree of authentic interaction. On the written level, Chambers and O'Sullivan (2004) show that consultation of a small specialized corpus, including 125,000 words from the French newspaper *Le Monde*, allowed a group of advanced L2 learners to improve the quality of their written texts.

Many of the authentic written documents presented to language learners include a significant proportion of complex lexical items. As an illustration of this, we extracted five articles from the web version of the French newspaper *Le Monde* (August 18, 2005; http://www.lemonde.fr/) in a variety of domains, ranging from international affairs, to technology, sports, and social phenomena. The articles contain a range of complex lexical items, which have been underlined in the paragraphs we have reproduced below, for which English glosses are included in Appendix A.

(6)   **Technology:**

Cette <u>entrée</u> en fanfare donna le coup d'envoi d'une <u>euphorie</u> autour de l'Internet, dont on <u>prédisait</u> qu'il allait <u>révolutionner</u> les modes de vie et créer une nouvelle économie. En Bourse, cette "<u>exubérance irrationnelle</u>", selon <u>l'expression</u> du président de la Réserve fédérale <u>américaine</u>, Alan Greenspan, s'est traduite par une <u>multiplication</u> par près de cinq de la valeur du Nasdaq entre 1995 et son pic en mars 2000: Des sociétés Internet <u>naissantes</u>, fondées par des <u>étudiants</u> dans des garages, qui dépensaient l'argent de leur <u>capitaux-risqueurs</u> avant d'avoir <u>concrétisé</u> la moindre vente, voyaient leurs <u>valorisations boursières</u> dépasser celles des géants de l'industrie.

(7)   **Sports:**

Il est sorti du stade de la Mosson, à Montpellier, mercredi 17 août, comme il était arrivé, deux jours plus tôt, au <u>rassemblement</u> de l'équipe de France, avant le match <u>amical</u> contre la Côte d'Ivoire: En courant, tête baissée, entouré de plusieurs gardes du corps. Zinédine Zidane est devenu presque aussi <u>insaisissable</u> en dehors du terrain que sur la pelouse. Vénéré comme la plus glamour des rock-stars, acclamé à coups de "Zizou, Zizou, Zizou!" par 41 500 spectateurs toujours aussi transis d'amour, le <u>meneur</u> de jeu du Real Madrid et capitaine <u>retrouvé</u> de l'équipe de France, plus qu'un <u>footballeur</u>, a été élevé au rang de <u>sauveur</u> de tout un peuple, mercredi 17 août, après avoir contribué à la <u>flatteuse</u> victoire (3–0) des Bleus face aux <u>Ivoiriens</u>, pourtant auteurs d'une belle prestation.

(8)   **International affairs:**

La <u>démonstration</u> de force et <u>d'efficacité</u> voulue par les <u>organisateurs</u> des <u>attentats</u> du mercredi 17 août, au Bangladesh, a été réussie. Quelque 350 bombes de faible <u>puissance</u> ont explosé dans tout le pays, en l'espace d'une heure, en fin de <u>matinée</u>, selon un bilan <u>policier</u> <u>revu</u> à la hausse tout au long de la <u>journée</u>. Une <u>cinquantaine</u> de villes ont été touchées par des déflagrations visant des bâtiments <u>administratifs</u>, des tribunaux, des clubs de la presse, des gares ou des stations de bus. Au moins deux morts et une <u>centaine</u> de blessés ont été recensés à l'issue de cette campagne <u>terroriste</u>, visiblement <u>calibrée</u> pour provoquer des pertes humaines limitées.

(9)   **French news:**

Le parquet de Metz, <u>destinataire</u> de la plainte, l'a <u>classée</u> "sans suite", estimant que les éléments manquaient pour "<u>caractériser</u> l'infraction". Quelques mois plus tôt dans une affaire du même type la <u>plaignante</u> avait renoncé à sa <u>procédure</u> et demandé à être mutée, le <u>surveillant</u> que Virginie mettait en cause avait reçu une lettre du <u>procureur</u> "attirant -son- attention sur -son- <u>comportement</u> <u>fréquemment</u> grossier, <u>méprisant</u>, voire injurieux à l'égard de cette <u>fonctionnaire</u> féminine".

(10)   **Social/media:**

Pour M. Gaultier, la campagne de Choc n'est qu' "un coup de <u>racolage</u>", et <u>l'évocation</u> de la lutte contre la drogue n'est qu' "un prétexte pour montrer une image puissante et vendre du papier". "Ma <u>réaction</u> n'est pas très positive", affirme de son côté Didier Jayle, président de la mission <u>interministérielle</u> de lutte contre la drogue et la <u>toxicomanie</u> (Mildt). "Cette personne est exhibée sans <u>humanité</u>, poursuit-il. Ce type d'images augmente la peur de ceux qui <u>diabolisent</u> déjà la drogue et risque d'être mise à distance par les autres. A part l'horreur que l'on ressent, que comprend-on?" Pour sa part, l'association de lutte contre le sida Act Up Paris dénonce cette campagne dans une <u>publication</u> que l'association nomme "X", "magazine dont le contenu <u>éditorial</u> repose <u>entièrement</u> sur des clichés <u>sélectionnés</u> pour satisfaire au <u>voyeurisme</u> le plus bas de son <u>lectorat</u>".

Table 5. Items from Le Monde, last week of June 2005, unattested by the Trésor de la langue française (based on Véronis 2005)

agroalimentaire altermondialiste angolais animateur-producteur anti-tabac
assurance-maladie attentat-suicide audiovisuel auriverde _auropunctata
autos ayatollah biodiversité cannabis chiite cibler cogneuses
communautariste communautarisée design deux-roues directeur-général djihad
droitise druze duffle-coat e-mail euro euro-arabe euros festives fractale
gays grenoblois hard haïtienne homophobie hurdler hutus indépendantiste
indépendantistes intercommunautaires internautes internet irakien
irakienne irakiennes irakiens islamiste islamistes isérois ivoirienne
jamaïquaine kha-nyou largage mbj md mds micro-ondes moghols méga-banques neurodégénérative
non-fumeurs pakistanais perf pixels porte-parole
prosyrien provisionnement président-directeur pédophile pédophilie raveurs
relutive rwandais rwandaises salafiste saoudien saoudite sarkozystes soul
supporteurs surfacturations surfacturé techno tek'noz teknival texan
tutsis téléchargement ultracompacts écologiquement écosystèmes

Importantly from the point of view of L2 acquisition, all these forms are, in principle, at least partially analyzable. In addition, some of them provide clues at other linguistic levels as well. For example, it is well-known that many learners of L2 French have significant problems with gender assignment and gender concord. This is no doubt due to a variety of factors (see Ayoun's and Herschensohn's respective chapters in this volume). However, a number of word formation mechanisms, suffixation in particular, provide unambiguous clues to gender assignment. The benefits to learners of recognizing complex words therefore extend beyond semantics.

Many of the complex words found in the passages above are already attested in standard French dictionaries. However, this is not always the case. Word formation is a generative device which constantly produces new (i.e., previously unattested) forms, and lexicographers will always be running second in the race to identify and analyze new lexical creations. A small illustration of this is provided by Véronis (2005) who presents a list of lexical items found in the online version of *Le Monde* of the last week of June 2005 which are not attested by the *Trésor de la langue française*. In all, 93 items of the sort were found (see Table 5).

Of these 93 items, 65 (or just under 70%) are based on one of the word formation devices we have been discussing here. If these data are representative of what is found in other authentic texts presented to learners, then two things seem clear. First, knowing what we do about the role and accuracy of morpho-lexical factors, especially word-formation, in accurate guessing of meaning, presenting L2 speakers with such material without having taught word formation and without supporting materials would seem to miss an important point. Second, simply pointing L2 learners toward traditional lexicographical resources like dictionaries will not provide them with sufficient means for understanding these authentic materials.

7.   A cognitive approach to word formation

There exists a longstanding debate in applied linguistics on the relative weight which should be given to teaching of the formal aspects of language, and that which should be devoted to communicative aspects. Over the years, the pendulum has swung back and forth, as Zimmerman (1997) shows in her historical overview. DeKeyser (2001), provides convincing evidence that both facets are important, and that language teaching should simultaneously bring L2 learners to analyze the elements they are learning, while acquiring the ability to proceduralize and apply their linguistic knowledge.

Many of the traditional presentations of word formation have tended to assimilate the phenomenon to application of syntactically-constrained rules. While this has led to significant insights in some areas, as, for example, the role of argument structure in complex lexical items, the approach to the data themselves has sometimes been summary, with small sets of examples used to justify large conclusions. From a pedagogical perspective, this is somewhat unfortunate, since the rules created in this fashion, by their overgenerality, have limited value when presented to learners, who require finer-grained information. However, there are exceptions, and these are beginning to form a solid foundation for language pedagogy. As an example, Panther and Thornburg (2001) provide a detailed analysis of the set of words in English which make use of the suffix *-er* and show that the usual core meaning of 'agent who performs the role defined by the verbal base' is first of all too general, since the relation of the agent to the verb is usually more specific, designating a profession or a usual practitioner (cf. 'teacher'), and since around the notion of 'event' implicit in such forms, there exists a set of semantic variants, including the obvious instruments (cf. 'mixer'), but also locations (cf. 'diner'), purpose-patients (cf. 'broiler'), events themselves (cf. 'rear-ender'), and others. Although the analysis is based on English, its implications for the teaching of second languages, including French, are clear: If we are to present derivation and compounding in a serious fashion, our models must be fine-grained, semantically motivated, and based on reasonably large sets of examples. Additional work in this vein has been done by Lieber (2004) who presents a discussion of some semantic components implicit in the English derivational system. The cognitive linguistics tradition in general also offers promise. For example, Langacker (1991), in a discussion of the distinction between nouns and verbs, in which nouns are presented as encapsulating the processes which verbs present explicitly, shows how this is related to the observed tendency for nominalization not to affect a verb's conceptual content, whereas creation of a denominal verb tends to add new semantic features. Compare for example *marcher* 'to walk' – *une marche* 'a walk' and *clou* 'a nail' – *clouer* 'to nail'. The meaning of *une marche* is relatively easy to deduce if one knows the base verb, but the meaning of *clouer* requires one to understand the device used to act upon the nail, and the result of the operation. Valuable materials also exist in French to some extent. For instance, Corbin (1987) provides a thorough discussion of word-formation devices in French, together with detailed lists of affixes, bases, and operations. In the next section, we will see how information of the sort can be used in a learning environment.

8. Computational approaches to the teaching and learning of L2 word formation

Despite nearly thirty years of existence, Computer-Aided Language Learning (CALL) has still to gain broad acceptance in the classroom, apart from the omnipresence of word processing software, email, and to a lesser extent, grammar checkers (see Pennington 2003 for discussion). For example, Barr (2004) surveyed the use of CALL in two British (Ulster, Cambridge) and one Canadian university (Toronto) and found relatively low uptake of CALL resources. In particular, no instances of computers for teaching or learning word formation or lexical creativity were mentioned.

Two promising exceptions lie in concordancing software (see e.g., Bley-Vroman 2003; Cosme 2003; Chambers & O'Sullivan 2004), and in the use of online dictionaries. For instance, in a series of experiments, de Ridder (2003) found that the provision of on-screen hyperlinked glosses for L2 texts appears to lead to improved vocabulary acquisition. In earlier work, Krantz (1991) studied dictionary lookup strategies of L2 learners of English in the context of their reading of a short text. The latter case is interesting, in that most of the words looked up by participants in the study were of Latinate origin, and by our counts based on Krantz's lists, approximately a third of those forms looked up at least five times were derivationally complex.

There is no doubt that paper and online dictionaries and corpus-based supporting materials will play a crucial role in the teaching of complex lexical items. However, both have their weaknesses. As we have seen, dictionaries will always be out of date to some extent. Corpus-based materials relying on current web data offer the potential for partly filling this gap. In particular, internet search engines provide a means of moving from a new word found in a text to a set of comparable examples found on the web. However, such an approach is not without problems, as the following example illustrates. We chose the lexical item *communautarisée* 'communitarized' from the Véronis list shown above, and entered it as a search parameter into Google (date of search, 02/01/2005). We reproduce here the first six hits:

(11) a. *Europe: une diplomatie <u>communautarisée</u>?*
      b. *Oui! la coopération judiciaire et policière peut être <u>communautarisée</u>.*
      c. *L'Union belge estime sans doute que le sport est une matière culturelle <u>communautari-</u><u>sée</u>. Je ne vois aucun inconvénient, si d'autres réunions se tiennent à …*
      d. *Ceux-ci, avec la politique commerciale, représentent la quasi-totalité des prérogatives de la sphère <u>communautarisée</u> de l'action extérieure européenne. …*
      e. *Il introduisit également une nouveauté en ne défendant pas seulement l'objectif d'une politique extérieure <u>communautarisée</u>, mais en proposant à l'Europe et, …*
      f. *<u>Communautarisée</u>, parce que le site permet de n'afficher son profil qu'à un nombre réduit de personnes (les amis de mes amis ou les amis des amis de mes amis …)*

It is important to note that the precise meaning of the base form varies from example to example, including 'the European Community' in examples (11a, b, d, e), 'the Belgian communities' (Flemish and Walloon) in example (11c), and 'the members of a particular internet group' in example (11f). Moreover, the meaning of the suffix itself varies from 'transfer of responsibility to the group designated by the base form' in the first five examples to 'limitation of access to the group designated by the base form' in the last example. We find here a confirmation of the cognitive desiderata discussed earlier. We are not claiming that such fine-grained analysis is impossible on the basis of corpus materials such as these: Clearly, we have just provided, in abridged form, the elements of just such an analysis. However, we would argue that it would be unrealistic to suppose that L2 learners would be capable of such analyses themselves, or would be willing to do them. If that is the case, then authentic corpus materials will need to be pre-analyzed by L2 teachers, or discussed in detail in class. This is not impossible, in fact it is probably desirable because of the advantages it provided in terms of exposure to a variety of authentic written materials. We would simply argue that other, complementary approaches exist as well. In the next section, we will discuss one of these.

9. Some illustrations of generation-based word-formation teaching and testing

In this section, we will present an additional tool for the teaching of L2 word formation in French, based on the notion of *generative CALL*, where utterances are not pre-stored, but generated on the fly by a computer. In other words, the computer contains only the grammar and lexicon of the language to be presented, and must synthesize each example presented to a learner. This means as well that everything which it is important to know about a particular lexical unit or combination of units must be represented in the metalanguage of the generative environment. Such a model requires a significant investment of resources under the surface, but the advantage of very fine control over generated utterances and over the analysis of learner input. We will illustrate this approach by means of VINCI, a large and complex program which has been under development for more than a decade, and which has been used to produce a wide range of utterances, some of considerable complexity, such as puns (Lessard & Levison 1992), riddles (Lessard & Levison 1993), limericks (Lessard & Levison 2005), and narrative texts (Levison & Lessard 2004a, 2004b).

In the following paragraphs, we present and discuss three examples of the use of VINCI to assist in the teaching and learning of various facets of word formation. These examples presuppose no particular understanding of the program itself, but are used to illustrate what the program, or other similar programs, can do. Readers interested in the underlying devices used, and a fuller description of VINCI itself, may consult the project website at http://www.cs.queensu.ca/Compling, which includes a fuller discussion of the examples presented here, the actual linguistic data used to generate them, and the program itself, which is freely available for download.

The metalanguage and operations provided by VINCI allow for a wide range of language teaching and testing activities. In the area of word formation, they permit, among other things, the generation and presentation of derived or compounded words, and the testing of a learner's capacity for producing new lexical forms by rule.

In this way, the system bridges the gap between basic lexical knowledge and the morphological complexity of authentic texts. We will present three examples of the use of the program, ranging from exercises designed to allow learners to practice learned relations and teachers or researchers to test levels of learner knowledge or performance, to open-ended activities where the computer provides a set of starting points for autonomous student activities, and finally to interactive exercises where the learner (or subject) interacts with the computer as interlocutor.

9.1 First example: Presentation and testing of derivational patterns

We will begin with the presentation of a mechanism for dealing with cohorts of complex lexical items, together with their base forms. Consider first the homonymous suffixes -*eur* (as added to an adjective to form a noun denoting the quality carried by the adjective; e.g., *lenteur* 'slowness', *longueur* 'length', *pâleur* 'paleness'), and -*eur* (as added to a verb to denote the agent who performs the action of the verb; cf. *coureur* 'runner', *mesureur* 'measurer', *vendeur* 'seller'). Distinguishing the two is important for a number of reasons, including the large semantic difference between them, but also the fact that the first suffix gives rise to feminine nouns, while the second produces masculine nouns. Using this sort of basic linguistic information, VINCI can generate at the simplest level sets of elements which follow some pattern, as in sequences of deverbal nouns in -*eur*:

(12) *acheteur* 'buyer', *coureur* 'runner', *mesureur* 'measurer', *vendeur* 'seller'

In a more complex model, such forms are presented individually on the screen, and the language learner is asked to provide the appropriate base form, thereby demonstrating his or her ability to decompose such units. Thus, a student seeing *acheteur* 'buyer' will be expected to type *acheter* 'to buy'. Alternatively, learners are presented with base forms, and are requested to provide the appropriate derived form. Such exercises may also be embedded in the more extended context of a phrase or sentence. For example, the computer may generate the utterance: *Cette voiture est lente. Cela me surprend* 'This car is slow. That surprises me'. Given this, the learner is expected to simplify the sentence and type: *La lenteur de cette voiture me surprend* 'The slowness of this car surprises me'. Note that in this case it is necessary to add the appropriate article to the derived form, thereby demonstrating knowledge of gender. At an even more complex level, examples of the two models of -*eur* (deverbal and de-adjectival) may be generated at random, encouraging the learner to distinguish the two. And finally, the mix of generated forms can be enriched by adding monomorphemic items to the list, so that a learner seeing *fleur* 'flower' will need to recognize that there is no adjectival or verbal base.

Similar exercises allow for the presentation of other prefixes or suffixes, for distinction between the two distinct senses of a prefix or suffix, as in the case of *contre-*, which has the meanings 'opposition' as in *contre-attaque* 'counter-attack', *contre-manifestation* 'counter-demonstration', and 'second or secondary' as in *contre-*

signature 'countersignature', *contre-lecture* 'second reading'. Another exercise involves an analysis of V+N compounds (as in *coupe-papier* 'paper cutter', *garde-malade* 'caregiver', *tire-bouchon* 'corkscrew'), where a number of important points can be made clear to the learner, including the fact that all such compounds are masculine, and (although the terminology used with students is simpler) the fact that they are exocentric head-final structures, where the first element represents a verb and the second element its direct object taken in the generic sense. Thus, learners come to see that a *garde-malade* is someone who cares for a sick person, while a *tire-bouchon* is something that pulls out a cork.

Generated forms such as those above may also be embedded into even longer, narrative, contexts (see Levison & Lessard 2004a, 2004b). In addition, although this is not discussed here (but see Levison, Lessard, & Walker 2000; as well as Levison, Lessard, Danielson, & Merven 2001), the VINCI environment provides a rich set of error analysis devices which allow the system to diagnose student errors and, if desired, to adjust subsequent productions on the basis of tendencies, including errors, found in previous student responses.

9.2 Second example: Playful use of word formation devices

An often neglected component of lexical acquisition and use concerns the playful use of language to explore possible words and possible worlds. The following exercise illustrates this in the context of learned compounds. The starting point for the exercise is a 180 item lexicon containing frequent Greek and Latin bases, such as *crypto-, lacto-, luso-, gyno-, télé-, -émie, -cide, -cratie, -phage, -vore*. The lexical entry for each of these forms includes a variety of information, including a definition, gender in the case of suffixal forms, and, since some normative sources criticize the combination of Greek with Latin bases, the language of origin. On the basis of this, it is possible to construct simple rules which generate possible forms. Some examples are: *Lactovore, lusocide, gynocratie, cryptoémie*. Relaxing the constraint on a common language of origin will produce additional forms such as *lusophage* or *télécide*. It is important to recognize that although some of the combinations generated will in fact correspond to attested lexical entries, the goal here is to construct starting points for descriptions of 'possible worlds' upon which students are asked to write short passages or hold discussions. So, for example, presented with the form *gynocratie*, a student – or possibly a group of students – would reflect on what a government by women would look like; or given *lactovore*, they would discuss the consequences of a milk-based diet. Of course, as a preliminary, students must determine the meaning of the learned bases, and of their combinations.

One of the crucial characteristics of learned formations such as these is that they are head-final. Furthermore, and this is crucial for the learning of French, the final element will determine the gender of the complex unit. Thus, for example, *gynocratie* is feminine. One means of making clear both the headedness and the gender of such forms is by means of a transformation to include an article and a gloss, where the order of the glossed elements is explicitly the reverse of the order of elements in the word itself. Such a device produces sequences like *la gynocratie* or *le télécide*, and definitions like *gynocratie – gouvernement par la femme*, or *télécide – assassinat à distance*.

9.3 Third example: Word formation in human-computer dialogues

Exercises such as those just described function primarily at the formal level and their communicative aspects are limited (although in the second of the two approaches, generated compound nouns can be used to elicit discussion among students). An alternative approach involves having learners engage in a dialogue with the computer. In particular, we have explored cases where the computer asks information of a learner. This has the advantage of leaving control of the dialogue in the hands of the computer, allowing for significantly greater predictability with respect to student input, while giving learners the illusion of power, since they may feel they are providing information to the computer. For example, in one model we have used previously, the computer plays the role of a customer who asks the location of the various products in a grocery store, and the learner, who must know this information and be able to use the relevant linguistic terminology, provides the response.

We describe here a variant of this model, where learners play the role of job counselors: The computer, which plays the role of a job-seeker, gives a description of some set of skills and preferences, and the learner must use these to recommend a job or profession.

The starting point for such a system is the set of 460 nouns in our current French lexicon which designate a wide range of occupations, including *agriculteur* 'farmer', *bibliothécaire* 'librarian', *boulanger* 'baker', *douanier* 'customs official', *expert-comptable* 'accountant', *fonctionnaire* 'civil servant', *guitariste* 'guitarist', *journaliste* 'journalist', *lexicologue* 'lexicologist', *mineur* 'miner', *navigateur* 'navigator', *parfumeur* 'perfume manufacturer', *plombier* 'plumber', *sage-femme* 'midwife', *téléphoniste* 'telephone operator', and so on, many of which make use of suffixation or compounding. Each noun carries a set of traits, including a classification of the type of occupation, such as *art, métier, profession*, and so on. In addition, since occupations involve some task, each provides information on actions typical of each occupation, as in *cuire.pain* ('bake bread') in the case of a baker. Each also includes a specification of the typical context in which the occupation is performed, (*intérieur* in the case of occupations performed indoors, *scène* in the case of performers, etc.), as well as in some cases an attribute qualifying the conditions of the occupation (*danger* in the case of a policeman, *matinal* in the case of a baker). Many entries contain pointers to other, related words, such as the location of an occupation (as in *hôpital* 'hospital' in the case of a doctor or a psychologist), and in some cases, the typical instrument of the person's occupation (such as *guitare* in the case of a guitarist). In some cases, information is also provided on other occupations from the same domain (such as *pâtissier* 'pastry chef' in the case of *boulanger* 'baker'), and possibly one or more synonyms (such as *docteur* in the case of *médecin*). Finally, as in previous examples, information is provided on the morphological status of nouns, as well as information on their base forms.

On the basis of this information, utterances are generated by the computer, which, in the role of job-seeker, describes its preferences, as in the following example:

(13)   *Je m'appelle Monique Mallet. J'ai dix-neuf ans. Je suis matinale. Je préfère travailler à l'intérieur. J'adore le pain. J'aime les boulangeries. Je veux un emploi qui me permettra de travailler avec mes mains. Qu'est-ce que vous me proposez?*
'My name is Monique Mallet. I'm 19 years old. I'm an early riser. I like working indoors. I adore bread. I like bakeries. I want a job that will let me work with my hands. What do you suggest?'

Note that the computer production is gender-marked. In this case, since the job-seeker is female, the third sentence is *Je suis matinale*. The language learner is expected to pick up these clues in the advice given, and propose the job of *boulangère*.

The production of the set of possible responses expected from the student follows essentially the same path as that used to produce the question. Among other things, variant syntactic structures are permitted as shown in (14):

(14)   a.   *Devenez X.*   'Become an X'
        b.   *Je vous propose le métier de X.*   'I suggest the job of X'
        c.   *Avez-vous songé à devenir X?*   'Have you thought about becoming a X'
        d.   *Vous feriez un bon X.*   'You would make a good X'

Depending on the complexity of typing desired, the computer can propose the first part of these strings, leaving the learner to add only the name of the occupation. Alternatively, the learner can be required to enter one of the entire response strings in 14. Also, whenever a lexical entry contains pointers to synonyms (as in the case of *médecin* above), or to other jobs in the same domain (as in the relation between *boulanger* and *pâtissier*), these elements are included in the list of possible student responses. A range of error analysis routines is applied to each utterance produced by the learner. The product of this final exercise is a continuously-varying set of utterances produced by the computer which provide semantic characterization of occupations, lexical items from the same field, and clues to derivational relations.

9.4   Combining word formation teaching approaches

The computational model just presented should be seen as one element in the arsenal available to the language instructor interested in teaching word formation as part of a course. It is possible to envisage a suite of activities which would together lead to better understanding and performance by L2 learners in this area. In many of these cases, it is likely that an approach based on operationalizing learning would be of value. For example, on the level of reception, learners could be presented with authentic texts containing complex wordforms which they would be asked to identify and describe. At the same time, individual word formation devices could be focused on by means of concordance data in order to bring to light both commonalities across different occurrences of the same device and variation based on context (cf. *communautariser* discussed earlier). As we have seen above, generative tools can provide a complement to this micro-analysis of the machinery of word-formation, as well as a controlled environment in which learners can practice their production and analysis skills. Finally, a return to authentic texts would allow these micro-level skills to be applied in a richer context. For example, given an authentic text, students could practice rewriting and transformation exercises in which complex lexical items are replaced by paraphrases using simple words, or where longer utterances are reduced to complex lexical items.

It would appear, however, that this would require a revision of existing pedagogical materials and the production of materials usable by both instructors and learners in order to obtain the metalinguistic terms and tools in order to discuss word formation coherently. This is not to argue for a full-fledged course in word-formation for every L2 learner; however, it is an argument for inclusion of a basic level of knowledge and terminology in all language courses beyond the most basic level.

10. Conclusions and future paths

The preceding sections have shown that:

- according to the data analyzed here, L2 learners of French appear to make less frequent use of word formation devices than do native speakers, both in oral and written language;
- there is evidence that word formation devices receive relatively little attention in syllabi, textbooks, and testing environments;
- there is some evidence that use of word-formation clues is a valuable aid to L2 readers in the interpretation of unknown lexical items;
- recent research in linguistics, particularly in the cognitive tradition, is beginning to provide more detailed models of word formation which might profitably be used in teaching word formation to L2 learners;
- lexicographical and corpus-based materials have demonstrated potential for enriching the set of word formation data available to students, although some gaps still remain;
- generative environments provide an additional approach which allows for focused presentation of the rule-governed aspects of word formation to second language learners.

However, there remain a number of significant gaps in our knowledge and practice. In particular, although we have seen evidence that at least some L2 learners fall short of L1 models in their use of word formation, both in speech and writing, and that some research shows L2 readers using word formation clues effectively, the precise nature and effect of word formation clues in L2 textual understanding remains essentially an open question. At another level, although we have solid evidence for the continuing creation of new lexical items at the level of the native speaker linguistic community (in other words, at the level of the lexicon), we know much less about the extent to which, and in what ways, individual native speakers generate new forms, and how much this varies from speaker to speaker (in other words, at the level of vocabulary). Although more is now known about the mental storage of complex lexical forms by native speakers, the details of mental storage of complex lexical items by L2 speakers is much less clear. There is also a fundamental gap in our understanding of the interplay between linguistic ability and metalinguistic knowledge in the area of word formation. For example, to what extent must native speakers be capable of consciously analyzing lexical items in order to understand or to produce new ones? Does this hold true for L2 speakers as well? If we compare L1 and L2 in other areas, it would seem that there exists a difference between the two sorts of speakers and that L2 speakers tend to require more explicit linguistic knowledge in order to function in a near-native fashion. However, again, our knowledge of L2 metalinguistic knowledge is limited (see e.g., Birdsong 1989) and the role of explicit knowledge in L1 and L2 word formation is yet little explored. It is also clear that the rate and kind of word formation varies from domain to domain (compare, for example, a technical article in physics with a recipe), and that native speakers trained in various domains adapt their production and reception appropriately. It remains to be determined to what extent L2 learners come to approach this level of competence. Similarly, word-formation devices vary in their relative frequency, as well as in the relative frequency of the lexical items to which they are attached. It is not yet clear to what extent L2 learning of word formation is influenced by, or takes account of, such frequency differences.

Clearly, much remains to be done. In particular, a number of particular areas stand out in which a generative approach would be useful. First, as a number of researchers (Hulstijn 1997, for example) have pointed out, the study of L2 phenomena is hampered by the multiplicity of intertwined factors involved in any instance of L2 activity, including the form, meaning and frequency of lexical items, their repetition within a text, their role in the presentation of new information and in the development of the text, and the interplay of the learner's previous knowledge and the information presented in the text. The simultaneous control of all these dimensions forms a significant challenge, and many experimental and teaching paradigms focus on only one or two dimensions at a time. An enriched generative environment, by its explicit control over many variables, offers a valuable tool in managing this complexity. However, as a prelude to this, one area in particular merits serious consideration: Calculation of the relative frequency, coverage (that is, the number of different lexical items to which they attach themselves), semantics, and productivity of the various French affixes based on large recent corpora of spoken and written productions in various domains of use. It is sometimes claimed that after a long period of deprecation, French language word formation is on the rise. If the goal of L2 teaching is to provide learners with as close an image as possible to authentic use of the language being taught, then such empirical data will be crucial. The analysis of existing and future corpora has the potential of providing this. Of course, L2 learner texts should also be studied to ascertain the extent to which such texts show convergence or divergence from L1 productions.

Another promising area for a generative approach lies in the the study of cognate forms between a learner's first and second languages as a means of bootstrapping lexical access (see for example Holmes & Guerra Ramos 1993). In the case of English and French, this advantage extends to a large set of affixes which the two languages share. There is a significant opportunity to test the contribution of such shared affixes in the ability to interpret new lexical items. However, this will require careful control for the influence of the lexical bases chosen. As well, as in the case of traditional cognates, formal similarity is a double-edged sword, in that the first language can sometimes distort the learner's perception of the meaning or use of an L2 form. In the case of affixes, our preliminary work (Lessard & Levison 2001) suggests that, at least with regard to their ability to judge relative productivity, less-advanced learners tend to be more influenced by their first language than more advanced learners. In fact, even in the case of physical objects with monomorphemic labels, it would be imprudent to assume an easy mapping between languages. Malt and Sloman (2003), for example, show that even such simple words as 'bottle' and 'dish' pose labelling problems for Polish L2 learners of English. Even greater difficulties can be anticipated in the case of derivationally complex forms.

Earlier in this chapter, it was pointed out that N+N, N+PREP+N, N+ADJ and other compounds not based on orthographic contiguity were not dealt with here. This is a significant gap in our knowledge of L2 language. In particular, it will be important to measure the similarities and differences between compounds, collocations and other formulaic utterances, at both the morphosyntactic and semantic levels. However, as Wray (2002) points out, relatively little research has been done on L2 formulaic sequences. This area will require a combination of corpus data (both L1 and L2), computational analysis, and generative modelling.

Finally, there is the vast domain of lexical creativity based on semantic adjustments to a base form. We are beginning to see the basis for the principled and detailed analysis of such phenomena through work based on the *generative lexicon* model (see Pustejovsky 1995), work in cognitive semantics (see e.g., Talmy 2000), and other linguistic approaches which restore the lexicon to a central place in linguistic analysis. The modelling of such phenomena provides another area where a generative approach may be of value.

Appendix A: English glosses for extended French examples

(6) Technology:
This triumphant entry gave rise to euphoria around the Internet, with some predicting that it would revolutionize ways of life and create a new economy. On the stock markets, this "irrational exuberance", to use the expression of the president of the American Federal Reserve, Alan Greenspan, translated itself into a five-fold increase in the value of the Nasdaq index between 1995 and its zenith in March 2000: newborn Internet companies, founded

by students in garages, who spent the money of their investment capitalists before making any sales, saw their value on the stock market surpass that of industry giants.

(7)   Sports:
He left the Mosson stadium at Montpellier, Wednesday August 17, as he had arrived two days earlier to meet the French team before the friendly match against the Ivory Coast: running, head down, surrounded by several bodyguards. Zinedine Zidane has become almost as untouchable off the pitch as on. Venerated like a rock star, with cries of "Zizou, Zizou"! by 41,500 loving spectators, the leader of Real Madrid and returning captain of the French team was elevated above the rank of soccer player to that of savior of a people on Wednesday August 17 after having contributed to the flattering victory of the Bleus against the Ivory Coast team, who nevertheless put on a fine performance.

(8)   International affairs:
The demonstration of strength and efficiency desired by the organizers of the attacks of Wednesday, August 17, was accomplished. Approximately 350 small bombs exploded over the country in the space of an hour toward the end of the morning, with police figures rising during the day. Around 50 cities saw damage to administrative buildings, courts, press clubs, railway and bus stations. At least two deaths and around a hundred injuries have been recorded during this terrorist attack, visibly designed to cause minimal human damage.

(9)   French news:
The Metz court, which received the complaint, dropped the case on the belief that there was insufficient evidence to characterize the infraction. Several months earlier in a similar case, the complainant dropped her case and asked to be transferred and the guard against whom Virginie presented her case received a letter from the prosecutor drawing his attention to his frequently indecent, contemptuous, insulting, indeed damaging behavior with respect to the female employee.

(10)   Social/media:
For Mr. Gaultier, the Choc campaign is only a "publicity stunt" and mention of the battle against drugs only "a pretext to show a positive image and sell papers". "My reaction is not very positive", stated Didier Jayle, president of the interministerial mission for combatting drugs and drug addiction. "This person is shown without humanity", he stated. "This type of images increases fear among those who diabolize drugs and risks being ignored by others. Apart from the horror it elicits, what else does it teach us?" The Act Up Association, which combats AIDS denounced the campaign in a publication named "X", "a magazine whose editorial content is based entirely on images selected to appeal to the lowest form of voyeurism of its readership".

(11)   a.   Europe: a communitarized diplomacy?
        b.   Yes! Judicial and police cooperation can be communitarized.
        c.   The Belgian Union no doubt believes that sport is a communitarized cultural issue. I see no problem, if other meetings decide ...
        d.   The latter, with commercial policy, represent almost all the prerogatives of the communitarized sphere of European foreign initiatives ...
        e.   He introduced a new approach in defending not only the objective of a communitarized foreign policy, but in proposing to Europe ...
        f.   Communitarized, because the site permits the showing of one's profile to only a few people (the friends of my friends, or the friends of my friends' friends ...)

Appendix B: A fuller description of the VINCI environment

VINCI is both a collection of metalanguages for natural language generation and an interpreter which takes some subset of a linguistic description based on these metalanguages and produces written or oral output. Embedded in an editing environment (IVI), it also includes facilities for links with 'driver programs' which may control aspects of generation at a higher level, as well as facilities for analyzing and diagnosing learner (or in the case of research, subject) input. In what follows, a brief description of the various metalanguages is provided. Fuller descriptions are available in publications by Lessard and Levison and on the VINCI website (www.cs.queensu.ca/CompLing).

The core metalanguage, and in many respects the 'glue' which holds the other metalanguages together, is a system of attributes. Attributes are structured in terms of classes and values, which may represent morphological, syntactic or semantic information, as illustrated by the following examples, where the metalanguage item appears on the left and an explanation, in brace brackets, on the right.

> Genre (masc, fém)　　　　　　　　　{Masculine or feminine gender}
> Verbtype (vi, vtd, vtdi, ...)　　　　　{Intransitive, transitive, ditransitive verbs}
> Casnom (humain, animal, vivant... }　{Human, animal, living things}

Attributes may be *partially ordered*, in the sense that any given value may presuppose one or more higher level values, as in the following example:

> humain<animé,　　　　　{Humans are included in the class of animates}
> animé<mobile,　　　　　 {Animates are mobile (can move around)}
> animé<tangible,　　　　　{Animates are tangible (can be touched)}
> animé<vivant...　　　　　 {Animates are alive}

Attributes may also be compounded and deconstructed, as in the following examples:

> humain.suj　　　{The compound of the values 'humain' and 'suj' (subject)}
> humain/suj　　　{The previous compound reduced to its first element}

A series of attribute classes and values may be included in the specification of a single lexical entry, as in the following examples:

> "forêt"|N|fém, Nombre, lieu, sauvage, d2, g10km, ...
>
> > {*Forêt* is feminine, may be singular or plural, is a wild (sauvage) place (lieu) with two dimensions (d2) and is approximately 10 km across (g10km)}
>
> "princesse"|N|fém, Nombre, humain, femelle, beau, intelligent, Cheveux, gentil...
>
> > {*Princesse* is feminine, may be singular or plural, is a female human, is beautiful ('beau') and intelligent, and has hair which in any particular instantiation, may be of any color specified by the class Cheveux}
>
> "tuer"|V|vtd, humain.suj, influencer, animé.objd, Temps...
>
> > {*Tuer* (kill) is a transitive verb which takes a human subject, represents an action of influencing an animate direct object, can take any verb tense... }

Similarly, combinations of attributes may be used in the context of morphology rules, as in:

> plur : #1 + "s";　{If a syntax-tree node carries the attribute 'plur', the string "s" should
> 　　　　　　　　　be added to the item in the first field of the lexical entry}
> sing : #1;　　　　{If it carries the attribute 'sing', then the first field alone is used}

For simplicity, we have ignored here a number of complex additional morphological devices such as tables, rules within lexical fields, and context-sensitive morphology, where the action to be performed takes account of earlier or later lexical items in the generated utterances, as when the definite article *le* is elided to *l'* if the following noun or adjective begins with a vowel. We have also ignored the fact that morphological data and rules may be constructed both for orthographic and phonetic strings.

Attributes play an important role in syntax rules, ensuring semantic and morphological agreement among the various parts of a generated utterance. The basis of VINCI syntax is an attribute grammar formalism, whereby nodes on a developing syntax tree may inherit traits from their parents and receive new traits as required. In addition, VINCI's use of *guarded syntax rules* permits the situation whereby the presence of a trait on a parent node determines the selection of a particular child node. For example, in the development of a noun phrase, if the parent node contains the value p1 or p2 (first or second person), the child node must be a pronoun (*je, tu, nous, vous*), whereas if the parent node contains the trait p3 (third person), the child node may be either a pronoun (*il, ils, elle, elles*) or a full noun phrase.

> ROOT = CHOOSE Pe : Personne, No : Nombre, Ge : Genre;
>> {Select some values for person (first, second or third), number (singular or plural), and gender (masculine or feminine)}
>
> NP[Pe, Ge, No] % {Define a noun phrase (NP) with the values chosen above} %

> NP = INHERIT Pe : Personne, No : Nombre, Ge : Genre;
>> {Inherit the values for person, gender and number from ROOT}
>
> < p1, p2 : PRON[pronper, Pe, No]
>> {Check the value of Personne on the parent (NP)
>> If the value is first or second (p1 or p2), then the child takes the form of a personal pronoun (PRON) with the appropriate person and number}
>
> <p3 : (DET[Ge, No] N[Ge, No] | PRON[pronper, Pe, No]) %
>> {If the value of Person on the parent is p3 (third person), then the child may either be a noun phrase with a determiner and a noun or it may be a pronoun}

The development of utterances in the VINCI environment differs from a number of traditional generative formalisms in another important respect as well. Along with the usual sequence (syntax, lexicon, morphology), VINCI may take as a starting point a *semantic expression* (see below), which is transformed into a set of lexical *preselections*. These are used to control and fill in the contents of subsequent syntactic productions. The following example shows a preselection which chooses a member of the set of all masculine singular nouns having the semantic trait 'humain'.

> PRESELECT a : N[masc, sing, humain] %

Preselection rules, like lexical entries in the dictionary and lexical search patterns, may include and take account of a wide range of information, including attributes (as we saw above), but also morphological rules, orthographic and phonetic specifications, and lexical pointers which specify related lexical items such as synonyms, antonyms, hyperonyms, holonyms, and so on. So, for example, the following preselection specifies a transitive verb with a human subject which describes the action of moving something, which begins with the letter *b* and which has the regular *-er* morphology. (For example, *bouger*.)

> PRESELECT a : V[vtd, humain.suj, déplacer]/1 = "b*"/5= $12%

The following preselection specifies an adjective which describes a positive degree of size and which has an antonym. One adjective chosen by this preselection rule would be *gros*, which has the opposite *petit*.

PRESELECT a : ADJ[grandeur, pos]/13=ant: %

More interestingly from a communicative point of view, VINCI may be used to generate narrative texts to which a learner or test subject responds not in terms of formal linguistic manipulations, but rather in terms of discussions of content. For example, we have shown in earlier work how VINCI may be used to generate short fairy tales in French or English. After having been presented with one of these tales, a learner may be asked questions related to the content of the narrative (see Levison & Lessard 2004a, 2004b for details):

> *Comment s'appelait la princesse?*   {What was the princess' name?}
> *Qui a tué le sorcier?*   {Who killed the sorcerer?}
> *Avec quoi?*   {With what?}

Finally, VINCI includes one other important element from the point of view of the study and enhancement of lexical creativity: Mechanisms for *lexical transformations*. In one form of these, known as *static lexical transformations*, a lexical search pattern is taken as the starting point for some rule-governed transformation. All items in an existing lexicon which satisfy the lexical search pattern will undergo the lexical transformation and a set of new, rule-governed, products will be produced and added to the base lexicon. Consider the following simple case:

rule 9
?|V|vtd|?|$12|?| _makes_ [#7 + "able"]|ADJ|qualité||$3|| %

This rule searches a lexicon for transitive *-er* verbs ($12 is a morphology rule for *-er* verbs) and adds the suffix *-able* to produce adjectives. The resulting adjectives have the attribute 'qualité' and are inflected for number but not gender ($3 is a rule which adds -s for plurals, but leaves the base uninflected for gender). Created forms based on one of our lexicons include *apportable* 'bringable', *attaquable* 'attackable', *comparable* 'comparable', *composable* 'composable', *doutable* 'doubtable', *fermable* 'closable', *exprimable* 'expressible', *jouable* 'playable', *mesurable* 'measurable', *posable* 'placable', *remboursable* 'refundable', *sautable* 'jumpable', *souhaitable* 'hope-able', *trompable* 'foolable', *tuable* 'killable', etc. Some of these are attested by dictionaries like the *Petit Robert*, while others may be found in documents. All are possible forms.

In the case of word formation, VINCI must make the distinction between existing lexical entries which are nonetheless analyzable (such as *enseignant* 'teacher') and possible new formations which are not attested in current dictionaries, such as, for example, *robodrome* in the sense of 'a racetrack for robots', on the model of *hippodrome* 'racetrack for horses' and *vélodrome* 'racetrack for bicycles'. Where a complex lexical form is already part of the language, this status is reflected by means of an attribute, and the base form or forms on which the derived or compounded form has been created will be captured by lexical pointers, as in the following example:

"enseignant"|N|Genre, Nombre, humain, attesté, … |…|bv: "enseigner"/V;|…

where the pointer bv refers to the *base verbale* or verbal base. On the other hand, it is not difficult to find ephemeral, or sometimes even relatively frequent forms in specialized terminologies which do not appear in the standard dictionaries. For example, the *Petit Robert* does not include the form *archéocratie* ('government by the aged'), but it can be found on the web. The decision on whether such forms will be marked as attested or not will depend on the use being made of the lexicon in each circumstance and the degree of normativity desired.

Similarly, we make use of a set of attributes to distinguish monomorphemic words (which carry the trait 'm_simple') from multimorphemic words, and within the latter class, subclasses of lexical structure, including prefixation, suffixation, composition, and so on, as the following examples illustrate.

> "table"|N|fém, Nombre, physobj, m_simple, ...|...
> "avancement"|N|masc, concept, m_suffixé, ...|...
> "taille-crayon"|N|masc, outil, m_composé_vn, ...|...

Furthermore, there exists a partial ordering among these attributes:

> m_suffixé<m_dérivé<m_complexe,   {A suffixed word is a derived word and also a complex word}
> m_composé_vn<m_composé<m_complexe   {A V+N compound is a compound and also a complex word}

so that more or less general classes may be selected.

Example

The presentation of cohorts of similar complex lexical entries, such as those based on a particular suffix, requires first the detailed representation of such entries, including their semantics, whether or not they are attested, what form of word formation they are based on, and what their base forms are. Sections of some typical lexical entries using deverbal and deadjectival nouns are reproduced below:

> "lenteur"|N|fém, Nombre, perceptible, attesté, m_suffixé|...|badj: "lent"/ADJ|...
> "longueur"|N|fém, Nombre, perceptible, attesté, m_suffixé|...|badj: "long"/ADJ|...
> "pâleur"|N|fém, Nombre, perceptible, attesté, m_suffixé|...|badj: "pâle"/ADJ|...
> "coureur"|N|masc, Nombre, humain, attesté, m_suffixé|...|bv: "courir"/ADJ|...
> "mesureur"|N|masc, Nombre, humain, attesté, m_suffixé|...|bv: "vendre"/ADJ|...
> "vendeur"|N|masc, Nombre, humain, attesté, m_suffixé|...|bv: "vendre"/ADJ|...

On the basis of these, a variety of syntax rules are possible. At the simplest level, a rule such as

> ROOT = N/1= "*eur"/14=badj %

will find and generate all nouns ending in -eur having an adjectival base.

At a more complex level, the following syntax rule:

> ROOT = N/1 = "*eur"/14=badj %
> QUESTION = ROOT %
> ANSWER = SHOW_BASE : ROOT %

when combined with the following transformation:

> SHOW_BASE = TRANSFORMATION
> N : 1/@14:badj; %

will present a learner with examples of deadjectival nouns in *-eur* and request their base form. So a student seeing *longueur* will type *long*. Of course the usual error analyses described above will apply. Inversely, the following rule:

ROOT = N/1 = "*eur"/14=badj %
QUESTION = SHOW_BASE : ROOT %
ANSWER = ADD_ARTICLE : ROOT %

combined with the following transformation:

ADD_ARTICLE = TRANSFORMATION
N[Nombre, Genre] : DET[déf, 1!Nombre, 1!Genre] 1 ; %

and the SHOW_BASE transformation shown above, will present the learner with the simple base forms and request the derived form, with the transformation ADD_ARTICLE prepending an article to the expected answer. Note that gender is taken into account in the choice of the article, so that learners will come to see the gender difference between the two forms of *-eur*.

A richer set of examples, together with the language generation software and language description files, may be found on the VINCI project's website.

CHAPTER 12

Growing up bilingual in French and French Sign Language*

Laurie Tuller, Marion Blondel and Nathalie Niederberger
Université François Rabelais, Tours / CNRS & Université de Rouen /
Lycée Français La Pérouse, San Francisco

Résumé
Ce chapitre présente l'acquisition du langage en contexte de surdité en s'appuyant sur l'exemple de l'espace francophone européen. Les auteures mettent en regard le français et la langue des signes française (LSF) à travers les différents cas de figures liés au contexte de surdité et les étapes successives de l'acquisition de ces deux langues naturelles. Ce va-et-vient entre les deux langues permet aux auteures à la fois de souligner les similarités entre le développement du français et de la LSF, mais aussi les différences liées aux modalités impliquées (visuo-gestuelle pour la LSF, audio-orale pour le français). Autrement dit, ce chapitre propose une exploration des différentes formes de bilinguisme français-LSF selon qu'il s'agit d'un apprenant sourd ou entendant, ou selon qu'il s'agit du français oral ou du français écrit, en accordant une attention toute particulière au contact et aux interactions entre deux langues empruntant deux canaux séparés.

Abstract
This chapter presents language acquisition in the context of deafness with a focus on French-speaking Europe. The authors look at both French and French Sign Language (LSF) via the different cases related to the context of deafness and the successive stages of language acquisition in these two natural languages. The comparison between the two languages underlines both similarities in acquisition of French and of LSF, and differences related to modality (visuo-gestural in LSF and audio-oral in French). Thus, this chapter proposes an exploration of the different forms of French-LSF bilingualism, which vary according to whether the learner is deaf or hearing, or whether French is oral or written, with particular attention to contact and interaction between two languages which use two different channels.

* Many thanks to an anonymous reviewer for helpful suggestions, and to Dalila Ayoun for her numerous, finecombed re-readings of this chapter, in which remaining shortcomings are ours alone. We remain indebted to the participants in our studies reported here, and to their families, for making this research possible.

1.   Introduction

French Sign Language – *LSF* (*Langue des signes française*) – is the natural sign language that is used in communities in France, Switzerland, and Belgium. 'French' in the appellation 'French Sign Language' refers to the fact that these communities are found in areas where French is the natural oral language.[1]

1.1   French Sign Language

As linguistic research since the 1960s has amply and persuasively demonstrated, natural sign languages are human languages, in every sense of the term, which arise in communities containing a substantial number of deaf persons. They are *not* merely spatial versions of surrounding oral languages. In other words, French Sign Language is not a transposition of French into gestures, but a separate language with its own lexicon, morphology, syntax, and, yes, phonology. Examples of structural differences between French and LSF which show the fundamental independence of these languages are given in (1) and (2). The examples in (1) illustrate the syntax of WH constructions in the two languages.

(1)   a.   *Qui   est   arrivé   hier* ?
           who   is   arrived   yesterday
           'Who arrived yesterday?'
      b.   YESTERDAY   WHO   ARRIVE[2]
           yesterday   who   arrive
           'Who arrived yesterday?'
      c.   **Est arrivé   qui   hier* ?
           arrived   who   yesterday
      d.   YESTERDAY   ARRIVE   WHO
           yesterday   arrive   who
           'Who arrived yesterday?'
      e.   **Qui   est   arrivé   qui   hier* ?
           who   is   arrived   who   yesterday
      f.   YESTERDAY   WHO   ARRIVE   WHO
           yesterday   who   arrive   who
           'Who arrived yesterday?'

Likewise, while French morphological agreement involves person, number and gender, with the latter restricted to a two-fold distinction (masculine, feminine), as illustrated in (2a–c), agreement in LSF involves encoding of a much richer variety of features.

---

1. LSF is mainly used in French-speaking countries in Europe. Quebec, for example, has a different sign language: LSQ (*langue des signes québécoise*).

2. We follow international conventions for presenting sign language data. LSF signs are given in capital letters in their English gloss.

These elements, which are referred to as "classifiers" in the sign language literature, are akin to noun classes. A few of the many possibilities are illustrated in (2d–g).

(2) a. *Max la   connaît bien cette   poésie.*
M   ACC-FEM know   well this-FEM poetry
'Max knows this poetry well'

b. *Max le   connaît bien ce   livre.*
M   ACC-MASC know   well this-MASC book
'Max knows this book well'

c. *Max les   connaît bien ces   livres.*
M   ACC-PL know   well these books
'Max knows these books well'

d. MAN "human being"-classifier-COME
'A man comes'

e. MAN TWO "dual"-classifier-COME
'Two men come'

f. CAR "vehicle"-classifier-COME
'A car comes'

g. BALL "round object"-classifier-COME
'A ball comes'

Sign languages are natural human languages not just because of their structures, however, but also because of the way they are acquired, the way they are produced and understood in the brain, the way they emerge and evolve historically, as well as the way they vary geographically and socially. As we will see in detail below, native sign language development in children looks like any other native language development. Major milestones occur at about the same ages. Early signs designate the same references as early words. More complex constructions, including those that require mastery of discourse phenomena, appear later than simpler constructions. Language development which begins after the so-called critical period for language acquisition has predictable effects, resembling those found in late language acquisition of oral languages (see Mayberry & Lock 2003 for a recent review of the literature). The neural underpinnings of sign language production and comprehension are those used for oral language, as aphasia, FMRI (functional magnetic resonance imaging) and other studies have shown (see Emmorey 2002: 271–314). One exciting research project stemming from work on sign language has been the documentation by Judy Kegl and colleagues[3] of the emergence and evolution of Nicaraguan sign language, which started out as an isolated domestic code, developed into a pidgin and creolized into a full-fledged sign language in the context of the creation of a school for the deaf. One of the interesting aspects of this work has been the parallels observed between the evolution of this sign language and that of Hawaiian English Creole (see e.g., Bickerton 1981). Study of synchronic variation in sign languages has revealed the same kinds of geographic

---

3. For a description of the project and a publications list, see http://www.unet.maine.edu/courses/NSLP/.

B'

Figure 1. Hanshape [B']

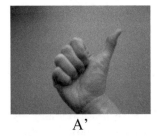

A'

Dh

Figure 2. Hanshapes [A'] and [Dh]

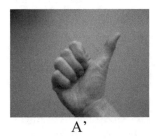

A'

Key

Figure 3. Hanshapes [A'] and [Key]

and social variables that are at work in synchronic variation in oral languages (see Woodward & De Santis 1977a, b; and De Santis 1977; cited in Woodward 1979; as well as Mottez 1976: 24–25 on variation in LSF). Within LSF, there is a fair amount of lexical variation, a couple of examples of which are given in (3).[4]

> (3) a. MOMMY
>   [B'] handshape touching the cheek twice (Switzerland)[5]
>   [B'] handshape touching the flank twice (one of the variants in France)

---

4. To the best of our knowledge, there are no recent studies which would provide a global picture of LSF variation.

5. Handshapes are commonly described in the sign language literature partly by use of symbols based on manual alphabets and numbers associated with diacritic symbols indicating whether the thumb

    b.   PUPIL
        [A'] handshape touching the right shoulder twice (Geneva, Switzerland)
        [Dh] with bent index on right cheek (Lausanne and Fribourg, Switzerland)
    c.   BOY
        [A'] handshape (thumb extended) going from one side of the forehead to the other side (Tours, France; Switzerland)
        [Key] handshape touching the temple with a twisting wrist movement (Poitiers, France)

The study of sign languages from the vantage points of psycholinguistics, neurolinguistics, sociolinguistics and historical linguistics all underline the fact that they are products of the human faculty for language. The same conclusion comes from looking at how they are used. Indeed, sign language speakers use sign languages for the same wide variety of functions that oral language speakers use oral languages for, from making jokes to abstract theorizing to poetry. The existence of sign language poetry has inspired a number of studies, most based on ASL. Among them, Klima and Bellugi (1976), Valli (1990) and Ormsby (1995) bring to light elements of linguistic structure that play a role in the structure of sign poetry. These include exploiting the phonological form of signs under repetition in ways comparable to those of spoken language poetry (rhyme, alliteration and assonance), the use of metaphor, and creative changes to the form of signs that smooth between-sign transitions in ways not found in ordinary signed discourse. Sutton-Spence (2005) offers a state-of-the-art analysis of signed poetry in various languages, including British Sign Language (BSL), Italian Sign Language (LIS), and LSF. In work centered on LSF, Blondel (2000) discovered visual-gestural equivalents to the key properties of oral nursery rhymes: Rhythmic patterns based in part on the alternation of accented and unaccented elements, balanced use of space, which is comparable to the melodic dimension of oral nursery rhymes and repetition of an element belonging to a particular structural class (handshape, movement, facial expression, and so on) which can be compared with assonance or alliteration. In (4), for instance, the repetition of the same handshape [3] or [6] in LSF corresponds to the assonance [wa] or rhyme [is]/[iz] in French.

(4) a.   *Un deux trois*   'one, two, three'
        Nous irons aux bois 'we'll go to the woods'
        Quatre cinq six   'four, five, six'
        Cueillir des cerises 'we'll pick cherries'
        […]
    b.   ONE TWO THREE   (underlined sign has [3] handshape)
        Cl "leaf wafting downwards" [3] handshape
        FOUR FIVE SIX   [6] handshape
        MUSHROOM MUSHROOM
        MUSHROOM MUSHROOM   [6] handshape […]

---

is extended or not for instance, partly by use of expressions fixed by usage such "flat hand", "key", and so on.

Summarizing, French Sign Language is a natural sign language with its own structure, not with a structure based on standard spoken French.

1.2   French and French Sign Language

Why include a chapter on French Sign Language in a volume devoted to French applied linguistics? Part of the answer to that question has already been provided: LSF, as we have just seen, is a natural language and as such can inform issues in L1 and L2 acquisition (including bilingualism) the same way any other natural language can. The rest of the answer has to do with what is special about bilingual acquisition of French Sign Language and French, a situation related to both the nature of deafness and the politics of deaf education. In most populations, congenital deafness affects between one or two out of every 1,000 people.[6] Deaf members of society are thus surrounded by hearing persons. Furthermore, it is generally estimated that between 90 to 95% of deaf children are born to hearing parents (see, e.g., Meier & Newport 1990). Thus, deaf persons overwhelmingly grow up in hearing families, with hearing parents and siblings. If 95% of deaf persons marry other deaf persons, 90% of these couples will have hearing children. This rapid review of the demography of deafness points to the fact that language "contact" between French and French Sign Language is not only very intimate, it also has a rather special character. We propose to explore here the topic of French-LSF contact from the point of view of the child language learner. An important aspect of language development in the case of deaf children concerns the language choices made not only by parents, but by the surrounding community. Will resources be allocated to make sign language instruction available to hearing parents of deaf children? Is instruction for deaf children available in sign language? Is classroom instruction in French made accessible via sign language interpretation? Via visual coding of French? These questions and many others will determine how deaf children grow up acquiring French, as well as if and how they grow up acquiring LSF.

French is not a run-of-the-mill L2 for deaf signers of LSF, as we shall see, and French-LSF bilingualism is not ordinary bilingualism at all. Not only is this bilingualism extra-ordinary for deaf children, principally because one language is immediately accessible and the other requires adaptive measures, but the multitude of variables involved in growing up deaf, or with deaf parents, means that there are a multitude of types of bilingualism involved. These variables include the following: Age, quality and

---

6. There are populations with considerably higher rates of deafness, a fact that has significant sociolinguistic implications. The most famous example is that of Martha's Vineyard (in the U.S.), which was populated by descendants of an isolated population in England in which frequent intermarriage increased prevalence of deafness. Up until the beginning of the 20th century, one out of every 155 children on Martha's Vineyard was born deaf and English-ASL (American Sign Language) bilingualism was widespread among the hearing for over 250 years (see Groce 1985). Non-genetic causes of hearing loss in children account for about 20–25%, and this percentage is on the decrease; genetic hearing loss accounts for the rest.

quantity of exposure to sign language; use of adaptive systems such as Cued Speech (visual encoding of oral language); exposure to reading via sign language, and so on. What happens when deaf children learn both LSF and French (oral or written)? What happens when hearing children learn French and LSF simultaneously? What happens when hearing children have deaf signing parents?

In order to address these questions, we first present a concise summary of what is known of the history of LSF and its relations to other sign languages, such as ASL and LSQ (Section 2). In order to delve into the question of bilingual language development, which is also bimodal in that it entails development of languages which use different modalities of linguistic perception and production (aural-oral and visual-gestural), a review of the findings of research on sign language acquisition is presented in Section 3, with references to findings on the acquisition of LSF, a domain which has so far received very little attention,[7] at least as far as natural, early language development is concerned. The remainder of the chapter is devoted specifically to bimodal, bilingual language development in both hearing (Section 4.1) and deaf children (Section 4.2).

2.   The boundaries of LSF

The first uses of the term *langue des signes française* 'French sign language' we have found is in Sallagoïty (1975), and in Mottez (1976:51–52): "[…] the familiar French sign language that we should simply call *French sign language*" (our translation).[8] To define the scope of LSF is as difficult as it is for a spoken language that has a recent or no writing system, or a spoken language that has only recently become institutionalized. The usual question is whether sign language variants should be considered distinct members of the same language family, or dialects of the same language. Compared to spoken languages, genetic links between sign languages have been little studied. It is all the more difficult to determine the area of a sign language given that deaf communities are not continuous, either genetically speaking or geographically speaking. In other words, a signer rarely shares her language as a first language with her parents or with her neighbors (see introduction above). These properties seem to be specific to deafness and sign languages.

2.1   A history shared with ASL history

It seems that sign languages have always existed, whenever deaf communities have been constituted. But the 'success' of a sign language variant is clearly linked to how a community of signers arises and extends over others. The history of sign languages is

---

7. See Blondel and Tuller (2000) for a critical review of published linguistic research on LSF.

8. «[…] *la langue familière française des signes que l'on devrait appeler tout simplement* la langue des signes française.»

therefore connected to the history of deaf communities, and especially to the history of the schools or institutions for the deaf.

In 1760 in France, Abbé de l'Epée founded the first school for the deaf where signs were used. His method spread over several schools in France and many schools abroad, during his life and after he died, through the training of deaf and hearing teachers coming from Germany, Poland, Austria, Italy, Spain, Sweden, Portugal, Denmark, Holland, Russia, and so on (Lane 1991[1984]: 74; Presneau 1998: 113). Note that Abbé de l'Epée is often mentioned as a reference for LSF (sometimes it is even said that he invented LSF), although he actually merely used some of the signs the deaf used among themselves, and added a group of signs to correspond with what he thought was missing in LSF when compared to French, such as signs for functional categories (*les signes méthodiques*). The real novelty was the idea of dispensing instruction via the medium of manual shapes based on the natural signs of the pupils, and the fact that this pedagogical method was widely publicized. Presneau (1998: 103) reminds us that Abbé de l'Epée and his followers gave "public lessons [...] to worthy and leading audiences, not only from Paris but also from abroad [...]" (our translation).[9]

In 1816, the young hearing teacher Thomas Gallaudet went from the U.S. to Paris, where he attended classes at the *Saint Jacques* school for the deaf, directed by Abbé de l'Epée and his followers (Lane 1991[1984]: 179). He had been sent to Europe in order to be trained to become the head of the first school for the deaf in Hartford, Connecticut. Gallaudet convinced the young deaf teacher Laurent Clerc to return with him and work as a teacher in Hartford. Clerc went to the United States and began his teaching with the *signes méthodiques* (which he did not use anymore after 1830), LSF, and the local sign language already used by the pupils (Lane 1991[1984]: 72–73). The first pupils of Clerc and Gallaudet came from ten different states, and classes were addressed both to deaf pupils directly and to teachers for the deaf who used then the same method in their state of origin, so that the 'contact signing' that resulted from contacts between LSF and local sign languages rapidly spread over the whole union. Hence, in spite of the fact that this was the French teaching method rather than just LSF that Clerc brought to the United States, it seems that this kind of propagation explains the proximity between the two sign languages. Along these lines, De Santis (1977) and Woodward and De Santis (1977a, 1977b) suggest that ASL was first a Creole resulting from contact between LSF and local sign languages of the United States at the beginning of the XIX century. It is suggested that this is how the French sign language family appeared. This family consists of a group of sign language variants that have historical links; among them one finds ASL, LSQ (*Langue des signes québécoise*, the sign language of francophone Quebec), and several European sign languages.

---

9. «[...] *les leçons publiques* [...] *devant un parterre de notables et de sommités, non seulement parisiens, mais aussi étrangers* [...]»

2.2 LSF and the French-speaking world

The success of the French teaching method and the spontaneous contacts between deaf communities (especially those in relatively close proximity) resulted in the existence of a homogeneous group of sign languages variants. Furthermore, as mentioned above, since signed and spoken languages are in close contact, one could logically think that the French-signing world would correspond geographically to the French-speaking world. In fact, the French-speaking world does not coincide exactly to the boundaries of LSF just as the English-speaking world does not correspond exactly to the boundaries of BSL (British Sign Language) or ASL. Secondly, even if sign language variants belong to a homogeneous group, that is, the same sign language family, it still remains difficult to say if they constitute separate languages or variants of a same language. Consider, for example, the title of Johnston (2002): "BSL, Auslan and NZSL: Three signed languages or one?" What about sign languages in Belgium or Switzerland, given the fact that only parts of these countries are francophone? Finally, drawing boundaries between sign languages is all the more complex since, even in contemporary France, lexical items between varieties of LSF are highly variable and seem to be based more on the history of the schools for the deaf than on geography (for instance, signed lexicons differ more between Poitiers and Tours, which are only 100 km apart, than between Paris and Tours, which are 230 km apart).

As for Belgium, several names exist for the sign language variant used in the Walloon area. According to the official decree recognizing sign language in October 2003, this variant is "the sign language of French-speaking Belgium" (*langue des signes de Belgique francophone, LSBF*). For Loncke (1987), "Belgian Sign Language" is a general expression including the dialects that came from old LSF and that are used by the deaf in Belgium. Nève (1996: 398), in his description of the "*Langue des signes française de Belgique francophone*" ('French Sign Language of French-speaking Belgium'), adds that "signed languages in Belgium – either French-, Dutch- or German-speaking – actually are dialects of the French sign language of Abbé de l'Epée (our translation)".[10] Indeed, according to Francophone Federation for the Deaf in Belgium (*Fédération francophone des sourds de Belgique*) sources, Joseph Henrion, who taught in the first school for the Deaf in Liège, was a pupil in Abbé de l'Epée's institution.

As for Switzerland, it seems that the situation corresponds to what happened in the United States with Laurent Clerc. In 1822, a young deaf man, Isaac Etienne Chomel, went to Geneva where he created the first class for deaf children. He became the first teacher, and then the first director of the school. He came from Paris, where Sicard (Abbé de l'Epée's successor) had been his teacher. Chomel brought with him the French method invented by Abbé de l'Epée. According to the archives of the School for the Deaf (*Centre pour Enfants Sourds de Montbrillant*) in Geneva, the deaf community of Geneva kept in touch with the deaf of Paris and Marseille. There are only a few lex-

---

10. «*les langues signées de Belgique – francophone, néerlandophone et germanophone, en ce qui concerne les langues orales et écrites – sont en fait des dialectes de la langue des signes française de l'Abbé de l'Epée*».

ical differences between the LSF used in Geneva and the LSF used in Paris, as far as we know (see e.g., MOMMY, described above in (3a)). According to Swiss Federation for the Deaf sources, sign language variants in the French-speaking part of Switzerland are usually called LSF.

Nevertheless, as in France, there is some dialectal variation in Swiss LSF, especially between Geneva and rural communities, which have had less contact with French communities. As is the case for deaf signers in France, even if these differences may hamper beginning signers, they do not prevent fluent signers from understanding each other. It seems that, if some of the deaf in these regions call their dialects *langues des signes de Suisse Romande* 'sign languages of French-speaking Switzerland', it is for the same reasons as those of the hearing people who proclaim their linguistic specificity. We should not be surprised to find the same sociolinguistic stakes for the deaf as are found for the hearing in the denomination for their language: The same degree of variation between two communities can be judged by the speakers to be either two dialects of the same language or two separate languages (from a sociolinguistic point of view, see Woll, Sutton-Spence, & Elton 2001). The separate language/dialect question is all the more vexed given the difficulty of doing quantitative studies, and hence their rarity: Both diachronic and synchronic signed databases are still missing for the majority of identified varieties of sign language.

As far as we know, the majority of studies addressing the question of dialects versus separate languages are based either on mutual intelligibility or on comparison between lexicons (lexicostatistics[11] and the glotto-chronological approach). Some exceptions include studies of phonological variation (mainly handshape variations, or change from bi- to uni-manual sign), and morphological or syntactic variations (negative incorporation, classifier constructions have been mentioned), but these phonological and morphosyntactic aspects more often serve to study sociolinguistic variation in a sign language than to distinguish two separate sign languages. The relatively recent cross-linguistic perspective on sign languages (see Baker, van den Bogaerde, & Crasborn 2003) should contribute to identifying aspects specific to a given sign language, and hence will contribute to distinguishing this sign language from others.

This overview concerning the boundaries of LSF has sought to make it clear that sign languages in general, and LSF in particular, are, at the same time, very *representative* of how difficult it is to draw clear boundaries for a language and very *atypical* in

---

11. Lexicostatistics, one method used, consists of comparing the core vocabulary of two languages in order to determine the degree of similarity. According to standard lexico-statistical guidelines, "dialects of the same language should have 81% to 100% rate of cognates, and languages belonging to the same language family should have a 36% to 81% rate of cognates" (Woodward 2000:25). To fit with sign languages characteristics, Woodward adapted the standard list used for oral languages for sign languages. Lexico-statistics was used to compare ASL, BSL, Auslan and NZSL, as we saw previously, but also in studies Woodward carried out on sign languages of India, Costa Rica, or Thailand and Vietnam, and so on.

the way they are transmitted, and hence in the way they are connected to both their speaking counterparts and to other sign languages.

3. Sign Language development

In this section, we briefly summarize aspects of the sign language development in children acquiring sign language naturally, as their L1, from their deaf signing parents. Sign language acquisition is currently an area of active research. A thorough review of the literature can be found in Emmorey (2002) (see also Chamberlain, Morford, & Mayberry 2000; and Morgan & Woll 2002, for recent volumes devoted to articles on sign language acquisition). The results presented here refer mainly to aspects of the development of ASL, which is currently the most studied sign language. However, the existing research on the acquisition of other sign languages (namely British Sign Language, Sign Language of the Netherlands, Japanese Sign Language, and Quebec Sign Language) has found very similar patterns of development (see for instance, Chamberlain et al. 2000; Coerts & Mills 1994; Dubuisson, Lelièvre, Parisot, & Vercaingne-Ménard 2001; Morgan & Woll 2003; Petitto, Katerlos, Levy, Gauna, Tétreault, & Ferraro 2001).

3.1 Early language milestones

A manual version of babbling has been observed in every known deaf community (Emmorey 2002). Manual babbling involves meaningless, cyclic, repetitive movements, produced in a limited spatial area equivalent to the signing space used by adult signers (Meier, Moreland, & Cheek 2000; Petitto & Marentette 1991). Manual babbling also shares handshapes and location features with the first meaningful signs.

The earliest production of signs was found in situations of imitation or in routine contexts by Bonvillian and Folven (1993) who studied the early development of ASL. They are later produced to label new objects or events. These steps are similar to the ones described for the acquisition of first words in oral languages. However, these authors have suggested that signs tend to be produced earlier than words. Very early sign production (between 8 to 11 months) was also reported by Anderson and Reilly (2002), in a group of 7 children, who were studied via an ASL version of the *MacArthur Communicative Development Inventory*. This study found, in a larger sample of 69 children (mean 16;7 months), that two-sign combinations first appeared between 12 and 22 months. This precociousness in sign production has been attributed to early motor control of the manual articulators, early maturation of the visual cortex, and the fact that caregivers can physically control child production (Meier & Newport 1990). However, this sign advantage is no longer generally accepted, most authors arguing that the earliest appearing signs are equivalent to early prelinguistic communicative gestures produced by hearing children (see Meier & Newport 1990; and Emmorey 2002 for a comprehensive discussion). In LSF, the case study of Illana, a hearing child born to a deaf father and a hearing mother and exposed to French and LSF from birth, shows no advantage in sign language, but rather a production of first signs and first words around the same age (see Section 4 for details).

3.2   Development of phonology

The first signs produced by young children are simplified versions (the so-called baby talk) of the equivalent adult signs. Their development has been argued to be related to the phases of motor control development (Boyes-Braem 1990; Dubuisson et al. 2001; Meier et al. 2000). First signs used are also frequent in the language, easy to perceive, and are phonologically unmarked (Emmorey 2002; Marentette & Mayberry 2000). At the phonological level, signs are composed of five parameters. The first parameters acquired are *location* of the sign, then *movement* and then *handshape* (Meier et al. 2000; Morford 2000). Later, children will reproduce the correct *orientation* of the hand as well as the *non-manual components* (facial expressions and head movements). The combination of the five parameters in one sign is mastered in ASL by the age of four (Emmorey 2002). Boyes-Braem (1990) describes four stages of development, which are illustrated in Figure 4 (see Boyes-Braem 1990: 112–115, for complete illustration). The first group of handshapes is produced around the age of 12 months and involves natural handshapes that children already use in their interaction with the world (such as closed fist, pointing gesture). Later development includes more complex handshapes that require better mastery of fine motor control, including finger differentiation and finger inhibition (stages 2, 3 and 4). Similar findings were observed for Quebec Sign Language (Dubuisson et al. 2001), British Sign Language and Finnish Sign Language (Boyes-Braem 1990).

3.3   Lexical development

Two studies focus on the composition of the early lexicon in ASL. The first study was conducted on 22 children followed longitudinally (Bonvillian & Folven 1993). The second study was based on parental reports of 69 children (Anderson & Reilly 2002). They both come to the conclusion that the semantic categories and the grammatical categories are very similar for ASL and English, with a high number of nouns, mostly referring to animals, vehicles and household. However, both studies mention that the size of the lexicon increases gradually; the vocabulary spurt typically observed in oral language development was not found. Anderson and Reilly (2002) also noticed that the percentage of predicates in the vocabulary of children learning ASL is consistently higher than in English-speaking children. They suggest that this phenomenon may be related to the high frequency of verb initial or verb final utterances in ASL.

Although sign languages differ from oral languages in the extent to which lexical items display iconicity (for obvious modality-related reasons), this difference has not been found to be related in a difference in lexical development in children (cf. Newport

Stage 1

Stage2

Stage3

Stage4

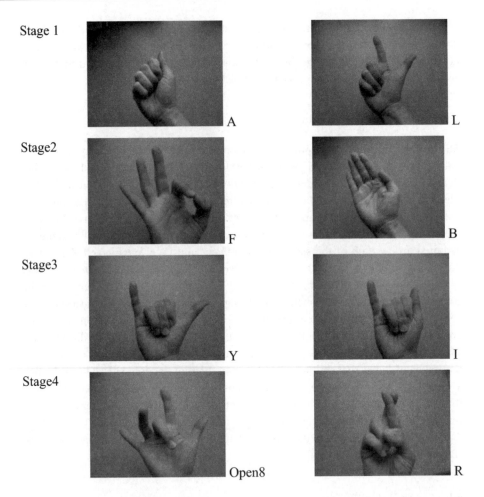

A

L

F

B

Y

I

Open8

R

Figure 4. Development of handshape according to Boyes-Braem's (1990) four stages

& Meier 1985). Thus, lexical items whose form imitates their meaning are not acquired earlier than non-iconic items, and, quite generally, the same items are found in early lexicons of signing and speaking children (see Section 4, for illustration of this fact).

3.4 Acquisition of morpho-syntax

In studies of morpho-syntactic aspects of sign language acquisition, a few areas have received considerable attention (for a review see Lillo-Martin 1999). These involve aspects that are characteristic of sign languages: (a) Pronouns, which form a complex system based on pointing gestures oriented toward (absent or present) participants; (b) Verb agreement, lexically restricted to certain verbs, and expressed through movement toward spatial participant loci; and (c) Classifier constructions (see discussion of (2) above), a complex grammatical gender system, in which physical properties of objects are incorporated into verbs in the form of agreement. The results of acquisition studies of these properties, which are briefly summarized here, show that major early milestones once again follow the chronology observed in oral language development, and that more complex aspects of the target language are mastered well after the primary language acquisition period (0–7 years), as in oral language acquisition.

3.4.1 *Acquisition of pronouns*

Beginning at about 9 months, deaf children (like hearing children) produce (non-linguistic) pointing gestures oriented towards people and objects. It is argued that these elements take on linguistic status little by little. Petitto (1987) presents data showing that some children learning sign language go through a stage (between ages 1;6 to 2;0) in which they make reversal errors (between "you" and "me"), something they would not do if these elements were merely deictic pointing gestures. Finally, by the age of 2–2;6, deaf children are able to use pointing gestures as pronouns by pointing towards referents which are physically present (Emmorey 2002). In the adult language, pronouns referring to persons/objects that are not present are produced by assigning to each of them a specific portion of the signing space (locus) using a combination of labelling and pointing. This kind of pronoun is more cognitively demanding; comprehension is reached by around age of 3 or 4, and errors continue in production until age 5 (Lepot-Froment 2000; Lillo-Martin 1991; Lillo-Martin & Klima 1990; Maller, Singleton, Supalla, & Wix 1999).

3.4.2 *Acquisition of verb agreement*

A sub-category of sign language verbs use the directionality of movement to encode within the verbal sign its subject (starting point) and object (ending point) (directional verbs). For instance, the LSF verb TELEPHONE is produced with a movement whose starting point and ending point will vary: "I call you" will be signed with a movement from the signer to towards the addressee, whereas "He called her" will be signed with a movement starting from the locus previously assigned to "he" towards the locus assigned to "she" (for a comprehensive linguistic description for LSF, see Moody 1983; or Schembri 2003 for a more general discussion on directional verbs in sign languages). In the early stages of development, children tend to use a frozen form for directional verbs or produce reversed movements. Agreement with physical referents is mastered in ASL around the age of 3–3;6 (Newport & Meier 1985). Then, a phase of overgeneralization has been observed where all the verbs (including non-directional ones) are modified. Verbal agreement is fully mastered by the age of 6 (Lillo-Martin, Bellugi, Struxness, & O'Grady 1985; Bellugi, van Hoek, Lillo-Martin, & O'Grady 1988), and, regarding forms involving multiple morphemes, by the age of 7–8 (Newport & Meier 1986).

3.4.3 *Acquisition of classifier constructions*

Classifier constructions, which have been compared to complex gender systems found in noun classes in Bantu (see Benedicto & Brentari 2004 for recent presentation and analysis of classifier constructions in ASL), are complex signs that contain simultaneous morpho-syntactic encoding of physical properties of an object, spatial relations between two objects and/or movement of one object through space (for the most recent description, see Emmorey 2003). Because of their linguistic complexity and the bi-manual coordination they involve, classifier constructions are usually mastered only around the age of 8–9 (Emmorey 2002). However, first attempts were found by Slobin, Hoiting, Kuntze, Lindert, Weinberg, Pyers, Anthony, Biederman and Thumann (2003) studying children in their third year, interacting with their caregiver in an experimental task involving small objects, both in California and the Netherlands.

3.5   Narrative development

3.5.1   *Cohesion and anaphoric devices*
The introduction of a new referent is created by assigning it a portion of the signing space by means of eye gaze, directional verbs or classifier constructions from/towards the assigned space. The best adult narrators usually combine all these devices in order to increase narrative cohesion (Anthony 2002). However, mastery of this set of complex devices is not reached until adolescence: Slobin et al. (2003) found that five-year-old narrators often forget to properly introduce referents, and Mann (2001) described an evolution between two groups of 8–11 year-olds and 12–13 year-olds: The younger children used mainly pointing and single classifier constructions, whereas the older children tend to integrate these devices in more complex role playing.

3.5.2   *Referential shift*
Sign languages use specific spatial-visual devices to express different physical/psychological perspectives within a single narration (Poulin & Miller 1994). A so-called referential shift (Emmorey 2002; Engberg-Pedersen 1993) is produced by body and eye gaze shifts. The narrator can thus leave a neutral perspective and temporarily take on the role of one of the characters in order to tell the story from his/her perspective, and then shift back to a neutral perspective, or even shift to another character's perspective. Referential shifts involve the use of classifier constructions, including body classifiers where the narrator's body parts become the character's/object's body. These linguistically and cognitively demanding devices are not fully mastered until late adolescence in ASL, although Maller et al. (1999) mentioned that children start to shift from neutral perspective to one character's perspective at the age of 3;6. A recent study on British Sign Language acquisition similarly shows that body classifiers are understood by only 40% of the 3 to 5 years-olds in an experimental setting, 70% of the 6 to 9 years-olds and 90% of the 9 to 12 years-olds. At this later age, still only 70% of the participants were able to produce those classifiers correctly (Morgan & Woll 2003).

Summarizing, studies of natural sign language acquisition have revealed remarkable similarities with oral language acquisition. However, as was pointed out above, early, monolingual acquisition of sign language undoubtedly represents the exception rather than the rule, as most children learning a sign language either do so simultaneously with acquisition of an oral language (in the case of hearing children), or as a late L2 in the context of atypical L1 acquisition of an oral language (in the case of most deaf children). We turn to these (much more frequent) cases of bimodal bilingual language development, concentrating on children, both hearing and deaf, who grow up acquiring both French and LSF.

4. Bimodal bilingual language development

4.1 Hearing children acquiring French and LSF

Hearing children with deaf parents form a heterogeneous group from the point of view of the nature of linguistic input in the home. Nevertheless, these individuals do have in common some form of bimodal bilingualism, and very often share some sort of common cultural identity. After presenting the varied linguistic situations of children of deaf parents (so-called CODAs), we concentrate for the remainder of the section on the case of balanced, early input. First, we present results of the study of production data of bilingual language development, looking at major linguistics milestones and other aspects of early development in both languages, as compared to early monolingual development in each of the languages. As we will see, there is ample evidence demonstrating clear similarities in development of the two languages. At the same time, close investigation of specific questions linked to the communication channel reveals areas which are specific to bilingual language development in two modalities, raising a number of questions concerning the status of early productions: What is the syntactic distribution between simultaneity and sequentiality? What is the status and role of pointing gestures in bimodal child production?

4.1.1 *Growing up as a "CODA"*
Children of deaf parents, referred as CODAs or Children of Deaf Adults, are "adults who acquired both signed and spoken languages naturally without explicit instruction" (Emmorey et al. 2003:2). It is all the more difficult to estimate their number in that studies addressing specificities of their outcome, to our knowledge, are few and recent (see e.g. Bishop & Hicks 2005). In France especially, it seems that CODAs have not yet formed organizations like those existing in the USA, although we know through individual accounts that most of them immediately identify with the description Emmorey et al. (2003:2) give: "Hearing adults who grew up in Deaf families constitute an important bilingual community. Many identify themselves as CODAs or Children of Deaf Adults who have a cultural identity defined in part by their bimodal bilingualism, as well as by shared childhood experiences in Deaf families".

One variable distinguishing hearing children exposed to both LSF and French is whether they grow up in a bilingual home (with one deaf-signing parent and one hearing-speaking parent for instance), or in a monolingual home (both parents are deaf and sign). When language input is distinct in the home and outside of the home, the next question is: Does exposure to the two languages begin at the same time? Nowadays, health and social services encourage deaf parents to find a hearing-speaking caregiver for their hearing child, so that the child is exposed to oral language as soon as possible, but this is not the case for the majority of older CODAs. However, the situation can be more complex than "one language at home, the other language outside of the home" since parents may adapt the way they sign to the hearing status of the child and, in a bilingual home, the nature of language input may depend in part on whether the hearing parent signs fluently or not. A final, important aspect is mentioned in some accounts of CODAs: Signing until recently was believed by many parents to be harmful to oral language development and thus deaf parents thought they had to speak to their children and sign only among themselves. Consequently their hearing children grew up with positive attitudes about French and negative attitudes about LSF (see *Surdités* 2000,[12] for an issue devoted to CODAs in France).

All these considerations mean that acquisition of LSF and French by hearing children cannot really be addressed as a homogeneous situation. Woll and Morgan (2002:293) mention that "some early research on hearing children in Deaf families [...] focus[ed] solely on spoken language skills and report[ed] these children to be at risk of language delay". The risk of misinterpreting the bilingual outcome is also mentioned by Emmorey et al (2003:10) in their study of ASL-English bilingual communication: "Such speech should not be viewed as 'bad English', but as a form of bilingual communication that is parallel to the code-mixing that occurs with unimodal bilinguals". To the best of our knowledge, there are no studies on the prevalence of delayed spoken language (or of its eventual long-term effects) among hearing children with deaf parents. In a review of published work on this topic, Schiff-Myers (1993) concludes that discrepancy between the speech heard from a deaf parent and that from other sources does not interfere with oral language acquisition, and that oral language can be learned with much less verbal input than is normally available.

We will focus here on balanced bilingual situations, drawing from a longitudinal study we have done on a hearing child simultaneously developing French and LSF. In this study (see Blondel, Lecourt, & Tuller 2004; Blondel & Tuller to appear; Lecourt 2003; Révérand 2004), Tuller, Blondel and collaborators collected 21 samples (of 30–60 minutes each) of spontaneous production from Illana, who is acquiring French and LSF in a natural setting. Her father is a deaf signer and a child of deaf parents; her mother is hearing, and a fluent signer. Illana was about 3 months old when she first attended a day-care center, an environment which is exclusively French-speaking, but she is also in frequent contact with her deaf grandfather and with other signers in the local deaf community. In other words, this child has been exposed to both LSF and French since birth, and therefore is a case of simultaneous bilingual acquisition. During recording sessions, which range from age 0;6;7 to 2;10;4, Illana mainly interacts

---

12. *Surdités. Enfants de parents sourds* 2, juin 2000. Paris: Association GESTES.

Table 1. Major developmental language milestones for Illana

Milestone	Age / Session for Illana	Data from acquisition literature
Pointing Gesture	8;05	Average age of 11 mo., but attested at 8 mo. (Butterworth 2003)
		First deictic gestures, 10–12 mo. (Caselli & Volterra 1990)
Oral Word	10;00	French monolinguals: 9–14 mo.
SIGN	11;00	Approximately 12 mo. (see Emmorey 2002 for review)
Oral Word + Oral Word	19;00	French-LSQ bilinguals: 17 mo. (LSQ) and 20 mo. (French) (Petitto et al. 2001; Holowka et al. 2002) French monolinguals: 17–26 mo.
SIGN + SIGN		

(in ordinary daily activities at home) with her father, her hearing bilingual mother, one or two hearing investigators and, more rarely, with her deaf, signing grandfather.

4.1.2 *Similarities in early language development*

Results of the longitudinal Illana corpus gathered and analyzed by Tuller et al. are consistent with the idea that bilingual (bimodal) language development gives rise to parallel progression in French and LSF. More precisely, the authors observed in Illana's language production the same major stages at comparable ages as those observed in other studies of language development, in mono- and bilingual contexts. Thus, beginning our survey with the earliest milestones, we videotaped during the 8;5 session a manual form of babbling previously mentioned to us by the child's parents. Interestingly, several of the more robust occurrences of manual babbling[13] were produced simultaneously with oral babbling. Oral babbling was recorded starting at the first session, at 6;7. However, the first session with a significant number of occurrences of canonical oral babbling is also at 8;5. Table 1 summarizes major stages in Illana's language development, and how they compare with results from the literature. Illana's first pointing gestures were identified at 8 months, which is consistent with the relevant literature. The onset of the one-word stage for Illana was at essentially the same time for both oral words (10 months) and signs (11 months), and fits squarely within the period in which first words appear in monolingual acquisition of French and in monolingual sign language acquisition (around 12 months). Likewise, the first occurrence of sequences of two signs was found in the same session as the first occurrence of two-word strings, and, once again, this timing is consistent with what is known about monolingual French acquisition, and with what is known about bilingual, bimodal language development (see also Petitto & Kovelman 2003).

An important result of study of bilingual acquisition is the evidence it has been argued to provide that children acquiring two languages seem to be constructing two

---

13. See Petitto and Marentette (1991), Meier and Willerman (1995) and Meier (2000) for criteria for the identification of gestural babbling.

Table 2. Illana's first lexical items (6;07–17;17)

LSF	French	Both languages	Emblems
BATH	*tiens* 'here'	'Daddy'	'no'
SOCCER	*voilà* 'there's'	'dog'	'yes'
GRANDPA	*cuillère* 'spoon'	'head'	'goodbye'
SLEEP	*Maman* 'Mommy'	'rabbit'	
BEAR	*Nin-nin*	'again'	
LIGHT	*chaussure* 'shoe'	'bread'	
SANTA-CLAUS	*caca* 'pooh-pooh'	'eat'*	
COOKIE	*chaussette* 'sock'	'pig'	
BIRD	*canard* 'duck'	'no'	
TORTOISE	*non* 'no'	'cat'	
WORK	*guili-guili* 'goochy-goochy-goo'	'drink'*	
BRAVO			
THANK-YOU**			
GIVE!**			

*PROTO-SIGN or PROTO-WORD. PROTO-SIGN refers to any symbolic gesture that does not correspond to, or even vaguely resemble, a conventional LSF sign. For example, Illana sticks her tongue out and several times in rapid succession with the clear meaning of 'eat'. Similarly, PROTO-WORD designates vocalizations that do not correspond to a conventional French word and nevertheless have a symbolic function such as *miam-miam* 'yum-yum/eat' or *guili-guili* 'goochy-goochy-goo'.
**HOME-SIGN. This term designates symbolic manual gestures that are not conventional LSF lexical items, but that are used as conventional items by all family members. The home-sign GIVE!' for instance, is a five-handshape sign with palm oriented upwards and with an opening-closing finger movement.

grammars, from the very beginning stages of lexical acquisition. This is shown notably by the proportion of words for the same referent in both languages from the beginning of the one-word stage (Holowka, Brosseau-Lapré, & Petitto 2002). We assessed the emerging lexicon from age 6;07–17;17 (the first 13 sessions of the Illana corpus), and found that roughly one-third of Illana's lexical items (excluding repetitions of adults) were exclusively in French, one-third exclusively in LSF and one-third were items found in both languages. Table 2, in which phonological deviations are glossed over, presents these early lexical items. Note that "emblems", gestural forms commonly produced by hearing-speaking people in the surrounding culture, such as waving goodbye, are also (parts of) adult signs in LSF.

Cross-language synonyms (words and signs with the same meaning) were observed from the very beginning of the one-word stage, a finding which suggests that Illana is indeed simultaneously developing two separate grammars, from early on.

As is the case for spoken 'baby talk', 'errors' or 'deviations' in signed 'baby-talk' displayed regular patterns: Forms produced by children differ from the target adult forms, but the approximation or substitution process is not at all random. During the previously mentioned early period (from age 6;07 to 17;17), Illana, for instance, uses one hand instead of both hands to sign BEAR, RABBIT, GLOVE, CAT and TORTOISE. Apparently, single-handed forms are less complex than the bi-manual forms. Secondly, Illana tends to produce manual and non-manual components of a single sign separately: For instance, she signs PIG either solely by wrinkling her nose (without any manual articulator), or solely with her extended index touching twice her nose (without the facial expression), whereas the adult sign for 'pig' requires simultaneous production of both of these components. Finally, we observed the so-far most documented child error in the literature: Handshape acquisition (for a state-of-the-art account, see Morford 2000). Indeed, phonological analysis of Illana's early signs (from age 6 to 18 months) revealed striking systematicity in the nature of the errors. As explained above, signs are composed of the contrastive parameters of handshape, movement, orientation, localization, and, for some signs, the use of two hands as well as the use of facial expression. Of these parameters, handshape has been found to be one of the most frequent sources of error (see Conlin, Mirus, & Meier 2000). Phonological analysis of the early signs produced by Illana showed that signs whose handshape was target-consistent were signs with the following three handshapes: [1] (index finger extended), as in MAMAN, [A] (closed fist), as in BATH or COOKIE, and [5] (all five fingers extended and spread), as in the sign BRAVO. Furthermore, target-deviant handshapes involved substitution of precisely one of these three handshapes for the (more complex) target handshape, as illustrated in Figure 5, where Illana's substitution is given on the left, and the target handshape involving two or three fingers or partial closure of the fist is given on the right.

In other words, the dominant handshapes in Illana's early production were the three forms [1], [A] and [5]. This result conforms to what has been found for monolingual sign language acquisition, where the [5], [1], [A] and [B] handshapes are the first produced by young children (Marentette & Mayberry 2000). The fact that the B handshape was not one of the early forms for Illana also mirrors the results of the sign language acquisition literature. Indeed, B handshape only appears in stage 2 of development in Boyes-Braem's 1990 description of ASL acquisition). In addition, Marentette and Mayberry (2000) report that the most common substitution found in their study of a child acquiring ASL was [5] in place of [B], and this substitution was also noted by Orlansky and Bonvillian (1988).

Marentette and Mayberry argue that the first primes acquired are those that are easy to produce, perceptually salient, and frequent in the target language (see also Boyes-Baem 1990). Articulatory ease of production for young children seems to involve; (1) Either fully extended or entirely folded fingers ([B] or [A], but not handshapes involving partially bent fingers such as [Bbc] above); (2) With the exception of the index finger, all fingers in the same position (thus [B], [1] and [A], but not [Ubc] or [1hc]); (3) Spread fingers rather than fingers held tightly together ([5] instead of [B]). Unsurprisingly, these are also the most frequent handshapes in the target language. Likewise, from a perceptual point of view these three handshapes are maximally contrastive – all fingers fully extended and spread versus all fingers folded into a fist, versus a single extended (index) finger, a result which is strongly reminiscent of the vowel triangle /i, u, a/ in oral languages, which also corresponds not only to maxi-

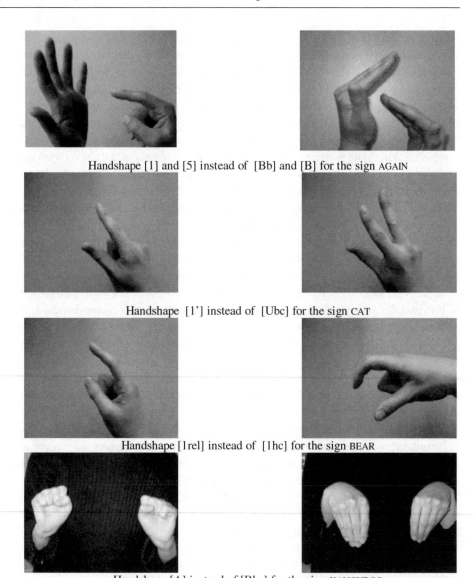

Handshape [1] and [5] instead of [Bb] and [B] for the sign AGAIN

Handshape [1'] instead of [Ubc] for the sign CAT

Handshape [1rel] instead of [1hc] for the sign BEAR

Handshape [A] instead of [Bbc] for the sign KANGUROO

Figure 5. Early handshape substitutions

mum perceptual saliency, but also to frequency in input, cross-linguistic markedness, and ease of articulation.

To sum up, simultaneous acquisition of French and French sign language looks like monolingual development of each of these languages, in terms of chronology, but also in terms of target-deviant productions. The study of Illana has shown that her language development resembles ordinary French development and ordinary sign language development despite the fact that she is hearing and that she is learning both

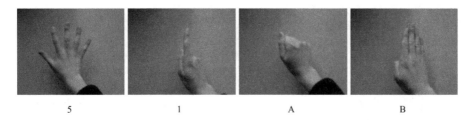

5   1   A   B

Figure 6. The [B], [1], [A] and [5] handshapes

languages at the same time. In this respect, bimodal bilingual development does not differ from bilingual development involving a single modality.

4.1.3 Modality and bilingual language development

However, the bilingual acquisition of a signed language and a spoken language is not completely analogous to the bilingual acquisition of two spoken languages (or two signed languages). The bimodality of this bilingualism makes it possible to investigate questions that cannot be addressed (or not in the same way) when studying monomodal bilingual language development. We will illustrate this by examining first of all code-mixing, a feature of all bilingual development, but which in bimodal bilingualism is particularly rich in that not only a single utterance can contain words in two different languages, but words may be produced simultaneously by virtue of the fact that each language uses different articulators (those of the oral channel and those of the gestural channel). How do young children take advantage of this added dimension? We then turn to the relation between prelinguistic gestures and linguistic production. A detailed study of the status of pointing gestures in the Illana corpus sheds new light on the role of pointing gestures in the early stages of language development.

Petitto et al. (2001), in a comparative study of French-English and French-LSQ bilingual language acquisition, argue that the phenomenon of (intra-sentential) code-switching stems not from a confused underlying representation, but rather supports the hypothesis of simultaneous development of two grammars. These authors show that the rate of code-switching for each child they studied correlates with the rate of code-switching found in their parents' speech, and that it also correlates with the language of the child's conversational partner. When children produce utterances with code-switching, the change in language does not occur sporadically, half in one language half in the other, but rather children produce an utterance in one of the languages (generally that of their interlocutor) in which they introduce, in a semantically appropriate fashion, one or two words from the other language. One of the fascinating aspects of bimodal code-mixing is the rich array of formal possibilities it allows due to the fact that oral articulation can be produced both sequentially to, and simultaneously with gestural articulation, which itself can involve hands, facial expression, and other body movements (head, shoulders, etc.). Indeed the frequent use of the term "code-mixing", rather than "code-switching", for the case of *bimodal*, bilingual production reflects this simultaneity.

In our case study of Illana (see in particular Lecourt 2003; and Révérand 2004), simultaneous production of a word with a sign appeared a few months after the first occurrences of isolated words and signs (10 and 11 months, respectively), at 14 months. These first occurrences of code-mixing all involved mixes in which the two elements had the same semantic content, as in (5):

(5)   a.   *chat*   'cat'
           CAT   (14;10)

      b.   *tête*   'head'
           HEAD   (14;10)

Shortly thereafter simultaneous combinations of two elements having different semantic content, as in (6), appeared:

(6)   a.   *Papa*   'Papa'
           AGAIN   (15;08)

      b.   *nin-nin nin-nin*   'Nin-nin Nin-nin'
           AGAIN AGAIN AGAIN   (15;27)

Interestingly, it was only when evidence of the two-word stage emerged in both LSF and in French, at 19 months, that *sequential* code-mixing also appeared. In example (7a), we see a sequence in which the word and the sign have the same semantic content. In (7b), the sequence involves a sign in LSF followed by a sequence in French which contains a word identical to the LSF sign ('doll').

(7)   a.   *chat* CAT   'cat cat'   (19;00)
      b.   DOLL [a] *pousser poupée*   'doll [a] push doll'   (19;00)

As combinations become more intricate in each of the two languages, more complex mixes emerge in which complete sentences are produced simultaneously in each of the two languages. Notice that in these cases, illustrated in (8), the simultaneous production involves lexical items with the same semantic content:

(8)   a.   *Oral*:   *ça fait do(do)*   'that does night'
           Right hand: PT_____   (pointing gesture)
           Left hand: SLEEP
                          'It goes night-night'   (22;17)

      b.   *Il boit. Ca y est*   'He drinks. That's it.'
           DRINK FINISHED
           'He's finished drinking'   (2;7;26)

In the examples in (9), we see mixes in which there is a partial over-lap in the semantic content of the French and the LSF. In (9a), both the French and the LSF contain the lexical item 'like/same', but while the former contains the complement ('Illana'), the latter contains the subject ('it'). The example in (9b) contains a complete sentence in both French (assuming that [E] is the determiner *le* 'the') and in LSF, but while the subject in French is a lexical phrase, it is a pronoun in LSF.

(9) a.   *comme Illana* 'same as Illana'
           PT SAME
           'It's the same as Illana'   (2;3;14)

     b. *Oral:*   *[E] perroquet pleure pas ?* '[E] parrot cry not'
        Head: NEGATION
        Manual: PT CRY NOT PT 'It cry not it'
                    'The parrot does not cry?'   (2;3;14)

Examples like those in (10) were rare, occurring only in files after age two and a half. In these mixes, the content of the French and LSF components of the utterance is entirely different. Whereas mixes up to this point all seem to involve partial or total repetition in one language of material expressed in the other language, in these particular later mixes, the utterance is formed with lexical items produced in only one of the two languages. As it was found for semantically congruent mixing, it appears that simultaneous mixing of semantically complementary material appears earlier than sequential mixing of such material:

(10) a.   *ma cabane* 'my playhouse'
           WANT
           'I want my playhouse'   (2;7;26)

     b. *Papa Papa* 'Papa Papa'
           CHATTER-BOX
           'Papa is a chatter-box'   (2;10;4)

     c. FISH *et une feuille* 'fish and a leaf'
           'There's a fish and a leaf'   (2;10;4)

Summarizing, language mixing in the Illana corpus, which contains files up to age 2;10;4, involves much more simultaneous mixing than sequential mixing. This result confirms the findings of Petitto et al. (2001:486–487) on two French/LSQ bilinguals, both of whom are older than Illana at her oldest session (one was taped between age 2;10;11 and 3;04;4, and the other from 3;09;00 to 4;03;24). 94% of these children's mixes were simultaneous. Furthermore, Illana's simultaneous mixes were much more likely to be semantically congruent than not, a result that also mirrors Petitto et al's conclusion on the basis of the two older children. These results are also very similar to those found by Emmorey et al. (2003): An analysis of production of eleven CODA adults revealed that 95% of their mixes were simultaneous, while 94% were semantically congruent. In other words, the emergence of code-mixing is not chaotic. We return to this property of bimodal code-mixing in Section 4.2.4 below. Rather, there appears to be an orderly progression, in which simultaneity precedes sequentiality, and semantic congruence precedes semantic complementarity. Although much remains to be understood about the development of bimodal code-mixing (and about adult bimodal code-mixing), we can conclude here that even very young children take advantage of the structural possibilities offered by bimodality, and they do so in an orderly way.

Another area in which bimodal bilingual language development provides interesting evidence is that of the role of prelinguistic gestures in the unfolding of more complex grammatical structures. Study of pointing gestures in monolingual oral language development has shown that these play a transitional role in the elaboration of two-word propositional combinations (see Capirci, Iverson, Pizzuto, & Volterra 1996; Goldin-Meadow & Butcher 2003). It is hypothesized that combinations of elements which are expressed in different modalities, viz. gesture and speech, precede expression of two elements in the same (spoken) modality. In young children, Goldin-Meadow and Butcher suggest that knowledge that isn't sufficiently developed in a single modality can be expressed by combining two modalities. Gesture, according to Goldin-Meadow and Butcher, provides the child with means to express information which is not yet expressed by speech. What about language development in a language in which linguistic articulation uses gesture? Is the transitional role of pointing gestures related to the fact that they involve a modality different from speech, or rather, is it related to the fact that these elements are non-linguistic communicative devices? Does language development give evidence for the (later) linguistic status of pointing gestures in sign language?

Bimodal bilingual language development provides a unique avenue in which to explore these questions. Blondel et al. (2004) and Blondel and Tuller (to appear) show, based on the Illana corpus, that the first occurrence of each new kind of combination (oral/gestural/mixed, simultaneous/sequential) *including* a pointing gesture precedes the comparable one *without* a pointing gesture. This was found to be the case at very early stages in which combinations were composed of prelinguistic vocalizations and gestures,[14] proto-signs, proto-words, as well as at later stages when combinations also included home-signs, French words, and LSF signs. Thus, combinations consisting of production (simultaneous and sequential) of a pointing gesture and prelinguistic vocalization or gesture were found early on (before age 11 months). At 13;13, more complex combinations appeared in which pointing gestures were produced simultaneously with proto-words, proto-signs, and words. These combinations, which all had as one of the combined elements a pointing gesture, were produced prior to the appearance at 14;10 of combinations in which both items were words or signs.

The development of sequential combinations shows the same progression. The first sequential combinations including a pointing gesture (PT) with a lexical item (either oral or signed), as in (11), precede the first sequential 'word + proto-word', 'SIGN + word', 'SIGN + SIGN' or 'word + word' combinations, as in (12).

(11) a. (14;10) PT + SIGN + PT   PT>*glass* + WATER + PT>*glass*
      b. (14;10) SIGN + PT   DOG + PT>*interviewer* + *father* + *herself*
      c. (14;10) PT + word   PT>*shampoo* + *tiens*! 'here!'

---

14. These terms are used to refer to early vocalizations and manual activities, including syllabic and non-syllabic babbling (vocal and manual) (see Petitto 1988; Meier & Willerman 1995).

(12) a. (15;27) word + proto-word *Maman guili-guili* 'Mommy goochy-goochy-goo'
       b. (19;00) word + SIGN   chat CAT
       c. (19;00) SIGN + SIGN   FISH EAT
       d. (19;00) word + word   *pousser Papa* 'push Daddy'

Goldin-Meadow and Butcher's (2003) study of the role of pointing gestures in the development of oral language concludes that gestures offer children a way to express information that is not yet expressed via speech. It is suggested that recourse to a different modality allows for production of early propositional combinations, and signals that production of genuine two-word propositions is imminent. Blondel and Tuller (op. cit.) show that Illana's pointing gestures are precursors not only to her later syntactic development in French, but also in LSF. Her earliest pointing gestures are argued to be entirely extra-linguistic, occurring several months before her first (proto-)words and (proto-)signs. The fact that emergence of propositions for Illana follows the same chronology in speech and in sign, with pointing gestures playing a role in transition to complete propositions in each language, would appear to indicate that the precursor role of pointing gestures has to do with their non-linguistic status at this stage, and not with the fact that they use a different modality from (oral) language.

Pointing gestures not only use the same modality as sign language, but these forms also correspond to what have been analyzed as pronouns (and definite determiners) in LSF and other sign languages. Thus, a first person singular pronoun corresponds to a PT to the speaker, second person to a PT to the addressee, and so on. Blondel and Tuller argued that early pointing gestures are non-linguistic. What evidence is there that their status changes? In fact, bimodal bilingual language development helps shed light on this question. The Illana corpus reveals that pointing gestures display several new properties (pointing gestures with an animate target produced with a verb; absent, animate reference, co-occurrence in the same utterance with a French pronoun) at exactly the same time (19 months) as pronouns appear in French and robust predicative relations emerge in LSF (as well as in French and in mixes). This constellation of facts strongly suggests that pointing gestures therefore have acquired pronominal status at this age, which corresponds to the age found by Petitto (1987) for the emergence of pronouns in monolingual acquisition of ASL (18 months). The close relationship between these new properties of pointing gestures and the emergence of syntax in LSF suggests that pointing gestures do indeed have grammatical status in this language. Indeed, if they were essentially pragmatic extra-linguistic elements, the fact that their evolution parallels the evolution of syntax would be entirely coincidental.

The study of the simultaneous development of French and LSF reveals the striking similarities between oral language development and visuo-gestural language development. Major linguistic milestones follow the same chronology, and the emergence of syntax follows the same pattern at the same age, with pointing gestures serving as a transition to mature propositional structure in each of the languages. Children with early complete access to both French and LSF develop each of these languages in an orderly way which follows known chronologies for monolingual acquisition of these languages. From the earliest stages, these children engage in code-mixing which exploits the bimodal nature of their bilingualism.

4.2 Acquisition of LSF and of French by deaf children

Deaf children can be divided in two distinct categories: Those born to deaf, signing parents (at most 10%), and those born to hearing parents (at least 90%), as mentioned in the introduction of this chapter. The linguistic situation of the two populations is therefore drastically different. While the first are learning a sign language as a natural first language in similar conditions to those in which hearing children are learning an oral language (see Section 2), the second will learn some oral language (depending on their degree of hearing loss) and maybe some sign language, depending on their parents' choice/proficiency and on availability of relevant community services. Indeed, these parents, in the best-case scenario, will start to learn a sign language after their child has been diagnosed for deafness; however, since diagnosis typically isn't made in France until the child is over a year old, sign language input will begin late. The heterogeneity in linguistic exposure found in this second group, which represents the vast majority of deaf children, presents a challenge for the study of language acquisition in this context.

In France and in the French-speaking part of Belgium, current deaf education policy does not promote systematic bilingual French/LSF programs. Depending on the schools, LSF might be taught as a first language, including grammar classes, it might be used by interpreters for deaf students integrated in mainstream classrooms, used in special education for some communicative settings, or even not provided at all (see Cuxac 1999; Millet 1990). Therefore, many deaf individuals discover LSF only much later in life, through their contacts with the deaf community. On the contrary, French is taught early in all programs, most of the time as a first language. Emphasis is given to written French, although deaf children generally receive regular training in oral French, through a specific type of instruction given by speech-language therapists. Oral French is often used as the language of communication/instruction in the classroom (Mugnier & Millet 2003). Language mixes are also frequent, especially French-based language combined with some signs, which is used as the main means of communication by most hearing teachers with deaf students (Millet 1999).

The situation is rather different in the French-speaking part of Switzerland, where bilingualism is promoted in public schools for the deaf. The curriculum includes LSF conversation and grammar classes, and French is approached as a second language taught by a team of deaf and hearing teachers. Oral French is also provided on a daily basis by speech-language therapists.

Summarizing, nearly all deaf children growing up in European francophone countries are exposed and trained, to some degree, in oral French, regardless of the type of educational environment they evolve in. Nearly all of them also come into at least some contact, at some point, with LSF. All of them will be confronted with written French, the language of the surrounding culture.[15] In other words, deaf children will be growing up acquiring both French and French Sign Language. What does this entail? We look first at how they develop LSF and what their LSF looks like. We then turn to the acquisition of written French (4.2.2) and oral French (4.2.3). Finally, we examine what is known about the interaction between acquisition in the two languages (4.2.4) and the types of language mixes produced by this population (4.2.5).

4.2.1 *Acquisition of LSF*

The acquisition of LSF by deaf children born to deaf native signer parents has only been studied marginally (see however Blondel & Tuller 2000, for a review of studies addressing this subject, and Section 3.1 for acquisition of LSF by hearing children born to deaf native signer parents). Niederberger (2004) studied the LSF proficiency of deaf children born to hearing parents and raised bilingually in oral/written French and LSF. These data provide a window on the acquisition of LSF, although the specific situation encountered by these children cannot be directly compared to a natural first language acquisition, as mentioned earlier.

The 39 participants in the Niederberger's study consisted of 26 girls and 13 boys, ages 8 to 17, severely or profoundly deaf and enrolled in bilingual programs in the French speaking/signing part of Switzerland. Their LSF skills were tested at the morpho-syntactic and narrative levels, using an assessment tool, the *TELSF, Test de LSF*, adapted from the *TASL, Test of ASL* (Niederberger, Aubonney, Dunant-Sauvin, Palama, Aubonney, Delachaux-Djapo, & Frauenfelder 2001; Prinz, Strong, & Kuntze 1994). Four psycholinguistic tasks were presented to each participant individually, in order to evaluate their ability to comprehend and produce LSF narratives and LSF classifier constructions, that encode physical properties of objects and spatial relations in complex verb forms (see 3.4.3 for details). Their answers were then compared to the answers of a control group of 12 deaf non-native signer adults from the deaf community of the same geographic area.

Data show that these learners are able to produce adequate classifiers in a task of story recall, although there is a lot of quantitative variation within the group. Similar quantitative variation is found among the deaf adults, but they produce significantly more classifier constructions than the children, which would seem to indicate that acquisition of classifiers continues through adolescence. Similarly, in a comprehension task requiring the selection of the appropriate classifier among a choice of four, the participants can easily differentiate classifiers based on semantic properties (fish/bird/human/vehicle) and size (small/big), but cannot take into account more subtle differences (such as 2 or 3 dimensional objects), that are easily understood by the adult participants.

At the narrative level, most children can understand a story in LSF and answer to basic or even elaborate questions about the plot. Only the youngest participants (age

---

15. LSF, like other sign languages, has no written form used by more than a handful of specialists.

8) cannot give a short accurate answer, and instead repeat a whole part of the story. Development of narrative production seems to still be in progress in this age bracket. Indeed, although all the participants are able to retell a story from a picture book, their narratives are still incomplete (notably, the end tends to be too short, without real closure), and do not fully contain the specific features of a sign language story, such as detailed character and space descriptions, role playing and role shifting. For example, to describe the situation "dog walking into the hallway", half of the participants use the standard sign followed by the citation form TO-WALK, whereas the other half of the participants use the appropriate form (DOG bimanual-[B]-handshape-classifier-TO-WALK) involving role-playing. Most of the participants do introduce referents correctly, but cannot maintain them properly and repeat the citation form of the sign rather than using pointing and eye gaze. However, most of them try to use these properties in some parts of their production. In contrast, the adult participants produce many more pointing gestures/eye gazes, and use a lot of referential shift devices while telling the same story.

The utterances produced within the narratives by the children are mostly grammatically correct, except for a few participants who sometimes produce strings of unconnected signs. However, only a few complex utterances were produced in this situation, whereas the adults tend to produce longer utterances involving more complex structures. Similarly, children produce mainly simple classifiers while adults integrate these in complex structures and role-playing.

Overall, this pattern of skills is very similar to what is described for deaf children of hearing parents who are learning ASL or LSQ. Indeed, Anthony (2002) and Vercaingne-Ménard, Godard and Labelle (2001) reported a similar lack of verb modulation and spatial referents, as well as the use of simple classifiers rather than classifiers embedded in complex structures. Thus, it seems that for this kind of deaf population, learning a sign language mostly from non-native signers at home and later in life at school, acquisition is stretched out over time, up to the end of the adolescence for the most complex parts of language, such as narratives and classifier constructions. These children, however, will eventually reach a good level of proficiency, as demonstrated by the data collected on the L2 non-native signer adult controls of the Swiss study.

Quality and timing of exposure to sign language and consequences on general development. The data collected in Switzerland support the claim that even inconsistent exposure to sign language can promote language acquisition for the deaf child (Slobin 2002). Slobin found that deaf children from the US and from the Netherlands can use their hearing parents' "poor" sign language input to build a more elaborate linguistic system (Schiff-Myers 1993 reaches the same conclusion for hearing children using the "poor" oral language of their deaf parents). These children's language will then be enriched through contacts at school with other deaf children and teachers (if any).[16]

---

16. The quality and consistency of sign language exposure through the first years at school seem to affect the level of linguistic proficiency, as shown by Niederberger (2004). Indeed, these data reveal

As mentioned earlier, systematic exposure to LSF is not generalized in France, but rather depends on the policy of individual schools (a few bilingual programs exist in France, for instance *Iris* in Toulouse, *Service d'Education Bilingue* in Poitiers, *CEBES*, *CELEM* and *Laurent-Clerc* in Paris). Because of their auditory deficit, but also often because of community education policy, some of the deaf children born to hearing parents do not have access to a comprehensive linguistic system (Millet & Mugnier 2004). The linguistic consequences of this unique situation have been well documented. Oral language acquisition usually is quite delayed (see 4.2.3 for a detailed description). In sign language, late exposure (after the age of seven) generally leads to a deficit in syntax and morphology (Mayberry 1993; Newport 1990), and a slower pace in sign processing (Emmorey & Corina 1990; cited in Emmorey 2002). This phenomenon is found for late L1 sign language learners only, whereas late L2 sign language learners do not show these deficits, as demonstrated by the study of Mayberry (1993) on 12 post-lingually deaf students whose L1 was English and who learned ASL during their adolescence.

Consequences for cognitive development have also been reported by de Villiers, de Villiers, Schick and Hoffmeister (2000) and, in France, by Courtin and Melot (2005) as well as Deleau (1997), who showed that French deaf children born to hearing parents generally present a two-year delay in development of theory of mind. The authors interpret this delayed language effect as specific to this population due to their limited access to linguistic input. Indeed, Courtin and Melot's data reveal that deaf children born to deaf signing parents do not show any delay in this area and even outperform hearing children on some Theory of Mind's tasks. De Villiers et al. found similar results in the United States, with deaf children of deaf signing parents outperforming deaf children of hearing parents, and bilingually raised deaf children outperforming orally raised deaf children.

4.2.2 *Acquisition of written French*

Major difficulties encountered by the deaf child. Learning to read and write is one of the biggest challenges that the deaf child has to face in his/her academic curriculum. Major difficulties have been reported by most studies over the years regardless of the type of educational methods provided (for a review, see Dubuisson & Daigle 1998; Lepot-Froment & Clerebaut 1996). For instance, Conrad (1979), in a well-known survey of over 300 deaf adolescents finishing high school in Great Britain, describes a general reading level comparable to 4th grade hearing students, although some rare students seem to perform at their age level (only 18 of the participants). Another study, conducted in the United States with 65 students, ages 16–18, insisted on the heterogeneity of performance, ranging from 2nd to 12th grade reading levels (Moores & Sweet 1990).

---

that study participants coming from one of the school programs outperform the participants enrolled in the two other programs, in the two LSF production tasks mentioned above (classifiers and narrative production tasks).This phenomenon has not been fully explained yet and would require a more in-depth analysis of the three participating school programs.

However, some researchers have argued that these comparisons are not relevant, and that deaf children should instead be compared to L2 readers, since these two groups are both learning to read in a language that they do not master yet (Dubuisson & Bastien 1998, see below). Indeed, lack of oral proficiency has been claimed to be responsible for most of the written difficulties encountered by deaf children. Alegria (1999) points out that, in order to read, deaf children need to acquire French language structures and lexical items that hearing children have already known for a number of years by the time they enter first grade.

An ongoing debate focuses on how to describe the difficulties of the deaf in reading and writing: Are these indications of a tremendous delay, or rather a specific deficit, limited to some areas of the written language (Lepot-Froment & Clerebaut 1996)? Reading difficulties are reported at various levels, particularly regarding world knowledge, vocabulary, and morpho-syntax (Lepot-Froment & Clerebaut 1996; Marschark 1993; Vercaingne-Ménard 2002; Wilbur 2000). Performance in grammar is patchy and tied to the contents explicitly taught in the classroom. At the vocabulary level, the lexicon is not only reduced in size, but more rigid, with a limited number of meanings attached to each entry, and without any connections among forms deriving from the same root (Gaustad 2000). Thus, word identification, which is based mainly on graphemic clues (since phonological information is often not available, Leybaert & Alegria 1986), is challenging. Consequently, the deaf child needs to learn every single word as a new entry. Many word identification errors are found, mostly among visually similar words (Dubuisson & Bastien 1998). These researchers also reveal that deaf learners are better readers of texts than of single sentences or words, and rely on the linguistic and extra-linguistic context to decipher written messages. However, Leybaert and Alegria point out that the efficiency of these strategies is limited, due to lack of knowledge of French.

Niederberger (1999) studied reading strategies used by four deaf children raised bilingually in LSF and French, ages 8–9, using a common test of reading skills for hearing children (the *LMC* test, Khomsi 1990). Results show a lot of inaccurate word identification (confusions between *qui* 'who' and *oui* 'yes' for example). Participants also frequently refused to read sentences that included unknown nouns and verbs, skipping the item without trying to decompose the unknown words into morphemes. When processing sentences, they relied on lexical strategies: The meaning was constructed on the basis of a few lexical items, and without taking into account grammatical morphemes such as verbal tense. These data are consistent with the pattern of difficulties described above. However, using a lexical probability task, Daigle and Armand (2004) demonstrated that deaf readers can use morphological strategies, although at a much later age (10–12 for the best readers, and only at the age of 13–15 for the less skilled readers).

Writing difficulties seem to be partially similar to those experienced by L1 learners, but even more similar to those of L2 learners. Nadeau and Machabée (1998) found errors on prepositions, auxiliary verbs, pronominal verbs, verbal morphology, gender, articles, pronouns and graphically similar words. Some errors were not found in the two other groups and were considered by the authors as *deaf specific*: Word order errors, redundancy (*je vu *visitrai* 'I seen will-visit'), verbal morphology (*le garcon suis triste* 'the boy am sad'), omission of obligatory complements. However, in Section 4.2.3 we will present an alternative interpretation of these so-called *deafisms*. Another characteristic of deaf productions is the accumulation of errors within sentences: Nadeau and Machabée give examples such as *Mon cousin voit meon transforme change bleu* 'My cousin sees (???) transforms changes blue', *Je veux couche le soleil pour mon corps bien* 'I want sets the sun for my body well'.

A different way to learn to read and write. Some researchers have focused on differences rather than on deficits, looking not only for weaknesses but also for strengths. They consider that deaf children have a specific way of learning how to read and write due to cultural commonality (Kuntze 1998; Padden 1993), or due to use of compensatory strategies (Alegria 1999; Denys & Alegria 1998). Padden studied 40 deaf children learning English spelling. She found that only 20% of misspellings were similar to the misspellings of hearing children. She suggests that hearing learners produce errors related to sound-letter correspondences, whereas deaf learners make visual errors of letter inversions, omissions and substitutions. Alegria (1999) reported in a summary of his studies, that, in French, deaf students similarly produce fewer phonological errors than hearing learners (approximately 30% vs. 90%), but more errors in the order of letters (approximately 7% vs. 1%).

Niederberger and Berthoud-Papandropoulou (2004) studied the use of French pronouns by a group of 11 bilingual French/LSF deaf children, ages 8 to 15. They showed in a completion task that deaf learners either write the targeted pronoun correctly or omit it, whereas control hearing 2nd grade learners often omit the plural marker on the subject pronoun (*il/ils* 'he, they-MASC' *elle/elles* 'she, they-FEM'). They interpret these different patterns of answers as evidence of use of different strategies. Hearing learners seem to initially use their knowledge of oral French, which induces them to produce morphological errors, since in most contexts singular and plural forms are pronounced identically. Deaf participants, on the other hand, do not seem to have recourse to oral French, as shown by the low performance in the oral part of the study, and by the absence of such errors. Niederberger and Berthoud-Papandropoulou suggest that deaf learners might instead use their knowledge of LSF in order to find the correct answer, since this language, unlike oral French, distinguishes singular pronouns (single pointing), numeral pronouns (pointing with two to five fingers in a small circle), and a generic plural pronoun (pointing by drawing a small circle). Indeed, in this completion task, some children were seen signing to themselves single, dual and plural LSF pronouns before writing down the answers in French.

Denys and Alegria (1998) studied the reading strategies implemented by eight deaf adults selected for their good reading performance. Participants showed exceptionally strong skills in word spelling, and a medium range performance in comprehension of sentences that could be processed lexically. On the contrary, in another reading task requiring a fine-grained syntactic analysis, their performance drastically dropped.

Niederberger (2004) studied the written French skills of the same group of 39 bilingual French/LSF deaf children presented earlier (see Section 4.2.1). Six tasks were used to evaluate their proficiency in narrative production and comprehension, morpho-syntactic production and comprehension, and in addition, in lexical strategies for sentence comprehension and word spelling judgment. Only 23 participants were able to complete all the tasks. The 16 remaining participants completed a subset of the tasks; they were mainly limited by their lack of vocabulary. Results were heterogeneous and correlated with the age of the students. However, all the participants showed the same areas of strengths and weaknesses: They performed well on word spelling judgment, lexical strategies in sentence comprehension, text comprehension, narratives structure, and punctuation, whereas morpho-syntactic production was lower than expected given their overall proficiency. Similar patterns of acquisition were described in other studies on written French by deaf children and adults in Quebec (Dubuisson & Bastien 1998; Vercaingne-Ménard 2002).

This pattern of written French acquisition thus seems characteristic of the deaf population. In particular, it appears to be very different from the pattern shown by a control group in the Swiss study of 20 2nd graders and 20 4th graders from the same geographic area. Deaf participants perform similarly to the 2nd graders in lexical strategies and text comprehension, whereas 2nd graders outperform deaf participants in morpho-syntax, and deaf participants outperform 2nd graders in word spelling judgment and, for those who can write a narrative, in narrative structure and punctuation.

Factors involved in learning to read and write achievement. A few researchers have attempted to explain the heterogeneity in reading/writing found among deaf children. For instance, Moores and Sweet (1990) list six factors: Cognitive development and world knowledge, school achievement, proficiency in grammar, conversational skills, speech and hearing skills, and finally, family demographics. Strong and Prinz (1997, 2000) add metalinguistic development, quality of the linguistic input in the family, and type of education provided at school. Parental hearing status also seems to play an important role, with second and third generation deaf children outperforming deaf children born to hearing parents (Chamberlain & Mayberry 2000; Wilbur 2000). Most of these studies reveal, across the effects of various factors, the importance of solid, early linguistic experience. For years, oral-based linguistic experience was considered to be the only necessary base to build reading and writing skills on. But data from deaf children born to deaf signing parents, and recent studies showing high correlations between sign language proficiency and reading and writing skills (Hoffmeister 2000; Niederberger 2004; Padden & Ramsey 2000; Prinz & Strong 1998) suggest that linguistic skills developed in sign language might provide an equivalent background. We return to these findings in the context of the interaction between language development in LSF and language development in French in Section 4.2.4. However, before examining that interaction, another component of language acquisition in French must first be considered: The acquisition of oral French.

4.2.3 *Acquisition of oral French*

Prelingual hearing loss, and especially the significant loss involved in severe and profound deafness, makes learning an oral language extremely difficult. This hearing loss involves not only raised hearing thresholds (intensity of incoming sound), but also considerable distortion of incoming sounds. Lip-reading, which is a natural cognitive skill in hearing people as well (see Campbell 1997), does not, when it is the sole, unaided input, allow for language acquisition. Most of the articulators used in speech are invisible (behind the lips), and much visible articulation is ambiguous (e.g., /p, b, m/). Furthermore, in order for caretakers to know they need to adopt various simple means to foster communicative development (facing the child, drawing attention to the mouth, etc.), they, of course, first need to know their child is deaf. Hearing loss is not detected in most deaf children until several months have passed. A Paris study of 140 children under the age of six conducted between 1990 and 1999 found that the average age of detection was 16 months for profound hearing loss, 23 months for severe hearing loss, and 37 months for moderate hearing loss (Garbédian 2004). A German study reported in Picard (2004) reported similar findings: Detection occurred just under age two for profound deafness, and two and a half years for severe deafness.[17] In other words, acquisition of an oral language begins late and proceeds slowly, requiring specialized intervention to develop both comprehension strategies (such as lip-reading skills), and production strategies (proprioceptive awareness of phonemic contrasts, etc.).

What is the end result? Deaf speakers, even quite competent ones, definitely sound different. A characteristic 'deaf accent' involves not only target-deviant phonemes, but, especially, a particular prosody and voice quality. Although the speech hurdle to oral language development is formidable, morpho-syntax is strikingly affected in the context of hearing impairment. We propose to concentrate on this aspect of language here, as it constitutes the area most acutely affected by hearing loss (with implications for other areas of language and cognitive development),[18] and one which has been studied from a comparative vantage point. Researchers on the oral language of the deaf unanimously agree that functional categories (and related syntactic processes), as opposed to lexical categories, are particularly subject to target-deviant production (see de Villiers, de Villiers, & Hogan 1994; Mogford 1993; Lepot-Froment & Clerebaut 1996, for reviews).

---

17. Universal neonatal hearing screening should change these statistics, but it is yet to be implemented throughout France, for example.

18. Conway (1990: 120), for example, in a discussion of semantic development, concludes that it is mastery of syntactic structures and grammatical processes which permit expression of complex semantic information that are lacking in the deaf. Jill de Villiers and colleagues (see de Villiers 2005; de Villiers & de Villiers 2000; de Villiers et al. 2000) have argued that delays in acquisition of complex syntax are responsible for a significant delay in children's development of aspects of the ability to reason about their own and other people's mental states.

Unsurprisingly, this pattern has been confirmed in study of the French of deaf speakers. Tuller (2000) presents an analysis of errors in a spontaneous language corpus of over 650 utterances (60 minutes of recording time) produced by a profoundly deaf 18-year-old whose first language is French. S. was diagnosed and fitted for (conventional) hearing aids at age one. His first contact with LSF was at age 14 in a residential school for the deaf; he reports being more comfortable communicating in French. His French is generally quite intelligible, and he can be considered an example of a very proficient deaf speaker of French. Interestingly, despite this apparent overall proficiency, 21% of his utterances in fact contain at least one error. Of the 130 errors identified, only 8.5% (11 tokens) involved lexical categories; all other errors involved functional categories (119 tokens). These figures are nearly identical to those reported by Volterra and Bates (1989) in a study of a very proficient deaf speaker of Italian: Functional category errors constituted 91.8% of total errors, this time in a written corpus of ten letters addressed to a close friend. Analysis of a one-hour sample of free speech from this same speaker revealed a similar distribution.

This qualitative similarity between errors in oral production and errors in written production has been reported by other researchers. Vincent-Durroux (1992) presents a study of the oral language of four French-speaking and four English-speaking profoundly deaf adolescents (age 12 to 15) who know no sign language. Comparing her results with those of a series of studies conducted by Dubuisson and colleagues in Montreal (see Dubuisson & Daigle 1998, for review, and discussion in the preceding section), she concludes that deaf subjects, whether oral or signing, produce French in essentially the same way – when they speak and when they write.

Explanations as to why functional categories are selectively impaired in the context of oral language acquisition by the deaf generally center on the fact that these items, due to their lack of phonetic saliency, are not readily accessible in language input to deaf persons, who rely principally on information obtained by lip-reading. As closed-class items tend to be short, they are produced rapidly and with less stress, and thus are less visible on the lips, meaning that linguistic input will selectively lack these items. Volterra and Bates (1989) observe that these items might also suffer a marked disadvantage in lexical retrieval due to their low semantic content, accounting for the co-occurrence of correct and incorrect forms and for good metalinguistic knowledge of grammatical rules in the face of relatively poor performance in spontaneous language. They point out that this disadvantage is partly offset for hearing speakers, by the high frequency of such items – precisely what is missing for deaf speakers. Insufficient input in general – and lack of sufficient exposure to essential grammatical elements in particular – leads to a delay in language acquisition, with the consequence that critical period effects can also be a contributing factor in the resulting grammar. De Villiers et al. (1994) note that although written language will supply input for grammatical items, once formal education has begun, it may very well be that deaf children start out by deciphering written language via their impoverished grammar, filtering out anything this grammar cannot handle. This would certainly partly explain the similarity in oral and written errors.[19]

These studies conclude that interference from knowledge of a sign language cannot offer a viable explanation for the observed constellation of errors since the same errors are found in speakers having had exposure (even natively) to a conventional sign language and those having had no exposure at all. One interpretation of this conclusion has been that the relevant property is deafness. Obviously, there is a trivial sense in which deafness is the root of language difficulties of the deaf (see Tuller 1999, for discussion): If these children were not deaf they would not, other things being equal, have the problems with oral language acquisition that they have. What researchers such as Dubuisson and Nadeau (1993) propose is, however, that the errors observed in so-called "Deaf French"[20] can be attributed at least in part to the way information is processed by deaf individuals, and, in particular, the way space and time are processed. This proposal is reminiscent of that made by O'Connor and Hermelin (1983) (cited in Mogford 1993) who suggest that comprehension strategies observed in the deaf result from learning language visually, which would entail coding of spatial information and would interfere with the acquisition of patterns that rely primarily on temporal ordering. This cognitive organization, which is proposed to be specific to deafness, would entail not only the use of certain structures in the French produced by deaf persons, but also the existence of these same structures in sign languages such as LSQ and LSF. Tuller (1999) notes that not all errors can be accounted for in this way, since, as Sero-Guillaume (1994) points out, there are 'deaf' errors in French which do not correspond to existing structures in LSF. The improbability of such a direct link between deafness and the morpho-syntactic properties of oral language produced by the deaf is also supported by comparative work in which 'Deaf French' is compared to French produced by other exceptional learners. Nadeau (1993) in fact observes numerous similarities with L2 French, though errors proposed to be specific to deaf learners of French are also presented. Comparison with learners for whom language development is disrupted for one reason or another provides another key test for the validity of this explanation.[21]

---

19. Anecdotal support for this suggestion is found in the following quote, from Millet (1990:29), from an interview of a deaf adolescent, who describes how he reads in French, "To learn, I look at the text, but I don't need to learn the little words, I take the important words; that's it and then I understand the text. To read a sentence, to understand a sentence, I take the important words, but not the words that aren't important, like 'that' or 'of', and after, I understand" (our translation).

20. The term 'Deaf French' comes from the use of the term 'Deaf English', first proposed by Charrow (1976:141), who suggested that 'deafisms' and commonality of errors found in deaf students provide grounds for the idea that "the deaf have a dialect of their own – a 'Deaf English' – different from Standard English".

21. Mogford notes that both Quigley, Power and Steinkamp (1977), the largest study of English syntax development of deaf pupils in the U.S. and Bishop (1983), a British study of 79 deaf pupils, point out

One line of investigation we have found to be productive has been comparison of language performance of deaf persons with that of individuals diagnosed for Specific Language Impairment (SLI), which is defined as developmental language impairment affecting children who are free from problems in all other areas (normal intelligence, no sensory or frank neurological deficits, etc.). Children with SLI have no hearing loss, but, like deaf children, their language development is delayed, resulting in severely impaired language. We compared the language of S, the 18-year-old deaf speaker of French presented above to that of M, a 19-year-old with a childhood diagnosis of SLI (see Audollent & Tuller 2003). The similarities are remarkable: 20.8% of the utterances of a spontaneous language corpus of over 800 utterances were erroneous, the same proportion found for S. As expected, while lexical categories are virtually error-free, functional categories have a significantly higher error rate, as was the case for S. More striking were the similarities found between the functional categories which were especially affected, versus those which were generally produced without error: The *passé composé* and *plus-que-parfait* verb tenses versus present and immediate future tenses, object pronouns versus subject pronouns and independent pronouns, and so on:

(13)   *Et si j'ai apprend ma guitare j'aurais pu jouer avec B.* [S]
        (target form: *avais appris*)
        'and if I had learned the guitar, I could have played with B'

(14)   *J'ai dit que je cherche un emploi vu qu'elle était au courant que je suis sorti de prison* [M]
        (target forms: *cherchais; étais sorti*)
        'I said that I was looking for a job since she knew that I had left prison'

(15)   *J'ai rencontré ___ à Tours comme ça.* [S]
        'I met (them) in Tours like that'

(16)   *J'ai ma marraine qui est au Canada et puis qui vient passer des vacances* [...]. *Alors j'ai vue ___. Et puis elle parle français.* [M]
        'I've got my godmother who's in Canada and who comes for vacation. So, I saw (her). And, well, she speaks French.'

The sentences in (13) and (14) illustrate difficulties with verb tense, while the sentences in (15) and (16) illustrate illegitimate omission of object pronouns, alongside correct production of pronoun subjects. Both speakers avoided complex syntax to the same degree: Only 28.5% of S's and 29.4% of M's sentences were complex (determined by presence of at least one subordinate clause), whereas a control native 18-year-old speaker of French who had benefited from typical language development, but who grew up in a similar socio-cultural setting, produced 48.5% complex sentences, which corresponds to proportions typically found in adult spontaneous language samples (around 50%).

These findings received additional support with our comparative studies of deaf children and SLI children. Using experimental elicited production and comprehension

---

that the strategies they observed are not exclusive to the deaf, but rather are observed in other groups with syntactic difficulties.

tasks targeting specific grammatical forms,[22] we found parallel patterns of selective vulnerability, and unexpected responses were identical for the group of 21 deaf children (11 were severely deaf and 10 were profoundly deaf), and 28 children with SLI (ages 5 to 13) (see Jacq & Tuller 1999; Jakubowicz, Tuller, & Rigaut 2000). While definite determiners and subject pronouns are generally well produced by all groups of children,[23] objects pronouns (reflexive *se* and accusative *le/la* 'him/her') were problematic for all groups of children. Notably, there was a very significant difference between production of homophonous definite determiners (which posed no problem) and accusative clitics (which were significantly impaired). The errors produced by both groups of deaf children were the same, with high rates of object omission, one of the striking properties found in our case studies of S and M, young adults whose French developed in the contexts of profound hearing loss and SLI, respectively.

The particular vulnerability of object pronouns in the acquisition of French is now widely recognized: They appear later in typical language acquisition (Hamann, Rizzi, & Frauenfelder 1996; Jakubowicz et al. 2000), they are problematic for children diagnosed with SLI (Jakubowicz, Nash, Rigaut, & Gérard 1998), as well as for children learning French as a second language (Paradis, Crago, & Genesee 2003). The fact that this is also one of the principal difficulties of deaf children learning French (including those with mild-to-moderate hearing loss, see Tuller & Jakubowicz 2004) would seem to indicate that there are certain aspects of French which are vulnerable when language acquisition is disrupted, whatever the cause for that disruption may be, and that therefore deafness, per se, does not seem to have specific grammatical consequences for the acquisition of oral French. A likely cause for these similarities is the fact that exceptional language development is protracted in time, meaning that language development is not complete at the end of the critical period for language acquisition, and that therefore alternative avenues are enlisted. Just what these latter may consist of and how they are enlisted is the subject of much current work in psycho- and neurolinguistics (see, e.g., Thomas 2005).

4.2.4 *Relationship between development in LSF and development in French*
In this section we will discuss two aspects of LSF and French interaction: First, the question of the relationship between development in LSF and development in French will be addressed, with a presentation of data from experimental and educational settings showing evidence of interaction and transfer across modalities. Then we will present examples of contact language phenomena between LSF and French produced by deaf children, involving various kinds of mixes along the monolingual-bilingual continuum (Grosjean 1996).

---

22. Experimental material was developed by C. Jakubowicz (see Jakubowicz et al. 1998).

23. The only exception was found in the most severely affected SLI children (and also the youngest), who had more difficulty with subject pronouns.

Developmental interaction between the two languages. Recent experimental studies have shown clear correlations between ASL and written English proficiency by bilingual deaf children and adults (Chamberlain & Mayberry 2000; Hoffmeister 2000; Mayberry & Lock 2003; Padden & Ramsey 1998; Prinz & Strong 1998; Strong & Prinz 1997). These results were later replicated by Niederberger (2004) (see also Niederberger & Frauenfelder 2005) in a study of 39 LSF and French deaf learners (see data presentation in Section 4.2.1. and 4.2.2 above). Scores obtained in tests of narrative production and comprehension as well as morpho-syntax in LSF were standardized and added to create a global indicator of LSF proficiency. Similarly, scores for narrative production and comprehension as well as morpho-syntax in French were added to create a written French indicator. Pearson correlation showed a strong link between the two sets of language skills (r = .485; p = .002). Moreover, results showed higher correlations in comprehension than in production, and at the narrative level rather than at the morpho-syntactic level, confirming data presented for ASL/English by Prinz et al. (2001) and Mayberry et al. (1999) (cited in Chamberlain & Mayberry 2000). Interestingly, strong correlations were also found between LSF narrative skills and oral French comprehension skills.

Data gathered in educational settings in Austria, New Zealand and Quebec have demonstrated that knowing a sign language can improve reading and writing achievement (Biederman 2003; Krausneker 2003; Vercaingne-Ménard 2002). In France, Millet showed in a first study that sessions in which LSF and French are explicitly compared helped young deaf adults enrolled in a literacy project to improve their written French: At the end of the training program, they continued to produce numerous errors, but these were qualitatively different. In particular, in a reading comprehension test, they no longer copied answers randomly from the text and seem more personally involved in their answers (Millet 1993). In a second study, Millet and Mugnier (2004) showed that a group of eight third graders improved their reading comprehension of a text after a special session in LSF focused on the meaning of this written text.

Although this cross-modality language development relationship is now attested by a number of studies, the nature of the specific mechanisms involved in this interaction still needs to be further analyzed. Some authors have suggested the role of linguistic transfer at a narrative level (Wilbur 2000), while others have underlined the role of metalinguistic skills (Chamberlain & Mayberry 2000). However, all the data collected so far attest to the fact that explicit sign language instruction is necessary to allow this transfer to occur. Indeed, good sign language conversational skills do not appear to be sufficient, in and of themselves, to improve reading and writing acquisition, as shown by the results of Moores and Sweet (1990). Mayberry and Lock (2003) demonstrate that one of the pertinent variables is age of sign language acquisition. They show that *early* experience with a sign language has a significant effect on later syntactic abilities in English (as tested by (written) grammatical judgment and sentence-to-picture matching tasks), complementing previous work showing that early L1 experience with an oral language (the case for individuals who become deaf during childhood) has significant effects on L2 acquisition of a sign language (Mayberry 1993).

How the two languages interact in production. As was seen in Section 4.1, children raised bilingually often produce language mixes. In the specific situation of bimodal bilingualism, both languages may appear in a single utterance not only alternatively, but also *simultaneously* (*code-blends*) (Emmorey et al. 2003; van den Bogaerde & Baker 2002). Although bimodal mixes are beginning to be documented for CODAs (see Section 4.1), bimodal oral/sign mixes produced by deaf individuals still need to be more deeply investigated. Loncke, Quertinmont, Martens and Dussart (1996) studied four deaf children, aged 9 to 13, learning French and Belgian Sign Language.[24] They found that all four children used more bimodal utterances (58%) than unimodal utterances (42%) while interacting with each other in an experimental setting. Furthermore, language mixes were more often simultaneous (74%) than sequential (26%). Most of the time, the two languages carried non-equivalent information (72%). Niederberger (2005) presented data on bimodal mixes produced by 12 bilingual LSF/French deaf children, aged 8 to 15, during an oral narrative production task. In this study, most of the utterances contained simultaneous redundant elements (88%); Simultaneous non-redundant elements were only found in 17% of the utterances and sequential non-redundant elements in 18% of the utterances. These data are very similar to those described in recent studies on CODAs (Emmorey et al. 2003; Petitto et al. 2001) and to the results presented in 4.1 on the Illana corpus. Most of the redundant elements were nouns and verbs, whereas non-redundant signed elements were mainly classifiers. The three kinds of mixes seem to have different purposes. Bimodal sequential mixes appear to be similar to the sequential mixes found in oral/oral bilingualism. In this narrative situation, bimodal bilingual individuals mainly switched from oral French into LSF when they could not find the appropriate word or construction, as shown in (17).

(17) <u>le a dit eh</u>! 'the said hey!'
     DUCK
     'the duck said hey!' (E35;10)

Simultaneous non-redundant mixes appear to be a creative combination of oral and sign language in order to efficiently express complex actions and relations between objects, as they are produced mainly at two specific points of the story, the complication and the resolution, as illustrated in (18a–b).

(18) a. <u>bateau brrrrrrrrrr</u> 'boat brrrrrrrr'
        BOAT (classifier) MOVE (high speed, forward)
        'the boat is moving forward very fast' (E10;18)
    b. <u>voiture /pa/</u> 'car (leaves?)'
        (classifier) MOVE (high speed, forward)
        'the car is moving forward very fast' (E10;20)

---

24. Although some authors call the sign language used in French-speaking Belgium 'French Sign Language', as presented in Section 2, Loncke and other authors prefer to differentiate it by using a specific name. This is a good example of the problems encountered in setting sign language boundaries in 'francophone' areas.

Finally, simultaneous redundant mixes, as in (19):

(19)   <u>après le mouton i(l) dit non</u>   'then the sheep says no'   (E26;24)
       AFTER SHEEP SAY NO

seem to be used in a variety of contexts, including semantic clarification of mispro-
nounced words (see Mugnier & Millet 2003), and narrative planning, but their high
rate in some narratives might also reflect the language mixes usually addressed to the
students by the hearing staff of the school. Further investigation clearly needs to be
conducted in other settings in order to better understand these phenomena.

5.   Conclusion

This chapter has proposed a critical assessment of empirical findings on bilingual
development of French and French sign language, presented within the wider background of acquisition research on sign language and on deafness. The L2 French that
is involved in this bilingual language development is not an ordinary L2 for deaf children in that (1) Early exposure to sign language is relatively rare and thus there is
often no real L1 for L2 French to build onto, and (2) Oral language development by
deaf children generally starts late and proceeds slowly and with great difficulty, and
thus L2 French is very rarely an early L2. Bilingual French/LSF acquisition is different from other cases of bilingual development involving French, for both deaf and
hearing children, in that the other language being acquired is a language which uses
a different modality (visuo-gestural instead of audio-oral). Contact between the two
languages is also rather unusual. Learning to read and write for a deaf child growing up
in a French-speaking country in Europe means learning to read and write in French,
whether French is a late, atypical L1, or a late atypical L2. For the vast majority of deaf
children in this situation, French is also the (first) language of their parents, siblings,
neighbors, and classmates. Likewise, hearing children who grow up in LSF at home, do
so in the midst of a wider language context which is overwhelmingly French. As can be
expected, this intense language contact leads to considerable language-mixing, which,
once again, presents peculiarities that cannot be found in ordinary language-mixing
due to the fact that co-articulation of the two languages is possible given that each
one uses a different modality. Thus, it is possible to sign and to speak literally at the
same time, but not to speak, say, French and English at the same time. In other words,
study of children growing up acquiring both French and French sign language offers an
interesting way of exploring research questions related to the development of French
(which aspects of the grammar of French are vulnerable when language development
does not proceed in a typical fashion? In what way does knowledge of spoken French
determine how written French is acquired?), as well as related to the general field of
language development (what is the link between non-verbal communicative behavior
and stages of linguistic development? In bilingual and L2 contexts, which features are
susceptible to being transferred?).

Through a mixture of literature review and presentation of our own research findings, we have shown that there is convergence on the existence of common properties between oral language acquisition and signed language acquisition on the one hand, and, on the other hand, between monomodal bilingualism and bimodal bilingualism. When language development begins early and when language input is fully accessible, as is the case for hearing children acquiring LSF and French, acquisition proceeds in an entirely ordinary fashion. Learning language in two different modalities presents no particular difficulties compared to learning two languages in the same modality, or, learning a single language. The case study of Illana, a young hearing child simultaneously acquiring French and LSF, provided evidence that there is development of separate linguistic systems from early stages, and that these two systems follow a strikingly parallel progression through the early stages of grammar development. Code-mixing in Illana, from very early on, is strikingly similar to what has been found for bilingual Swiss-French/LSF older children and for bilingual English-ASL adults, reinforcing the idea that code-mixing in young children is not a chaotic mixture of two languages, but follows readily observable patterns, even in the case of code-mixing which involves two modalities and thus exploits the possibility of simultaneous production of elements from both languages. Prelinguistic gestures in Illana's production are found to play a role in the emergence of the syntax of LSF, a language whose modality uses gestures, analogous to the findings for the emergence of syntax in oral language, suggesting that it is the fact that these gestures are non-linguistic which allows them to play this role, rather than the fact that they use a modality different from the linguistic modality in the case of audio-oral languages.

Late exposure to LSF, and late as well as partial exposure to French – the unmarked case for deaf children growing up in French and in LSF – give rise to protracted language development and deficits, particularly in the area of morpho-syntax, in both of these languages. Particular grammatical items stand out as being especially vulnerable – classifiers in LSF, and object pronouns in French. In the case of French, these correspond to the same elements which are difficult for young monolingual typically developing French children and which have been identified as markers of specific language impairment in children experiencing atypical language development, suggesting that observed morpho-syntactic difficulties are primarily related to the structure of French itself, rather than to specific properties of deafness. On the other hand, children approaching written French with LSF as a first/primary language, do so in at least some ways that set them apart from typically-developing L1 French-speakers (absence of errors based on homophony, etc.). However, once again, expressive morpho-syntax is the area of written French that remains the most affected by problems for deaf children (unlike hearing francophone children acquiring written French). Late exposure to language input leads not only to documented language deficits, but also to delay in other areas of cognitive development (such as Theory of Mind). Taken together these results underline the conclusion that it is not the bilingualism of the language situation of deaf children that is the defining characteristic of their language development, but rather the fact that language exposure, even L1 language exposure, for most of these children begins late, and, in the case of French, remains degraded.

Although sign language research has progressed considerably in the last several decades, research on language development in the context of deafness is relatively young, at least in the case of development of French and of French sign language. Language development and deafness is an area which provides a rich array of research due to the variables inherent in this situation: Age of exposure to language input; quality, quantity and modality of language input. We have argued here that exploration of language development in this context contributes to better understanding of the structure of French, the structure of LSF, and the nature of language development. There is, however, another issue involved in discovering just how deaf children, and hearing children in deaf families, grow up acquiring both French and LSF, which has a distinctively more applied dimension. While countries such as France have embraced the global trend toward full scholastic integration of deaf children, there has been little study of how these children are in fact developing language (oral, written and signed) in this context, and how their language development is related to development of other skills. Professionals, families and deaf students themselves are increasingly explicit about formulating demands for relevant language assessment and objective evaluation of teaching methods. Construction of such tools relies on careful psycholinguistic studies and thorough linguistic analysis.

CHAPTER 13

Using electronic corpora in SLA research[*]

Florence Myles
University of Newcastle upon Tyne

Résumé

La première partie de ce chapitre introduit la linguistique de corpus et les nouvelles méthodologies qu'elle a développées, avant de présenter les raisons pour lesquelles les chercheurs en acquisition de langue seconde (L2) ne les utilisent guère, malgré leurs nombreux avantages. Une deuxième partie passe brièvement en revue la façon dont les corpus ont été utilisés en acquisition de langue seconde, principalement dans le contexte de corpus écrits d'apprenants avancés d'anglais L2, car il n'en existe fort peu d'autres. La dernière partie du chapitre illustre la façon dont l'informatique peut être utilisée pour faciliter les recherches en L2, en présentant l'étude de cas d'une série de projets dont le but est de construire une banque de corpus oraux de français L2 (www.flloc.soton.ac.uk), et en illustrant comment le logiciel CHILDES (http://childes.psy.cmu.edu) peut être utilisé afin de répondre à des questions de recherche spécifiques.

Abstract

The first part of this chapter introduces corpus linguistics and the powerful methodologies used in the field, before discussing the reasons why they have been largely ignored by SLA researchers, and making the case for the need to adopt them to advance SLA research. A second section briefly reviews the way in which corpora have been used in SLA research, primarily in the context of written corpora of advanced learners of English, as very little else exists. The final part of the chapter will demonstrate the way in which computerized methodologies can be used, by presenting the case study of a project which constructed a database of French Learner Language Oral Corpora (FLLOC, www.flloc.soton.ac.uk), and by illustrating how the software tools used within the context of this project (the CHILDES system, http://childes.psy.cmu.edu) can be used to address specific research questions.

---

[*] This chapter draws on two earlier articles (Myles 2005b; Myles & Mitchell 2004). I am very grateful for the very useful comments of an anonymous reviewer and of the editor of this volume. Any remaining weaknesses are my own entirely.

1.   Introduction

The field of corpus linguistics has been growing at a very fast pace over the last two decades or so, and the new computer-assisted methodologies elaborated to assist language research have had a major impact in many areas of applied linguistics, such as lexicography and pedagogic grammar. Good illustrations are the COBUILD/Bank of English project (Sinclair 1987, 1991),[1] www.cobuild.collins. co.uk), CANCODE (Carter 1997, 1998),[2] www.cambridge.org/elt/corpus/cancode.htm), as well as publications such as the *Longman Grammar of Spoken and Written English* (Biber, Johansson, Leech, Conrad, & Finegan 1999). By comparison, second language acquisition (SLA) research has remained until recently relatively unaffected by new technologies. There are a number of reasons for this, which we review below, but it is now imperative that the field takes advantage of larger datasets using new technologies for data management and analysis, if further progress is to be made in testing competing theoretical positions, and developing stronger empirical grounding for SLA theory.

The first part of this chapter introduces corpus linguistics and the powerful methodologies associated with it, before discussing the reasons why they have been largely ignored by SLA researchers, and making the case for the need to adopt them to advance SLA research. In a second section, we briefly review the way in which corpora have been used in SLA research, primarily in the context of written corpora of advanced learners of English, as very little else exists. The final part of the chapter demonstrates how computerized methodologies can be used, by presenting a case study of a project whose aim was to construct a database of French Learner Language Oral Corpora (FLLOC, available at http://www.flloc.soton.ac.uk),[3] and by illustrating how the software tools used within the context of this project (the CHILDES system devised and housed at Carnegie Mellon University http://childes.psy.cmu.edu) can be used to address specific research questions.

---

1.   The COBUILD corpus runs to hundreds of millions of words of English text from British, US, Australian and Canadian sources (including textbooks, novels, newspapers, guides, magazines, and websites). The corpus has been automatically word-class tagged, and a 200-million-word corpus has been parsed.

2.   CANCODE comprises 5 million words of spoken English, collected in Britain between 1995 and 2000.

3.   Thanks are due to the other members of the research team involved in the FLLOC project: Rosamond Mitchell, Sarah Rule, Emma Marsden, Mischa Tuffield and Vladimir Mircevski.

2. Corpus linguistics: Relevance to SLA research

2.1 Corpus linguistics

The term 'corpus linguistics' is relatively easy to define, as the branch of linguistics focusing on the analysis of corpora. Corpora can be defined as large samples of (electronically-stored) naturally occurring language, in either oral or written form, although, as they are much easier and cheaper to collect, written corpora are both much more common and larger, and oral corpora are only relatively recently making an appearance (native small corpora since the early eighties, and larger ones – more than a million words – much more recently). Corpus linguistics usually focuses on describing languages as they are being used, in a 'bottom up' fashion, by contrast with 'top down' theoretically motivated analyses. This is not a necessity of course, as 'top down' hypotheses can also be tested on corpora, and we will return to this point later. But much emphasis in the work of corpus linguists has been placed on showing that we can learn a lot about language(s), and the way they work by studying how they are used in real life. These empirically grounded descriptions have taught us many facts about language which more theoretically motivated approaches failed to capture, because of their tendency to remove from 'real' language its imperfections, and to study the sanitized language of an ideal speaker/hearer in order to get to its underlying structure. For example, an unexpectedly large amount of language has been found to be formulaic in nature (e.g., many greetings, closing and opening remarks), rather than being generated on-line as generativists might claim (Wray 2002).

Traditionally, in corpus linguistics, large corpora of native languages have been collected in order to find patterns of use through computerized searches. This approach has been particularly fruitful in the context of studies of lexical patterning, as it is very easy to search for words or collocations (sequences of words which frequently co-occur), and study their contexts, or in discourse analysis studies, for the study of written genres on a very large scale (Stubbs 1996), or of spoken genres (Biber 1988; Carter & McCarthy 2004). Many concordancing packages are available, making the process of searching for words very straightforward; they also provide statistical analyses (e.g., WordSmith www.lexically.net/wordsmith, Scott 1999; see Section 2.4).

This approach has been less extensively used for grammatical analyses, which are more complex, although progress is being made, and many taggers and/or parsers are now available, such as the University of Lancaster's CLAWS tagger (www.comp.lancs.ac.uk/computing/research/ucrel/claws/), or the ENGCG parser (http://www.lingsoft.fi/doc/engcg/intro/). An overview of these developments and their overall impact in applied linguistics is offered by Hunston (2002), but need not concern us here, as she does not review their impact on SLA research.

Corpus linguistics has been very well received as a pedagogical tool (Aston, Bernardini, & Stewart 2004; Granger, Hung, & Petch-Tyson 2002; Hunston 2002; Pennington & Stevens 1992), as it enables learners to explore authentic language in a guided way, finding out patterns for themselves which should hopefully lead to better retention. Again, the domain of application is primarily lexical/collocational. Teachers have used corpus linguistics methodologies to address the vexed pedagogical question of idiomatic use, which is difficult to teach prescriptively (Barlow 1996; Davies 2004; Hunston 2002). Advanced learners in particular are very used to their teachers telling them they have used the wrong expression, or that what they have produced does not sound quite right, or that native speakers would say it another way, all very good reasons of course, but difficult to prove to learners. Getting them to find out for themselves how expressions are used, can help them focus on the all important issue of usage in language, for which there are no grammar books or prescriptive rules that learners can learn by heart (for a recent review of the use of corpora in language teaching, see e.g., Aston, Bernardini, & Stewart 2004). The agenda here remains the same as in mainstream corpus linguistics, that is the description of patterns of language in use, which is why it has been much used as a tool in this field. But the purpose of the present chapter is to review the use of corpora in SLA research, and we will not examine in more detail the use of corpus linguistics in applied linguistics or language teaching research.

By contrast with the above two fields, SLA research has been rather slow in making use of computerized methodologies to assist its endeavors. There are a number of reasons for this, which will be explored more fully shortly. One of the main reasons is that, as SLA is a relatively new field of research, the emphasis has been on theory-building and the testing of hypotheses about the nature of L2 grammars. In an initial phase, this could be done using relatively small datasets, not necessarily consisting of production data (e.g., grammaticality judgment tests have been a common elicitation method). As corpus linguistics lends itself particularly well to work of a descriptive and therefore a-theoretical nature, putting much emphasis on frequency data, it was not seen as particularly useful for addressing those kinds of questions. Finding out patterns about L2 lexical use was not of primary concern to researchers, who were more concerned about the development of the L2 grammar. The fact that corpus linguistics and the methodologies it has developed tend to be corpus-driven (i.e., hypothesis-finding or bottom up) rather than corpus-based (hypothesis testing or top down), was a disincentive to SLA researchers (Barlow 2005; Granger 1998; Tognini-Bonelli 2001):

> In a corpus-based approach, a search is selected to find data that are relevant to a particular hypothesis. On the other hand, in a corpus-driven approach large amounts of data derived from corpus analysis are used in the formulation of grammatical descriptions.
>
> In practice, researchers may well make use of a combination of approaches, but there are biases in practice such that broadly speaking the experimental/generative tradition favors hypothesis-driven, corpus-based approaches, while corpus linguists have a preference for a hypothesis-finding, corpus-driven methodology.   (Barlow 2005:344)

Additionally, the cost of oral data collection was seen as prohibitive by many researchers.

2.2 Corpus linguistics in L1 and L2 acquisition research

2.2.1 *Corpus linguistics in L1 acquisition research*

Corpus linguistics, narrowly defined as a hypothesis-finding methodology concerned with finding patterns of language usage through the use of concordancers on large datasets, has been relatively little used in first language acquisition research, for the same reasons as in SLA research. Large oral corpora are very costly to collect and transcribe, and the emphasis in L1 acquisition research is also generally on hypothesis-testing rather than hypothesis-finding.

However, in L1 acquisition, the need for corpora and for making use of new technologies has been recognized for some 25 years, and acquisitionists have developed their own tools for analyzing child language data. The CHILDES tools, elaborated for storing, managing and analyzing data, are now standard in the field, and have enabled huge strides in answering some of the questions the field is addressing (MacWhinney 2000a, 2000b; Sokolov & Snow 1994). The CHILDES system will be explained in some detail below, as it is used in the case study oral French L2 database described later.

2.2.2 *Corpus linguistics in L2 acquisition research*

In L2 acquisition research, corpus linguistics has made very little inroad for a number of reasons. First, as mentioned above, this is a relatively new field, which has been engaged primarily to-date in the initial phase of theory building. Observations made in the seventies about patterns of development in L2 acquisition required theoretical frameworks to investigate them (Dulay & Burt 1973, 1974, 1975; Dulay, Burt, & Krashen 1982). For example, one observation which revolutionized the way in which the whole enterprise of second language learning and teaching was viewed was the fact that there are many similarities in the developmental sequences followed by L2 and L1 learners. Also, the fact that learners were shown to produce L2 language structures which are unlike both their L1 and the L2 they are learning, required explanation. The following phase saw the in-depth study of small groups of learners from various first language backgrounds in order to carry out preliminary tests of some of the hypotheses generated by the theorizing. What we want to argue here is that the field has now reached a level of maturity whereby we need much larger datasets in order to test more fully some of the hypotheses of interest to the field. In the same way as the L1 acquisition field (much older by comparison) started with small scale studies (e.g., diary studies of one child in the first part of the 20th century, such as Brandenburg 1915; Chamberlain & Chamberlain 1904; Grégoire 1937, 1947; Leopold 1939, 1947, 1949a, 1949b; or a little later, the famous Brown's (1973) studies of 3 children), and graduated to much larger databases of child language from the 1980s onwards, the field of SLA now needs to follow suit.

2.3   Why do we need corpora and computerized tools in SLA research?

One of the most important resources in SLA research, alongside a clear theoretical framework, is a good quality dataset to work on, that is carefully transcribed according to agreed and transparent conventions, and clearly documented (e.g., tasks used, level of learners, etc.). The language produced by learners, whether spontaneously or by means of various elicitation procedures, remains our main window into trying to understand how second languages are acquired. On one hand, we can test competing hypotheses which make different predictions about the grammar constructed by learners, while on the other hand, through detailed analysis of learners' L2 productions, capture both general trends in learner development, and what is variable in this development. This work crucially relies on good quality data, from large sets of learners, whose profiles are clearly documented.

The question then arises of what type of dataset is best suited to address this developmental agenda. We would argue that fairly spontaneous oral data is a better window into the learner's underlying interlanguage system than written data, which may be complicated by monitoring processes of various kinds (e.g., use of dictionaries, conscious application of learned rules, etc., Ädel 2005). Of course, oral productions are not totally exempt of the conscious application of learned rules, but are less likely to be, given the demands of on-line processing in oral communication. Additionally, longitudinal corpora are also a better window into development over time, as the same learners can be studied at regular intervals during the acquisition process. For these reasons, although there are some large cross-sectional electronic corpora of L2 English writing already in existence, including the pioneering International Corpus of Learner English (Granger, Dagneaux, & Meunier 2002), and the 10 million-word Longman Learners' Corpus, consisting of written work produced by L2 learners of English from a wide range of L1s and levels (see www.longman. com/dictionaries/corpus/lclearn.html), this work will only very briefly be reviewed here, so that we may concentrate instead on presenting the case study of the creation and analysis of a French oral learner corpora database.

The collection of oral data is both expensive and labor intensive. Learners need to be identified and access negotiated, tasks need to be carefully designed in order to elicit the kind of data which will allow to answer the specific research questions being asked, and then must be administered, recorded and transcribed, before analysis can take place. For these reasons, unsurprisingly, researchers have traditionally only managed to collect small datasets. Even a very ambitious project, such as the 1980s European Science Foundation (ESF) project (Perdue 1993), which involved learners from 11 source and target languages, reports in detail on the linguistic development of very small numbers of learners in each setting (for some language pairs, only 3 or 4 learners), thus making it difficult to evaluate the generalizability of the ESF theoretical claims (Perdue 1995; Perdue & Klein 1997). Similarly, the influential claims of Lardiere (1998a, 1998b, 2000) about the 'end state' of second language acquisition are based on the study of a single Chinese learner of English, Patty, tested over a period of some eighteen years. Although this dataset is undoubtedly extremely valuable, given its lon-gitudinal nature and the time-span of the data collection, it needs to be complemented by other similar datasets.

It is too often the case in the SLA literature that conclusions are reached on the basis of the L2 production of very small numbers of learners, leading to what may be premature generalization. The need for basing SLA analyses on both larger samples and a greater range of language pairs, has been argued for by an increasing number of researchers in the field (Ellis 2002b; Rutherford & Thomas 2001).

It is therefore crucially important that much larger and diverse corpora of oral in-terlanguage data should be collected and shared for use in SLA research. Information technology can assist researchers in a number of ways at this stage: In the elicita-tion, storage and management of data, and above all, its accessibility. We will now briefly outline these contributions of new technologies to oral data collection, before discussing and illustrating more fully the main potential contribution of computer technology to SLA research, that is, its role in supporting data analysis.

2.3.1 *Data storage and management*

It is now extremely easy to collect oral data digitally and to store them on a com-puter in the shape of digital sound files, usually of much better quality and durability than analogue data. Computers can also help in the elicitation of data, for example through web-based or computer-based elicitation tasks (Ayoun 2000). Many soft-ware programs are freely available to assist transcription, for example the University of Michigan's *SoundScriber* (www.lsa.umich.edu/eli/micase/soundscriber.html), and editing software such as *Adobe Audition* (www.adobe.com/special/products/audition/syntrillium.html) make it easy to manipulate the sound files in a number of ways, for instance, to locate a particular excerpt, to edit files for anonymization purposes, or to time pauses.

2.3.2 *Data accessibility*

Undoubtedly, one of the main advantages of using new technologies in order to handle large datasets of oral L2 data is accessibility to the wider research community, via a web interface. The advantages of sharing large L2 corpora are summarized below:

– Before embarking on expensive and time-consuming data collection, SLA re-searchers have the option of using existing L2 corpora to pursue a range of focused research agendas. Decisions as to the necessity for new data collection will depend on the nature of the research questions being asked, and on the corpora available.
– Electronic datasets are durable, and can be analyzed in different ways by separate research teams. This means that such datasets will be much more fully exploited than if used by the original creators alone.
– With full access to the original dataset, it will become easier to scrutinize and cross-check the interpretation of L2 phenomena made by other researchers.

- Different research groups, with varying expertise and research agendas, can contribute different types of secondary material to a database, such as annotated files. For example, one group of researchers could tag the same oral L2 corpus for its morpho-syntactic categories, while another group could annotate prosodic or phonological features, and yet another sociolinguistic and/or discourse features, thus greatly enhancing the database.
- Sharing datasets should act as a stimulus to the field to agree a common format for corpora in order to ensure comparability. This common format should not only deal with annotations such as transcription conventions and tagging, but also learner profiles (what features should be encoded, how learners' levels should be determined etc.).[4]
- Agreeing transcription procedures will allow not only to facilitate the use of other researchers' data without having to learn new conventions every time, but, crucially, it will allow the field to address more systematically the problems involved in representing in written form oral interlanguage data with all its non-standard features. For example, how do you transcribe the [e] ending very commonly used as the default form for verbs in early French interlanguage data? Should it be *jouer/joué*? What do you do when learners mispronounce a form, such as the definite article which very often sounds something between *le* ('the', masculine, singular) and *la* ('the', feminine, singular) in early interlanguage data?

It is important to note here that data-sharing practices are much more likely to become commonplace if the software being used for analysis procedures is free, and access to learner databases themselves is made available without charge to researchers and students. In some areas of applied linguistics, the construction of corpora has been undertaken as a commercial or semi-commercial venture (e.g., the various corpora supported by ELT publishers), and in such cases access to software and/or to corpora is often restricted, or may be available only through subscription. (The *Cambridge Learner Corpus*, for example, is only available for use to authors and staff of Cambridge University Press, and the *International Corpus of Learner English* is relatively expensive to purchase.) We believe that for the SLA research community to make full use of corpora and associated software, access to both should be unrestricted. The CHILDES project is a longstanding example of good practice in terms of open access, and it is crucially important that applied linguists and SLA researchers adopt similar access procedures, as more and more L2 learner corpora become available.

But if the use of new technologies for data storage and management is self-evidently beneficial for data accessibility, the most important benefit of such tools is undoubtedly for data analysis. The next section is going to briefly review corpus linguistics methodologies, and how they have been used in SLA research.

---

4. I am grateful to an anonymous reviewer for pointing this out.

2.4 Data analysis: What kinds of tools are available?

Hunston (2002) divides the general types of analysis which the overall development of corpus linguistics has made possible into 'word-based' and 'category-based' methods.

Word-based methods involve the identification of words or sequences of words (or rather, letter strings separated by blanks) within a corpus in order to perform a variety of operations upon them, through the use of concordancers such as *WordSmith Tools* (Scott 1999). Concordancing, that is the identification and collation of all examples of a given word or phrase within the corpus, together with their immediate context (typically, a line of text with the target word in the middle), allows for a variety of further analyses such as the identification and statistical analysis of lexical collocates of the target word or phrase, or of the grammatical relations it enters into (see Hunston 2002: Chapters 3 and 4). Other word-based methods include the use of software to calculate the mean length of utterances (MLU) in a given corpus, to work out the frequencies of lexical types and tokens in a corpus[5] (and the type/token ratio), or to identify 'keywords' within a text (Hunston 2002: 67–68).

Category-based methods involve some form of annotation of the corpus before-hand, allocating the words it contains to different categories proposed by researchers and program writers, which can then be used as the basis for corpus searches and statistical procedures in the same way as with concordancers (Hunston 2002: 79–94). Researchers may choose to annotate corpora manually, semi-automatically or auto-matically, depending on a range of factors, from the size of the corpus, the level of accuracy and refinement of annotation required, and the software tools available (Hunston 2002: 82–83). Part-of-speech (POS) taggers are one of the most common category-based programs used, typically achieving over 90 per cent accuracy in assign-ing grammatical categories to the words in a native corpus (e.g., CLAWS or the *Bank of English* tagger). For example, the latest version of CLAWS has now been used to POS tag the 100 million words of the *British National Corpus* (UCREL 2004). Computer programs have also been written in order to parse previously tagged corpus texts, that is, to label sentences, clauses and phrases of different syntactic types (see e.g., Leech & Eyes 1997; quoted in Hunston 2002: 84). However, the output of parsers still typically requires editing and correction by researchers.

Apart from tagging POS to support the analysis of morphology and syntax, category-based methods have been developed to annotate corpora for a wide variety of other features, such as semantic content and discourse functions (see e.g., Garside, Leech, & McEnery 1997 for examples). Some researchers have also undertaken manual tagging of L2 corpora: For instance, the work of Granger and her colleagues who have annotated written corpora of learner English and of learner French for error analy-sis purposes using an error editor to automate the entering of error tags (Dagneaux, Dennes, & Granger 1998; Granger, Vandeventer, & Hamel 2001).

---

5. *Lexical types* refer to the number of different words in a corpus, whereas *tokens* refers to the total number of words (e.g. the word *the* counts as one type, but might have numerous tokens).

2.5   How have these tools been used in SLA research?

The SLA research community remains rather slow to make use of software for the analysis of large learner corpora (see e.g., Aston et al. 2004; Granger et al. 2002, for an overview of existing work), and this in spite of slowly increasing availability of electronic datasets (e.g., the small number of L2 oral datasets becoming available via CHILDES, discussed later). One of the reasons for this is arguably the (non) availability of (or lack of familiarity with) software suitable for SLA purposes, as well as the fact that applied linguistics students are seldom trained in the use of computerized methodologies. For some research agendas, programs such as concordancers can be very effective and useful. However, as we have seen, this type of program only supports searches for words, phrases or morphemes, rather than more abstract features such as grammatical categories, or phonological patterns. (Concordancers can of course re-trieve grammatical categories if the corpus has been tagged, but they do not include tools for tagging the corpus automatically.) For this reason, they have been used pri-marily by acquisitionists working on discrete words or discourse (e.g., Aijmer 2002; Flowerdew 2004; Hasselgren 2002; Lenko-Szymanska 2004; Nesselhauf 2004). Given that a great majority of SLA researchers to date have been concerned primarily with the acquisition of morpho-syntax, for which concordancers have limited use, it is no surprise that they have largely ignored corpus linguistics tools.

The 1990s saw two attempts to develop analysis software specifically to deal with L2 data: COALA developed by Pienemann (1992), and COMOLA by Jagtman and Bongaerts (1994). These programs, however, did not seem to capture the imagination of the SLA community, perhaps because it was not yet ready to embrace such method-ologies, and they have now been discontinued. No POS tagging software is currently available which has been specifically designed for SLA data. Limited attempts have been made to use standard taggers (i.e., designed for native data) in order to annotate SLA data (e.g., Granger & Rayson 1998), but their use on deviant L2 data is prob-lematic (Granger 2002: 18). By contrast, in the field of L1 acquisition, software for the storage, management, sharing and analysis of data (the CHILDES system), has been constantly developed and updated since the early 1980s, and is now very widely used.

Very little recent corpus-based L2 research has made use of more sophisticated tools than concordancers. In a recent review of such work, Myles (2005b) only found a handful of studies making use of tools such as POS taggers or CHILDES (Borin & Prütz 2004; Housen 2002; Tono 2004). Additionally, the L2 remains En-glish in all cases, and the corpora are all written (except in one case, where a large written corpus is complemented by a small oral one). All learners are ad-vanced. This is due of course to the computerized written corpora currently avail-able to the research community, which are largely limited to the ICLE corpus (http://www.i6doc.com, (Granger et al. 2002) and the Longman Learners' corpus (http://www.longman.com/dictionaries/corpus/lclearn.html). Most of the studies are rather unambitious in their use of new technology, and remain descriptive, document-ing differences between L2 productions and the target language, rather than attempting to provide an explanatory account. Barring a few exceptions, these studies are also not very well informed by SLA theory, and tend to assume that finding out differences in use between learners and native speakers will have direct pedagogical implications, which of course is not necessarily the case. Such research is undoubtedly useful, as we need good descriptions of learner interlanguage on which to base our explanatory accounts of its development. However, corpus linguists and SLA specialists must now work more closely together in order to ensure that the methodologies used best serve the research agendas of current interest to the field.

The second part of this chapter will present a case study of the creation and exploitation of a database of oral French L2 corpora, illustrating how new technologies can assist SLA research.

3. The FLLOC database: A case study

This last section outlines an ongoing research initiative by a team of researchers including the present author,[6] which has led to the construction of a database of oral French L2 corpora, available from the internet and comprising transcripts, soundfiles, and morphosyntactically tagged transcripts (http://www.flloc.soton.ac.uk). This database will be used to give an example of the possibilities offered by computerized methodologies, in the context of French SLA. After a brief presentation of the software and database, we will illustrate how the various tools available in CHILDES can assist in investigating specific research questions across large datasets. For more details of the database and its methodology, see Marsden, Myles, Rule and Mitchell (2003), Myles and Mitchell (2004), Rule, Marsden, Myles and Mitchell (2003).

3.1 The CHILDES system

Like many L2 researchers, we have been engaged for a number of years in the collection of data to address specific research agendas. For example, in the early 90s, our research team collected a very large longitudinal corpus from classroom learners of French, comprising some 60 children studied over a period of over two years (12 to 14 year-old), who were tested once a term using a battery of 1:1 oral tasks with a researcher and pair tasks (Mitchell & Dickson 1997). This corpus comprises some 650 transcripts (around 720,000 words), and we became acutely aware that this extremely rich dataset could never be exploited to its full potential by our own research team, as we were only able to analyze a relatively small subset of the database manually (Mitchell & Martin 1997; Myles 2003, 2005a; Myles, Hooper, & Mitchell 1998; Myles, Mitchell, & Hooper 1999). Moreover, the dataset was not easy to share with other researchers. In

---

6. Other members of the team include or have included: Rosamond Mitchell, Sarah Rule, Emma Marsden, Annabelle David, Vladimir Mircevski, Mischa Tuffield.

the context of a new project, we therefore decided to investigate the possibility of using computerized methodologies to manage, store, share and analyse the data (Myles 2002). After investigating the various options available, we came to the conclusion that the CHILDES system was the most suitable option, especially as SLA-specific adaptations seemed quite easy to incorporate into the system. There were many reasons for this choice: The system is sophisticated and well supported; it is used as a standard within the L1 research community; it is constantly updated and refined; it is relatively flexible and capable of being adapted to specific needs; the policy of open access adopted by CHILDES makes accessibility and data-sharing very straightforward. Additionally, CHILDES offers a large suite of software including both word-based and category-based programs which can be used to carry out concordancing, frequency counts, and so on. Most importantly for us given our research interests, CHILDES also makes available POS taggers for a range of languages (currently 11 languages, with more in preparation).[7] The POS taggers are relatively easy to modify according to specific criteria and research needs. In its latest version, the CHILDES system is also XML compatible.[8]

The CHILDES system was originally conceived in the early eighties to assist first language acquisition research, but it is also now used for research into language disorders and in a limited way for second language research (Housen 2002; Malvern & Richards 2002; Malvern, Richards, Chipere, & Durán 2004; Paradis, Corre, & Genesee 1998). The CHILDES tools have been used in well over 1300 published studies ranging from all aspects of L1 acquisition to computational linguistics, language disorders, narrative structures, literacy development, phonological analyses and sociolinguistics (MacWhinney 2000a, 2000b). All CHILDES tools are freely available on the internet (http://childes.psy.cmu.edu).

CHILDES consists of three integrated components:

– The database, TALKBANK, consists primarily of child speech recordings and transcriptions in a wide range of languages, but it also includes some language disorder data and bilingual data. It is a condition of using CHILDES tools that any data transcribed and analyzed with them becomes part of the Talkbank database. A small but increasing number of SLA datasets is now available in Talkbank, including:

   – The Ionin corpus (Russian immigrant children learning English; 22 participants aged 2:4 to 12:5).

---

7. Cantonese, Chinese, Danish, Dutch, English, French, German, Hebrew, Italian, Japanese and Spanish.

8. EXtensible Markup Language (XML) was designed to meet the challenges of large-scale electronic publishing, and is now playing an increasingly important role in the exchange of a wide variety of data on the Web and elsewhere.

- The Reading corpus (34 oral GCSE examinations taken by 16 year-old English learners of French within the UK education context; group of 15 native controls).
- The LIDES corpus (The Language Interaction Data Exchange System – LIPPS project: Language Interaction in Plurilingual and Plurilectal Speakers). The researchers involved have used their own list of coding conventions based on the CHILDES conventions. For example, they specifically tag each word/morpheme to indicate its language (http://talkbank.org/data/LIDES/). The LIPPS research team have produced a coding manual which is available to other researchers.
- Part of the FLLOC database described in this chapter (the rest will be integrated into Talkbank in the near future).

- CHAT (Codes for the Human Analysis of Transcripts) are the transcription procedures, which must be adhered to in order to ensure compatibility with the CLAN analysis programmes.
- CLAN (Computerized Language Analysis) consists of 37 commands for carrying out various operations such as tagging, searches and counts, along with a range of 'switches' that can be used to customize each command. This is a powerful and flexible software package that can carry out rapid and detailed analyses, and is designed to recognize the tagging conventions of CHAT.

3.2 Transcription and tagging

3.2.1 *Headers and tiers*

All files must start with a *header* which contains information about the file (e.g., task, participants), and which is crucial for requesting the CLAN programs to carry out analyses on individual or batches of files, specific speakers, and so on.

Transcripts following the CHAT system are organised in tiers: The main (or speaker) tier always starts with *, and contains the language produced during the interaction. In addition to this main tier, 'dependent tiers' can optionally be added on separate lines, which always start with %, and contain any coding of the data, as well as any commentary. Examples of such tiers are the *%err* tier (on which errors are coded), the *%mor* tier (containing morpho-syntactic tagging), the *%com* tier (commentary) or the *%pho tier* (phonological coding). Many more are listed and exemplified in the CHAT manual available online (http://childes.psy.cmu.edu). The advantage of organizing the data in this way is that, in view of their own research agenda, researchers can add whatever tiers are necessary for their data analysis. Some tiers are generated automatically (e.g., the morphosyntactic tagging), while others are generated by hand coding (e.g., the error coding); either way, the new levels of coding can then be added to the database for use by other researchers. The data do not become increasingly cluttered, however, as transcripts can be viewed and handled without the various dependent tiers. Once coding is complete, the various CLAN commands can be applied to any of the tiers.

The transcription conventions are specified in the CHILDES manual and must be adhered to for the CLAN programs to run successfully on the data. It is however possible to add various adaptations, for instance, for SLA specific purposes.[9]

3.2.2 *The %mor tier*

A tool we found particularly useful in CLAN is the MOR program which generates morpho-syntactic tagging of the speaker line (semi-)automatically. Versions of MOR have been produced for a range of languages (eleven so far), with the MOR tagger for French developed by Christophe Parisse in 2001. Below is an excerpt from a transcript with an added MOR tier from the Linguistic Development Corpus (see database content below). The extract comes from the file of a year 10 learner (15 year old; 3 ½ years of classroom French) carrying out an elicitation task focusing on the use of negation. *N27 is the speaker line for the learner and *FLO the speaker line for the researcher.

(1)   *N27:   elle ne pas fumer .
      %mor: pro:subj|elle&FEM&_3S adv:neg|ne adv:neg|pas v:inf|fumer .
      *FLO: mmm .
      *N27:   um elle chanter .
      %mor: co|um pro:subj|elle&FEM&_3S v:inf|chanter .
      *FLO: mmm .
      *N27:   um # elle [/] # elle ne pas fait du golf .
      %mor: co|um pro:subj|elle&FEM&_3S adv:neg|ne adv:neg|pas
              v:mdllex|faire&PRES&3SV prep:art|du&MASC&SING n|golf&_MASC .
      *FLO: très bien .
      *N27:   elle [/] # elle [/] elle boit du thé .
      %mor: pro:subj|elle&FEM&_3S v|boire&PRES&3SV prep:art|du&MASC&SING
              n|thé&_MASC .
      *FLO: mmm.
      *N27:   euh elle fait de tennis .
      %mor: co|euh pro:subj|elle&FEM&_3S v:mdllex|faire&PRES&3SV prep:art|de
              n|tennis&_MASC&_SINGPL .
      Note: for details of the transcription conventions, see http://www.flloc.soton.ac.uk

The %mor line can be generated very quickly on large batches of files, in the following three steps: First, the MOR command tags the data with all possible options (e.g., *pas* will be tagged as both a noun and a negator); second, the POST command disambiguates over 90% of the data automatically; finally, a manual disambiguator allows you to assign a category to the instances POST has not been able to decide on. Other CLAN commands then enable searches for morpho-syntactic strings to be carried out directly on this output.

---

9.   For details of how this has been achieved in the context of the case study database, see Marsden et al. (2003); Myles and Mitchell (2004); Rule et al. (2003).

3.3 CLAN commands

A full list of the programs currently available in CLAN can be found in the Appendix. There are currently 37 programs available, and most researchers will only use a few of these, depending on their research needs. We will only illustrate here a few of the CLAN commands, selected for their potential usefulness for SLA research, and illustrating different types of analysis (e.g., lexical, morphological, syntactic). In each case, we will illustrate the working of the programs with small scale analyses conducted on the FLLOC database.

3.3.1 *Word-based analyses: MLU*

The mean length of utterance is a common measure of a child's developmental level in the early stages of L1 acquisition. It is particularly useful for short utterances (MLUs of 5 and under), and has been little used in SLA research for two reasons: (a) Learners who are well beyond the very early stages are usually the object of study; and (b) L2 learners in the early stages of acquisition tend to rely on sometimes lengthy rote-learned phrases which can skew the results (Myles et al. 1998, 1999). However we have found it useful as a rough measure in studying development among early L2 learners. For example, the following MLUs were found for the same instructed L2 French learner (coded *01) undertaking a conversational task with an adult researcher at two years' interval (at ages 12 and 14):

(2) From file <01A7iiPRD.cha>
       MLU for Speaker: *01A:
       Number of: utterances = 98, morphemes = 232
       Ratio of morphemes over utterances = **2.367**
       Standard deviation = 1.847

(3) From file <01L9viJVH.cha>
       MLU for Speaker: *01L:
       Number of: utterances = 33, morphemes = 197
       Ratio of morphemes over utterances = **5.970**
       Standard deviation = 3.504

The MLU for learner *01 has increased from 2.36 to 5.97 when performing the same task at two years' interval. Scaled up for use with group data, calculations of MLU can give a rough general measure of the level of complexity of beginner learners' interlanguage at different stages.

3.3.2 *Word-based analyses: Lexical richness*

CLAN incorporates typical concordancing programs which can be used for the lexical analysis of a corpus. As well as various concordancing searches (KWAL, COMBO), which will be illustrated later, programs such as FREQ and FREQPOS compute the frequency of the words produced in a file or batch of files, according to sentence position in the case of FREQPOS.

Table 1. FREQ output for Learner *04, conversation task, age 12 (from file <04L9LAJ.cha>)

51 le	2 maison	1 journaliste
14 euh	2 ok	1 livre
14 um	2 peint	1 magasin
11 et	2 pêche	1 magazine
10 garçon	2 regarder	1 monde
8 monster@sd	2 vrai	1 ou
5 grand_mère	1 aller	1 parler
4 en	1 arriver	1 part
4 family@sd	1 avec	1 peint@g
4 lake@sd	1 bateau	1 photos
4 mère	1 beaucoup	1 pour
4 petit	1 courses	1 prendre
4 ville	1 de	1 prennent
4 à	1 demande	1 rester
3 bouées	1 elle@g	1 surprise
3 dans	1 est@g	1 surprise@g
3 fille	1 fait	1 télé
3 la	1 faux	1 un
3 lac	1 font	1 vacances
2 aussi	1 il	1 voient
2 des	1 ils	1 voiture
2 dessin	1 jardin	

65 Total number of different word types used
211 Total number of words (tokens)
0.308 Type/Token ratio
Notes:
@g indicates a word repeated from the researcher's output
@sd indicates an English noun

In Table 1 we present the output of FREQ applied to a story retelling task for Learner *04 (year 9, age 13), arranged in descending order (various switches allow for different presentation formats, e.g. in alphabetical order, ascending or descending order of frequency, etc.).

The program gives the total number of word types, word tokens, and type/token ratio at the bottom of each frequency output. Such frequency data can be used in a variety of ways, for instance, as a progress measure, or as the basis for further analyses of categories of words known/used, of contexts of use, and so on. It can be fed into a statistical package such as STATFREQ. Again, these analyses can be scaled up to include several files for the same learner (e.g., to compare output from year to year for each learner), or batches of files from entire groups of learners (e.g., to compare lexical output from whole year groups). For a much more sophisticated measure of lexical diversity using CHILDES see Malvern and Richards (2002), as well as Malvern et al. (2004).

3.3.3 *Word-based analyses: Concordancing*

COMBO is the CLAN program which searches for (complex) string patterns. It can be applied to any of the tiers, enabling the search of both words or strings of words, and of morpho-syntactic patterns as we will illustrate shortly. A simple search for the word *mère* 'mother' as a search string on the learner tier, carried out for Learner *04 for the same file as that used in Table 1 above, is shown below:

(4)   combo +t*L04 +s "mère" 04L9LAJ.cha

Combo:	CLAN search command
+ t*L04:	specifies the tier (in this case we only want to do a word-based search on the main tier for Learner *04, excluding the researcher's utterances)
+s:	start of the search string
"word":	word searched for
04L9LAJ.cha:	name of file the search is carried out on (which contains info about learner, task, year and researcher)

The output of this command is as follows:

(5)   From file <04L9LAJ.cha>

  *** File "04L9LAJ.cha": line 14.

  *L04:   um le (1)mère livre le maga(zine) le euh .

  *** File "04L9LAJ.cha": line 38.

  *L04:   le (1)mère et le petit garçon euh # .

  *** File "04L9LAJ.cha": line 44.

  *L04:   euh le (1)mère et le garçon # fait des courses [*] à la ville .

  *** File "04L9LAJ.cha": line 59.

  *L04:   le (1)mère et le petit garçon um [^ eng: how do you say see?] .

  Strings matched 4 times

The output indicates the file which has been searched (this is a particularly very useful feature when the analysis has been carried out on batches of files), then lists all utterances in which the string has been found, indicating at the end how many times the string has been found.

3.3.4 *Category-based analyses: Morpho-syntax*

Once morpho-syntactic tagging has been completed as illustrated above, complex searches can then be carried out directly on the morpho-syntactic output. For example, all instances of verbs in the infinitive can be retrieved, or all relative pronouns, and so on. More complex strings can also be searched for: Such as all instances of a negator directly followed by a verb in the infinitive, or all adjectives following a noun, or all masculine determiners followed by a feminine noun, and so on. The possibilities are as diverse as the research questions.

The following COMBO command is written to search directly on the morpho-syntactic output, that is, the *%mor* tier, for instances of incorrect assignment of gender concord, in this case, instances where a masculine determiner is followed by a feminine noun. For illustrative purposes the command has again been written for a single file (learner *47 undertaking a picture narrative task):

(6)   combo +t%mor +s"det*MASC*^n*FEM*" 47L11FLO.mor.pst

+t%mor:	indicates the tier the search is carried out on
*:	indicates any metacharacter (some symbols might follow the MASC code on the *mor* output)
MASC:	the code for masculine
^:	followed by
n:	the code for noun
FEM:	the code for feminine
47L11FLO.mor.pst:	the name of the file. '.mor.pst' is the file extension after it has been 'mored' and 'posted' (POST is the disambiguation program).

The output is as follows:

From file <47L11FLO.mor.pst>

*** File "47L11FLO.mor.pst": line 11.

*L47:   la famille en vacances euh le grand_mère et les enfants euh euh et le lac et la maison de Wales [/] Wales .

%mor: det|la&FEM&SING n|famille&_FEM prep:art|en n|vacance&_FEM-_PL co|euh (1)det|le&MASC&SING (1)n|grand_mère&_FEM conj|et det|les&PL adj|enfant&_PL co|euh co|euh conj|et det|le&MASC&SING n|lac&_MASC conj|et det|la&FEM&SING n|maison&_FEM prep|de n:prop|Wales .

*** File "47L11FLO.mor.pst": line 40.

*L47:   um le mère um regarder le magasin euh .

%mor: co|um (1)det|le&MASC&SING (1)n|mère&_FEM co|um v:inf|regarder det|le&MASC&SING n|magasin&_MASC co|euh .

*** File "47L11FLO.mor.pst": line 47.

*L47:   le grand_mère peint <le mons(tre)> [//] le monster@s:d du lac .

%mor: (1)det|le&MASC&SING (1)n|grand_mère&_FEM v|peindre&PRES&3SV det|le&MASC&SING n:eng|monster det|du&MASC&SING n|lac&_MASC .

*** File "47L11FLO.mor.pst": line 65.

*L47:   um le mère et les garçons um faire les courses regarder le magasin .

%mor: co|um (1)det|le&MASC&SING (1)n|mère&_FEM conj|et det|les&PL n|garçon&_MASC-_PL co|um v:mdllex|faire&INF det|les&PL n|course&_FEM-_PL v:inf|regarder det|le&MASC&SING n|magasin&_MASC .

*** File "47L11FLO.mor.pst": line 71.

*L47:   ok um le grand_mère peint le en xxx .

%mor: co|ok co|um (1)det|le&MASC&SING (1)n|grand_mère&_FEM v|peindre&PRES&3SV det|le&MASC&SING prep|en |xxx .

*** File "47L11FLO.mor.pst ": line 79.

*L47:   un bouée deux bouées um treize bouées et quatre bouées [?] .

%mor: (1)det|un&MASC&SING (1)n|bouée&_FEM num|deux n|bouée&_FEM-
        _PL co|um num|treize n|bouée&_FEM-_PL conj|et num|quatre
        n|bouée&_FEM-_PL .

*** File "47L11FLO.mor.pst ": line 136.

*L47:   <le famille> [/] um le famille [^ eng: how do you say leave] ?

%mor: co|um (1)det|le&MASC&SING (1)n|famille&_FEM ?

Strings matched 7 times

This search shows that learner 47 produced 7 instances of masculine determiners followed by feminine nouns in this task. Complementary searches for other combinations of masculine and feminine attribution on nouns, determiners, and adjectives make it very easy to find patterns of gender attribution and agreement across large amounts of data, either from individual learners or whole groups of learners. Given current theoretical interest in gender assignment and agreement (see e.g., Ayoun this volume; Franceschina 2001; Hawkins 1998b; Hawkins & Franceschina 2004; Myles 1995; Prévost & White 2000; Sokolik & Smith 1992), it is crucially important that we have access to large oral corpora, preferably longitudinal, representing a range of L1/L2 pairs which vary in terms of gender being an inherent property of nouns as in Romance languages or not. We can then trace the development of gender assignment in different learner populations, and assess the significance of parametric differences in functional features on the basis of plentiful and varied evidence, rather than very small groups of learners.

Let us illustrate with one further example the use of Combo to search for a category-based complex string in order to address a specific research agenda of current theoretical interest. Rule and Marsden (2006) investigated the development of negatives in relation to finite and non-finite verbs in the emerging grammars of early learners of French. Differences in negative placement in French and English are a result of the verb raising past the negative in French but not in English because Infl is strong in French but weak in English. Therefore, the French negative particle *pas* occurs after a finite lexical verb in French (1), but in English 'not' cannot occur after a finite lexical verb (2) and the dummy auxiliary 'do' needs to be inserted (3). The verb will not raise over negation in French if it is non-finite (4) (for more details concerning verb raising in French see Ayoun 2005a; Hawkins 2001; Herschensohn this volume).

(7)   *Jean ne regarde pas la television*

(8)   *'Jean (ne) watches not the television'

(9)   *John does not watch television*

(10) *Jean regarde la télévision pour ne pas s'endormir*
      'John watches television to not sleep' (i.e., in order not to fall asleep)

Rule and Marsden therefore traced all occurrences of the following in the data:

- *pas* followed immediately by infinitive
- *pas* followed immediately by verb in present
- verb in present followed immediately by *pas*
- infinitive followed immediately by *pas*

This could be done extremely easily, across the whole corpus, using a COMBO directly on the %MOR tier (for further details, see Rule 2004; Rule & Marsden 2006).

We hope to have demonstrated through these examples how the CHILDES tools can serve a wide range of current research agendas. Remember our criticism of the current SLA literature often making wide ranging claims on the basis of very small numbers of learners, and therefore making it difficult to generalize to other learners and/or language pairs. More systematic use of computerized methodologies applied to large and varied electronic corpora will enable us to become much more confident about our observations, and therefore about possible explanations for these observations. For example, the current debate about the relationship between the acquisition of morphology and syntax in second language learners, both in Initial State and in End State grammars (for a review, see Herschensohn this volume), will only be resolved by tracing the development of a wider range of learners from a variety of L1/L2 backgrounds. Moreover, longitudinal corpora such as that of Patty (Lardiere 1998a, 1998b, 2000) or that of Chloe (Herschensohn this volume), are extremely rare and valuable, as they allow to follow development over time; therefore, they must be shared and complemented by other similar and contrasting datasets. Additionally, some theoretically interesting properties are quite rare in spontaneous learner productions (e.g., adverbs, which raise interesting questions about the verb-raising parameter), and having access to a variety of large corpora increases the chance of finding enough tokens of that property to draw useful conclusions.

After this brief illustration of the possibilities offered by the CHILDES system to assist L2 analysis, let us now turn to a short description of the database which supported these analyses.

3.4 The database (www.flloc.soton.ac.uk)[10]

The FLLOC website contains an electronic database of French Learner Language Oral Corpora, representing classroom learners at different levels, freely available to the research community. Each corpus in the database includes digital sound files and transcripts formatted using CHILDES conventions, as well as transcripts which have been tagged morpho-syntactically. The database also comprises a search facility which enables researchers to select the sound files and transcripts they wish to access, according

---

10. This project was supported by grants from the Economic and Social Research Council (RES000220070) and the Arts and Humanities Research Board (RE-AN9657/APN15456). A further project funded by the Arts and Humanities Research Council (REF112118) is adding a new longitudinal corpus of AS/A level learners (16–18 years-old) to complete the database.

to criteria such as the level of the learners, the elicitation task used, the sex of the participants, and so on.

The corpora included in the database have all been digitized and edited to ensure anonymity, and the transcripts have been (re)formatted according to the CHILDES system. Details of the CHILDES tools are given on the website, and any additional transcription conventions that have been used are specified in the context of each project (e.g., SLA-specific adaptations). Additionally, most of the transcripts have been tagged using the French MOR program and these tagged transcripts are also available on the website.

The corpora included in the database have all been donated by SLA researchers in the United Kingdom and in Europe, so that they can be easily accessible to the research community. There are currently five corpora in total, representing instructed learners of L2 French from complete beginners to final year university undergraduates, undertaking a range of interactive and narrative tasks, mostly on a one-to-one basis with a researcher. A further longitudinal corpus of AS and A level students (UK context; age 16–18) is currently being collected. The database currently includes approximately 1,350,000 words, representing 1375 transcripts and accompanying soundfiles, as well as morphosyntactically tagged files in most cases, as follows:

- *Progression Corpus*: 60 learners in years 7, 8 and 9 in the UK context (beginners at outset of data collection; age 12–14; longitudinal over 2 ¼ years; range of 1:1 narrative and interactive tasks, e.g., story retelling, information gap, structured conversation etc. – $\simeq$ 720,000 words, 650 transcripts and soundfiles, approximately 10 to 15 minutes each).
- *Linguistic Development Corpus:* 20 learners in each of years 9, 10 and 11 in the UK (post-beginners; age 14–16; cross-sectional; four 1:1 tasks each, some repeated from above project – $\simeq$ 214,000 words, 240 transcripts/soundfiles, around 10 to 15 minutes each).
- *Reading Corpus:* 34 learners (post-beginners; age 16; UK GCSE oral examination; 26 native controls – $\simeq$ 41,400 words, 60 transcripts).
- *Salford Corpus:* 12 university undergraduate learners in the UK (intermediate to advanced; longitudinal; narrative and interactive tasks – $\simeq$ 332,000 words, 300 transcripts and soundfiles; approximately 5 to 10 minutes each).
- *Brussels Corpus:* 125 Dutch learners of French (intermediate; narrative task; 18-year olds – $\simeq$ 41,800 words, 125 transcripts).

Each corpus is accompanied by a project description, which includes details of the learners and the tasks used, any additional transcription conventions used, plus an overview of the files contained in the database. How each corpus is organized is also specified (e.g., longitudinal corpora are organized chronologically, whereas cross-sectional corpora are organized by task). All files (sound files, transcripts and tagged transcripts) can be directly downloaded for use by bona fide researchers who sign up to an explicit users' code.

To our knowledge, this is the only French L2 oral database currently available to the research community on the web.

4. Conclusion

So, what can we conclude about the current use of computerized methodologies in SLA research? Some progress has undoubtedly been made, and there are now some L2 corpora available. But there are too few, and the kind of studies that are being undertaken are too closely dependent on what corpora are at hand, and what software tools are readily available and user-friendly. For reasons explored earlier, the kind of corpora which are currently available are not necessarily those most suited to the investigation of SLA acquisition processes; they are nearly always written, cross-sectional, and overwhelmingly from advanced learners of English. Although these corpora clearly have their place in the range of SLA studies the field needs to undertake, especially at the level of lexis, discourse and pragmatics, and are of interest to university teachers of advanced learners, they need to be supplemented by a much more diverse range of corpora, both in terms of the level of the learners and of the range of languages. To advance its research agenda, the field now needs good quality longitudinal oral corpora, in a number of different L1/L2 combinations. Furthermore, these corpora need to be shared systematically across the research community, as they represent one of its most valuable resources.

Additionally, the field needs to become much more ambitious in its use of new technologies, which should be serving its own agenda, rather than dictating it. The possibilities offered by the computerized analysis of corpora are considerable, as we hope to have demonstrated. SLA researchers, however, need to ensure that not only the corpora they collect, but the computerized tools they use, are adapted to their research agendas, rather than the other way round, that is, adapting their research questions to the corpora or the tools readily available as is too often the case. Some sophisticated tools can now be used, and it is high time that the pioneering work of L1 acquisitionists in this area is emulated by L2 researchers, so that our collective goal of better explaining second language acquisition becomes more firmly grounded in rich empirical data.

5. Directions for future research

As will have become clear from reading this chapter, much remains to be done. Very few L2 studies make use of computerized methodologies to analyse L2 corpora. When they do, it is overwhelmingly in the context of written productions of advanced L2 English. Moreover, these studies often remain limited, and fail to be theoretically informed.

The needs of the field are therefore endless, and can be summarized as follows:

- The collection of good quality corpora, in a range of L1/L2 pairs, preferably oral and longitudinal, is an urgent requirement;
- These corpora need to be made available to the research community via the web, preferably free of charge;
- SLA researchers and postgraduate students need to be trained in the use of appropriate software;
- Conventions need to be agreed for the transcription and annotation of L2 data, and for the documentation of learner profiles and corpora databases.

Some initial steps have been made in this direction, but considerably more remains to be done.

Appendix

CLAN commands (source: CHILDES on-line manual, http://childes.psy.cmu.edu/manuals/CLAN.pdf, pp. 37–38)

Command	Function
CHAINS	Tracks sequences of interactional codes across speakers.
CHECK	Verifies the accuracy of CHAT conventions in files.
CHIP	Examines parent-child repetition and expansion.
CHSTRING	Changes words and characters in CHAT files.
COLUMNS	Refor R Formats the transcripts into columnar form.
COMBO	Searches for complex string patterns.
COOCUR	Examines patterns of co-occurence between words.
DATES	Uses the date and birthdate of the child to compute age.
DIST	Examines patterns of separation between speech act codes.
DSS	Computes the Developmental Sentence Score.
FLO	Reformats the file in simplified form.
FREQ	Computes the frequencies of the words in a file or files.
FREQMERG	Combines the outputs of various runs of FREQ.
FREQPOS	Tracks the frequencies in various utterance positions.
GEM	Finds areas of text that were marked with gem markers.
GEMFREQ	Computes frequencies for words inside gem markers.
GEMLIST	Lists the pattern of gem markers in a file or files.
KEYMAP	Lists the frequencies of codes that follow a target code.
KWAL	Searches for word patterns and prints the line.
MAKEDATA	Converts data formats for CHAT files across platforms.
MAKEMOD	Adds a %mod line for the target SAMPA phonology
MAXWD	Finds the longest words in a file.
MLT	Computes the mean length of turn.
MLU	Computes the mean length of utterance.
MODREP	Matches the child's phonology to the parental model.
MOR	Inserts a new tier with part-of-speech codes.

(*continued*)

Command	Function
PHONFREQ	Computes the frequency of phonemes in various positions.
POST	Probabilistic disambiguator for the %mor line
POSTLIST	Displays the patterns learned by POSTTRAIN
POSTTRAIN	Trains the probabilistic network used by POST
RELY	Measures reliability across two transcriptions.
SALTIN	Converts SALT files to CHAT format.
STATFREQ	Formats the output of FREQ for statistical analysis.
TEXTIN	Converts straight text to CHAT format.
TIMEDUR	Uses the numbers in sonic bullets to compute overlaps.
VOCD	Computes the VOCD lexical diversity measure.
WDLEN	Computes the length of utterances in words.

## CHAPTER 14

Creole studies

Patrick-André Mather
Universidad de Puerto Rico, Río Piedras

Résumé

Dans le présent chapitre, nous nous proposons d'examiner différents modèles sur la genèse des langues créoles qui ont été proposés ou défendus au cours des 40 dernières années par des linguistes francophones en Europe (notamment Chaudenson, Hazael-Massieux et Manessy), et en Amérique du Nord (notamment Lefebvre et Valdman), à savoir les modèles substratistes, universalistes et superstratistes (ou "eurogénétiques"). Nous examinerons les questions liées aux processus cognitifs responsables de la créolisation, notamment les processus d'acquisition et d'appropriation des langues première et seconde, mais aussi les facteurs externes telle l'histoire socio-économique des colonies où les langues créoles ont vu le jour. Ensuite, nous aborderons les débats théoriques et idéologiques relatifs aux rôles respectifs des langues européennes et africaines dans la genèse des créoles, étant donné que ces questions ont été, et demeurent, très controversées parmi les créolistes francophones. Enfin, nous présenterons l'un des modèles de créolisation les plus courants, ou modèle "gradualiste", à la lumière des recherches récentes parmi les créolistes francophones et autres. Pour l'illustrer, nous comparerons des structures de différents créoles français et de français langue seconde.

Abstract

This chapter summarizes and discusses models of creole genesis that have developed over the past 40 years among Francophone (and other) linguists both in Europe (e.g., Chaudenson, Hazael-Massieux, Manessy) and in North America (e.g., Lefebvre, Valdman). It covers internal factors, such as the cognitive processes involved in creolization, but also external factors such as the socio-economic histories of the plantation colonies where these languages emerged. In addition, ideological debates concerning the respective roles of European and African languages in the genesis of creoles will be addressed, as these are and have been very controversial among French-speaking creolists over the past few decades. Finally, one widely accepted model of creolization, the so-called Gradualist Model, is discussed in the light of recent research among Francophone and other creolists.

1.   Introduction

In this chapter we discuss the origin of French-lexifier creoles, and the role of both
L1 and L2 acquisition in the genesis of these languages. Creoles are languages born
in the 17th and 18th centuries in European plantation colonies, through contact between European superstrate languages (mainly French, English, Dutch, Portuguese
and Spanish) and various substrate languages spoken by slaves and indentured laborers (e.g., from West Africa in the case of Caribbean creoles). Creoles are by definition
mixed languages: While their lexicon is mainly derived from their respective European
superstrates (e.g., French), their morpho-syntax is a combination of substrate features
(e.g., West African), superstrate features, and innovations resulting from processes of
first (L1) and second (L2) language acquisition. Typically, creoles are highly analytic
languages, with a fixed SVO word-order, invariant preverbal tense, mood and aspect
(TMA) markers, and little, if any, inflectional morphology. Creole studies is relevant
for theories on language genesis and change, for models of L1 and L2 acquisition,
and for sociolinguistics since creoles often co-exist with their respective lexifier languages in what is often termed diglossia (Ferguson 1959). Creolistics is thus concerned
with explaining mechanisms of language change, and teasing apart the respective roles
of substrates, superstrates and languages universals in the genesis of creole languages,
that is, of L1 and L2 acquisition. In the following, we first present the traditional model
of creole genesis that until recently was widely used in textbooks, a two-step model of
pidginization and subsequent creolization. Second, we discuss briefly the history and
geographical distribution of French-lexifier creoles. Then, we outline the main competing hypotheses on the origin of creoles, namely the substratist, superstratist and
universalist views of creole genesis, which place different emphases on the respective
roles of the L1, the L2, and universals of acquisition. Finally, we explore the Gradualist
Model of creole genesis, which is currently the most widely accepted among Francophone creolists, and which views creole genesis as the result of L2 acquisition of French
over several generations, with limited access to native speakers of French.

2.   The emergence of creole studies and the nativization hypothesis

Most creolists draw a sharp distinction between pidgins and creoles. For example, Hall
(1966:xii) states: "For a language to be a true pidgin, two conditions must be met: Its
grammatical structure and its vocabulary must be sharply reduced [...], and also the
resultant language must be native to none of those who use it". Hymes (1971b:65–90)
defines a pidgin as a simple code which "evolves as a response to a limited need for
communication" and which encodes only "the most basic functions of communication [...] the result being impoverished or absent morphology [...] limited lexical
stock; a constrained number of adpositions; non-expression of the copula; and lack
of sentential embedding". One frequently cited example of a pidgin is Russenorsk (described in Broch 1927; and Broch & Jahr 1984), a trade pidgin created and used in

the 19th century by Norwegian and Russian fishermen. Russenorsk had a limited vocabulary, mainly SVO word order, no inflectional or derivational morphology, and a single multiple-use preposition. The following example is provided by Broch and Jahr (1984:41):

(1) *Kor   ju   stannom pa gammel ras?*
     where you   stay   on old   time
     'Where did you stay last year?'

For the purposes of this chapter, we will adopt this 'classic' definition of a pidgin, as summarized by DeGraff (1999:6): "Pidgins [...] are simplified, lexically and structurally reduced, unstable nonnative systems, with variable and inconsistent patterns, created and used for limited communication among adults who are native speakers of mutually unintelligible languages". This definition excludes so-called "expanded pidgins" like Tok Pisin, since the latter are as structurally and lexically complex as any language, creole or other.[1] Traditionally, a creole is defined as a pidgin that has become the native language of a speech community (Hall 1966:xiii). Once a pidgin is acquired as a native language by children, one says it has been creolized. According to this theory, concomitant with nativization of the pidgin, there is structural expansion and complexification: As the incipient creole takes on all the functions of a first language, it complexifies and acquires the various grammatical and stylistic resources needed for the language to function as the main language of a community, such as means to express tense, mood and aspect, embedded structures, topicalization of certain phrases, and so on. Thus, according to the traditional model of creole genesis (which views a creole as a nativized pidgin), it seems logical to assume that children are the main agents of creolization, which is viewed fundamentally as a process of L1, rather than L2, acquisition. The main proponent of this model is Bickerton (1981, 1999), which we discuss below in Section 3.3.

The traditional model of creole genesis, which views a creole as a nativized pidgin, was until recently widely assumed to apply to most plantation creoles in the Caribbean and in the Indian Ocean. We will see in the following sections that most Francophone creolists dispute the claim that creoles were made by children, and their argument is based in part on the absence of any evidence of a pidgin stage in French plantation colonies.

It is difficult to provide a precise definition of *creole* since there is much controversy surrounding the origin, development and typological features shared by creole languages. According to Thomason (2001:159–160):

> Creoles develop in contact situations that typically involve more than two languages (...); they typically draw their lexicon, but not their grammar, primarily from a single language, the lexifier language (...). The grammar of a creole, like the grammar of a

---

1. Tok Pisin is the official name of New Guinea Pidgin English, which evolved as a contact language in the 18th and 19th centuries and has recently acquired native (e.g., L1) speakers. It is also an official language in Papua New Guinea.

pidgin, is a crosslanguage compromise of the languages of its creators, who may or may not include native speakers of the lexifier language.

It should be added that most creoles share several typological characteristics, such as a fixed SVO word order, reduplication, little or no inflectional morphology (in particular no morphological markings for gender or plurality, invariant verbs), and a series of preverbal tense, mood and aspect markers instead of verbal suffixes. In short, creoles are highly analytical languages, and in this sense are typologically close to Kwa languages from West Africa, and quite different from French, which even in its non-standard, spoken varieties has some inflectional morphology and a more variable word-order. Thus, while the lexicon of French-lexifier creoles is largely derived from French, the morphosyntax and semantics is the product of independent developments, possibly with considerable transfer from West African (and other) substrates.

3.   An overview of French-lexifier creoles

The colonization of various territories by the French during the 17th and 18th centuries led to the emergence of various creolized varieties of French. These varieties fall into two main groups.

The first group of creoles emerged in the Americas during the late 17th and early 18th centuries: The creoles spoken to this day in Guadeloupe, Martinique, Dominica, St Lucia and French Guyana are to a large extent mutually intelligible, and are sometimes referred to collectively as *créole antillais* (see examples below and in Section 5.3). There are two other French creoles in the same area: Haitian, which is a more radical creole and not mutually intelligible with *créole antillais,* and Louisiana Creole, which is closer to Standard French than both Haitian and *créole antillais* (see also Caldas this volume). The following examples are taken from Poullet and Telchid (1990: 248–250):

(2)   Louisiana Creole: *To bezwen monjé kêkjoz oubyen to va tonbé malad.*
      Guadeloupean Creole: *Ou bizwen manjé kèchoz sansa ou ké tonbé malad.*
      French: *Tu dois manger quelque chose sinon tu vas tomber malade.*
                                        'You must eat something, otherwise you will become sick'

(3)   Haitian Creole: *Nan nuit la m'té blijé changé pozisyon*
      Guadeloupean Creole: *Adan lannuit-la an té oblijé chanjé pozisyon*
      French: *Dans la nuit, j'ai été obligé de changer de position.*
                                        'During the night, I had to change position'

Haitian is a more radical creole for several reasons. One is the fact that the country has been linguistically and culturally isolated from France since its independence in 1800, with only 5% of the population being able to speak French fluently. This contrasts with other French creoles in the Caribbean, which often co-exist with French (as in Martinique, Guadeloupe and French Guyana).

The second group of French-lexifier creoles, referred to as *Isle de France* creoles, are spoken on islands in the Indian Ocean that were settled in the 18th century from

Mauritius. Mauritian is a radical creole spoken on Mauritius, with closely related varieties in Rodrigues and the Seychelles. A more acrolectal variety (i.e., a variety closer to French in terms of its morpho-syntax, most notably its verbal inflectional morphology) is spoken on the French island of *Réunion* (see Mather 2001). These islands were settled in the same way as the Caribbean islands, except that slaves and laborers were brought in mainly from East (rather than West) Africa, Madagascar (during the initial phase of settlement, or *société d'habitation*), and many Indian contract laborers were subsequently brought in after the abolition of slavery. Structurally, *Isle de France* creoles are quite similar to Caribbean Creoles, with the exception of *Réunionnais* which is sometimes referred to as a 'semi-creole' because it represents a partial, rather than complete, restructuring of French and retains some French morphology like gender and tense inflection (see Holm 2004: 19).

The following are sentences in Haitian, Guadeloupean and Mauritian creoles, along with their translations in English and French.

(4) Haitian Creole (Holm 2000: 91; adapted from Valdman 1970: 260):
Te   gen   you tan   zannimo te   gen   you wa   ki   te   you nonm trè
ANT have a   time animals ANT have a   king who ANT a   man   very
entèlijan epi trè   malen.
clever   and very cunning
Il était une fois des animaux qui avaient un roi très intelligent et très malin
'There once were animals who had a king who was a very clever and very cunning man.'

(5) Guadeloupean Creole (Poullet & Telchid 1990: 57):
Yè   maten,   Man Elvina té   tousèl an kaz   a-y,   sé timoun
Yesterday morning, Mrs. Elvina ANT alone in house at-her, be children
a-y-la   pa té   la,   yotout té   soti.
at-her-DET not ANT there,   all   ANT gone.
Hier matin, Madame Elvina était toute seule dans sa maison, ses enfants n'étaient pas là, ils étaient tous sortis
'Yesterday morning, Mrs. Elvina was alone in her house, her children weren't there, they were all gone'

(6) Mauritian Creole (Adone 1994):
Mo ti   ava fin kapav etidye si mo pa ti   mizer
I   ANT MOD PERF able study if I   not PAST poor
J'aurais pu étudier si je n'étais pas pauvre
'I could have studied if I were not poor'

The three examples above illustrate the main characteristics of creoles: Although most of the lexicon and some structures can be traced back to (non-standard) French (with some phonological changes), the sentence structure and word-order are markedly different. For instance, several French verbs, modals and past participles (such as *été* 'been', *était* 'was', *va* 'go', *fini* 'finished') were reanalyzed as invariant, pre-verbal markers expressing tense, mood and aspect. Creoles are thus typologically distinct languages, and despite similarities in the lexicon, cannot be considered dialects of French.

4. Competing models: Substratists, superstratists, universalists

Creolists disagree on the cognitive processes at work during creole genesis, and on the respective role of susbstrates (in particular, African languages), of the superstrate (French) and of language universals (e.g., Universal Grammar). Generally speaking, substratists argue that creole genesis can be largely accounted for as the result of *second* language acquisition with restricted access to the lexifier language (here, French), and with massive transfer from the African substrates. Superstratists also believe that creole genesis is a special case of L2 acquisition, but argue that French was gradually restructured by successive generations of L2 speakers (incoming slaves/laborers acquiring French from earlier slaves), accelerating changes that were already ongoing in French (e.g., morphological simplification). On the other hand, Universalists (e.g., Bickerton) argue that creole genesis is a special case of *first* language acquisition in the absence of robust input. In other words, children created creoles using the 'macaronic' pidgin of their parents, and using the default semantic and syntactic settings of Universal Grammar. As such, if one adopts the Bickertonian view of creole genesis (which is not endorsed by most Francophone creolists such as Bollée, Manessy, Mufwene, Neumann-Holschuh, Valdman), creoles represent somewhat of a challenge from the parameter-setting language acquisition perspective that calls for clear, abundant and unambiguous input. According to Bickerton (1977:49), creolization is "L1 acquisition with restricted input". This restricted input, according to Bickerton's model, was a macaronic pidgin. How can children set parameters using this degenerate input? One possible solution proposed by Bickerton is the Language Bioprogram Hypothesis, equated with Universal Grammar, and defined "in terms of a set of parameters [...] each parameter having a finite (and small) number of possible settings [...] [constituting] the list of preferred settings that the child, in the absence of contrary evidence, would assume to be appropriate" (Bickerton 1984:178). As pointed out by Ayoun (2003:15), Bickerton claims that the unmarked setting is the most likely to be chosen, "a result indicative of some strong predisposition of the organism to adopt that setting" (Bickerton 1999:59). Default settings are chosen as a last resort, that is, when no evidence suggests that another setting should be adopted. Bickerton (1999) defends the Language Bioprogram by claiming that it consists in a set of default settings that come into play when "no preexisting TMA [tense, modality, aspect] or sequence markers get incorporated into the creole grammar. These settings are not triggered lexically – they are triggered by the *absence* of TMA markers" (p. 61).

Contra Bickerton, Lightfoot (1999) claims that children scan the input for cues and set their parameters accordingly. Some parameters may be set to the marked setting, whereas others will be set to the unmarked setting. More specifically, Lightfoot (1999:433) shows that children set parameters according to cues in unembedded domains: "Learners do not try to match the input; rather, they seek certain abstract structures in the input [...], looking only at structurally simple domains [...]. The output of the grammar is entirely a by-product of the cued parameter settings". This is a strong departure from input-matching models, and allows for creolization (in the sense of nativization of a macaronic pidgin) without necessarily appealing to Bickerton's Bioprogram. A corollary is that creoles, if indeed they are the product of L1 (rather than L2) acquisition using restricted input, do not necessarily represent the unmarked parameter settings.

We will now look at each of the three main competing models of creole genesis, keeping in mind that each attributes a different role to L1 acquisition, L2 acquisition and, for the latter, to L1 transfer versus universals of L2 acquisition. The reader should note that the following section presents an overview of various competing theories, which do not necessarily represent the author's own view of creole genesis, which will be presented in Sections 4 and 5.

4.1 Substratist theories

According to substratists (e.g., Koopman 1986; Alleyne 1986), the structure of creoles is due largely to the transfer of substratum structures into the incipient creole. As a universalist, Bickerton has repeatedly challenged substratists to provide an account of exactly how substrate features made their way into the incipient creoles. Lefebvre (1986, 1998) and Lumsden (1999) have met this challenge by proposing a mental process of relexification whereby substratum (West African) lexical entries are relabeled using phonetic strings from the European lexifier language. In other words, in Lefebvre's view, Haitian is a West African (specifically, Fongbe) language used with French phonetic strings. Or, French words used in a Fongbe grammatical mold. One example is in the similar use and combination of preverbal TMA markers in both Haitian and Fongbe, as illustrated by the following example:

(7) *Mari t' ap   prepare pat*   [Haitian]
    Mari ko ná   da   wo   [Fongbe]
    Mary ANT DEF-FUT prepare dough
    'Mary would have prepared dough'   (Lefebvre 1998: 124–125)

This is in striking contrast to French, which uses auxiliaries and inflectional suffixes, as illustrated below:[2]

(8) *Marie aurait préparé de la pâte*
    'Mary would have prepared dough'

In addition to relexification, Lefebvre (1998) argues that two other processes were at work during the genesis of Haitian: Reanalysis and dialect leveling, both of which are claimed to feed on the output of relexification. There exist some interesting parallels between relexification in creole genesis, and L1 transfer in L2 acquisition theory.

A case in point is Schwartz and Sprouse (1996), who believe that L2 learners have full access to Universal Grammar, but contrary to Epstein, Flynn and Martohardjono

---

2. DeGraff (2002), in an extensive review of Lefebvre's work, disputes her analysis of the data and argues that some of these constructions can also be derived from non-standard French forms.

(1996), they argue that the L1 also plays a major role. More specifically, they claim that learners initially assume that their L1 in its entirety (with the exception of the phonetic matrices of lexical items) constitutes the starting point in L2 acquisition. In Schwartz and Sprouse's (1996) Full Access/Full Transfer model, learners start off with their L1 grammar, and then gradually restructure their interlanguage guided by principles and parameters of Universal Grammar. In this model, L1 and L2 acquisition differ both in their initial state and often in their final state, mainly because of the L1. To support this hypothesis, researchers must show that (a) L2 learners use the analysis of their L1 as their first hypothesis of L2 input, and (b) learners with different L1s show different development paths. With respect to (b), Schwartz (1996) shows that Korean and Turkish learners of German, whose L1 is verb final, initially posit that German is also verb-final, whereas Romance and Arabic learners, whose L1s are VX, first assume that German is also VX.

What is appealing about the Full Transfer/Full Access model is that it makes precise claims about L1 transfer, and in particular, that transfer is found in earlier stages of development, and that transfer errors precede developmental errors (which are consistent with Universal Grammar but cannot be traced back to the L1 or the L2). This position mirrors Lefebvre's (1986, 1998) relexification hypothesis, in which the creators of Haitian used their entire L1 grammar and inserted the phonetic matrices of the L2 (French). It should be noted, contra Lefebvre and Schwartz and Sprouse, that some L2 acquisition researchers have shown (e.g., Juffs 1996; Montrul 1997) that the Full Transfer /Full Access model is an oversimplification. For example, Montrul (1997: 265) shows that in the initial stages of acquisition of the L2 lexicon, learners overgeneralize the causative/inchoative alternation to unergative and unaccusative verbs. In doing so, they rely on a kind of universal semantic template and make the same developmental errors as L1 learners. L1 transfer errors do occur, but in later stages, and affect inflectional morphology, such as overt vs. zero verb markings. This is consistent with a modular view of L1 transfer, that is, certain areas of grammar are more susceptible to transfer than others.

Lumsden (1999: 129) argues that relexification is not limited to creole genesis, but that it "is also visible in lexical transfer errors that are typical of incomplete second language acquisition by adults". He adds that "the concrete evidence for relexification in adult L2 learning is found in examples of lexical transfer" (ibid.: 131). Based on work by Lefebvre (1986, 1998), it is also argued that relexification applies only to lexical categories, namely nouns, verbs, adjectives and prepositions. Whether or not one adheres to Lefebvre and Lumsden's relexification hypothesis for Haitian creole, relexification itself may very well be the mental process underlying substratum influence in both L2 acquisition and creole genesis. Some historical linguists have observed (e.g., Rayfield 1970; Thomason & Kaufman 1988) that shift-induced interference is mainly structural, while the lexicon is that of the target language. In other words, it may often appear that learners are using words from the L2 with the L1 grammatical mold. In fact, lexical entries encode not only the phonological forms and the semantics of words, but also case assignment and subcategorization properties which are reflected in the sentence structure, in addition to semantic information (e.g., argument structure; see Pinker 1989). If learners only acquire the surface, phonetic form of some L2 words but use the properties of the corresponding L1 lexical entry, then the result does account for shift-induced interference. Lumsden (1999: 131) expresses this idea as follows:

> A person who already has a native language may create a new vocabulary of lexical categories by linking the semantic and syntactic representations of his native language lexicon with new phonological representations that are derived from the phonetic strings of a target language.

Of course, relexification only applies when learners fail to acquire all the properties of a particular L2 lexical entry. In many instances, some L1 words are relexified with L2 phonetic strings, while in other cases all the properties of a particular L2 word are acquired, not just the phonetic shape. It follows that the more restricted the access to the L2,[3] the greater the role of relexification in creole genesis. Thus, relexification will rarely apply wholesale, as Lefebvre (1998) believes it does for Haitian, and in most cases it will account only for those structures which seem to be borrowed from substratum languages, while other L2 acquisition processes are also at work (see examples of relexification below in Section 5).

4.2 Superstratist theories

With some notable exceptions (e.g., Lefebvre, Valdman), most francophone creolists minimize the role of African languages in the genesis of creoles, and some even reject the notion that creoles are mixed languages. For example, Chaudenson (2002: 3ff.) denounces "erroneous ideas" often found within the creolistics literature:

> *Une littérature scientifique largement dépassée contribue à maintenir dans le public des idées fausses comme la 'mixité' des créoles, le rôle majeur des langues africaines, l'intercompréhension des créoles français* [...].
> 'A largely outdated scientific literature has helped maintain among the general public misguided ideas such as the 'mixed' identity of creoles, the major role of African languages, or the mutual intelligibility of French creoles'.   [translation mine]

Chaudenson and other francophone creolists (e.g., Bollée, Manessy, Mufwene, Neumann-Holschuh, Valdman) subscribe to the notion that creoles are European languages that have evolved in a particular or accelerated way due to exceptional social and demographic circumstances, and have thus become autonomous langages. Chaudenson (2002: 5) labels his model "*le modèle eurogénétique*", since he believes that creolization is the result of the spontaneous acquisition (i.e., acquisition in an informal setting without corrective feedback) of popular, regional varieties of 17th century

---

3. The "restricted access" hypothesis has been disputed by several creolists, including Chaudenson and Mufwene.

French, which had already undergone some restructuring and koineization in French colonies. According to Chaudenson (2002:7):

> *La disproportion entre les populations blanche et noire, quand s'installent les 'sociétés de plantation' entraîne, pour la plupart des nouveaux arrivants, une forme de rupture avec le modèle linguistique central; ce sont les stratégies d'apprentissage linguistique qui, s'exerçant sur les variétés elles-mêmes approximatives des esclaves chargés désormais de l'encadrement, vont conduire à l'émergence et à l'institutionnalisation des systèmes nouveaux que sont les créoles.*
>
> 'The disproportion between the white and black populations when the first plantations are set up, leads for most new arrivals to a break with the central linguistic model; language acquisition strategies, applied to the already approximate varieties of the slaves in charge of the new arrivals, lead to the emergence and to the institutionalization of new linguistic systems, creole languages'.   [translation mine]

Contrary to the classical model of creole genesis, there is strong evidence (e.g., Chaudenson 1989; Mufwene 1997) that many, if not most plantation creoles in the Caribbean and in the Indian Ocean never had a 'pidgin' stage which can be clearly differentiated from a creole. For French-lexifier creoles, there is evidence that most plantation creoles never had a pidgin stage at all: Bollée (1977a, b, c) for instance shows that creolization is possible without a prior pidgin stage, using evidence from Indian Ocean French creoles. This suggests that the classical definition of a creole as a 'nativized pidgin' needs to be revised to account for the gradualist scenario, which views creoles as the result of the acquisition of successive L2 varieties of French over several generations, as will be explained below.

There is also an ongoing debate about the rate of creole genesis. According to several studies on the genesis of Atlantic and Indian Ocean creoles (Arends 1986, 1989; Baker 1990, 1993; Chaudenson 1979, 1989, 1992; Mufwene 1990, 1997; Plag 1993; Singler 1986, 1988, 1990, 1993, 1996), most plantation creoles developed over a period of several generations, up to one century. According to this gradualist model, during the first period of colonization, European settlers had very few slaves; the latter lived in close contact with their white masters, and little creolization occurred. As the number of slaves increased, especially during the 18th-century sugar boom, the L2 European varieties acquired by the new slaves were increasingly divergent from the lexifier as these speakers had less and less access to native speakers of the lexifier language. In line with Chaudenson (1989) and Mufwene (1990) for example, Arends (1993:376) believes that creolization is a process which is "gradual rather than sudden, over several generations", and that it is a process of L2 (rather than L1) acquisition by adults. DeGraff (1999) argues that both L1 and L2 acquisition are involved.

This hypothesis is compatible with the gradualist theory of creolization as advocated inter alia by Chaudenson (see references above), although the latter downplays, and perhaps underestimates, the role of substratum transfer in the emergence of the creole grammar. In sum, creole genesis may occur whenever L2 speakers of French (or any other lexifier language) have limited direct access to the lexifier languages (be it the standard or non-standard, colonial varieties). This amounts to saying that gradual creolization (Chaudenson 1989; Mufwene 1997; contra Bickerton 1977, 1981, 1999) is no different from shift-induced language change in the target language, except that in the former, access to the target language is more restricted than in the latter. In other words, in normal shift-induced language change, speakers shift gradually to the target language and have access to native speakers of that language, and only some substratum features (mainly phonological) make it into the new variety. In creole genesis however, language shift is more rapid and learners have little or no access to L1 speakers, therefore substratum features have a better chance of fossilizing and becoming part of the new, restructured variety, that is, of the emerging creole.

While there is compelling evidence that creolization in French plantation colonies in the Indian Ocean and the Caribbean is the result of successive waves of slaves acquiring increasingly divergent varieties of the target language, no one was there to record the process, although there are some textual attestations of early stages of creolization in both *Réunion* and Haiti for example (see references in Lefebvre 1998:397). What is needed is data on the acquisition of L2 French by speakers of languages believed to have been spoken by slaves in the plantation colonies. Such data are available in Lafage (1985), Manessy (1994), and Mather (2005). Some examples are provided in Section 6 below.

4.3 Universalist theories

As noted above, Bickerton (1977, 1981, 1999) draws a sharp distinction between pidgins and creoles. Ever since Bickerton first formulated his theory on creole genesis, the Bioprogram Hypothesis has created a great deal of excitement and controversy among creolists. Bickerton (1981) is an ambitious attempt to answer three questions concerning the "roots of language": (1) How were creole languages formed and, in particular, how do children create a full-fledged natural language with severely impoverished input?; (2) How do children acquire languages?; and (3) How did the human language faculty emerge? The Bioprogram, which has been equated to Universal Grammar by for instance DeGraff (1999), is defined as an innate faculty which ensures that, given linguistic input, humans will develop a specific type of grammar in the same way they develop a particular skeletal structure. A creole language is the realization of the 'default' instructions of the Bioprogram *qua* Universal Grammar with minimal language-specific idiosyncrasies. This 'default' language would appear as part of the normal development of each child, but in most cases the 'default' settings are over-run by the idiosyncrasies of the language used in the country where each child is born. According to Bickerton (1981), the incorrect hypotheses made by children are similar to structures found in creole grammars. Thus, in the absence of sufficient input from the speech of adults (when these adults speak a rudimentary pidgin, for example), children automatically use the default grammatical features of Universal Grammar. Bickerton views the many similarities between creoles in different regions of the world as evidence for his theoretical model.

Regarding the linguistic content of the Bioprogram, Bickerton (1981) proposes four basic semantic distinctions, which correspond to four different syntactic constructions in creoles: (a) Specific/non-specific (e.g., determiners); (b) State/process; (c) Punctual/non-punctual (e.g., verb aspect); and (d) Causative/non-causative.

For example, Hawaiian Creole English uses the definite article *da* for specific NPs known to the listener and the indefinite article *wan* for specific NPs unknown to the listener. Other NPs have no articles or markers of plurality. The following examples are cited in Romaine (1988:260–261):

(9)   *Hi get   da hawaian   waif*
      He have a   Hawaiian wife
      'He has a Hawaiian wife'

(10) *Hi get   wan blaek buk*
      He have one black book
      'He has a black book'

(11) *Yang   fela   dei   no   du daet*
      Young fellow they NEG do that
      'Young fellows don't do that'

(12) *Bat nobadi gon get jab*
      But nobody FUT get job
      'But nobody will get a job'

(13) *Hu   go daun frs   is luza*
      Who go down first is loser
      'The one who goes down first is the loser'

The distribution of *da* and *wan* in HCE is markedly different from that of 'the' and 'a' in English, as evidenced in the above examples. Bickerton (1981:56) claims that most creoles have a system identical to that of HCE, citing examples from Guyanese Creole which are remarkably similar to HCE.[4]

Bickerton (1981) studies in detail the tense, aspect and mood systems of creoles. He proposes that verbs express three different oppositions which are realized as preverbal particles, in that order: (a) The tense opposition [anterior]; (b) The aspectual opposition [punctual]; and (c) The modality distinction [irrealis]. These express basic semantic primitives which, according to Bickerton (1981), are a human universal linguistic prototype, and emerge as default settings in the children who are the creators of creoles, on the basis of a 'macaronic' pidgin. In the case of HCE, the markers are *bin* (anterior), *go* (irrealis) and *stei* (punctual).

More recently, Bickerton (1999) reiterates the hypothesis that creolization is the result of L1 acquisition with impoverished pidgin input, and compares the pidgin-to-creole cycle with the utterances of children before and after their second birthday,

---

4. Mufwene (1986) disputes the SPECIFIC/NONSPECIFIC distinction in the case of Gullah, showing also partial similarity to English. M. Dijkhoff contradicts Bickerton with Papiamentu data from complex nominals.

showing that at age two there is an "explosion of syntax". Thus, neither pidgins nor the language of "under-twos" make use of syntax: "It is as if children pass from a pidgin stage to a creole stage in a matter of days or weeks at most (ibid.: 64)", and the "course of syntactic acquisition is consistent with the abrupt coming-on-line of a specific neurological module devoted to syntactic processing" (ibid.: 65). He also argues that children must be the creators of creoles, using impoverished pidgin input, since "adults can only acquire a language if input is rich and robust". This argument is based, crucially, on the premise that the initial stages of creole genesis is some kind of "macaronic" pidgin with little grammatical structure, and that the innate Bioprogram enables children to restructure this input into a UG-consistent grammar, presumably with very little owed to their parents' L1(s). Thus, according to Bickerton (1981, 1999), similarities among creoles are due, primarily, to the universal operation of the Bioprogram among children exposed to different pidgins throughout the world.

Although Bickerton's model was certainly revolutionary when first proposed almost 30 years ago, it has been criticized on several grounds. On the one hand, there is little or no evidence of a 'pidgin' stage for French-lexifier creoles. On the other hand, the assumption is that the children who created creoles were somehow clean-slates in that they did not have access to any robust linguistic input. This seems unlikely since many children were probably bilingual or even trilingual, that is, acquired their parents' L1(s) in addition to the pidgin/creole used in the wider community.

In addition, there are several problems with Bickerton's interpretation of his data. Based on work by Clark (1979) and Goodman (1985), McWhorter (1997: 55ff.) provides some evidence against the Bioprogram: In particular, he argues that Bickerton's Hawaian pidgin speakers were probably not the originators of Hawaiian Creole English (HCE). In fact, they were not pidgin speakers, but rather second language speakers of HCE. McWhorter's argument is based on written accounts from the middle of the 19th century, which provide evidence that there was an English-based pidgin in Hawaii much earlier than hypothesized by Bickerton, even though a Hawaiian-based pidgin may have been dominant in the mid-19th century in terms of numbers of speakers. This argument is particularly damaging to the Bioprogram since Hawaii provides the only evidence for Bickerton's model. If Bickerton's pidgin data prove to be from the wrong period, then his entire hypothesis falls apart.

4.4 Mixed views

Recently, there has been much cross-fertilization among various areas of research. Some L2 acquisition researchers have worked on similarities and differences among L2 acquisition and pidgins and creoles, including Mufwene (1990, 1997), Odlin (1992), Selinker and Lakshmanan (1992), Arends (1993), Manessy (1994), DeGraff (1996), Wekker (1996), Winford (1998), Siegel (1999), and DeGraff (1999). Furthermore, there is now much more detailed data and historical documentation on a variety of creoles. In L2 acquisition, one interesting avenue which is relevant for creole genesis is the study of untutored learning situations, which led to a better understanding of the nature of interlanguages within immigrant speech communities. There has also been considerable work on the role of the L1 in L2 acquisition, for example Perdue (1993), and Véronique (1994). Starting in the 1980s, creolists have also started to synthesize universalist and substratist views (e.g., Mufwene 1986; Muysken & Smith 1986; Thomason & Kaufman 1988).

In his article in the International Encyclopedia of the Social and Behavioral Sciences (2002), Mufwene expressed the need for more cross-fertilization among different theoretical models:

> Few creolists subscribe nowadays to one exclusive genetic account, as evidenced by the contributions to Mufwene (1993). The 'complementary hypothesis' (Corne 1999; Mufwene 2001) seems to be an adequate alternative, provided we can articulate the ecological conditions under which the competing influences (between the substrate and superstrate languages, and within each group) may converge or prevail upon each other. This position was well anticipated by Schuchardt (1909, 1914) in his accounts of the geneses of *Lingua Franca* and of Saramaccan. More and more research is now underway uncovering the sociohistorical conditions under which different Creoles have developed, for instance, Arends (1995), Chaudenson (1992:21), Corne (1999), and Mufwene (2001).

DeGraff (1996), who also researched creole genesis and L2 acquisition, suggests that insufficient exposure to the target language leads to creolization: "It could be hypothesized that creolization occurs when the PLD (primary linguistic data, say, from a pidgin and/or the contact languages) adequately meet threshold T, due to the learner's age, length of exposure, extended use, and so on" (DeGraff 1996:724). For DeGraff, transfer through relexification, followed by the Bioprogram (i.e., Universal Grammar) 'filling the gaps', leads to creolization. DeGraff's idea is interesting in that it draws on both the universalist and the substratist positions. However, the two other hypotheses put forth by DeGraff are highly controversial: Most creolists do not believe that relexification (as defined in Muysken 1981; Lefebvre 1986, 1998) is a major factor in pidginization or creolization, and the Bioprogram hypothesis is very controversial as well, as already mentioned. It would therefore seem premature to take these two concepts wholesale and claim that they apply to other creoles.

5. Creole genesis: A particular case of L2 French acquisition over several generations?

As we have mentioned above, over the past twenty-five years, many creolists (and not only French or Francophone creolists) have argued that creole genesis is best described as a gradual process involving successive stages in the acquisition of L2 French or L2 English (e.g., Arends 1995; Chaudenson 1981, 1989; Migge 1998; Singler 1996). This theory can be called the L2 acquisition/gradualist model of creole genesis. Though most plantation creoles arose in the 17th and 18th centuries, today many co-exist with their European lexifier language, and there are a series of intermediate registers or "lects" between the acrolectal creole varieties, close to the lexifier language, and basilectal varieties, whose grammar has diverged considerably from that of the lexifier. According to the gradualist model, the acrolectal varieties pre-date the mesolectal and basilectal varieties. Creole genesis is viewed as a gradual process away from the lexifier language, toward increasing basilectalization, as successive generations of African slaves acquired increasingly divergent varieties of, and introduced substratum features into, the emerging contact language (see Chaudenson 2001; Mufwene 2001).

According to Chaudenson (2002: 8ff.) and others, three elements must be considered to account for the genesis of creoles. First, the French input heard by the slaves was not 20th century standard French, but 17th and 18th century non-standard varieties of French. Several researchers on French lexifier creoles (e.g., Alleyne 1996: 35–40) have shown that the *français populaire* 'popular French' at that time was characterized by a heavy reliance on periphrastic verbal constructions, and avoided the standard synthetic forms for the future and the past, for instance. This is crucial since most creolists agree that creole preverbal TMA (tense, mood and aspect) markers are in fact derived from colloquial French periphrastic constructions, as noted above in Section 2. As Alleyne (1996: 35) points out:

> *Il est important de constater que le français possède, et possédait dans le passé, au moins deux modalités syntaxiques – l'une standard, conservatrice, bourgeoise; l'autre innovatrice, dynamique, populaire.*
>
> 'It is worth noting that French has, and had in the past, at least to syntactic modalities – a standard, upper class conservative one, and an innovative, dynamic and working-class one'. [translation mine]

The 'popular' (i.e., working-class) French alluded to by Alleyne is characterized mainly by phonological and lexical differences, and by a greater reliance on analytical, periphrastic constructions to encode tense, mood and aspect, as opposed to the standard inflected forms (e.g., colloquial *je vais manger* vs. Standard French *je mangerai* 'I will eat'). This does not imply that colloquial and standard French were typologically different languages; but there were important stylistic differences, and the analytical structures of spoken French were more widely used, and because of their analyticity and reduced inflection, they more closely resembled the TMA markers of Kwa languages spoken by West African slaves. Chaudenson (2003) lists several constructions that show where the creoles' periphrastic constructions were selected from, and also shows that the verbal inflectional system was not that similar to modern French. Alleyne (1996: 35) adds:

> *La différenciation dialectale, telle qu'elle existe sur le territoire francais, a été observée principalement sur le plan phonologique et lexical [...] il y a beaucoup moins de particularités régionales sur le plan syntaxique.*
>
> 'Dialectal differences which exist in France have been observed mainly in the area of phonology and the lexicon... there are much fewer regional differences in the syntax'. [translation mine]

Second, Chaudenson (e.g., 2002:9) claims that in the last centuries, there have been evolutionary processes affecting specific aspects of French morphosyntax. The idea is that in normal L1 or L2 acquisition, these evolutionary processes are blocked, or at least slowed down, by pressure from the standard used in school (see Train this volume). In the absence of standardizing pressures, evolutionary processes are unrestricted and one gets the kind of accelerated language change evidenced by creoles.

Finally, Chaudenson (2002:10ff.) points out that there exist a number of acquisition strategies and processes that gradually enabled creole languages to emerge as autonomous languages, given very specific historical circumstances. Chaudenson (1989, 1995) distinguishes two phases in the settlement of plantation colonies: The *société d'habitation* (small farming units), and the *société de plantation* (large-scale sugar plantations). In the *société d'habitation*, the white population formed a majority, the farms were small and the number of slaves limited. At this time, superstrate and substrate speakers lived in close contact. It is likely that L2 varieties of French, similar perhaps to current L2 varieties spoken in West Africa, developed during this phase. At this initial stage, what occurred was a simple case of shift-induced language change. However, the *sociétés de plantation*, which were created during the sugar boom, required large numbers of slaves. Depending on the island colony, the sugar boom generally occurred during the first decades of the 18th century. In this new society, the slaves of the first generation, who had acquired an L2 variety of French during the first phase of settlement, are assumed to have become the intermediaries between the white masters and the new slaves who had no direct contact with L1 speakers of French. This particular situation is what distinguishes creole genesis from 'normal' L2 acquisition: The L2 variety of the first slaves became the target language of the incoming slaves, whose pidginized variety in turn became the target of the more recent arrivals (Chaudenson 1989:74). Creole genesis is a very specific process which requires the particular social and historical conditions that existed in the early 18th century in plantation colonies founded by Europeans.

Thus, creole genesis can be compared to a kind of L2 acquisition 'in reverse', in the sense that while the early stages of creole genesis were quasi 'normal' L2 acquisition, the end-stage produced a language (basilectal or radical creole) markedly different from the European lexifier. By contrast, in successful L2 acquisition, the end-stage of acquisition is closer to the target language than the initial stages. Thus, the phylogenesis of creoles (as E(xternalized)-languages in the sense of Chomsky (1986), that is, a language shared by a community of speakers) is a mirror image of the ontogenesis of an L2 grammar as constructed/represented in the mind of the individual speaker (or I(nternalized)-language). In particular, there is more L1 transfer in early stages of L2 acquisition, as there are more substratum features in the basilectal varieties of plantation creoles, which are more recent than acrolectal varieties.

If one recognizes that creole genesis is a particular instance of language change due to external causes (since two or more languages are interacting), it follows that creolization cannot be fully understood without reference to theories of L2 acquisition. Similarly, regular language change which is not due to language contact could conceivably be subsumed under a general theory of L1 acquisition. In the following section, we provide some evidence that creole genesis is a particular case of L2 acquisition under exceptional circumstances.

6.   On the development of creoles: Evidence from L2 French

Three kinds of evidence can help support the claim that creole genesis is best described as a succession of (increasingly 'deviant' from French) L2 varieties of French, acquired over several generations. First, current research in L2 acquisition may yield valuable insights into the cognitive mechanisms of creolization, including L1 transfer, selective acquisition of L2 structures, as well as reanalysis and fossilization of interlanguage structures. In the following, evidence of this kind will be adduced to illustrate parallels between creolistics and SLA theory. Second, case studies of West African L2 French can give us an idea of the initial stages of creolization, which Chaudenson (1995) and Singler (1996) defined as quasi normal L2 acquisition. Third, the creole continua that exist to this day on several former plantation colonies, including the islands of *Réunion* and Martinique, may very well represent a survival of the successive stages of creole genesis in the 17th and 18th centuries, with the acrolectal varieties being the oldest, and the mesolectal and basilectal varieties representing successive developments (see discussion in Chaudenson 2001; and Mufwene 2001).

Although most of the lexicon is of French origin, there are some *faux amis* ('false friends' or deceptive cognates). Some words have undergone phonological changes, sometimes reflecting archaic or regional pronunciations. For example, *voir* 'to see' is pronounced [vwe], *peine* 'sorrow' becomes [pen]. A number of other words of African, Indian, Caribbean and Spanish origin have also been added to this French lexical base. The following examples compare L2 French with structures in French-lexifier creoles, and illustrate how the initial stages of creole genesis may have been quasi-normal L2 acquisition of French, with some transfer from the L1s (here, West African languages, in particular Ewe and Fongbe).

6.1 The position of determiners within the NP

The position of the specifier, adjectives and complements within the noun phrase is a salient syntactic feature, and is readily identifiable in both creoles and L2 varieties of European languages. As noted by Lefebvre (1998:94), the definite article is post-nominal in both Haitian and Fongbe (one of the main West African substrate languages in Haitian creole):

(14)   *M manje krab la*   (Haitian Creole)
      I   eat   crab DET
      'I ate the crab (in question/that we know of)'

(15)   *N du ason o*   (Fongbe)
      I   eat crab DET
      'I ate the crab (in question/that we know of)'

As shown in the following examples, determiners are invariably post-nominal in dialects of Ewe (to which Fongbe belongs):

(16)   *nyonù – à*
      woman – the(SING)

(17)   *nyonù – wó*
      woman – the(PLUR)   (Ewe; Lafage 1985:242)

(18)   *molu a   bi   vò*
      rice DET cooked already
      'The rice is already cooked'   (Gengbe; Kangni 1989:15)

(19)   textit*tèkplo a   lè   xo   à   mè*
      table   DET be-at room DET inside
      'The table (in question) is in the room'   (Gengbe; Kangni 1989:15)

(20)   *àwù yà   zɛ*
      suit DEM torn
      'This suit is torn'   (Gengbe; Kangni 1989:15)

(21)   *èkplo nwa sì*
      table DEM old
      'This table is old'   (Gengbe; Kangni 1989:15)

Interestingly, there are examples of postposed determiners in the L2 French of L1 Ewe speakers, as illustrated in the examples below:

(22)   *N'y a   qu'à pousser auto-là*
      NEG have only push   car there
      'All you need to do is to push the car'   (L2 French, L1 Ewe; Lafage 1985:409)

(23)   *Femme là,   c'est méchant*
      Woman there, it is evil
      'The woman is evil'
      Standard French: *La femme est méchante.*
      'The woman is evil'   (Lafage 1985:407)

(24)   *Patron là il a   dit...*
      Boss   the he has said
      Standard French: *Le patron, il a dit.*
      'The boss said'   (Lafage 1985:412)

(25)   *La police va   arrêter voleurs là*
      The police will arrest thieves the/there
      Standard French: *La police va arrêter les voleurs.*
      'The police will arrest these thieves'   (Lafage 1985:416)

While it is true that the French demonstrative *-là* can be suffixed to a noun (especially in overseas varieties like Québec French, and in non-standard varieties of metropolitan French), it must be used in addition to the preposed definite article (in Québec French) or demonstrative (in Standard French), and it has a demonstrative meaning which is more marked than in Haitian, Fongbe, and the L2 French example above. This suggests that the substrate data influenced the reanalysis of the French structure, as evidenced by the Haitian and L2 French data.

6.2 Use (and omission) of noun determiners

In many French-lexifier creoles, preposed French determiners have been reanalyzed as part of the root noun, as in the following examples from Mauritian (Baker & Corne 1986: 170):

(26) a. *Zanfan*   *les enfants*   'child'
      b. *dilo*   *de l'eau*   'water'
      c. *lera*   *le rat*   'rat'
      d. *lamer*   *la mer*   'sea'

There are apparently over 550 such examples in Mauritian. Baker and Corne (1986: 170–172) claim that this 'agglutination' of the French article is due to Bantu substrate influence. Indeed, Bantu nouns have unstressed class prefixes, so when Bantu speakers tried to learn L2 French, they may have reanalyzed French articles as unstressed prefixes.

Though this reanalysis is not surprising (it is also found in child L1 varieties of French), it is significant that West African L2 speakers of French also tend to amalgamate the article and the noun, even though Kwa languages do not have class prefixes. Therefore, this reanalysis can occur regardless of whether there are class prefixes in the L1. Consider the following examples from *français populaire* ('popular French') by L1 Ewe speakers:

(27) *Y'a*   *un*   *l'école.*
      There's   a   the-school
      'There is a school'   (Lafage 1985: 410)

(28) *C'est*   *beaucoup*   *l'auto*   *pour*   *Lomé.*
      It's   many   the-car   for   Lomé
      'There are many cars in Lome'   (ibid.)

(29) *Des*   *nenfants,*   *le*   *zoiseau.*
      DET   children,   DET   bird   (Lafage 1985: 409)

Similar examples are found in Caribbean creoles: According to Baker and Corne (1986: 170), there are between 100 and 200 words with 'agglutinated' articles in each of the French-lexifier Caribbean creoles, compared with 550 for Indian Ocean creoles, which suggests that L1 transfer from Bantu languages reinforced the tendency to 'agglutinate' articles. If West African L2 speakers of French reanalyze articles as part of the noun, it is not surprising that the creators of French-lexifier creoles also used this reanalysis. Here, Baker and Corne's argument for L1 influence is that articles in most West African languages are postposed, not preposed as in French, leading to a reanalysis of French articles as part of the noun. In other words, the L1 grammar could not parse Det + Noun strings, so it simply assumed that they were bare nouns.

Given that articles are always postposed in Ewe and Fongbe, and that indefiniteness in both languages is usually expressed by a bare noun, Ewe learners of French tend to omit articles, as in the following examples (Lafage 1985:256):

(30)   *C'est pas poulet*
       C'est pas un poulet.
       It is not chicken
       'It's not a chicken'

(31)   *Il a tué pintade*
       Il a tué une pintade.
       He has killed bird
       'He has killed a bird'

(32)   *Donner cadeau*
       Donner un cadeau.
       (to) Give present
       'To give a present'

To have a general idea of how creolization can be the end-result of a succession of interlanguage varieties of European lexifier languages, one can mention the use of the French adverb *là* ('there'), which is also used in NPs as an enclitic to intensify the demonstrative article: *Cet homme-là* ('this man'). Manessy (1984:45) notes that, in West African French, *là* is used much more frequently than in Standard French, and can follow nouns, verbs or sentences, and is often used as the normal form of the definite or demonstrative article:

> *En français d'Afrique la distribution de cette marque d'insistance [-là] est très large: On la trouve en fait après n'importe lequel des constituants de l'énonciation.*
> 'In African French, this mark of emphasis (-*la*) has a very wide distribution: It can be found after any constituent of the utterance'.   [translation mine]

The word *là* is used as a determiner in noun phrases such as *ballon là* (the/this ball), and this shift and expansion in the use of *là* in West African L2 French is probably the first step in an evolution which led to the French Caribbean creoles where *là* has been reanalyzed a post-nominal definite article.

6.3 The origin of tense-mood-aspect markers

As mentioned above, creole grammar is very different from standard French grammar. Creoles are highly analytical systems with little or no inflectional morphology, and their verbal system is characterized by preverbal markers indicating tense, mood and aspect, instead of the inflectional suffixes typical of French verbs. Thus, French is a much more synthetic language than French-lexifier creoles. Here are a few examples of tense, mood and aspect markers from Guadeloupean Creole:

(33) Tense:
I té manjé
He PAST eat
Il avait mangé
'he had eaten'

(34) Mood:
Ou ké ri
You IRR laugh
tu vas rire
'you will laugh'

In (34), *ké* ('irrealis') expresses an action which is being envisaged but not yet accomplished.

(35) Aspect:
I ∅ travay
S/he work
Il/elle a travaillé
's/he has worked'

In (35), the absence of a particle (or zero particle) expresses the perfective aspect, whereas in (36) *ka* expresses imperfective aspect.

(36) *An ka palé*
I PROG talk
Je parle / je suis en train de parler
'I'm talking'

These markers can also be combined to express, for example, the conditional with *Té* (past) + *ké* (irrealis):

(37) *Si an té palé, yo té ké fe mwen pé*
If I PAST talk, they PAST IRR make me shut-up
Si j'avais parlé, ils m'auraient fait taire
'If I had talked, they would have made me shut up'

Similarly, *té* (past) combined with *ka* (progressive) yields the imperfect:

(38) *I té ∅ dit pa té ka pwan jé*
S/he PAST said not PAST PROG take game
Il/elle avait dit qu'il/elle n'acceptait pas les plaisanteries
'S/he had said that s/he didn't accept jokes'

Finally, *ké* (irrealis) combined with *ka* (progressive) yield the future progressive:

(39) *Lé ou ké rivé an ké ka manjé*
Time you IRR arrive I IRR PROG eat
Quand tu arriveras, je serai en train de manger
'When you arrive I will be eating'

Preverbal tense-mood-aspect markers are among the most common features of plantation creoles, and although they exist in many of the substrate languages (in particular the African language Ewe), they are also attested in creoles (e.g., Mauritian) where such substrate influence is unlikely. In addition, they are not robustly attested in any L2 acquisition studies, and they therefore remain problematic for the L2 acquisition account of creole genesis. Myhill (1991:13) claims that "a number of patterns of tense/aspect marking can be found in data from both creoles and second language acquisition", but admits that there is still little data on tense/aspect marking in L2 acquisition.

The evidence for TMA markers in L2 English is very thin, and (to the best of my knowledge) non-existent in L2 French studies. Why is this? One possibility is that current (West African) L2 French is analogous to the early stages of creole genesis, when slaves (still) had access to the European lexifier language. Perhaps it is only in later stages (when access to the lexifier was more restricted) that periphrastic constructions, stripped of their inflectional endings, were reanalyzed (by children and/or adults) as bare preverbal markers. If this hypothesis is correct, then TMA markers emerged only after the shift to large-scale sugar plantations, and therefore cannot be found in current varieties of L2 French,[5] which represent an earlier stage of creolization, as claimed by Mather (2005), using data from Baker (1995).

According to Baker (1995:6–7), in the French-lexifier creole Antillais, the preverbal past, future and progressive markers are first attested 36 years, 115 years and 115 years respectively after the islands were settled. For Sranan, we have 68 years, 68 years and 115 years respectively for the same TMA markers. And in Mauritian, the preverbal completive, past, future and progressive markers are first attested 13 years, 58 years, 56 years and 101 years respectively after the initial settlement of the island colony.

In sum, according to Baker (1995), features not attested in L2 French, namely TMA markers, typically appear at least 50 years after the initial settlement, that is, after the shift from small-scale farming to large-scale sugar plantations. It is precisely from this point on that, according to Chaudenson (1989), slaves no longer had direct access to native varieties of the lexifier language, and the more basilectal features of creoles emerged. Thus, Baker's (1995) evidence offers a plausible explanation for the absence of preverbal TMA markers in the initial stages of creole genesis and, hence, in West African L2 French, since both represent a stage where learners have access to the European lexifier language.

Another possibility (compatible with the first explanation) is that it is *first* language learners (i.e., children) who created the TMA markers found in most plantation creoles, as they reanalyzed the inflectionless auxiliaries and modals of the previous generation of speakers as bare verbal markers, that is, as a base-generated functional category. After all, even though it is probably adults who introduced most grammat-

---

5.   It should be noted that the French models in Africa have not been the same as they were in plantation settings. The kinds/patterns of social interactions involved were not the same either. This is a partial consequence of the distinction Mufwene (2001) makes between the (plantation) settlement colonies and the exploitation colonies of Africa.

ical features into the incipient creoles, children too may have played a role, and TMA markers may be a case in point. This is consistent with DeGraff's (1999: 495) proposal of a 'cascade' effect: "With respect to creole genesis, adults (beyond age 15, say) might be the primary agents of *potential innovations* in L2 a[cquisition], whereas children play the role of *stabilizers* or *regulators*" [original emphases].

7.   Conclusion

In this chapter, we have seen that creoles are relatively new languages that arose mainly in the context of European plantation colonies in the 17th and 18th centuries in the Caribbean, Indian Ocean and Pacific Ocean. However, there is still no consensus on the exact steps in the development of these contact languages, nor on the respective role of the European lexifier or the African substrate languages.

Traditionally, creolists have been classified according to the relative weight given to substrates, superstrates and universals of L1 or L2 acquisition. More recently, more hybridist or complementary positions have been developed, where there is a role for all three. In terms of the social context of creole genesis, most Francophone creolists have abandoned the traditional "pidgin-creole life cycle hypothesis", and adopted a more gradualist model where creole languages gradually moved away from their European models, in the direction of increasing basilectalization, that is, increasingly divergent varieties of creoles. According to this hypothesis, creolization is essentially a process of L2 acquisition with little or no corrective feedback, over several generations of L2 speakers of French (or other European languages).

Whether one believes creoles to be the product of L1 or L2 acquisition, creolistics has obvious implications for other fields of inquiry. In terms of L1 acquisition, Bickerton's Bioprogram suggests that creoles should be acquired more rapidly and with fewer errors than non-creole languages, a prediction that has recently begun to be tested and borne out by Adone (1994), among others.

In terms of L2 acquisition, Siegel (1998) provides one of the most insightful accounts of the link between transfer in L2 acquisition and substratum effects in creole genesis. He points out that L1 transfer is a common process in all stages of L2 acquisition, and that individual transfer is the ultimate source of substrate features in pidgins, creoles and other contact varieties. Siegel (1998) reviews the constraints proposed in L2 acquisition studies and in creolistics, and applies them to Melanesian Pidgin, which exhibits strong substrate influence. He uses Andersen's (1990) "cognitive operating principles" for L2 acquisition, and focuses on the six following principles: Markedness, perceptual salience, transparency, simplicity, frequency and congruence. Siegel (1998) then applies these principles to specific features transferred from Oceanic substrates into Melanesian Pidgin English. He concludes that congruence and perceptual salience best account for those features transferred from substrate languages, and for English forms reanalyzed to fit substrate patterns. Cognitive principles and learning strategies have been shown in the L2 acquisition literature to play a role in cross-linguistic influence, and Siegel (1998) convincingly demonstrates their usefulness in explaining substratum influence in pidgin/creole genesis.

Over the next few years there will no doubt be a better understanding of the mechanisms of creolization as researchers study the origin and emergence of preverbal TMA markers in untutored L2 acquisition.

8.   Directions for future research

There are several current trends for future research in creole studies. In the areas of L1 and L2 acquisition for example, one might wonder whether the supposedly unmarked characteristics of creoles (according to e.g. Bickerton) are reflected in the relative ease or speed of acquisition of creoles by children (as L1s) and by adults. Adone (1994) conducted a valuable and insightful study on the L1 acquisition of Mauritian Creole syntax, but studies on the L1 acquisition of other creoles would be useful for comparison, as pointed out by Muysken & Law (2001). In terms of the lexicon, Lefebvre (1998) has made the case that the lexical semantic structure of Haitian reflects West African patterns, in particular FonGbe. Again, in the substratist perspective, more systematic comparisons between the lexicons of creoles and their putative substrates are needed to reinforce the substratist argument. In terms of syntax, comparing various stages of untutored L2 acquisition of European lexifier languages (particularly French and English) might yield interesting results in terms of the historical development of invariant preverbal tense, mood and aspect markers in creoles. This would give more weight to the gradualist/L2 acquisition model of creole genesis.

CHAPTER 15

Issues in French applied linguistics in West Africa

Remi Sonaiya
Obafemi Awolowo University

Résumé

Ce chapitre passe en revue un certain nombre de questions auxquelles ont été confronté des chercheurs concernant l'enseignement de la langue française en Afrique et qui demeurent pertinentes. Ces questions touchent également les autres langues européennes présentes sur le continent, surtout l'anglais. Le chapitre commence par soulever la problématique de la présence des langues européennes en Afrique en général et de leur co-existence difficile avec les langues locales, et présente le contexte de la pratique de la linguistique appliquée en Afrique comme n'étant pas neutre. Le français en Afrique est analysé à partir de la perspective de la "mission civilisatrice" et de la politique élitiste des colonisateurs qui a mené à son "échec". Dans les anciennes colonies, des variétés non-standard et les langues locales font concurrence au français standard. En discutant l'apprentissage du français en tant que langue seconde ou étrangère, la question des méthodes non-adaptées aux réalités socio-culturelles africaines est soulevée ainsi que ses conséquences sur la société africaine. L'analphabétisme croissant en langue française est analysé comme résultant directement de la politique élitiste pratiquée par les Français en Afrique et du maintien du statut quo par les gouvernements africains après les indépendances, ainsi que du manque de locuteurs natifs comme enseignants et des problèmes relatifs à la standardisation. Finalement, le français est considéré comme une langue pouvant remplir des fonctions spécifiques dans la société africaine, étant donné que le multilinguisme est déjà bien ancré dans les comportements verbaux africains. Ce chapitre aborde également le français dans des pays anglophones. La Côte d'Ivoire représente les pays francophones, alors que le Nigéria illustre le cas des pays anglophones.

Abstract

This chapter reviews some of the long-standing issues which researchers have had to grapple with regarding the teaching of French in Africa. Certainly, they are not relevant for French alone, but equally concern the other European languages spoken on the continent, especially English. The chapter begins by discussing the problem of the presence of European languages in Africa and of their difficult co-existence with the local languages. The context for the practice of applied linguistics in Africa is thus presented as non-neutral. French in Africa is analyzed from the perspective of the "civilizing mission" and elitist policy of the colonizers, a policy which has only helped to ensure its "failure". In the former colonies, non-standard varieties and the indigenous languages compete with standard French. In the discussion of French as a second or foreign language, the issue of methods which are badly adapted to African socio-cultural realities is raised and its consequences for African societies discussed. Increasing illiteracy in French is analyzed as a direct result of the elitist policy practiced by the French in Africa and which was continued by African governments after independence. The lack of native speakers as teachers and the problems related to standardization also contribute to illiteracy. The conclusion reached is that French is a language which could play some specific roles in the African society, especially given the fact that multilingualism is a mark of African verbal behavior. French in Anglophone countries is also briefly discussed. Côte d'Ivoire is taken to represent the Francophone countries, while Nigeria illustrates the situation in Anglophone countries.

1.   Historical background: Socio-political and linguistic issues

As indicated by Lodge (this volume), French in Africa is certainly one of the "plural stories" of French – a story which, justifiably or otherwise, many voices on the African continent believe is not being properly told. Therefore, before entering into the specific details of the teaching and learning of the French language in West Africa, it is important to raise the issues which are of general concern on the continent, not only among the intellectual elite, but to governments as well, and to show what role foreign languages in general are being perceived as playing in these issues.

One fundamental point of concern right now has to do with the unacceptable level of under-development in most African countries. That is, after almost fifty years of independence from colonial rule in most countries (for example, Ghana 1958; Senegal 1959; Togo 1960; Nigeria 1960), the continent is still confronted with fratricidal wars, famine and hunger, debilitating diseases, and a glaring incapacity of the governments to meet the basic needs of the citizens, especially in the provision of drinking water, housing, electricity, health care, education and roads. Efforts at confronting these issues and seeking solutions are leading to the creation of an army of both governmental and non-governmental organizations all across the continent. Suffice it to mention, in this respect, the New Partnership for African Development (NEPAD), which enjoys the financial support of most of the world's great powers and upon which a considerable degree of hope is being pinned.

The persistence of the kinds of problems outlined above have led some to conclude that so far, education has failed in Africa. Education, it is generally assumed, is supposed to lead to the application of knowledge which should bring about an improvement in the lives of the people. Since this seems not to be the case in Africa, the challenge has been to seek out the reasons for this failure, and to propose ways of reversing the situation.

The relevant issue for us here, however, is not so much a concern about the condition of Africa itself, but the kinds of discussions it is engendering on the continent, especially among academics. This is where the West comes in, and once the West comes in, the issue of western languages follows automatically. Voices condemning the role of the West and the great responsibility that falls upon the West's shoulders concerning the under-development of Africa continue to be heard. Such voices cry out not only against the economic subjugation of Africa by the West, but equally against what is perceived as the continent's cultural and linguistic domination. From Walter Rodney's outright accusation in the title of his 1982 book, *How Europe underdeveloped Africa*, to the issues raised in respect of the continued dominance of European languages in the running of affairs on the continent, it is clear that Africans are still struggling to come to terms with the burden of their history.

I will dedicate some space in this first section to the issue of language on the African continent – a most complex issue on which volumes have already been written – because without a clear picture of the linguistic situation of Africa and the politics of language, it will be impossible for us to speak in meaningful sociolinguistic terms about the role of French within the African society.

As mentioned above, Africans are still trying to come to terms with the burden of their history – and for our specific purposes here, with the linguistic burden of their colonial history. A basic dilemma has to do with our experience of schooling. The case of Govan Mbeki (Prah 1998:xi–xii) is typical of most educated Africans:

> In my days through primary school all the Xhosa I learned in the classroom was to recite a poem in Xhosa. It was only at secondary school that I was taught the grammar of the language. Through all my schooling days, therefore, Xhosa, my language, had little or no relevance to my education, except that when I pursued it to course II at University I failed it.

Along similar lines, Nelson Mandela described the great embarrassment he felt when the queen of Basutoland addressed him in Sesotho and he could not respond, which made her ask: "What kind of lawyer and leader will you be who cannot speak the language of your own people?" These incidences are clearly understood in light of the fact that within the African educational system European languages, that is, the languages of the colonizers, were maintained as the sole languages of education during the colonial period. However, what continues to be of great concern to a number of African scholars (Bokamba 1991; Djité 2000, 2004; Ngalasso 1989, among others) is the fact that even after independence, not only are European languages still being maintained within the educational system, but very little is being done to develop African languages which had suffered over a century of neglect. This state of affairs is what Djité (2004:1) refers to as "the most painful and absurd interface between Africa and the rest of the world": The fact that Africa is the only continent in the world in which language-in-education "is largely exogenous to the society it seeks to serve". It is only in more recent times that mother tongue education is starting to be practiced in a few countries but, even then, it tends to be restricted mainly to primary schools. When it is taught beyond the primary school, it is usually treated as any other subject (Prah 1998:xii).

Attempts have been made in some countries, mostly former French colonies, to reverse the colonial language-in-education policies and give preference to local languages. In 1959, for example, Madagascar chose to make Malagasy the sole official language. However, the country found it extremely difficult to handle the rivalry between the different dialects and bring about standardization (*Le Robert, dictionnaire historique de la langue française* 1992:29). French has, therefore, remained the *de facto* official language. Other countries chose different mixes of official bilingualism instead, depending on their particular historical and socio-political circumstances: Cameroon opted for French and English, Chad and Mauritania combined French with Arabic, while small and relatively monolingual countries like Burundi and Rwanda were able to have a local language (Kirundi & Kinyarwanda, respectively) co-exist with French as official languages.

In my opinion, the fact that the majority of educated Africans have been schooled in languages other than their own constitutes a significant psychological burden, at least among those who have a penchant for deep reflection. Some researchers have suggested that this reality is responsible, at least in part, for the apparent failure of education in Africa. Thus, Savané (1993) and Sonaiya (2004) suggest that a schism was created separating school life from the rest of everyday living: School was where you were forbidden to speak your own language, and forced to speak the colonial master's language. Of course, it meant that you could not truly be yourself in school, since you could not freely express your innermost feelings and ideas. Your school experience was constantly an enactment of the statement credited to the Boer leader, Steyn, in 1913, that "the language of the conqueror in the mouth of the conquered is the language of slaves" (cited in Prah 1998:2). As such, school must have been robbed of much of its meaning which, in turn, would have meant that a significant portion of the learning that was going on there was primarily by rote, as Savané (1993) points out, since its relationship to real life might not have been evident for most of the learners.

Sonaiya (2003) states that "the continued learning and use of European languages in Africa still poses considerable problems", and it is only with a proper understanding of the dynamics of this reality that the question of Africans as learners and users of European languages may be correctly dealt with. The same article also points out that this issue is one which preoccupies African literary writers to a significant degree. For example, Ngugi Wa Thiongo (formerly known as James Ngugi) finally abandoned the use of English as his medium of expression out of a deep conviction regarding the inability of this language to adequately express his thoughts and emotions: "I think English is only a stopgap; it will not be used always. It is not a language that expresses the people's culture. I see it as a temporary phenomenon that is dying" (Egejuru 1980:54). He was obviously mistaken, for the use of English has continued to gain more ground on the continent, although reservations might be expressed on the issue of standards.

Others who did not go so far as Ngugi still expressed feelings of alienation as a result of being constrained to use a language that was not truly theirs. Egejuru (1980) reports on interviews conducted with some African writers and states that many of them admit to using European languages out of compulsion, not by choice. Camara

Laye, for example, views foreign languages as being "indispensable as a means of communication with the outside world" (1980:36), while Ousmane Sembène notes that in order to "get acquainted with universal literature I am obliged to use the French language which is my exile because deep down I exile myself when I use French" (1980:39). This point is re-echoed in Prah (1998:2) who says regarding the language dynamics in Africa:

> It is in language that people find their mental home, their definitional relationship to the external world. What this also means is that people can hardly be themselves in an idiom in which they have difficulty understanding or expressing themselves. They can barely be creative and innovative in a language they have to struggle with in order to command expression.

These are some of the underlying issues which needed clarification before a discussion of the role of any foreign language in Africa could be properly undertaken. European languages, especially French and English, are not present in Africa as they are in many other parts of the world, and this informs how they evolve, as well as how they are perceived.

In the remaining sections of this chapter I examine, to start with, issues relating generally to applied linguistics in West Africa, specifically the distinction to be made between applied linguistics as a formal discipline and applied linguistic practices. The point is made that applied linguistics in Africa cannot be viewed in a neutral manner, given the existing tension between the European languages and the local languages.

2. Applied linguistics in West Africa

Tracing the historical contexts in which applied linguistics emerged in Africa, Makoni and Meinhof (2004:78) suggest that since language and Empire have always gone hand-in-hand, "there is no historical period of African colonial and postcolonial encounters with the West and where ethnic groups have been in contact within a polity, which did not include some version of applied linguistics". They then go on to propose a distinction between applied linguistics as a formal discipline and applied linguistic 'activities'.

Historically, the Portuguese were the first Europeans to undertake voyages of discovery along the African coast starting from the 15th century; however, systematic exploration of the interior was carried out mainly in the 19th century. Applied linguistic activities were a part of this systematic exploration, and they were carried out largely by missionaries who developed dictionaries, readers and other language learning materials, and equally engaged in the translation into local languages of the Bible and other Christian literature (for example, Thomas Jefferson Bowen's *Grammar and Vocabulary of the Yoruba Language* (1858), Rev. J. G. Cristaller's *Grammar of the Asante and Fante Language called Tshi* (1875), later followed by his *Dictionary* (1933), the Christian Missionary Society's *Yoruba Hymn Book* (1925)). However, applied linguistics as a formal discipline did not emerge until the late 1950s and early 1960s, coinciding with the attainment of political independence in many African countries.

Makoni and Meinhof (2004) claim that applied linguistics as a discipline "has not yet systematically confronted its own colonial legacy as other disciplines in Africa such as anthropology [...] which has shown considerable reflexivity under the pervasive influence of colonial and postcolonial theories" (2004:79). Part of the reflexivity which is required should begin with a full consciousness of the consequences of the fundamental change which occurred with respect to applied linguistic activities between the colonial and postcolonial periods: That is, while the primary focus during the colonial era was the development of African language materials for the use of Europeans, applied linguistics as a discipline has concentrated primarily on the teaching and learning of European languages by Africans. Activities relating to the teaching, learning and analysis of African languages tend to be embedded within the African Studies programs of the universities which offer them. The importance of this fact is that the term 'applied linguistics' then came to be restricted to the teaching and learning of European languages. As Makoni and Meinhof (2004:79) point out, in South Africa, applied linguistics was conceptualized as being synonymous with, and limited to, the teaching of the English language.

It is clear from the foregoing that applied linguistics in Africa (and possibly in other countries of the third world with a history of colonization like India, for instance) cannot be viewed in a neutral fashion. There is always a tension in the background, which can be perceived either negatively or positively, created by the competition between the European languages and the local languages. The peculiarity of the African situation, which greatly increases its complexity, is the fact that colonization itself was preceded by a period of enslavement. There is, therefore, a whole historical baggage which European languages in Africa carry, and which affects the practice of applied linguistics on the continent, especially since the effects of the history still persist not only in the language-in-education policies of many African states but, more importantly, in their day-to-day realities. While some states' policies appear to give more prominence to the teaching of local languages – to the detriment of European languages – the reality is that very few of them have attained the degree of indigenization of the language-in-education system which they had hoped for.

Mauritius is a Francophone country where the official linguistic policies have remained unchanged in spite of the important economic and linguistic changes under way in the region. In contrast, Morocco has made Arabization its main language policy since after independence; however, in practice, the situation remains the same, for questions are still being asked, even after 40 years of independence, whether the policy has been effective or not. The conclusion to be drawn from the situation in many African countries is that regardless of the official language policy in the books, the practical reality tends to be one of continued primacy being given to the former colonial languages. That is, Africa seems incapable of shaking off, so to speak, these European languages. How should this situation be perceived?

3.   African multilingualism and the appropriation of the French language

An issue which is now being raised more and more in some African countries concerning European languages has to do with the status to be ascribed to the languages themselves. In recent times, for example, new Englishes have become an object of study as several researchers are focusing attention on issues relating to the domestication or appropriation of the English language by non-native populations (see, e.g., Bamgbose, Banjo, & Thomas 1997; Platt, Weber, & Liam 1984). Voices are now being heard which take exception to the position according to which all the linguistic woes of the continent are blamed on the imposition of European languages and the concomitant neglect of African languages. For instance, Djité (2004: 9) asks pointedly: "Is it indeed possible, nearly half a century on, to speak of the language of the former colonizer as being imposed?"

Djité's reasoning is worth examining, and it coincides with that expressed in Sonaiya (2003, 2004) in which it is suggested that a new, more positive attitude towards the European languages needs to be adopted. Djité also questions the assumption that "a speech community is empowered only when it operates in its own mother tongue, when that mother tongue is actively promoted and used through the educational system" as well as the corollary argument which maintains that "using another language, and especially languages of the former colonizers, leads to disempowerment of the speech community" (Djité 2004: 9). Here is the argument Djité (2004: 9) advances to justify the position he takes:

> Indeed, language choice and language use in the developing world show very active agents, especially within the masses. Language practices in this part of the world have always been marked by multilingualism. Language diversity and the necessity of communicating across language boundaries have always fostered a desire to learn the language of the neighbor, the language of the playground, the language of the marketplace.

What Djité is saying, in effect, is that Africans have always learned and used other people's languages, a practice dictated by the linguistic diversity prevalent in the region. He claims, moreover, that this practice has been further encouraged at independence through internal and international migration, urbanization and even through exogamous marriages. That is, people are constantly adapting their language practices and repertoires to the ever-changing realities in the societies in which they live, taking on local or European languages as dictated by their immediate circumstances or by their aspirations. Multilingualism, involving local languages, has always been practiced in Africa, and now a new multilingualism is evolving, dictated by new facts of life. For Djité (2004: 10), "the language of the former colonizer, or popular varieties of this language, is very much part and parcel of this new multilingualism, and growing sections of the speech communities now perceive this language as one of their own".

Several researchers have been focusing on this phenomenon of the appropriation of the French language, particularly as it relates to *Côte d'Ivoire*. Kouadio (1999: 301) writes of "the global phenomenon of appropriation of French by Ivorian speakers", claiming that this has given rise to "a variety of French which is about to reach a relative autonomy". Simard (1994) employs the term of Ivorization to characterize the phenomenon, and both this author and Sampson (1997) maintain that popular Ivorian French is a language in the process of becoming creolized. In a recent article, Boutin (2004) discusses verbal complementation in Ivorian French and shows how it diverges significantly from the standard language. She then concludes that the popular French spoken in Côte d'Ivoire should be considered a variety of the original language – not a subnormative variety but, rather, "a national form of the language in its own right, with its rules, its recurrent structures and its specificities" (Boutin 2004:33). This rather peculiar situation of Côte d'Ivoire, including the manner in which demographic changes have been impacting language practices, will be examined in greater detail in the following section. It should be noted here, however, that the French spoken in Côte d'Ivoire could be viewed as a continuum, covering varieties ranging from the *nouchi* spoken by the young people to the Ivorian academic French.[1]

A similar argument to Djité's (cited above), although not based on a historical perspective, could be made based on the point that various languages may and do perform different functions or serve various purposes in the life of an individual. It therefore becomes unnecessary to require that every acquired language be an identity language, like Ngugi Wa Thiongo (see Section 1) would demand. An individual probably needs just a single identity language, as argued by Amin Maalouf (1998) in *Les identités meurtrières*. However, the same individual needs other languages, at least two in Maalouf's opinion, to meet other social and psychological needs. Adopting a functionalist approach to understanding foreign language learning and use might help to resolve some longstanding and thorny issues still confronting Africans in respect of the continued use of their former colonizers' languages.

4.   French in West Africa

In discussing French in West Africa, I will be examining facts relative to Côte d'Ivoire primarily, taking the country as largely representative of other Francophone West African countries although equally unique in a certain sense. There will be a brief discussion at the end of the section on French in Nigeria as well, to illustrate and provide an insight into what obtains in English-speaking countries.

According to the *Rapport sur l'état de la francophonie*,[2] the statistics for French in Africa are impressive: Official language in twelve African countries (Benin, Burkina Faso, Central African Republic, Congo-Brazzaville, Côte d'Ivoire, Gabon, Guinea, Mali, Niger, Réunion, Senegal and Togo); co-official language in eight others (French

---

1.   I am grateful to Béatrice Boutin for calling my attention more closely to this point.

2.   Cited under http://french.about.com/library/bl-whatisfrench.htm

and Kirundi in Burundi; French and English in Cameroon; French and English in Congo-Kinshasa; French and Arab in Djibouti; French and Spanish in Equatorial Guinea; French and Arab in Mauritania; French, English and Kinyarwanda in Rwanda; French and Arab in Chad). French is equally a language of significant importance in several countries, especially in North Africa (Morocco, Algeria and Tunisia). Even in a non-francophone country like Nigeria, French has been accorded a special status, in acknowledgment of the fact that all its immediate neighbors are French-speaking (Niger and Chad to the north, Benin Republic to the west, and Cameroon to the east), as well as a testimony to the leading role that Nigeria plays in the West African sub-region.

In terms of the number of native speakers, both Comrie's (1998) article for *Encarta Encyclopedia* and the SIL *Ethnologue* (1999) list French as the eleventh largest in the world – although the numbers given vary – put at 72 million and 79.5 million, respectively. The significant difference observable is due to the fact that the SIL figures include the 7.5 million speakers of Haitian Creole. In Weber's (1997) listing, French occupies the thirteenth position, coming after Punjabi and Javanese, which are not included on the two other lists. However, when the category referred to by Weber as secondary speakers is considered (and this is the group to which speakers of French in Africa belong), French tops the list with 190 million speakers. Adding this to the number of native speakers, we have a total of 265 million speakers, making it the fifth most commonly spoken language in the world.

The issue of the actual number of French speakers in African countries is somewhat of an enigma. The population of French speakers given for most African countries in *Ethnologue* (2005)[3] is merely in thousands: Benin: 16,700; Gabon: 37,500; *Côte d'Ivoire*: 17,470. If these figures are correct, then they begin to raise fundamental questions regarding the appropriateness of even referring to these countries as Francophone, since only a negligible percentage of the population speaks the official language. For example, in the case of *Côte d'Ivoire* with a population of 18.9 million,[4] it means that less than 1% of the population is French-speaking. It is very likely that these figures refer to those who speak the standard French of France. However, as mentioned already, there has been an appropriation of European languages by African populations, and many of them now consider these languages as their own.

Nonetheless, it is in light of such considerations that Louis-Jean Calvet (2002:284) in his book, *Linguistique et colonialisme* asks pointedly in the chapter on French in Africa: *"Quelle francophonie?"* (Which Francophony?) After presenting figures regarding the levels of literacy in some of the languages spoken in African countries, he concludes that the percentage of West Africans who speak French could be put at 5% of the population (2002:286). His verdict (Calvet 2002:287) is that these countries are taken to be French-speaking primarily *"par la grace du discours officiel et de quelques*

---

3. See www.ethnologue.com/show_language.asp?code=fra

4. See www.mbendi.co.za/land/af/ga/p0005.htm

décrets" ('thanks to the official discourse and to a handful of decrees').The elitist type of education carried out by France in its former colonies explains the phenomenon of high levels of illiteracy in their West African colonies, and will be discussed more fully below.

It is useful at this point to compare the different systems of government practiced by the two major colonial powers in West Africa. The French, through their policy of assimilation, sought to make Frenchmen of the populations in their colonies while the British established a system of indirect rule, governing the people through the traditional institutions which were already in place. One would imagine, therefore, that there must have been more direct, unmediated contact between the colonizers and the local populations in the French colonies; however, this does not seem to have translated into a higher degree of awareness of the language among the African populations. While the local languages were encouraged in the British colonies, they were practically forbidden in all official interactions in the French colonies.

The motivating force of the entire policy of assimilation, as practiced by the French, was to civilize the supposedly uncivilized African populations, and there was no doubt, it seemed, in the minds of the French colonial administration, that this was precisely what was needed. A major tool in this so-called civilizing venture was the French language itself, and the colonial administration brought its whole weight to bear on enforcing its use – of course, to the detriment of the local languages. The gravity of the consequences of these policies on the African populations may probably never be fully comprehended. However, Djité (2000: 29) quotes a former Ivorian Minister of National Education as having stated the following during the 4th Congress of the *Parti Démocratique de Côte d'Ivoire* in 1981:

> [...] the school, instead of being a factor of development, as its true vocation should be, has reached a point where it is tearing apart the fabric of our society and alienating the individual. It has become an obstacle to harmonious evolution and political equilibrium, for it does not integrate the child into the traditional environment, but gives him/her a means to escape it, without providing him/her with what s/he needs to find his/her place in the mainstream of modern society.

In the following section we examine the role of French in the educational system, basing our judgments primarily on the situation in *Côte d'Ivoire*, and show the paradox in which it is shrouded. That is, while French remains the official language in *Côte d'Ivoire*, as well as in several other countries in West Africa, it has not been mastered by a significant percentage of the population, nor is it the language most commonly used in daily interactions (Djité 2000, 2004). While a fairly large percentage of the people have smatterings of the language, knowledge of standard French is primarily restricted to the educated elite minority. Heine's prediction in 1977 that "by the year 2000, about 60 per cent of the African population will still be ignorant of the language which is used to govern, administer and educate them" (cited in Djité 2000: 31) is thus most unfortunately borne out.

5.   French in the educational system of former colonies of West Africa

Djité (2000) presents an excellent summary of French in *Côte d'Ivoire*, especially within the context of language planning in Africa, and I have benefited greatly from his work in writing this chapter. In all their former colonies, the French have continued to be very active in promoting the teaching of the French language. Right from the colonial period, great emphasis was placed on the effective teaching of French throughout the educational system. Djité (2000: 28) reports that while the decree of 1 May 1924 encouraged the systematic use of standard French and specified the domains in which the use of local languages would be accepted, the Brazzaville Conference of 8 February 1944 made a recommendation "supporting French as the exclusive language for all teaching in schools, and for any pedagogical use of local languages in the classroom to be completely forbidden in both public and private schools throughout all French-speaking Africa".

Key instruments for the promotion of the French language in Africa are the *Alliance Française* and the *Agence Intergouvernementale de la Francophonie* – AIF (formerly known as *Agence de Coopération Culturelle et Technique* – ACCT).[5] While the former offers French courses to the general public, the latter is more directly involved with the educational system, working through the well-known *coopérants* – often, young 'experts' sent from France to work with the locals, and to supervise activities related to French interests. The primary responsibilities of the AIF are the development of French teaching materials and the training of language teachers in the latest teaching methodologies developed by French researchers.

In the teaching of French at the different levels of the educational system, very little effort, if any, was made to adapt the content of the manuals or the pedagogical methods to African realities. The young African children who were selected to be educated were to be turned into Frenchmen, as stated above; thus, they were subjected to the same materials and methods with which their fellow students in France were being trained. The story is frequently told of African school children being made to memorize and recite texts which could, at best, only be described as alienating, because they contain phrases such as *nos ancêtres, les Gaulois* ('our ancestors, the Gallic').

The intention of the colonial administration was crystal clear. Bokamba (1991) quotes a General Inspector of Education as having said that "[t]he objective [was] not to protect the originality of the colonized, but to elevate them to our level", while the decree that was promulgated on 22 August 1945 states the following:

> The main objective of teaching at primary school level is to influence, direct and speed up the evolution of the African population. This teaching shall only be dispensed in the French language.   (Djité 2000: 28)

---

5.   The ACCT now has an Anglophone equivalent – the Center for French Teaching and Documentation (CFTD) – whose activities will be examined in the discussion of French in Nigeria.

Thus, the method employed in the teaching of French in Africa was not based on the recognition of the learners' linguistic and cultural particularities; that is, complete abstraction was made of all that had to do with their context of learning.

In recent times, the issue of context of learning has been receiving a certain degree of attention in the applied linguistic literature (e.g., Akinyemi 2005; Banda 2003; Byram, Gribkova, & Starkey 2002; Hu 2002). This situation is certainly not unconnected with the fact that the learner has emerged, more recently, as the center of focus in language learning – his/her specific needs, learning preferences as well as the context of learning are being seen as important factors to take into account. Byram et al. (2002: 4) propose an intercultural dimension to language learning, whose essence is "to help language learners to interact with speakers of other languages on equal terms, and to be aware of their own identities and those of their interlocutors". Some researchers are equally expressing more and more skepticism about the universal applicability of teaching methods because, as Sonaiya (2002: 107) claims, "teaching methods are cultural products". For example, Hu (2002) discusses Communicative Language Teaching (CLT) which was imported for teaching English in China and asserts that it has failed to make the expected impact because it is fundamentally in conflict with the Chinese culture of learning. He states:

> [...] CLT and the Chinese culture of learning are in conflict in several important respects, including the philosophical assumptions about the nature of teaching and learning, perceptions of the respective roles and responsibilities of teachers and students, learning strategies encouraged, and qualities valued in teachers and students.
> (Hu 2002: 93)

Thus, the French approach to education in Africa can probably be described as a *tabula rasa* approach – where the position of the educators was to assume that the learners arrived in school as completely blank slates. No recognition was given to the languages they already spoke, nor to the culture to which they belonged. Since neither the languages nor the culture were recognized, there was no question raised about the appropriateness of the teaching methods being applied. If the methods were right for French children, they had to be for Africans as well, since the main objective was to "raise" the level of the Africans and "speed up their evolution", as indicated in the quotations given above. Robert Train's chapter (this volume) on language ideology and foreign language pedagogy sheds more light on this issue.

The impact of the school experience of Africans on the African society is yet to be fully researched and analyzed (but cf. Savané 1993; and Sonaiya 2004 for preliminary results). All the same, one may wonder whether learners who have been subjected to such constraints could develop into effective users of the languages so acquired. Even when they obviously display a high degree of competence in their use of the language, there might be hidden emotional and psychological costs to the acquisition which these learners may have to bear forever. The cases already mentioned of writers who liken the experience of writing in a foreign language to being in exile is indicative of a deep sense of un-ease regarding the use of these languages. Furthermore, many

Africans are saddened by their inability to read and write their own languages as well as they do those of their former colonizers. Other, more apparent consequences of France's policy regarding the teaching of French in the colonies, however, are more direct and measurable. One such consequence has to do with the widespread nature of illiteracy.

6. On the question of illiteracy

Two aspects of the language policy of France in Africa are pertinent to the question of illiteracy in the former French colonies, such as *Côte d'Ivoire*. First, the fact that education was elitist, that is, made available to only a handful of the population, and second, that French was imposed as the sole language of education in an obviously multi-lingual environment. The effect produced was that only a very small minority of the population attained competence in Standard French (for a non-standard variety soon developed), and that minority found itself shut off from the rest of the mostly illiterate population. The situation in all the colonies, therefore, was that the vast majority of the population was incapable of speaking the official language of the country. That is, they were illiterate in the language in which they were supposed to be conducting all their (official) affairs on a daily basis. Unfortunately, the situation is still the same today, and Djité (2000:33) claims that "illiteracy in French is near crisis level". (This should be understood as illiteracy in standard French.)

In practical terms, this illiteracy means that the people do not possess the skills required to access the information contained in official documents and speeches, nor are they able to express their own thoughts and ideas directly to those in positions of authority over them. It means that the majority of the people depend on the small minority to serve as intermediaries between them and the government in conducting all their official businesses (for example, filling out passport and visa application forms, registering their small businesses, etc.). While public officials sometimes use a non-standard variety in addressing the people, access to written official information can only be gained through knowledge of the standard variety.

Before the beginning of the serious economic crisis which befell African countries in the late 1980s and early 1990s, the economic life of the people seemed to have managed to move along fairly smoothly. Most of the elite who had been educated in the French system got ready employment and, although a class society evolved, there were no serious disturbances to the stability of the countries. However, as the economic downturn set in and rising unemployment became a fact of life, the unemployed elite (with a French education) have become disillusioned, as both they and the general populace have come to see that mastery of Standard French and education no longer automatically give the assurance of employment and a high standard of living. Thus, there is very little motivation for the people to strive to attain literacy in French. As Djité (2000:34) puts it, "the poorly-educated are ill-prepared to add Standard French, while the educated ones who are unemployed realize that it is not likely to alleviate their current predicament in any significant way". Many young people are opting out of school, choosing instead to seek their fortunes in other activities like trading or even farming.

In *Côte d'Ivoire*, the rise of illiteracy in Standard French has been directly proportional to the spread of two *lingua francae*, Popular French and Dyula. A phenomenon that has contributed significantly to this spread is the increase in migrations in the West African sub-region. *Côte d'Ivoire* is peculiar in this regard, for it boasts a very high population of foreigners, including Liberians, Sierra Leoneans, Ghanaians, Malians, and even a significant number of Nigerians. While economic ties between a particular region of Yorubaland, in South-Western Nigeria (including the towns of Ejigbo and Shaki), have existed for many decades, in more recent years there has been an exodus of young Nigerians from other parts of the country as well, in search of employment opportunities and better living conditions. Many of them are reported to be setting up small businesses in different regions of *Côte d'Ivoire*, as mechanics, hairdressers, tailors, and so on. These immigrants, while they keep swelling the population of the country, are not acquiring Standard French, however; instead, they are learning Popular French and Dyula, the languages which facilitate their easy integration into the Ivorian society.

Furthermore, since the African languages had been neglected in the educational system, literacy programs cannot be easily conducted in them, since instruction materials are not readily available in the local languages. In any case, given that the policy has not changed in any significant manner (that is, French is still recognized as the language of instruction within the educational systems of most of the Francophone countries), this means that if people are not acquiring literacy in standard French, then they are not likely to be acquiring it in any other language either.

Another element which needs to be mentioned in connection with the increasing illiteracy in Standard French is the fact that French is now being taught in the educational institutions not by native (French) speakers, as the case used to be, but by non-natives. This is the prevailing situation not only in Francophone Africa but in the Anglophone countries as well, and it is causing a certain degree of concern because of the falling levels of competence even among those who are supposed to have been well educated in these foreign languages. An interesting article titled "The English language in Nigeria: The case of a vanishing model?" was recently published by a university lecturer (Adesanoye 2004) who analyzed the texts of the inaugural lectures given over a ten-year period by professors in one of the Nigerian universities and showed them to have been riddled with serious grammatical errors. The point which the author sought to make was that "[w]e have no moral – or for that matter, intellectual – right to expect unblemished English language performance from our students when we ourselves are not prepared to show the way" (Adesanoye 2004: 255).

Somehow, the departure of the Europeans from African educational institutions (precipitated at first by a certain desire to Africanize the faculty, and later, by the economic difficulties which came upon the continent) also coincided with the general fall in educational standards. However, while concern over fallen standards in disciplines in the sciences and in technology, for example, have led to efforts aimed at reversing the situation, such has not been the case with languages. With respect to the foreign languages used as official languages and languages of instruction, a certain kind of African pride would wish to argue that these are not our own languages, and that we are not under any compulsion to use them exactly as their owners do. In fact, someone who approximates the native speakers of these languages too closely (particularly in terms of phonetics) might be accused of having been brainwashed by the Europeans, and of possessing a slavish mentality.

This brings us to the issue of the domestication or appropriation of European languages by Africans, and how this might be related to the matter of standards. If Africans now desire to appropriate the languages of their former colonizers, up to what point would they be free to do so, while maintaining some kind of recognizable standard? The problem is that many of the non-natives who are teaching foreign languages in Africa are themselves not using the standard varieties of these languages, and deviations from the norm are noticeable, on the phonetic/phonological as well as grammatical levels. There is evidence of interference from their mother tongues, and this seems to worsen from one generation of teachers to the next, as one mother tongue influence compounds the previous one. In Nigeria, for example, various kinds of deviant pronunciations are currently being noticed in the society at large as well as on radio and television which were not known a decade ago. Studies need to be conducted into these phenomena.

The question, of course, in respect of standards, is how to determine which variety of a language should be considered as the standard. However, this is not really the issue with respect to French in Africa; we are not so much concerned whether it is Parisian French which should be taken as the standard or not. The issue, rather, is whether we can now start to accept, say, Popular French as the standard; that is, whether we have a right to do with an imported or imposed language as we wish, and then insist that it is our own version of the language. Before presenting some of the different viewpoints on this issue, let us first briefly discuss the Popular French in *Côte d'Ivoire*.

7. Popular French in *Côte d'Ivoire*

Popular Ivorian French has been discussed both in the sociolinguistic as well as applied linguistic literature (cf. in particular, the important contributions of Gabriel Manessy). In recent times, as already mentioned, researchers have come to view it as illustrative of a high degree of appropriation of a foreign language by a given community, such that a process of creolization is being attested (Sampson 1997). Boutin (2003) has argued that Ivorian Popular French be regarded as a *bona fide* variety of the French language.

I wish to make a distinction, right from the start, between Popular Ivorian French and *Nouchi*, which is another name by which it is often called. Although I recognize the two as (roughly) referring to the same reality, I will use the term of Popular Ivorian French (PIF), as does Simard (1994), instead of *Nouchi*. The reason for this is two-fold: First, scholarly works on the language do not refer to it as *Nouchi* (for example, Djité 2000; and Boutin 2003); second, I believe it is possible to make some kind of distinction, be it ever so minor, between the two. *Nouchi* has a connotation of playfulness or lack of seriousness, an attitude of deliberately experimenting with language, and a marked tendency toward slang. It is more of the young people's version of PIF. The *Nouchi* website (www.nouchi.com) is interactive, and even encourages contributions of individually coined words and expressions. It claims to be dedicated to the promotion of "*l'expression africaine sur Internet*" ('African expression on the Internet'), and invites the cybernaut to explore the resources of Africanized French *with a smile* (emphasizing its playful dimension). A dictionary is available on the site to assist novices.

Manessy, in a 1984 article, presents evidence for the existence of "colonial French" in Africa, right from the early days of the colonial enterprise. He interprets data from a 1916 manual for officers of colonial troops which include examples of the type of French spoken by the "sharpshooters" (African soldiers in the French army). Manessy shows that their language is very similar to that currently spoken in Francophone Africa by the uneducated, with the major difference being the preponderance of military jargon in the soldiers' language. PIF, therefore, has its origins in the language contact situation which came into being in the wake of the arrival of French people in West Africa.

Manessy, as a creolist, "was interested in the ways approximate use in contact situations develops into consistent creole languages" (Tabouret-Keller & Gadet 2003:9), and he went on to draw a distinction between vehicularization and vernacularization. The basic need for communication in a contact situation where there is pressure from the norm (that is, the language with the upper hand, so to speak) gives rise to vehicularization, a process geared primarily towards optimizing the potentialities of the linguistic system. With vernacularization, on the other hand, the language is more settled, and starts to develop more complex and diversified means of expression which go beyond the strict communicative function. It could clearly be asserted that the Popular French of *Côte d'Ivoire* has passed through these two stages and is now considered – at least by many – a language in its own right.

It is not possible, within the limits of this chapter, to fully discuss the characteristics of Popular Ivorian French; however, a brief insight into its functioning will be presented.[6] While there are original African creations in French which are used in several Francophone countries (for example, *poulet bicyclette* 'chicken bicycle' for the local scavenging chicken, *deuxième bureau* 'second office' for a man's second wife), PIF clearly goes beyond this kind of coinage. It has become a whole new way of using language, involving grammar as much as it does vocabulary. It also represents a rich

---

6.   For a more detailed account see, for example, Sampson (1997), Kouadio (1999), Boutin (2002, 2004).

combination of different languages, drawing primarily from French as well as from the African languages spoken in *Côte d'Ivoire* and even elsewhere (e.g., *tchatcher* 'to chat' is said to have been derived from Spanish *chacharear*, according to Walter 1988). Boutin (2003:34) claims that PIF has become the endogenous norm, and that it is being acquired as a first language by about 25% of the Ivorian population. It was in response to this phenomenon that Chaudenson (1992) proposed the term of *nativisation* ('nativization').

One of the characteristics of PIF, as described by Boutin (2003:34) is that it is neither the French of France, nor that spoken by academicians, nor is it to be regarded as the type of interlanguage French spoken by learners. At the beginning of its development during the first two decades after independence, language teachers would have spent some time seeking to correct what they must have perceived as erroneous and representing clear departures from the normal usage. Over time, however, these peculiar usages became accepted through the process of vernacularization, with the Ivorian community insisting on them as evidence of its appropriation of the French language.

A few examples will suffice to provide a general flavor of PIF here. Apart from the typically *Nouchi* slang words (like *môgô* 'guys'), systematic studies of the differences between standard French and PIF can and have been made (Boutin 2002, 2003; Kouadio 1999; Sampson 1997). The first two following examples are from Djité (2000:34), while the last two are from the *Nouchi* website:

Popular Ivorian French	Standard French	English
C'est versé à Abidjan.	*C'est chose courante à Abidjan.*	It's a common thing in Abidjan.
I' veut mouiller mon pain.	*Il veut me créer des ennuis.*	He wants to get me into trouble.
Découvrirez ces recettes...	*Découvrez ces recettes...*	Discover these recipes...
Libérez vous de tout vos	*Libérez-vous de toutes vos*	Free yourself from all your
frustrations.	*frustrations.*	frustrations.

Here are some general comments on the particularities of PIF using these examples:

- Dropping of the 'I' of the 3rd person subject pronoun in *I' veut mouiller mon pain*. This is very commonly done, especially when the following verb is one that begins with a consonant.
- Simplification of the rules of standard French in some contexts: For instance, both the third and fourth examples involve the imperative, but *découvrirez* is erroneously conjugated, while *libérez* is correct. It would appear that the general rule in PIF is to form the imperative using the infinitive as the stem, except for verbs ending in '-er', where one would have had, for example, *libérerez*. Why this form is not generally acceptable might be due to the repetition of /re/ that is involved.
- Non-compliance with the rules of agreement, as in *tout vos frustrations*, where *tout* does not agree in number and gender with *frustrations*. It must be borne in mind that PIF is first and foremost a spoken language, originally used by the uneducated, even though certain forms of it are now being integrated into the more standard

variety (Simard 1994). In PIF, qualifiers tend to have a single form, such that the phonetic differences indicative of number and gender are obliterated. Thus, *tout*, *toute*, *tous* and *toutes* are all realized as /tu/. This raises some issues in terms of standardization, which will be addressed below.

– Use of imagery, as seen in *C'est versé à Abidjan* and *I' veut mouiller mon pain*. In the first case, *versé* might have been arrived at from *répandu* 'spilled', which would have been the one of the standard French options in this context. The image which might have been exploited is that of some kind of liquid having been poured on the ground, such that the ground is now covered by it. The verb which normally would be used for such an act of pouring in standard French is *verser*, while *répandu* (< *répandre* 'to spill, scatter, spread') would describe the resultant state. Twisting the situation around in an interesting manner, PIF chooses the active verb to describe a state of affairs (the fact that something is common). The literal translation of the second sentence is: 'He wants to soak my bread' (throw it into water). The idea is clear; someone who does that is creating difficulties for the other person.

A question that arises with respect to the growing importance of PIF is that of standardization, particularly regarding its written form. Boutin (2003) decries the fact that while linguistic analyses have been carried out on the French spoken in Québec, Belgium and Switzerland, such has not been the case with respect to African French. She desires that studies be conducted analyzing the African variety of French and comparing it with the standard. However, this can only be possible when Popular French itself will have become standardized. As of now, there still exists some amount of individual variation in several domains (as the different contributions on the *Nouchi* website demonstrate), although certain constructions, like some of those examined in Boutin (2003) are becoming relatively stable (e.g., *Où Yao est sorti?* instead of *D'où Yao est sorti?* 'Where did Yao come out from?'). It will be important to carefully study this individual variation and closely monitor its development, if PIF is to find a place in the educational system.

In bringing this section to a conclusion, I would like to return to the issue of how the tensions among the competing languages in *Côte d'Ivoire* may be properly managed. Dumont (1990) advocates that French should now be considered an African language – and I wonder if he means standard French – due to the level of appropriation which has occurred. Others, like several of the authors already cited, would maintain that it is the African version of French that should now be accorded proper recognition. Still other voices are advocating the inclusion of African languages in the educational system, although not necessarily demanding that the European languages be abandoned. How should all these positions be harmonized?

While recognizing the seemingly daunting problems associated with the use of European languages in Africa, some positive and constructive positions are nonetheless being advanced (e.g., Djité 2000, 2004; Camara Laye in Egejuru 1980: 36). The Nigerian novelist, Chinua Achebe (cited in Djité 2004: 11) once wondered: "Is it right that a man should abandon his mother tongue for someone else's? It looks like a dreadful betrayal and produces a guilty feeling...". His conclusion, however, was the following: "[...] for me there is no other choice. I have been given the language, and I intend to use it".

I wish to associate myself with the opinions of those who, like Achebe, believe that the better option for Africans is to put to full use that which they already possess. In Sonaiya (2005), for example, I propose that translators in Africa could play the role of mediators of literacy in their societies, making accessible to their people the information that is available on the global scene, and which is mostly expressed in the major languages of the world. In so doing, they would be helping to bring about a reduction in the level of exclusion suffered by the continent's non-literate inhabitants. In the same vein, I believe that the trend towards increased illiteracy in French in Africa needs to be arrested and reversed. Africa is grossly under-represented on the international scene, except when it is a question of receiving aid from the rest of the world to fight one disaster or another. The possession of a global language, like French, should be exploited in presenting African perspectives on issues, even if not in African languages.

As has been mentioned earlier, multilingualism is one of the characteristics of the linguistic terrain in many African countries. While efforts should be made to correct the disadvantaged status of African languages on the continent, the functions that the European languages can perform within our societies should not be ignored either. As Djité (2000: 36) points out, it is "[t]he exclusive promotion of Standard French in Côte d'Ivoire [which] has contributed to a number of linguistic and social distortions and inequities (e.g., elite closure, illiteracy in French, an imbalance between school and real life, high school drop-out rates, high rates of unemployment)". This means that the promotion of local languages in Africa could actually be very beneficial to promoting Standard French, an objective that the French have always longed to achieve.

8.   French in Anglophone Africa

In order to give a more complete picture of French in sub-Saharan Africa, it will be useful to equally examine what obtains in non-Francophone countries, using Nigeria as an example. While French is normally learned as a second language in Francophone countries, it has the status of a foreign language in a country like Nigeria, where it is learned mostly as a third, but in some cases fourth, language. Typically therefore, Nigerian learners of French are bilingual, having already acquired their mother tongues as well as English, the country's official language.

While French has been taught in Nigerian secondary schools and universities since the 1960s, it does not have an official status, nor has its teaching been pursued with any special attention until very recently. What brought about a change in this state of affairs was that in 1994, for reasons which were not fully disclosed, the then Head of State, the late General Sanni Abacha, decreed, in true military fashion, that French would become, "with immediate effect", the second official language of the country. Unfortunately, the necessary structures for the practical execution of such a decree had not been put in place: Where were the teachers who would ensure the teaching of the language at every level of the educational system? Where were the hundreds of translators who would be needed to ensure that every single document would be brought out both in French and English? And so on. Therefore, the general impression within the country was that the decree was more of a political move than a well thought-out language policy, for it came at a time when the General was ostracized by most of the international community, especially Britain and the United States. Since France seemed to have shown friendliness at that time, General Abacha probably thought that a way to demonstrate appreciation was to turn Nigeria into a bilingual country overnight.

While nothing came out of this decree – and Abacha even wanted the language teachers to be brought in straight from France, for he would have none of these Francophones whose French accents were already corrupted by their mother tongues! – it nevertheless started a serious discussion within the country about the importance of the French language to Nigeria. These events occurred at a time when Nigerians themselves were becoming more sensitive to the opportunities that knowledge of French could open up for them. On the international scene, Olusegun Obasanjo (now President of the Federation) had earlier lost the bid for the United Nations' Secretary-General's position to Boutros Ghali. It is said that Obasanjo failed to get the full backing of the African countries because the Francophone block felt that a non French-speaking person could not adequately represent them or defend their interests. Similar scenarios were being played out at other levels: Nigerians were applying for international jobs and were being rejected solely because of their lack of competence in French.

On the economic level as well, the need for knowledge of French was becoming more and more evident. The trading profile between Nigeria and her neighbors was rapidly changing. In the couple of decades following independence, the former colonies maintained close economic ties to their former colonial masters and there were very few industries in the African nations. Nigerians who went to neighboring Benin Republic, for example, did so more out of a desire for the exotic. This situation, however, has greatly changed: Industries have developed, especially in Nigeria, and Nigerian products are being exported more and more to countries in the West-African sub-region, particularly petroleum by-products, textiles and pharmaceutical products. Efforts at sub-regional integration are also yielding fruit, for there is greater ease of movement of goods across the borders. For example, used vehicles which arrive from Europe in large numbers at the Cotonou port are then re-exported to Nigeria, where there are greater numbers of prospective buyers.

As a result of all these activities, there is greater awareness in the country concerning the usefulness of French. In fact, an interesting by-effect of the importation of used vehicles into the country is that foreign languages are now present on our roads, since the inscriptions on the majority of the vehicles are not painted over. As part of a larger project on foreign languages in the Nigerian society, a small investigation was conducted in which questionnaires were administered so as to ascertain what perceptions the general public as well as owners of such vehicles (i.e., with inscriptions) had.[7] Based on the answers provided by the respondents to the 50 questionnaires administered around the motor parks in Ile-Ife, it is clear that there is increased awareness of foreign languages among the Nigerian population. While most of them do not recognize the languages (they are mainly Dutch, German and French), and certainly have no idea of what the inscriptions mean, some of them are nonetheless very proud to own such vehicles. Asked whether they would wish to learn a foreign language and to identify which one, over 90% of those who responded in the affirmative chose French, giving as the main reasons for their choice the opportunities for business and communication in West Africa.

It was mentioned earlier that there have been migrations from Anglophone countries into Francophone lands. There has equally been a reverse flow. For instance, many of the French teachers in Nigerian secondary schools and colleges of education are Togolese, Beninese, Ivorian or Nigerians who had lived in those countries and have now returned home. The interesting effect of this fact is that the French spoken in Nigeria now, for the most part, has a distinctly French West African accent. It is primarily in the universities that we have Nigerian French teachers who were trained in France and Canada, and these are mostly those occupying the higher cadres as senior lecturers, associate professors and professors. Their younger colleagues have not had the same opportunities for foreign training which is costly, and the kinds of scholarships that were available up until about twenty years ago have all but dried up. A clear difference in level of competence is thus observable between the two categories of university teachers, and a palliative is now being sought in short-term courses in Francophone countries for the younger lecturers.

As for the teaching of the French language in the country, what obtains is similar to that which has already been identified for the Francophone countries. Two primary instruments for the promotion of the French language are the *Alliance Française* and the recently established *Center for French Teaching and Documentation* (CFTD). The *Alliance Française* caters to the general public; anyone who wishes to learn French is free to enroll. Up until 2003 there was only one CFTD in the country, located in the town of Jos in northern Nigeria. A second one has now been opened in Ibadan, so as to cater to the needs in the southern part of the country. The Center's primary activity is the conduct of training programs for French teachers, mostly at the secondary school level, although some have been organized for university French teachers as well, and to serve as a resource center for researchers.[8]

---

7.   See Appendix at the end of the chapter.

8.   This author and her two colleagues spent a month at the CFTD in Jos while writing the second level of their French teaching method. This is the first method written by Nigerians which has enjoyed the financial support of the French government.

The CFTD organizes courses aimed primarily at familiarizing teachers with the recent developments in French language teaching, and training them in the use of the methods developed in France. As in the case of Francophone countries, the question is hardly ever raised regarding the appropriateness of these materials for the Nigerian socio-linguistic and socio-cultural context. However, Nigerian researchers, primarily those in the universities, are starting to develop their own methods, deemed to be better-suited to the realities of the Nigerian learners.

The first of such methods developed by Nigerians is *Je démarre!: Méthode de français pour débutants* (Sonaiya, Mojola, & Amosu 1997) and *J'Avance!: Méthode de français, niveau II* (Sonaiya, Mojola, & Amosu 1999). According to the authors, the manuals were written in response to the scarcity of suitable and affordable materials for teaching French in tertiary institutions in Nigeria. Manuals imported from France (and which had been used for several decades) have become more and more expensive over the years, in addition to their Europe-centered content being inappropriate for Nigerian learners. A need was felt to include African realities alongside those of France, so that learning could take place in an environment where all that was encountered was not completely foreign to the learner.

Another resource center in the country is the library of the Nigerian French Language Village in the town of Badagry. French major students of tertiary institutions in Nigeria are required to spend a year at the French Village, a replacement of the Year Abroad program which required such students to spend the third year of their studies in a university located in a French-speaking country. The high costs in terms of foreign exchange led to the cancellation of the program when the economy of the nation took a downward turn in the late 1980s.

French, along with Arabic, has now been conferred with a special status in Nigeria's current language policy on education. This has led to the establishment of so-called pilot schools in all the different states of the country as well as a pilot university in each of the six geo-political regions of the country. These pilot institutions are receiving special attention from the Nigerian government as well as substantial assistance from the French government in a collaborative venture. The objective is to gradually increase the quality of French instruction in some Nigerian educational institutions, with the hope that this will have a multiplier effect over time. If this language policy were to be vigorously pursued and French were to become a *de facto* second foreign language – even if not a second official language – Nigeria, with a population of over 130 million (one in four Africans is a Nigerian) would be significantly swelling the ranks of French-speakers all over the world.

9. Conclusion

Several questions concerning the presence of the French language in West Africa have been raised in this chapter. The intention was to give the reader a broad perspective on the points considered rather than present an in-depth analysis of some particular issue. In this concluding section, I review some of the issues which have been covered and suggest ways in which they could point towards new research directions.

A point which has been raised in this chapter and which deserves to be underscored is the fact that most of the governments which took over in African countries after the official departure of the former European powers did not seriously reconsider what their language policies should be in respect of the language of their former colonizers and their own local languages. That is, in spite of the important socio-political change which the attainment of independence represented, there was no serious or deliberate pursuit of a linguistic change which would have responded in a better way to the realities of their people and contributed to a greater sense of well-being among them.

The situation is still the same today, to a large extent. That is, although very important socio-economic and demographic changes are leading to the evolution of important socio-linguistic phenomena, such as the rise of pidgins and creoles in African countries, African governments are not seriously re-considering their language policies. For example, discussions on the choice of national languages have been going on in practically every African country since the attainment of independence, but only very few of them have taken any definite steps in that respect (for example, Burundi, Rwanda and Tanzania). In practically every country in West Africa, the former colonial languages have remained as the sole official languages.

Unfortunately, in some paradoxical twist of circumstances, the monopoly which is enjoyed by these languages has not succeeded in ensuring their spread. Instead, as has been shown, illiteracy in these languages is increasing. This state of affairs needs to be urgently addressed, for Africans to stop being excluded from full participation in the global community. In fact, developments in other parts of the world, in France in particular, may be instructive for African countries in helping them gain a different perspective on this issue.

The concept of *Francophonie* has been a strong unifying notion among France and its former colonies, and one might wonder whether loyalty to it might partly explain the reluctance, in Francophone countries, to espouse any language policy which would seem to undermine the status of French (although a similar tendency exists in the Anglophone countries as well). However, there is increasing promotion of multilingualism in France itself now (part of it attributable, certainly, to the formation of the European Union). Under François Mitterrand the idea of opening up the country linguistically was widely discussed as well as the need to make foreign languages an important aspect of the education of young people. This might have been a direct response to the Forum of Reflection set up by the UNESCO in 1993 to outline principles that should guide the organization's activities in the coming decades. The members of the committee which constituted the Forum identified the knowledge of other languages as a key component of education. Rather than persist in a mind-frame which locks them up in a historical past, Francophone countries should seek to recognize and develop a functional approach to their language-in-education policies.

One is bound to wonder whether African nations have not been ignoring, to their own detriment, a property which they already possess and which could have been used for the development of their society. That is, why are Africans not actively promoting bilingual education in their various countries? Since the policies practiced so far have not yielded the desired results (that is, education has not led to significant development in African societies, as argued in Sonaiya 2003), one would think that the time has come to make changes to those policies.

The attempts at mother-tongue education have equally not yielded the desired results. Djité (2000) captures the sentiment well when he explains that the masses are suspicious of mother-tongue education and believe that the plan of the elite is to trick them into settling for a sub-standard type of education. This is understandable, since education in the official language is perceived by all as representing the key that opens doors of greater opportunities and makes for upward mobility in the society. Whether this is actually borne out in real life or not is a different matter. It appears that it would now be reasonable to pursue bilingual education. Certainly, much work would need to be done in this respect, in order to be clear how such a policy would be executed. Both language planners and social scientists would need to work hand-in-hand in order to determine not only the linguistic content and progression of such a multilingual education, but also what the most culturally acceptable practices would be.

Moreover, more studies need to be conducted in order to determine what impact the language of education in Africa has had on the general development of the continent. Quite a few researchers, including the present author, strongly suspect that there is more than mere coincidence to the underdevelopment of the African continent, and the fact that it is the only place in the world where the majority of the population is being schooled in languages other than their own. French in Africa is not likely to disappear in the near future. However, it appears the language may come into newer and more specific roles, engaging positively with other languages on the continent and, most likely, thereby working to ensure its own *épanouissement*.

Appendix

Project: Foreign Languages in the Nigerian Society

Questionnaire: Foreign languages on vehicles
Respondent's sex: / / Male / / Female Age: / / Below 30 yrs / / Above 30 yrs
1. How do you view vehicles with foreign languages on them?
/ / I like them / / I don't like them / / I am indifferent to them
2. What are the languages on those vehicles? Start with the most common.

3. Do you ever try to pronounce what is written on the vehicles? / / Yes / / No
4. Do you know anyone personally who has such a vehicle? / / Yes / / No

5. If yes, what do you think is the owner's attitude to the language on the vehicle? (e.g. proud of it, sees it as helpful for easy identification, etc.)

_____

6. Are the owners of such vehicles at times called by what is written on their vehicle? / / Yes / / No
7. Should the government force owners to paint their vehicles if they have foreign languages written on them? / / Yes / / No Give the reason for your answer:

_____

8. Do you think that there is a greater awareness of foreign languages in Nigeria today because of the presence of such vehicles? / / Yes / / No
9. Would you like to learn a foreign language? / / Yes / / No If yes, which one(s)?

_____

10. What purpose(s) would you use the language(s) for?

_____
_____

Thank you very much.

EPILOGUE

French in Louisiana

A view from the ground*

Stephen J. Caldas
University of Louisiana at Lafayette

Résumé

Ce chapitre commence par un survol de la longue histoire de la langue française en Louisiane à partir du XVIIième siecle. Ensuite, l'auteur décrira la situation actuelle du français parlé dans l'état parmi les locuteurs natifs blancs, noirs et créoles, et expliquera les efforts déployés pour raviver la langue française dans 'l'état des bayous'. Ces efforts se traduisent surtout par la création de programmes d'immersion dans les écoles publiques. Les données évaluatives qui indiquent le succès de ces programmes sont examinées. Ce chapitre présente les données du dernier récensement américain ainsi que des informations tirées de documents historiques. L'auteur fera également part de ses propres expériences en tant qu'un habitant dans une partie de la Louisiane où jusqu'à 50% des habitants sont francophones, et où ses enfants étaient inscrits dans un programme d'immersion française. Il présente les résultats des observations de ses enfants élevés dans un contexte bilingue.

Abstract

This chapter will first provide a broad overview of the long history of the French language in Louisiana, which dates to the seventeenth century. Then, the author will describe the present condition of French speaking in the state among Black, Creole, and White native speakers of the language. Finally, the author will describe ongoing efforts to revive the French language in the Bayou State, efforts which center mostly on the establishment of French immersion programs in public schools. Empirical data that indicate the degree to which these programs have been successful will be presented. In addition to using historical documents and U.S. Census data, the author will draw on his own first-hand experiences as a resident in the most francophone community of the most francophone parish in Louisiana where both Cajun and Creole French are spoken by up to 50% of the local residents. He will also draw upon his own participant-observation study to rear his children to be French/English bilingual and biliterate in Louisiana, as well as his children's experiences in Louisiana school French immersion programs.

---

* I'm deeply indebted to Nicole Boudreaux and Michelle Haj-Broussard for providing information for this chapter, as well as to the two anonymous reviewers of this manuscript who provided very useful, informative, and detailed critiques.

1.   Introduction

In 1718 Jean-Baptiste Le Moyne, Sieur de Bienville founded the City of New Orleans on the first high ground along the banks of the Mississippi. Unfortunately, this so-called high ground was not high enough. As soon as levees were built (from the French word *levée de terre*, or 'raised ground') to keep the Mississippi River from annually flooding the city, not only was the river kept out, but so was the rich silt which had created the spit of land on which the city sat in the first place. Thus, the new French city began sinking almost as soon as it was founded. Like the sinking city of New Orleans, surrounded on all sides by water and forbidding swamps, the French language in Louisiana was likewise planted in soil that would become linguistically hostile as English and Spanish slowly encroached from all sides. From the very start, extinction was always looming just over the horizon for both the city and its first European language.

For New Orleans, the inevitable hit on August 29, 2005. Indeed, I am writing these words within weeks of Louisiana's – and America's – greatest natural disaster. Hurricane Katrina devastated literally tens of thousands of square miles in Southeast Louisiana, flooding the largely below sea-level New Orleans, and displacing more than a million state residents. Some of the displaced evacuees will eventually return to the state, but many have nothing to return to, and will likely never come home. Katrina was followed three weeks later by Hurricane Rita along the Southwestern Louisiana coastline, devastating much of the Cajun lowland country stretching from Terrebonne Parish to the Sabine Pass along the Texas-Louisiana border.

Rita was very destructive, but the vast majority of those forced from their homes by the flooding did not have to leave Cajun country to find shelter. Katrina, on the other hand, emptied much of the New Orleans area of its population, scattering evacuees to all 50 states (El Nasser & Overberg 2005). As officials try to measure the consequences of so huge a disruption and dislocation in the lives of so many people, it occurred to me that had Hurricane Katrina hit the state just 100 miles further west, an additional casualty of the storm might have been serious, perhaps irreversible damage to what remains of the varieties of French which are still spoken after almost 300 years.

Successive waves of settlers to Louisiana brought several varieties of French to the region. The first varieties were the French Canadian dialects introduced directly by settlers who came to the new French territory in the wake of Robert Cavalier de la Salle's trip down the Mississippi to its mouth in 1682 (Picone 1997). Another wave followed very closely, introducing the French and French-based Creole spoken by White settlers and slaves from the Caribbean (Picone 1997). About 9,000 French and Creole speakers fleeing the Haitian revolution of 1803, including White landowners and their Black bondsmen, injected their unique varieties of Caribbean French and Creole into the rich Louisiana linguistic mix. Today, vestiges of the Haitian dialect have been identified in the Creole still spoken around Breaux Bridge, Louisiana (Brasseaux & Conrad 1992). The Acadians who began arriving in Louisiana following their deportation from Nova Scotia by the British between 1755 and 1759 introduced another dialect of French to the then Spanish territory of Louisiana, a variety now termed Cajun French. Other varieties of French came to the state via *Québécois* immigrants and successive waves of immigration from France, especially during the nineteenth century.

By the turn of the twenty-first century, essentially only two varieties of French are still spoken in the state to any extent, Cajun and Creole (moreover, there is some debate about whether Creole is a language in its own right, but see Mather this volume). There is also a variety of French spoken in Terrebonne parish among the Houma Indians (Picone 1997). These varieties continue to survive because there are still insular, tight-knit communities in southwest and south central Louisiana (proverbial 'high ground') where a relatively large proportion of residents can still speak French.

The number of native speakers of these Louisiana dialects dwindles everyday due to natural mortality, and these languages are only still spoken where there remain small pockets of a 'critical mass' of French speakers who are able to converse with each other in these French dialects. These tiny linguistic communities, one of which I consider myself fortunate to live in, seem so fragile that I am not sure they could survive a demographic upheaval of the magnitude of Katrina. Along with Louisiana's disappearing marshland, the United States is in the slow process of losing one of its greatest cultural and linguistic treasures, and most Americans are not even aware that it exists. In this chapter, I would like to share with the reader both the empirical data, and my first-hand experience observing French in Louisiana as it is still spoken in the early twenty-first century by Cajuns and Creoles. I also provide a brief historical overview of the peoples who still speak these interesting dialects. Finally, I discuss Louisiana's efforts to preserve French, which are centered mostly in its school French immersion programs. I share empirical data that suggest the degree to which these programs have been successful in meeting their goals.

2.   America's best-kept secret

As a testament to just how well-kept the secret of French in Louisiana is, even though 50% of my ancestry is Acadian, and I have been formally studying French in Louisiana for two and a half decades, I was not really aware of the extent to which there were still relatively vibrant communities of native French speakers in southwest Louisiana until I moved to this part of the state in 1994. As a youth, I lived mostly outside of Louisiana, as a consequence of life in a peripatetic military family, though I attended high school in New Orleans. Except for perhaps my Cajun grandmother, I never heard one Cajun or Creole word uttered when I lived in the Crescent City, and indeed, cannot recall even hearing a Cajun accent during my high school years. For those who may not know, native New Orleaneans speak English with an accent more akin to Brooklyn or Boston than to nearby Baton Rouge. I attended university in Baton Rouge, where I met my *Québécoise* wife who came south to learn English. She was the catalyst that awakened my interest in the French language, an interest that may have otherwise remained dormant.

Even though my wife and I subsequently reared our own children to speak French in Louisiana (documented in Caldas & Caron-Caldas 1992, 1997, 1999, 2000, 2002; and Caldas 2006), we had been living for many years near the state capital of Baton Rouge, about 50 miles east of Lafayette. There are few French speakers in Baton Rouge. Indeed, most native Baton Rougeans speak English with just a touch of a southern accent. The French-speaking Cajuns and Creoles I talk about in this chapter decidedly do not speak English with southern accents. Native French-speaking Louisianans speak English with a very strong and unique French accent. Indeed, it is so pronounced that I have almost always been able to identify French-speaking Cajuns and Creoles by the way that they speak English. However, it is also true that there are many speakers of Cajun English who have pronounced 'Cajun' accents simply as a consequence of being surrounded by other speakers of Cajun English.

Until the last thirty years or so, comparatively little scholarly research had been conducted on French-speaking Louisiana (Brown 1993). Now, it seems that there is a rush to document this wonderfully unique phenomenon and its associated culture before it is too late, with so much high quality research being conducted that there is no space in this chapter to cite it all. I encountered the heart of French-speaking Louisiana when I took a position at the University of Louisiana (then the University of Southwestern Louisiana) located in Lafayette. Lafayette is the self-proclaimed 'hub city' of French Louisiana, an area of the state commonly known as Acadiana. The term Acadiana was created in the mid-twentieth century from the fusion of the words 'Acadia' and 'Louisiana'. *Acadie* ('Acadia' in English) is the name of the region in Nova Scotia that was the center of the Acadian community in Canada prior to the forced deportation of Acadians by the British in the eighteenth century. First, I would like to briefly examine the historical connections between the original *Acadie* in Canada, and the Cajun people and language of present day Acadiana. Then, I would like to trace the parallel development in Louisiana of the French-speaking Black[1] Creoles. Finally, I will visit efforts to preserve French in the state, focusing on school French immersion programs.

2.1 *Acadie*

The Cajuns (*Cadiens* in Louisiana French) of Louisiana are distant cousins of the present day Acadians (*Acadiens* in French Canada,) who populate hundreds of French-speaking communities in the Canadian maritime provinces of Nova Scotia, New Brunswick, and Prince Edward Island, as well as northern Maine. In fact, about 1,000,000 residents of the 7,000,000 inhabitants of the French-speaking Province of *Québec* have Acadian ancestors as well. I have spent time in New Brunswick, the Cana-

---

1. The 'Creoles' of Louisiana are a mixed race category of persons, so my referring to them as 'Black Creoles' is a shorthand way of distinguishing these persons from the several other historical groups in the state who have referred to themselves as 'Creoles' but did not have African ancestry.

dian province with the largest concentration of Acadians, and I am happy to report that French speaking there is alive and well. In fact, the French-speaking community in New Brunswick, especially along the Acadian peninsula in the northeast part of the province, is much more dynamic than is Louisiana's. Most New Brunswick francophones attend school in French, are French literate, and have access to much French-speaking media, such as francophone television stations and daily newspapers published in French. Plus, these northern Acadians tend to live in communities that are predominantly French-speaking, and live their lives speaking mostly French, though most New Brunswick Acadians are French-English bilinguals (Boudreau 1996). By contrast, most native French-speaking Louisianans cannot read or write any variety of French. (More on French schooling in Louisiana below.) Moreover, the vast majority of Cajuns less than fifty years of age do not speak French at all (Henry & Bankston 2002).

There are, however, commonalities between the two Acadian communities, one set in southern Louisiana and the other in eastern Canada. In addition to their common ancestry, there are many linguistic similarities between the Acadian and Cajun varieties of French (Ancelet 2004a, 2004b, 2005). Also, both groups of Acadians share the memory of their tragic historical saga, which the Acadians still in Canada and their cousins in Louisiana both refer to as *Le Grand Dérangement*. This term is literally, and somewhat euphemistically, translated into 'the Great Upheaval'. However, the forced British deportation of the Acadians in the late eighteenth century should more realistically be interpreted something as an enormous catastrophe. In terms of the magnitude of disruption in the lives of entire communities, *Le Grand Dérangement* has some similarities to the massive dislocations caused by Hurricanes Katrina and Rita. However, these storms were natural catastrophes, whereas *Le Grand Dérangement* was man-made.

2.2 *Le Grand Dérangement* and Acadian history

An understanding of life in *Acadie* prior to *Le Grand Dérangement* can better help us understand why Cajuns still speak French at all after so long a separation from their French-speaking roots in Canada, and even more distant roots in France. First of all, the name 'Cajun' itself is a derivation of the name *Acadien*. Even though many do not speak French, Cajuns are well aware of their ancestry, and the least educated Cajun can tell you that his people were forced out of Canada. It is this strong ethnic identity, which is very much alive (Henry & Bankston 2002), that helped the Acadians weather so many adversities, natural and otherwise. Though the French first settled Nova Scotia in 1604, the British burned this settlement in 1613 (Faragher 2005). Thus, the first French citizens to settle the New World, and eventually identify themselves as Acadians, initially began arriving in what is today Nova Scotia in 1632. There is an apocryphal account that the explorer Verrazzano had named this part of North America "Arcadia" more than three quarters of a century before the arrival of the French settlers, because the pastoral lay of the land reminded him so much of the legendary Arcadia region of Greece, though some believe the word may actually comes from the Indian Micmac *Kadi* (Faragher 2005). Arcadia became *Acadie* in French, which in Louisiana morphed into 'Acadia', and finally, 'Acadiana'.

The Acadian people were farmers, livestock raisers, and fishermen, living peacefully off the land while the French and British slowly colonized North America. Unfortunately, their land happened to be near the center of the conflict between the two competing European colonial superpowers that France and England were, and Nova Scotia changed hands more than once between these two countries as they struggled to dominate the continent. With the Treaty of Utrecht in 1713, most of *Acadie* fell under the British sphere of control. By the time of the outbreak of the Seven Years War (also known in the U.S. as the French and Indian War) in the 1750s, the Acadians had developed a strong ethnic identity quite distinct from the rest of French North America. They were avowed neutrals, pledging not to take sides with either European power, a stance that irked both the French and the British. However, the British were especially suspicious of this large colony of French-speaking Catholics among them, and during the war ordered the Acadians to pledge their allegiance to the king of England. The Acadians categorically refused, and the British military governor of Nova Scotia, Charles Lawrence, implemented a plan that had been around for decades in the form of his infamous order to deport all the Acadian settlers to the eastern seaboard of the British colonies of North America, to England, and back to France.

In what is now classified as a classic example of ethnic cleansing (Faragher 2005), the British systematically rounded up the Acadian settlers, burned their homes and churches, and forced them aboard British ships for long sea voyages that many hundreds, if not thousands, of Acadians would not survive. It is estimated that a quarter of the Acadian deportees shipped to England in 1756 died within a year from a smallpox epidemic. Indeed, 700 Acadians forcibly bound for France in 1758 died in two shipwrecks alone (Landry & Lang 2001). Two of my mother's ancestors deported in 1758, one from Isle Royale (now Cape Breton, Nova Scotia), and the other from Isle Saint Jean (now Prince Edward Island) survived the long winter sea voyage and landed in Saint Malo, France. There, the two deportees met, married, and gave birth in exile to a son who would eventually migrate to Louisiana with thousands of other Acadian exiles. Many other Acadians who survived the forced deportation found themselves scattered among more hostile populations not particularly happy to have these new French-speaking, Catholic refugees who looked and spoke a lot like the enemy they were fighting. One of the least hospitable destinations of many deportees was the puritanical English Protestant colony of Massachusetts, which counted 1,043 Acadians by 1763 (Landry & Lang 2001).

After the Treaty of Paris in 1763 formally ended the Seven Years War and the precipitating ostensible cause of *Le Grand Dérangement* in the first place (many believe the whole episode was a land grab), some Acadians quietly infiltrated back into what is today New Brunswick because it was still largely unsettled and wild. These refugees joined other Acadians who had been hiding out in New Brunswick throughout the deportation nightmare. Some Acadians also trickled back into Nova Scotia and Prince Edward Island only to find that their prime lands had been quickly seized and resettled by English, Scottish, and American colonists. The returning refugees once again set up shop as farmers, fishermen, and raisers of livestock, though their new lands were often not as fertile or desirable as the ones taken from them (Landry & Lang 2001). Many returning Acadians were so terrorized by the British deportation, that they lived in fear in the Canadian woods for years (where many more died of starvation, exposure, and illness), rather than make their presence known to the Canadian British authorities. Thousands of Acadians eventually found their way back to France, either voluntarily or on British ships, but even there, they did not feel at home. They had been separated from the mother country for a century and a half by that time, and many no longer fit comfortably in the more formalized and rigidly structured French society, in part because their language had already evolved to be quite distinct from the French dialects of that day (Ancelet 2004, 2005).

The folklorist and Cajun researcher Barry Ancelet noted that the Acadian language, well-established in North America by the 1630s, evolved in relative isolation from the French spoken on the continent. Ancelet points out that the continental variety of French was subsequently influenced and standardized by *L'Académie Française*, and the written and spoken French of the European Enlightenment writers in ways that only tangentially affected Acadian French. Indeed, Brasseaux (1987) notes that Acadian French started out as a different variant of French in the first place, since it was a non-standard dialect spoken in the region of France from which most Acadians migrated in the early seventeenth century, notably from the north of Poitou in the area around *Loudun* and *Lachaussée*, and toward the west around *St. Onge* and the *Vendée* region.

Examples of some Cajun French expressions, and their counterparts spoken on the other side of the Atlantic, highlight the differences between these two varieties of French. Cajuns say *magasin* for 'barn.' The French say *grange*. A raccoon in Cajun is a *chaoui*, whereas in France the same animal is referred to as a *raton laveur*. (See the Index for a glossary of more Cajun terms and expressions, along with their French counterparts.)

The Acadians had also gotten used to a degree of freedom and independence that was not typical for persons of their class in the hierarchical France of the late eighteenth century. The French tended to look down upon these Acadian refugees, and indeed the North American French population in general, as rather unrefined backwoods hicks. Vestiges of this condescending French attitude can still be seen in the language today. In modern *Québécois* French, the expression "*Il est colon!*" ('He's a colonist!') translates into something like 'He's a backwards idiot!'

However, an outlet would be provided to those restless Acadians ready and willing to migrate yet one more time. The Treaty of Paris not only ended hostilities between England and France, it also ceded much of the Louisiana territory – which had belonged to France – over to Spain, another British rival. The Spanish were anxious to colonize Louisiana with industrious and loyal Catholic citizens as a buffer against the expanding Protestant English (and ultimately American) colonies to the east. The former French colony had never really thrived under largely inefficient and often corrupt

French rule, in part because there were probably as many opportunists looking for a quick buck, as there were settlers desiring to establish families and raise much needed crops to feed the growing population of New Orleans (Hall 1992; Taylor 1984).

Thus, the Spanish, who were generally much better administrators of Louisiana than were the French, wisely decided to offer homesteads to those displaced Acadians who would be willing to settle the humid subtropical lowlands and prairies along the northern Gulf of Mexico in what is today southern Louisiana. In one of the greatest migrations of its time, thousands of Acadians from along the Atlantic rim stretching from the American English colonies up to the maritime provinces of Canada, across to England and France, and back down and across to the Caribbean Islands ultimately made their way to Louisiana. In 1785, 1600 Acadian exiles in France took the Spanish up on their generous offer and boarded seven ships bound for New Orleans (Landry & Lang 2001). This exodus emptied France of two-thirds of its temporary Acadian refugee population.

The Acadians arrived in a territory that though ostensibly Spanish, was inhabited mostly by French speakers, albeit a population speaking yet another variety of French different from the Acadian language. Still, the Acadian influx simply strengthened the French-speaking identity of Louisiana (while expanding the variability of the language), and through their large, stable families ensured the hegemony of French in Louisiana for a century or more to come. Indeed, so strong was the French-speaking culture in the state, that the few Spanish who did live in Louisiana were largely assimilated by the French-speaking population. As a testimony to just how hegemonic French was during the Spanish period and later, one can still find families with names like Romero, Hernandez, Ramirez, Nunez, Perez and Martinez, whose families date to the Spanish rule of Louisiana, but that today speak fluent French, but no Spanish. This situation is now, of course, changing, as new families from Central and South America, who carry these very same surnames, immigrate once again to the former Spanish colony. Indeed, one of the interesting linguistic consequences of the disasters caused by Hurricanes Katrina and Rita is a huge influx of Spanish-speaking Central American workers into the affected areas to clean up the mess (AP 2005). Some, if not many of these immigrants, will no doubt stay in Louisiana. It's extremely doubtful that this newest wave of Hispanic immigrants will learn to speak French. What's easier to imagine is that native Spanish speakers will soon outnumber native French speakers in a state that has until now resisted the large Latino demographic transition that is sweeping much of the rest of the United States (discussed in detail in Caldas & Bankston 2005).

Louisiana was once again briefly a French colony from 1800 to 1803, when cash-strapped Napoleon sold the Louisiana territory to Thomas Jefferson's United States for 15 million dollars.[2] The size of the U.S. more than doubled with a pen stroke, as all or

---

2. In today's dollars, at a conservative estimate of $500 per acre, the Louisiana territory would cost $256 billion, still a bargain by any stretch of the imagination.

parts of 15 modern states were added to the growing country. Still, many of the new American citizens wanted to remain French. In fact, so proud were the Louisianans to be temporarily French again (if even for three years of almost complete neglect by the mother country), that many Louisianans mightily protested the transfer to the United States, taking down the American flag as soon as it was run-up in the French Quarter of New Orleans and hoisting once again the Tricolor of France. New Orleaneans wept openly and bitterly in the streets at news of the territory's transfer to the United States. When Louisiana became a state in 1812, it was the first and last state admitted as part of the United States in which native English-speakers were in the minority (Crawford 1992). When the new monolingual English-speaking Louisiana governor Claiborne took over the state's reigns, he complained that "not one in fifty of the old inhabitants appear to me to understand the English language" (cited in Crawford 1992:40).

Many of the Acadian French-speaking communities outside of New Orleans were relatively isolated, some only accessible by boat, with inhabitants only infrequently making trips to the city to buy and sell goods. This is precisely why the major native variety of French still spoken in Louisiana today is Cajun French. The other French-speaking communities in Louisiana have long ago assimilated into the majority English-speaking population, especially those francophone communities that lived in New Orleans. Incidentally, such was the importance of New Orleans that Cajuns still refer to the city in French as La Ville ('the city'), as if there were not any other cities in Louisiana.

The tight-knit, rural French-speaking communities of south Louisiana clung tenaciously to their language and heritage, and for a very long time often viewed themselves as French even more than they did as Americans, referring to English-speaking Louisianans as les Américains ('the Americans'). During the American Civil War of the 1860s, some French-speaking Louisianans in Acadiana hung French flags from their porches when Union soldiers marched through their towns, to differentiate themselves from non French-speaking Southerners. One Union soldier in Cajun Country in 1863 wrote in his diary "A great many of the people of this section were French, or claimed to be, and when we were marching through, claimed French protection by hanging out French flags" (Bradshaw 1998:16). However, on the other side of that great divide, there were French-speaking Louisianans loyal to the Southern cause who formed regiments called the Zouaves, dressing in flamboyant French military uniforms (there were also northern Zouave regiments in the Civil War, most notably out of New York City).

As an indication of just how strong Cajun ethnicity remains, and how they viewed themselves as being unique from the rest of the state's inhabitants, one can still find elderly Cajuns who refer to non-Cajun English-speakers as les Américains (Picone 2003). Indeed, at the turn of the twenty-first century, there were still a few elderly native-born Louisianans who spoke only French, though they would likely be ninety years of age or older. Throughout the nineteenth century, and until about roughly 1920, entire communities in South Louisiana were filled with White Cajuns and Black Creoles who coexisted together without speaking any English. When the legendary Huey Long campaigned for governor in 1924 and 1928, he needed the aid of a French interpreter when he gave his stump speeches in Acadiana (Williams 1969). The Cajuns, a previously often ignored political constituency, appreciated Long's interest in them, and their vote ensured his election in 1928.

Cajuns still respond warmly to those who make an honest attempt to communicate with them in their language. After Hurricane Rita devastated the southwestern part of the state, two politicians, one of them a Cajun, visited a hard hit rural Cajun area where French is still spoken. When the Anglophone politician asked a group of survivors if they needed help, the group simply stared blankly at him, as if they did not understand him. The second politician, a Cajun state representative, then asked the group the same question in French. The group immediately came to life, happily chatting with the representative in a mixture of French and English (A language barrier 2005).

3. The true heart of French Louisiana

So, what exactly is the status of Cajun French-speaking in Louisiana at the turn of the twenty-first century, two hundred and fifty years after *Le Grand Dérangement* ultimately destined thousands of Acadian refugees to call this new *Acadie* their home? First, a geographical description of the Acadiana region of south Louisiana may help the reader better visualize where these French-speakers reside. Acadiana is comprised of twenty-two parishes (also known as counties in the rest of the country) which form a roughly triangular shaped territory with one point anchored in the southeastern part of the state near (but not including) New Orleans, rising northwestward to a point just south of Alexandria in the central part of the state, and descending southwestward to a point in the southwestern corner of the state near the Louisiana-Texas border. Within these twenty-two parishes reside the vast majority of those Louisianans who are native French speakers. These twenty-two parishes also constitute the bulk of Catholic Louisiana. The rest of the state is largely monolingual English-speaking Protestant, with Southern Baptists constituting the largest Protestant denomination in Louisiana.

The greatest concentration of French speakers is in the roughly eight or so parishes of south-central Louisiana that surround the hub city of Lafayette. If there is a French-speaking epicenter, U.S. Census Bureau figures would indicate that it is probably in the rural parish of St. Martin just east of Lafayette, where the author currently resides. St. Martin Parish has the highest concentration of French speakers in the state, with fully 30.5% of the population five years of age and older[3] indicating on the 2000 census that they spoke a language other than English at home. Indeed, according to 2000 U.S. Census figures, St. Martin Parish has a higher proportion of French speakers than any other county in the entire United States, northern Maine included. Since only 0.9% of

---

3. All figures indicated for speakers of a language at home other than English are for the population five years of age and older.

the parish was foreign-born, and only .08% of the population indicated that they were of Hispanic or Latino origin, we can safely deduce that the vast majority, perhaps 99% or more of these persons, were speaking French at home (U.S. Census 2000).

In 2000, 46.7% of the 1,505 residents in my CDP (Census Designated Place) spoke a language other than English at home, though only 2.4% were foreign born, and zero residents entered the CDP between 1990 and 2000 (U.S. Census 2000). In fact, 12.2% of my rural community indicated on the 2000 Census that "they did not speak English very well".

However, most of the French-speaking population throughout Acadiana, as well as the Cajun/Creole community in which I live, is over forty years of age, and more likely over fifty or sixty years of age (Henry & Bankston 2002). Since I have been fortunate to become acquainted with Cajuns and Creoles of the most authentic stock possible (more on Creoles shortly), I have also had the exceptional experience of meeting a few people less than 40 years of age who learned to speak French in a Cajun or Creole home. Their cases are so exceptional that I can remember each one. One boy, now in his twenties, is a sugar cane farmer who spends almost all of his time with his French-speaking father among French-speaking Creole and Cajun laborers raising their finicky tropical crop. Incidentally, this same farming family has begun to bring in Spanish-speaking immigrants to do this same backbreaking work that they had been hiring locals to do, once again suggesting the demographic future of the state. While this young man is able to speak French, his three sisters (all older than him, and not involved in farming) cannot speak it (but can understand it), indicating the importance of social milieu in assuring the continuity of a spoken tongue (a point extensively researched in Caldas 2006). Another case was a 36-year-old Black Creole I picked up hitchhiking one day near Breaux Bridge, east of Lafayette. What was memorable about this young man, apart from the fact that he was a fluent Creole speaker, was that as we chatted in French he was surprised that I did not know the meaning of what for him was obviously a very common Creole French word I had never heard before. The impression I came away with from our brief ride together was that this young man had very little understanding of the existence of the French speaking world beyond his own limited one, and seemed to assume that many more people in Louisiana spoke his dialect of French than is actually the case.

There is empirical evidence to suggest that only primarily older Louisianans are native French speakers, and as they die off, so does their native variety of French (as indicated by the U.S. Census Bureau). For example, whereas 46.7% of the members in my rural community indicated that they spoke a language other than English in their home in 2000, the figure in 1990 was 59.7%. This represents a decrease of more than one-fifth of the population of French speakers in the most francophone part of Louisiana in only one decade. The decrease in French speakers at the parish-level (St. Martin Parish) went from 47.3% of the population in 1980, to 39.4% in 1990, to 30.5% in 2000. From a more subjective perspective, this means that I am accutely aware, and enjoy, each moment that I hear spontaneous French conversations in public in my small community, knowing that I am witnessing the very end of two rare and disappearing dialects. For those sociolinguists who argue that "language is culture" (Fishman 1985), I may also have a front row seat on the extinction of an entire culture – or two cultures (one Creole, one White) – as well.

Let me make clear that when I do hear individuals conversing in French in my rural community, rarely do I hear only French spoken. More often than not there is a high degree of code-switching back and forth between English and French, with more English than French spoken in a typical bilingual conversation. I do not believe that I have yet met an individual unable to speak English, though I have met elderly French-speakers who speak better French than they do English. However, among those Cajuns and Creoles older than seventy years of age in my community (born before 1935), many, if not most, will tell you that they entered the first grade unable to speak English. These same individuals will tell you that many of their parents (born before 1915 or so) were unable to speak English, and needed their children to translate for them.

3.1 The Hub City

French is not spoken uniformly in public across even the most francophone parishes in Acadiana. For example, though the city of Lafayette, with a population of about 110,000 in 2000, is often considered the heart of French Louisiana, one rarely hears French spoken publicly within the city limits. The reasons for this are telling of the Cajun people and their perspective on their variety of French. On the 2000 U.S. Census, 18.3% of the population of Lafayette parish indicated that they spoke a language other than English at home. Given that only 2.5% of the population was foreign-born, and only 1.7% of the population indicated that they were of Hispanic origin, we can safely conclude that the vast majority of those who spoke a language other than English were speaking French. Thus, there are obviously many French-speaking Cajuns who call Lafayette home, but they have adjusted to the relatively cosmopolitan atmosphere of the city that also includes many non French-speakers and many individuals with no French ancestry at all. Indeed, though decidedly a somewhat subjective observation, those Cajuns living in Lafayette seem to have a much less pronounced Cajun accent when they speak English than do those Cajuns living just 10 miles outside the city limits. I have spent hundreds of hours observing high school classrooms in both Lafayette and the surrounding parishes. I was struck by the almost southern California valley-speak accents of the majority of the teens I heard conversing in classrooms and on the school grounds of Lafayette's large, suburban-type high schools. The majority of the pupils in these schools are native to the area, and sport names like Comeaux, Daigle, Guidry, Leger, Lemoine, Savoie, and Thibodeaux. However, in the nearby towns of Opelousas, Breaux Bridge, Erath and Abbeville, one is much more likely to hear teens with these same last names speaking with a more pronounced Cajun accent.

I experienced several incidents in Lafayette that gave me some insight into how Cajuns perceive their language and culture, and which might explain the apparent city-country linguistic differences I observed. Upon assuming my new teaching position in the city, I initiated several conversations with Cajuns I met working in local retail stores who had accents indicating they spoke French. For one, they always seemed delighted to speak French with me. Once, however, a saleswoman in her sixties asked me if I were surprised that she spoke French. I answered "no", that I knew that many residents of the city spoke the language. She answered that many people could speak French, but wouldn't. I have since heard several other city residents validate her comment. One of my Cajun graduate students from the country south of Lafayette told me that in her youth she heard people saying that they were moving to Lafayette to "get themselves a brick house". The implication was they were moving "up" to a higher socio-economic, cosmopolitan area. Another graduate student told me that Cajuns living in Lafayette did not want to appear countrified, and so avoided speaking with a Cajun accent.

3.2 The beginning of the end

First of all, if what I have already written has not made this point clear, there is now almost no intergenerational transfer of French taking place in Louisiana, the *sin qua non* of language maintenance in a society (Landry, Allard & Henry 1996:465). Given the shrinking percentage of Cajuns and Creoles who still speak French, and the fact that most of those who do are over fifty years of age, is telling of the effectiveness of the state's early efforts to assimilate these populations into the English-speaking majority. There were essentially two forces, one legal and one social, which worked together to undermine the once vibrant French-speaking communities in the state. The legal assault on French in Louisiana actually dates back to the Reconstruction Constitution of 1864, immediately following the collapse of the Confederate rebellion in the state. The northern government sought to diminish all nonconformity in the state, and imposed a new state constitution that mandated only English be used in the state's public schools (see Estaville 1990). As Picone (1997) notes, the real death knell of French, though, was the passage of a compulsory education law in 1916, closely followed by the re-writing of the state's constitution in 1921. Lawmakers effectively codified popular prejudice against non-English speakers in the then new state constitution in Article 12, Section 12 that stated that: "The general exercises in the public schools shall be conducted in the English language" (West 1977:696). French was the primary language of instruction in many Acadian south-Louisiana schools when this constitutional prohibition was passed, and the lawmakers knew this. The 1921 state constitution effectively nullified a Louisiana law passed in 1847 that actually *authorized* bilingual instruction (Crawford 1997).

This prohibition against teaching in French was written into law as a consequence of a growing social force. The United States became increasingly isolationist following the end of WWI, evidence of which can be seen in President Wilson's failure to convince the American people to sign onto the League of Nations, originally his idea. In the wake of hundreds of thousands of American casualties in a bloody European war, and the growing "Red" menace of the new communist state in the Soviet Union, American sentiment grew increasingly distrustful of all things "foreign". The country had turned decidedly inward and isolationist by the early 1920s. The Acadians of south

Louisiana were not following suit, hence the anti-French legislation. In some other parts of the country, this post-war xenophobia manifested itself as anti-Norwegian, anti-Swedish, anti-Native American, and anti-German (the language of the enemy). Places like Nebraska passed legislation forbidding the teaching of classes in German.

3.3 Humiliation as powerful social force

Many Cajuns and Creoles are simply ashamed of their French, and are very hesitant to speak it around non-French speakers (or French speakers from outside the state), though there is now no legislation forbidding the speaking of French, and *au contraire*, there is a desperate attempt in the state to save the language (more on this below). I feel very fortunate to have been accepted into these almost secret linguistic societies, and to have been a witness to completely natural communications in French between native French Louisiana interlocutors. The root of their hesitancy to speak French is the legacy of a half-century of active social humiliation heaped onto French-speaking Acadians and Creoles. Humiliation is a powerful weapon, and has yielded the casualty of a linguistic inferiority complex. From roughly the 1920s to the early 1960s, monolingual French speakers in Louisiana were berated, punished, and shamed for speaking French in school. They were beaten, compelled to kneel on rice, forced to write lines, and generally ridiculed if a French word or phrase accidentally escaped their lips while on school grounds, in both public and Catholic schools (Incidentally, Acadians in northern Maine were recipients of the same harsh treatment for speaking French in school [Decker 1997].) Acadians were also teased for their unusual accents when speaking English. It was during the 1940s or 1950s that the ethnically derisive term 'coonass', of potentially racist and vulgar origins, was coined by outsiders to refer to Cajuns (Dormon 1983). However, in what is revelatory of their *joie de vivre* and self-deprecating good sense of humor, rather than be offended by the term, many Cajuns simply co-opted the expression as a tongue-in-cheek reference to their ethnicity.

For these legal and social reasons, French is essentially only still spontaneously spoken in the small, socially homogenous villages and towns in the countryside of south-central and southwest Louisiana. Most of the inhabitants of these relatively isolated areas either speak French, or more likely are the children or grandchildren of French speakers. They are comfortable speaking French with others who share their language and unique perspective on life. Some Cajuns and Creoles are not even comfortable speaking French with non-Cajun or non-Creole French speakers. For example, it is a rare conversation that I have with a Cajun or Creole in which he or she does not offer an apology for his or her 'bad' French. I have heard natives of France and even *Québec* refer to Cajun and Acadian French in disdainful and condescending terms, so I suppose it should not be surprising that Cajuns have to some extent internalized these negative stereotypes of their language.

So why didn't the last Louisiana generation to speak French fluently also rear their children to speak their ancestral language? As others (e.g., Picone 1997), I think that the short answer to this question is that they did not want to pass along to their children what they believed to be a social and educational handicap. Recall that the last generation, whose members are now mostly older than 50, were ridiculed for speaking French, and some still are. Of course, like many social realities, the truth is more complex than this. Cajuns were a largely poor and under-educated country people, many of whom could write neither English nor French. Moreover, according to historical accounts, such was also the case with their ancestors in New Brunswick. In the fifty years that followed *Le Grand Dérangement*, even members of the well educated Catholic clergy in neighboring French-speaking Québec looked down upon the dispersed Acadians, some going so far as to blame the Acadians for their own deportation! Missionary Lefebvre de Bellefeuille argued that "the greatest fault of the parishioners of Caraquet [Acadian town in NE New Brunswick] is that they are ignorant, Acadian, and that the cause of their unhappiness is their sin" (Landry & Lang 2000: 138) [translation mine]. And this unflattering assessment of the Acadians was coming from a fellow French Catholic. One can only imagine what English Protestants thought of the deportees who were shipped in large numbers to the British colonies.

In Louisiana, the Acadian language and accent were associated with disadvantage and poverty, and still are. A few years ago, I had a conversation with the daughter of an elderly French-speaking woman who told me that her mother so closely associated the French accent (which was heavy) with ignorance, that she could not understand why then bilingual Cajun governor Edwin Edwards was not ashamed to speak publicly with such heavily accented English (S. Starling, personal communication, November 12, 1991). The last generation reared to speak French in Louisiana was so humiliated not only because of how they spoke, but also because of who they were, that they were ashamed of their supposedly bad French, and saw little need to speak it. Just as a sidebar, I have often been told by members of the first monolingual English-speaking Cajun generation that some of the few times they heard their parents speaking French was when the parents did not want their children to understand them.

4. Creoles

I would now like to briefly discuss the other population of French-speaking individuals in Acadiana, who today identify themselves as 'Creoles', and who also usually consider themselves African Americans. Additionally, most of these Louisiana Creoles are, like their Cajun counterparts, Catholics. The term Creole is polysemous, and has taken on different meanings since Columbus first bumped into the Americas (Neuman 1985). In the eighteenth and nineteenth centuries a 'Creole' often referred to an individual of White ancestry born in the New World to European parents who usually came over from Portugal, Spain, or France. There was a 'Latin' and 'aristocratic' connotation to the term, and it was used to differentiate one from someone with a 'common' Anglo Saxon heritage (see Henry & Bankston 1998, for an excellent historical treatment of the term Creole, and its present application to French-speaking Louisiana Blacks). This former sense of the term 'Creole' is almost never used anymore in Louisiana.

4.1 Current definition of a Louisiana 'Creole'

Today, the term 'Creole' in Louisiana usually refers to individuals with mixed Black and White ancestries who are also francophone and Catholic. Many, if not most Louisiana Creoles trace their lineage back to *les gens de couleur libre* ('free people of color') prior to the Civil War. Some have a mixture of both free and slave ancestry. Louisiana French and Spanish tradition – custom and law prior to the territory becoming American – exerted social and legal pressure on White men to provide freedom to their Black mistresses who bore them children, as well as freedom and an education to the offspring of these miscegenous relationships (Brasseaux, Fontenot, & Oubre 1996). Quite simply, the race line in colonial Louisiana was as indefinite and permeable as it was anywhere in the New World (and certainly much less than in the rest of the south), with people of color arbitrarily promoted to the status of Whites, and often holding high positions of authority (Hall 1992).

Many of the social White elite in New Orleans as well as the gentry in the plantation system had separate households for their Black mistresses and the children they bore for their White suitors. These children were often freed from bondage by their biological fathers, and reared as very well educated 'free persons of color', who went on to have quite successful businesses of their own. Indeed, many free persons of color were themselves slave owners (Brasseaux et al. 1996). *Les gens de couleur libres* were not just confined to New Orleans. For example, many Creoles of the Cane River region trace their lineage to Marie Thérèse Coincoin of the Melrose Plantation just outside of Natchitoches, Louisiana, in the northwestern part of the state. Marie Thérèse Coincoin and the sons she bore by her slave-owner Thomas Pierre Metoyer were set free by Metoyer, and established themselves along the Cane River (which was the Red River before it changed course around 1837 [Picone 2003]). Their offspring are sometimes referred to as the 'Cane River People'. Also, from as early as the eighteenth century there was a growing population of free Blacks in what are today the south-central and southwestern parts of the state, at the time rivaling in size the free Black population in New Orleans (Brasseaux, Fontenot, & Oubre 1996). When Louisiana was under French and Spanish rule, *les gens de couleur libres* occupied a middle ground racial status between Whites and Blacks. The Spanish, in particular, were interested in expanding the number of this category of persons. After the Louisiana Territory was purchased from France by the U.S., 'free people of color' was the term used to refer to "any racial mixture of less than one half Negro" (Oubre & Leonard 1983:72).

4.2 Creole identity

The Creoles of Louisiana developed a very strong group identity centered on their freedom, their education, their Catholic religion, their typically lighter skin tone, and the French language. They did not identify very closely with their Black cousins in chains, and indeed, had very little in common with first uneducated slaves, and after the Civil War, with uneducated or undereducated freedmen. In his famous 1972 novel

The Autobiography of Miss Jane Pittman, Ernest Gaines writes about the distance that French-speaking Creoles put between themselves and Blacks, and how the ability to speak French was used as a gate-keeping mechanism to distinguish genuine Creoles from others. Though fiction, Gaines' novel depicts well the social situation of Blacks and Creoles in Pointe Coupée Parish, Louisiana after the Civil War.

Creoles resisted White America's attempts to classify them as Blacks, much preferring to be called 'French'. However, they ultimately lost the battle in the racially charged and polarized atmosphere of the Jim Crow period. In the infamous Supreme Court case of Plessy v. Ferguson that established the odious "Separate but Equal" doctrine of legal (*de jure*) segregation, the light-skinned Creole Homer Plessy, who was removed from a "Whites only" train car, had argued that he was indeed a White man (Plessy v. Feruguson 1896). However, the so-called "one drop" rule was *de rigueur* in much of the country by the late nineteenth century, the rationale being that if a person had even one drop of Negro blood, then he or she was Black.

Though Whites in the twentieth century may have seen Creoles as Blacks, Creoles themselves continued to see themselves differently. They had their own churches, they tended to marry within their group, and they continued to speak French. One of my Creole graduate students told me that while attending a dinner party in New Orleans and talking with another Creole mother, she took out pictures of her children to show the other woman. My graduate student said that as soon as the other woman saw how light-skinned her children were, she exclaimed that their children should get together at an upcoming Creole picnic in New Orleans. "I believe that my children definitely passed the color test and hair test with this mother" (personal communication, October 19, 2005, Bobbie DeCuir).

Visitors to Louisiana may indeed notice that some of those individuals who consider themselves Creoles do indeed seem to have a more *café au lait* skin complexion than most individuals who classify themselves as African American. Historically, Creoles themselves have used skin tone as well as the ability to speak French as markers of their distinctiveness. The "brown paper bag test" was a well-known screening technique used at Creole socials to differentiate Creoles from non-Creoles. In fact, Henry Louis Gates, Jr., the chairman of the Afro-American Studies Department at Harvard, revealed in his book *The Future of the Race* (1996) that "bag parties" were held at his alma mater, Yale, as late as the late 1960s. He said that the practice traveled north from some of "the brothers" from New Orleans, and consisted in sticking a brown paper bag on the door. Anyone with a darker skin tone than the bag was denied entrance to the party.

Closer to home and much more recently, another of my graduate students in Lafayette shared the following story with me:

> Once I had an African American colleague (who had a medium dark skin tone) from New Orleans tell me that I could pass the "bag test". He was surprised when I didn't know to what test he was referring since I was from south central Louisiana, where there is a large population of Creoles, whose physical profile was similar to my own. He

said that because I could pass the bag test, I didn't have to worry about being excluded from any of the prominent social events in New Orleans.

(Gail Bonhomme, personal communication, October 24, 2005)

Another young woman, a fair skinned (non-Creole) African American from Miami, Florida, who taught school in rural St. Martin Parish, shared the following telling incidents with me. She said she was shocked upon arriving in Acadiana and having lighter skinned Creole Blacks counsel her "not to cut her hair or get too much sun", so she wouldn't be mistaken for darker skinned Blacks. "I was totally freaked out and thought I was losing my mind!", she exclaimed, especially after a darker skinned yard worker at the University of Louisiana at Lafayette was surprised that she, a lighter skinned Black, would even speak with him. Her confusion deepened when she mistook lighter skinned Blacks at the university for Whites, who politely pointed out they were African Americans (reported in Bankston & Caldas 2002: 107).

It is important to note that Louisiana Creole French likely also has its roots among Black slaves on French-speaking Louisiana plantations (Campbell, in press). According to Campbell, Louisiana Creole French, which he also refers to as *Gombo* or *Negro French*, is "moribund", and only spoken in three areas of Louisiana. And having worked in all three, I can report that Creole French is really only a viable language in the three contiguous parishes of St. Martin, St. Landry, and Lafayette, where by 1990 there were somewhere in the neighborhood of 22,000 to 28,000 Creoles (Dormon 1992). Thus, I was able to observe the rare phenomenon of native Louisiana Creoles conversing spontaneously with each other in native Louisiana French.

4.3 Current Creole French

The author lives in one of the largest concentrations of French-speaking Creoles in the state (and in contrast, has yet to meet a native New Orleanean Creole who was also a native French speaker). In fact, the dialect of Creole spoken just east of Lafayette likely has vestiges of Haitian French, which dates to the influx of 9,000 Haitian refugees, 6,000 of whom were Black (and most likely slaves with their masters), who fled to Louisiana from Saint Domingue during the island's 1803 revolution (Brasseaux & Conrad 1992). This author's experience has been that French speaking among Louisiana's francophone Creoles seems as common as it is among the state's Cajun population. Thus, if it is truly a "moribund language", as Campbell assesses it, the outlook is equally dim for Cajun French. In Breaux Bridge, a town of about 7,000 Cajuns and Creoles six miles to the east of Lafayette, many French Creole expressions have diffused into the local Cajun French (which Campbell classifies as the more prestigious of the two languages), and I have frequently witnessed the two populations, Creole and White, conversing easily with each other. In fact, Picone (2003) suggests that the language of many Louisiana Creoles is in fact Cajun French. In what could be considered a metaphor for cross-linguistic pollination, the Acadiana musical styles of Cajun and Zydeco (Creole) share many similarities as well, as they both developed alongside each other in the same rural environment. Both musical styles incorporate the accordion, but interestingly, Cajun music is mostly sung in French, whereas Zydeco is either sung in a mixture of French and English, or is sung exclusively in English (Ancelet 1996; Olivier & Sandmel 1999).

However, the Cajun and Creole French-speaking populations are far from being integrated. In Breaux Bridge, up until 2004, the Creoles had their own separate Mardi Gras festival, apart from the (mostly White) Breaux Bridge Cajun Mardi Gras. In some communities, like Cecilia just to the northeast of Breaux Bridge, the Creoles have their own separate Catholic church, which sits only 300 yards from the Cajun Catholic church. I attended the White Catholic church on several occasions, and never saw a single person of color seated among the small group of Cajun parishioners, though according to the 2000 U.S. Census, 41.5% of Cecilia's population identified itself as Black.

It is in little country communities like the aforementioned Cecilia, which are peopled almost entirely with Cajuns and Creoles, that one is most likely to hear French spoken unabashedly in public in Louisiana. Whereas I have only rarely heard French spoken publicly in Lafayette, and have heard French spoken occasionally in public places in the small city of Breaux Bridge, I have heard French spoken more often than not when I have ventured into Cecilia, both amongst and between Cajuns and Creoles. However, it was by persons aged 40 and older.

5.   French immersion and the revival of French in Louisiana

Though native varieties of Louisiana French seem bound for imminent extinction, there is a movement underway in the state to preserve its French-speaking heritage (Caldas 1998). One can date the beginning of this movement to the creation by the state legislature, in 1968, of the Council for the Development of French in Louisiana (CODOFIL). According to the CODOFIL's website, the organization is empowered to "do any and all things necessary to accomplish the development, utilization, and preservation of the French language *as found in Louisiana* [emphasis mine] for the cultural, economic and touristic benefit of the state" (What is CODOFIL? n.d., §1).

According to the state archivist of Louisiana, the state has never passed legislation declaring either English or French to be Louisiana's official language (F. Hardy, personal communication, January 9, 2006). However, as part of the language revival, the state has been moving on the legal front to help preserve French-speaking. In 1974, Article XII, §4 of Louisiana's revised constitution strengthened the state's hand in preserving French when it declared:

> The right of the people to preserve, foster, and promote their respective historic, linguistic and cultural origins is recognized.

Louisiana also passed legislation that states:

> When advertisements are required to be made in relation to judicial process, or in the
> sale of property for unpaid taxes, or under judicial process or any other legal process
> of whatever kind, they shall be made in the English language and may in addition be
> duplicated in the French language. State and local officials and public institutions are
> reconfirmed in the traditional right to publish documents in the French language in
> addition to English.   (from Louisiana's Revised Statutes, 43:204)

Louisiana has been making a concerted effort to preserve a tradition that prior to the
Civil War included printing documents in English and French as a matter of course.[4]
Indeed, Louisiana Governor Jacques Villeré (1816–1820) did not even speak English,
and the state's legislature was required to operate in English and French out of necessity. As noted above, in 1847 the state legislature even passed a law authorizing
bilingual instruction (Crawford 1997).

5.1 The mandate

Though the mandate of CODOFIL stipulates doing all things necessary to preserve
the French language "as found" in the state, the reality is that the organization's most
successful efforts to preserve French in Louisiana are not centered on preserving Cajun or Creole varieties of French. The most effective efforts of CODOFIL are targeted
at school French immersion programs, where school subjects are taught to children
in the French language from as early as kindergarten, and in some school districts
continue through high school. Whereas there is evidence that the children in these
programs who may spend the majority of a school day immersed in French are doing
well academically (Bankens & Akins 1989; Caldas & Boudreaux 1999; Haj-Broussard
2003), the vast majority of French immersion students are not learning the Louisiana
varieties of French spoken by their grandparents (Ancelet 1988). Rather, they are being taught in French by teachers who are mostly brought into the state from other
French-speaking countries. In fall 2003, for example, CODOFIL coordinated efforts
to bring to Louisiana 108 teachers from Belgium, 107 teachers from France, 67 from
French-speaking Canadian provinces, 28 from francophone Africa, and 6 from Haiti
(D. Côté, personal communication, April 30, 2004). By 2005, there were an estimated
3000 Louisiana students enrolled in French immersion programs in 30 schools across
the state (N. Boudreaux, personal communication, January 3, 2006).

Still, these students are generally not learning to speak local varieties of the language, but rather the modern varieties spoken by their distant cousins from around
the francophone world (French immersion, n.d.). Moreover, although the explicit and
implicit goal of the Louisiana school French immersion programs is to perpetuate the

---

4. The government of Québec, Canada, has taken much interest in the fate of French in Louisiana
in general, and in its written French record in particular, as evidenced in Hardy, F., Turner, B., and
Clifton, D. "La Louisiane", in *Les Archives des Francophones Nord-Américaines II, Québec Archives, Vol.
36, No. 2, pp. 23–37.*

speaking of French outside of the classroom environment (Boudreaux 1998), based on my long-term first hand observations of French immersion students in Lafayette, these students' French conversations do not appear to extend beyond their French immersion classrooms (Caldas 2006). My daughters were enrolled in Louisiana French immersion programs for six years of their K-12 schooling experience. I credit their programs with giving them the solid foundation upon which they have continued to build a substantial degree of literacy in the language. However, I never observed even one conversation in French, however brief, between my daughters and their French immersion peers, who were all able to speak French, but did not do so outside of class (Caldas 2006). During this same time frame, however, my daughters spoke French to each other, but only outside the context of their Louisiana friendship networks, which were constituted almost entirely by children in their French-immersion program.

5.2 American peer pressure

An interesting phenomenon I noted and documented in the French immersion program in the school district of Lafayette involved student social identity in the program, and how this identity affected language choice. First of all, the French immersion students formed a tight-knit identifiable sub-group, like Eckert's (1989) "jocks" and "burnouts", or Foley's (1990) "socially prominent", that they and others sometimes labeled "the Frenchies". However, the primary identifiable characteristics of the Frenchies was not that they spoke French, but that they (at the time of my observations in the late 1990s) came from middle and upper-middle class White families, and in general accepted the hegemony of the school. A disproportionately large number of the Frenchies were identified as "academically gifted". There seemed to be a normative structure among the Frenchies that did not legitimate speaking French outside of the classroom. In fact, it seemed that even *within* these ostensibly French-only classrooms that students preferred to speak English among themselves when not closely monitored by their francophone teachers (Caldas 2006).

5.3 Non-native accents

Let me make it clear that there is much research to support the efficacy of foreign language immersion as perhaps the best pedagogical tool for teaching students to speak another language (Genesee 1987; Harley, Allen, Cummins, & Swain 1990; Lambert & Tucker 1972). However, as effective as school foreign language immersion is as a teaching strategy, there seemed to be yet another unintended consequence of the program I observed, at least for my own children and other children in bilingual families with whom I communicated. I noted that while my daughters were in the program, they tended to pick up their French immersion peers' American accents when speaking French, in addition to their classmates' Anglicisms. Another francophone couple who are second language experts, and who also spoke French at home to their children, noticed that two of their children who were in the same program were also picking up an American accent when they spoke French, and were also using Anglicisms that they picked up from their immersion classmates. These included saying things like *jaune voiture* ('yellow car') instead of *voiture jaune*, and *il a donné à moi,* ('he gave to me') instead of *il m'a donné*, and *je cherche pour le livre* ('I'm looking for the book'), instead of *je cherche le livre* (D. Cheramie, personal communication, July 11, 2003). This couple also had an older son who did not attend a French immersion program, and who did not pick up an American accent, nor speak French using English grammatical structures.

In an interesting twist to how French immersion classmates potentially influence how their peers learn to pronounce in French, in the rural parish of St. Martin, which appears to be one of the last bastions of native French speaking in the U.S., it seems that most students speak English with a more pronounced Cajun accent. A fellow researcher who enrolled one of her two sons in this Cajun parish's French immersion program noted that her son learned to speak French not with her French (from Grenoble) accent, but with a Cajun accent. She did not attribute his Cajun accent to the classroom French spoken by her son's peers, but rather to their Cajun English accents! Her other son learned to speak French with an accent similar to the region in France to which he returned often for vacations (personal communication, N. Boudreaux, September 21, 2004).

I do not think that my observations are an indictment of the Louisiana French immersion programs I observed as much as they are telling of how children in these programs are learning to speak French. Since our son only spent one semester in a French immersion classroom when he was in the fourth grade, we were able to compare his developing French with that of his sisters. Interestingly, like the son of the couple mentioned above, our son seemed to develop accentless fluency (or French with a *Québécois* accent) quicker than his sisters who spent six years sitting next to Anglophones learning French. In short, Louisiana's French immersion programs are creating French/English bilingual-biliterate children. However these programs do not seem to be perpetuating a society of individuals who speak French outside of an academic setting. Nor are these programs preserving native varieties of traditional Louisiana French, except perhaps in those rare instances where the French immersion teacher speaks the native variety in his or her classroom.

5.4 French immersion and academic achievement

Louisiana's immersion programs seem to be having more success boosting student academics than they are in perpetuating spontaneous French speaking outside of the classroom. In Caldas and Boudreaux (1999), we discovered that students in the state's French immersion programs were doing significantly better on the math and English language arts components of Louisiana's high stakes (LEAP) test (which are administered only in English) than students enrolled in English-only instruction. Indeed, using multiple regression statistical modeling, we found that immersion students in poverty, and African American students, were doing disproportionately well on the LEAP test

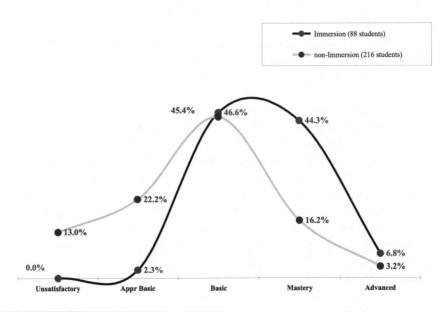

LEAP 2005 4th grade Language Arts
Immersion/Non Immersion (2 schools)

Figure 1. LEAP 2005 4th grade language arts (immersion vs. non-immersion)

compared to non-immersion African American students and low socioeconomic status students. In more recent research on the academic effects of the French immersion program in the southwestern part of the state, Haj-Broussard (2003) also found that her sample of French immersion students performed significantly better on both the math and English language arts components of the LEAP test than did regular education students. Though African Americans traditionally perform significantly less well on the LEAP test than Whites, Haj-Broussard found that African American immersion students in her sample performed as well as White regular education students on the mathematics component of the LEAP.

On the most recent 2005 LEAP test results available from the two elementary schools in Lafayette with the largest number of immersion students, the 88 immersion fourth graders performed much better than their 171 non-immersion peers. As is graphically represented in Figure 1, whereas fully 95.7% of the fourth grade immersion students scored at the passing level of basic or above on the LEAP test, only 64.8% of their non-immersion counterparts passed this high stakes test.

In five Acadiana parishes which house school French immersion programs, immersion students on average also scored significantly better than non-immersion students on the third grade norm-referenced Iowa Test of Basic Skills (ITBS – administered only in English). Figure 2 graphically represents the composite percentile scores for the 2002 ITBS.

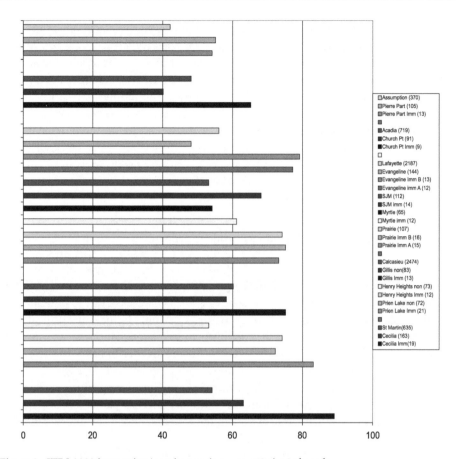

Figure 2. ITBS 2002 immersion/non immersion – composite 3rd grade

Shown are the average composite percentile rankings of immersion classrooms and the entire school housing a French immersion program in each of the Acadiana parishes with the program. Also shown is the parish average percentile ranking. Numbers of students included in each average are listed in parentheses in the legend, along with the name of each immersion school and the name of each parish. ImmA and ImmB designations indicate more than one immersion class in the same school. Since the average scores for each immersion school also include the immersion students, school figures would be even lower if the immersion students were not included. Thus, the spread in scores between the immersion and non-immersion students is even greater than depicted.

A total of 11 of the 12 immersion classrooms in the ten schools had higher average composite percentile rankings on the 2002 ITBS than either the schools in which they were housed or the parish average. Only one immersion classroom in one school (ImmA at Prairie Elementary in Lafayette) did not have a higher composite average than the overall school average (73 v. 74). However, had the immersion students been removed from the school average, it is possible that even this classroom would have had a higher average ranking than the school (73rd percentile).

When results on each component of the 2002 ITBS are analyzed individually, 9 of the 12 immersion classrooms have higher average percentile rankings in every ITBS subtest than the schools in which they are housed. On the Reading subtest, every immersion classroom outscored their schools. On the Math subtest, every immersion classroom but one outscored its school, with one classroom (the aforementioned Prairie Elementary classroom in Lafayette) having the same average percentile ranking as its school. On the Science subtest, two classrooms had lower scores than their schools, and on the Sources of Information subtest, three classrooms of the 12 had lower rankings than their schools.

5.5 Reasons for immersion students' academic success

So, we see that French immersion students in Acadiana are doing markedly better on a national norm-referenced test administered in English than their classmates who have been exposed to more English language instruction. What factors can account for their enhanced academic performance? One possible explanatory factor is that students self-select into these programs, and they are likely to have more concerned and involved parents than regular education students (N. Boudreaux, personnal communication, January 3, 2006). As noted earlier, the immersion program in Lafayette did seem to include a disproportionate number of high SES, high-achieving students when my daughters were enrolled. Apart from SES and more engaged parents, however, there may be other factors that also help explain the academic success of students in south Louisiana's French immersion program.

Haj-Broussard's (2003) qualitative research revealed that her sample of French immersion students had a more positive view of the school, enjoyed higher self-esteem, and were more collaborative (especially the African American girls). She discovered that the French immersion teachers in her study were less rigid than the regular education teachers, challenged their students more, and encouraged more autonomy than did the non-immersion teachers. Her findings were corroborated by Nicole Boudreaux, the President of the Louisiana Consortium of Immersion Schools and French Immersion, who is also the Coordinator and Lead Teacher of French Immersion in Lafayette Parish, with many years of experience as an immersion teacher. Ms. Boudreaux attributes the differing student attitudes of immersion students with fostering greater academic achievement. She cites four factors that account for the differing orientation of immersion students towards school and academics (from interview with N. Boudreaux on January 3, 2006):

1. The greater involvement of immersion parents in their children's lives.
2. The differing teaching formation of foreign French teachers which encourages more independent thinking and creativity in their students.

3. The academic environment of immersion classrooms, which often have no texts and require that immersion teachers create their own materials, and reflect more deeply on their instructional practices.
4. Differing classroom chemistry in immersion classrooms: Students must depend more on each other in order to succeed academically in another language that their parents and other adults usually do not speak.

In short, in Louisiana's French immersion programs we see students becoming not only bilingual-biliterates, but perhaps more well-rounded and open than non-immersion students. However, in general we do not see Cajun or Creole French varieties being passed onto the state's youth, and we do not see students speaking significant amounts of French outside the classroom. In the case of those students who already speak French, we may also see the French immersion classroom experience morphing student accents and grammar to conform to non-native/non-standard American peer-speak.

6.   Concluding thoughts about Louisiana French

Unfortunately, the Cajun and Creole languages of south Louisiana, as living, dynamic tongues, are not likely to survive another fifty years, if that long. It is not easy for me to make this prognostication. Every time I read the obituary section in the local newspaper, and see that an eighty year old with a name like Hypolite Boudreaux or Marie LeBlanc has died, I sadly revise downward the number of living native Louisiana French speakers. Perhaps other Louisiana academics or Francophiles might chide me for my lack of faith in the ability of the state and its people to save our unique languages. I would point out that unfortunately, the changing state demographics do not give us much cause to hope that our traditional languages will survive.

At present the best way that the state has for ensuring that French continues to be spoken is through its French immersion school programs. As noted earlier, these programs not only produce bilingual-biliterates, but also higher than average performing students who may also be more intellectually curious and well-rounded than their non-immersion peers. However, I have not seen any evidence to suggest that they are going to reproduce a society that uses French in its everyday transactions in the way that Spanish is used in San Diego or Acadian French is spoken in Caraquet, New Brunswick. Moreover, most of the children in these programs are learning the varieties of French currently spoken in *Québec*, Belgium, Sub-Saharan Africa or France, not the Cajun or Creole French of many of their ancestors. That Louisiana French is not being taught in the state's French immersion school programs has been a point of contention since the language revival first blossomed in the late 1960s (Ancelet 1988). It does not seem likely that Louisiana French will replace the continental variety used in immersion classrooms anytime soon, and even if Cajun French were to become the medium of instruction, it appears unlikely that such a move would perpetuate Cajun French speaking outside of the classroom anyway.

6.1 Directions for future research

The fact that Louisiana does have a vigorous foreign language school immersion program can be a boon for ongoing research on the effects of such programs on student outcomes. Research already conducted in Louisiana and elsewhere has demonstrated that students in these programs tend to perform well academically. However, apart from Haj-Broussard (2003) and Caldas and Boudreaux (1999), what has been studied in much less depth is the extent to which SES and race/ethnicity (or their interaction) account for the enhanced academic performance of foreign language immersion students. Or, looked at differently, what is the unique effect of foreign language immersion programs on academic achievement, controlling for important extraneous factors?

Using large-scale databases of individual student data (Louisiana has 3000 immersion students) and Ordinary Least Squares Regression, or better yet, Hierarchical Linear Modeling, could help give us quantitative answers to this critical question. More qualitative research (like Haj-Broussard's), including classroom observations and longitudinal ethnographic studies, could provide more clarification into the teacher, classroom and peer dynamics of immersion programs. Are teachers and students in these programs truly more independent and creative? Do immersion students truly work together more collaboratively than their non-immersion peers? To what extent are immersion students speaking the target language outside of the classroom setting? Do immersion students who share a heritage with the target language (e.g., Cajuns and Creoles in Louisiana) perform better than immersion students who do not? These are all important questions which future research will hopefully address.

6.2 Lessons learned

Fortunately, there are historians like Carl Brasseaux and Mathé Allain, folklorists like Barry Ancelet, and sociologists like Jacques Henry, all of the University of Louisiana at Lafayette, who have devoted their lives to documenting Louisiana's rich French speaking heritage for future generations to read and marvel at. Though the number of native Louisiana French speakers declines with each passing day, the slow demise of so rich a linguistic heritage need not simply render us saddened and nostalgic. There are a few lessons for us to learn. The first is to recognize both the power and the limitation of schools to squelch and preserve minority languages. We can date the demise of French in Louisiana to the 1921 constitutional prohibition against teaching in any language other than English. Of course, it takes more than just legal fiat to change the lifestyle of an entire people. Teachers and principals, products of the same xenophobic social environment that allowed so heinous a law to be passed in the first place, not only zealously enforced this statute, but also actively persecuted young children who dared utter a French word on campus. One can only imagine the uproar and litigation that would result today from physically punishing a young Latino child on an American schoolyard for daring to speak a Spanish word during recess.

One positive outcome of 'political correctness' – if I can use this expression as a neutral term to describe an intellectual movement of the last two to three decades – has been to sensitize Americans to differing cultural and linguistic points of view. It is simply unfortunate that this sensitivity to the value of cultural and linguistic unique- ness was almost entirely absent in Louisiana during most of the twentieth century. Rather than being recognized as torchbearers of a unique linguistic tradition on the North American continent, native French speakers in Louisiana were, quite frankly, belittled and humiliated for their distinctiveness. May we be receptive to the very ex- pensive lessons we have learned from the Louisiana experience. Everyone's language and culture are (or at least, it seems to me, should be) precious to them, as these social attributes define, in large part, who we are. Therefore, given the almost inseparably close bonds between language and culture, no individual, group, or government can morally defend any efforts that belittle or demean these dimensions of an individual's or group's identity. French-speaking in Louisiana survived more than three centuries filled with wars, disease, the massive influx of non-French-speaking settlers, and the continual battering by hurricanes. However, in spite of valiant stubbornness, French- speaking in the Bayou State does not appear likely to survive the governmental and social pressures originally determined to extinguish it.

Appendix

Table 1. Sample of English, Cajun/Creole French, and Standard French terms and expressions

English	Cajun/Creole French	Standard French
coat	*capot* (n, m)	*manteau* (n, m)
glass (drinking)	*pinte* (n, f)	*verre* (n, m)
I'm leaving.	*j'su gone* (Expression in rural St. Martin Parish in Creole and Cajun.)	*je m'en vais*
it's going well	*ça se plume* (Cajun and Creole)	*ça va bien*
shrimp	*chevrette* (n, f)	*crevette* (n, f)
slowly	*doucement* (adv.)	*lentement* (adv.)
wheelbarrow	*birouette* (n, f)	*brouette* (n, f)
you're welcome	*pas de quoi*	*de rien*

References

Achiba, M. (2003). *Learning to Request in a Second Language: Child interlanguage pragmatics.* Clevedon: Multilingual Matters.

Adamson, H. D. & Regan, V. (1991). The acquisition of community speech norms by Asian immigrants learning English as a second language. *Studies in Second Language Acquisition, 13,* 1–22.

Ädel, A. (2005). Involvement and detachment in writing: The effects of task setting and intertextuality. Paper presented at the AAACL6/ICAME 26, Ann Arbor, MI.

Adesanoye, F. A. (2004). The English language in Nigeria: The case of a vanishing model? In K. Owolabi & A. Dasylva (Eds.), *Forms and Functions of English and Indigenous Languages in Nigeria: A festschrift in honor of Ayo Banjo* (pp. 239–257). Ibadan: Group Publishers.

Adone, D. (1994). *The Acquisition of Mauritian Creole.* Amsterdam: John Benjamins.

Ager, D. (1990). *The Sociolinguistics of Contemporary French.* Cambridge: CUP.

Ager, D. (1999). *Identity, Insecurity and Image. France and language.* Clevedon: Multilingual Matters.

Ahmed, S. M. (1990). Psychometric properties of the boredom proneness scale. *Perceptual and Motor Skills, 71,* 963–966.

Aijmer, K. (2002). Modality in advanced Swedish learners' written interlanguage. In S. Granger, J. Hung, & S. Petch-Tyson (Eds.), *Computer Learner Corpora, Second Language Acquisition and Foreign Language Learning* (pp. 55–76). Amsterdam: John Benjamins.

Ajzen, I. & Fishbein, M. (1980). *Understanding Attitudes and Predicting Social Behavior.* Englewood-Cliffs, NJ: Prentice Hall.

Akinyemi, A. (2005). Integrating culture and second language teaching through Yoruba personal names. *The Modern Language Journal, 89,* 115–126.

A language barrier. (2005). *The Daily Advertiser,* September 28, 2A.

Alario, F.-X. & Caramazza, A. (2002). The production of determiners: Evidence from French. *Cognition, 82*(3), 179–223.

Alcón Soler, E. (2005). Does instruction work for learning pragmatics in the EFL context? *System, 33*(3), 417–435.

Alcón Soler, E. & Martínez Flor, A. (Eds.). (2005). Pragmatics in instructed language learning. Special issue, *System, 33*(3).

Alegria, J. (1999). La lecture chez l'enfant sourd: Conditions d'acquisition. *Language et Pratiques, 23,* 27–46.

Allen, P., Swain, M., Harley, B., & Cummins, J. (1990). Aspects of classroom treatment: Toward a more comprehensive view of second language education. In B. Harley, P. Allen, J. Cummins, & M. Swain (Eds.), *The Development of Second Language Proficiency* (pp. 57–81). Cambridge: CUP.

Alleyne, M. (1986). Substratum influences – Guilty until proven innocent. In P. Muysken & N. Smith (Eds.), *Substrata versus Universals in Creole Genesis* (pp. 301–315). Amsterdam: John Benjamins.

Alleyne, M. (1996). *Syntaxe historique créole.* Paris: Editions Karthala.

Allport, G. W. & Odbert, H. S. (1936). Trait names: A psycho-lexical study. *Psychological Monographs, 47,* No. 211.

Ancelet, B. J. (2004a). La place du français local dans l'enseignement de la langue. *Entre Nous (Bulletin pédagogique du Centre provincial de ressources pédagogiques de la Nouvelle-Ecosse), 100,* 14–16.

Ancelet, B. J. (2004b). Valoriser la variabilité pour préserver une identité linguistique. *Entre Nous* (*Bulletin pédagogique du Centre provincial de ressources pédagogiques de la Nouvelle-Ecosse*), 99, 8–12.

Ancelet, B. J. (2005). Recherche sur la langue acadienne: Le cas de la Nouvelle-Écosse. *Entre Nous* (*Bulletin pédagogique du Centre provincial de ressources pédagogiques de la Nouvelle-Ecosse*), 101, 10–13.

Ancelet, B. (1996). Zydeco/Zarico: The term and the tradition. In J. Dormon (Ed.), *The Creoles of the Gulf Coast* (pp. 126–143). Knoxville, TN: University of Tennessee Press.

Ancelet, B. (1988). A perspective on teaching the 'Problem Language' in Louisiana. *The French Review, 61*(3), 345–356.

Andersen, R. W. (1990). Models, processes, principles and strategies: Second language acquisition inside and outside the classroom. In B. Van Patten & J. F. Lee (Eds.), *Second Language Acquisition and Foreign Language Learning* (pp. 45–68). Clevedon: Multilingual Matters.

Anderson, B. (2001). Adjective position and interpretation in L2 French. In J. Camps & C. R. Wiltshire (Eds.), *Romance Syntax, Semantics, and L2 Acquisition* (pp. 27–41). Amsterdam: John Benjamins.

Anderson, B. (2002). The fundamental equivalence of native and interlanguage grammars: Evidence from argument licensing and adjective position in L2 French. PhD dissertation, Indiana University, Bloomington.

Anderson, B. (in press a). Learnability and parametric change in the nominal system of L2 French. *Language Acquisition.*

Anderson, B. (in press b). Pedagogical rules and their relationship to frequency in the input: Observational and empirical data from the L2 French classroom. *Applied Linguistics.*

Anderson, B. R. (1991). *Imagined Communities: Reflections on the Origin and Spread of Nationalism* (revised edition). London: Verso.

Anderson, S. R. (1982). The analysis of French schwa: Or, how to get something for nothing. *Language, 58,* 534–573.

Anderson, D. & Reilly, J. (2002). The MacArthur communicative development inventory: Normative data for American Sign Language. *Journal of Deaf Studies and Deaf Education, 7*(2), 83–106.

Andriamamonjy, P. (2000). Le rôle du genre grammatical au cours de la reconnaissance de noms. *L'Année psychologique, 100,* 419–442.

Antes, T. (1993). The effect of enhanced input on the acquisition of phonological gender markers in first year French. PhD dissertation, Cornell University.

Anthony, M. E. (2002). The role of American Sign Language and conceptual wholes in facilitating language, cognition, and literacy. PhD dissertation, University of California, Berkeley.

Antón, M. (1999). The discourse of a learner-centered classroom: Sociocultural perspectives on teacher-learner interaction in the second-language classroom. *The Modern Language Journal, 83,* 303–318.

Antón-Méndez, I. (1999). Gender and number processing in Spanish. PhD dissertation, University of Arizona, Tucson.

Antón-Méndez, I., Nicol, J., & Garrett, M. (2002). The relation between gender and number agreement processing. *Syntax, 5,* 1–25.

Appadurai, A. (1996). *Modernity at Large: Cultural dimensions of globalization, public worlds,* Vol. 1. Minneapolis, MN: University of Minnesota Press.

Apple, M. W. (2000). *Official Knowledge: Democratic education in a conservative age* (2nd ed.). London: Routledge.

Apple, M. W., Kenway, J., & Singh, M. (Eds.). (2005). *Globalizing Education: Policies, pedagogies, and politics.* Bern: Peter Lang.

Arceneaux, J. (1980). Schizophrénie linguistique. In B. J. Ancelet (Ed.), *Crise sur le bayou* (pp. 16–17). Montréal: Les Editions Intermède.

Archibald, J. (1998). The acquisition of second language phrasal stress: A pilot study. In S. J. Hannahs & M. Young-Scholten (Eds.), *Focus on Phonological Acquisition* (pp. 263–289). Amsterdam: John Benjamins.

Arends, J. (1986). Genesis and development of the equative copula in Sranan. In P. Muysken & N. Smith (Eds.), *Substrata versus Universals in Creole Genesis* (pp. 103–127). Amsterdam: John Benjamins.

Arends, J. (1989). Syntactic developments in Sranan: Creolization as a gradual process. PhD dissertation, University of Nijmegen.

Arends, J. (1993). Towards a gradualist model of creolization. In F. Byrne & J. Holm (Eds.), *Atlantic Meets Pacific: A global view of pidginization and creolization* (pp. 371–380). Amsterdam: John Benjamins.

Arends, J. (1995). Demographic factors in the formation of Sranan. In J. Arends (Ed.), *The Early Stages of Creolization* (pp. 233–277). Amsterdam: John Benjamins.

Arnauld, A. & Lancelot, C. (1660). *Grammaire de Port-Royal*. Paris: Le Petit.

Arnaud, P. J. L. & Sauvignon, S. J. (1997). Rare words, complex lexical units and the advanced learner. In J. Coady & T. Huckin (Eds.), *Second Language Vocabulary Acquisition: A rationale for pedagogy* (pp. 157–173). Cambridge: CUP.

Aron, R. (1955). *L'opium des intellectuels, liberté de l'esprit*. Paris: Calmann-Lévy.

Aronoff, M. (1976). *Word Formation in Generative Grammar*. Cambridge, MA: The MIT Press.

Associated Press. (2005). Immigrants fill N.O. cleanup jobs. *Daily Advertiser*, October 8, 3-A.

Aston, G., Bernardini, S., & Stewart, D. (2004). *Corpora and Language Learners*. Amsterdam: John Benjamins.

Audollent, C. & Tuller, L. (2003). La dysphasie: Quelles séquelles en français? *ANAE, 74–75*, 264–270.

Auger, J. (2003). Linguistic norm vs. functional competence: Introducing Québec French to American Students. In C. Blyth (Ed.), *The Sociolinguistics of Foreign-Language Classrooms: Contributions of the native, the near-native, and the non-native speaker* (pp. 79–104). Boston, MA: Heinle.

Auger, J. & Valdman, A. (1999). Letting French students hear the diverse voices of francophony. *The Modern Language Journal, 83*, 403–412.

Auroux, S. (1994). *La révolution technologique de la grammatisation: Introduction à l'histoire des sciences du langage*. Liège: Mardaga.

Austin, J. L. (1976 [1962]). *How To Do Things With Words. The William James Lectures Delivered at Harvard University in 1955*. J. O. Urmson & M. Sbisà (Eds.) (2nd ed.). New York, NY: OUP.

Authier, J.-M. (19920. Is French a null subject language in the DP? *Probus, 4*, 1–16.

Ayoun, D. (1999). Verb movement in French L2 acquisition. *Bilingualism, 2*, 103–125.

Ayoun, D. (2000). Computer-based and web-based elicitation tasks in second language acquisition. *Language Learning and Technology, 3*, 78–98.

Ayoun, D. (2001). The role of negative and positive feedback in the second language acquisition of *passé composé* and *imparfait*. *The Modern Language Journal, 85*, 226–243.

Ayoun, D. (2003). *Parameter Setting in Language Acquisition*. Cambridge: Continuum.

Ayoun, D. (2004). The effectiveness of written recasts in the second language acquisition of aspectual distinctions in French: A follow-up study. *The Modern Language Journal, 88*, 31–55.

Ayoun, D. (2005a). Verb movement in the L2 acquisition of English by adult native speakers of French. In S. Foster-Cohen, P. Garcia Mayo, & J. Cenoz (Eds.), *EUROSLA Yearbook 5* (pp. 35–76). Amsterdam: John Benjamins.

Ayoun, D. (2005b). The development of future expression in L2 French. Talk given at the Second Language Research Forum, Columbia University, New York, October 8–10.

Ayoun, D. (2005c). Tense and aspect in L2 French from a universal grammar perspective. In D. Ayoun & R. Salaberry (Eds.), *Tense and Aspect in Romance Languages: Theoretical and applied perspectives* (pp. 79–127). Amsterdam: John Benjamins.

Ayoun, D. & Salaberry, R. (Eds.). (2005). *Tense and Aspect in Romance Languages: Theoretical and applied perspectives*. Amsterdam: John Benjamins.

Ayres-Bennett, W. (1990). Variation and change in the pronunciation of French in the seventeenth century. In J. N. Green & W. Ayres-Bennett (Eds.), *Variation and Change in French* (pp. 151–179). London: Routledge.

Ayres-Bennett, W. (1996). *A History of the French Language Through Texts*. London: Routledge.

Ayres-Bennett, W. (2004). *Sociolinguistic Variation in Seventeenth-Century France. Methodology and case-studies*. Cambridge: CUP.

Baayen, R. H. & Renouf, A. (1991). Productivity and English derivation: A corpus-based study. *Linguistics, 29*, 801–843.

Babin, J.-P. (2000). *Lexique mental et morphologie lexicale.* Bern: Peter Lang.

Bachman, L. F. (1990). *Fundamental Considerations in Language Testing.* Oxford: OUP.

Bachman, L. F. & Palmer, A. S. (1996). *Language Testing in Practice. Designing and developing useful language tests.* Oxford: OUP.

Bahns, J., Burmeister, H., & Vogel, T. (1986). The pragmatics of formulas in L2 learner speech: Use and development. *Journal of Pragmatics, 10*(6), 693–723.

Bailey, K. M. (1983). Competitiveness and anxiety in adult second language learning: Looking *at* and *through* the diary studies. In H. W. Seliger & M. H. Long (Eds.), *Classroom-Oriented Research in Second Language Acquisition* (pp. 67–103). Rowley, MA: Newbury House.

Baker, A., van den Bogaerde, B., & Crasborn, O. (2003). *Cross-linguistic Perspectives in Sign Language Research. Selected papers from TISLR 2000.* Hamburg: Signum.

Baker, S. C. & MacIntyre, P. D. (2000). The role of gender and immersion in communication and second language orientations. *Language Learning, 50*, 311–341.

Baker, P. (1990). Off Target? (Column). *Journal of Pidgin and Creole Languages, 5*, 107–119.

Baker, P. (1993). Assessing the African contribution to French-based creoles. In S. Mufwene (Ed.), *Africanisms in Afro-American Language Varieties* (pp. 123–155). Athens, GA: University of Georgia Press.

Baker, P. & Corne, C. (1986). Universals, substrata and the Indian Ocean creoles. In P. Muysken & N. Smith (Eds.), *Substrata versus Universals in Creole Genesis* (pp. 163–183). Amsterdam: John Benjamins.

Ball, R. (1997). *The French Speaking World: A practical introduction to sociolinguistic issues.* London: Routledge.

Bamgbose, A., Banjo, A., & Thomas, A. (Eds.). (1997). *New Englishes: A West African perspective.* Trenton, NJ: African World.

Banda, F. (2003). A survey of literary practices in Black and Colored communities in South Africa: Towards a pedagogy of multiliteracies. *Language, Culture and Curriculum, 16*, 106–129.

Bankens, B. & Akins, D. (1989). *French Immersion Comparative Data Stanford 7-Plus Achievement Test at Prien Elementary School* (Research report No. 90-017-422-04). Calcasieu Parish School Board, Lake Charles, LA.

Bankston, C. L. & Caldas, S. J. (2002). *A Troubled Dream: The promise and failure of School Desegregation in Louisiana.* Nashville, TN: Vanderbilt University Press.

Banniard, M. (1992). *Viva Voce.* Paris: Institut des études augustiniennes.

Bardovi-Harlig, K. (1992). The telling of a tale: Discourse structure and tense use in learners' narratives. In L. F. Bouton & Y. Kachru (Eds.), *Pragmatics and Language Learning* [Monograph series Vol. 3] (pp. 144–161). Urbana-Champaign, IL: University of Illinois at Urbana-Champaign, Division of English as an International Language.

Bardovi-Harlig, K. (1999a). Researching method. In L. F. Bouton (Ed.), *Pragmatics and Language Learning* [Monograph series Vol. 9] (pp. 237–264). Urbana-Champaign, IL: University of Illinois at Urbana-Champaign, Division of English as an International Language.

Bardovi-Harlig, K. (1999b). Exploring the interlanguage of interlanguage pragmatics: A research agenda for acquisitional pragmatics. *Language Learning, 49*(4), 677–713.

Bardovi-Harlig, K. (2001). Evaluating the empirical evidence. Grounds for instruction in pragmatics? In K. R. Rose & G. Kasper (Eds.), *Pragmatics in Language Teaching* (pp. 13–32). Cambridge: CUP.

Bardovi-Harlig, K. & Hartford, B. S. (1993). Learning the rules of academic talk: A longitudinal study of pragmatic change. *Studies in Second Language Acquisition, 15*, 279–304.

Bardovi-Harlig, K., Hartford, B. S., Mahan-Taylor, R., Morgan, M. J., & Reynolds, D. W. (1991). Developing pragmatic awareness: Closing the conversation. *ELT Journal, 45*(1), 4–15.

Bardovi-Harlig, K. & Dörnyei, Z. (1998). Do language learners recognize pragmatic violations? Pragmatic versus grammatical awareness in instructed L2 learning. *TESOL Quarterly, 32*(2), 233–259.

Barlow, M. (1996). Corpora for theory and practice. *International Journal of Corpus Linguistics, 1*, 1–37.

Barlow, M. (2005). Computer-based analyses of learner language. In R. Ellis & G. Barkhuizen (Eds.), *Analyzing Learner Language* (pp. 335–357). Oxford: OUP.

Barnes, B. (1990). Apports de l'analyse du discours à l'enseignement de la langue. *The French Review, 64*(1), 95–107.

Baroni, M. (2003). Distribution-driven morpheme discovery: A computational-experimental study. In G. Booij & J. van Marle (Eds.), *Yearbook of Morphology 2003* (pp. 213–248). Dordrecht: Kluwer.

Barr, D. (2004). *ICT – Integrating Computers in Teaching*. Bern: Peter Lang.

Barron, A. (2002). Interlanguage pragmatics/cross-cultural pragmatic references – A selection. English Department, University of Bonn. Retrieved [9.8.2005] from http://www.uni-bonn.de/www/Barron/intercultural_pragmatic _bibliography.html

Barron, A. (2003). *Acquisition in Interlanguage Pragmatics. Learning how to do things with words in a study abroad context*. Amsterdam: John Benjamins.

Bartning, I. (1997). L'apprenant dit avancé et son acquisition d'une langue étrangère. Tour d'horizon et esquisse d'une caractérisation de la variété avancée. *Acquisition et Interaction en Langue Etrangère, 9*, 9–50.

Bartning, I. (1999). L'attribution et l'accord du genre des déterminants et des adjectifs en français parlé – apprenants avancé vs apprenants préavancés. Paper presented at the EuroSLA 9 Conference, Lund, June 10–12, 1999.

Bartning, I. (2000). Gender agreement in L2 French: Pre-advanced vs advanced learners. *Studia Linguistica, 54*, 225–237.

Basbøll, H. (1978). Schwa, jonctures et syllabification dans les représentations phonologiques du français. *Acta Linguistica Hafniensa, 16*, 147–182.

Basbøll, H. (1988). Sur l'identité phonologique du schwa français et son rôle dans l'accentuation et dans la syllabation. In S. Paul Verluyten (Ed.), *La phonologie du schwa français* (pp. 15–41). Amsterdam: John Benjamins.

Battye, A. & Roberts, I. (1995). Introduction. In A. Battye & I. Roberts (Eds.), *Clause Structure and Language Change* (pp. 3–28). New York, NY: OUP.

Bauer, L. (2001). *Morphological Productivity*. Cambridge: CUP.

Bauer, L. & Nation, I. S. P. (1993). Word families. *International Journal of Lexicography, 6*, 253–279.

Bauer, L. & Trudgill, P. (1998). *Language Myths*. London: Penguin.

Bauman, R. (1986). *Story, Performance and Event: Contextual studies of oral narrative*. Cambridge: CUP.

Bauman, R. & Briggs, C. (2003). *Voices of Modernity: Language ideologies and the politics of inequality*. Cambridge: CUP.

Bayley, R. & Preston, D. (Eds.). (1996). *Second Language Acquisition and Linguistic Variation*. Amsterdam: John Benjamins.

Bayley, R. & Regan, V. (Eds.). (2004). *The Acquisition of Sociolinguistic Competence*. Special issue, *Journal of Sociolinguistics, 8*(3).

Bayley, R. & Regan, V. (2004). Introduction: The acquisition of sociolinguistic competence. *Journal of Sociolinguistics, 8*(3), 323–338.

Béal, C. (1992). Did you have a good week-end? Or why there is no such thing as a simple question in cross-cultural encounters. *Australian Review of Applied Linguistics, 15*(1), 23–52.

Beaudoin, M. (1998). Découpage syllabique en français comme langue seconde. *Canadian Modern Language Review, 54*(3), 354–375.

Beck, M.-L. (1998). L2 acquisition and obligatory head movement: English-speaking learners of German and the local impairment hypothesis. *Studies in Second Language Acquisition, 20*, 311–348.

Beebe, L. M. (1983). Risk-taking and the language learner. In H. W. Seliger & M. H. Long (Eds.), *Classroom-Oriented Research in Second Language Acquisition* (pp. 29–66). Rowley, MA: Newbury House.

Beebe, L. M. (1988). Five sociolinguistic approaches to second language acquisition. In L. Beebe (Ed.), *Issues in Second Language Acquisition: Multiple Perspectives* (pp. 43–75). Rowley, MA: Newbury House.

Beebe, L. M. & Cummings, M. C. (1996 [1985]). Natural speech act data versus written questionnaire data: How data collection method affects speech act performance. In S. M. Gass & J. Neu (Eds.), *Speech Acts Across Cultures. Challenges to communication in a second language* (pp. 65–86). Berlin: Mouton de Gruyter.

Beeching, K. (2001). Repair strategies and social interaction in spontaneous spoken French: The pragmatic particle *enfin. Journal of French Language Studies, 11*(1), 23–40.

Bell, A. (1984). Style as audience design. *Language in Society, 13*, 145–204.

Bellugi, U., van Hoek, K., Lillo-Martin, D., & O'Grady, L. (1988). The acquisition of syntax and space in young deaf signers. In D. Bishop & K. Mogford (Eds.), *Language Development in Exceptional Children* (pp. 132–149). Edinburgh: Churchill-Linvingstone.

Belz, J. A. (2002). The myth of the deficient communicator. *Language Teaching Research, 6*(1), 59–82.

Belz, J. A. & Kinginger, C. (2002). The cross-linguistic development of address form use in telecollaborative language learning: Two case studies. *Canadian Modern Language Review, 59*(2), 189–214.

Belz, J. A. & Thorne, S. L. (Eds.). (2006). *Internet-Mediated Intercultural Foreign Language Education*. Boston, MA: Heinle.

Benati, A. (2004). The effects of processing instruction and its components on the acquisition of gender agreement in Italian. *Language Awareness, 13*, 67–80.

Benedicto, E. & Brentari, D. (2004). Where did all the arguments go? Argument-changing properties of classifiers in ASL. *Natural Language and Linguistic Theory, 22*(4), 743–810.

Bensoussan, M. & Laufer, B. (1984). Lexical guessing in context in EFL reading comprehension. *Journal of Research in Reading, 7*, 15–31.

Bentrovato, S., Devescovi, A., D'Amico, S., Wicha, N., & Bates, E. (2003). The effect of grammatical gender and semantic context on lexical access in Italian using a timed word-naming paradigm. *Journal of Psycholinguistic Research, 32*, 417–430.

Berliner, D. C. (2005). Our impoverished view of educational reform. *Teachers College Record*: http://www. tcrecord.org. [cited 3 August 2005]. ID Number: 12106.

Bernstein, B. (2000). *Pedagogy, Symbolic Control and Identity: Theory, research, critique* (revised edition). Lanham, MD: Rowman & Littlefield.

Bernstein, J. (1991). DPs in French and Walloon: Evidence for parametric variation in nominal head movement. *Probus, 3*, 101–126.

Bernstein, J. (1993). The syntactic role of word markers in null nominal constuctions. *Probus, 5*, 5–38.

Bertelson, P. & Mousty, P. (1991). La reconnaissance tactile des mots dans la lecture du Braille. In R. Kolinsky, J. Morais, & J. Segui (Eds.), *La reconnaissance des mots dans les différentes modalités sensorielles: Etudes de psycholinguistique cognitive* (pp. 307–320). Paris: Presses Universitaires de France.

Best, C. T. (1994). The emergence of native-language phonological influences in infants: A perceptual assimilation model. In J. Goodman & H. C. Nussbaum (Eds.), *The Development of Speech Perception: The transition from speech sounds to spoken words* (pp. 167–224). Cambridge, MA: The MIT Press.

Best, C. T. (1995). A direct realist view of cross-language speech perception. In W. Strange (Ed.), *Speech Perception and Linguistic Experience: Issues in cross-language research* (pp. 171–206). Baltimore, MD: York Press.

Bialystok, E. (1993). Symbolic representation and attentional control in pragmatic competence. In G. Kasper & S. Blum-Kulka (Eds.), *Interlanguage Pragmatics* (pp. 43–57). New York, NY: OUP.

Biber, D. (1988). *Variation Across Speech and Writing*. Cambridge: CUP.

Biber, D., Johansson, S., Leech, G., Conrad, S., & Finegan, E. (1999). *Longman Grammar of Spoken and Written English*. London: Longman.

Bickerton, D. (1977). Pidginization and creolization: Language acquisition and language universals. In A. Valdman (Ed.), *Pidgin and Creole Linguistics* (pp. 49–69). Bloomington, IN: Indiana University Press.

Bickerton, D. (1981). *Roots of Language*. Ann Arbor, MI: Karoma.

Bickerton, D. (1984). The language bioprogram hypothesis. *Behavioral & Brain Sciences, 7*, 173–221.

Bickerton, D. (1999). How to acquire language without positive evidence: What acquisitionists can learn from creoles. In DeGraff (Ed.), *Language Creation and Language Change: Creolization, diachrony, and development* (pp. 49–74). Cambridge, MA: The MIT Press.

Bidot, E. (1925). *La clef du genre des substantifs français (méthode dispensant d'avoir recours au dictionnaire)*. Poitiers: Imprimerie Nouvelle.

Biederman, Y. M. (2003). Literacy Learning in a Bilingual School for Deaf Students: Negotiating between New Zealand Sign Language and English. PhD dissertation, University of California, Berkeley.

Bijvoet, E. (2002). Near nativeness and stylistic lexical competence in Swedish of first and second generation Finnish immigrants to Sweden. *The International Journal of Bilingualism, 6*(1), 39–51.

Billmyer, K. & Varghese, M. (2000). Investigating instrument-based pragmatic variability: Effects of enhancing discourse completion tests. *Applied Linguistics, 21*(4), 517–552.

Birdsong, D. (1989). *Metalinguistic Performance and Interlinguistic Competence*. Berlin: Springer Verlag.

Birdsong, D. (In press). Nativelike pronunciation among late learners of French as a second language. In O.-S. Bohn & M. Munro (Eds.), *Second Language Speech Learning: The role of language experience in speech perception and production*. Amsterdam: John Benjamins.

Bishop, M. (1983). Comprehension of English syntax by profoundly deaf children. *Journal of Child Psychology and Psychiatry, 24*, 415–434.

Bishop, M. & Hicks, S. (2005). Orange eyes: Bimodal bilingualism in hearing adults from deaf families. *Sign Language Studies, 5*, 188–230.

Blake, R. J. & Zyzik, E. C. (2003). Who's helping whom: Learner/heritage-speakers' networked discussion in Spanish. *Applied Linguistics, 24*(4), 519–544.

Bley-Vroman, R. (1983). The comparative fallacy in interlanguage studies: The case of systematicity. *Language Learning, 33*, 1–17.

Bley-Vroman, R. (1990). The logical problem of foreign language learning. *Linguistic Analysis, 20*, 3–49.

Bley-Vroman, R. (2003). Corpus linguistics and second language acquisition: Rules and frequency in the acquisition of English multiple wh-questions. In P. Leistyna & C. F. Meyer (Eds.), *Language and Computers, Corpus Analysis: Language structure and language use* (pp. 255–272). Amsterdam: Rodopi.

Block, D. (1999). Who framed SLA research? Problem framing and metaphoric accounts of the SLA research process. In L. Cameron & G. Low (Eds.), *Researching and Applying Metaphor* (pp. 135–148). Cambridge: CUP.

Blommaert, J. (2005). *Discourse: A critical introduction*. Cambridge: CUP.

Blondel, M. (2000). Poésie enfantine en langues des signes: Modalité visuo-gestuelle vs modalité audio-orale. PhD dissertation, Université François–Rabelais, Tours.

Blondel, M. & Tuller, L. (2000). La recherche sur la LSF: Un compte rendu critique. *Recherches Linguistiques de Vincennes, 29*, 29–54.

Blondel, M., Lecourt, I., & Tuller, L. (2004). Les pointés et l'acquisition de la morphosyntaxe en LSF. *Silexicales, 4*, 17–32.

Blondel, M. & Tuller, L. (To appear). Pointing in bimodal, bilingual acquisition: A longitudinal study of a LSF-French bilingual child. In J. Quer (Ed.), *Leading Research in Sign Language: Selected Papers from TISLR 2004*. Seedorf: Signum Verlag.

Blum-Kulka, S. (1982). Learning to say what you mean in a second language: A study of the speech act performance of learners of Hebrew as a second language. *Applied Linguistics, 3*(1), 29–59.

Blum-Kulka, S., House, J., & Kasper, G. (1989). *Cross-Cultural Pragmatics: Requests and apologies*. Norwood, NJ: Ablex.

Blum-Kulka, S. & Olshtain, E. (1986). Too many words: Length of utterance and pragmatic failure. *Studies in Second Language Acquisition, 8*, 165–180.

Blyth, C. (1995). Redefining the boundaries of language use: The foreign language classroom as a multilingual speech community. In C. Kramsch (Ed.), *Redefining the Boundaries of Language Study* (pp. 145–183). Boston, MA: Heinle.

Bogaards, P. & Laufer, B. (Eds.). (2004). *Vocabulary in a Second Language: Selection, acquisition and testing.* Amsterdam: John Benjamins.

Bogaerde, B. van den & Baker, A. (2002). Are young deaf children bilingual? In G. Morgan & B. Woll (Eds.), *Directions in Sign Language Acquisition* (pp. 183–206). Amsterdam: John Benjamins.

Boivin, M. C. (1998). Case feature checking and its consequences. Evidence from *en*-cliticization in French. In J.-M. Authier, B. E. Bullock, & L. A. Reed (Eds.), *Formal Perspectives on Romance Linguistics. Selected papers from the 28th linguistic symposium on Romance languages* (pp. 39–56). Amsterdam: John Benjamins.

Bokamba, E. (1991). French colonial language policies in Africa and their legacies. In D. Marshall (Ed.), *Language Planning: Focusschrift in honor of Joshua A. Fishman on the occasion of his 65th Birthday*, Vol. 3 (pp. 175–215). Amsterdam: John Benjamins.

Bollée, A. (1977a). *Le créole français des Seychelles. Esquisse d'une grammaire – textes – vocabulaire.* Tübingen: Niemeyer.

Bollée, A. (1977b). *Zur Entstehung der französischen Kreolendialekte im Indischen Ozean. Kreolisierung ohne Pidginisierung* [Kölner Romanistische Arbeiten. Neue Folge, Heft 51]. Geneva: Librairie Droz.

Bollée, A. (1977c). Remarques sur la genèse des parlers créoles de l'Océan Indien. In J. Meisel (Ed.), *Langues en contact – Pidgins – Creoles – Languages in Contact* (pp. 137–149). Tübingen: Narr.

Bolton, W. (1982). *A Living Language: The history and structure of English.* New York, NY: Random House.

Bonfiglio, T. P. (2002). *Race and the Rise of Standard American.* Berlin: Mouton de Gruyter.

Bonvillian, J. D. & Folven, R. J. (1993). Sign language acquisition: Developmental aspects. In M. Marschark & M. D. Clark (Eds.), *Psychological Perspectives on Deafness* (pp. 229–265). Hillsdale, NJ: Lawrence Erlbaum.

Borer, H. (1984). *Parametric Syntax.* Dordrecht: Foris.

Borin, L. & Prütz, K. (2004). New wine in old skins? A corpus investigation of L1 syntactic transfer in learner language. In G. Aston, S. Bernardini, & D. Stewart (Eds.), *Corpora and Language Learners* (pp. 67–87). Amsterdam: John Benjamins.

Bork, H. D. (1975). 'Néo-français' = français avancé? Zur Sprache Raymond Queneaus. *Romanische Forschungen, 87,* 32–35.

Borkin, A. & Reinhart, S. M. (1978). Excuse me and I'm sorry. *TESOL Quarterly, 12*(1), 57–69.

Bosque, I. & Picallo, C. (1996). Postnominal adjectives in Spanish DPs. *Journal of Linguistics, 32,* 349–385.

Boudreau, A. (1996). Les mots des jeunes Acadiens et Acadiennes du Nouveau-Brunswick. In L. Dubois & A. Boudreau (Eds.), *Les Acadiens et leur(s) Langue(s)* (pp. 137–150). Moncton N-B: Les Éditions d'Acadie.

Boudreaux, N. (1998). A Formative Evaluation of the French Immersion Program in the Cecilia Schools of Saint Martin Parish. MA thesis, University of Louisiana at Lafayette.

Bouhours, D. (1675). *Remarques nouvelles sur la langue françoise.* Paris: Mabre-Cramoisy.

Bourdieu, P. (1982). *Ce que parler veut dire: L'économie des échanges linguistiques.* Paris: Fayard.

Bourdieu, P. & Passeron, J.-C. (1970). *La reproduction: Eléments pour une théorie du système d'enseignement.* Paris: Editions de Minuit.

Bourhis, R. Y. & Sachdev, I. (1984). Vitality perceptions and language attitudes: Some Canadian data. *Journal of Language & Social Psychology, 3,* 97–126.

Bourhis, R. Y., Giles, H., & Rosenthal, D. (1981). Notes on the construction of a subjective vitality questionnaire for ethnolinguistic groups. *Journal of Multilingual and Multicultural Development, 2,* 145–155.

Boutin, B. A. (2003). La norme endogène du français de Côte d'Ivoire: Mise en évidence des règles différentes du français de France concernant la complémentation verbale. *Sud Langues, 2,* 33–46.

Boutin, B. A. (2004). *Description de la variation: Etudes transformationnelles des phrases du français de Côte d'Ivoire.* Villeneuve sur Ascq: Presses Universitaires du Septentrion.

Bouton, L. F. (1988). A cross-cultural study of ability to interpret implicatures in English. *World Englishes, 7,* 183–196.

Bovet, L. (1988). Le français en Suisse romande. *Présence francophone, 29,* 7–26.

Bowen, T. J. (1858). *Grammar and Vocabulary of the Yoruba Language*. Washington, DC: The Smithsonian Institute.

Bowers, C. A. & Flinders, D. J. (1990). *Responsive Teaching: An ecological approach to classroom patterns of language, culture, and thought*. New York, NY: Teachers College Press.

Boyes-Baem, P. (1990). Acquisition of the handshapes in American Sign Language: A preliminary analysis. In V. Volterra & C. Erting (Eds.), *From Gesture to Language in Hearing and Deaf Children* (pp. 107–127). Berlin: Springer.

Boyle, J. (1997). Imperialism of the English language in Hong Kong. *Journal of Multilingual and Multicultural Development, 18*, 169–181.

Bradshaw, J. (1998). The Civil War: Autumn 1863, Return to South Louisiana. *Daily Advertiser,* History of Acadiana Supplement, *16*, 16.

Brandenburg, G. (1915). The language of a three-year-old child. *Pedagogical Seminary, 22*, 89–120.

Brasseaux, C. A. (1987). *The Founding of New Acadia: The beginnings of Acadian life in Louisiana, 1765–1803*. Baton Rouge, LA: Louisiana State University Press.

Brasseaux, C. A. & Conrad, G. R. (1992). *The Road to Louisiana: The Saint Domingue refugees*. University of Southwestern Louisiana at Lafayette: Center for Louisiana Studies.

Brasseaux, C. A., Fontenot, K. P., & Oubre, C. F. (1996). *Creoles of Color in the Bayou Country*. Oxford, MS: University Press of Mississippi.

Broch, I. & Jahr, E. H. (1984). Russenorsk: A new look at the Russo-Norwegian pidgin in Northern Norway. In P. S. Ureland & I. Clarkson (Eds.), *Scandinavian Language Contacts* (pp. 21–65). Cambridge: CUP.

Broch, O. (1927). Russenorsk. *Archiv für slavische Philologie, 41*, 209–262.

Broeder, P., Extra, G., van Hout, R., & Voionmaa, K. (1993). Word formation processes in talking about entities. In C. Perdue (Ed.), *Adult Language Acquisition: Cross-linguistic perspectives*, Vol. 2 (pp. 41–72). Cambridge: CUP.

Brown, B. (1993). The social consequences of writing Louisiana French. *Language in Society, 22*, 67–101.

Brown, P. & Levinson, S. (1987). *Politeness: Some universals in language usage*. Cambridge: CUP.

Brown, R. (1973). *A First Language: The early stages*. Cambridge, MA: Harvard University Press.

Bruck, M., Jakimik, J., & Tucker, R. (1971). Are French immersion programs suitable for working-class children? A follow-up investigation. *Word, 1–2–3*, 311–341.

Bruhn de Garavito, J. & White, L. (2002). L2 acquisition of Spanish DPs: The status of grammatical features. In A.-T. Pérez-Leroux & J. Liceras (Eds.), *The Acquisition of Spanish Morphosyntax: The L1/L2 connection* (pp. 153–178). Dordrecht: Kluwer.

Brunel, C. (1926). *Les plus anciennes chartes en langue provençale*. Paris: Picard.

Brunel, C. (1952). *Les plus anciennes chartes en langue provençale*, Supplément. Paris: Picard.

Brunot, F. (1966). *Histoire de la langue française*. Paris: A. Colin.

Bullock, B. E. (2002). Constraining the vagaries of glide distribution in varieties of French. In C. R. Wiltshire & J. Camps (Eds.), *Romance Phonology and Variation* (pp. 11–25). Amsterdam: John Benjamins.

Bullock, B. E. & Gerfen, C. (2005). The preservation of schwa in the converging phonological system of Frenchville (PA) French. *Bilingualism, 8*, 117–130.

Butterworth, G. (2003). Pointing is the royal road to language for babies. In S. Kita (Ed.), *Pointing: Where language, culture and cognition meet* (pp. 9–34). Mahwah, NS: Lawrence Erlbaum.

Bybee, J. (2001). *Phonology and Language Use*. Cambridge: CUP.

Bygate, M. (2004). Some current trends in applied linguistics: Towards a generic view. *AILA Review, 17*, 6–22.

Byram, M. (1997). *Teaching and Assessing Intercultural Competence*. Clevedon: Multilingual Matters.

Byram, M., Gribkova, B., & Starkey, H. (2002). *Developing the Intercultural Dimension in Language Teaching: A practical introduction for teachers*. Strasbourg: Council of Europe.

Caldas, S. J. (1998). How to suppress childhood bilingualism... And bring it back to life again. *Learning Languages, 4*, 15–23.

Caldas, S. J. (2006). *Rearing Bilingual-Biliterate Children in Monolingual Cultures*. Clevedon: Multilingual Matters.

Caldas, S. J. & Bankston, C. L. (2005). *Forced to Fail: The paradox of school desegregation*. Westport, CT: Praeger.

Caldas, S. J. & Boudreaux, N. (1999). Poverty, race, and foreign language immersion: Predictors of academic achievement. *Learning Languages, 5*, 4–15.

Caldas, S. J. & Caron-Caldas, S. (1992). Rearing bilingual children in a monolingual culture: A Louisiana experience. *American Speech, 67*, 290–296.

Caldas, S. J. & Caron-Caldas, S. (1997). Cultural influences on French/English language dominance of three bilingual children. *Language, Culture, and Curriculum, 10*, 139–155.

Caldas, S. J. & Caron-Caldas, S. (1999). Language immersion and cultural identity: Conflicting influences and values. *Language, Culture, and Curriculum, 12*, 42–58.

Caldas, S. J. & Caron-Caldas, S. (2000). The influence of family, school and community on 'bilingual preference': Results from a Louisiana/Quebec case study. *Applied Psycholinguistics, 21*, 365–381.

Caldas, S. J. & Caron-Caldas, S. (2002). A sociolinguistic analysis of the language preferences of adolescent bilinguals: Shifting allegiances and developing identities. *Applied Linguistics, 23*, 490–514.

Calvet, L.-J. (1999). *Pour une écologie des langues du monde*. Paris: Plon.

Calvet, L.-J. (2002). *Linguistique et colonialisme*. Paris: Payot et Rivages.

Cameron, D. (1990). Demythologizing sociolinguistics: Why language does not reflect society. In J. Joseph & T. Taylor (Eds.), *Ideologies of Language* (pp. 79–93). London: Routledge.

Cameron, D. (1995). *Verbal Hygiene*. London: Routledge.

Cameron, D. (2002). Globalization and the teaching of 'communication skills'. In D. Block & D. Cameron (Eds.), *Globalization and Language Teaching* (pp. 67–82). London: Routledge.

Cameron, D. & Coates, J. (Eds.). (1989). *Women in their Speech Communities*. London: Longman.

Campbell, R. (1997). Reading the lips: Speculation on the nature and role of lipreading in cognitive development of deaf children. In M. Marschark, P. Simple, D. Lillo-Martin, R. Campbell, & V. Everhart (Eds.), *Relations of Language and Thought: The view from sign language and deaf children* (pp. 110–146). Oxford: OUP.

Campbell, J. B. & Hawley, C. W. (1982). Study habits and Eysenck's theory of extraversion-introversion. *Journal of Research in Personality, 16*, 139–146.

Campbell, L. (In press). Sociolinguistics in the USA. In P. Trudgill (Ed.), *Handbook of Sociolinguistics* (2nd ed.). Berlin: Mouton de Gruyter.

Camproux, C. (1953). *Histoire de la littérature occitane*. Paris: Payot.

Canale, M. (1983). From communicative competence to communicative language pedagogy. In J. C. Richards & R. W. Schmidt (Eds.), *Language and Communication* (pp. 2–27). London: Longman.

Canale, M. & Swain, M. (1980). Theoretical bases of communicative approaches to second language teaching and testing. *Applied Linguistics, 1*(1), 1–47.

Capirci, O., Iverson, J. M., Pizzuto, E., & Volterra, V. (1996). Gestures and words during the transition to two-word speech. *Journal of Child language, 23*, 645–673.

Caput, J.-P. (1972). *La langue française. Histoire d'une institution*, T. 1, 842–1715. Paris: Larousse.

Carey, S. T. (1991). The culture of literacy in majority and minority language schools. *Canadian Modern Language Review, 47*, 950–976.

Carroll, R. (1987). *Evidences invisibles: Américains et Français au quotidien*. Paris: Editions du Seuil.

Carroll, S. (1989). Second language acquisition and the computational paradigm. *Language Learning, 39*, 535–594.

Carroll, S. (2000). *Input and Evidence: The raw materials of second language acquisition*. Amsterdam: John Benjamins.

Carroll, S. E. (2004). Segmentation: Learning how to 'hear words' in the L2 speech stream. *Transactions of the Philological Society, 102*(2), 227–254.

Carstens, V. (2000). Concord in minimalist theory. *Linguistic Inquiry, 31*, 319–355.

Carstens, V. (2003). Rethinking complementizer agreement: Agree with a case-checked goal. *Linguistic Inquiry, 34*, 393–412.

Carter, R. (1997). Speaking Englishes, speaking cultures: Using CANCODE. *Prospect, 12*, 4–11.

Carter, R. (1998). Orders of reality: CANCODE, communication, and culture. *English Language Teaching Journal, 52*, 43–56.

Carter, R. & McCarthy, M. (2004). Talking, creating: Interactional language, creativity and context. *Applied Linguistics, 25*, 62–88.

Carton, F. (1974). *Introduction à la phonétique du français*. Paris: Bordas.

Casagrande, J. (1983). La syllabe dans l'optique de la loi de position, ou procès et sentence de douteuses notions. *General Linguistics, 23*, 246–264.

Casagrande, J. (1984). *The Sound System of French*. Washington, DC: Georgetown University Press.

Caselli, M. C. & Volterra, V. (1990). From communication to language in hearing and deaf children. In V. Volterra & C. J. Erting (Eds.), *From Gesture to Language in Hearing and Deaf Children* (pp. 263–277). Berlin/New York: Springer.

Cedergren, H. & Simoneau, L. (1985). La chute des voyelles hautes en français de Montréal 'As-tu entendu la belle syncope?' In M. Lemieux & H. Cedergren (Eds.), *Les tendances dynamiques du français parlé à Montréal*, Vol. 1 (pp. 57–144). Montréal: Office de la langue française.

Cenoz, J. & Valencia, J. F. (1993). Ethnolinguistic vitality, social networks and motivation in second language acquisition: Some data from the Basque country. *Language, Culture and Curriculum, 6*, 113–127.

Cerguiglini, B. (1991). *La naissance du français*. Paris: Presses Universitaires de France.

Cerquiglini, B. (1995). *L'accent du souvenir*. Paris: Editions de Minuit.

Cerquiglini, B. (2004). *La genèse de l'orthographe française (XIIe–XVIIe siècles)*. Paris: Champion.

Chamberlain, A. & Chamberlain, I. (1904). Studies of a child. *Pedagogical Seminary, 11*, 264–291, 452–283.

Chamberlain, C. & Mayberry, R. I. (2000). Theorizing about the relation between American Sign Language and reading. In C. Chamberlain, J. P. Morford, & R. I. Mayberry (Eds.), *Language Acquisition by Eye* (pp. 221–259). Mahwah, NJ: Lawrence Erlbaum.

Chamberlain, C., Morford, J. P., & Mayberry, R. I. (2000). *Language Acquisition by Eye*. Mahwah, NJ: Lawrence Erlbaum.

Chambers, J. K. (2003). *Sociolinguistic Theory: Linguistic variation and its social significance* (2nd ed.). Malden, MA: Blackwell.

Chambers, A. & O'Sullivan, I. (2004). Corpus consultation and advanced learners' writing skills in French. *ReCALL, 16*(1), 158–172.

Charette, M. (1991). *Conditions on Phonological Government*. Cambridge: CUP.

Charrow, V. R. (1976). A psycholinguistic analysis of 'Deaf English'. *Sign Language Studies, 7*, 139–150.

Chastain, K. (1975). Affective and ability factors in second language learning. *Language Learning, 25*, 153–161.

Chaudenson, R. (1979). *Les Créoles français*. Paris: Fernand Nathan.

Chaudenson, R. (1989). *Créoles et enseignement du français*. Paris: L'Harmattan.

Chaudenson, R. (1992). *Des îles, des hommes, des langues*. Paris: L'Harmattan.

Chaudenson, R. (1995). *Les créoles*. Paris: Presses Universitaires de France.

Chaudenson, R. (1999). Les français d'outre-mer. In J. Chaurand (Ed.), *Nouvelle histoire de la langue française* (pp. 345–375). Paris: Seuil.

Chaudenson, R. (2002). La genèse des créoles. In C. Bavoux & D. de Robillard (Eds.), *Linguistique et créolistique: Univers créoles 2* (pp. 1–15). Paris: Anthropos.

Chaudenson, R. (2003). *La créolisation: Théorie, applications, implications*. Paris: L'Harmattan.

Chaudenson, R., Mufwene, S., & Pargman, S. (2001). *Des îles, des hommes, des langues*. London: Routledge.

Chaurand, J. (Ed.). (1999). *Nouvelle histoire de la langue française*. Paris: Seuil.

Cheek, J. M. & Buss, A. H. (1981). Shyness and sociability. *Journal of Personality and Social Psychology, 41*, 330–339.

Chern, C.-L. (1993). Chinese students' word-solving strategies in reading in English. In T. Huckin, M. Haynes, & J. Coady (Eds.), *Second Language Reading and Vocabulary Learning* (pp. 67–85). Norwood, NJ: Ablex.

Chevalier, J.-C. (1968). *Histoire de la syntaxe*. Geneva: Droz.

Chevaux, F. & Meunier, F. (2004). Cross-modal semantic priming and gender-marked context in French. Paper presented at the 10th Annual Conference on Architectures and Mechanisms of Language Processing, September 16–18, Université d'Aix-en-Provence.

Chomsky, N. (1965). *Aspects of the Theory of Syntax*. Cambridge, MA: The MIT Press.

Chomsky, N. (1986). *Knowledge of Language*. New York, NY: Praeger.

Chomsky, N. (1995). *The Minimalist Program*. Cambridge, MA: The MIT Press.

Chomsky, N. (2000). Minimalist inquiries: The framework. In R. Martin, D. Michaels, & J. Uriagereka (Eds.), *Step by Step: Essays on minimalist syntax in honor of Howard Lasnik* (pp. 89–155). Cambridge, MA: The MIT Press.

Chomsky, N. (2001). Derivation by phase. In M. Kenstowicz (Ed.), *Ken Hale: A life in language* (pp. 1–52). Cambridge, MA: The MIT Press.

Chomsky, N. (2002). *On Nature and Language*. Cambridge: CUP.

Cichocki, W., House, A. B., Kinlock, A. M., & Lister, A. C. (1999). Cantonese speakers and the acquisition of French consonants. In J. Leather (Ed.), *Phonological Issues in Language Learning* (pp. 95–121). Oxford: Blackwell.

Cinque, G. (1994). On the evidence for partial N-movement in the Romance DP. In G. Cinque, J. Koster, J.-Y. Pollock, L. Rizzi, & R. Zanuttini (Eds.), *Paths Towards Universal Grammar* (pp. 85–110). Washington, DC: Georgetown University Press.

Clachar, A. (1998). Differential effects of linguistic imperialism on second language learning: Americanization in Puerto Rico. *International Journal of Bilingual Education and Bilingualism, 1*, 102–119.

Clahsen, H. (1988). Parameterized grammatical theory and language acquisition: A study of the acquisition of verb placement and inflection by children and adults. In S. Flynn & W. O'Neil (Eds.), *Linguistic Theory in Second Language Acquisition* (pp. 47–75). Dordrecht: Kluwer.

Clahsen, H., Eissenbeiss, S., & Vainikka, A. (1994). The seeds of structure: A syntactic analysis of the acquisition of case marking. In T. Hoekstra & B. D. Schwartz (Eds.), *Language Acquisition Studies in Generative Grammar* (pp. 85–118). Amsterdam: John Benjamins.

Clahsen, H. & Felser, C. (2006). Grammatical processing in language learners. *Applied Psychlolinguistics, 27*, 3–42.

Clahsen, H. & Hong, U. (1995). Agreement and null subjects in German L2 development: New evidence from reaction-time experiments. *Second Language Research, 11*, 57–87.

Clahsen, H. & Muysken, P. (1986). The availability of Universal Grammar to adult and child learners: A study of the acquisition of German word order. *Second Language Research, 5*, 93–119.

Clahsen, H. & Muysken, P. (1989). The UG paradox in L2 acquisition. *Second Language Research, 5*, 1–29.

Clark, E. V. (1993). *The Lexicon in Acquisition*. Cambridge: CUP.

Clark, E. V. (1998). Lexical creativity in French-speaking children. *Cahiers de psychologie cognitive/Current Psychology of Cognition, 17*(2), 513–530.

Clark, R. (1979). In search of Beach-la-Mar. *Te Reo, 22*, 3–64.

Clément, R. (1980). Ethnicity, contact and communicative competence in a L2. In H. Giles, W. P. Robinson, & P. M. Smith (Eds.), *Language: Social psychological perspectives* (pp. 147–154). Oxford: Pergamon Press.

Clément, R. (1984). Aspects socio-psychologiques de la communication inter-ethnique et de l'identité culturelle. *Recherches sociologiques, 15*, 293–312.

Clément, R. (1986). Second language proficiency and acculturation: An investigation of the effects of language status and individual characteristics. *Journal of Language and Social Psychology, 5*, 271–290.

Clément, R. (1994). The acquisition of French as a second language in Canada: Towards a research agenda. In J. W. Berry & J. A. Laponce (Eds.), *Ethnicity and Culture in Canada: The research landscape* (pp. 410–434). Toronto: University of Toronto Press.

Clément, R., Baker, S. C., Josephson, G., & Noels, K. (2005). Media effects on ethnic identity among linguistic majorities and minorities: A longitudinal study of a bilingual setting. *Human Communication Research, 31*, 399–422.

Clément, R., Baker, S. C., & MacIntyre, P. D. (2003). Willingness to communicate in a second language: The effects of context, norms and vitality. *Journal of Language and Social Psychology, 22*, 190–209.

Clément, R. & Gardner, R. C. (2001). Second language mastery. In W. P. Robinson & H. Giles (Eds.), *Handbook of Language and Social Psychology* (pp. 489–504). London: Wiley.

Clément, R., Gardner, R. C., & Smythe, P. C. (1977). Motivational variables in second language acquisition: A study of francophones learning English. *Canadian Journal of Behavioral Science, 9*, 123–133.

Clément, R., Gardner, R. C., & Smythe, P. C. (1980). Social and individual factors in second language acquisition. *Canadian Journal of Behavioral Science, 12*, 293–302.

Clément, R. & Kruidenier, B. G. (1983). Orientations in second language acquisition: The effects of ethnicity, milieu and target language on their emergence. *Language Learning, 33*, 273–291.

Clément, R. & Kruidenier, B. G. (1985). Aptitude, attitude and motivation in second language proficiency: A test of Clément's model. *Journal of Language and Social Psychology, 4*, 21–37.

Clément, R. & Noels, K. A. (1991). Langue, statut et acculturation: Une étude d'individus et de groupes en contact. In M. Lavallée & F. Larose (Eds.), *Identité, culture et changement social: Actes du 3ième colloque de l'Association pour la recherche interculturelle* (pp. 315–326). Paris: L'Harmattan.

Clements, G. N. & Keyser, S. J. (1983). *CV Phonology. A generative theory of the syllable* [Linguistic Inquiry Monograph Nine]. Cambridge, MA: The MIT Press.

Clifford, M. M. (1991). Risk taking. Theoretical, empirical, and educational considerations. *Educational Psychologist, 26*, 263–297.

Coates, J. (1986). *Women, Men and Language*. London: Longman.

Cobb, T. & Horst, M. (2004). Is there room for an academic word list in French? In P. Bogaards & B. Laufer (Eds.), *Vocabulary in a Second Language: Selection, acquisition and testing* (pp. 15–38). Amsterdam: John Benjamins.

Coerts, J. & Mills, A. (1994). Early sign combinations of deaf children in sign language of the Netherlands. In I. Ahlgren, B. Bergman, & M. Brennan (Eds.), *Perspectives on Sign Language Usage: Papers from the Fifth international symposium on sign language Research*, Vol. 2 (pp. 319–331). Durham: ISLA.

Cohen, A. D. (1997). Developing pragmatic ability: Insights from the accelerated study of Japanese. In H. M. Cook, K. Hijirida, & M. Tahara (Eds.), *New Trends & Issues in Teaching Japanese Language & Culture* [Technical Report 15] (pp. 133–159). Honolulu, HI: Second Language Teaching and Curriculum Center, University of Hawai'i at Manoa.

Cohen, Y. & Norst, M. J. (1989). Fear, dependence and loss of self-esteem: Affective barriers in second language learning among adults. *RELC Journal, 20*, 61–77.

Colé, P., Pynte, J., & Andriamamonjy, P. (2003). Effect of grammatical gender on visual word recognition: Evidence from lexical decision and eye movement experiments. *Perception & Psychophysics, 65*(3), 407–419.

Colin, J.-P. (2003). Le lexique. In M. Yaguello (Ed.), *Le grand livre de la langue française* (pp. 391–456). Paris: Seuil.

Collentine, J. & Freed, B. F. (2004). Learning context and its effects on second language acquisition: Introduction. *Studies in Second Language Acquisition, 26*, 153–171.

Collins, J. (1996). Socialization to text: Structure and contradiction in schooled literacy. In M. Silverstein & G. Urban (Eds.), *Natural Histories of Discourse* (pp. 203–228). Chicago, IL: The University of Chicago Press.

Comrie, B. (1998). The world's major languages. *Encarta Encyclopedia*.

Conlin, K., Mirus, C., & Meier, R. (2000). The acquisition of first signs: Place, handshape, and movement. In C. Chamberlain, J. Morford, & R. Mayberry (Eds.), *Language Acquisition by Eye* (pp. 51–69). Mahwah, NJ: Lawrence Erlbaum.

Conrad, R. (1979). *The Deaf School Child*. London: Harper and Row.

Content, A., Mousty, P., & Radeau, M. (1990). BRULEX. Une base de données lexicales informatisée pour le français écrit et parlé. *L'Année Psychologique, 90*, 551–566.

Conway, D. (1990). Semantic relationships in the word meanings of hearing-impaired children. *Volta Review, 92*, 339–349.

Cook, V. (1992). Evidence for multicompetence. *Language Learning, 42*, 557–591.

Cook, V. (1997). Monolingual bias in second language acquisition research. *Revista Canaria de Estudios Ingleses, 34*, 35–50.

Cook, V. (1999). Going beyond the native speaker in language teaching. *TESOL Quarterly, 33*, 185–210.

Cook, V. (2002). Language teaching methodology and the L2 user perspective. In V. Cook (Ed.), *Portraits of the L2 User* (pp. 325–343). Clevedon: Multilingual Matters.

Cook, V. (Ed.). (2002). *Portraits of the L2 User*. Clevedon: Multilingual Matters.

Cook-Gumperz, J. (Ed.). (1986). *The Social Construction of Literacy*. New York, NY: CUP.

Coquebert-Montbret, E. (1835). *Mélanges sur les langues, dialectes et patois*. Paris: Bureau de l'Almanach du Commerce.

Corbett, G. (1991). *Gender*. Cambridge: CUP.

Corbett, G. (2003). Agreement: Terms and boundaries. In W. Griffin (Ed.), *The Role of Agreement in Natural Language: Proceedings of the 2001 Texas linguistic society conference, Austin, Texas, 2–4 March 2001* (pp. 109–122). Austin, TX: Texas Linguistic Society.

Corbin, D. (1987). *Morphologie dérivationnelle et structuration du lexique* (2 Vols.). Tübingen: Niemeyer.

Corson, D. (2001). *Language Diversity and Education*. Mahwah, NJ: Lawrence Erlbaum.

Cosme, C. (2005). A corpus-based perspective on information packaging in English and French. Implications for advanced L2 instruction. Paper presented at the 5th *PALC Conference*.

Coulmas, F. (1981). Introduction: Conversational routine. In F. Coulmas (Ed.), *Conversational Routine. Explorations in standardized communication situations and prepatterned speech* (pp. 1–17). The Hague: Mouton.

Council for the Development of French in Louisiana. (n.d.). *What is CODOFIL?* Retrieved October 15, 2005 from http://www.codofil.org/english/index.html

Council for the Development of French in Louisiana. (n.d.). *French immersion*. Retrieved October 15, 2005 from http://www.codofil.org/english/education.html#immersion

Courtin, C. & Melot, A.-M. (2005). Metacognitive development of deaf children: Lessons from the appearance-reality and false belief tasks. *Developmental Science, 8*, 16–25.

Coveney, A. (1996). *Variability in Spoken French*. Exeter: Elm bank Publications.

Coxhead, A. (2000). A new academic word list. *TESOL Quarterly, 34*(2), 213–238.

Crawford, J. (1992). *Hold Your Tongue*. New York, NY: Addison-Wesley.

Crawford, J. (1997). *Language legislation in Louisiana*. Retrieved January 8, 2006 from http://ourworld.compuserve.com/homepages/JWCRAWFORD/can-la.htm

Cristaller, J. G. (1875). *A Grammar of the Asante and Fante Language Called Tshi*. Basel: Basler Mission.

Cristaller, J.G . (1933). *Dictionary of the Asante and Fante Language Called Tshi*. Basel: Basler Mission.

Crookes, G. & Schmidt, R. W. (1991). Motivation: Reopening the research agenda. *Language Learning, 41*, 469–512.

Crowley, T. (1990). That obscure object of desire: A science of language. In J. E. Joseph & T. J. Taylor (Eds.), *Ideologies of Language* (pp. 27–50). London: Routledge.

Crystal, D. (2003). *A Dictionary of Linguistics and Phonetics* (5th ed.). Oxford: Blackwell.

Cummins, J. (2000). Immersion education for the millennium: What we have learned from 30 years of research on second language immersion. http://www.iteachilearn.com/cummins/immersion2000.html

Cummins, J. & Swain, M. (1986). *Bilingualism in Education*. London: Longman.

Cuxac, C. (1999). L'accès au français écrit dans le cadre d'une éducation bilingue de l'enfant sourd. *Language et Pratiques, 23*, 16–26.

Dagneaux, E., Dennes, S., & Granger, S. (1998). Computer-aided error analysis. *System, 26*, 163–174.

Dahan, D., Swingley, D., Tanenhaus, M., & Magnuson, J. (2000). Linguistic gender and spoken-word recognition in French. *Journal of Memory and Language, 42*, 465–480.

Daigle, D. & Armand, F. (2004). Le traitement morphologique en lecture chez des sourds gestuels québécois. *LIDIL, 30*, 117–131.

Daly, J. A. & McCroskey, J. C. (Eds.). (1984). *Avoiding Communication: Shyness, reticence, and communication apprehension*. Beverly Hills, CA: Sage.

Dannequin, C. (1988). Les enfants baillonnés (gagged children): The teaching of French as mother tongue in elementary school. *Language and Education, 1*(1), 15–31.

Dansereau, D. (1995). Phonetics in the beginning and intermediate oral proficiency-oriented French classroom. *The French Review, 68*, 638–651.

Darder, A. (2005). Schooling and the culture of dominion: Unmasking the ideology of standardized testing. In G. E. Fischman, P. McLaren, H. Sunker, & C. Lankshear (Eds.), *Critical Theories, Radical Pedagogies, and Global Conflicts* (pp. 207–222). New York, NY: Rowman & Littlefield.

Davies, A. (2003). *The Native Speaker: Myth and reality*. Clevedon: Multilingual Matters.

Davies, A. & Elder, C. (Eds.). (2004). *The Handbook of Applied Linguistics*. Malden, MA: Blackwell.

Davies, M. (2004). Student use of large, annotated corpora to analyze syntactic variation. In G. Aston, S. Bernardini, & D. Stewart (Eds.), *Corpora and Language Learners* (pp. 257–269). Amsterdam: John Benjamins.

Deci, E. L. & Ryan, R. M. (1985). *Intrinsic Motivation and Self-determination in Human Behavior*. New York, NY: Plenum.

Deci, E. L. & Ryan, R. M. (2002). *Handbook of Self-Determination Research*. New York, NY: The University of Rochester Press.

Deci, E. L., Vallerand, R. J., Pelletier, L. G., & Ryan, R. M. (1991). Motivation in education: The self-determination perspective. *The Educational Psychologist, 26*, 325–346.

Decker, B. (1997). The other Acadians: In Northern Maine, Acadians struggle to preserve culture. *The Daily Advertiser*, August 31, A1.

Dees, A. (1985). Dialectes et scriptae à l'époque de l'ancien français. *Revue de linguistique romane, 49*, 87–117.

DeGraff, M. (1996). UG and acquisition in pidginization and creolization. *Behavioral and Brain Sciences, 19*, 724.

DeGraff, M. (1999). Creolization, language change, and language acquisition: A Prolegomenon. In M. DeGraff (Ed.), *Language Creation and Language Change: Creolization, diachrony, and development* (pp. 1–46). Cambridge, MA: The MIT Press.

DeGraff, M. (2002). Relexification: A re-evaluation. *Anthropological Linguistics, 44*(4), 321–411.

DeKeyser, R. M. (2001). Automaticity and automatization. In P. Robinson (Ed.), *Cognition and Second Language Instruction* (pp. 125–151). Cambridge: CUP.

Dekydtspotter, L., Donaldson, B., Edmonds, A. C., Liljestrand Fultz, A., & Petrush, R. A. (2005). Intermodular interactions in English–French relative clause attachment disambiguation. Paper presented at Boston University Conference on Language Development.

Dekydtspotter, L. & Hathorn, J. C. (2005). *Quelque chose... de remarquable* in English-French acquisition: Mandatory, informationally encapsulated computations in second language interpretation. *Second Language Research, 21*, 291–323.

Dekydtspotter, L. & Outcalt, S. D. (2005). A syntactic bias in scope ambiguity resolution in the processing of English-French cardinality interrogatives: Evidence for informational encapsulation. *Language Learning, 1*, 1–37.

Dekydtspotter, L. & Petrush, R. A. (2006). On the acquisition of *ne ... que* 'only' in English-French. Paper presented at Generative Approaches to Second Language Acquisition (GASLA) 8, Bamff, Alberta, Canada.

Dekydtspotter, L. & Sprouse, R. A. (2001). Mental design and (second) language epistemology: Adjectival restrictions of *wh*-quantifiers and tense in English-French interlanguage. *Second Language Research, 17*, 1–35.

Dekydtspotter, L., Sprouse, R. A., & Anderson, B. (1997). The interpretive interface in L2 acquisition: The process-result distinction in English-French interlanguage grammars. *Language Acquisition, 6*, 297–332.

Dekydtspotter, L., Sprouse, R. A., & Gibson, E. (2001). The interpretation of two kinds of relative clauses in English-French interlanguage. *Proceedings of the Annual Boston University Conference on Language Development, 25*, 227–237.

Dekydtspotter, L., Sprouse, R. A., & Swanson, K. A. B. (2001). Reflexes of mental architecture in second-language acquisition: The interpretation of *combien* extractions in English-French interlanguage. *Language Acquisition, 9*, 175–227.

Dekydtspotter, L., Sprouse, R. A., & Thyre, R. (1999/2000). The interpretation of quantification at a distance in English-French interlanguage: Domain specificity and second-language acquisition. *Language Acquisition, 8*, 1–36.

Delattre, P. (1938). L'accent final en français: Accent d'intensité, accent de hauteur, accent de durée. *The French Review, 12*, 3–7.

Delattre, P. (1940). Le mot est-il une entité phonétique en français? *Le français moderne, 8*, 47–56.

Deleau, M. (1997). L'attribution d'états mentaux chez des enfants sourds et entendants: Une approche du rôle de l'expérience langagière sur une théorie de l'esprit. *Bulletin de Psychologie*, L (427), 48–56.

Delfitt, D. & Schroten, J. (1991). Bare plurals and the number affix in DP. *Probus, 3*, 155–185.

Dell, F. (1980). *Generative Phonology and French Phonology* (Translated by Catherine Cullen). Cambridge: CUP.

Dell, F. (1984). L'accentuation dans les phrases en français. In F. Dell, D. Hirst, & J.-R. Vergnaud (Eds.), *Forme sonore du langage: Structure des représentations en phonologie* (pp. 65–122). Paris: Hermann.

Dell, F. (1995). Consonant clusters and phonological syllables in French. *Lingua, 95*, 5–26.

Dell, F. & Selkirk, E. (1978). On a morphologically governed vowel alternation in French. In S. J. Keyser (Ed.), *Recent Transformational Studies in European Languages* (pp. 1–51). Cambridge, MA: The MIT Press.

Denys, M. & Alegria, J. (1998). Comment lisent les personnes sourdes qui lisent bien: Analyse cognitive des mécanismes de lecture de huit cas. Paper presented at the 2nd international colloquium *ACFOS surdité et Accès à la langue écrite: De la recherche à la pratique*, Paris, October 1998.

De Ridder, I. (2003). *Reading from the Screen in a Second Language*. Antwerp: Garant.

De Santis, S. (1977). Elbow to handshift in French and American sign language. Paper presented at NWAVE Conference, Georgetown University, Washington, DC.

Desrochers, A. & Brabant, M. (1995). Interaction entre facteurs phonologiques et sémantiques dans une épreuve de catégorisation lexicale. *Revue canadienne de psychologie expérimentale, 49*, 240–263.

Desrochers, A. Paivio, A., & Desrochers, S. (1989). L'effet de la fréquence d'usage des noms inanimés et de la valeur prédictive de leur terminaison sur l'identification du genre grammatical. *Canadian Journal of Psychology, 43*, 62–73.

Desrochers, A. & Paivio, A. (1990). Le phonème initial des noms inanimés et son effet sur l'identification du genre grammatical. *Canadian Journal of Psychology, 44*, 44–57.

de Swart, H. (1992). Intervention effects, monotonicity and scope. In C. Baker & D. Dowty (Eds.), *Proceedings of the Second Conference on Semantics and Linguistic Theory* (pp. 387–406). Columbus, OH: Ohio State University, Dept. of Linguistics.

de Villiers, J. & de Villiers, P. (2000). Linguistic determinism and the understanding of false beliefs. In P. Mitchel & K. Riggs (Eds.), *Children's Reasoning & the Mind* (pp. 191–228). Hove: Psychology Press.

de Villiers, J., de Villiers, P., & Hogan, E. (1994). The central problem of functional categories in English syntax of oral deaf children. In H. Tager-Flushberg (Ed.), *Constraints on Language Acquisition: Studies of atypical children* (pp. 9–47). Hillsdale, NJ: Lawrence Erlbaum.

de Villiers, P. (2005). The role of language in theory-of-mind development: What deaf children can tell us. In J. W. Astington & J. A. Baird (Eds.), *Why Language Matters for Theory of Mind* (pp. 266–297). New York, NY: OUP.

de Villiers, P., de Villiers, J., Schick, B., & Hoffmeister, R. (2000). Theory of mind development in signing and non-signing deaf children: The impact of sign language on social-cognition. Paper presented at the Seventh International Conference on Theoretical Issues in Sign Language Research, Amsterdam, July 2000.

Dewaele, J.-M. (1994). Variation synchronique des taux d'exactitude. Analyse de fréquence des erreurs morpholexicales dans trois styles d'interlangue française. *International Review of Applied Linguistics, 32*(4), 275–300.

Dewaele, J.-M. (1995a). Variation synchronique dans l'interlangue: Analyse critique du Modèle du Caméléon de E. Tarone. *ITL Review of Applied Linguistics, 109–110,* 1–18.

Dewaele, J.-M. (1995b). Style-shifting in oral interlanguage: Quantification and definition. In L. Eubank, L. Selinker, & M. Sharwood Smith (Eds.), *The Current State of Interlanguage* (pp. 231–238). Amsterdam: John Benjamins.

Dewaele, J.-M. (1999). Word order variation in interrogative structures of native and non-native French. *ITL Review of Applied Linguistics, 123–124,* 161–180.

Dewaele, J.-M. (2001). Une distinction mesurable: Corpus oraux et écrits sur le continuum de la deixis. *Journal of French Language Studies, 11,* 179–199.

Dewaele, J.-M. (2002a). Using sociostylistic variants in advanced French IL: The case of *nous/on*. In S. Foster-Cohen, T. Ruthenberg, & M.-L. Poschen (Eds.), *EUROSLA Yearbook 2* (pp. 205–226). Amsterdam: John Benjamins.

Dewaele, J.-M. (2002b). Variation, chaos et système en interlangue française. *Acquisition et Interaction en Langue Etrangère, 17,* 143–167.

Dewaele, J.-M. (2004a). Retention or omission of the 'ne' in advanced French IL: The variable effect of extralinguistic factors. *Journal of Sociolinguistics, 8*(3), 433–450.

Dewaele, J.-M. (2004b). *Vous* or *tu*? Native and non-native speakers of French on a sociolinguistic tightrope. *International Review of Applied Linguistics, 42*(4), 383–402.

Dewaele, J.-M. (2004c). Blistering Barnacles! What language do multilinguals swear in?! *Estudios de Sociolingüística, 5*(1), 83–106.

Dewaele, J.-M. (2004d). Colloquial vocabulary in the speech of native and non-native speakers: The effects of proficiency and personality. In P. Bogaards & B. Laufer (Eds.), *Learning Vocabulary in a Second Language: Selection, acquisition and testing* (pp. 127–153). Amsterdam: John Benjamins.

Dewaele, J.-M. (2004e). The acquisition of sociolinguistic competence in French as a foreign language: An overview. In F. Myles & R. Towell (Eds.), *The Acquisition of French as a Second Language*, Special issue of *Journal of French Language Studies, 14,* 301–319.

Dewaele, J.-M. (2005a). Investigating the psychological and the emotional dimensions in instructed language learning: Obstacles and possibilities. In L. Ortega (Ed.), *Reconceptualizing research on L2 learning across education contexts*, Special issue of *The Modern Language Journal, 89*(3), 367–380.

Dewaele, J.-M. (Ed.). (2005b). *Focus on French as a Foreign Language: Multidisciplinary approaches.* Clevedon: Multilingual Matters.

Dewaele, J.-M. & Furnham, A. (1999). Extraversion: The unloved variable in applied linguistic research. *Language Learning, 49,* 509–544.

Dewaele, J.-M. & Furnham, A. (2000). Personality and speech production: A pilot study of second language learners. *Personality and Individual Differences, 28,* 355–365.

Dewaele, J.-M. & Mougeon, R. (Eds.). (2002). *L'appropriation de la variation en français langue étrangère.* Special issue of *Acquisition et interaction en langue étrangère, 17.*

Dewaele, J.-M. & Pavlenko, A. (2002). Emotion vocabulary in interlanguage. *Language Learning, 52*, 265–324.

Dewaele, J.-M. & Planchenault, G. (2006). Dites-moi tu?! La perception de la difficulté du système des pronoms d'adresse en français. In M. Faraco (Ed.), *Regards croisés sur la classe de langue: Pratiques, méthodes et théories* (pp. 153–171). Aix-en-Provence: Publications de l'Université de Provence.

Dewaele, J.-M. & Regan, V. (2001). The use of colloquial words in advanced French interlanguage. In S. Foster-Cohen & A. Nizegorodcew (Eds.), *EUROSLA Yearbook 1* (pp. 51–68). Amsterdam: John Benjamins.

Dewaele, J.-M. & Regan, V. (2002). Maîtriser la norme sociolinguistique en interlangue française: Le cas de l'omission variable de 'ne'. *Journal of French Language Studies, 12*, 123–148.

Dewaele, J.-M. & Véronique, D. (2000). Relating gender errors to morphosyntactic and lexical systems in advanced French interlanguage. *Studia Linguistica, 54*(2), 212–224.

Dewaele, J.-M. & Véronique, D. (2001). Gender assignment and gender agreement in advanced French interlanguage: A cross-sectional study. *Bilingualism, 4*, 275–297.

Dickerson, L. J. (1975). The learner's interlanguage as a system of variable rules. *TESOL Quarterly, 9*, 401–407.

Djité, P. (2000). Language planning in Côte d'Ivoire. *Current Issues in Language Planning, 1*, 11–46.

Djité, P. (2004). Living on borrowed tongues? A view from within. Paper presented at the 30th International LAUD Symposium, University of Koblenz-Landau, Germany, April 19–22.

Donato, R. (1994). Collective scaffolding in second language learning. In J. P. Lantolf & G. Appel (Eds.), *Vygotskyan Approaches to Second Language Research* (pp. 33–56). Norwood, NJ: Ablex.

Donovan, L. A. & MacIntyre, P. D. (2004). Age and sex differences in willingness to communicate, communication apprehension, and self-perceived competence. *Communication Research Reports, 21*, 420–427.

Dormon, J. (1983). *The People Called Cajuns: An introduction to an ethnohistory*. Lafayette, LA: University of Louisiana Center for Louisiana Studies.

Dormon, J. (1992). Louisiana's 'Creoles of color': Ethnicity, marginality and identity. *Social Science Quarterly, 73*, 615–626.

Dörnyei, Z. (2001). *Teaching and Researching Motivation*. Harlow: Longman.

Dörnyei, Z. (2003). *Attitudes, Orientations, and Motivations in Language Learning*. Malden: Blackwell.

Dörnyei, Z. (2005). *The Psychology of the Language Learner: Individual differences in second language acquisition*. London: Lawrence Erlbaum.

Dörnyei, Z. & Kormos, J. (2000). Problem-solving mechanisms in L2 communication: A psycholinguistic perspective. *Studies in Second Language Acquisition, 20*, 349–385.

Dörnyei, Z. & Otto, I. (1998). Motivation in action: A process model of L2 motivation. *Working Papers in Applied Linguistics (Thames Valley University, London), 4*, 43–69.

Doughty, C. (2003). Instructed SLA: Constraints, compensation, and enhancement. In C. Doughty & M. H. Long (Eds.), *The Handbook of Second Language Acquisition* (pp. 256–310). Oxford: Blackwell.

Doughty, C. & Williams, J. (Eds.). (1998). *Focus on Form in Classroom Second Language Acquisition*. Cambridge: CUP.

Dubois, C.-G. (1970). *Mythe et langage au seizième siècle*. Bordeaux: Editions Ducros.

Dubois, J. (1531). *In linguam gallicam isagoge, una cum eiusdem grammatica latino-gallica*. Paris: Robert Estienne.

Dubois, J. & Dubois, C. (1971). *Introduction à la lexicographie: Le dictionnaire*. Paris: Larousse.

Dubuisson, C. & Bastien, M. (1998). Que peut-on conclure des recherches portant sur la lecture par les sourds? In C. Dubuisson & D. Daigle (Eds.), *Lecture, écriture et surdité* (pp. 73–101). Montreal: Les Editions Logiques.

Dubuisson, C. & Daigle, D. (1998). *Lecture, écriture et surdité: Visions actuelles et nouvelles perspectives*. Montréal: Les Éditions Logiques.

Dubuisson, C. & Nadeau, M. (1993). Analyse de la performance en français écrit des apprenants sourds oralistes. *Revue de l'ACLA, 16*, 79–91.

Dubuisson, C., Lelièvre, L., Parisot, A.-M., & Vercaingne-Ménard, A. (2001). Acquisition of handshape in Quebec Sign Language (LSQ). Paper presented at the 7th international conference on Theoretical Issues in Sign Language Research, Amsterdam.

Duffield, N., White, L., Bruhn de Garavito, J., Montrul, S., & Prévost, P. (2003). Clitic placement in L2 French: Evidence from sentence matching. *Journal of Linguistics, 38*, 487–525.

DuFon, M. A. (1999). The acquisition of linguistic politeness in Indonesian as a second language by sojourners in naturalistic interactions. PhD dissertation, University of Hawai'i at Manoa, HI.

DuFon, M. A. (2000). The acquisition of negative responses to experience questions in Indonesian as a second language by sojourners in naturalistic interactions. In B. Swierzbin, F. Morris, M. E. Anderson, C. A. Klee, & E. Tarone (Eds.), *Social and Cognitive Factors in Second Language Acquisition. Selected proceedings of the 1999 Second Language Research Forum (SLRF)* (pp. 77–97). Somerville, MA: Cascadilla.

Dugas, L. G. (1999). Attrition of pronunciation accuracy among advanced American learners of French. PhD dissertation, Indiana University, Bloomington.

Dulay, H. & Burt, M. (1973). Should we teach children syntax? *Language Learning, 23*, 245–258.

Dulay, H. & Burt, M. (1974). Natural sequences in child second language acquisition. *Language Learning, 24*, 37–53.

Dulay, H. & Burt, M. (1975). A new approach to discovering universals of child second language acquisition. In D. Dato (Ed.), *Developmental Psycholinguistics* (pp. 209–233). Washington, DC: Georgetown University Press.

Dulay, H., Burt, M., & Krashen, S. (1982). *Language Two*. New York, NY: OUP.

Dumas, D. (1987). *Nos façons de parler: Les prononciations en français québécois*. Québec: Presses de l'Université du Québec.

Dumont, P. (1990). *Le français, langue africaine*. Paris: L'Harmattan.

Durand, J. (1985). On a recent tridimensional analysis of French liaison. *Folia linguistica, 20*, 477–491.

Eckert, P. (1989). *Jocks and Burnouts: Social categories and identity in the high school*. New York, NY: Teachers College Press.

Eckman, F. R. (1977). Markedness and the Contrastive Analysis hypothesis. *Language Learning, 27*, 315–330.

Edmondson, W. & House, J. (1991). Do learners talk too much? The waffle phenomenon in interlanguage pragmatics. In R. Phillipson, E. Kellerman, L. Selinker, M. Sharwood Smith, & M. Swain (Eds.), *Foreign/Second Language Pedagogy Research: A commemorative volume for Claus Faerch* (pp. 273–287). Clevedon: Multilingual Matters.

Edmondson, W., House, J., Kasper, G., & Stemmer, B. (1984). Learning the pragmatics of discourse: A project report. *Applied Linguistics, 5*(2), 113–127.

Egejuru, P. A. (1980). *Towards African Literary Independence*. Westport, CT: Greenwood Press.

Ehrman, M. (1990). Owls & doves: Cognition, personality, and learning success. In J. E. Alatis (Ed.), *Georgetown University Roundtable on Languages and Linguistics 1990* (pp. 413–437). Washington, DC: Georgetown University Press.

Ehrman, M. (1996). An exploration of adult language learner motivation, self-efficacy, and anxiety. In R. L. Oxford (Ed.), *Language Learning Motivation: Pathways to the new century* (pp. 81–104). Honolulu, HI: University of Hawai'i Press.

Eisenstein, E. L. (1983). *The Printing Revolution in Early Modern Europe*. Cambridge: CUP.

Eisenstein, M. & Bodman, J. (1993). Expressing gratitude in American English. In G. Kasper & S. Blum-Kulka (Eds.), *Interlanguage Pragmatics* (pp. 64–81). Oxford: OUP.

Ellis, N. (1995). Consciousness in second language acquisition: A review of field studies and laboratory experiments. *Language Awareness, 4*, 123–146.

Ellis, N. (2002a). Frequency effects in language processing: A review with implications for theories of implicit and explicit language acquisition. *Studies in Second Language Acquisition, 24*, 143–188.

Ellis, N. (2002b). Reflections on frequency effects in language processing. *Studies in Second Language Acquisition, 24*(2), 297–339.

Ellis, R. (1992). Learning to communicate in the classroom. A study of two language learners' requests. *Studies in Second Language Acquisition, 14,* 1–23.

Ellis, R. (1994). *The Study of Second Language Acquisition.* Oxford: OUP.

El Nasser, H. & Overberg, P. (2005). Katrina exodus reaches all states: Big social networks help some relocate. *USA TODAY,* September 29, A.1.

Ely, C. M. (1986). An analysis of discomfort, risk-taking, sociability, and motivation in the L2 classroom. *Language Learning, 36,* 1–25.

Emmorey, K. (2002). *Language, Cognition and the Brain: Insights from sign languages.* Mahwah, NJ: Lawrence Erlbaum.

Emmorey, K. (2003). *Perspectives on Classifier Constructions in Sign Languages.* Mahwah, NJ: Lawrence Erlbaum.

Emmorey, K. & Corina, D. (1990). Lexical recognition in sign language: Effects of phonetic structure and morphology. *Perceptual and Motor Skills, 71,* 1227–1252.

Embick, D. & Noyer, R. (2001). Movement operations after syntax. *Linguistic Inquiry, 32,* 555–595.

Emonds, J. (1978). The verbal complex V'-V in French. *Linguistic Inquiry, 9,* 151–175.

Encrevé, P. (1983). La liaison sans enchaînement. *Actes de la Recherche en Sciences Sociales, 46,* 39–66.

Encrevé, P. (1988). *La liaison avec et sans enchaînement.* Paris: Editions du Seuil.

Engberg-Pedersen, E. (1993). *Space in Danish Sign Language.* Hamburg: Signum Verlag.

Englebert, A. (1984). Esquisse d'une histoire de la négation en français. *Travaux de Linguistique, 11,* 7–25.

Epstein, S., Flynn, S., & Martohardjono, G. (1996). Second language acquisition: Theoretical and experimental issues in contemporary research. *Behavioral and Brain Sciences, 19,* 677–714.

Errington, J. (2001). Colonial linguistics. *Annual Review of Anthropology, 30,* 19–39.

Ervin-Tripp, S. (1974). Is second language learning like the first? *TESOL Quarterly, 8,* 111–127.

Estaville, L. (1990). The Louisiana French language in the nineteenth century. *Southern Geographer, 30,* 107–120.

Estienne, H. (1578 [1980]). *Deux dialogues du nouveau langage françois* (Edition critique par P. M. Smith). Geneva: Slatkine.

Estienne, H. (1582 [1999]). *Hypomneses de Gallica lingua peregrinis eam discentibus necessariae* (Edited and translated by J. Chomarat). Paris: Champion.

Estienne, R. 1549. *Dictionnaire françois-latin.* Paris: Robert Estienne.

Eubank, L. (1993/1994). On the transfer of parametric values in L2 development. *Language Acquisition, 3,* 183–208.

Eubank, L. (1996). Negation in early German-English interlanguage: More valueless features in the L2 initial state. *Second Language Research, 12,* 73–106.

Eubank, L. & Grace, S. (1998). V-to-I inflection in non-native grammars. In M. L. Beck (Ed.), *Morphology and its Interface in Second Language Knowledge* (pp. 69–88). Amsterdam: John Benjamins.

Evans, M. & Fisher, L. (2005). Measuring gains in pupils' foreign language competence as a result of participation in a school exchange visit: The case of Y9 pupils at three comprehensive schools in the UK. *Language Teaching Research, 9,* 173–192.

Eysenck, M. W. (1979). Anxiety, learning, and memory: A reconceptualization. *Journal of Research in Personality, 13,* 363–385.

Eysenck, H. J. & Eysenck, S. B. G. (1975). *Manual of the Eyesenck Personality Questionnaire (Junior and Adult).* London: Hodder and Stoughton.

Eysenck, S. & Zuckerman, M. (1978). The relationship between sensation-seeking and Eysenck's dimensions of personality. *British Journal of Psychology, 69,* 483–487.

Fagyal, Z. & Moisset, C. (1999). Sound change and articulatory release: Where and why are high vowels devoiced in Parisian French. In J. Ohala, Y. Hasegawa, M. Ohala, D. Glanville, & A. Bailey (Eds.), *Proceedings of the XIVth International Congress of Phonetic Sciences* (pp. 309–312). Berkeley, CA: University of California Press.

Fairclough, N. (1992). The appropriacy of 'appropriateness'. In N. Fairclough (Ed.), *Critical Language Awareness* (pp. 33–56). London: Longman.

Falsgraf, C. & Majors, D. (1995). Implicit culture in Japanese immersion classroom discourse. *Journal of the Association of Teachers of Japanese, 29*(2), 1–21.

Faragher, J. M. (2005). *A Great and Noble Scheme: The tragic story of the expulsion of the French Acadians from their American homeland.* New York, NY: Norton.

Farina, D. M. (1984). The morphological rule of learned backing and lexical phonology. *Studies in the Linguistic Sciences, 14*, 31–56.

Fauchet, C. (1581). *Recueil de l'origine de la langue et poésie françoise.* Paris: R. Estienne.

Felix, S. (1985). More evidence on competing cognitive systems. *Second Language Research, 1*, 47–72.

Finkbeiner, M. & Nicol, J. (2003). Semantic category effects in second language word learning. *Applied Psycholinguistics, 24*(3), 369–383.

Firth, A. & Wagner, J. (1997). On Discourse, communication and (some) fundamental concepts in SLA. *The Modern Language Journal, 81*(3), 277–300.

Fishman, J. A. (1972). *Language and Nationalism: Two integretative essays.* Rowley, MA: Newberry House.

Fishman, J. A. (1985). *The Rise and Fall of the Ethnic Revival: Perspectives on language and ethnicity.* New York, NY: Mouton.

Flege, J. (1987). The production of 'new' and 'similar' phones in a foreign language: Evidence for the effect of equivalence classification. *Journal of Phonetics, 15*, 47–65.

Flege, J. & Hillenbrand, J. (1987). Limits on phonetic accuracy in foreign language speech production. In G. Ioup & S. H. Weinberger (Eds.), *Interlanguage Phonology* (pp.176–203). Cambridge, MA: Newbury House.

Flowerdew, L. (2004). The problem-solution pattern in apprentice vs. professional technical writing: An application of appraisal theory. In G. Aston, S. Bernardini, & D. Stewart (Eds.), *Corpora and Language Learners* (pp. 125–135). Amsterdam: John Benjamins.

Foley, D. E. (1990). *Learning Deep in the Capitalist Heart of Tejas Culture.* Philadelphia, PA: University of Pennsylvania Press.

Fouché, P. (1959). *Traité de prononciation française.* Paris: Klincksieck.

Francard, M. (1990). *Ces Belges qui parlent français.* Louvain-la-Neuve: Université Catholique de Louvain.

Franceschina, F. (2001). Morphological or syntactic deficits in near-native speakers? An assessment of some current proposals. *Second Language Research, 17*, 213–247.

Franceschina, F. (2005). *Fossilized Second Language Grammars: The acquisition of grammatical gender.* Amsterdam: John Benjamins.

Freed, A. F. & Greenwood, A. (1996). Women, men, and type of talk: What makes the difference? *Language in Society, 25*, 1–26.

Freed, B., Segalowitz, N., & Dewey, D. (2004). Context of learning and second language fluency in French. *Studies in Second Language Acquisition, 26*, 275–301.

Frenck-Mestre, C. (2002). An on-line look at sentence processing in the second language. In R. R. Heredia & J. Altarriba (Eds.), *Bilingual Sentence Processing* (pp. 217–236). New York, NY: Elsevier.

Frenck-Mestre, C. & Pynte, J. (1997). Syntactic ambiguity resolution while reading in second and native languages. *Quarterly Journal of Experimental Psychology, 50*(A), 119–148.

Frendreis, J. & Tatalovich, R. (1997). Who supports English-only language laws? Evidence from the 1992 national election study. *Social Science Quarterly, 78*, 334–368.

Friedemann, M.-A. & Rizzi, L. (Eds.). (2000). *The Acquisition of Syntax.* Harlow: Longman.

Friederici, A. D., Garrett, M. F., & Jacobsen, T. (Eds.). (1999). Editorial and introduction to Part I of the special issue *Processing of Grammatical Gender. Journal of Psycholinguistic Research, 28*, 455–456.

Gadet, F. (1996). *Le français ordinaire* (2nd ed.). Paris: Armand Colin.

Gadet, F. (2003). La variation: Le français dans l'espace social, régional et international. In M. Yaguello (Ed.), *Le grand livre de la langue française* (pp. 91–152). Paris: Seuil.

Gaines, E. J. (1982). *The Autobiography of Miss Jane Pittman.* New York, NY: Bantam.

Garbédian, E. N. (2004). Le dépistage universel est-il envisageable en France ? Paper presented at the 8ème *Journée d'ORL et chirurgie cervico-faciale pédiatrique,* Faculté de médecine de Tours.

Gardette, P. (1983). Le franco-provençal, son histoire, ses origines. In B. Horiot, M.-R. Simoni, & G. Straka (Eds.), *Etudes de géographie linguistique* (pp. 569–584). Paris: Klincksieck.

Gardner, R. C. (1979). Social psychological aspects of second language acquisition. In H. Giles & R. St. Clair (Eds.), *Language and Social Psychology* (pp. 132–147). Oxford: Blackwell.

Gardner, R. C. (1983). Learning another language: A true social psychological experiment. *Journal of Language and Social Psychology, 2,* 219–239.

Gardner, R. C. (1985). *Social Psychology and Second Language Learning.* London: Edward Arnold.

Gardner, R. C. (1990). Attitudes, motivation, and personality as predictors of success in foreign language learning. In T. S. Parry & C. W. Stansfield (Eds.), *Language Aptitude Reconsidered* (pp. 179–221). Englewood Cliffs, NJ: Prentice-Hall.

Gardner, R. C., Day, B., & MacIntyre, P. D. (1992). Integrative motivation, induced anxiety, and language learning in a controlled environment. *Studies in Second Language Acquisition, 14,* 197–214.

Gardner, R. C., Lalonde, R. N., & Moorcroft, R. (1985). The role of attitudes and motivation in second language learning: Correlational and experimental considerations. *Language Learning, 35,* 207–227.

Gardner, R. C. & Lambert, W. (1959). Motivational variables in second language acquisition. *Canadian Journal of Psychology, 13,* 266–272.

Gardner, R. C. & Lambert, E. (1972). *Attitudes and Motivation in Second Language Learning.* Rowley, MA: Newbury House.

Gardner, R. C. & MacIntyre, P. D. (1991). An instrumental motivation in language study: Who says it isn't effective? *Studies in Second Language Acquisition, 13,* 57–72.

Gardner, R. C. & Smythe, P. C. (1975). *Second language acquisition: A social psychological approach.* Research Bulletin No. 332. London, Ontario: Department of Psychology, University of Western Ontario.

Gardner, R. C., Smythe, P. C., Clément, R., & Gliksman, L. (1976). Second language learning: A social psychological perspective. *Canadian Modern Language Review, 32,* 198–213.

Gardner, R. C., Smythe, P. C., & Lalonde, R. N. (1984). *The nature and replicability of factors in second language acquisition.* Research Bulletin No. 605. London, Ontario: Department of Psychology, University of Western Ontario.

Garside, R., Leech, G., & McEnery, T. (Eds.). (1997). *Corpus Annotation: Linguistic information from computer text corpora.* London: Longman.

Garvin, P. L. & Mathiot, M. (1968). The urbanization of the Guaraní language: A problem in language and culture. In J. A. Fishman (Ed.), *Readings in the Sociology of Language* (pp. 365–374). The Hague: Mouton.

Gascoigne, C. (2003). A catalogue of corrective moves in French conversation. *The French Review, 77,* 72–83.

Gaskell, M. G., Spinelli, E., & Meunier, F. (2002). Perception of resyllabification in French. *Memory and Cognition, 30*(5), 798–810.

Gass, S., Bardovi-Harlig, K., Magnan, S. S., & Walz, J. (Eds.). (2002). *Pedagogical Norms for Second and Foreign Language Learning and Teaching: Studies in honor of Albert Valdman.* Amsterdam: John Benjamins.

Gates, H. L. (1996). *The Future of the Race.* New York, NY: Knopf.

Gaustad, M. G. (2000). Morphographic analysis as a word identification strategy for deaf readers. *Journal of Deaf Studies and Deaf Education, 5,* 60–80.

Gauthier, P. & Lavoie, T. (1995). *Français de France et Français du Canada.* Lyon: Université Lyon III.

Gazier, A. (1880). *Lettres à Grégoire sur les patois de la France (1790–1794).* Paris: Durand.

Gee, J. P. (1990). *Social Linguistics and Literacies: Ideology in discourse.* London: Falmer Press.

Gendron, J.-D. (1966). *Tendances phonétiques du français parlé au Canada*. Québec: Presses de l'Université Laval.

Genesee, F. (1987). *Learning Through Two Languages: Studies of immersion and bilingual education*. New York, NY: Newbury House.

Genesee, F. (1998). A case study of multilingual education in Canada. In J. Cenoz & F. Genesee (Eds.), *Beyond Bilingualism: Multilingualism and multilingual education* (pp. 243–258). Clevedon: Multilingual Matters.

Gerbner, G. (1969). Toward cultural indicators: Analysis of mass mediated public message systems. *AV Communication Review, 17*, 137–148.

Gess, R. & Herschensohn, J. (2001). Shifting the DP parameter: A study of anglophone French L2ers. In C. R. Wiltshire & J. Camps (Eds.), *Romance Syntax, Semantics and their L2 Acquisition* (pp. 105–119). Amsterdam: John Benjamins.

Giles, H., Bourhis, R. Y., & Taylor, D. (1977). Towards a theory of language in ethnic group relations. In H. Giles (Ed.), *Language, Ethnicity and Intergroup Relations* (pp. 307–348). London: Academic Press.

Gilliéron, J. & Edmont, E. (1904–1911). *Atlas linguistique de la France*. Paris: Champion.

Giroux, H. A. (1981). *Ideology, Culture, and the Process of Schooling*. Philadelphia, PA: Temple University Press.

Gliksman, L., Gardner, R. C., & Smythe, P. C. (1982). The role of the integrative motive on students' participation in the French classroom. *Canadian Modern Language Review, 38*, 625–647.

Golato, A. (2003). Studying compliment responses: A comparison of DCTs and recordings of naturally occurring talk. *Applied Linguistics, 24*, 90–121.

Golato, P. S. (1998). Speech segmentation strategies of adult bilingual speakers of French and English: A second look at the limits of bilingualism. PhD dissertation, University of Texas, Austin.

Goldberg, L. R. (1993). The structure of phenotypic personality traits. *American Psychologist, 48*, 26–34.

Goldberg, E. & Noels, K. A. (2006). Motivation, ethnic identity and post-secondary education choices of graduates of intensive French language high school programs. *Canadian Modern Language Review, 62*, 423–447.

Goldin-Meadow, S. & Butcher, C. (2003). Pointing toward two-word speech in young children. In S. Kita (Ed.), *Pointing: Where language, culture, and cognition meet* (pp. 85–108). Mahwah, NJ: Lawrence Erlbaum.

Goodman, M. (1985). Review of Bickerton (1981). *International Journal of American Linguistics, 51*, 109–137.

Gossen, C.-T. (1967). *Französische Skriptastudien*. Vienna: Österreichische Akademie der Wissenschaften.

Gougenheim, G. (1935). *Eléments de phonologie française*. Paris: Les Belles Lettres.

Gougenheim, G. (1967). *L'élaboration du français fondamental (1er degré)*. Paris: Didier.

Grabe, W. (Ed.). (2000). Applied linguistics as an emerging discipline. *Annual Review of Applied Linguistics, 2*.

Gradol, D. & Swann, J. (1989). *Gender Voices*. Cambridge: Blackwell.

Granfeldt, J. (2000). The acquisition of DP in bilingual and second language French. *Bilingualism, 3*, 263–280.

Granfeldt, J. (2005). The development of gender attribution and gender agreement in French: A comparison of bilingual first and second language learners. In J.-M. Dewaele (Ed.), *Focus on French as a Foreign Language* (pp. 164–190). Clevedon: Multilingual Matters.

Granfeldt, J. & Schlyter, S. (2004). Cliticisation in the acquisition of French as L1 and L2. In P. Prévost & J. Paradis (Eds.), *The Acquisition of French in Different Contexts* (pp. 333–370). Amsterdam: John Benjamins.

Granger, S. (1998). *Learner English on Computer*. London: Addison Wesley Longman.

Granger, S. (2002). A bird's eye view of learner corpus research. In S. Granger, J. Hung, & S. Petch-Tyson (Eds.), *Computer Learner Corpora, Second Language Acquisition and Foreign Language Teaching* (pp. 3–33). Amsterdam: John Benjamins.

Granger, S., Dagneaux, E., & Meunier, F. (2002). *The International Corpus of Learner English. Handbook and CD-ROM.* Louvain-la-Neuve: Presses Universitaires de Louvain.

Granger, S., Hung, J., & Petch-Tyson, S. (2002). *Computer Learner Corpora, Second Language Acquisition and Foreign Language Teaching.* Amsterdam: John Benjamins.

Granger, S. & Rayson, P. (1998). Automatic lexical profiling of learner texts. In S. Granger (Ed.), *Learner English on Computer* (pp. 119–131). London: Addison Wesley Longman.

Granger, S., Vandeventer, A. & Hamel, M.-J. (2001). Analyse de corpus d'apprenants pour l'ELAO basé sur le TAL. *Traitement automatique des langues, 42,* 609–621.

Greenberg, J. H. (1978). How does a language acquire gender markers? In J. H. Greenberg, C. A. Ferguson, & E. A. Moravcsik (Eds.), *Universals of Human Language III: Word structure* (pp. 47–82). Stanford, CA: Stanford University Press.

Grégoire, A. (1937). *L'apprentissage du langage,* Vol. 1. *Les deux premières années.* Paris: Droz.

Grégoire, A. (1947). *L'apprentissage du langage,* Vol. 2. *La troisième année et les années suivantes.* Paris: Droz.

Grevisse, M. (1980 [1936]). *Le bon usage* (11th ed.). Gembloux: Duculot.

Grice, H. P. (1975). Logic and conversation. In P. Cole & J. Morgan (Eds.), *Speech Acts: Syntax and semantics,* Vol. 3 (pp. 41–58). New York, NY: Academic Press.

Grillo, R. (1989). *Dominant Languages: Language and hierarchy in Britain and France.* Cambridge: CUP.

Grimshaw, J. (1990). *Argument Structure.* Cambridge, MA: The MIT Press.

Groce, N. E. (1985). *Everyone Here Spoke Sign Language: Hereditary deafness on Martha's Vineyard.* Cambridge, MA: Harvard University Press.

Grondin, N. & White, L. (1993). Functional categories in child L2 acquisition of French. *McGill Working Papers in Linguistics, 9,* 121–145.

Grosjean, F. (1996). Living with two languages and two cultures. In I. Paradis (Ed.), *Cultural and Language Diversity and the Deaf Experience* (pp. 20–37). Cambridge: CUP.

Grosu, A. & Landman, F. (1998). Strange relatives of the third kind. *Natural Language Semantics, 6,* 125–170.

Guilbault, C. P. G. (2002). The acquisition of French rhythm by English second language learners. PhD dissertation, University of Alberta, Canada.

Guilbert, L. (1965). *La formation du vocabulaire de l'aviation.* Paris: Larousse.

Guilbert, L. (1967). *Le vocabulaire de l'astronautique.* Paris: Larousse.

Guilbert, L. (1975). *La créativité lexicale.* Paris: Larousse.

Guilford, J. (1999). L'attribution du genre aux emprunts à l'anglais. *La Linguistique, 35,* 65–85.

Guillelmon, D. & Grosjean, F. (2001). The gender marking effect in spoken word recognition: The case of bilinguals. *Memory and Cognition, 29,* 503–511.

Guimond, S. & Tougas, F. (1994). Sentiments d'injustice et actions collectives: La privation relative. In R. Y. Bourhis & J. P. Leyens (Eds.), *Stéréotypes, discrimination et relations intergroupes* (pp. 201–231). Liège: Mardaga.

Guiraud, P. (1956). *L'argot* [Que Sais-Je?]. Paris: Presses Universitaires de France.

Guiraud, P. (1966). *Le moyen français* [Que Sais-Je?]. Paris: Presses Universitaires de France.

Guiraud, P. (1968). *Le jargon de Villon ou le gai savoir de la coquille.* Paris: Gallimard.

Hackman, D. J. (1977). Patterns in purported speech acts. *Journal of Pragmatics, 1,* 143–154.

Haj-Broussard, M. (2003). Language, identity and the achievement gap: Comparing experiences of African-American students in a French immersion and a regular education context. PhD dissertation, Louisiana State University, Baton Rouge.

Hale, K. (1996). Can UG and L1 be distinguished in L2 acquisition? *Behavioral and Brain Sciences, 19,* 728–730.

Hall, G. M. (1992). *Africans in Colonial Louisiana: The development of Afro-Creole culture in the eighteenth century.* Baton Rouge, LA: Louisiana State University Press.

Hall, J. K. (1998). Differential teacher attention to student utterances: The construction of different opportunities for learning in the IRF. *Linguistics and Education, 9,* 287–311.

Hall, R. A. (1966). *Pidgin and Creole Languages.* Ithaca, NY: Cornell University Press.

Halle, M. & Marantz, A. (1993). Distributed morphology and the pieces of inflection. In K. Hale & S. J. Keyser (Eds.), *The View from Building, 20* (pp. 111–176). Cambridge, MA: The MIT Press.

Hamers, J. F. & Blanc, M. (1988). *Bilinguality and Bilingualism.* Cambridge: CUP.

Hamann, C., Rizzi, L., & Frauenfelder, U. (1996). The acquisition of subject and object clitics in French. In H. Clahsen (Ed.), *Generative Perspectives on Language Acquisition* (pp. 251–260). Amsterdam: John Benjamins.

Hammerly, H. (1989). French immersion (Does it work?) and the development of Bilingual Proficiency Report. *Canadian Modern Language Review, 45,* 567–578.

Hannahs, S. J. (1995a). The phonological word in French. *Linguistics, 33,* 1125–1144.

Hannahs, S. J. (1995b). *Prosodic Structure and French Morphophonology* [Linguistische Arbeiten 337]. Tübingen: Max Niemeyer.

Hannahs, S. J. & Young-Scholten, M. (Eds.). (1998). *Focus on Phonological Acquisition.* Amsterdam: John Benjamins.

Hansen, A. B. (1994). Etude du E caduc – stabilisation en cours et variations lexicales. *Journal of French Studies, 4,* 25–54.

Hardison, D. (1992). Acquisition of grammatical gender in French: L2 Learner accuracy and strategies. *Canadian Modern Language Review, 48*(2), 292–306.

Harley, B. (1979). French gender 'rules' in the speech of English-dominant, French-dominant and monolingual French-speaking children. *Working Papers in Bilingualism, 19,* 129–156.

Harley, B. (1992). Aspects of the oral second language proficiency of early immersion, late immersion, and extended French students at grade 10. In R. J. Courchêne, J. I. Glidden, J. St. John, & C. Thérien (Eds.), *Comprehension-Based Second Language Teaching* (pp. 371–388). Ottawa: Ottawa University Press.

Harley, B. (1998). The role of form-focused tasks in promoting child L2 acquisition. In C. Doughty & J. Williams (Eds.), *Focus on Form in Classroom Second Language Acquisition* (pp. 156–174). New York, NY: CUP.

Harley, B., Cummins, J., Swain, M., & Allen, P. (1990). The nature of language proficiency. In B. Harley, P. Allen, J. Cummins, & M. Swain (Eds.), *The Development of Second Language Proficiency* (pp. 7–25). Cambridge: CUP.

Harley, B., Allen, P., Cummins, J., & Swain, M. (Eds.). (1990). *The Development of Second Language Proficiency.* Cambridge: CUP.

Harley, H. & Ritter, E. (2002). Structuring the bundle: A universal morphosyntactic feature geometry. In H. J. Simon & H. Wiese (Eds.), *Pronouns – Grammar and Representation* (pp. 23–40). Amsterdam: John Benjamins.

Harris, J. (1983). *Syllable Structure and Stress in Spanish: A nonlinear analysis* [Linguistic Inquiry Monograph 8]. Cambridge, MA: The MIT Press.

Harris, J. (1991). The exponence of gender in Spanish. *Linguistic Inquiry, 22,* 27–62.

Harris, M. (1978). *The Evolution of French Syntax.* London: Longman.

Harris, R. (1980). *The Language-Makers.* Ithaca, NY: Cornell University Press.

Hartford, B. S. & Bardovi-Harlig, K. (1992). Experimental and observational data in the study of interlanguage pragmatics. In L. F. Bouton & Y. Kachru (Eds.), *Pragmatics and Language Learning* [Monograph series 3] (pp. 33–52). Urbana-Champaign, IL: University of Illinois at Urbana-Champaign, Division of English as an International Language.

Harwood, J., Giles, H., & Bourhis, R. Y. (1994). The genesis of vitality theory: Historical patterns and discoursal dimensions. *International Journal of the Sociology of Language, 10,* 167–206.

Hasan, R. (1996). The ontogenesis of ideology: An interpretation of mother child talk. In C. Cloran, D. Butt, & G. Williams (Eds.), *Ways of Saying, Ways of Meaning: Selected papers of Ruqaiya Hasan* (pp. 133–151). London: Cassell.

Hasselgren, A. (2002). Learner corpora and language testing: Smallwords as markers of learner fluency. In S. Granger, J. Hung, & S. Petch-Tyson (Eds.), *Computer Learner Corpora, Second Language Acquisition and Foreign Language Teaching* (pp. 143–173). Amsterdam: John Benjamins.

Haugen, E. (1959). Language planning in modern Norway. *Anthropological Linguistics, 1*, 8–21.

Haugen, E. (1972 [1966]). Dialect, Language, Nation. In A. S. Dil (Ed.), *The Ecology of Language: Essays by Einar Haugen* (pp. 237–254). Stanford, CA: Stanford University Press.

Hausmann, F.-J. (1979). Wie alt ist das gesprochene Französisch? *Romanische Forschungen, 91*, 431–444.

Hawkins, R. (1998a). The inaccessibility of formal features of functional categories in second language acquisition. Paper presented at the Pacific Second Language Research Forum, Tokyo.

Hawkins, R. (1998b). Explaining the difficulty of French gender attribution for speakers of English. Paper presented at the 8th annual EUROSLA Conference, Paris.

Hawkins, R. (2001). *Second Language Syntax: A generative introduction*. Cambridge: Blackwell.

Hawkins, R. (2004). The contribution of the theory of universal grammar to our understanding of the acquisition of French as a second language. *Journal of French Language Studies, 14*, 257–280.

Hawkins, R. & Chan, C. Y. (1997). The partial availability of Universal Grammar in second language acquisition: The 'failed functional features hypothesis'. *Second Language Research, 13*, 187–226.

Hawkins, R. & Franceschina, F. (2004). Explaining the acquisition and non-acquisition of determiner-noun gender concord in French and Spanish. In P. Prévost & J. Paradis (Eds.), *The Acquisition of French in Different Contexts* (pp. 175–206). Amsterdam: John Benjamins.

Hawkins, R. & Towell, R. (1992). Second language acquisition research and the second language acquisition of French. *Journal of French Language Studies, 2*, 97–121.

Hawkins, R., Towell, R., & Bazergui, N. (1993). Universal Grammar and the acquisition of French verb movement by native speakers of English. *Second Language Research, 9*, 189–233.

Hay, J. & Baayen, H. (2003). Parsing and productivity. In G. Booij & J. van Marle (Eds.), *Yearbook of Morphology 2002* (pp. 203–235). Dordrecht: Kluwer.

Haynes, M. (1993). Patterns and perils of guessing in second language reading. In T. Huckin, M. Haynes, & J. Coady (Eds.), *Second Language Reading and Vocabulary Learning* (pp. 46–64). Norwood, NJ: Ablex.

Haznedar, B. (2001). The acquisition of the IP system in child L2 English. *Studies in Second Language Acquisition, 23*, 1–39.

Haznedar, B. (2003). The status of functional categories in child second language acquisition: Evidence from the acquisition of CP. *Second Language Research, 19*, 1–41.

Haznedar, B. & Schwartz, B. D. (1997). Are there optional infinitives in child L2 acquisition? In E. Hughes, M. Hughes, & A. Greenhill (Eds.), *Proceedings of the 21st Annual Boston University Conference on Language Development* (pp. 257–268). Somerville, MA: Cascadilla.

Hécaen, H. (1968). L'aphasie. In A. Martinet (Ed.), *Le langage* (pp. 85–89). Paris: Gallimard.

Hedgcock, J. & Lefkowitz, N. (2000). Overt and covert prestige in the French language classroom: When is it good to sound bad? *Applied Language Learning, 11*, 75–97.

Held, G. (1995). *Verbale Höflichkeit. Studien zur linguistischen Theorienbildung und empirische Untersuchung zum Sprachverhalten französischer und italienischer Jugendlicher in Bitt- und Dankessituationen*. Tübingen: Narr.

Heller, M. (1999). *Linguistic Minorities and Modernity: A sociolinguistic ethnography*. London: Longman.

Heller, M. (2002). Globalization and the commodification of bilingualism in Canada. In D. Block & D. Cameron (Eds.), *Globalization and Language Teaching* (pp. 47–63). London: Routledge.

Henry, J. M. & Bankston, C. L. (2002). *Blue Collar Bayou: Louisiana Cajuns in the new economy of ethnicity*. Westport, CT: Praeger.

Henry, J. M. & Bankston, C. L. (1998). Propositions for a structuralist analysis of Creolism. *Current Anthropology, 39*(4), 558–566.

Herman, J. (1991). Spoken and written Latin in the last centuries of the Roman Empire. A contribution to the linguistic history of the western provinces. In R. Wright (Ed.), *Latin and the Romance Languages in the Early Middle Ages* (pp. 29–43). London: Routledge.

Herman, J. (2000). *Vulgar Latin* (translated from the French by R. Wright). University Park, PA: Pennsylvania State University Press.

Herschensohn, J. (2000). *The Second Time Around: Minimalism and L2 acquisition*. Amsterdam: John Benjamins.

Herschensohn, J. (2001). Missing inflection in L2 French: Accidental infinitives and other verbal deficits. *Second Language Research, 17*, 273–305.

Herschensohn, J. (2003). Verbs and rules: Two profiles of French morphology acquisition. *Journal of French Language Studies, 13*, 23–45.

Herschensohn, J. (2004). Functional categories and the acquisition of object clitics in L2 French. In P. Prévost & J. Paradis (Eds.), *The Acquisition of French in Different Contexts* (pp. 207–242). Amsterdam: John Benjamins.

Herschensohn, J. (2006). Français langue seconde: From functional categories to functionalist variation. *Second Language Research, 22*, 95–113.

Higgins, E. T. (1998). Promotion and prevention: Regulatory focus as a motivational principle. *Advances in Experimental Social Psychology, 30*, 1–46.

Hill, A. B. (1975). Extraversion and variety-seeking in a monotonous task. *British Journal of Psychology, 66*, 9–13.

Hill, T. (1997). The development of pragmatic competence in an EFL context. PhD dissertation, Temple University, Philadelphia.

Hoffman-Hicks, S. D. (1999). The longitudinal development of French foreign language pragmatic competence: Evidence from study abroad participants. PhD dissertation, Indiana University, Bloomington.

Hoffmeister, R. J. (2000). A piece of the puzzle: ASL and reading comprehension in deaf children. In C. Chamberlain, J. P. Morford, & R. I. Mayberry (Eds.), *Language Acquisition by Eye* (pp. 143–163). Mahwah, NJ: Lawrence Erlbaum.

Hölker, K. (1988). *Zur Analyse von Markern. Korrektur- und Schlußmarker des Französischen*. Stuttgart: Franz Steiner Verlag Wiesbaden.

Holm, J. (2000). *An Introduction to Pidgins and Creoles*. Cambridge: CUP.

Holm, J. (2004). *Languages in Contact: The partial restructuring of vernaculars*. Cambridge: CUP.

Holmes, V. M. & Dejean de la Bâtie, B. (1999). Assignment of grammatical gender by native speakers and foreign learners of French. *Applied Psycholinguistics, 20*(4), 479–506.

Holmes, J. & Guerra Ramos, R. (1993). False friends and reckless guessers: Observing cognate recognition strategies. In T. Huckin, M. Haynes, & J. Coady (Eds.), *Second Language Reading and Vocabulary Learning* (pp. 86–108). Norwood, NJ: Ablex.

Holowka, S., Brosseau-Lapré, F., & Petitto, L. A. (2002). Semantic and conceptual knowledge underlying bilingual babies' first signs and words. *Language Learning, 55*(2), 205–262.

Holtus, G., Metzeltin, M., & Schmitt, C. (1988). *Lexikon de Romanistischen Linguistik* (6 Vols.). Tübingen: Niemeyer.

Hope, T. E. (1971). *Lexical Borrowing in the Romance Languages*. Oxford: Blackwell.

Horwitz, E. K., Horwitz, M. B., & Cope, J. A. (1986). Foreign language classroom anxiety. *The Modern Language Journal, 70*, 125–132.

House, J. (1993). Toward a model for the analysis of inappropriate responses in native/nonnative interactions. In G. Kasper & S. Blum-Kulka (Eds.), *Interlanguage Pragmatics* (pp. 161–195). Oxford: OUP.

House, J. (1996). Developing pragmatic fluency in English as a foreign language. Routines and metapragmatic awareness. *Studies in Second Language Acquisition, 18*, 225–252.

House, J. (1997). Kommunikative Bewußtheit und Fremdsprachenlernen. *Fremdsprachen Lehren und Lernen, 26*, 68–87.

House, J. & Kasper, G. (2000). How to remain a non-native speaker. In C. Riemer (Ed.), *Kognitive Aspekte des Lehrens und Lernens von Fremdsprachen. Festschrift für Willis J. Edmondson zum 60. Geburtstag* (pp. 101–118). Tübingen: Narr.

Housen, A. (2002). A corpus-based study of the L2 acquisition of the English verb system. In S. Granger, J. Hung, & S. Petch-Tyson (Eds.), *Computer Learner Corpora, Second Language Acquisition and Foreign Language Learning* (pp. 77–116). Amsterdam: John Benjamins.

Howard, M. (2001). The effects of study abroad on the L2 learner's structural skills. Evidence from advanced learners of French. In S. Foster-Cohen & A. Nizegorodcew (Eds.), *EUROSLA Yearbook 1* (pp. 123–142). Amsterdam: John Benjamins.

Howard, M. (2002a). Prototypical and non-prototypical marking in the advanced learner's aspectuo-temporal system. In S. Foster-Cohen, T. Ruthenberg, & M.-L. Poschen (Eds.), *EUROSLA Yearbook 2* (pp. 87–113). Amsterdam: John Benjamins.

Howard, M. (2002b). Les interrelations entre les facteurs contextuels et l'emploi des temps du passé. Une étude d'apprenants avancés du français. *Revue française de linguistique appliquée, 7*(2), 31–42.

Howard, M. (2004a). On the interactional effect of linguistic constraints on L2 variation. The case of past time marking. *International Review of Applied Linguistics, 42*, 321–336.

Howard, M. (2004b). Variation and second language acquisition: A preliminary study of advanced learners of French. *SKY Journal of Linguistics, 17*, 143–165.

Howard, M. (2005a). The emergence and use of the *plus-que-parfait* in advanced French interlanguage. In J.-M. Dewaele (Ed.), *Focus on French as a Foreign Language: Multidisciplinary perspectives* (pp. 63–87). Clevedon: Multilingual Matters.

Howard, M. (2005b). L'acquisition de la liaison en français langue seconde. Une analyse quantitative d'apprenants avancés en milieu guidé naturel. *Corela – cognition, représentation, langage 3*, http://edel. univ-poitiers.fr/corela

Howard, M. (2005c). L'emploi de l'imparfait par l'apprenant de français. In E. Labeau & P. Larrivée (Eds.), *Nouveaux développements de l'imparfait*, Special issue of *Cahiers Chronos, 14*, 175–197.

Howard, M. (2005d). On the role of context in the development of learner language: Insights from the study abroad research. *ITL Review of Applied Linguistics, 148*, 1–20.

Howard, M., Lemée, I., & Regan, V. (2006). The L2 acquisition of a phonological variable: The case of /l/ deletion in French. *Journal of French Language Studies, 16*(1), 1–24.

Hu, G. (2002). Potential cultural resistance to pedagogical imports: The case of communicative language teaching in China. *Language, Culture and Curriculum, 15*(2), 93–105.

Hulk, A. (1991). Parameter setting and the acquisition of word order in L2 French. *Second Language Research, 7*, 1–34.

Hulk, A. & Tellier, C. (1998). Conflictual agreement in Romance nominals. In J.-M. Authier, B. E. Bullock, & L. A. Reed (Eds.), *Formal Perspectives on Romance, Linguistics* (pp. 179–195). Amsterdam: John Benjamins.

Hulk, A. & Tellier, C. (2000). Mismatches: Agreement in qualitative constructions. *Probus, 12*, 33–65.

Hull, A. (1988). The first person plural form: *Je parlons. French Review, 62*, 242–247.

Hulstijn, J. H. (1997). Second-language acquisition research in the laboratory: Possibilities and limitations. *Studies in Second Language Acquisition, 19*, 131–143.

Hunnius, K. (1975). Archaische Züge des langage populaire. *Zeitschrift für Französische Sprache und Literatur, 85*, 145–161.

Hunston, S. (2002). *Corpora in Applied Linguistics*. Cambridge: CUP.

Hymes, D. (Ed.). (1971). *Pidginization and creolization of languages: Proceedings of a conference held at the University of the West Indies, Mona, Jamaica, April 1968.* Cambridge: CUP.

Hymes, D. H. (1972). On communicative competence. In J. B. Pride & J. Holmes (Eds.), *Sociolinguistics* (pp. 269–293). Harmondsworth: Penguin.

Hymes, D. H. (1974). *Foundations of Sociolinguistics: An ethnographic approach.* Philadelphia, PA: University of Pennsylvania Press.

Hymes, D. H. (1992). The concept of communicative competence revisited. In M. Pütz (Ed.), *Thirty Years of Linguistic Evolution* (pp. 31–58). Amsterdam: John Benjamins.

Insee. (1999). *Enquête familiale.* Paris: Insee-Ined.

Irmen, L. & Rossberg, N. (2004). Gender markedness of language. The impact of grammatical and nonlinguistic information on the mental representation of person information. *Journal of Language and Social Psychology, 23*(3), 272–307.

Irvine, J. T. & Gal, S. (2000). Language ideology and linguistic differentiation. In P. V. Kroskrity (Ed.), *Regimes of Language: Ideologies, polities, and identities* (pp. 35–83). Santa Fe, NM: School of American Research Press.

Jacq, G. & Tuller, L. (1999). Spécificités morphosyntaxiques du français de l'enfant sourd: Une étude comparative. *Glossa, 69*, 4–14.

Jaffe, A. (1999). *Ideologies in Action: Language Politics on Corsica*. Berlin: Mouton de Gruyter.

Jagtman, M. & Bongaerts, T. (1994). Report – COMOLA: A computer system for the analysis of interlanguage data. *Second Language Research, 10*(1), 49–83.

Jakubowicz, C. & Faussart, C. (1998). Gender agreement in the processing of spoken French. *Journal of Psycholinguistic Research, 27*, 597–617.

Jakubowicz, C., Nash, L., Rigaut, C., & Gérard, C. L. (1998). Determiners and clitic pronouns in French-speaking children with SLI. *Language Acquisition, 7*, 113–160.

Jakubowicz, C., Tuller, L., & Rigaut, C. (2000). Phonologically weak items in abnormal acquisition of French. In S. C. Howell, S. A. Fish, & T. Keith-Lucas (Eds.), *Proceedings of the 24th Annual Boston University Conference on Language Development* (pp. 450–461). Somerville, MA: Cascadilla.

Jaworski, A. (1994). Pragmatic failure in a second language: Greeting responses in English by Polish students. *International Review of Applied Linguistics in Language Teaching, 32*, 41–55.

Jeffrey, B. (2002). Performativity and primary teacher relations. *Journal of Education Policy, 17*(5), 531–546.

Jochnowitz, G. (1973). *Dialect Boundaries and the Question of Franco-Provençal*. The Hague: Mouton.

Johnson, J. S. & Newport, E. L. (1989). Critical period effects in second language learning: The influence of maturational state on the acquisition of English as a second language. *Cognitive Psychology, 21*, 60–99.

Johnson, W. (1987). Lexical levels in French phonology. *Linguistics, 25*, 889–913.

Johnston, T. (2002). BSL, Auslan and NZSL: Three signed languages or one? In A. Baker, B. van den Bogaerde, & O. Crasborn (Eds.), *Cross-linguistic Perspectives in Sign Language Research: Selected papers from TISLR 2000* (pp. 47–69). Hamburg: Signum Verlag.

Johnstone, B. (1996). *The Linguistic Individual: Self-expression in language and linguistics*. New York, NY: OUP.

Joseph, J. E. (1987). *Eloquence and Power*. London: Francis Cairns.

Joseph, J. E. (1988). New French: A pedagogical crisis in the making. *The Modern Language Journal, 72*(1), 31–36.

Joseph, J. E. (2004). *Language and Identity: National, ethnic, religious*. New York, NY: Palgrave.

Juffs, A. (1996). Semantics-syntax correspondences in second language acquisition. *Second Language Research, 12*, 177–221.

Julia, D. & Revel, J. (2002). Postface. In M. de Certeau, D. Julia, & J. Revel (Eds.), *Une politique de la langue. La révolution française et les patois: L'enquête de Grégoire* (pp. 413–441). Paris: Gallimard.

Kager, R. (1999). *Optimality Theory*. Cambridge: CUP.

Kail, M. (2004). On-line grammaticality judgments in French children and adults: A crosslinguistic perspective. *Journal of Child Language, 31*, 713–737.

Kanagy, R. (1999). Interactional routines as a mechanism for L2 acquisition and socialization in an immersion context. *Journal of Pragmatics, 31*, 1467–1492.

Kanagy, R. & Igarashi, K. (1997). Acquisition of pragmatic competence in a Japanese immersion kindergarten. In L. F. Bouton (Ed.), *Pragmatics and Language Learning* [Monograph series 8] (pp. 243–265). Urbana- Champaign, IL: University of Illinois at Urbana-Champaign, Division of English as an International Language.

Kangni, A.-E. (1989). *La syntaxe du Gɛ. Etude syntaxique d'un parler Gbe (Ewe): Le Gɛdu Sud-Togo*. Frankfurt: Peter Lang.

Kaplan, R. B. (Ed.). (2002). *The Oxford Handbook of Applied Linguistics*. Oxford: OUP.

Karmiloff-Smith, A. (1979). *A Functional Approach to Child Language: A study of determiners and reference.* Cambridge: CUP.

Karmiloff-Smith, A. (1986). Some fundamental aspects of language development after age 5. In P. Fletcher & M. Garman (Eds.), *Language Acquisition* (pp. 307–323). Cambridge: CUP.

Kasper, G. (1981). *Pragmatische Aspekte in der Interimsprache. Eine untersuchung des Englischen fortgeschrittener deutscher Lerner.* Tübingen: Narr.

Kasper, G. (1984). Pragmatic comprehension in learner-native speaker discourse. *Language Learning, 34,* 1–20.

Kasper, G. (1986). Discourse regulation in interlanguage communication. In A. Trosborg (Ed.), *Communicative Competence in Foreign Language Learning and Teaching* (pp. 64–84). Aarhus: Aarhus University Press.

Kasper, G. (1992). Pragmatic transfer. *Second Language Research, 8*(3), 203–231.

Kasper, G. (1993). Interkulturelle Pragmatik und Fremdsprachenlernen. In J.-P. Timm & H. J. Vollmer (Eds.), *Kontroversen in der Fremdsprachenforschung* (pp. 41–77). Bochum: Brockmeyer.

Kasper, G. (1997). Can pragmatic competence be taught? Honolulu, University of Hawai'i at Manoa, Second Language Teaching and Curriculum Center. Retrieved [9.8.2005] from: http://www.nflrc.hawaii.edu/NetWorks/NW06/

Kasper, G. (1998a). Interlanguage pragmatics. In H. Byrnes (Ed.), *Learning Foreign and Second Languages. Perspectives in research and scholarship* (pp. 183–208). New York, NY: Modern Language Association of America.

Kasper, G. (1998b). Datenerhebungsverfahren in der Lernersprachenpragmatik. *Zeitschrift für Fremdsprachenforschung, 9*(1), 85–118.

Kasper, G. (2000). Data collection in pragmatics research. In H. Spencer-Oatey (Ed.), *Culturally Speaking. Managing rapport through talk across cultures* (pp. 316–341). London: Continuum Press.

Kasper, G. (2001a). Classroom research on interlanguage pragmatics. In K. R. Rose & G. Kasper (Eds.), *Pragmatics in Language Teaching* (pp. 33–60). Cambridge: CUP.

Kasper, G. (2001b). Four perspectives on L2 pragmatic development. *Applied Linguistics, 22*(4), 502–530.

Kasper, G. (2004). Speech acts in (inter)action: Repeated questions. *Intercultural Pragmatics, 1*(1), 125–133.

Kasper, G. & Blum-Kulka, S. (1993). Interlanguage pragmatics: An introduction. In G. Kasper & S. Blum-Kulka (Eds.), *Interlanguage Pragmatics* (pp. 3–17). Oxford: OUP.

Kasper, G. & Dahl, M. (1991). Research methods in interlanguage pragmatics. *Studies in Second Language Acquisition, 13,* 215–247.

Kasper, G. & Rose, K. R. (1999). Pragmatics and SLA. *Annual Review of Applied Linguistics, 19,* 81–104.

Kasper, G. & Rose, K. R. (2002). *Pragmatic Development in a Second Language.* Oxford: Blackwell.

Kasper, G. & Schmidt, R. W. (1996). Developmental issues in interlanguage pragmatics. *Studies in Second Language Acquisition, 18,* 149–169.

Katz, S. (2003). Near-native speakers in the foreign-language classroom: The case of Haitian immigrant students. In C. Blyth (Ed.), *The Sociolinguistics of Foreign-Language Classrooms: Contributions of the native, the near-native, and the non-native speaker* (pp. 131–160). Boston, MA: Heinle.

Kaye, J. D. & Lowenstamm, J. (1984). De la syllabicité. In F. Dell, D. Hirst, & J.-R. Vergnaud (Eds.), *Forme sonore du langage* (pp. 123–159). Paris: Hermann.

Kecskes, I. (1999). Situation-bound utterances from an interlanguage perspective. In J. Verschueren (Ed.), *Pragmatics in 1998. Selected papers from the 6th International Pragmatics Conference,* Vol. 2 (pp. 299–309). Antwerp: International Pragmatics Association.

Kecskes, I. (2003). *Situation-bound Utterances in L1 and L2.* Berlin: Mouton de Gruyter.

Kerbrat-Orecchioni, C. (2001). *Les actes de langage dans le discours. Théorie et fonctionnement.* Paris: Nathan.

Khomsi, A. (1990). *Epreuve d'évaluation de la compétence en lecture: Lecture de mots et compréhension.* Paris: Edition du Centre de Psychologie Appliquée.

Kim, Y. Y. (1988). *Communication and Cross-cultural Adaptation: An integrative theory.* Philadelphia, PA: Multilingual Matters.

Kimura Y., Nakata Y., & Okumuram, T. (2001). Language learning motivation of EFL learners in Japan: A cross-sectional analysis of various learning milieus. *JALT Journal, 23*, 47–68.

Kinginger, C. (2000). Learning the pragmatics of solidarity in the networked foreign language classroom. In J. K. Hall & L. S. Stoops Verplaetse (Eds.), *Second and Foreign Language through Classroom Interaction* (pp. 23–46). Mahwah, NJ: Lawrence Erlbaum.

Kinginger, C. (2002). Genres of power in language teacher education: Interpreting the experts. In S. J. Savignon (Ed.), *Interpreting Communicative Language Teaching: Contexts and concerns in teacher education* (pp. 193–207). New Haven, CT: Yale University Press.

Kinginger, C. (2004). Alice doesn't live here anymore: Foreign language learning and identity reconstruction. In A. Pavlenko & A. Blackledge (Eds.), *Negotiation of Identities in Multilingual Contexts* (pp. 219–242). Clevedon: Multilingual Matters.

Kinginger, C. & Belz, J. A. (2005). Socio-cultural perspectives on pragmatic development in foreign language learning: Microgenetic case studies from telecollaboration and residence abroad. *Intercultural Pragmatics, 2*(4), 369–421.

Kinginger, C. & Farrell, K. (2004). Assessing development of meta-pragmatic awareness in study abroad. *Frontiers: The interdisciplinary journal of study abroad, 10*, 19–42.

Kinginger, C. & Farrell, K. (2005). Gender and emotional investment in language learning during study abroad. *CALPER Working Papers Series, 2*, 1–12.

Klausenburger, J. (1978). French linking phenomena: A natural generative analysis. *Language, 54*(1), 21–40.

Klein, W. & Perdue, C. (1992). *Utterance Structure. Developing grammars again.* Amsterdam: John Benjamins.

Klein, W. & Perdue, C. (1997). The basic variety (or: Couldn't natural languages be much simpler?). *Second Language Research, 13*, 301–347.

Kleinmann, H. H. (1977). Avoidance behavior in adult second language acquisition. *Language Learning, 27*, 93–17.

Klima, E. & Bellugi, U. (1976). Poetry and song without sound. *Cognition, 4*, 45–97.

Kloss, H. (1967). 'Abstand' languages and 'Ausbau' languages. *Anthropological Linguistics, 9*(7), 29–41.

Knittel, M. L. (2005). Some remarks on adjective placement in the French NP. *Probus, 17*(2), 185–226.

Koch, P. & Oesterreicher, W. (1990). *Gesprochene Sprache in der Romania: Französisch, Italienisch, Spanisch.* Tübingen: Niemeyer.

Kocourek, R. (1992). *La langue française de la technique et de la science: Vers une linguistique de la langue savante.* Wiesbaden: Brandstetter.

Koeneman, O. & Neeleman, A. (2001). Predication, verb movement, and the distribution of expletives. *Lingua, 111*, 189–233.

Kohn, A. (2000). *The Case Against Standardized Testing: Raising the scores, ruining the schools.* Portsmouth, NH: Heinemann.

Koike, D. A. & Pearson, L. (2005). The effect of instruction and feedback in the development of pragmatic competence. *System, 33*(3), 481–501.

Koopman, H. (1986). The genesis of Haitian: Implications of a comparison of some features of the syntax of Haitian, French and West African languages. In P. Muysken & N. Smith (Eds.), *Substrata versus Universals in Creole Genesis* (pp. 231–258). Amsterdam: John Benjamins.

Kouadio, N'G. J. (1990). Le nouchi abidjanais, naissance d'un argot ou mode linguistique passagère? In E. Gouaini & N. Thiam (Eds.), *Des langues et des villes; actes du colloque international de Dakar* (pp. 373–383). Paris: Didier-Erudition.

Kouadio, N'G. J. (1999). Quelques traits morphosyntaxiques du français écrit en Côte d'Ivoire. In *Cahiers d'études et de recherches francophones, Langues, 2*(4), 301–314.

Koutsogiannis, D. & Mitsikopoulou, B. (2004). The Internet as a global discourse environment: A commentary on *Second Language Socialization in a Bilingual Chat Room* W.S.E. Lam & *Second Language Cyberhetoric: A study of Chinese L2 writers in an online usenetgGroup*, J. Bloch. *Language Learning & Technology, 8*(3), 83–89. Available at http://llt.msu.edu/vol8num3/koutsogiannis/

Koven, M. (1998). Two languages in the self/the self in two languages: French-Portuguese bilinguals' verbal enactments and experiences of self in narrative discourse. *Ethos, 26*, 410–455.

Koven, M. (2006). Feeling in two languages: A comparative analysis of a bilingual's affective displays in French and Portuguese. In A. Pavlenko (Ed.), *Bilingual Minds: Emotional experience, expression, and representation* (pp. 84–117). Clevedon: Multilingual Matters.

Kraft, B. & Geluykens, R. (2002). Complaining in French L1 and L2. A cross-linguistic investigation. In S. Foster-Cohen, T. Ruthenberg, & M.-L. Poschen (Eds.), *EUROSLA Yearbook 2* (pp. 227–242). Amsterdam: John Benjamins.

Kramsch, C. (1993). *Context and Culture in Language Teaching.* Oxford: OUP.

Kramsch, C. (1997). The privilege of the nonnative speaker. *PMLA, 112*, 359–369.

Kramsch, C. (1998). The privilege of the intercultural speaker. In M. Byram & M. Fleming (Eds.), *Language Learning in Intercultural Perspective: Approaches through drama and ethnography* (pp. 16–31). New York, NY: CUP.

Kramsch, C. (2000). Second language acquisition, applied linguistics, and the teaching of foreign languages. *The Modern Language Journal, 84*(3), 311–326.

Kramsch, C. & Thorne, S. L. (2002). Foreign language learning as global communicative practice. In D. Block & D. Cameron (Eds.), *Language Learning and Teaching in the Age of Globalization* (pp. 83–100). London: Routledge.

Krantz, G. (1991). *Learning Vocabulary in a Foreign Language: A study of reading strategies.* Göteborg: Acta Universitas Gothoburgensis.

Krausneker, V. (2003). Deaf second language learning in elementary school: Report from a sociolinguistic research study in the first bilingual class in Vienna, Austria. Paper presented at the European Days of Deaf *Education*, Orebro, Sweden, May 2003.

Kristol, A. M. (1989). Le début du rayonnement parisien et l'unité du français du moyen âge: Le témoignage des manuels d'enseignement du français écrits en Angleterre entre le XIIIe et le début du XVe siècle. *Revue de linguistique romane, 53*, 335–367.

Kuntze, M. (1998). Literacy and deaf children: The language question. *Topics in Language Disorders, 18*(4), 1–15.

Labeau, E. (2005). Beyond the aspect hypothesis: Tense-aspect development in advanced L2 French. In S. Foster-Cohen, M. del Pilar García-Mayo, & J. Cenoz (Eds.), *EUROSLA Yearbook 5* (pp. 77–101). Amsterdam: John Benjamins.

Labov, W. ([1969] 1972a). The logic of nonstandard English. In P. P. Giglioli (Ed.), *Language and Social Context* (pp. 179–215). Harmondsworth: Penguin Books.

Labov, W. (1972b). *Sociolinguistic Patterns.* Philadelphia, PA: University of Pennsylvania Press.

Labov, W. (2001). The anatomy of style-shifting. In P. Eckert & J. R. Rickford (Eds.), *Style and Sociolinguistic Variation* (pp. 85–108). Cambridge: CUP.

Lado, R. (1957). *Linguistics Across Cultures: Applied linguistics for language teachers.* Ann Arbor, MI: University of Michigan.

Lado, R. (1964). *Language Teaching, a Scientific Approach.* New York, NY: McGraw-Hill.

Lafage, S. (1985). *Français écrit et parlé en pays Éwé (Sud-Togo).* Paris: Société d'études linguistiques et anthropologiques de France.

Lakshmanan, U. & Selinker, L. (1994). The status of CP and the tensed complementizer *that* in the developing L2 grammars of English. *Second Language Research, 10*, 25–48.

Lalonde, R. N. & Gardner, R. C. (1984). Investigating a causal model of second language acquisition: Where does personality fit? *Canadian Journal of Behavioral Science, 16*, 224–237.

Lambert, P. Y. (1997). *La langue gauloise.* Paris: Errance.

Lambert, W. E. (1975). Culture and language as factors in learning and education. In A. Wolfgang (Ed.), *Education of Immigrant Students* (pp. 55–83). Canada: Ontario Institute for Studies in Education, Toronto.

Lambert, W. E. (1978). Cognitive and socio-cultural consequences of bilingualism. *Canadian Modern Language Review, 34*, 537–547.

Lambert, W. E. & Tucker, G. R. (1972). *The St. Lambert Experiment*. Rowley, MA: Newbury House.

Landry, N. & Lang, N. (2001). *Histoire de l'Acadie*. Québec: Septentrion.

Landry, R. & Allard, R. (1992). Ethnolinguistic vitality and the bilingual development of minority and majority group students. In W. Fase, K. Jaspaert, & S. Kroon (Eds.), *Maintenance and Loss of Minority Languages* (pp. 223–251). Amsterdam: John Benjamins.

Landry, R., Allard, R., & Henry, J. (1996). French in South Louisiana: Towards language loss. *Journal of Multilingual and Multicultural development, 17*(6), 442–468.

Landry, R. & Bourhis, R. Y. (1997). Linguistic landscape and ethnolinguistic vitality: An empirical study. *Journal of Language and Social Psychology, 16*, 23–49.

Lane, H. L. (1991 [1984]). *Quand l'esprit entend: Histoire des sourds-muets*. Paris: Odile Jacob.

Langacker, R. (1991). *Foundations of Cognitive Grammar*, Vol. 2. Stanford, CA: Stanford University Press.

Lantolf, J. & Pavlenko, A. (2001). (S)econd (L)anguage (A)ctivity Theory: Understanding second language learners as people. In M. Breen (Ed.), *Learner Contributions to Language Learning: New directions in research* (pp. 141–158). London: Longman.

Lapkin S. (Ed.). (1999). *French Second Language Education in Canada: Empirical studies*. Toronto: University of Toronto Press.

Lapkin, S., Swain, M., & Smith, M. (2002). Reformulation and the learning of French pronominal verbs in a Canadian French Immersion context. *The Modern Language Journal, 86*, 485–507.

Lardiere, D. (1998a). Case and tense in the fossilized steady state. *Second Language Research, 14*, 1–26.

Lardiere, D. (1998b). Dissociating syntax from morphology in a divergent end-state grammar. *Second Language Research, 14*, 359–375.

Lardiere, D. (2000). Mapping features to forms in second language acquisition. In J. Archibald (Ed.), *Second Language Acquisition and Linguistic Theory* (pp. 102–129). Oxford: Blackwell.

Lasnik, H. (1999). Verbal morphology: Syntactic structure meets the minimalist program. In H. Lasnik (Ed.), *Minimalist Analysis* (pp. 97–119). Malden, MA: Blackwell.

Lave, J. & Wenger, E. (1991). *Situated Learning: Legitimate peripheral participation*. New York, NY: CUP.

Le Dû, J., Le Berre, Y., & Brun-Trigaud, G. (2005). *Lectures de l'atlas linguistique de la France*. Paris: Comité des travaux historiques et scientifiques.

Leaver, B. L. & Shekhtman, B. (Eds.). (2002). *Developing Professional-Level Language Proficiency*. Cambridge: CUP.

Lecourt, I. (2003). Emergence de la morphosyntaxe du français en contexte de bilinguisme bimodal: Etude de cas. MA thesis, University François-Rabelais, Tours.

Leech, G. (1988 [1983]). *Principles of Pragmatics*. London: Longman.

Leech, G. & Eyes, E. (1997). Syntactic annotation: Treebanks. In R. Garside, G. Leech, & T. McEnery (Eds.), *Corpus Annotation: Linguistic information from computer text corpora* (pp. 34–52). London: Longman.

Leeman, J. (2003). Recasts and second language development: Beyond negative evidence. *Studies in Second Language Acquisition, 25*, 37–63.

Lefebvre, C. (1986). Relexification in creole genesis revisited: The case of Haitian Creole. In P. Muysken & N. Smith (Eds.), *Substrata versus Universals in Creole Genesis* (pp. 279–300). Amsterdam: John Benjamins.

Lefebvre, C. (1998). *Creole Genesis and the Acquisition of Grammar: The case of Haitian creole*. Cambridge: CUP.

Lemée, I. (2002). Acquisition de la variation socio-stylistique dans l'interlangue d'apprenants hibernophones de français L2: Le cas de *on* et *nous*. *Marges Linguistiques, 4*, 56–67.

Lenko-Szymanska, A. (2004). Demonstratives as anaphora markings in advanced learners' English. In G. Aston, S. Bernardini, & D. Stewart (Eds.), *Corpora and Language Learners* (pp. 89–107). Amsterdam: John Benjamins.

Léon, P. (1966). Apparition, maintien et chute du 'e' caduc. *La Linguistique, 2*, 111–122.

Léon, P. (1987). Voyelles/consonnes: Hiérarchie phonématique. *Canadian Journal of Linguistics, 32*(3), 235–244.

Leopold, W. (1939). *Speech Development of a Bilingual Child: A linguist's record. Vocabulary growth in the first two years*, Vol. 1. Evanston, IL: Northwestern University Press.

Leopold, W. (1947). *Speech Development of a Bilingual Child: A linguist's record. Sound learning in the first two years*, Vol. 2. Evanston, IL: Northwestern University Press.

Leopold, W. (1949a). *Speech Development of a Bilingual Child: A linguist's record. Grammar and general problems in the first two years*, Vol. 3. Evanston, IL: Northwestern University Press.

Leopold, W. (1949b). *Speech Development of a Bilingual Child: A linguist's record. Diary from age two*, Vol. 4. Evanston, IL: Northwestern University Press.

Leow, R. (1997). Attention, awareness and foreign language behavior. *Language Learning, 47*, 467–505.

Leow, R. (1999a). The role of attention in second/foreign language classroom research: Methodological issues. In F. Martínez-Gil & J. Gutiérrez-Rexac (Eds.), *Advances in Hispanic Linguistics: Papers from the 2nd Hispanic Linguistic Symposium* (pp. 60–71). Somerville, MA: Cascadilla.

Leow, R. (1999b). Attention, awareness, and *focus on form* research: A critical overview. In J. Lee & A. Valdman (Eds.), *Meaning and Form: Multiple perspectives* (pp. 69–98). Boston, MA: Heinle.

Leow, R. (2000). A study of the role of awareness in foreign language behavior: Aware vs unaware learners. *Studies in Second Language Acquisition, 22*, 557–584.

Leow, R. (2001). Do learners notice enhanced forms while interacting with the L2? An online and off-line study of the role of written input enhancement in L2 reading. *Hispania, 84*, 496–509.

Lepot-Froment, C. (2000). L'acquisition d'une langue des signes: Données empiriques et questions apparentées. In M. Kail & M. Fayol (Eds.), *L'acquisition du language* (pp. 193–229). Paris: Presses Universitaires de France.

Lepot-Froment, C. & Clerebaut, N. (1996). *L'Enfant sourd: Communication et langage*. Bruxelles: De Boeck & Larsier.

Levelt, W. J. M. (1989). *Speaking. From intention to articulation*. Cambridge, MA: The MIT Press.

Levinson, S. C. (1983). *Pragmatics*. Cambridge: CUP.

Lessard, G. & Levison, M. (1992). Computational modelling of linguistic humour: Tom Swifties. Paper presented at the ALLC/ACH Joint Annual Conference, Christ Church, Oxford.

Lessard, G. & Levison, M. (1993). Computational modelling of riddling strategies. Paper presented at the ACH/ALLC Joint Annual Conference, Georgetown University, Washington, DC.

Lessard, G. & Levison, M. (2001). Lexical creativity in L2 French. *IRAL, 39*, 245–257.

Lessard, G. & Levison, M. (2005). Computational generation of limericks. *Literary and Linguistic Computing 20*(1), supplement: 89–105.

Lessard, G., Levison, M., Maher, D., & Tomek, I. (1994). Modelling second language learner creativity. *Journal of Artificial Intelligence in Education, 5*(4), 455–480.

Levison, M. & Lessard, G. (2004a). Computer-based analysis and testing of second language acquisition in a naturalistic context: the VINCI environment. In J. Colpaert, W. Decoo, M. Simons, & S. van Bueren (Eds.), *CALL and Research Methodologies* (pp. 217–223). Antwerp: Universiteit Antwerpen.

Levison, M. & Lessard, G. (2004b). Generated narratives for computer-aided language teaching. In L. Lemnitzer, D. Meurers, & E. Hinrichs (Eds.), *COLING Workshop on eLearning for Computational Linguistics and Computational Linguistics for eLearning* (pp. 26–31). Geneva.

Levison, M., Lessard, G., Danielson, A. M., & Merven, D. (2001). From symptoms to diagnosis. In K. Cameron (Ed.), *CALL – The Challenge of Change* (pp. 53–59). Exeter: Elm Bank Publications.

Levison, M., Lessard, G., & Walker, D. (2000). A multi-level approach to the detection of second language learners errors. *Literary and Linguistic Computing, 15*, 313–322.

Levy, E. S. (2004). Effects of language experience and consonantal context on perception of French front rounded vowels by adult American English learners of French. PhD dissertation, The City University of New York.

Levy, Y. (1983). It's frogs all the way down. *Cognition, 15*, 75–93.

Lewis, M. (1997). Pedagogical implications of the lexical approach. In J. Coady & T. Huckin (Eds.), *Second Language Vocabulary Acquisition: A rationale for pedagogy* (pp. 255–270). Cambridge: CUP.

Leybaert, J. & Alegria, J. (1986). Processus de lecture chez l'enfant sourd: Une approche psycholinguistique. In J. Alegria (Ed.), *Vivre sourd aujourd'hui... et demain?* [Sociologie et Surdité; Psychologie et surdité 1] (pp. 93–116). Bruxelles: Mecaprint.

Liddicoat, A. L. & Crozet, C. (2001). Acquiring French interactional norms through instruction. In K. R. Rose & G. Kasper (Eds.), *Pragmatics in Language Teaching* (pp. 125–144). Cambridge: CUP.

Lieber, R. (2004). *Morphology and Lexical Semantics.* Cambridge: CUP.

Liljestrand Fultz, A. (2006). Prosody in lexical and syntactic disambiguation in English-French interlanguage. Ms., Indiana University.

Lillo-Martin, D. (1991). *Universal grammar and American Sign Language: Setting the null argument parameters.* Dordrecht: Kluwer.

Lillo-Martin, D. (1999). Modality effects and modularity in language acquisition: The acquisition of American Sign Language. In T. Bhatia & W. Ritchie (Eds.), *Handbook of Language Acquisition* (pp. 531–567). San Diego, CA: Academic Press.

Lillo-Martin, D., Bellugi, U., Struxness, L., & O' Grady, M. (1985). The acquisition of spatially organized syntax. *Papers and Reports on Child Language Development, 24,* 70–78.

Lillo-Martin, D. & Klima, E. S. (1990). Pointing out differences: ASL pronouns in syntactic theory. In S. D. Fisher & P. Siple (Eds.), *Theoretical Issues in Sign Languages Research* (pp. 191–210). Chicago, IL: University of Chicago Press.

Lin, Y. & Rancer, A. S. (2003). Sex differences in intercultural communication apprehension, ethnocentrism, and intercultural willingness to communicate. *Psychological Reports, 92,* 195–200.

Linell, P. (2005). *The Written Language Bias in Linguistics: Its nature, origins and transformations.* London: Routledge.

Lippi-Green, R. (1997). *English with an Accent: Language, ideology, and discrimination in the United States.* London: Routledge.

Liskin-Gasparro, J. E. (1998). Linguistic development in an immersion context: How advanced learners of Spanish perceive SLA. *The Modern Language Journal, 82,* 159–176.

Lloyd, P. (1979). On the definition of Vulgar Latin. *Neuphilologische Mitteilungen, 80,* 110–122.

Lockerbie, I., Molinaro, I., Larose, K., & Oakes, L. (2005). *French as the Common Language in Quebec.* Quebec: Nota bene.

Lodge, R. A. (1985). *Le plus ancien registre de comptes des Consuls de Montferrand.* Clermont-Ferrand: Mémoires de l'Académie des Sciences de Clermont-Ferrand.

Lodge, R. A. (1993). *French, from Dialect to Standard.* London: Routledge.

Lodge, R. A. (1996). Stereotypes of vernacular pronunciation in 17th–18th century Paris. *Zeitschrift für Romanische Philologie, 112,* 205–231.

Lodge, R. A. (1999). Colloquial vocabulary and politeness in French. *Modern Language Review, 94,* 355–365.

Lodge, R. A. (2004). *A Sociolinguistic History of Parisian French.* Cambridge: CUP.

Loncke, F. (1987). Belgian. In J. V. van Cleve (Ed.), *Gallaudet Encyclopaedia of Deaf People & Deafness* (pp. 59–60). New-York, NY: McGraw-Hill.

Loncke, F., Quertinmont, S., Martens, K., & Dussart, I. (1996). Les jeunes sourds et la pratique de la communication bimodale. In C. Lepot-Froment & N. Clerebaut (Eds.), *L'Enfant sourd: Communication et langage* (pp. 317–346). Bruxelles: De Boeck & Larsier.

Long, M. H. (1983). Does instruction make a difference? *TESOL Quarterly, 17,* 359–382.

Long, M. H. (1988). Instructed interlanguage development. In L. Beebe (Ed.), *Issues in Second Language Acquisition: Multiple perspectives* (pp. 115–141). Rowley, MA: Newbury House.

Long, M. H. (1990). Maturational constraints on language development. *Studies in Second Language Acquisition, 12,* 251–285.

Long, M. H. & Doughty, C. J. (2003). SLA and cognitive science. In C. J. Doughty & M. H. Long (Eds.), *The Handbook of Second Language Acquisition* (pp. 866–870). Oxford: Blackwell.

Longobardi, G. (1994). Reference and proper names: A theory of N-movement in syntax and logical form. *Linguistic Inquiry, 25*, 609–665.

Lucy, J. A. (1993). Reflexive language and the human disciplines. In J. A. Lucy (Ed.), *Reflexive Language: Reported speech and metapragmatics* (pp. 9–32). Cambridge: CUP.

Luke, A. (2004). Two takes on the critical. In B. Norton & K. Toohey (Eds.), *Critical Pedagogies and Language Learning* (pp. 21–29). Cambridge: CUP.

Lumsden, J. S. (1992). Underspecification in grammar and natural gender. *Linguistic Inquiry, 23*, 469–486.

Lumsden, J. S. (1999). Language acquisition and creolization. In M. DeGraff (Ed.), *Language Creation and Language Change. Creolization, diachrony and development* (pp. 129–157). Cambridge, MA: The MIT Press.

Lusignan, S. (1987). *Parler vulgairement.* Paris-Montréal: Vrin.

Lusignan, S. (2004). *La langue des rois au moyen âge.* Paris: Presses Universitaires de France.

Lyster, R. (1994). The effect of functional-analytic teaching on aspects of French immersion students' sociolinguistic competence. *Applied Linguistics, 15*, 263–287.

Lyster, R. (1996). Question forms, conditionals, and second-person pronouns used by adolescent native speakers across two levels of formality in written and spoken French. *The Modern Language Journal, 80*, 165–180.

Lyster, R. (2004). Research on form-focused instruction in immersion classrooms: Implications for theory and practice. *Journal of French Language Studies, 14*, 321–341.

Lyster, R. & Rebuffot, J. (2002). Acquisition des pronoms d'allocution en classe de français immersif. *Acquisition et Interaction en Langue Etrangère, 17*, 51–72.

Maalouf, A. (1998). *Les identités meurtrières.* Paris: Bernard Grasset.

Mack, M., Bott, S., & Boronat, C. B. (1995). Mother, I'd rather do it myself, maybe: An analysis of voice-onset time produced by early French-English bilinguals. *IDEAL, 8*, 23–55.

MacIntyre, P. D. (1999). Language anxiety: A review of the literature for language teachers. In D. J. Young (Ed.), *Affect in Foreign Language and Second Language Learning: A practical guide to creating a low-anxiety classroom atmosphere* (pp. 24–45). Boston, MA: McGraw-Hill.

MacIntyre, P. D. (2005). Willingness to communicate in the second language: Individual and intergroup process. Paper presented at the Language Learning Round Table of the EUROSLA Conference, Dubrovnik, Croatia.

MacIntyre, P. D., Babin, P. A., & Clément, R. (1999). Willingness to communicate: Antecedents and consequences. *Communication Quarterly, 47*, 215–229.

MacIntyre, P. D., Baker, S., Clément, R., & Conrod, S. (2001). Willingness to communicate, social support and language learning orientations of immersion students. *Studies in Second Language Acquisition, 23*, 369–388.

MacIntyre, P. D., Baker, S., Clément, R., & Donovan, L. (2002). Sex and age effects on willingness to communicate, anxiety, perceived competence, and L2 motivation among junior high school French immersion students. *Language Learning, 52*, 537–564.

MacIntyre, P. D., Baker, S., Clément, R., & Donovan, L. A. (2003). Talking in order to learn: Willingness to communicate and intensive language programs. *Canadian Modern Language Review, 59*, 589–607.

MacIntyre, P. D. & Charos, C. (1996). Personality, attitudes, and affect as predictors of second language communication. *Journal of Language and Social Psychology, 15*, 3–26.

MacIntyre, P. D., Clément, R., Dörnyei, Z., & Noels, K. A. (1998). Conceptualizing willingness to communicate in a L2: A situational model of L2 confidence and affiliation. *The Modern Language Journal, 82*, 545–562.

MacIntyre, P. D. & Donovan, L. A. (2004). Desire for control and communication-related personality variables. *Psychological Reports, 94*, 581–582.

MacIntyre, P. D., Donovan, L. A., & Standing, L. (2004). Extraversion and willingness to communicate in second language learning. Paper presented at the annual conference of the Canadian Psychological Association, Saint John's NL, June 2004.

MacIntyre, P. D. & Gardner, R. C. (1989). Anxiety and second-language learning: Toward a theoretical clarification. *Language Learning, 39*, 251–275.

MacIntyre, P. D. & Gardner, R. C. (1991). Investigating language class anxiety using the focused essay technique. *The Modern Language Journal, 75*, 296–304.

MacIntyre, P. D. & Gardner, R. C. (1994a). The effects of induced anxiety on cognitive processing in computerized vocabulary learning. *Studies in Second Language Acquisition, 16*, 1–17.

MacIntyre, P. D. & Gardner, R. C. (1994b). The subtle effects of language anxiety on cognitive processing in the second language. *Language Learning, 44*, 283–305.

MacIntyre, P. D., MacMaster, K., & Baker, S. (2001). The convergence of multiple models of motivation for second language learning: Gardner, Pintrich, Kuhl and McCroskey. In Z. Dörnyei & R. Schmidt (Eds.), *Motivation and Second Language Acquisition* (pp. 461–492). Honolulu, HI: Second Language Teaching and Curriculum Center, University of Hawai'i at Manoa.

MacIntyre, P. D., Noels, K. A., & Clément, R. (1997). Biases in self-ratings of second language proficiency: The role of language anxiety. *Language Learning, 47*, 265–287.

MacWhinney, B. (2000a). *The CHILDES Project: Tools for analyzing talk*, Vol. 1: *Transcription format and programs* (3rd ed.). Mahwah, NJ: Lawrence Erlbaum.

MacWhinney, B. (2000b). *The CHILDES Project: Tools for analyzing talk*, Vol. 2: *The database* (3rd ed.). Mahwah, NJ: Lawrence Erlbaum.

Maeshiba, N., Yoshinaga, N., Kasper, G., & Ross, S. (1996). Transfer and proficiency in interlanguage apologizing. In S. M. Gass & J. Neu (Eds.), *Speech Acts Across Cultures. Challenges to communication in a second language* (pp. 155–187). Berlin: Mouton de Gruyter.

Makoni, S. & Meinhof, U. (2004). Western perspectives in applied linguistics in Africa. In S. M. Gass & S. Makoni (Eds.), *World Applied Linguistics* (pp. 77–104). Amsterdam: John Benjamins.

Makoni, S. & Pennycook, A. (2005). Disinventing and (re)constituting languages. *Critical Inquiry in Language Studies, 2*(3), 137–156.

Malherbe, F. de (1630). *Les œuvres de M. de Malherbe.* Paris: Chappellain.

Malinowski, B. (1923). The problem of meaning in primitive languages. In C. K. Odgen & I. A. Richards (Eds.), *The Meaning of Meaning: A study of the influence of language upon thought and of the science of symbolism* (pp. 296–336). New York, NY: Harcourt Brace Jovanovich.

Mallen, E. (1990). Clitic movement inside noun phrases. *Studia Linguistica, 44*, 1–29.

Mallen, E. (1997). A minimalist approach to concord in noun phrases. *Theoretical Linguistics, 23*, 49–77.

Maller, S. J., Singleton, J. L., Supalla, S., & Wix, T. (1999). The development and psychometric properties of the American Sign Language Proficiency Assessment (ASL-PA). *Journal of Deaf Studies and Deaf Education, 4*(4), 255–269.

Malt, B. C. & Sloman, S. A. (2003). Linguistic diversity and object naming by non-native speakers of English. *Bilingualism, 6*(1), 47–67.

Malvern, D. & Richards, B. (2002). Investigating accommodation in language proficiency interviews using a new measure of lexical diversity. *Language Testing, 19*(1), 85–104.

Malvern, D., Richards, B., Chipere, N., & Durán, P. (2004). *Lexical Diversity and Language Development: Quantification and assessment.* Basingstoke: Palgrave.

Manessy, G. (1984). Français-tirailleur et français d'Afrique. *Cahiers de l'Institut de Linguistique de Louvain, 9*(3–4), 113–126.

Manessy, G. (1994). Modalités d'appropriation d'une langue seconde. In D. Véronique (Ed.), *Créolisation et acquisition des langues* (pp. 211–224). Aix-en-Provence: Publications de l'Université de Provence.

Mann, W. (2001). Referential Cohesion in Deaf Children's ASL Narratives. MA thesis, San Francisco State University.

Marantz, A. (1997). No escape from syntax: Don't try morphological analysis in the privacy of your own lexicon. *University of Pennsylvania Working Papers in Linguistics, 4*, 201–225.

Marchello-Nizia, C. (1979). *Histoire de la langue française aux XIVe et XVe siècles.* Paris: Bordas.

Marentette, P. & Mayberry, R. I. (2000). Principles for an emerging phonological system: A case study of early ASL acquisition. In C. Chamberlain, J. P. Morford, & R. I. Mayberry (Eds.), *Language Acquisition by Eye* (pp. 71–90). Mahwah, NJ: Lawrence Erlbaum.

Marinova-Todd, S. (1994). The critical period in second language acquisition: The case of gender. MA·thesis, York University.

Markman, B., Spilka, I., & Tucker, R. (1975). The use of elicited imitation in search of an interim French grammar. *Language Learning, 25*(1), 31–41.

Mar-Molinero, C. (2000). *The Politics of Language in the Spanish-Speaking World: From colonisation to globalisation, the politics of language.* London: Routledge.

Markus, H. & Nuirius, P. (1986). Possible Selves. *American Psychologist, 41*(9), 954–969.

Marschark, M. (1993). *Psychological Development of Deaf Children.* New York, NY: OUP.

Marsden, E., Myles, F., Rule, S., & Mitchell, R. (2003). Using CHILDES tools for researching second language acquisition. In S. Sarangi & T. van Leeuwen (Eds.), *Applied Linguistics and Communities of Practice,* Vol. 18 (pp. 98–113). London: BAAL/Continuum.

Martin, D. (1997). Toward a new multilingual language policy in education in South Africa: Different approaches to meet different needs. *Educational Review, 49*, 129–139.

Martin, H.-J. (1999). *Livre, pouvoir et société à Paris au XVIIIe Siècle.* Geneva: Droz.

Martin, P. (2002). Le système vocalique du français du Québec: De l'acoustique à la phonologie. *La Linguistique, 38*(2), 71–88.

Martineau, F. & Mougeon, R. (2003). Sociolinguistic research on the origins of *ne* deletion in European and Quebec French. *Language, 79*, 118–152.

Martinet, A. (1969). *Le français sans fard.* Paris: Presses Universitaires de France.

Martinet, A. (1972). La nature phonologique d'e caduc. In A. Valdman (Ed.), *Papers in Linguistics and Phonetics to the Memory of Pierre Delattre* (pp. 393–399). The Hague: Mouton.

Martinet, A. & Walter, H. (1973). *Dictionnaire de la prononciation française dans son usage réel.* Paris: France-Expansion.

Martínez Flor, A. (2004). The effect of instruction on the development of pragmatic competence in the English as a foreign language context: A study based on suggestions. PhD dissertation, Universitat Jaume I, Castellón.

Martínez Flor, A. & Fukuya, Y. J. (2005). The effects of instruction on learners' production of appropriate and accurate suggestions. *System, 33*(3), 463–480.

Martohardjono, G. (1993). Wh-movement in the acquisition of a second language: A cross-linguistic study of three languages with and without movement. PhD dissertation, Cornell University.

Masgoret, A.-M. & Gardner, R. C. (2003). Attitudes, motivation and second language learning: A meta-analysis of studies conducted by Gardner and associates. In Z. Dörnyei (Ed.), *Attitudes, Orientations, and Motivations in Language Learning* (pp. 167–210). Oxford: Blackwell.

Mastromonaco, S. (1999). Liaison in French as a second language. PhD dissertation, University of Toronto.

Mather, P.-A. (2000). Creole Genesis: Evidence from West African L2 French. In D. Gilbers, J. Nerbonne, & J. Schaeken (Eds.), *Languages in Contact* (pp. 247–261). Amsterdam: Rodopi.

Mather, P.-A. (2001). On the origin and linguistic status of Réunionnais. *Te Reo – Journal of the New Zealand Linguistics Association, 44*, 83–107.

Mather, P.-A. (2005). Noun phrases in L2 French and Haitian: Clues on the origin of plantation creoles. *Journal of Universal Language, 6*, 53–84.

Mather, P.-A. (In press). Second language acquisition and creolization: Same (I) processes, different (E) results. *Journal of Pidgin and Creole Languages, 22*(1).

Matoré, G. (1985). *Le vocabulaire et la société médiévale.* Paris: Presses Universitaires de France.

Matoré, G. (1988). *Le vocabulaire et la société du XVIe siècle.* Paris: Presses Universitaires de France.

Mauger, C. 1706). *Nouvelle grammaire françoise.* Rouen: Besogne.

Maurais, J. (1987). *Politique et aménagement linguistiques.* Québec: Conseil de la langue française.

Maurand, G. (1981). Situation linguistique d'une communauté rurale en domaine occitan. *International Journal of the Sociology of Language, 29*, 99–119.

Mayberry, R. I. (1993). First-language acquisition after childhood differs from second-language acquisition: The case of American Sign Language. *Journal of Speech and Hearing Research, 36*, 1258–1270.

Mayberry, R. I., Chamberlain, C., Waters, G., & Doehring, D. (1999). Reading development in relation to signed language and structure. Manuscript in preparation.

Mayberry, R. I. & Lock, I. (2003). Age constraints on first versus second language acquisition: Evidence for linguistic plasticity and epigenesis. *Brain and Language, 87*, 369–384.

McCarthy, J. J. (Ed.). (2004). *Optimality Theory in Phonology: A reader.* Oxford: Blackwell.

McCroskey, J. C., Burroughs, N. F., Daun, A., & Richmond, V. P. (1990). Correlates of quietness: Swedish and American perspectives. *Communication Quarterly, 38*, 127–137.

McCroskey, J. C. & Richmond, V. P. (1990). Willingness to communicate: Differing cultural perspectives. *The Southern Communication Journal, 56*, 72–77.

McCroskey, J. C. & Richmond, V. P. (1991). Willingness to communicate: A cognitive view. In M. Booth-Butterfield (Ed.), *Communication, Cognition, and Anxiety* (pp. 19–37). Newbury Park, CA: Sage.

McLaughlin, J., Osterhaut, L., & Kim, A. (2004). Neural correlates of second-language word learning: Minimal instruction produces rapid change. *Nature Neuroscience, 7*, 703–704.

McWhorter, J. (1997). *Towards a New Model of Creole Genesis.* New York, NY: Peter Lang.

McWhorter, J. (1998). Identifying the creole prototype: Vindicating a typological class. *Language, 74*(4), 788–818.

Meier, A. J. (1998). Apologies: What do we know? *International Journal of Applied Linguistics, 8*(2), 215–231.

Meier, R. P. & Newport, E. L. (1990). Out of the hands of babes: On a possible sign advantage in language acquisition. *Language, 66*, 1–23.

Meier, R. P., Moreland, C. J., & Cheek, A. (2000). Motoric constraints in infant sign production. Paper presented at the 7th conference on Theoretical Issues in Sign Language Research, Amsterdam, July 2000.

Meier, R. P. & Willerman, R. (1995). Prelinguistic gesture in deaf and hearing infants. In K. Emmorey & J. Reilly (Eds.), *Language, Gesture, and Space* (pp. 391–409). Hillsdale, NJ: Lawrence Erlbaum.

Meisel, J. (1997). The acquisition of the syntax of negation in French and German: Contrasting first and second language development. *Second Language Research, 13*, 227–263.

Meisel, J. (1999). Parametric change in language development: Psycholinguistic and historical perspectives on second language acquisition. *LynX, 6*, 18–36.

Meisel, J. (2000). Revisiting Universal Grammar. *Revista de Documentacao de Estudo em Linguistica Teorica e Aplicata, 16*, 129–140 (Special Issue).

Meisel, J., Clahsen, H., & Pienemann, M. (1981). On determining developmental stages in natural second language acquisition. *Studies in Second Language Acquisition, 3*(2), 109–135.

Mel'čuk, I. A. (1958). Statistics and the relationship between gender of French nouns and their endings. In V. J. Rozencvejg (Ed.), *Essays on Lexical Semantics I* (pp. 11–42). Stockholm: Skriptor.

Mey, J. (1985). *Whose Language? A study in linguistic pragmatics.* Amsterdam: John Benjamins.

Migge, B. (1998). Substrate influence in creole formation: The origin of *give*-type serial verb constructions in the Surinamese Plantation Creole. *Journal of Pidgin and Creole Languages, 13*(2), 215–266.

Millet, A. (1990). La place de la LSF dans l'intégration scolaire des enfants sourds. Rapport de recherche, Programme 1988 d'action spécifique Sciences humaines et sociales: Thème Aide à l'intégration d'enfants handicapés en milieu scolaire. Laboratoire LIDILEM, University of Grenoble.

Millet, A. (1993). Surdité: Déficience sensorielle innée et mutité linguistique acquise. *TRANEL, 19*, 145–158.

Millet, A. (1999). Bilinguisme et apprentissages linguistiques chez des jeunes apprenants sourds. *Recherches sur la Langues des Signes, 1*, 125–135.

Millet, A. & Mugnier, S. (2004). Français et langue des signes française: Quelles interactions au service des compétences langagières? Etude de cas d'une classe d'enfants sourds de CE2. *Repères, 29*, 207–232.

Milner, J. (1977). A propos des génitifs adnominaux en français. In C. Rohrer (Ed.), *Actes du colloque franco-allemand de linguistique théorique* (pp. 67–107). Tübingen: Niemeyer.

Milner, J. (1982). *Ordres et raisons de langue*. Paris: Editions du Seuil.

Milroy, J. (2001). Language ideologies and the consequences of standardization. *Journal of Sociolinguistics, 5*, 530–555.

Milroy, J. & Milroy, L. (1999). *Authority in Language* (3rd ed.). London: Routledge.

Mischel, W. (1999). *Introduction to Personality* (6th ed.). Fort Worth, TX: Harcourt Brace.

Mitchell, R. & Dickson, P. (1997). *Progression in Foreign Language Learning. Report of a project funded by the economic and social research council, 1993–1996* [Occasional Paper no. 45]. Southampton: Centre for Language in Education.

Mitchell, R. & Martin, C. (1997). Rote learning, creativity and 'understanding' in classroom foreign language teaching. *Language Teaching Research, 1*(1), 1–27.

Mogford, K. (1993). Oral language acquisition in the prelinguistically deaf. In D. M. V. Bishop & K. Mogford (Eds.), *Language Development in Exceptional Circumstances* (pp. 110–131). Hillsdale, NJ: Lawrence Erlbaum.

Monfrin, J. (1963). Humanisme et traductions au moyen âge. *Journal des Savants*, 161–190.

Montrul, S. (1997). Transitivity alternations in second language acquisition: A cross-linguistic study of English, Spanish and Turkish. PhD dissertation, McGill University, Montreal.

Moody, B. (1983). *La langue des signes: Histoire et grammaire, 1*. Paris: Ellipses.

Moores, D. & Sweet, C. (1990). Factors predictive of school achievement. In D. Moores & K. Meadow-Orlans (Eds.), *Education and Developmental Aspects of Deafness* (pp. 154–201). Washington, DC: Gallaudet University Press.

Moreau, M.-L. (1998). De l'imaginaire linguistique à la politique linguistique: A la recherche d'un standard pour le diola (Casamance, Sénégal). In C. Canut (Ed.), *Imaginaires linguistiques en Afrique: Actes du colloque de l'INALCO. Attitudes, représentations et imaginaires linguistiques en Afrique. Quelles notions pour quelles réalités? (9 novembre 1996)* (pp. 109–118). Paris: L'Harmattan.

Morford, J. P. (2000). Delayed phonological development in ASL: Two case studies of deaf isolates. *Recherches Linguistiques de Vincennes, 29*, 121–142.

Morgan, G. & Woll, B. (2002). *Directions in Sign Language Acquisition*. Amsterdam: John Benjamins.

Morgan, G. & Woll, B. (2003). The development of reference switching encoded through body classifiers in British Sign Language. In K. Emmorey (Ed.), *Perspectives on Classifiers Constructions in Sign Language* (pp. 297–310). Mahwah, NJ: Lawrence Erlbaum.

Morin, C.-Y. (1989). Changes in the French vocalic system in the 19th century. In M. E. H. Schouten & P. T. van Reenen (Eds.), *New Methods in Dialectology* (pp. 185–197). Dordrecht: Foris.

Morin, C.-Y. (1994). Les sources historiques de la prononciation du français au Québec. In R. Mougeon & E. Béniak (Eds.), *Les origines du français québécois* (pp. 199–236). Sainte Foy: Les Presses de l'Université Laval.

Morin, Y.-C. (1974). Règles phonologiques à domaine indéterminé: Chute du cheva en français. *Cahier de Linguistique, 4*, 69–88.

Morin, Y.-C. (1978). The status of mute 'e'. *Studies in French Linguistics, 1*(2), 79–140.

Morin, Y.-C. (1982). Cross-syllabic constraints and the French 'e muet'. *Journal of Linguistic Research, 2*(3), 41–56.

Morin, Y.-C. (1987). French data and phonological theory. *Linguistics, 25*, 815–843.

Morin, Y.-C. (1988). Disjunctive ordering and French morphology. *Natural Language and Linguistic Theory, 6*, 271–282.

Morris, C. W. (1938). Foundations of the theory of signs. In O. Neurath, C. Carnap, & C. Morris (Eds.), *International Encyclopedia of Unified Science* (pp. 77–138). Chicago, IL: University of Chicago Press.

Moses, J. (2002). The development of future expression in English-speaking learners of French. PhD dissertation, Indiana University, Bloomington.

Mottez, B. (1976). A propos d'une langue stigmatisée, la langue des signes. Ms., Ecole des Hautes Etudes en Sciences Sociales, Centre d'Etudes des Mouvement Sociaux, Paris.

Mougeon, R. & Béniak, E. (1995). *Les origines du français québécois*. Sainte Foy: Les Presses de l'Université Laval.

Mougeon, R. & Dewaele, J.-M. (Eds.). (2004). Variation in second language acquisition. *International Review of Applied Linguistics, 42*(4) (Special issue).

Mougeon, R., Nadasdi, T., & Rehner, K. (2002). État de la recherche sur l'appropriation de la variation par les apprenants avancés du FL2 ou FLE. *Acquisition et Interaction en Langue Etrangère, 17*, 7–50.

Mougeon, R. & Rehner, K. (2001). Variation in the spoken French of Ontario French immersion students: The case of *juste* vs. *seulement* vs. *rien que*. *The Modern Language Journal, 85*, 398–415.

Mougeon, R., Rehner, K., & Nadasdi, T. (2004). The learning of spoken French variation by immersion students from Toronto. *Journal of Sociolinguistics, 8*, 408–432.

Mougeon, R., Rehner, K., & Nadasdi, T. (2005). Learning to speak everyday (Canadian) French. *Canadian Modern Language Review, 61*, 543–561.

Mufwene, S. (1986). Les langues créoles peuvent-elles être définies sans allusion à leur histoire? *Études Créoles, 9*, 135–150.

Mufwene, S. (1986). The Universalist and Substrate hypotheses complement one another. In P. Muysken & N. Smith (Eds.), *Substrata versus Universals in Creole Genesis* (pp. 129–162). Amsterdam: John Benjamins.

Mufwene, S. (1990a). Creoles and Universal Grammar. *Linguistics, 28*(4), 783–807.

Mufwene, S. (1990b). Transfer and the substrate hypothesis in creolistics. *Studies in Second Language Acquisition, 12*(1), 1–23.

Mufwene, S. (1994b). On decreolization: The case of Gullah. In M. Morgan (Ed.), *Language and the Social Construction of Identity in Creole Situations* (pp. 63–99). Los Angeles, CA: Center for Afro-American Studies, UCLA.

Mufwene, S. (1997a). Jargons, pidgins, creoles, and koines: What are they? In A. Spears & D. Winford (Eds.), *The Structure and Status of Pidgins and Creoles* (pp. 35–70). Amsterdam: John Benjamins.

Mufwene, S. (1997b). What research on creole genesis can contribute to historical linguistics. Paper presented at the XIIIth International Conference on Historical Linguistics, Düsseldorf, Germany, August 13, 1997.

Mufwene, S. (2001). *The Ecology of Language Evolution*. Cambridge: CUP.

Mufwene, S. (2005). *Créoles, écologie sociale, évolution linguistique: Cours donnés au Collège de France durant l'automne 2003*. Paris: L'Harmattan.

Mugnier, S. & Millet, A. (2003). L'oral et les enfants sourds: Des textes officiels à la classe. Paper presented at the Colloque Oral, Grenoble, France.

Mühlhäusler, P. (1996). *Linguistic Ecology: Language change and linguistic imperialism in the Pacific region*. London: Routledge.

Müller, S. (2004). 'Well you know that type of person': Functions of *well* in the speech of American and German students. *Journal of Pragmatics, 36*(6), 1157–1182.

Muysken, P. & Law, P. (2001). Creole studies. A theoretical linguist's field guide. *Glot International, 5*(2), 47–57.

Muysken, P. & Smith, N. (Eds.). (1986). *Substrata versus Universals in Creole Genesis*. Amsterdam: John Benjamins.

Myhill, J. (1991). Typological text analysis: Tense and aspect in creoles and second languages. In T. Huebner & C. A. Ferguson (Eds.), *Crosscurrents in Second Language Acquisition and Linguistic Theories* (pp. 93–121). Amsterdam: John Benjamins.

Myles, F. (1990). Error and order in the acquisition of French as a second language. PhD dissertation, University of Sheffield.

Myles, F. (1995). Interaction between linguistic theory and language processing in SLA. *Second Language Research, 11*(3), 235–266.

Myles, F. (2002). *Linguistic Development in Classroom Learners of French: A cross-sectional study* (No. End of ESRC award report R000223421). Southampton: University of Southampton.

Myles, F. (2003). The early development of L2 narratives: A longitudinal study. *Marges Linguistiques, 5*, 40–55.

Myles, F. (2004). French second language acquisition research: Setting the scene. *Journal of French Language Studies, 14*, 211–232.

Myles, F. (2005a). The emergence of morpho-syntactic structure in French L2. In J.-M. Dewaele (Ed.), *Focus on French as a Foreign Language* (pp. 88–113). Clevedon: Multilingual Matters.

Myles, F. (2005b). Interlanguage corpora and second language acquisition research. *Second Language Research, 21*(4), 373–391.

Myles, F., Hooper, J., & Mitchell, R. (1998). Rote or rule? Exploring the role of formulaic language in classroom foreign language learning. *Language Learning, 48*(3), 323–363.

Myles, F., Mitchell, R., & Hooper, J. (1995). Interrogative chunks in French L2: A basis for creative construction? *Studies in Second Language Acquisition, 21*, 49–80.

Myles, F., Mitchell, R., & Hooper, J. (1999). Interrogative chunks in French L2: A basis for creative construction? *Studies in Second Language Acquisition, 21*(1), 49–80.

Myles, F. & Mitchell, R. (2004). Using information technology to support empirical SLA research. *Journal of Applied Linguistics, 1*(2), 69–98.

Myles, F. & Towell, R. (Eds.). (2004). The Acquisition of French as a Second Language. *Journal of French Language Studies/Journal International de Langue et de Linguistique Françaises, 14*(3) (Special issue).

Nadasdi, T., Mougeon, R., & Rehner, K. (2003). Emploi du 'futur' dans le français parlé des élèves d'immersion française. *French Language Studies, 13*, 195–219.

Nadeau, M. (1993). Peut-on parler de 'français sourd'? *Revue de l'ACCLA, 15*, 65–84.

Nadeau, M. & Machabée, D. (1998). Dans quelles mesures les erreurs des sourds sont comparables à celles des entendants? In C. Dubuisson & D. Daigle (Eds.), *Lecture, écriture et surdité* (pp. 169–194). Montréal: Editions Logiques.

Naiman, N., Frohlich, M., Stern, H. H., & Todesco, A. (1978). *The Good Language Learner.* Toronto: Ontario Institute for Studies in Education.

Nassaji, H. (2003). L2 Vocabulary learning from context: Strategies, knowledge sources and their relationship with success in L2 lexical inferencing. *TESOL Quarterly, 37*(4), 645–670.

Nation, I. S. P. (2001). *Learning Vocabulary in Another Language.* Cambridge: CUP.

Nesselhauf, N. (2004). How learner corpus analysis can contribute to language teaching: A study of support verb constructions. In G. Aston, S. Bernardini, & D. Stewart (Eds.), *Corpora and Language Learners* (pp. 109–124). Amsterdam: John Benjamins.

Neuman, I. (1985). *Le Créole de Breaux Bridge, Louisiane: Etude morphosyntaxique, textes, vocabulaire.* Hamburg: Helmut Buske.

Nève, F.-X. (1996). *Essai de grammaire de la Langue des Signes Français.* Genève: Bibliothèque de la faculté de philosophie et lettre de l'Université de Liège.

Newmeyer, F. J. (1986). *The Politics of Linguistics.* Chicago, IL: University of Chicago Press.

Newport, E. L. (1990). Maturational constraints on language learning. *Cognitive Science, 14*, 11–28.

Newport, E. L. & Meier, R. P. (1985). The acquisition of American Sign Language. In D. Slobin (Ed.), *The Crosslinguisitc Study of Language Acquisition 1* (pp. 881–938). Hillsdale, NJ: Lawrence Erlbaum.

Ngalasso, M. M. (1989). Le dilemne des langues africaines. *Notre Librairie, 98*, 15–21.

Nicot, J. (1606). *Trésor de la langue françoise.* Paris: Douceur.

Niederberger, N. (1999). Représentations des pratiques sociales de l'écrit et apprentissage de la lecture chez les enfants sourds. Paper presented at the Commission Romande de Réflexion sur l'Enseignement du Français, ECES, Lausanne.

Niederberger, N. (2004). Capacités langagières en langue des signes française et en français écrit chez l'enfant sourd bilingue: Quelles relations? PhD dissertation, University of Geneva.

Niederberger, N. (2005). Use and functions of French Sign Language by deaf children during an oral French production task. Paper presented at the 9th International Conference on the Study of Child Language, Berlin, July 2005.

Niederberger, N., Aubonney, M., Dunant-Sauvin, C., Palama, G., Aubonney, S., Delachaux-Djapo, S., & Frauenfelder, U. H. (2001). *TELSF, Test de la Langue des Signes Française.* Geneva: Laboratoire de Psycholinguistique Expérimentale, Université de Genève and Centre pour Enfants Sourds de Montbrillant, SMP, Geneva.

Niederberger, N. & Berthoud-Papandropoulou, I. (2004). Utilisation des pronoms personnels en français écrit par des enfants sourds bilingues: Un parcours spécifique d'apprentissage? *LIDIL, 30,* 27–38.

Niederberger, N. & Frauenfelder, U. H. (2005). Linguistic proficiency of the deaf bilingual child in French Sign Language and written French: What is the relation between the two? In A. Brugos, M. Clark-Cotton, & S. Ha (Eds.), *Proceedings of the 29th Boston University Conference on Language Development* (pp. 413–423). Somerville, MA: Cascadilla.

Niezgoda, K. & Röver, C. (2001). Pragmatic and grammatical awareness: A function of the learning environment? In K. R. Rose & G. Kasper (Eds.), *Pragmatics in Language Teaching* (pp. 63–79). Cambridge: CUP.

Ninio, A. & Snow, C. E. (1996). *Pragmatic Development.* Boulder, CO: Westview.

Ninio, A. & Wheeler, P. (1984). Functions of speech in mother-infant interaction. In L. Feagans, C. Garvey, & R. Golinkoff (Eds.), *The Origins and Growth of Communication* (pp. 196–207). Norwood, NJ: Ablex.

Noels, K. A. (2001a). Learning Spanish as a second language: Learners' orientations and perceptions of teachers' communicative style. *Language Learning, 51,* 107–144.

Noels, K. A. (2001b). New orientations in language learning motivation: Towards a model of intrinsic, extrinsic and integrative orientations. In Z. Dörnyei & R. Schmidt (Eds.), *Motivation and Second Language Acquisition* (pp. 43–68). Honolulu, HI: Second language Teaching and Curriculum Center, University of Hawai'i at Manoa.

Noels, K. A. (2003). Learning Spanish as a second language: Learners' orientations and perceptions of their teachers' communication style. In Z. Dörnyei (Ed.), *Attitudes, Orientations and Motivations in Language Learning* (pp. 97–136). Oxford: Blackwell.

Noels, K. A. (2005a). Orientations to learning German: Heritage language learning and motivational substrates. *Canadian Modern Language Review, 62,* 285–312.

Noels, K. A. (2005b). Fostering self-determination and intrinsic motivation in heritage-and non-heritage learners of German. Ms., University of Alberta.

Noels, K. A. & Clément, R. (1996). Communicating across cultures: Social determinants and acculturative consequences. *Canadian Journal of Behavioral Science, 28,* 214–228.

Noels, K. A. & Clément, R. (1998). Language in education: Bridging educational policy and social psychological research. In J. Edwards (Ed.), *Language in Canada* (pp. 102–124). Cambridge: CUP.

Noels, K. A., Clément, R., & Pelletier, L. G. (1999). Perceptions of teacher communicative style and students' intrinsic and extrinsic motivation. *The Modern Language Journal, 83,* 23–34.

Noels, K. A., Clément, R., & Pelletier, L. G. (2001). Intrinsic, extrinsic and integrative orientations of French Canadian learners of English. *Canadian Modern Language Review, 57,* 424–442.

Norris, J. & Ortega, L. (2000). Effectiveness of L2 instruction: A research synthesis and quantitative meta-analysis. *Language Learning, 50,* 417–528.

Norton, B. (2000). *Identity and Language Learning: Gender, ethnicity and educational change.* Harlow: Pearson Education.

Norton, B. (2001). Non-participation, imagined communities and the language classroom. In M. P. Breen (Ed.), *Learner Contributions to Language Learning: New directions in research* (pp. 159–171). Harlow: Longman.

Noske, R. (1988). La syllabification et les règles de changement de syllabe en français. In S. P. Verluyten (Ed.), *La phonologie du schwa français* (pp. 43–88). Amsterdam: John Benjamins.

Noske, R. (1993). *A Theory of Syllabification and Segmental Alternation. With studies on the phonology of French, German, Tonkawa and Yawelmani* [Linguistische Arbeiten 296]. Tübingen: Niemeyer.

O'Connor, N. & Hermelin, B. (1983). The role of general ability and specific talents in information processing. *British Journal of Developmental Psychology, 1*, 389–403.

Odlin, T. (1992). Transferability and linguistic substrates. *Second Language Research, 8*, 171–202.

Ohta, A. S. (1995). Applying sociocultural theory to an analysis of learner discourse: Learner-learner collaborative interaction in the zone of proximal development. *Issues in Applied Linguistics, 6*, 93–121.

Ohta, A. S. (2001). A longitudinal study of the development of expression of alignment in Japanese as a foreign language. In K. R. Rose & G. Kasper (Eds.), *Pragmatics in Language Teaching* (pp. 103–120). New York: CUP.

Ohta, A. S. (2005). Interlanguage pragmatics in the zone of proximal development. *System, 33*(3), 503–517.

Olivier, R. & Sandmel, B. (1999). *Zydeco!* Jackson, MS: University Press of Mississippi.

Omar, A. S. (1992). Conversational openings in Kiswahili: The pragmatic performance of native and non-native speakers. In L. F. Bouton & Y. Kachru (Eds.), *Pragmatics and Language Learning* [Monograph series 3] (pp. 59–73). Urbana-Champaign, IL: University of Illinois at Urbana-Champaign, Division of English as an International Language.

Omar, A. S. (1993). Closing Kiswahili conversations: The performance of native and non-native speakers. In L. F. Bouton & Y. Kachru (Eds.), *Pragmatics and Language Learning* [Monograph series 4] (pp. 104–125). Urbana-Champaign, IL: University of Illinois at Urbana-Champaign, Division of English as an International Language.

Onwuegbuzie, A. J., Bailey, P., & Daley, C. E. (1999). Relationships between anxiety and achievement at three stages of learning a foreign language. *Perceptual and Motor Skills, 88*, 1085–1093.

Onwuegbuzie, A. J., Bailey, P., & Daley, C. E. (2000). The validation of three scales measuring anxiety at different stages of the foreign language learning process: The input anxiety scale, the processing anxiety scale, and the output anxiety scale. *Language Learning, 50*, 87–117.

Orlansky, M. & Bonvillian, J. (1988). Early sign language acquisition. In M. D. Smith & J. L. Locke (Eds.), *The Emergent Lexicon: The child's development of a linguistic vocabulary* (pp. 263–292). New York, NY: Academic Press.

Ormsby, A. (1995). The poetry and poetics of American Sign Language. PhD dissertation, Stanford University.

Osgood, C. E. & Sebeok, T. A. (1954). *Psycholinguistics: A survey of theory and research problems.* Bloomington, IN: Indiana University Press.

Ortega, L. (1999a). Language and equality: Ideological and structural constraints in foreign language education in the U.S. In T. Huebner & K. A. Davis (Eds.), *Sociopolitical Perspectives on Language Policy and Planning in the USA* (pp. 243–266). Amsterdam: John Benjamins.

Ortega, L. (1999b). Rethinking foreign language education: Political dimensions of the profession. In K. A. Davis (Ed.), *Foreign Language Teaching and Language Minority Education* (pp. 21–39). Honolulu, HI: Second Language Teaching and Curriculum Center, University of Hawai'i at Manoa.

Oubre, C. & Leonard, R. (1983). Free and proud: St Landry's Gens de couleur. In V. Baker & J. Kreamer (Eds.), *Louisiana Tapestry: The Ethnic Weave of St Landry Parish* (pp. 70–81). Lafayette, LA: University of Louisiana, Lafayette Center for Louisiana Studies.

Padden, C. (1993). Lessons to be learned from the young deaf orthographer. *Linguistics and Education, 5*, 71–86.

Padden, C. & Ramsey, C. (1998). Reading ability in signing deaf children. *Topics in Language Disorders, 18*, 30–46.

Padden, C. & Ramsey, C. (2000). American Sign Language and reading ability in deaf children. In C. Chamberlain, J. P. Morford, & R. I. Mayberry (Eds.), *Language Acquisition by Eye* (pp. 165–189). Mahwah, NJ: Lawrence Erlbaum.

Paden, W. D. (1998). *An Introduction to Old Occitan.* New York, NY: MLA.

Padilla, R. V. (2005). High-stakes testing and educational accountability as social constructions across cultures. In A. Valenzuela (Ed.), *Leaving Children Behind, How Texas-style Accountability Fails Latino Youth* (pp. 249–262). Albany, NY: State University of New York Press.

Pagé, M. (2006). Propositions pour une approche dynamique de la situation du français dans l'espace linguistique québécois. In P. Georgeault & M. Pagé (Eds.), *Le français, langue de la diversité québécoise* (pp. 27–76). Montréal: Québec Amérique.

Panther, K.-U. & Thornburg, L. (2001). A conceptual analysis of English -er nominals. In M. Putz, S. Niemeyer, & R. Dirven (Eds.), *Applied Cognitive Linguistics II: Language pedagogy* (pp. 149–200). Berlin: Mouton de Gruyter.

Paradis, M. (2004). *A Neurolinguistic Theory of Bilingualism*. Amsterdam: John Benjamins.

Paradis, J., Corre, M. L., & Genesee, F. (1998). The emergence of tense and agreement in child L2 French. *Second Language Research, 14*(3), 227–256.

Paradis, J. & Crago, M. (2004). Comparing L2 and SLI grammars in child French: Focus on DP. In P. Prévost & J. Paradis (Eds.), *The Acquisition of French in Different Contexts* (pp. 89–107). Amsterdam: John Benjamins.

Paradis, J., Crago, M., & Genesee, F. (2003). Object clitics as a clinical marker of SLI in French: Evidence from French-English bilingual children. In B. Beachley, A. Brown & F. Conlin (Eds.), *BUCLD 27 Proceedings* (pp. 638–649). Somerville, MA: Cascadilla.

Paris, G. (1888). Les parlers de France. *Revue des patois gallo-romans, 2*, 161–175.

Parodi, T., Schwartz, B. D., & Clahsen, H. (1997). On the L2 acquisition of the morpho-syntax of German nominals. *Essex Research Reports in Linguistics, 15*, 1–43.

Pater, J. (1998). Metrical parameter missetting in second language acquisition. In S. J. Hannahs & M. Young-Scholten (Eds.), *Focus on Phonological Acquisition* (pp. 235–261). Amsterdam: John Benjamins.

Pavlenko, A. (2002a). Bilingualism and emotions. *Multilingua, 2*(1), 45–78.

Pavlenko, A. (2002b). Poststructuralist approaches to the study of social factors in L2. In V. Cook (Ed.), *Portraits of the L2 User* (pp. 277–302). Clevedon: Multilingual Matters.

Pavlenko, A. (2003a). I never knew I was bilingual: Re-imagining teacher identities in TESOL. *Journal of Language, Identity, and Education, 2*, 251–268.

Pavlenko, A. (2003b). 'Language of the enemy': Foreign language education and national identity. *International Journal of Bilingual Education and Bilingualism, 6*(5), 313–331.

Pedersen, N. L., Plomin, R., McClearn, G. E., & Friberg, L. (1988). Neuroticism, extraversion, and related traits in adult twins reared apart and reared together. *Journal of Personality & Social Psychology, 55*, 950–957.

Peeters, B. (1999). 'Salut! Ça va? Vous avez passé un bon weekend?' *Journal of French Language Studies, 9*(2), 239–257.

Pennington, M. C. (2003). The impact of the computer in second language writing. In B. Kroll (Ed.), *Exploring the Dynamics of Second Language Writing* (pp. 287–310). Cambridge: CUP.

Pennington, M. & Stevens, V. (Eds.). (1992). *Computers in Applied Linguistics*. Clevedon: Multilingual Matters.

Pennycook, A. (1998). *English and the Discourses of Colonialism*. London: Routledge.

Pennycook, A. (2000). Lessons from colonial language practices. In G. Dueñas & I. Melis (Eds.), *Language Ideologies: Critical perspectives on the official English language movement*, Vol. 2: *History, theory, and policy* (pp. 195–220). Mahwah, NJ: Lawrence Erlbaum.

Pennycook, A. (2003). Global Englishes, Rip Slyme, and performativity. *Journal of Sociolinguistics, 7*(4), 513–533.

Pennycook, A. (2004). Performativity and language studies. *Critical Inquiry in Language Studies, 1*(1), 1–19.

Perdue, C. (Ed.). (1993). *Adult Language Acquisition: Cross-linguistic perspectives*, Vol. 1: *Field methods*. Cambridge: CUP.

Perdue, C. (1995). *L'Acquisition du français et de l'anglais par des adultes. Former des énoncés*. Paris: CNRS Editions.

Perdue, C. & Klein, W. (1997). The basic variety (or: Couldn't natural languages be much simpler?). *Second Language Research, 13,* 301–347.

Pesetsky, D. & Torrego, E. (2001). T-to-C Movement: Causes and consequences. In M. Kenstowicz (Ed.), *Ken Hale: A life in language* (pp. 355–426). Cambridge, MA: The MIT Press.

Petitto, L. A. (1987). On the autonomy of language and gesture: Evidence from the acquisition of personal pronouns in American Sign Language. *Cognition, 27,* 1–52.

Petitto, L. A. (1988). Language in the pre-linguistic child. In F. S. Kesel (Ed.), *The Development of Language and Language Researchers* (pp. 187–221). Hillsdale, NJ: Lawrence Erlbaum.

Petitto, L. A., Katerlos, M., Levy, B. G., Gauna, K., Tétreault, K., & Ferraro, V. (2001). Bilingual signed and spoken language acquisition from birth: Implications for the mechanisms underlying early bilingual language acquisition. *Journal of Child Language, 28,* 453–496.

Petitto, L. A. & Kovelman, I. (2003). The bilingual paradox: How signing-speaking bilingual children help us resolve bilingual issues and teach us about the brain's mechanisms underlying all language acquisition. *Language Learning, 8*(3), 5–18.

Petitto, L. A. & Marentette, P. (1991). Babbling in the manual mode: Evidence for the ontogeny of language. *Science, 251,* 1483–1496.

Pfister, M. (1993). Scripta et koiné en ancien français aux XIIe et XIIIe siècles. In P. Knecht & Z. Marzys (Eds.), *Formation spontanée de koinés et standardization dans la Gallo-Romania et son voisinage* (pp. 17–41). Neuchâtel: Université de Neuchâtel; Geneva: Droz.

Phillips, J. K. (1999). Introduction: Standards for world languages – On a firm foundation. In J. K. Phillips & R. M. Terry (Eds.), *Foreign Language Standards: Linking research, theories, and practices* (pp. 1–14). Lincolnwood, IL: National Textbook Company.

Phillipson, R. (1992). *Linguistic Imperialism.* Oxford: Oxford University Press.

Phillipson, R. (2003). *English-Only Europe? Challenging Language Policy.* London: Routledge.

Picallo, M. C. (1991). Nominals and nominalizations in Catalan. *Probus, 3,* 279–316.

Picard, M. (1987). *An Introduction to the Comparative Phonetics of English and French in North America.* Amsterdam: John Benjamins.

Picard, M. (2004). Perte auditive acquise chez l'enfant. Paper presented at the North American Conference on Deafness Screening and Intervention in Early Childhood. Available at http://www.inspq.qc.ca (Institut National de santé publique, Québec).

Picone, M. D. (1997). Enclave dialect contraction: An external overview of Louisiana French. *American Speech, 72,* 117–153.

Picone, M. D. (2003). Anglophone slaves in Francophone Louisiana. *American Speech, 78*(4), 404–433.

Pienemann, M. (1992). COALA: A computational system for interlanguage analysis. *Second Language Research, 8*(1), 59–92.

Piller, I. (2002). Passing for a native speaker: Identity and success in second language learning. *Journal of Sociolinguistics, 6*(2), 179–206.

Pinker, S. (1989). *Learnability and Cognition: The acquisition of argument structure.* Cambridge, MA: The MIT Press.

Plag, I. (1993). *Sentential Complementation in Sranan: On the formation of an English-based creole language.* Tübingen: Niemeyer.

Platt, J., Weber, H., & Liam, H. M. (1984). *The New Englishes.* London: Routledge.

Plénat, M. (1987). On the structure of rime in Standard French. *Linguistics, 25,* 867–887.

Plessy v. Ferguson, 163 U.S. 537 (1896).

Ploog, K. (2002). *Le français à Abidjan.* Paris: CNRS.

Poerck, G. de (1963). Les plus anciens textes de la langue française comme témoins d'époque. *Revue de linguistique romane, 27,* 1–34.

Pollock, J.-Y. (1989). Verb movement, Universal Grammar and the structure of IP. *Linguistic Inquiry, 20,* 365–424.

Pollock, J.-Y. (1997). *Langage et cognition. Introduction au programme minimaliste de la grammaire générative.* Paris: Presses Universitaires de France.

Poole, D. (1992). Language socialization in the second language classroom. *Language Learning, 42,* 593–616.

Pope, M. K. (1952). *From Latin to Modern French.* Manchester: Manchester University Press.

Porcher, L. (1995). *Le Français langue étrangère, émergence et enseignement d'une discipline.* Paris: Hachette Education.

Posner, R. (1966). *The Romance Languages: A linguistic introduction.* New York, NY: Doubleday.

Posner, R. (1997). *Linguistic Change in French.* Cambridge: CUP.

Poulin, C. & Miller, C. (1994). On narrative discourse and point of view in Quebec Sign Language. In K. Emmorey & J. Reilly (Eds.), *Sign, Gesture and Space* (pp. 117–131). Hillsdale, NJ: Lawrence Erlbaum.

Poullet, H. & Telchid, S. (1990). *Le créole sans peine (guadeloupéen).* Paris: Assimil.

Prah, K. K. (Ed.). (1998). *Between Distinction and Extinction.* Johannesburg: Witwatersrand University Press.

Pratt, M. L. (2003). Building a new public idea about language. *Profession,* 110–119.

Pratt, M. L. (2004). Language and national security: Making a new public commitment. *The Modern Language Journal, 88*(2), 289–291.

Presneau, J.-R. (1998). *Signes et institution des sourds aux XVIIIe–XIXe siècles.* Seyssel: Champ Vallon.

Preston, D. (1989). *Variation and Second Language Acquisition.* Oxford: Blackwell.

Preston, D. (2000). Three kinds of sociolinguistics and SLA: A psycholinguistic perspective. In B. Swierzbin, F. Morris, M. E. Anderson, C. E. Klee, & E. Tarone (Eds.), *Social and Cognitive Factors in Second Language Acquisition* (pp. 3–30). Somerville, MA: Cascadilla.

Prévost, P. (2004). The semantic and aspectual properties of child L2 root infinitives. In P. Prévost & J. Paradis (Eds.), *The Acquisition of French in Different Contexts* (pp. 305–331). Amsterdam: John Benjamins.

Prévost, P. & Paradis, J. (Eds.). (2004). *The Acquisition of French in Different Contexts.* Amsterdam: John Benjamins.

Prévost, P. & White, L. (2000a). Truncation and missing inflection in second language acquisition. In M. A. Friedmann & L. Rizzi (Eds.), *The Acquisition of Syntax* (pp. 202–235). London: Longman.

Prévost, P. & White, L. (2000b). Missing surface inflection or impairment in second language acquisition? Evidence from tense and agreement. *Second Language Research, 16*(2), 103–133.

Price, G. (1971). *The French Language Present and Past.* London: Arnold.

Price, M. L. (1991). The subjective experience of foreign language anxiety: Interviews with highly anxious students. In E. K. Horwitz & D. J. Young (Eds.), *Language Anxiety* (pp. 101–108). Englewood Cliffs, NJ: Prentice-Hall.

Prinz, P., Kuntze, M., & Strong, M. (2001). Variable factors in the relationship between American Sign Language (ASL) proficiency and English literacy acquisition in deaf children. In M. Almgren, A. Barrena, M.-J. Ezerzabarrena, I. Idiazabal, & B. Mc Whinney (Eds.), *Proceedings of the 8th Conference of the International Association for the Study of Child Language* (pp. 1429–1440). Somerville, MA: Cascadilla.

Prinz, P. & Strong, M. (1998). ASL proficiency and English literacy within a bilingual deaf education model of instruction. *Topics in Language Disorders, 18*(4), 47–60.

Prinz, P., Strong, M., & Kuntze, M. (1994). *The Test of ASL.* San Francisco CA: State University and California Research Institute.

Pritchard, D. F. L. (1952). An investigation into the relationship between personality traits and ability in modern languages. *British Journal of Educational Psychology, 22,* 147–148.

Prodeau, M. (2005). Gender and number in French L2: Can we find out more about the constraints on production in L2? In J.-M. Dewaele (Ed.), *Focus on French as a Foreign Language* (pp. 114–134). Clevedon: Multilingual Matters.

Prujiner, A., Deshaies, D., Hamers, J., Blanc, M., Clément, R., & Landry, R. (1984). *Variation du comportement langagier lorsque deux langues sont en contact.* Québec: International Centre for Research on Language Planning.

Pustejovsky, J. (1995). *The Generative Lexicon*. Cambridge, MA: The MIT Press.

Quigley, S. P., Power, D. J., & Steinkamp, M. W. (1977). The language structure of deaf children. *The Volta Review, 79*, 73–84.

Ramage, K. (1990). Motivational factors and persistence in foreign language study. *Language Learning, 40*, 189–219.

Rampton, B. (1990). Displacing the 'native speaker': Expertise, affiliation and inheritance. *ELT Journal, 44*, 338–343.

Rampton, B. (1997). Retuning in applied linguistics. *International Journal of Applied Linguistics, 7*(1), 3–25.

Rampton, B. (1999). Deutsch in Inner London and the animation of an instructed foreign language. *Journal of Sociolinguistics, 3*(4), 480–504.

Ranney, S. (1992). Learning a new script: An explanation of sociolinguistic competence. *Applied Linguistics, 13*, 25–50.

Rayfield, J. R. (1970). *The Languages of a Bilingual Community*. The Hague: Mouton.

Reagan, T. G. (2002). *Language, Education, and Ideology: Mapping the landscape of U.S. schools*. Westport, CT: Praeger.

Regan, V. (1995). The acquisition of sociolinguistic native speech norms. In B. Freed (Ed.), *Second Language Acquisition in a Study Abroad Context* (pp. 245–267). Amsterdam: John Benjamins.

Regan, V. (1996). Variation in French interlanguage: A longitudinal study of sociolinguistic competence. In R. Bayley & D. Preston (Eds.), *Second Language Acquisition and Linguistic Variation* (pp. 177–201). Amsterdam: John Benjamins.

Regan, V. (1997). Les apprenants avancés, la lexicalisation et l'acquisition de la compétence sociolinguistique: Une approche variationniste. *Acquisition et interaction en langue étrangère, 9*, 193–210.

Regan, V. (2004). The relationship between the group and the individual and the acquisition of native speaker variation patterns: A preliminary study. *International Review of Applied Linguistics, 42*, 335–348.

Regan, V. (2005). From speech community back to classroom: What variation analysis can tell us about the role of context in the acquisition of French as a foreign language. In J.-M. Dewaele (Ed.), *Focus on French as a Foreign Language: Multidisciplinary approaches* (pp. 191–209). Clevedon: Multilingual Matters.

Rehner, K. (2005). *Developing Aspects of Second Language Discourse Competence*. Muenchen: Lincom.

Rehner, K. & Mougeon, R. (1999). Variation in the spoken French of immersion students: To *ne* or not to *ne*, that is the sociolinguistic question. *The Canadian Modern Language Review, 56*, 124–154.

Rehner, K. & Mougeon, R. (2003). The effect of educational input on the development of sociolinguistic competence by French immersion students: The case of expressions of consequence in spoken French. *The Journal of Educational Thought/Revue de la Pensée Educative, 37*, 259–281.

Rehner, K., Mougeon, R., & Nadasdi, T. (2003). The learning of sociolinguistic variation by advanced FSL learners: The case of *nous* versus *on* in immersion French. *Studies in Second Language Acquisition, 25*, 127–157.

Révérand, E. (2004). Etude des énoncés bimodaux en contexte de bilinguisme bimodal: Etude de cas. MA thesis, University François-Rabelais, Tours.

Rézeau, P. (Ed.). (2001). *Dictionnaire des régionalismes de France: Géographie et histoire d'un patrimoine linguistique*. Brussels: De Boeck/Duculot.

Richter, M. (1983). A quelle époque a-t-on cessé de parler latin en Gaule? A propos d'une question mal posée. *Annales ESC, 3*, 439–448.

Rickford, J. R. & McNair-Knox, F. (1994). Addressee – and topic – influenced style shift. A quantitative sociolinguistic study. In D. Biber & E. Finegan (Eds.), *Sociolinguistic Perspectives on Register Variation* (pp. 235–276). Oxford: OUP.

Riding, R. J. & Banner, G. E. (1986). Sex and personality differences in second language performance in secondary school pupils. *British Journal of Educational Psychology, 56*, 366–370.

Rintell, E. M. & Mitchell, C. J. (1989). Studying requests and apologies: An inquiry into method. In S. Blum-Kulka, J. House, & G. Kasper (Eds.), *Cross-Cultural Pragmatics: Requests and apologies* (pp. 248–272). Norwood, NJ: Ablex.

Ritchie, W. C. & Bhatia, T. K. (Eds.). (1996). *Handbook of Second Language Acquisition*. New York, NY: Academic Press.

Ritter, E. (1991). Two functional categories in noun phrases: Evidence from modern Hebrew. In S. Rothstein (Ed.), *Syntax and Semantics, 25: Perspectives on Phrase Structure* (pp. 37–62). New York, NY: Academic Press.

Ritter, E. (1993). Where's gender? *Linguistic Inquiry, 24*, 795–803.

Roberts, I. (1998). *Have/Be* raising, Move F, and Procrastinate. *Linguistic Inquiry, 23*, 113–125.

Robertson, R. (1995). Globalization. Time-space and homogeneity-heterogeneity. In M. Featherstone, S. Lash, & R. Robertson (Eds.), *Global Modernities* (pp. 25–44). Thousand Oaks, CA: Sage.

Robinson, D., Gabriel, N., & Katchan, O. (1994). Personality and second language learning. *Personality and Individual Differences, 16*, 143–157.

Rodney, W. (1982). *How Europe Underdeveloped Africa*. Howard University Press.

Rogoff, B. (1990). *Apprenticeship in Thinking: Cognitive development in social context*. New York, NY: OUP.

Rohlfs, G. (1970). *Le Gascon, études de philologie pyrénéenne* [ZRP Beiheft 85]. Tübingen: Niemeyer.

Romaine, S. (1988). *Pidgin and Creole Languages*. New York: Longman.

Ronjat, J. (1913). *Le dévelopement du langage observé chez un enfant bilingue*. Paris: Champion.

Ronjat, J. (1932–1941). *Grammaire historique des parlers provençaux modernes*, 4 Vols. Montpellier: Société des langues romanes.

Rosa, E. & O'Neill, M. (1999). Explicitness, intake, and the issue of awareness. *Studies in Second Language Acquisition, 21*, 511–556.

Rose, K. R. (2000). An exploratory cross-sectional study of interlanguage pragmatic development. *Studies in Second Language Acquisition, 22*, 27–67.

Rose, K. R. (2005). On the effects of instruction in second language pragmatics. *System, 33*(3), 385–399.

Rose, K. R. & Kasper, G. (Eds.). (2001). *Pragmatics in Language Teaching*. New York, NY: CUP.

Rose, K. R. & Ng, C. (2001). Inductive and deductive approaches to teaching compliments and compliment responses. In K. R. Rose & G. Kasper (Eds.), *Pragmatics in Language Teaching* (pp. 145–170). Cambridge: CUP.

Rossillon, P. (1995). *Atlas de la langue française*. Paris: Bordas.

Rothwell, W. (2001). *OED, MED, AND:* The making of a new dictionary of English. *Anglia. Zeitschrift für Englische Philologie, 119*, 527–553.

Rule, S. (2004). French interlanguage corpora: Recent developments. In F. Myles & R. Towell (Eds.), *The Acquisition of French as a Second Language* [Special issue of the *Journal of French Language Studies*] (pp. 343–356). Cambridge: CUP.

Rule, S. & Marsden, E. (2006). The acquisition of functional categories in early French L2 grammars: The use of finite and non-finite verbs in negative contexts. *Second Language Research, 22*(2), 188–218.

Rule, S., Marsden, E., Myles, F., & Mitchell, R. (2003). Constructing a database of French interlanguage oral corpora. In D. Archer, P. Rayson, A. Wilson, & T. McEnery (Eds.), *Proceedings of the Corpus Linguistics 2003 Conference* [UCREL Technical Papers No. 16] (pp. 669–677). Lancaster: University of Lancaster.

Rutherford, W. & Thomas, M. (2001). The Child Language Data Exchange System in research on second language acquisition. *Second Language Research, 17*(2), 195–212.

Ruwet, N. (1972). *Théorie syntaxique et syntaxe du français*. Paris: Editions du Seuil.

Ryon, D. (2005). Language death studies and local knowledge: The case of Cajun French. In A. S. Canagarajah (Ed.), *Reclaiming the Local in Language Policy and Practice* (pp. 55–72). Mahwah, NJ: Lawrence Erlbaum.

Sabourin, L. (2001). L1 effects on the processing of grammatical gender in L2. In S. Foster-Cohen & A. Nizegorodcew (Eds.), *EUROSLA Yearbook 1* (pp. 159–169). Amsterdam: John Benjamins.

Sabourin, L., Stowe, L. A., & Haan, G. J. (2006). Transfer effects in learning a second language grammatical gender system. *Second Language Research, 22*, 1–29.

Sacks, H., Schegloff, E. A., & Jefferson, G. (1974). A simplest systematics for the organization of turn-taking in conversation. *Language, 50*(4), 696–735.

Salien, J.-M. (1998). Quebec French: Attitudes and pedagogical perspectives. *The Modern Language Journal, 82*(1), 95–102.

Sallagoïty, P. (1975). The sign language of Southern France. *Sign Language Studies, 7*, 181–202.

Sallinen-Kuparinen, A., McCroskey, J. C., & Richmond, V. P. (1991). Willingness to communicate, communication apprehension, introversion, and self-reported communication competence: Finnish and American comparisons. *Communication Research Reports, 8*, 55–64.

Sampson, K. (1997). L'influence des langues africaines sur l'évolution du français en Afrique. *Afrikanistische Arbeitspapiere, 52*, 45–59.

Sampson, R. (1999). *Nasal Vowel Evolution in Romance.* Oxford: OUP.

Sapir, E. (1925). Sound patterns in language. *Language, 1*, 37–51.

Sasaki, M. (1998). Investigating EFL students' production of speech acts: A comparison of production questionnaires and role plays. *Journal of Pragmatics, 30*, 457–484.

Savané, A. (1993). L'école des citoyens. *SOURCES.* Paris: UNESCO.

Savignon, S. (1972). *Communicative Competence: An experiment in foreign-language teaching.* Philadelphia, PA: Center for Curriculum Development.

Sawyer, M. (1992). The development of pragmatics in Japanese as a second language: The sentence-final particle *ne.* In G. Kasper (Ed.), *Pragmatics of Japanese as a Native and Foreign Language* [Technical Report No. 3] (pp. 83–125). Honolulu, HI: Second Language Teaching & Curriculum Center, University of Hawai'i at Manoa.

Sax, K. (2003). Acquisition of stylistic variation in American learners of French. PhD dissertation, Indiana University, Bloomington.

Scarcella, R. (1983). Discourse accent in second language performance. In S. Gass & L. Selinker (Eds.), *Language Transfer in Language Learning* (pp. 306–326). Rowley, MA: Newbury House.

Schachter, J. (1988). Second language acquisition and its relationship to Universal Grammar. *Applied Linguistics, 9*, 219–235.

Schachter, J. (1989). Testing a proposed universal. In S. Gass & J. Schachter (Eds.), *Linguistic Perspectives on Second Language Acquisition* (pp. 73–88). Cambridge: CUP.

Schane, S. (1968). *French Phonology and Morphology.* Cambridge, MA: The MIT Press.

Schauer, G. A. (2004). 'May you speak louder maybe?'. In S. H. Foster-Cohen, M. Sharwood Smith, A. Sorace, & M. Ota (Eds.), *EUROSLA Yearbook 4* (pp. 253–273). Amsterdam: John Benjamins.

Scheer, T. (2004). *A Lateral Theory of Phonology.* Berlin: Mouton de Gruyter.

Schembri, A. (2003). Rethinking classifiers in signed languages. In K. Emmorey (Ed.), *Perspectives on Classifier Constructions in Sign Languages* (pp. 3–34). Mahwah, NJ: Lawrence Erlbaum.

Schieffelin, B. B. & Ochs, E. (1986). Language socialization. *Annual Review of Anthropology, 15*, 163–91.

Schiffman, H. F. (1996). *Linguistic Culture and Language Policy.* London: Routledge.

Schiff-Myers, N. B. (1993). Hearing children of deaf parents. In D. M. V. Bishop & K. Mogford (Eds.), *Language Development in Exceptional Circumstances* (pp. 47–61). Hove: Psychology Press.

Schmidt, R. (1983). Interaction, acculturation and the acquisition of communicative competence: A case study of an adult. In N. Wolfson & E. Judd (Eds.), *Sociolinguistics and Language Acquisition* (pp. 137–174). Cambridge, MA: Newbury House.

Schmidt, R. (1990). The role of consciousness in second language learning. *Applied Linguistics, 11*, 129–158.

Schmidt, R. (1993a). Consciousness, learning and interlanguage pragmatics. In G. Kasper & S. Blum-Kulka (Eds.), *Interlanguage Pragmatics* (pp. 21–42). New York, NY: OUP.

Schmidt, R. (1993b). Awareness and second language acquisition. *Annual Review of Applied Linguistics, 13*, 206–226.

Schmidt, R. (1995). Consciousness and foreign language learning: A tutorial on the role of attention and awareness in learning. In R. Schmidt (Ed.), *Attention and Awareness in Foreign Language Learning* (pp. 1–63). Honolulu, HI: Second Language Teaching and Curriculum Center, University of Hawai'i at Manoa.

Schmidt, R. (2001). Attention. In P. Robinson (Ed.), *Cognition and Second Language Instruction* (pp. 3–32). Cambridge: CUP.

Schmidt, R., Boraie, D., & Kassabgy, O. (1996). Foreign language motivation: Internal structure and external connections. In R. L. Oxford (Ed.), *Language Learning Motivation: Pathways to the new century* (pp. 14–87). Honolulu, HI: University of Hawai'i Press.

Schmidt, R. & Frota, S. N. (1986). Developing basic conversational ability in a second language: A case study of an adult learner of Portuguese. In R. Day (Ed.), *Talking to Learn* (pp. 237–326). Rowley, MA: Newbury House.

Schmitt, N. (Ed.). (2002). *An Introduction to Applied Linguistics*. London: Arnold.

Schmitt, N. (Ed.). (2004). *Formulaic Sequences*. Amsterdam: John Benjamins.

Schmitt, N. & Zimmerman, C. B. (2002). Derivative word forms: What do learners know? *TESOL Quarterly, 36*(2), 145–171.

Schriefers, H. & Jescheniak, J. D. (1999). Representation and processing of grammatical gender in language production: A review. *Journal of Psycholinguistic Research, 28*, 575–600.

Schumann, J. H. (1978). *The Pidginization Process: A Model for Second Language Acquisition*. Rowley, MA: Newbury House.

Schwartz, B. D. (1993). On explicit and negative evidence effecting and affecting competence and linguistic behaviors. *Studies in Second Language Acquisition, 15*, 147–163.

Schwartz, B. D. (1996). Now for some facts, with a focus on development and an explicit role for the L1. Comment on Epstein et al. (1996). *Behavioral and Brain Sciences, 19*, 739–740.

Schwartz, B. & Sprouse, R. (1994). Word order and nominative case in non-native language acquisition: A longitudinal study of (L1 Turkish) German interlanguage. In T. Hoekstra & B. Schwartz (Eds.), *Language Acquisition Studies in Generative Grammar: Papers in honor of Kenneth Wexler from the 1991 GLOW workshops* (pp. 317–368). Amsterdam: John Benjamins.

Schwartz, B. D. & Sprouse, R. (1996). L2 cognitive states and the Full Transfer/Full Access model. *Second Language Research, 12*, 40–72.

Schwartz, B. D. & Sprouse, R. A. (2000). When syntactic theories evolve: Consequences for L2 acquisition research. In J. Archibald (Ed.), *Second Language Acquisition and Linguistic Theory* (pp. 156–186). Oxford: Blackwell.

Schwarzer, R. (1986). Self-related cognition in anxiety and motivation: An introduction. In R. Schwarzer (Ed.), *Self-Related Cognition in Anxiety and Motivation* (pp. 1–17). Hillsdale, NJ: Lawrence Erlbaum.

Scollon, R. (2004). Teaching language and culture as hegemonic practice. *The Modern Language Journal, 88*(2), 271–274.

Scollon, R. & Scollon, S. B. K. (2001). *Intercultural Communication: A discourse approach* (2nd ed.). Malden, MA: Blackwell.

Scott, M. (1999). *WordSmith Tools*. Oxford: OUP.

Scovel, T. (1978). The effect of affect on foreign language learning: A review of the anxiety research. *Language Learning, 28*, 129–142.

Scullen, M. E. (1997). *French Prosodic Morphology. A unified account*. Bloomington, IN: IULC.

Searle, J. R. (1969). *Speech Acts. An essay in the philosophy of language*. Cambridge: CUP.

Searle, J. R. (1976). A classification of illocutionary acts. *Language in Society, 5*, 1–23.

Searle, J. R., Kiefer, F., & Bierwisch, M. (1980). Introduction. In J. R. Searle, F. Kiefer, & M. Bierwisch (Eds.), *Speech Act Theory and Pragmatics* (pp. vii–xii). Dordrecht: Reidel.

Séguin, H. (1969). Les marques du genre dans le lexique français écrit contemporain: Compilation des cas et essai de classement. PhD dissertation, Université de Montréal.

Seguin, J.-P. (2003). Enchaînement et usage du point. In B. Combettes (Ed.), *Evolution et variation en français préclassique. Etudes de syntaxe* (pp. 69–137). Paris: Champion.

Séguy, J. (1973). Les atlas linguistiques de la France par régions. *Langue française, 18*, 65–90.

Selinker, L. (1972). Interlanguage. *International Review of Applied Linguistics, 10*, 209–231.

Selinker, L. & Lakshmanan, U. (1992). Language transfer and fossilization: The multiple effects principle. In S. Gass & L. Selinker (Eds.), *Language Transfer in Language Learning* (pp. 197–216). Amsterdam: John Benjamins.

Selkirk, E. O. (1978). The French foot: On the status of mute e. *Studies in French Linguistics, 1*(2), 141–150.

Selkirk, E. O. (1980). *The Phrase Phonology of English and French* [MIT doctoral dissertation 1972]. New York, NY: Garland.

Sero-Guillaume, P. (1994). Les sourds et l'acquisition du français. In P. Geneste & P. Sero-Guillaume (Eds.), *Les sourds, le français et la langue des signes (Bulletin CNFIJS)* (pp. 51–74). Chambery: Université de Savoie.

Sharwood Smith, M. & Truscott, J. (2005). Stages or continua in second language acquisition: A Mogul solution. *Applied Linguistics, 22*(2), 219–240.

Shelton, J. (1996). Second language acquisition of grammatical gender and agreement in French. PhD dissertation, University of Essex, England.

Shohamy, E. (2001). *The Power of Tests: A critical perspective of the uses of language tests.* London: Longman.

Shohamy, E. (2005). The power of tests over teachers: The power of teachers over tests. In D. J. Tedick (Ed.), *Second Language Teacher Education: International perspectives* (pp. 101–111). Mahwah, NJ: Lawrence Erlbaum.

Siegel, J. (1999). Transfer constraints and substrate influence in Melanesian Pidgin. *Journal of Pidgin and Creole Languages, 13*, 1–44.

Silverstein, M. (1998). The uses and utility of ideology: A commentary. In B. B. Schieffelin, K. A. Woolard, & P. V. Kroskrity (Eds.), *Language Ideologies: Practice and Theory* (pp. 123–145). Oxford: OUP.

Simard, Y. (1994). Les Français de Côte d'Ivoire. *Langue Française, 104*, 20–36.

Sinclair, J. (Ed.). (1987). *Looking Up: An account of the COBUILD project.* London: Harper Collins.

Sinclair, J. (1991). *Corpus Concordance Collocation.* Oxford: OUP.

Singler, J. V. (1986). Short note. *Journal of Pidgin and Creole Languages, 1*, 141–145.

Singler, J. V. (1988). The homogeneity of the substrate as a factor in pidgin/creole Genesis. *Language, 64*, 27–51.

Singler, J. V. (1990). On the use of socio-historical criteria in the comparison of creoles. *Linguistics, 28*, 645–669.

Singler, J. V. (1993). African influence upon Afri-American language varieties: A consideration of sociohistorical factors. In S. Mufwene (Ed.), *Africanisms in Afro-American Language Varieties* (pp. 235–253). Athens, GA: University of Georgia Press.

Singler, J. V. (1996). Theories of creole genesis, socio-historical considerations, and the evaluation of evidence: The case of Haitian creole and the relexification hypothesis. *Journal of Pidgin and Creole Languages, 11*, 185–230.

Singleton, D. (1999). *Exploring the Second Language Mental Lexicon.* Cambridge: CUP.

Siskin, H. J. (1999). The invalid revalidated: Caring for the language of Molière. *Profession, 1999*, 18–24.

Skehan, P. (1989). *Individual Differences in Second Language Learning.* London: Edward Arnold.

Slobin, D. I. (2002). *Can a Deaf Child Learn from Hearing Parents?* Berkeley, CA: University of California. Report of Research NSF Award (summary of the research conducted for 4 years with N. Hoiting).

Slobin, D. I., Hoiting, N., Kuntze, M., Lindert, R. B., Weinberg, A., Pyers, J., Anthony, M. E., Biederman, Y. M., & Thumann, H. (2003). A cognitive/functional perspective on the acquisition of 'classifiers'. In K. Emmorey (Ed.), *Perspectives on Classifier Constructions in Sign Languages* (pp. 271–296). Mahwah, NJ: Lawrence Erlbaum.

Smart, J. C., Elton, C. F., & Burnett, C. W. (1970). Underachievers and overachievers in intermediate French. *The Modern Language Journal, 54*, 415–442.

Smedts, W. (1988). De beheersing van de nederlandse woordvorming tussen 7 en 17. In F. Van Besien (Ed.), *First Language Acquisition* [ABLA Papers 12]. Antwerp: Association Belge de Linguistique Appliquée/Universitaire Instelling Antwerpen.

Smith, C. L. (2003). Vowel devoicing in contemporary French. *Journal of French Language Studies, 13*, 177–194.

Smith, N. & Tsimpli, I.-M. (1995). *The Mind of a Savant: Language learning and modularity.* Oxford: Blackwell.

Snyder, W., Senghas, A., & Inman, K. (2001). Agreement morphology and the acquisition of Noun-drop in Spanish. *Language Acquisition, 9*, 157–173.

Sokolik, M. & Smith, M. (1992). Assignment of gender to French nouns in primary and secondary language: A connectionist model. *Second Language Research, 8*(1), 39–58.

Sokolov, J. & Snow, C. (Eds.). (1994). *Handbook of Research in Language Development Using CHILDES.* Hillsdale, NJ: Lawrence Erlbaum.

Sonaiya, R. (2002). Autonomous language learning in Africa: A mismatch of cultural assumptions. *Language, Culture and Curriculum, 15*(2), 106–116.

Sonaiya, R. (2003). The globalisation of communication and the African foreign language user. In *New Language Bearings In Africa: A fresh quest.* Special Issue of *Language, Culture and Curriculum, 16*(2), 146–154.

Sonaiya, R. (2004). The apparent failure of education to produce development in Africa: What next? Paper presented at the Goethe Institute Workshop on Faculty Development, Lagos, Nigeria, Oct. 22–23, 2004.

Sonaiya, R. (2005). Re-defining the stakes in the teaching of translation. Paper presented at the International Conference on Translation and Interpretation, University of Lagos, Nigeria, July 10–15, 2005.

Sorace, A. (2005). Interfaces in L2 language development. Keynote lecture given at GALA 2005, Siena, Italy.

Soutet, O. (2002). De la double représentation du subjonctif présent en psychomécanique. *Cahiers Chronos, 7*, 99–116.

Spa, J. J. (1989). [ʌ, e, ɛ]: La solution paracyclique. *Lingvisticæ investigationes, 13*(1), 147–178.

Spada, N. (1997). Form-focused instruction and second language acquisition: A review of classroom and laboratory research. *Language Teaching, 29*, 1–25.

Spaëth, V. (1998). *Généalogie de la didactique du français langue étrangère, L'enjeu africain.* Paris: CIRELFA/Agence de la Francophonie/Didier Érudition.

Spilka, I. (1976). Assessment of second-language performance in immersion programs. *The Canadian Modern Language Review, 32*, 543–561.

Steele, J. (2001). Phonetic cues to phonological acquisition: Evidence from L2 syllabification. In A. H.-J. Do, L. Dominguez, & A. Johansen (Eds.), *Boston University Conference on Language Development 25 Proceedings* (pp. 732–743). Somerville, MA: Cascadilla.

Steele, J. (2002a). Representation and phonological licensing in the L2 acquisition of prosodic structure. PhD dissertation, McGill University.

Steele, J. (2002b). L2 learners' modification of target language syllable structure: Prosodic licensing effects in interlanguage phonology. In A. James & J. Leather (Eds.), *New Sounds 2000: Proceedings of the fourth international symposium on the acquisition of second-language speech* (pp. 315–324). Klagenfurt: University of Klagenfurt.

Stein, P. (1987). Kreolsprache als Quelle fur das gesprochene Französisch des 17. und 18. Jh. *Archiv für das Studium der Neueren Sprachen und Literaturen, 224*, 52–66.

Stemberger, J. P. (1985). CV phonology and French consonants: A concrete approach. *Journal of Linguistics, 21*, 453–457.

Stevens, F. (1984). *Strategies in Second Language Acquisition.* Quebec: Eden Press.

Steward, D. (2004). The Master's Degree in the modern languages since 1966. *ADFL Bulletin, 36*(1), 61–80.

Stewart, W. A. (1968). A sociolinguistic typology for describing national multilingualism. In J. Fishman (Ed.), *Readings in the Sociology of Language* (pp. 531–545). The Hague: Mouton.

Street, B. V. (1984). *Literacy in Theory and Practice.* Cambridge: CUP.

Street, B. V. (1995). *Social Literacies: Critical Approaches to Literacy in Development, Ethnography and Education*. London: Longman.

Strong, M. & Prinz, P. (1997). A study of the relationship between American Sign Language and English literacy. *Journal of Deaf Studies and Deaf Education, 2*, 37–46.

Strong, M. & Prinz, P. (2000). Is American Sign Language skill related to English literacy? In C. Chamberlain, J. P. Morford, & R. I. Mayberry (Eds.), *Language Acquisition by Eye* (pp. 131–141). Mahwah, NJ: Lawrence Erlbaum.

Strozer, J. (1994). *Language Acquisition After Puberty*. Washington, DC: Georgetown University Press.

Stubbs, M. (1996). *Text and Corpus Analysis*. Oxford: Blackwell.

Surridge, M. & Lessard, G. (1984). Pour une prise de conscience du genre grammatical. *The Canadian Modern Language Review, 42*, 43–52.

Sutton-Spence, R. (2005). *Analyzing Sign Poetry*. New York, NY: Palgrave.

Swain, M. (2000). French Immersion research in Canada: Recent contributions to SLA and applied linguistics. *Annual Review of Applied Linguistics, 20*, 199–212.

Swain, M. & Burnaby, B. (1976). Personality characteristics and second language learning in young children: A pilot study. *Working Papers on Bilingualism, 11*, 115–128.

Swain, M. & Lapkin, S. (1990). Aspects of the sociolinguistic performance of early and late French Immersion students. In R. C. Scarcella, E. S. Anderson, & S. D. Krashen (Eds.), *Developing Communicative Competence in a Second Language* (pp. 41–54). New York, NY: Newbury House.

Swain, M. & Lapkin, S. (2005a). The evolving socio-political context of immersion education in Canada: Some implications for program development. *International Journal of Applied Linguistics, 15*, 169–186.

Swain, M. & Lapkin, S. (2005b). Multilingualism through immersion? In D. Wolff (Ed.), *Mehrsprachige Individuen – Vielsprachige Gesellschaften* (pp. 191–206). Bern: Peter Lang.

Swales, J. M. (1997). English as Tyrannosaurus rex. *World Englishes, 16*(3), 373–382.

Swiggers, P. (1990). Ideology and the 'clarity' of French. In J. E. Joseph & T. J. Taylor (Eds.), *Ideologies of Language* (pp. 112–130). London: Routledge.

Tabouret-Keller, A. & Gadet, F. (2003). A French taste for theories. *International Journal of the Sociology of Language, 160*, 3–16.

Tachibana, Y., Matsukawa, R., & Zhong, Q. X. (1996). Attitudes and motivation for learning English: A cross-national comparison of Japanese and Chinese high school students. *Psychological Reports, 79*, 691–700.

Taft, M. & Meunier, F. (1998). Lexical representation of gender: A quasiregular domain. *Journal of Psycholinguistic Research, 27*, 23–45.

Takahashi, S. (1996). Pragmatic transferability. *Studies in Second Language Acquisition, 18*, 189–223.

Takahashi, S. (2001). The role of input enhancement in developing pragmatic competence. In K. R. Rose & G. Kasper (Eds.), *Pragmatics in Language Teaching* (pp. 171–199). Cambridge: CUP.

Takahashi, T. & Beebe, L. M. (1987). The development of pragmatic competence by Japanese learners of English. *JALT Journal, 8*(2), 131–155.

Talmy, L. (2000). *Toward a Cognitive Semantics*. Cambridge, MA: The MIT Press.

Taraban, R. (2004). Drawing learners attention to syntactic context aids gender-like category induction. *Journal of Memory and Language, 51*, 202–216.

Tarone, E. (1988). *Variation in Interlanguage*. London: Edward Arnold.

Tarone, E. (1989). On chameleons and monitors. In M. R. Eisenstein (Ed.), *The Dynamic Interlanguage* (pp. 3–15). New York, NY: Plenum Press.

Tarone, E. (1997). Analyzing IL in natural settings: A sociolinguistic perspective on second-language acquisition. *Communication and Cognition, 30*, 137–149.

Tarone, E. & Swain, M. (1995). A sociolinguistic perspective on second language use in immersion classrooms. *The Modern Language Journal, 79*, 166–178.

Tateyama, Y. (2001). Explicit and implicit teaching of pragmatic routines. In K. R. Rose & G. Kasper (Eds.), *Pragmatics in Language Teaching* (pp. 200–222). Cambridge: CUP.

Tateyama, Y., Kasper, G., Mui, L. P., Tay, H.-M., & Thananart, O. (1997). Explicit and implicit teaching of pragmatic routines. In L. F. Bouton (Ed.), *Pragmatics and Language Learning* [Monograph series 8] (pp. 163–177). Urbana-Champaign, IL: University of Illinois at Urbana-Champaign, Division of English as an International Language.

Taylor, J. G. (1984). *Louisiana: A history.* New York, NY: W.W. Norton.

Taylor, T. J. (1990). Which is to be master? The institutionalization of authority in the science of language. In J. E. Joseph & T. J. Taylor (Eds.), *Ideologies of Language* (pp. 9–26). London: Routledge.

Taylor, T. J. (2000). Language constructing language: The implications of reflexivity for linguistic theory. *Language Sciences, 22,* 483–499.

Taylor-Browne, K. (1984). The acquisition of grammatical gender by children in French immersion programs. MA thesis, University of Calgary.

Thomas, A. (1998). La liaison et son enseignement: Des modèles orthoépiques à la réalité linguistique. *Canadian Modern Language Review, 54*(4). Available at http://www.utpjournals.com/jour. ihtml?lp=product/cmlr/544/544-Thomas.html

Thomas, A. (2002). La variation phonétique en français langue seconde au niveau universitaire avancé. *Acquisition et Interaction en Langue Etrangère, 17,* 101–121.

Thomas, A. (2004). Phonetic norm versus usage in advanced French as a second language. *International Review of Applied Linguistics, 42,* 365–382.

Thomas, M. S. C. (2005). Characterizing compensation. *Cortex, 41,* 434–442.

Thomason, S. G. (2001). *Language Contact: An introduction.* Washington, DC: Georgetown University Press.

Thomason, S. G. & Kaufman, T. (1988). *Language Contact, Creolization, and Genetic Linguistics.* Berkeley, CA: University of California Press.

Thráinsson, H. (2003). Syntactic variation, historical development, and minimalism. In R. Hendrick (Ed.), *Minimalist Syntax* (pp. 152–191). Oxford: Blackwell.

Tobias, S. (1986). Anxiety and cognitive processing of instruction. In R. Schwarzer (Ed.), *Self-Related Cognition in Anxiety and Motivation* (pp. 35–54). Hillsdale, NJ: Lawrence Erlbaum.

Tognini-Bonelli, E. (2001). *Corpus Linguistics at Work.* Amsterdam: John Benjamins.

Tomlin, R. S. & Villa, V. (1994). Attention in cognitive science and SLA. *Studies in Second Language Acquisition, 16,* 183–203.

Tono, Y. (2004). Multiple comparisons of IL, L1 and TL corpora: The case of the L2 acquisition of verb subcategorization patterns by Japanese learners of English. In G. Aston, S. Bernardini, & D. Stewart (Eds.), *Corpora and Language Learner* (pp. 45–66). Amsterdam: John Benjamins.

Tory, G. 1529). *Champ fleury.* The Hague: Mouton (Johnson Reprint Corporation).

Towell, R. (1987). A discussion of the psycholinguistic bases for communicative language teaching in a foreign language teaching situation. *British Journal of Language Teaching, 25,* 91–101.

Towell, R. (2004). Research into the second language acquisition of French: Achievements and challenges. *Journal of French Language Studies, 14,* 357–375.

Towell, R. & Hawkins, R. (1994). *Approaches to Second Language Acquisition.* Clevedon: Multilingual Matters.

Towell, R., Hawkins, R., & Bazergui, N. (1996). The development of fluency in advanced learners of French. *Applied Linguistics, 17,* 84–119.

Train, R. W. (2000). Getting past the ideology of 'the language': The standardization of French and Spanish, and its implications in foreign-language pedagogy. PhDdissertation, University of California, Berkeley.

Train, R. W. (2002). Foreign language standards, standard language and the culture of standardization: Some implications for foreign language and heritage language education. Paper presented at the First UC Language Consortium Conference on Language Learning and Teaching, at University of California, Irvine. Available at http://uccllt.ucdavis.edu/hli/papers.htm

Train, R. W. (2003). The (non)native standard language in foreign language education: A critical perspective. In C. Blyth (Ed.), *The Sociolinguistics of Foreign Language Classrooms: Contributions of the native, the near-native and the non-native speaker* (pp. 3–39). Boston, MA: Heinle.

Train, R. W. (2006). A critical look at technologies and ideologies in internet-mediated intercultural foreign language education. In J. A. Belz & S. L. Thorne (Eds.), *Internet-Mediated Intercultural Foreign Language Education* (pp. 245–282). Boston, MA: Heinle.

Tranel, B. (1981). *Concreteness in Generative Phonology: Evidence from French.* Berkeley, CA: University of California Press.

Tranel, B. (1984). Closed syllable adjustment and the representation of schwa in French. In C. Brugman & M. Macaulay (Eds.), *Proceedings of the 10th Annual Meeting of the Berkeley Linguistics Society* (pp. 65–75). Berkeley, CA: University of California Press.

Tranel, B. (1988). A propos de l'ajustement de *e* en français. In S. P. Verluyten (Ed.), *La phonologie du schwa français* (pp. 89–131). Amsterdam: John Benjamins.

Tranel, B. (1996a). French liaison and elision revisited: A unified account within Optimality Theory. In C. Parodi, C. Quicoli, M. Saltarelli, & M. L. Zubizarreta (Eds.), *Aspects of Romance Linguistics* (pp. 433–455). Amsterdam: John Benjamins.

Tranel, B. (1996b). Exceptionality in optimality theory and final consonants in French. In K. Zagona (Ed.), *Grammatical Theory and Romance Languages* (pp. 275–292). Amsterdam: John Benjamins.

Tranel, B. (2000). Aspects de la phonologie du français et la théorie de l'optimalité. *Langue Française, 126,* 39–72.

Trévise, A. & Noyau, C. (1984). Adult Spanish speakers and the acquisition of French negation forms: Individual variation and linguistic awareness. In R. Andersen (Ed.), *Second Languages: A cross-linguistic perspective* (pp. 165–189). Rowley, MA: Newbury House.

Trosborg, A. (1995). *Interlanguage Pragmatics. Requests, complaints and apologies.* Berlin: Mouton de Gruyter.

Trudeau, D. (1992). *Les inventeurs du bon usage (1529–1647).* Paris: Minuit.

Trudgill, P. (1986). *Dialects in Contact.* Oxford: Blackwell.

Tsimpli, I.-M. & Roussou, A. (1991). Parameter resetting in L2? *University College London Working Papers in Linguistics, 3,* 149–169.

Tucker, G., Lambert, W., & Rigault, A. (1969). Students' acquisition of French gender distinctions: A pilot investigation. *International Review of Applied Linguistics, 7,* 51–55.

Tucker, G., Lambert, W., Rigault, A., & Segalowitz, N. (1968). A psychological investigation of French speakers' skill with grammatical gender. *Journal of Verbal Learning and Verbal Behavior, 7,* 312–316.

Tucker, G., Lambert, W., & Rigault, A. (1977). *The French Speaker's Skill with Grammatical Gender: An example of rule-governed behavior.* The Hague: Mouton.

Tuller, L. (1999). Le grammatical et l'extra-grammatical: Remarques sur quelques 'particularités' morphosyntaxiques des langues des sourds. In F. Cordier & J.-E. Tyvaert (Eds.), *Recherches en linguistique et psychologie cognitive* 11: *Actes des journées scientifiques* (pp. 81–97). Reims: Presses Universitaires.

Tuller, L. (2000). Aspects de la morphosyntaxe du français des sourds. *Recherches Linguistiques de Vincennes, 29,* 143–156.

Tuller, L. & Jakubowicz, C. (2004). Développement de la morphosyntaxe du français chez des enfants sourds moyens. *Le Langage et l'Homme, 39,* 191–208.

Tyne, H. (2005). La maîtrise du style en français langue seconde. PhD dissertation, University of Surrey and Sorbonne nouvelle, Nanterre.

UCREL. (2004). *CLAWS Part-of-Speech Tagger for English.* Available at http://www/comp.lancs.ac.uk/computing/research/ucrel/claws.

Uritescu, D., Mougeon, R., & Handouleh, Y. (2002). Le comportement du schwa dans le français parlé par les élèves des programmes d'immersion française. In C. Tatilon & A. Baudot (Eds.), *La Linguistique fonctionnelle au tournant du siècle. Actes du Vingt-quatrième Colloque international de linguistique fonctionnelle* (pp. 335–346). Toronto: Éditions du GREF.

Uritescu, D., Mougeon, R., Rehner, K., & Nadasdi, T. (2004). Acquisition of the internal and external constraints of variable schwa deletion by French immersion students. *International Review of Applied Linguistics in Language Teaching, 42*(4), 349–364.

U. S. Census Bureau (1990). *Census of Population and Housing: Louisiana*. STF-3A Magnetic Computer Tape. Washington, DC: Bureau of the Census.

U. S. Census Bureau (2000). *Census of Population and Housing*. Washington, DC: Government Printing Office.

U. S. House of Representatives (2003). *National Security Language Act*. 108th Congress, H. R. 3676.

Ushioda, E. (2001). Language learning at university: Exploring the role of motivational thinking. In Z. Dornyei & R. Schmidt (Eds.), *Motivation and Second Language Acquisition* (pp. 93–125). Honolulu, HI: Second Language Teaching and Curriculum Center, University of Hawai'i at Manoa.

Väänänen, V. (1967). *Introduction au latin vulgaire*. Paris: Champion.

Vainikka, A. & Young-Scholten, M. (1996a). Gradual development of L2 phrase structure. *Second Language Research, 12,* 7–39.

Vainikka, A. & Young-Scholten, M. (1996b). The early stages in adult L2 syntax: Additional evidence from Romance speakers. *Second Language Research, 12,* 140–176.

Vainikka, A. & Young-Scholten, M. (1998). Morphosyntactic triggers in adult SLA. In M. L. Beck (Ed.), *Morphology and its Interface in L2 Knowledge* (pp. 89–113). Amsterdam: John Benjamins.

Valdés, G. (1998). The construct of the near-native speaker in the foreign language profession: Perspectives on ideologies about language. *Profession*, 151–160.

Valdman, A. (1970). *Basic course in Haitian Creole*. Bloomington, MI: Indiana University Press.

Valdman, A. (1979). *Le français hors de France*. Paris: Champion.

Valdman, A. (1982). Français standard et français populaire: Sociolectes ou fiction? *The French Review, 56*(2), 218–227.

Valdman, A. (1983). Creolization and second-language acquisition. In R. W. Andersen (Ed.), *Pidginization and Creolization as Language Acquisition* (pp. 212–234). Rowley, MA: Newbury House.

Valdman, A. (1992). Authenticity, variation, and communication in the foreign language classroom. In C. Kramsch & S. McConnell-Ginet (Eds.), *Text and Context: Cross-disciplinary perspectives on language study* (pp. 79–97). Lexington, MA: D.C. Heath.

Valdman, A. (1993). *Bien entendu! Introduction à la prononciation française*. New York, NY: Prentice Hall.

Valdman, A. (2000). Comment gérer la variation dans l'enseignement du français langue étrangère aux Etats-Unis. *The French Review, 73,* 648–666.

Valdman, A. (2003). The acquisition of sociostylistic and sociopragmatic variation by instructed second language learners: The elaboration of pedagogical norms. In C. Blyth (Ed.), *The Sociolinguistics of Foreign Language Classrooms: Contributions of the native, the near-native, and the non-native speaker* (pp. 57–78). Boston, MA: Heinle Thomson.

Valdman, A. (2004). Réflections sur l'histoire de l'AILA. *AILA Review, 17,* 2–5.

Valdman, A., Auger, J., & Piston-Hatien, D. (2005). *Le français en Amérique du Nord. Etat présent*. Québec: Les Presses de l' Université Laval.

Valdman, A., Salazar, R. J., & Charbonneaux, M. A. (1964). *A Drillbook of French Pronunciation*. New York, NY: Harper.

Valenzuela, A. (Ed.). (2005). *Leaving Children Behind. How Texas-style accountability fails Latino youth*. Albany, NY: State University of New York Press.

Valli, C. (1990). The nature of the line in ASL poetry. In W. H. Edmondson & F. Karlsson (Eds.), *SLR '87: Papers from the fourth international symposium on sign language Research* (pp. 171–182). Hamburg: Signum Verlag.

Valois, D. (1991). The internal syntax of DP and adjective placement in French and English. *NELS, 21,* 367–382.

van Dijk, T. A. (1998). *Ideology: A Multidisciplinary Approach*. London: Sage.

VanPatten, B. & Oikkenon, S. (1996). The causative variables in processing instruction: Explanation versus structured input activities. *Studies in Second Language Acquisition, 18,* 225–243.

Varan, D. (1998). The cultural erosion metaphor and the transcultural impact of media systems. *Journal of Communication, 48,* 58–85.

Varney, J. (1933). *Pronunciation of French, Articulation and Intonation.* Ann Arbor, MI: Edwards Brothers.

Vaugelas, C. V. de (1647). *Remarques sur la langue française* (Ed. J. Streicher). Geneva: Slatkine Reprints, 1970.

Vendryès, J. (1921). *Le langage. Introduction linguistique à l'histoire.* Paris: Renaissance du livre.

Vercaingne-Ménard, A. (2002). *Expérimentation d'une approche bilingue à l'Ecole Gadbois: Année scolaire 2001–2002.* Montreal: Ministère de l'Education, Québec, Canada.

Vercaingne-Ménard, A., Godard, L., & Labelle, M. (2001). The emergence of narrative discourse in two young deaf children. In V. Dively (Ed.), *Sign Languages: Discoveries from international research* (pp. 120–132). Washington, DC: Gallaudet University Press.

Verluyten, S. P. (Ed.). (1988). *La phonologie du schwa français.* Amsterdam: John Benjamins.

Véronique, D. (2005). Syntactic and semantic issues in the acquisition of negation in French. In J.-M. Dewaele (Ed.), *Focus on French as a Foreign Language: Multidisciplinary approaches* (pp. 114–134). Clevedon: Multilingual Matters.

Véronique, D. & Stoffel, H. (2003). The acquisition of negation in French L2 by adult Moroccan Arabic speakers. *Marges Linguistiques, 5,* 242–259.

Véronis, J. (2005). Lexique: Nuage de mots d'aujourd'hui. *Technologies du langage.* Retrieved on February 2, 2005 from http://aixtal.blogspot.com/2005/07/lexique-nuage-de-mots-daujourdhui.html

Vigliocci, G., Butterworth, B., & Garrett, M. (1996). Subject-verb agreement in Spanish and English: Differences in the role of conceptual factors. *Cognition, 61,* 261–298.

Vihman, M. M., Davis, B. L., & DePaolis, R. (1995). Prosodic analysis of babbling and first words: A comparison of English and French. In K. Elenius & P. Branderud (Eds.), *Proceedings of the 13th International Congress of Phonetic Sciences,* Vol. 4 (pp. 14–21). Stockholm: KTH and Stockholm University.

Vincent-Durroux, L. (1992). La langue orale des sourds profonds oralistes: Etude comparative (anglais/français). PhD dissertation, University of Paris IV.

Vizmuller-Zocco, J. (1985). Linguistic creativity and word formation. *Italica, 62,* 305–310.

Volterra, V. & Bates, E. (1989). Selective impairment of Italian grammatical morphology in the congenitally deaf: A case study. *Cognitive Neuropsychology, 6,* 273–308.

Vuchic, R. (1993). A study of noun phrase agreement in French as a second language: An autosegmental model. PhD dissertation, University of Delaware.

Wagner, R. L. & Pinchon, J. (1991). *Grammaire du français classique et moderne.* Paris: Hachette.

Walker, D. C. (1975). Word stress in French. *Language, 51*(4), 887–900.

Walker, D. C. (1996). The new stability of unstable-e in French. *Journal of French Language Studies, 5,* 85–107.

Walker, D. C. (2001). *French Sound Structure.* Calgary: University of Calgary Press.

Walter, H. (1988). *Le français dans tous les sens.* Paris: R. Laffont.

Walter, H. (1990). Une voyelle qui ne veut pas mourir. In J. N. Green & W. Ayres-Bennett (Eds.), *Variation and Change in French* (pp. 27–36). London: Routledge.

Walter, H. (1998). *Le français d'ici, de là, de là-bas.* Paris: J-C Lattès.

Walter, H. (2000). *Le français d'ici, de là, de là-bas.* Paris: LGF – Livre de Poche.

Walz, J. (1986). Is oral proficiency possible with today's French textbooks? *The Modern Language Journal, 70*(1), 13–19.

Warden, M. (1997). The effect of form-focused instruction on control over grammatical gender by French immersion students in grade 11. PhD dissertation, University of Toronto, Canada.

Warga, M. (2001). Pragmatische Aspekte im Zweitsprachenerwerb. Eine Untersuchung zu Gesprächs-wörtern auf der Basis eines Korpus aus Gesprächsaufzeichnungen von Anfangslernern des Französischen. In C. Gronemann, C. Maaß, S. A. Peters, & S. Schrader (Eds.), *Körper und Schrift. Beiträge zum 16. Nachwuchkolloquium der Romanistik* (pp. 265–277). Bonn: Romanistischer Verlag.

Warga, M. (2004). *Pragmatische Entwicklung in der Fremdsprache. Der Sprechakt Aufforderung im Französischen.* Narr: Tübingen.

Warga, M. (2005). 'Je serais très merciable': Formulaic vs. individual speech in learners' request closings. *Revue Canadienne de Linguistique Appliquée, 8*(1), 67–91.

Wartburg, W. von (1923–1983). *Französisches etymologisches Wörterbuch,* 24 Vols. Bonn: Klopp.

Weber, E. (1976). *Peasants into Frenchmen: The modernization of rural France 1870–1914.* Stanford, CA: Stanford University Press.

Wechsler, S. (In press). 'Elsewhere' in gender resolution. In K. Hanson & S. Inkelas (Eds.), *The Nature of the Word-Essays in Honor of Paul Kiparsky.* Cambridge, MA: The MIT Press.

Weinreich, U. (1953). *Languages in Contact: Findings and problems.* The Hague: Mouton.

Wekker, H. (1996). Creolization and the acquisition of English as a second language. In H. Wekker (Ed.), *Creole Languages and Language Acquisition* (pp. 139–149). Berlin: Mouton de Gruyter.

Welles, E. B. (2004). Foreign language enrollments in United States institutions of higher education, Fall 2002. *ADFL Bulletin, 35*(2–3), 7–26.

West's Louisiana Statutes Annotated (1977). *Treaties and Organic Laws, Early Constitutions,* Volume 3, *U.S. Constitution and index.* St. Paul, MN: West Publishing.

White, L. (1991). Adverb placement in second language acquisition: Some effects of positive and negative evidence in the classroom. *Second Language Research, 7,* 133–161.

White, L. (2003). *Second Language Acquisition and Universal Grammar.* Cambridge: CUP.

White, L. (2004). 'Internal' versus 'external' universals. *Studies in Language, 28*(3), 704–706.

White, L., Valenzuela, E., Kozlowska-Macgregor, M., & Leung, Y.-K. (2004). Gender and number agreement in non-native Spanish. *Applied Psycholinguistics, 25,* 105–133.

White, L. & Genesee, F. (1996). How native is near-native? The issue of ultimate attainment in adult second language acquisition. *Second Language Research, 12,* 233–265.

White, S. (1989). Backchannels across cultures: A study of Americans and Japanese. *Language in Society, 18,* 59–76.

Wieczorek, J. A. (1994). The concept of 'French' in foreign language texts. *Foreign Language Annals, 27*(4), 487–497.

Wilbur, R. (2000). The use of ASL to support the development of English and literacy. *Journal of Deaf Studies and Deaf Education, 5*(1), 81–104.

Wildner-Bassett, M. E. (1984). *Improving Pragmatic Aspects of Learners' Interlanguage. A Comparison of methodological approaches for teaching gambits to advanced adult learners of English in industry.* Tübingen: Narr.

Wildner-Bassett, M. E. (1986). Teaching 'polite noises': Improving advanced adult learners' repertoire of gambits. In G. Kasper (Ed.), *Learning, Teaching and Communication in the Foreign Language Classroom* (pp. 163–178). Aarhus: Aarhus University Press.

Wilkinson, S. (2001). Noticing discourse: A point of departure for (re)designing the conversation course. *Foreign Language Annals, 34*(6), 523–533.

Williams, G. (1996). Language planning as discourse. In R. Singh (Ed.), *Towards a Critical Sociolinguistics* (pp. 281–304). Amsterdam: John Benjamins.

Williams, T. H. (1969). *Huey Long.* New York, NY: Knopff.

Wilmet, M. (1997). *Grammaire critique du français.* Louvain-la-Neuve: Duculot.

Wilson, G. (1978). Introversion/extraversion. In H. London & J. E. Exner (Eds.), *Dimensions of Personality* (pp. 217–261). New York, NY: John Wiley.

Wilson, R. G. & Lynn, R. (1990). Personality, intelligence components and foreign language attainment. *Educational Psychology, 10,* 57–71.

Withgott, M. M. (1982). Segmental evidence for phonological constituents. PhD dissertation, University of Texas, Austin.

Wodak, R., de Cillia, R., Reisigl, M., & Liebhart, K. (1999). *The Discursive Construction of National Identity* [Critical Discourse Analysis Series]. Edinburgh: Edinburgh University Press.

Wolfson, N. (1976). Speech events and natural speech: Some implications for sociolinguistic methodology. *Language in Society, 5,* 189–209.

Woll, B. & Morgan, G. (2002). Conclusions and directions for future research. In G. Morgan & B. Woll (Eds.), *Directions in Sign Language Acquisition* (pp. 291–299). Amsterdam: John Benjamins.

Woll, B., Sutton-Spence, R., & Elton, F. (2001). Multilingualism: The global approach to sign languages. In C. Lucas (Ed.), *The Sociolinguistics of Sign Languages* (pp. 8–32). Cambridge: CUP.

Wong, J. (2000). The token 'yeah' in nonnative speaker English conversation. *Research on Language and Social Interaction, 33*(1), 39–67.

Woolard, K. A. & Schieffelin, B. B. (1994). Language Ideology. *Annual Review of Anthropology, 23*, 55–82.

Woodward, J. (1979). Quelques aspects sociolinguistiques des langues des signes américaine et francaise. In F. Grosjean & H. Lane (Eds.), *La langue des signes* (pp. 78–91). Paris: Larousse.

Woodward, J. (2000). Sign languages and sign language families in Thailand and Viet Nam. In K. Emmorey & H. Lane (Eds.), *The Signs of Language Revisited: An Anthology to honor Ursula Bellugi and Edward Klima* (pp. 23–47). Mahwah, NJ: Lawrence Erlbaum.

Woodward, J. & De Santis, S. (1977a). Two to one it happens: Dynamic phonology in two sign languages. *Sign Language Studies, 17*, 329–346.

Woodward, J. & De Santis, S. (1977b). Negative incorporation in ASL and LSF. *Language in Society, 6*, 379–388.

Wray, A. (2000). Formulaic sequences in second language teaching: Principle and practice. *Applied Linguistics, 21*(4), 463–489.

Wray, A. (2002). *Formulaic Language and the Lexicon.* Cambridge: CUP.

Wright, R. (1982). *Latin and Early Romance.* London: Francis Cairns.

Wüest, J. (1995). Les scriptae françaises II. Picardie, Hainaut, Artois, Flandres. In G. Holtus, M. Metzeltin, & C. Schmitt (Eds.), *Lexikon de Romanistischen Linguistik*, t. II, 2 (pp. 300–314). Tübingen: Niemeyer.

Yaguello, M. (2000). X comme XXL: La place des anglicismes dans la langue. In B. Cerquiglini, J.-C. Corbeil, J.-M. Klinkenberg, & B. Peeters (Eds.), *Le français dans tous ses états* (pp. 353–361). Paris: Flammarion.

Yaguello, M. (Ed.). (2003). *Le grand livre de la langue française.* Paris: Seuil.

Yashima, T. (2000). Orientations and motivation in foreign language learning: A study of Japanese college students. *JACET Bulletin, 31*, 121–133.

Yashima, T. (2002). Willingness to communicate in a second language: The Japanese EFL context. *The Modern Language Journal, 86*, 55–66.

Yashima, T., Zenuk-Nishide, L., & Shimizu, K. (2004). The influence of attitudes and affect on willingness to communicate and second language communication. *Language Learning, 54*(1), 119–152.

Yoshimi, D. (2001). Explicit instruction and JFL learners' use of interactional discourse markers. In K. R. Rose & G. Kasper (Eds.), *Pragmatics in Language Teaching* (pp. 223–244). Cambridge: CUP.

Young, D. (1986). The relationship between anxiety and foreign language oral proficiency ratings. *Foreign Language Annals, 19*, 439–445.

Young, D. (1991). The relationship between anxiety and foreign language oral proficiency ratings. In E. K. Horwitz & D. J. Young (Eds.), *Language Anxiety* (pp. 57–63). Englewood Cliffs, NJ: Prentice-Hall.

Young, R. (1999). Sociolinguistic approaches to SLA. *Annual Review of Applied Linguistics, 19*, 105–132.

Young-Scholten, M. (1993). *The Acquisition of Prosodic Structure in a Second Language* [Linguistische Arbeiten 304]. Tübingen: Niemeyer.

Yu, M.-C. (1999). Universalistic and culture-specific perspectives on variation in the acquisition of pragmatic competence in a second language. *Journal of Pragmatics, 9*(2), 281–312.

Yule, G. (1996). *Pragmatics.* Oxford: OUP.

Zampini, M. L. (1998). L2 Spanish spirantization, prosodic domains, and interlanguage rules. In S. J. Hannahs & M. Young-Scholten (Eds.), *Focus on Phonological Acquisition* (pp. 209–234). Amsterdam: John Benjamins.

Zéphir, F. (1996). *Haitian Immigrants in Black America: A sociological and sociolinguistic portrait.* Westport, CT: Bergin & Garvey.

Zimmerman, C. B. (1997). Historical trends in second language vocabulary instruction. In J. Coady & T. Huckin (Eds.), *Second Language Vocabulary Acquisition: A rationale for pedagogy* (pp. 5–19). Cambridge: CUP.

Zipf, G. K. (1935). *The Psycho-biology of Language: An introduction to dynamic philology*. Boston, MA: Houghton Mifflin.

Zuengler, J. (1993). Explaining NNS interactional behavior: The effect of conversational topic. In G. Kasper & S. Blum-Kulka (Eds.), *Interlanguage Pragmatics* (pp. 184–195). Oxford: OUP.

Zufferey, F. (1987). *Recherches linguistiques sur les chansonniers provençaux*. Geneva: Droz.

English-French Glossary
Glossaire

Acadia, Acadian	*Acadie, acadien(ne)*
acculturation model	*modèle d'acculturation*
acquisition	*acquisition, appropriation*
additive bilingualism	*bilinguisme additif*
address term	*appellatif*
affective variables	*variables affectives*
agreement	*accord*
ambiguous, ambiguity	*ambigu, ambiguïté*
amotivation	*manque de motivation*
anaphora	*anaphore*
anxiety	*anxiété*
apocope	*apocope*
apophonous	*apophone (alternance vocalique)*
appropriate topics of conversation	*sujets de conversation appropriés*
arabization	*arabisation*
arbitrary gender	*genre arbitraire*
attention to form	*accent sur la forme*
auditory deficit	*déficit auditif*
aural-oral	*audio-oral*
autonomy	*autonomie*
bimanual	*bimanuel*
bimodal, bimodality	*bimodal, bimodalité*
Cajun English	*anglais cajun*
Cajun French	*français cajun*
computer-aided language learning (CALL)	*enseignement des langues assisté par ordinateur (ELAO)*
check(ing)	*vérifier, vérification*
Classical Latin	*latin classique*
classifier	*classificateur*
clue (syntactic, semantic, etc.)	*indication syntaxique, sémantique*
codification	*codification*
coerce, coercion	*contraindre, coercition/contrainte*
cognate	*mot apparenté, congénère*
cognize, cognition	*avoir conscience de, cognition/connaissance*
collocation	*collocation*
Colloquial Latin	*latin familier*
colloquial words	*expressions familières*
Communicative Language Teaching (CLT)	*didactique de langue communicative*

compound	*composé*
compounding	*composition*
computarized	*informatisé*
computational component	*composant de calcul*
concord(ance)	*concordance*
consonant	*consonne*
constructs	*concepts*
control group	*groupe témoin*
conversation analysis	*analyse conversationnelle*
conversational implicature	*implicature conversationnelle*
conversational routines	*routines conversationnelles*
coronal	*coronale*
corpus linguistics	*linguistique de corpus*
cross-linguistic pollination	*pollinisation multi-linguistique*
cued speech	*langage parlé complété (LPC)*
database	*banque de données*
data collection	*recueil de données*
deaf community	*communauté sourde*
deaf, deafness	*sourd, surdité*
derivational rule	*règle dérivationnelle*
determiner	*déterminant*
developmental sequence	*séquence développementale*
diglossia	*diglossie*
(high and low functions)	*(fonction élevée, basse)*
diphthongization	*diphtongaison*
deixis	*deixis*
directional verb	*verbe directionnel*
discourse analysis	*analyse du discours*
discourse competence	*compétence discursive*
discourse completion task (DCT)	*tâche de réalisation discursive*
discourse marker	*marqueur discursif/de discours*
dyad, dyadic	*paire, binaire*
elicitation task	*tâche empirique/de recueil de données*
elision	*élision*
emic	*émique*
endogenous	*endogène*
ending	*terminaison*
epicene nouns	*(noms) épicènes*
ethnic cleansing	*épuration linguistique*
etic	*étique*
extrinsic motivation	*motivation externe*
eye gaze	*direction du regard*
facial expression	*expression du visage*
Failed Feature Hypothesis	*Hypothèse des Traits en Faillite*
features	*traits*
findings	*résultats*
flexional ending	*terminaison flexionnelle ou désinence*
formal expression	*expression formelle*

formulaic (expressions/language/sequence)	*formulaïque, préfabriqué (expressions, langage, séquence)*
free variation	*variation libre*
fricative	*fricative, affriquée*
Full Access Hypothesis	*Hypothèse de l'accès total*
Full Transfer Hypothesis	*Hypothèse du transfert total*
functional categories	*catégories fonctionnelles*
gambits	*gambits, subterfuges*
gender assignment	*attribution du genre*
gestual channel	*canal gestuel*
gesture	*geste*
glide	*semi-consonne*
gloss	*traduction interlinéaire*
grammatical aspect	*aspect grammatical*
grammatical gender	*genre grammatical*
grammatical homonyms	*homonymes grammaticaux*
greeting behavior	*comportement de salutation*
handshape	*configuration manuelle*
head final compound	*composé à tête finale*
head initial compound	*composé à tête initiale*
hearing loss	*perte auditive*
hearing status	*statut auditif*
hearing	*entendant*
heritage language	*langue patrimoniale*
home-sign	*code signé familial/langue des signes domestique*
iconicity	*iconicité*
identity language	*langue identitaire*
idiomatic expression	*formation synaptique, expression idiomatique*
idiosyncrasy	*idiosyncrasie, particularité*
illiteracy	*analphabétisme*
illocution	*illocution*
illocutionary force	*force illocutoire, illocutionnelle*
impair	*affaiblir, compromettre, diminuer*
impairment	*affaiblissement*
Inf(lectional) features	*traits flexionnels*
input enhancements	*mises en relief de l'input*
instantiate	*exemplifier*
instructed language learning	*apprentissage d'une langue en instruction*
instructed learners	*apprenants en instruction*
interaction	*interaction*
interface	*interface*
interlanguage	*interlangue*
interpretive	*interprétif, interprétive*
interrogative structures	*structures interrogatives*
introversion–extraversion	*introversion–extraversion*
isogloss	*isoglosse*
koine	*koiné*
language learning	*apprentissage d'une langue*

language acquisition	*appropriation d'une langue*
language learning process	*processus d'apprentissage d'une langue*
language maintenance	*maintien linguistique*
language planning	*plannification linguistique*
learner	*apprenant*
learnability	*apprenabilité*
learned compound	*composé savant*
learning	*apprentissage*
leave-taking behavior	*comportement de prise de congé*
lexical base	*base lexicale*
lexical creativity	*créativité lexicale*
lexical gender	*genre lexical*
lexical renewal	*renouveau lexical*
lexical roots	*racines lexicales*
lexical variants	*variantes lexicales*
linguistic aptitude	*aptitude linguistique*
lip reading	*lecture labiale*
liquid	*liquide*
local languages	*langues autochtones*
(inter)locutor	*(inter)locuteur*
manual articulators	*articulateurs manuels*
manual babbling	*babillage manuel*
manual shapes	*formes manuelles*
mapping	*application*
matching	*appareillement, assortiment*
merge	*fusion, amalgame*
metalanguage	*métalangage*
microgenetic analysis	*analyse microgénétique*
micro-stylistic variation	*variation micro-stylistique*
mild-to-moderate hearing loss	*perte auditive légère-moyenne*
Missing Surface Inflection hypothesis	*hypothèse des flexions de surface manquantes*
MLU (mean length of utterance)	*LME (longueur moyenne d'énoncé)*
morphosyntactic variants	*variantes morphosyntaxiques*
motives, motivation	*motifs, motivation*
nasal	*nasale*
native speaker	*locuteur natif*
nativization	*nativisation*
naturalistic learners	*apprenants en milieu naturel*
naturalistic language learning	*apprentissage d'une langue en milieu naturel*
non-manual component	*composante non manuelle*
non-native speaker	*locuteur non natif*
noticing hypothesis	*hypothèse de la perception*
noun raising	*mouvement nominal*
Oc	*oc (oui en langues d'Oc)*
Oïl	*oïl (oui en langues d'Oïl)*
omission	*omission*
oral channel	*canal oral*
oral language	*langue orale*

outcomes	*résultats*
palatalization	*palatalisation*
parameter	*paramètre*
parasynthesis	*parasynthèse*
parseur	*analyseur syntaxique*
pattern	*modèle, schéma*
pedagogical norm	*norme pédagogique*
perception of difficulty	*perception de la difficulté*
phoneme system	*système phonématique*
phonological feature	*trait phonologique*
phonological lexicon	*lexique phonologique*
phonological variants	*variantes phonologiques*
phonotactic constraint	*contrainte phonotaxique*
phrasal phonology	*phonologie de phrase*
pointing gestures	*pointés (ou gestes de pointage)*
Popular Ivorian French or *Nouchi*	*français populaire ivoirien, nouchi*
postlingually	*postlingual*
pragmatics	*pragmatique*
prelingual	*prélingual*
primes	*configurations manuelles*
processing instruction	*instruction favorisant le traitement de l'input*
proficiency	*compétence*
profound deafness	*surdité profonde*
pronouns of address	*pronoms d'appel, appellatifs*
query preparatory-strategies	*stratégies préparatoires de requête*
recast	*reformulation*
referential shift	*changement/glissement de perspective*
register	*registre*
reliable, reliability	*fiable, fiabilité*
rhythm	*rythme*
rounded	*arrondi*
saliency	*saillance, trait saillant*
schwa	*schwa, cheva, e-muet, e-instable, e-caduc*
segmental inventory	*inventaire segmental*
self-determination	*auto-détermination*
self-confidence	*confiance en soi*
self-efficacy	*efficacité personnelle*
semantic shift	*glissement sémantique*
semantically congruent	*sémantiquement congruent*
sequential	*séquentiel*
severe deafness	*surdité sévère*
sign language	*langue des signes*
sign	*signe*
signer	*signeur*
signing space	*espace du signeur*
simultaneous	*simultané*
Specific Language Impairment (SLI)	*Troubles spécifiques du développement du langage (dysphasie)*

speech-language therapist	*orthophoniste / logopédiste / logopède*
sonority sequencing	*classement sonore/de sonorité*
sociolinguistic competence	*compétence sociolinguistique*
source language	*langue source*
spatial locus	*localisation spatiale*
speech act analysis	*analyse de l'acte de la parole/discursif*
speech act theory	*théorie de l'acte de la parole/discursif*
speech act performance	*performance de l'acte de la parole/discursif*
spread	*écarté*
standardization	*standardisation*
stop	*occlusive, plosive*
stress	*accent, accentuation*
Structure Building Hypothesis	*hypothèse de construction structurale*
structured input	*input structuré*
study abroad programs	*programmes de séjour linguistique à l'étranger*
subject pronouns	*pronoms sujet*
subtractive bilingualism	*bilinguisme soustractif*
superstratum	*superstrat*
suprasegmental	*suprasegmental(e)*
syllabicity	*syllabicité*
syllable	*syllabe*
(syllable) coda	*coda*
(syllable) nucleus	*noyau*
(syllable) onset	*attaque*
syllable structure	*structure syllabique*
syntactic variants	*variantes syntaxiques*
tagger, tagging	*tagger/taggueur ou marqueur/marquage*
target language	*langue cible*
teacher-fronted teaching	*enseignement dominé par l'enseignant*
tense	*temps*
turn-taking	*tour de rôle*
Type 1 variation	*variation de Type 1*
Type 2 variation	*variation de Type 2*
typological drift	*dérive typologique*
unimanual	*unimanuel*
unimodal	*unimodal*
uninterpretable functional features	*traits fonctionnels non-interprétables*
utter	*dire, prononcer, articuler*
utterance	*énoncé, propos, mots*
VARBRUL	VARBRUL
variants	*variantes*
variationist sociolinguistics	*sociolinguistique variationiste*
vehicularization	*véhicularisation*
vernacularization	*vernacularisation*
verb raising	*mouvement verbal*
vernacular	*vernaculaire*
visual coding	*encodage visuel*
visuo-gestural	*visuo-gestuel*

vocal cords	*cordes vocales*
voice	*voisement*
voice onset time (VOT)	*durée d'établissement du voisement*
voiced	*voisé, sonore*
voiceless	*non-voisé, sourd*
vowel	*voyelle*
Willingness to Communicate (WTC)	*volonté de communiquer (VDC)*
Vulgar Latin	*latin vulgaire*
word family	*famille lexicale*
word formation	*formation des mots*
XML	*langage XML*

Name index

Subject index